Historical Introduction to Modern Psychology

REVISED EDITION

Gardner Murphy

HARCOURT, BRACE & WORLD, INC.
NEW YORK, CHICAGO, AND BURLINGAME

TO MY MOTHER

CONTENTS

Preface to the Revised Edition   vii

Preface to the First Edition   x

Part One
The Antecedents of Modern Psychology

1. THE INTELLECTUAL BACKGROUND   3

2. THE SEVENTEENTH CENTURY   17

3. THE EIGHTEENTH CENTURY   30

4. THE EARLY NINETEENTH CENTURY   49

Part Two
The Rise of the Research Spirit

5. SOME INTELLECTUAL ANTECEDENTS
   OF EXPERIMENTAL PSYCHOLOGY   67

6. THE BEGINNINGS OF EXPERIMENTAL PSYCHOLOGY   79

7. BRITISH PSYCHOLOGY IN THE MID-NINETEENTH
   CENTURY   99

8. THE THEORY OF EVOLUTION   111

9. PSYCHIATRY FROM PINEL AND MESMER
   TO CHARCOT   127

10. GERMAN PHYSIOLOGICAL PSYCHOLOGY
    IN THE AGE OF HELMHOLTZ   137

11. WUNDT AND EXPERIMENTAL PSYCHOLOGY   149

12. EARLY STUDIES OF MEMORY   174

13. THE INFLUENCE OF NEUROLOGY, 1860–1910   184

14. WILLIAM JAMES   192

15. STRUCTURAL AND FUNCTIONAL TYPES
OF PSYCHOLOGY   210

16. THE WÜRZBURG SCHOOL   225

17. EXPERIMENTS ON THE ACQUISITION OF SKILL   234

Part Three

Contemporary Psychological Systems

18. BEHAVIORISM   251

19. MODERN CONCEPTIONS OF ASSOCIATION   269

20. GESTALT   284

21. FIELD THEORY   297

22. SIGMUND FREUD   307

23. THE RESPONSE TO FREUD   331

Part Four

Some Representative Research Areas

24. THE MEASUREMENT OF INTELLIGENCE   351

25. PHYSIOLOGICAL PSYCHOLOGY   373

26. CHILD PSYCHOLOGY   389

27. SOCIAL PSYCHOLOGY   402

28. PERSONALITY   419

29. AN INTERPRETATION   430

Bibliography   447

Index of Names   449

Index of Subjects   458

PREFACE TO THE REVISED EDITION

IN REVISING this volume, the primary aim has simply been to bring the picture of the modern period up to date. The narrative has not been essentially altered as it relates to the period up to and through the work of Wundt and James—very roughly, through the nineteenth century. With the spread of the newer experimental and clinical conceptions during this century, however, the perspective originally given in 1929 now appears distorted. In consequence, the need has been very evident not only for supplementary material on the developments from 1929 to the present, but for a radical reconstruction in the whole approach. The result has been that the procedure followed has been fundamentally different from that used in revising the first part of the book. In the first half, a little has been added here and there about philosophical background, especially the enduring importance of Greek philosophy, but for the most part the changes are simply by way of clarification and removal of errors. Every chapter, however, dealing with the modern period has been rewritten, and in many instances there is only a vague aroma remaining from the earlier presentation.

In dealing with the modern era, a distinction has been attempted between theoretical systems on the one hand and research areas on the other. In Part Three, six chapters are devoted to some important theoretical systems of the modern period, with just enough reference to specific findings to make the conceptions vital and intelligible. In Part Four, several research areas are presented that seem to give a fair conception of the newer types of investigation which should change the complexion of psychology as a whole. Several other research areas, and in fact several other theoretical systems, might well be recorded as equally important.

Indeed, the aim of the book as a whole would collapse if an attempt were made to survey all the research areas, or to present all the theoretical systems. The book would be too long, and in numerous instances the author would find himself writing about things with which he has no firsthand experience at all. Moreover, there exist today adequate surveys, both in the psychological journals and in books, dealing with the theories and research areas which are of interest to large groups of psychologists. It is hoped that the *primary* sources in the footnotes, the *secondary* sources (References) at the ends of chapters, and the bibliography at the end of the text will adequately guide the reader who is hungry for more.

At the same time, it is appropriate to indicate some of the fields the omission of which might otherwise appear extraordinary. Nothing much is said here about the development since the third quarter of the nineteenth century of the psychology of the sensory processes. Anyone familiar with the degree of specialization involved, and the huge mass of material, will know why this is so. But the reader who wants a real perspective should follow the psychological journals to see how much he is missing. Of even greater importance as far as the masses of data are concerned is the relative neglect of the field of psychological testing, and all the specialized investigations which deal with the standardization and the interrelations of test data, as well as the rich theoretical systems, such as factor analysis, which have emerged in the psychological interpretation of such findings. Again, the specialist will not be surprised to find that it is deemed impossible to summarize all this in a few pages, and he knows where the appropriate surveys are to be found. But the less specialized student must be warned that he is not here seeing all of modern psychology. Several other obvious omissions need perhaps only to be named: industrial and vocational psychology; the applied psychology of illumination, noise, food, drugs, and sleep; abnormal psychology as a discipline apart from physiological or psychoanalytic or personality psychology; comparative psychology, as apart from the use of animals in the documentation of general psychological theory. Finally, what is said here about learning theory is hardly more than a clue to where the clues may be found to the clues to learning.

A year ago, I had serious misgivings as to the problem of "objectivity" in describing present-day trends. Would not the task be shot through with my own autisms and useful only as a documentation of the helplessness of the individual in extricating himself from the toils of his own personality? What saved me from this morass was the generosity of the Department of Psychology at the University of California, which asked me to talk for two hours about ways in which the history of psychology might be written. When I got through, they told me that to write this narrative at the present time could be nothing more than one person's perspective. I should simply forget my troubles, write on things as I saw them, and make no apology. I swallowed, and smiled, and went ahead.

Finally, it should be emphasized that psychology is in rapid motion and that to observe it through one's own binoculars as one stands on a moving and rolling deck involves resolutely forgetting what *is* at a given moment, and thinking only of the type and the direction of motion. Methods discovered and facts reported are of incidental interest. But the thing that really counts is transition, change, redirection, fresh groping. If the book fails at every count in giving a good snapshot, I shall not be worried at all—if it still succeeds in any degree in conveying directions in which psychology is growing.

I am most grateful for the very attentive reading and helpful criticism given me by E. R. Hilgard, who read the revised manuscript; likewise for critical and most helpful reading of galley proofs by Egon Brunswik, Allan Fromme, Ernest Haggard, and Leo Postman; and for help in the task of documentation given me by Robert Schweers.

G. M.

City College, New York
July 1948

PREFACE TO THE FIRST EDITION

PSYCHOLOGY, in the sense of reflection upon the nature and the activities of mind, is a very ancient discipline; one which reached great heights in ancient Greece, and has continued (in intimate relation with philosophy) with every phase of European civilization. During the nineteenth century this literary and philosophic psychology underwent profound changes, chiefly as a result of the progress of biology, from which both concepts and methods were freely borrowed. Many of its greatest students began to rely upon experimental and mathematical method, believing that psychology could become a science akin to other biological sciences. It is the purpose of this volume to trace the course of those changes in the nineteenth and twentieth centuries which have thus tended to transform psychology and to give it its present character.

To see our contemporary psychology in perspective becomes each year more difficult. A sketch of the development of the science since the beginning of the nineteenth century should help to some extent to give such a perspective. No purpose would be served, however, in seeking to duplicate the existing historical studies of psychology. Brett's three-volume *History of Psychology* presents a comprehensive and eminently readable account of psychology from the time of the ancients through the nineteenth century; the third volume of this work has proved of immense value in the present study. But, simply because our purposes have been different, the duplication of material is not great. Brett's work shows the interconnections of nineteenth-century psychology with that of earlier periods, with emphasis upon many problems that have not as yet been found amenable to just that experimental approach which chiefly concerns the present work. Moreover, about half of the material in the present volume belongs to the twentieth century, material excluded by the chronological limits which Brett imposed on his own work (Preface, Vol. II, p. 5). The nearer a decade is to our own time, the more attention I have given it; the plan might remind one of Mercator's projection.

I have, indeed, attempted a brief account of certain phases of psychological history from the seventeenth century to the beginning of the nineteenth century, in order to make the psychology of the early nineteenth century intelligible. No one could be more keenly aware than I am of the complete inadequacy of this sketch. Its purpose is not to present a unified picture of psychology during the seventeenth and eighteenth centuries, but to throw into relief a few movements whose influence was still strong at the opening of the nineteenth century. With the nineteenth century, and especially with the beginnings of experimental psychology, the quantity of psychological writing becomes so vast that a panoramic survey rather than a minute inspection of individuals and movements is all that can well be attempted. Even so, I have doubtless failed at many points; I shall be very grateful to readers who will call my attention to errors, whether great or small.

The scope of "psychology" has enlarged so much in the past few generations, and the present usage of the term varies so much with individual points of view, that the limits of our present work need to be defined. The reader will find an apparent overemphasis upon the results of research work as opposed to the progress of psychological theory. This is due, in part, to an attempt to reflect adequately the trend toward empirical, especially experimental, method. I have, however, another reason for the relative neglect of psychological theory within the period of contemporary psychology. A survey of psychological literature within any decade since the founding of Wundt's laboratory would show that very little of the speculative material has survived. Here and there a striking exception appears; a man of great magnitude impresses his outlook upon a whole generation, while some experimentalists weave their findings and their interpretations into a vital unity which stimulates and directs further research. But in general the framework of the science is constituted by its empirical methods and results; and though I trust I have not unduly neglected the thought of the builders, it is upon the character of the building that I would lay emphasis.

The central purpose I have kept before me in the treatment of the more recent phases of psychology is to show the constantly widening range of experimental and quantitative method, to include ever more complicated problems. As each new field is conquered, and as methods become standardized and research titles numbered by the hundreds, it ceases to be capable of treatment in a general volume such as this. The reader will find, for example, practically nothing about studies of sensation since the work of Helmholtz; nothing about psychophysics since Fullerton and Cattell; nothing about association tests since Jung's first work. In part I have imposed these limitations on the work because it was the only way in which justice could be done to the many fields of psychology; in part I have done so simply because good historical treatment is already available for each thoroughly established special field.

My intention, then, is to present in rough chronological order the conquest by scientific method of one research field after another. In accordance with this line of attack it is quite impossible to afford any just treatment to the philosophical forms of psychology, or to the problems of epistemology and theory of value. Much significant work ordinarily regarded as psychological must quite arbitrarily be excluded, if any sort of unified purpose is to be achieved. A single illustration will show where I have tried to set the boundary. In *The Analysis of Mind* (p. 15) Russell clearly indicates his purpose: "I am interested in psychology not so much for its own sake, as for the light that it may throw on the problem of knowledge." This does not prevent his making valuable psychological observations; but it is natural that a man's chief interest should determine the field of his chief contribution. This holds good of much contemporary philosophical work in which psychology is a tool rather than an end. And on the other hand, the *philosophy* of mind bears a relation to the history of psychology very similar to the relation which the philosophy of physical sciences bears to the history of these sciences; that is, wherever such philosophical contributions *shape the course* of the science, they may be regarded as a part of its history. The line of exclusion is of course an arbitrary one; some sort of line must nevertheless be drawn.

But whereas contemporary British, French, and American psychology can be portrayed in some degree of detachment from prevalent philosophical systems, no such separation is possible in relation to contemporary German psychology. Germany is witnessing in many quarters a widespread revolt against experimentalism, and a recourse to methods which are as fully philosophical as they are psychological. In the two concluding chapters, Dr. Heinrich Klüver describes the outlook and the methods of a number of schools of contemporary German psychology, which are more or less interwoven with contemporary philosophy.

It will not be possible to treat of the *applications* of psychology. Such applications do, of course, yield at times new psychological principles. It is only when they do so that they can be considered here.

Some years ago, I was puzzled by the reflection that there existed no historical approach to that contemporary psychology which arose in the nineteenth century as a result of the interaction of experimental physiology, psychiatry, the theory of evolution, and the social sciences, constantly working upon certain materials from the history of philosophy, and guided by progress in the physical sciences and statistical method. Now, having made the attempt, I am no longer puzzled. Probably no one who has mastered the vast materials necessary for such an undertaking would have the courage to make a beginning. Perhaps it is just as well that the first venture in this direction should be made by one who because he sees but few paths, trudges the more cheerfully on the way. For the strange silences and vast lacunae which mark these pages I may therefore make no apology. For the sins of deliberate omission, however, I cannot so easily be comforted. The sins become more and more grievous as the work approaches present-day psychology. When one considers that the *Psychological Index* carries thousands of titles annually, one may well ask by what right a mere handful of these are mentioned. I can but mention three factors influencing my decisions. First, where a movement is represented by many titles I have preferred to quote one individual's research, making his methods and results clear, rather than to indulge in generalizations which the reader would find difficult to verify. Secondly, I have chosen as best I could in terms of the importance which attaches to each problem; an elaborate investigation extending a known principle might well be omitted, while a brief and inadequate treatment of a significant new problem might receive attention. Thirdly, and perhaps most important of all, I have chosen in accordance with my own conception of psychology and my own personal interests. When beginning to prepare the volume I fondly dreamed of an absolutely impersonal and objective record of modern psychological history. Fairness in presenting the work and the opinions of others I have hoped to attain; but I am convinced that the tasks of selection and emphasis make a purely objective record, at least for the present author, quite impossible.

Much as I am indebted to Brett's volumes, I am even more deeply grateful for his generous aid in reading the present volume in manuscript, in rectifying errors, and in giving valuable suggestions. The same generous gift of time and counsel has been given by Professors Margaret Floy Washburn, K. S. Lashley, Horace B. English, Harry L. Hollingworth, Albert T. Poffenberger, and Robert S. Woodworth. I cannot adequately express the degree of my indebtedness to each of them. To my students for whom this material was first prepared I owe constant inspiration; especially to Shailer Lawton and George Schoonhoven. For assistance in preparing the manuscript I thank Dr. Georgene Hoffman Seward, Miss H. A. Dandy, Miss Louise Sobye, and Mrs. Enrica Tunnell; Harvey W. Culp, Donald W. Eckley, Walter A. Hall, and Sam Rubinson; and, most of all, my wife and my mother.

G. M.

October 1928

PART ONE

The Antecedents of Modern Psychology

Chapter 1

THE INTELLECTUAL
BACKGROUND

Their fine ways of explaining Nature mechanically charmed me.
LEIBNITZ

F ROM color theories to defense mechanisms, from the functions
of a white rat's vibrissae to the mystic's sense of unutterable
revelation, from imaginary playmates to partial correlations—
wherein lies that unity of subject matter which leads us to speak,
compactly enough, of "contemporary psychology"? From behaviorism or Gestalt psychology to psychoanalysis or the objective measurement of character, the eye wanders over an interminable range of
experiments, measurements, hypotheses, dogmas, disconnected facts,
and systematic theories. In a sense it is true to say that through all
this vast mélange the very birth cry of the infant science is still re-
sounding. In another sense psychology is as old as civilization, and
this seething multitude of investigations and opinions springs from
a rich and variegated history. The complexity of contemporary
psychology suggests that its understanding may well require the
use of that *genetic* method which it has itself repeatedly demanded in
recent years. Whatever difficulties there may be in finding unity in
the various psychological disciplines, there is at least one unity to
which we can cling for orientation and perspective, for appreciation
and synthesis; and this is the tranquil unity of history.

The centuries since Descartes and Hobbes have woven together
the psychology of antiquity and the physical science of the Renaissance, the nineteenth-century triumphs of biological science and
the twentieth-century genius for measurement, while a multitude of
social forces, as well as strokes of individual genius, have shown
unities of method and conception underlying all the problems of
psychology, and indeed of life itself. For experimental psychology

sprang from the conception of a fundamental unity between psychology and physiology, and behaviorism from an attempt to make that unity more complete; psychoanalysis is an insistence on the fundamental unity of normal and abnormal, and of conscious and unconscious motives; Gestalt psychology strives to understand those Aristotelian "forms" which contribute the patterns of both the things of the physical world and the data of immediate experience.

Yet each of these movements toward unity is itself but a more comprehensive and systematic expression of movements that have been with us at least since the seventeenth century: behaviorism, for example, a refinement of Descartes' automatism and Hobbes's mechanism; the emphasis on the unconscious, a reminiscence of Leibnitz's idea of perceptions of which we are not aware; experimental psychology itself an application of that experimental and quantitative conception of nature which Galileo and Newton so brilliantly set forth. The venerable antiquity of psychology shows through the gloss of its newness, and makes the finality of each new emphasis seem a little less absolute. Not, indeed, that there is great usefulness in asserting that each achievement of science gives but a new name to the discovery of some Hellenic thinker. But psychology has made its recent rapid advances only because of the richness of its own history, and because of the centuries of general scientific progress which lie immediately behind us.

THE BACKGROUND IN GREEK PHILOSOPHY

A historical approach to contemporary psychology necessitates at the outset a glance at the psychology of preliterate peoples, followed by a study of the great traditions handed down from the world of Greek life and thought, and of the manner in which they have been understood and used by the men of the modern era.[1]

Among the efforts of primitive men to understand their world, their efforts at the construction of a psychology must be included. The motions of the heavenly bodies are no more impressive than are

[1] The scope and purpose of this volume do not permit anything more than the most fragmentary references to the psychology of the ancient and of the medieval world. The reader who would grasp the psychology of the Renaissance in its relation to the previous history of psychology should read a comprehensive history of philosophy, and, in conjunction with it, Dessoir, M., *Outlines of the History of Psychology* (1912) or Vols. I–II of Brett, G. S., *A History of Psychology* (1914–21). In this and in later footnotes, foreign titles appear in English if the work has been translated; but all dates are the dates of original publications. (In the References at ends of Chapters, dates are the dates of available library editions.)

the rhythms of waking and sleeping, the rise and fall of emotion; the deviations from normality which invite the labors of the shaman stimulate also the speculations of the philosopher.

While primitive cultures differ as much in their psychology as they do in their basketry and pottery, or their kinship systems, they show a general preoccupation with one recurrent problem—the nature and attributes of the soul. The dramatic difference between a sleeping and a waking man invites the thought that something has gone out and then returned. The awakening man may recount a battle in which he took part while, manifestly, his body lay still upon the ground. In illness, especially in delirium or coma, something seems to disappear which may, upon recovery, reappear. The conception of a psychic entity—a detachable soul, we may say—makes sense to him. And such an opinion is greatly strengthened by the fact that those who dream and those who go into and out of coma or delirium or trance may encounter those who have died. Apparitions, hallucinatory forms, of the deceased are also familiar. Although lacking solidity, the apparition seems to perceive and to understand. The opening lines of Homer's *Iliad* refer to the souls which in combat have departed to Hades; and when Achilles is visited in the nether world, he is still, in a sense, the Achilles once known.

The conceptions summarized here are usually called "dualistic," for they make of soul and body two distinct things; two things capable, indeed, of continuous interaction, but sharply and ultimately distinct as substances. There is a physical body and there is a ghost or detachable soul. Primitive psychology therefore usually has a place for the survival of the soul after bodily death, though the further abstraction of immortality—that is, permanent existence—is usually sketchy or completely absent. The applied psychology of primitive man includes devices for luring or coercing the soul to return to the body from which it has wandered, and devices for strengthening the soul and enabling it to withstand life's difficulties.

All of these conceptions are perfectly evident in the religious systems of the Greeks in the first millennium before Christ: the Olympian religion, the mystery religions, and the speculative religious systems of the classical period. We shall, in commenting upon these three, emphasize both the thought and the language of Gilbert Murray's *Five Stages of Greek Religion*. When the curtain rises on the drama as revealed by the Homeric poems, a band of vigorous, magnificent "swashbuckling" warriors from the Danube basin is besieging a prosperous city on the east shore of the Aegean, and the gods and goddesses of their pantheon take a fully human role in the

fracas. Within a few centuries, however, these long-haired bucca-
neers who produced such epic poetry have settled in the Greek
Peninsula, and have melted, both biologically and culturally, into
the dark-skinned native population, a people of majestic architecture
and sculpture, and vast, dark, inexpressible thoughts, as betokened
by the worship of nature in all its awesome aspects. The resulting
cultural unity is neither naïve and childlike nor dark and mystical,
but radiant, magnificent, subtle, inquisitive, and buoyant, turning
ever to new problems with an audacity matched only by the
capacity to give order and system to all that emerges.

The result is Greek philosophy, with its systems of interpretation
of nature and, within these, its types of interpretation of the human
body and soul. It is to be expected that the primitive "ghost soul,"
as Dessoir calls it, should appear in their speculations, and that early
Greek psychology should take the form of a relatively sophisticated
study of the doings of souls and of the laws of their behavior. When
therefore we find, along with those philosophers who reduce everything to water, or to fire, or to motion, or to numbers, those who
reduce everything to mind, we may view it as an attempt to reconcile the traditional mind-body dualism with a monism which insists
that mind is at the root of everything, all of nature making one
harmonious whole. When, moreover, the Orphic mysteries provide
expressly for the welfare of the soul, both within the body and after
its departure, and when they encourage belief in the independent
existence and collaboration of souls with one another after death,
and when, finally, Plato tells us that souls perceive more clearly and
reach to higher realities when freed of the body, we are encountering
the refinement, rather than the abandonment, of the rudiments of
primitive psychology.

But now we must look more closely at the rise of *types of psychology* among the thinkers of Hellas; in particular, at three conceptions of the mind developed by Greek thinkers which are found still
embedded in the tissue of our modern psychological doctrine: the
conceptions associated with the names of Democritus, Plato, and
Aristotle.[2]

The primary effort of the Greek philosophers in the sixth and
seventh centuries B.C. was to find a central substance or principle
from which all else could be derived. Material substances were sometimes chosen; sometimes the primary clue, as we have noted, was
motion. Extraordinary indeed was the material atomism of Democ-

---

[2] A very rich source is Stratton, G. M., *Theophrastus and the Greek Physiological
Psychology before Aristotle* (1917).

ritus. Democritus, impressed with the beauty and the clarity of mechanical explanations of nature, conceived the world to be made up of tiny atoms or particles in motion, their interaction being responsible for all that we observe. The particles which make up the soul are very small and smooth, but they are material particles, for all that; and since they are dispersed at death, there is no survival.

But in protest against all such orderly attempts to understand the world, there arose a skepticism which denied the possibility of knowing ultimate things, or even of knowing about the knowing process itself. The Sophists found in human experience a meaningless flow of experiences behind which neither outer reality nor any stable inner principle could be found. It was in this period of conflict between absolutists, who knew the final answers, and Sophists, who doubted whether any answers could ever be found, that Socrates with his conversational, critical method appeared—a man of extraordinary warmth and humanity, extraordinary tenacity in the quest for truth, who, as he appears in the dialogues written by his pupil Plato, confronts the Sophists and the skeptics and erects the architecture within which most subsequent Western philosophy and psychology develop.

Plato introduces us to a clarification and a full defense of the already ancient belief that soul and body are fundamentally different things ("psychophysical dualism"). While with primitive man and with the early Greeks, the *immaterial* soul had been confusedly regarded as possessing some qualities of a more or less *physical* nature—for example, it could be seen—the Platonic conception sharpens the distinction between soul and body, making them absolutely distinct kinds of things. The soul, moreover, being immaterial, may apprehend an ideal world, and it survives the death of the body. Among its manifest powers of transcending the concrete immediacy of physical objects is its capacity to deal with abstract relationships; the world of mathematics (as the Pythagoreans had earlier said) is a higher, more real world than the world of the senses; true philosophers must be mathematicians. As seen through Plato's eyes, the Socratic dialogues demonstrate the reality of the soul and the reality of knowledge about those things most precious and congenial to it; namely, the *universals* which transcend all concrete particulars—the beauty, the goodness, the mathematical relationships which represent the eternal and the ultimately real. The primitive man's ghost soul, winnowed and chastened in the fire of critical inquiry as to the nature of material and immaterial things, emerges as a real immaterial entity capable of knowing what is real.

We might expect, in this connection, a rich yield of psychological observation, based both upon introspection and upon studies of human behavior. This is not actually a task of primary interest to Plato. Since Plato's chief interest is in ultimates, we must not expect to find in him a rich yield of psychological detail. But such a yield was already coming from the medical men of the period. And an abundance of concrete psychological detail, in an ingenious new theoretical formulation, appears in the work of Plato's pupil Aristotle.

Aristotle was the sort of universal genius who makes three-paragraph summaries seem peculiarly lightheaded and perverse. His pertinence for the history of psychology lies in three contributions. First, in his orderly, architectural construction of a system of knowledge in which the study of the soul may be brought into relation, both empirically and rationally, with the study of living organisms. Second, in his definition of the nature of the soul and its activities in such fashion as to make the soul an expression of the living creature, and the living creature an expression of the soul, extirpating every rudiment of the dualism of soul and body which primitive man on the one hand, and his great master Plato on the other hand, had so carefully defined. Third, in his settling down to the workaday task of describing and interpreting human experience and behavior in concrete terms. The first and second contributions appear in the *De anima*.[3] The third task, appearing in the *Parva naturalia*, is expressed in vivid and readable accounts of youth and old age; of waking, sleeping, and dreaming; of the psychology of men and of women; of the processes of remembering and recognizing; and of that world of occult phenomena to which divination and prophetic dreams seemed to point; while in his volume on the orator (*De oratore*) he deals with the emotions the orator strives to sway, and in his *Ethics* and *Politics* he deals with problems of self-control and with interpersonal relations.

Aristotle was dissatisfied with the great gulf his master had placed between soul and body. Yet at the same time he could find little value in the mechanical theories of Democritus. He aimed to discover the intimate relation of mental and physical processes, yet to define the mental so as to show its differences from the physical. His solution lay in terms of a conception of *functions* carried out by the living organism. The raw stuff, or matter, of which a thing is made does not tell us what it is, nor what it does; but gives it *form*,

[3] Some of Aristotle's books are best known to the English-speaking world under their Latin titles.

and we can define it in terms of what it can do. Matter and form are always found together, but it is only through form that the potentialities inherent in matter can be actualized. The organs of the body would be mere matter were it not for the form which specifies how they must respond. Each of them can be said to have its own form; or, in a sense, its own soul. When the eye sees, we may say that seeing is its soul; the eye of a statue has no soul, for it does not see. The *potential* seeing which is an attribute of our eyes, even as we lie asleep, becomes *actual* when we open them and look at our environment. In the same way the potentiality of being seen is inherent in the objects around us; this potentiality is actualized when we see them. The living organism and the objects of its environment come together, are mutually responsive, actualized in reference one to the other.

We may properly use the term "soul" not only for the function of each organ, but for the living organism as a whole; the soul or mind is the *form* of the whole organism. The mind is not isolated from the thing known. In knowing, "the mind is the object." This gives us a functional definition of mind or soul. *Mind is a process;* it is defined in terms of what it does. The environmental world can be fully defined only in terms of what we do as a response to it, just as we ourselves must be defined in terms of our interactions with it. Organism and environment are not independent but are two aspects of an interacting system of events.

Aristotle proceeds to a close study of the senses; of learning and memory; of emotion; of imagination and reasoning. Most influential of all his specific teachings is to the effect that we remember things by virtue of "contiguity, similarity, and contrast" (reference to contiguity and similarity had been made by Plato). We think of Paul because he was with Peter, or because he is like Peter, or because he contrasts with Peter. This doctrine of *association* later became the doctrine that all the operations of the mind depend upon associations laid down in experience.

During the great philosophical days of Socrates, Plato, and Aristotle, the Greek city-state, heart and core of Greek civilization, had undergone one mortal crisis after another. Sparta had overwhelmed Athens; Thebes had crushed Sparta. Thereupon Philip of Macedon and his son Alexander, whom Aristotle personally had tutored, had reduced the Greek world to vassalage, then spread through the world whatever was Greek in the civilization they knew. As the period of insecurity, or even despair, set in—a "failure of nerve," as Gilbert Murray calls it—those who had learned to philosophize went on philosophizing. Now, however, instead of the exultation of spirit which marked the absolutists, and the breezy casualness which marked the Sophists and the skeptics, there set in a long period of intellectual disillusionment, in which the primary aim was to find comfort through philosophy in a world whose reassuring marks of stability had disappeared.

Take, for example, the simple pleasure-pain philosophy which Socrates had espoused in the "Gorgias," in which we learn that the good man, though he be humiliated or tortured, has a kind of happiness which makes him, in a literal sense, more fortunate than the base man who is rewarded by mere wealth and status. In the period of disillusion and skepticism, this exuberant idealism seems a sort of forced heroics. The calm and honest Epicurus, looking sadly at the ruins of what was Greek civilization, prefers to say simply that men, born into a world of sorrow, will do well to find as much happiness as they can, and to make happiness, while they can achieve it, their goal. The struggle of Aristotle to unify soul and body becomes, for others, a threat to the hope of immortality; they return to a body-mind dualism which will offer some hope that after passing through this vale of tears they may find eternal happiness. While at Alexandria, intellectual center of the world in the succeeding centuries, great strides were soon thereafter made in the physical and biological sciences, the Mediterranean world settled slowly into a period of rigidity and increasing hopelessness. This, of course, was not the viewpoint of the Roman gentleman of the first century B.C., nor, indeed, of the emperors and their courts at any time; but from our vantage point, it is clear that the Roman Empire represented a slow but steady crushing of elemental emotional and aesthetic expression. The fire on the Greek hearth flickered more and more uncertainly, and after the defeat of the Maccabees, the Hebrew struggle for national freedom went the same way, while countless peoples about the Mediterranean, assimilating Roman civilization, learned also to acquiesce in the stolidity, the dead-level respectability, of Roman commerce and law. We should not expect "observations on man," psychologies worthy of the name, to appear.

It is thoroughly consonant with our expectations that the one kind of psychology which did take shape after the demise of the Greek creative spirit was that of the Church Fathers, based upon despair regarding this world, including despair regarding the goodness and the value of the living body, and appropriately saturated with two dominant motifs: first, Plato's mind-body dualism, and second, a moralistic prejudice against everything in human nature which seemed to bespeak a relation to the animal kingdom. Hence the intense preoccupation with problems of sin, guilt, restitution, and authority. Partly, of course, it was because Christianity spoke to men and women who had but little to live for: slaves, soldiers, fishermen, and the lowest level of artisans and farmers. The conception that the whole world was sick had, however, permeated every class. The need for the effacement of sin and for a sense of purification and reunion with the divine, known everywhere through the Mediterranean world through the flourishing mystery religions, was much more fully and adequately expressed in the Christian communion, through which oneness with the Son of God and the renewal of childlike intimacy with a loving Father was patently available to every earnest seeker, be he slave or emperor. The psychology of the Church Fathers, slowly taking shape in the writings of Paul, Origen, and Augustine, dominated philosophy until the full revival of Aristotelianism in the twelfth and thirteenth centuries. It was a psychology anchored in Platonic dualism, in the sense of guilt and the need of restitution, and in the conception of the will—both the will of God and the will of man—as cardinal instruments for weal or woe. The will, of course, transcended, as did everything else in the inner nature of the soul, those principles of explanation which held generally for natural objects.

The rediscovery of Aristotle in the twelfth and thirteenth centuries led to an interest in naturalism. The alert concern with physical and medical realities, so characteristic of the age, led to the revival of a scientific way of looking at nature. The human soul became articulated with other things encountered in everyday experience. Aristotle's psychology became the center of that vast new enterprise which sought to reconstruct the philosophy of the Church Fathers in a naturalistic direction. This is stating the issue, of course, not as a man of the thirteenth century would have stated it, but as it looks to us today.

The immediate practical test of the new Aristotelian philosophy, as shown definitely in the work of Thomas Aquinas, was its capacity to reconcile the humanity, urbanity, and naturalism of Aristotle with the body-mind dualism of Plato and the Church Fathers, and to make a theologically acceptable treatise representing a union of ancient wisdom with those special doctrines upon which the salvation of the Christian soul depended. But once Aristotle had been rediscovered, and once he had been made the heart of scientific enterprise, the clock could not be set back; and from this time forward it is Aristotle very much more than Plato and the Church

Fathers who shows the way to that modern psychology, that essentially Greek psychology, which took shape in the Renaissance
period. For Greek psychology, especially the psychology of Aristotle, was brought into sharper focus, and became central in the
renewed efforts of men to understand man's own nature.

SCIENCE IN THE RENAISSANCE

Our problem now is to take closer account of the intellectual
temper of that new dawn of science and discovery which began with
the end of feudalism, and to study the manner in which this new
intellectual temper made use of the great traditions. The manorial
system, with its self-sufficient economic units, disintegrated as the
military power of the knight in armor was successfully challenged,
and as traffic in commodities such as wool rapidly enlarged the area
within which commerce was feasible. Travel by land and by sea
became safer and more profitable. Moreover, the Crusaders of the
twelfth and thirteenth centuries had discovered and carried back to
Europe much of the civilization of the Near East, in which many
elements of classical culture had been embedded. New phases of culture showed themselves; the new universities of the thirteenth century promoted the study of the classics, and a great artistic revival,
the Proto-Renaissance, spread over southern Europe. The true
Renaissance may be said to have begun as early as the fourteenth
century, and reached its greatest height in the sixteenth.

It gloried in explorations of all kinds, both physical and intellectual. But perhaps the realm of geographical discovery is as representative and enlightening as any. A beautiful epitome of the whole
movement is found in the coinage of the Spanish Empire, changing
as a result of the explorations of Columbus. In the days before the
discovery of America, some of the coins of Spain bore the words
Ne Plus Ultra: There Is Nothing Beyond. Spain and the Pillars of
Hercules were the edge of the world. Then came Columbus and the
age of the explorers. The inscription was changed. *Ne* was removed,
and the words read *Plus Ultra*. There *was* "more beyond."

For everywhere men sought for the new, both in the new appreciation of the culture of antiquity, and in the search for new knowledge
and new possessions, material and immaterial. Among the more
obvious expressions of the movement was the search for new routes
to the Far East, and the beginning of the building of empires to
include the "New World," the colonization of which was one of the
great achievements of the sixteenth and seventeenth centuries. As

the Holy Roman Empire slowly decayed, the new nation-states which came into being reached out for lands and wealth in the far corners of the world. During this period of discovery and expansion, the economic changes mentioned above went on at an accelerated pace, and Europe was caught in the vast upheaval of that Commercial Revolution which followed upon the collapse of the manorial system, the growth of towns, and the development of trade by land and sea, deriving from new routes to the East and from the general improvement in the means of communication. The political revolution in which Cromwell was the leader and Charles I was executed, and even more definitely the Revolution of 1688, in which the House of Orange was called to the throne, marked the emancipation of the commercial classes in Britain. This was the end of the traditional "divine right of kings," and the beginning of the self-assertion of a middle class, the great trading class which grew up as these economic changes occurred.

The spirit of unrest and of discovery became more and more conspicuous in the interests, spirit, and modes of thought of those who devoted themselves to art, to letters, to philosophy, and to practical affairs. In science a revival had begun as early as the twelfth century. The first great achievement was that of Copernicus (1543). His doctrine that the earth and the planets moved in circles about the sun (the revival of a theory dating from the third century B.C.) was the beginning of modern astronomy. In him and in his immediate successors can be seen the struggle and the ultimate union of the two great forces which generated modern science: the belief in a logically and aesthetically perfect "natural order" from which the laws of nature can be deduced, and the determination to put every theory to an empirical test, a test permitting a decision through direct observation.

For after Copernicus came Tycho Brahe, who spent his life recording with scrupulous exactness such observations on the motions of the heavenly bodies as the best instruments of his time permitted. The Copernican system did not fit his observations, and he did not guess that the reason for the inconsistency lay in the fact that the orbit of the earth's motion about the sun is not a circle but an ellipse. Even Tycho, the observer, believed that heavenly bodies must of necessity move in perfect curves, and to him the perfect curve was the circle. Nevertheless, in the hands of Tycho and his immediate successors, science was beginning to take on a definitely empirical cast, the spirit of indifference to the perfection of theory, and eagerness for accurate data as the first step toward a sound hypothesis. In the work of Kepler there was a combination of the work of these two predecessors. He succeeded in showing that Copernicus was essentially correct, but that the figures accumulated by Tycho necessitated the assumption of elliptical rather than circular orbits. With Kepler came into being the first great fusion of inductive with mathematical method.

A somewhat similar step was being taken by Gilbert in England in the study of magnetism. For him, direct observation was the basic method; he varied the conditions of observation in a way genuinely deserving the modern term "experimental." The foundation was being laid for the development of experimental science; and in many branches of physical science such investigations were soon under way. The work done by Gilbert was admired by Galileo, an ardent believer in the Platonic (and the Pythagorean) doctrine that mathematics is the clue to nature's laws, who nevertheless had the most extraordinary genius for the invention of methods for empirical demonstration of such laws. At the end of the sixteenth century and in the opening decades of the seventeenth, Galileo extended the experimental method and went far beyond Gilbert both in the range and in the importance of his observations. Galileo and his followers concerned themselves primarily with the fundamental problems of mechanics and optics.

In all this group we can distinguish the leaders and the trumpeters, those collecting data and those blaring forth to the world what had been and what was to be done. Francis Bacon became the great herald of the new empirical spirit as it fought its way among the many forces of the Renaissance. He failed, unfortunately, to grasp the significance of many inductive studies going on about him, such as those of Gilbert; nevertheless, as a systematizer and an interpreter he contributed much to the rapid spread of enthusiasm for empirical methods.

The greatest combination of mathematical with empirical method in the seventeenth century was that effected by the genius of Sir Isaac Newton. Newton's work consisted both in the development of new mathematical methods and in the continuation of the work of Kepler in the elaborate logical use of experimental results. He utilized the empirical data of others as well as his own, but contributed important original experiments, such as those with the prism demonstrating that white light may be split up so as to yield the spectral colors. Newton contributed much also to the philosophy of science, giving expression to a system of thought which could be used coherently in the advancement of knowledge. He sought to clarify those fundamental conceptions with which, as he conceived it, science must deal: space, time, mass, motion, force, and so on. Thus he well exemplified three different kinds of scientific work in the seventeenth century: the use of mathematical method; the impulse to vary conditions—that is, to experiment; and the study of the philosophical significance of the new acquisitions.

A few words about the organization of science. The only nation which had organized a definite means of scientific co-operation by the second half of the seventeenth century was France, and its work was confined chiefly to the city of Paris. The French Academy of Sciences began to receive royal support in 1671, which furthered the collaboration of investigators. The new impetus to scientific work given by the French Crown is in striking contrast to the situation in Britain. Newton worked practically alone. He helped to form a Royal Society, which was intended to give better means of co-operation, but he remained far greater than his own circle; and pitifully inadequate funds were granted by the Crown. The same condition existed in the German states. Germany, of course, was not a political unit, and naturally enough there was even less co-operation among its scattered men of science than in France and Great Britain, although the German university system was destined in the eighteenth century to serve as a center for the awakening interest in scientific effort. Galileo, in Italy, had worked alone, and under the suspicion of Church and State. The energies of Spain and Portugal were being expended in explorations and conquests in the New World. So if we are inclined to ask why a given "discovery" was announced when the facts were already known to contemporary investigators, the answer is that almost until the beginning of the nineteenth century scientific progress throughout western Europe was, with few exceptions, the fruit of the efforts of individuals, frequently working without knowledge of kindred efforts in their own and other lands, and destined to be forgotten until some scientist or scholar of a later day stumbled upon their work.

This holds strikingly true in the biological sciences. The revival of classical medicine, particularly in the Italian universities, was proceeding actively in the sixteenth century, and the desire to describe accurately, to understand in terms of observation rather than by speculative and deductive methods, was just as marked in biological science as in other fields, though generalizations were more difficult. The empirical movement was active generally, and led in the seventeenth century to the spread of epoch-making clinical and postportem studies in anatomy. The reader will remember, for instance,

Rembrandt's painting "The Anatomy Lesson," a representation of the then novel and amazing art of dissecting the human body. The same clinical spirit was manifested in the study of mental diseases; Burton's *Anatomy of Melancholy* (1621) gave descriptions of familiar types of insanity. But the greatest discovery in the field of medicine was Harvey's demonstration in 1628 of the circulation of the blood. Before the time of Harvey the prevalent doctrine was Galen's theory of red and blue blood, each type of blood being supposed to pulsate back and forth. Harvey demonstrated by actual experimentation that the blue blood became red in the course of circulation. And, almost at the same time, this discovery was paralleled in the field of instrumentation by the great improvement of the microscope in the hand of the Dutchman Leeuwenhoek, opening new fields to biological science.

REFERENCES

Aristotle, *Aristotle's Psychology,* trans. by W. A. Hammond (1902)

Baldwin, J. M., *History of Psychology: A Sketch and an Interpretation,* Putnam, 1913

Boring, Edwin G., *A History of Experimental Psychology,* Century, 1929

Brett, George S., *A History of Psychology,* 3 vols., London, 1914–1921

Dennis, Wayne, ed., *Readings in the History of Psychology,* Appleton-Century, 1948

Dessoir, Max, *Outlines of the History of Psychology,* Macmillan, 1912

Fuller, B. A. G., *A History of Philosophy,* rev. ed., 2 vols. in 1, Holt, 1945

Hulin, W. S., *A Short History of Psychology,* Holt, 1934

Pillsbury, Walter B., *The History of Psychology,* Norton, 1929

Russell, Bertrand, *History of Western Philosophy,* Simon and Schuster, 1946

Spearman, Charles E., *Psychology down the Ages,* Macmillan, 1937

Chapter 2

THE SEVENTEENTH CENTURY

Heraclitus . . . says . . . that it is by something in motion that what is in motion is known; for he, like most philosophers, conceived all that exists to be in motion. ARISTOTLE

THE SCIENTIFIC MOVEMENT of the seventeenth century was empirical; its appeal was primarily to observation rather than to authority. Its most fruitful concepts were mechanical; that is to say, they dealt with the movement of bodies in space.

The development of objective observation had immediate and definite effects on psychology. Much of the psychology which resulted from this new spirit of inquiry was, of course, the restatement or the reinterpretation of the psychology of antiquity. A considerable amount of original psychological work was, however, done in the seventeenth and eighteenth centuries. The psychology of these centuries, though influenced by specific discoveries, especially those pertaining to mechanics, was not so much guided by *specific* scientific developments as by the general trend toward empiricism, and the desire to understand man in those aspects of nature which are open to direct observation.

DESCARTES

The first great name in the psychology of the Renaissance was that of Descartes. He was an international figure whose contributions ranged from mathematics to physiology. He was interested in the nervous system, the study of which had begun to make new strides. Concerning himself especially with the sensory and motor functions of nerves and with the significance of these functions for psychological theory, he attempted a description of the relation of nervous processes to mental processes and behavior.[1]

[1] *The Passions of the Soul* (1650).

He utilized the current notion of "spirits" which by their motion within the nerve substance bring about the movements of the body. He sought to show how such conduction within the body could account for automatic and habitual acts. Descartes distinguished first between animal and human behavior. He held that animals were simply machines: their bodies were controlled by physical laws. If this were true, then there must be specific mechanisms provided for these acts. Nervous and muscular reactions followed predictably from the stimulation of the sense organs; incoming and outgoing pathways provided fixed channels for the arousal of the animal's whole repertory of acts. This conception of the *reflex* is the groundwork which psychologists of a physiological turn of mind have used ever since on which to build up an explanation of the more complicated activities of life. Modern mechanistic psychology grew out of this seventeenth-century conception—greatly stimulated, of course, by progress in the science of mechanics in the hands of Newton and his followers.

But the explanation of *human* acts seemed to require another approach. These acts Descartes divided into two groups, those of a mechanical nature and those of a rational nature. The rational acts were utterly distinct from the mechanical, and made possible judgment, choice, and will. This theory thus involved a sharp cleavage between animal functions and higher functions. Descartes retained the soul as an entity outside the spatial order; it was "unextended." The lucidity of his treatment helped to make clear the opposition between strict dualists who accepted his distinction and monists, like Spinoza, who believed that soul and body are ultimately one—two *aspects* of one reality.[2]

Descartes himself recognized serious difficulties in his position. If mind and matter were totally different things, how could there be a working relation between the two? How could the body act upon the soul, and vice versa? This question caused much trouble; he had to look about for the point of interaction, the "seat of the soul." Some of the ancients had placed the soul in one place, some in another. But medical studies had begun to point clearly to the importance of the brain. The trouble with the brain for Descartes's purposes was that it is "paired," right and left, and divided more finely into smaller structures which are arranged symmetrically on either side. But the pineal gland, the functions of which were unknown, is deeply embedded in the center of the brain. There is only one pineal gland; and it necessarily follows, thought Descartes, that it is the

[2] *Ethics* (1677).

seat of the soul. This gland acted to transmit physical stimuli to the soul, and to transmit impulses from the soul to the body. The soul's control of the body was through mechanical regulation of the connections between sensory and motor impulses in the nerves; the connection between the different sensory and motor impulses was controlled by the movements of the pineal gland. "This gland is variously affected by the soul . . . it impels the spirits which surround it toward the pores of the brain, which discharge them by means of the nerves upon the muscles." [3] This assumption reduced the problem of the action of the soul directly to control through the pineal gland, but no theory was vouchsafed as to the way in which an immaterial entity could exercise such mechanical effects. This dualism, or fundamental distinction between soul and body, so emphatically outlined by Descartes, has been the center of many psychological systems. But the acuteness of the difficulty was perhaps more apparent after Descartes's bold selection of the organ through which interaction was effected.

One other feature of Descartes's work, significant for later psychology, is the analysis of the emotions. The "passions" are treated almost like mechanical events; they are explained through motion in the brain, the blood, the "spirits," and the vital organs. Descartes's account of the "passions of the soul" reduces the complexity of emotional life to six elementary passions: wonder, love, hate, desire, joy, sadness. This process of dissecting human nature into elemental emotional experiences or impulses, which in their combination give all possible modes of emotion, is so fascinating that it has never ceased to occupy psychologists.[4] Yet the emotions listed by Descartes were described as though they were intellectual functions. Love, he believed, depends upon one's calculation of the pleasure an object may bring, and hate depends upon expected evil. The nonrational was translated into terms of the rational. The nineteenth-century "economic man," who avoided pain and sought pleasure, grew slowly and inevitably from this type of rationalism.

The two great successors to Descartes in France in the hundred years which followed are associated respectively with Descartes's idea of the nature of emotion and with his conception of the machinelike nature of the reflex response. Malebranche so fully understood the *physiological definition of emotion* that he may be regarded as a fore-

[3] *The Passions of the Soul*, Pt. I, Art. XXXIV.

[4] Among the better-known attempts are those of Hobbes, Cabanis, Gall, Lotze, James, McDougall, and Watson.

runner of the James-Lange theory (page 198).[5] La Mettrie showed that if animals are automata the same logic applies to men.[6] Descartes's interpretation of behavior in machine terms must be ruthlessly followed through to the end, granting man no immunities. La Mettrie used the term "machine" very broadly; he gave abundant consideration to the role of chemical as well as of mechanical processes in the body.

In the meantime, the extraordinary Spinoza, grinding away at lenses in the Netherlands, unknown to the world, was working out a philosophy of mind and body rich in ideas of a strangely modern cast—ideas far too modern to have any effect on his seventeenth-century contemporaries. Mind and body are aspects of one reality, so that physiology and psychology are utterly fused; memory is a sequence of mental events corresponding to a sequence of bodily events (arising from earlier impressions made on the body). The emotions and the motives of mankind are deeply irrational and often operate unconsciously so as to lead to self-deception. Spinoza's posthumously published *Ethics* (1677) was destined to sink deep into the minds of philosophers. But the intellectualistically minded men of his own era were not interested in the notion of unconscious motivation, and the unknown lens-grinder had no such easy access to an audience as had Descartes.

LEIBNITZ

In Germany in the meantime, soon after Descartes had worked out his application of physics and its methods to psychology, a somewhat similar approach was made by another mathematical genius, Leibnitz.[7] He likewise sought an answer to the problem of the relation of mind to body. Leibnitz held, as did Spinoza, that it was impossible to accept the doctrine of an immaterial soul acting upon a material body. The relation of mind and body was actually stated by Leibnitz in terms nearly as dualistic as those of Descartes, but dispensing altogether with the troublesome concept of interaction. There is, Leibnitz taught, a body which follows its own laws; that is, the laws of mechanics. The acts of a human body are just as mechanical as are those of an animal. We must explain *all* acts of the human body in terms of known physical causes. Mental acts and sequences must on the other hand be explained in terms of mental

[5] *Recherche de la vérité* (1674).
[6] *Man a Machine* (1748).
[7] *A New System of Nature* (1695).

causes. The soul carries on its acts without any direct reaction upon the body. Mental life displays an orderly sequence of events, while bodily life does the same; but these two never interact. His analogy was that of two clocks so constructed that they always perfectly agree, though neither acts upon the other.[8] Thus if we know what time it is by one clock, we know what time it is by the other. Mind and body *seem* to interact simply because of a "pre-established harmony" between them. We can understand mental changes only by understanding the preceding mental changes, and we can understand physical changes only by understanding the preceding physical changes; there is no causal connection between mental and physical. This doctrine made irrelevant the whole conception of interaction between mind and body, and sought to do away with all those apparent contradictions involved in asking how a mental event occurs in consequence of a physical event. We have in Leibnitz's system a "parallelism" of mind and body to which many shades of contemporary parallelism bear close resemblance. Through Descartes's interactionism, Spinoza's monism, and Leibnitz's parallelism, the seventeenth century outlined three of the major body-mind theories which dominated eighteenth- and nineteenth-century thought.

Mental events were themselves classified and graded for Leibnitz according to their degree of clearness, ranging from the most definitely conscious to those which were most vague and obscure. This led to a distinction which remained prominent in German psychology and is now widely recognized: We may be totally unconscious of our obscure perceptions. Others are, at the same time, clearly grasped, or *apperceived*.[9] Perception is an internal condition "representing external things," and *apperception* is "*consciousness* or the reflective knowledge of this internal state." [10]

ENGLISH EMPIRICISM: HOBBES

But significant as were the psychological systems of these men, probably the most important stream of tradition for us to consider in order to understand the psychology of the eighteenth and early nineteenth centuries is the English "empiricism" of Hobbes and his successors. The starting point for Hobbes, even more obviously than for the other thinkers we have considered, was the social and intel-

[8] *Second Explanation of the System of the Communication between Substances* (1696).

[9] Aristotle had distinguished between "having" and "observing" an experience.

[10] *The Principles of Nature and of Grace* (1714). Perception is a condition of a monad, a psychic individuality or soul. Monads are irreducible psychic entities.

lectual environment in which he lived. He was, in particular, engaged in the study of the great political upheaval going on about him, that surging-forward of the commercial classes which weakened the grip of the nobility upon its exclusive power and prerogatives. Charles I was executed in 1649; and Hobbes published his *Leviathan* in 1651. It was the "heroic" age of Cavaliers and Roundheads, the lyrics of Lovelace, the leader sleeping in his armor, and the echo of wars across the Channel. But Hobbes bitterly hated both the commercial and the political revolution; he was a royalist, and his conception of life was aristocratic. The organization of society was for him based upon the authority of some individuals over others. The "natural" state of man (without organized society) would be "solitary, poor, nasty, brutish, and short." [11]

Nevertheless, he was an observer who, in spite of his prejudices, was singularly detached; and this in a hyperpolitical age in which every thinking Englishman was startled to witness the disruption of the time-honored order.[12] Though he was in a sense a part of this upheaval, he was still a spectator rather than a participant.[13] He observed in a spirit in which few before him had observed; even Machiavelli and Sir Thomas More, his great predecessors in political theory during the Renaissance, had had a case to prove and a practical goal to win. He sought to understand the revolution and the human nature which lies behind both war and peace. He was the first "social psychologist" among the moderns, and the principles which he laid down were epoch-making both for social and for individual psychology.

Hobbes drew the distinction between original nature and the products of experience.[14] Some human acts he attributed to innate constitution; but most specific activities he regarded as acquired. He started out to catalogue the inherited tendencies, but quickly lost interest; hunger, thirst, and sex impulses were mentioned and passed over in a moment, being such obvious things that their psychology did not interest him. But in relation to social life, he gives a much fuller exposition of the principles of motivation. In this exposition, based largely on Aristotle's *Rhetoric*,[15] he described

[11] *Leviathan*, Pt. I, Chap. 13.

[12] Milton, for example, attached greater importance to his political writings than to his poetry; it was his great regret that he was snatched away from politics by his blindness. The political intensity and bitterness of the age reverberates even in Gray's stately rhythms three generations later.

[13] He took refuge in France during some of the stormiest years.

[14] *Leviathan*, Pt. I, Chap. 6.

[15] That is, the list of motives which the orator must sway.

human motives not as purely impulsive forces, but as strivings based on expectation of pleasure and pain.[16] First and foremost came fear, fear conceived not as a blind impulse but as perception of pain inherent in an object, causing withdrawal from it. Fear is dependent upon calculation of evil results. The desire for honor is another dominant motive; it is based on the recognition of pleasure which must accrue from standing well with one's fellows.

Now these elements of human nature (hunger, thirst, sex tendencies, fear, desire for honor, and, through all, the search for pleasure and the avoidance of pain) are the mainsprings of social conduct, and the basis for social organization. Each individual in human society was conceived by Hobbes to have proclivities which he wished to satisfy, and pains which he wished to avoid. Without society, each individual, alone, would directly seek pleasure and avoid pain. He would be obliged to engage in warfare with his neighbors in order to take from them the things he wished for himself, and to ward off the attacks which they in turn made upon him. Man is competitive, and if alone in his self-defense is necessarily miserable through the constant seizure of his possessions or the ceaseless task of self-defense. The only hope for men lies in the organization of commonwealths in which each man agrees to forego the pleasures of robbery in order to avoid attack from others.[17] In social groups each individual is prevented by the community from attacking his neighbor. A rational social organization thus prevents the selfishness of original nature from making for general chaos. Hobbes, like Machiavelli, insisted that the mainsprings of human conduct were self-interested, and that the most important was fear. Moralists had pointed out the essential baseness of humanity, and Augustine's and Calvin's emphasis on man's sinfulness was an expression rather than a cause of the age-long grudge which Western thought has cherished against man's moral nature. And this conception has been acceptable to penologists and to practical statesmen for centuries. Fear has been the central note of deterrent punishment, as of international politics and diplomacy.

Another mechanism of social control lay in the establishment of a nobility and of other special groups to whom honor was given in greater or lesser degree. Hobbes believed that gratification derived

[16] This simple hedonism was not particularly original. Many of the ancients assumed it; its elements were present also in More's *Utopia*. As was noted above, Descartes made a similar assumption.

[17] A similar conception of the commonwealth had been traced (by Glaucon) in Plato's *Republic*.

from high station, as well as from approval of one's acts, was a necessary part of the social order. But royalty is a very special form of noble rank, for the sovereign personalizes or represents society as a whole. The revolt against the sovereign is a contradiction in terms. The sovereign is the representative of all; by receiving supreme power he protects society against marauders. The king therefore rules, not through an abstract "divine right," but by the collective values he holds within himself as representative of the commonwealth. Hobbes believed the overthrow of the sovereign to be vicious as well as ultimately futile. Subsequent events, especially the expulsion of the Stuarts, were not such as his scheme of society demanded, and the fact tended in some measure to discredit his theory of the state.

But there was here a system of ideas of immense importance, ideas rooted in the thought of antiquity and now revived in opposition to the doctrines of the Middle Ages. There was first the idea that human acts result from an objectively knowable human nature; that man is made in such a way that analysis may make possible prediction and control. Society can so organize itself as to control individuals and create for itself a complex but reasonably stable system of social relations. We shall see later how the "political economists," especially Bentham, continued another branch of Hobbes's thought, namely, "psychological hedonism," the doctrine that self-interest is the basis of conduct.

This description of social life, moreover, was supplemented by a systematic philosophical inquiry and by a keen analysis of the principles of general psychology. Philosophically, Hobbes was captivated by the desire to reduce everything to *motion*. He was delighted by Galileo's mechanical experiments, and believed that through such methods the ultimate nature of "things natural" was to be discerned. This systematic (and dogmatic) emphasis on motion, even where motion could not be demonstrated, perhaps justifies the question whether Hobbes really was as purely "empirical" as is alleged. "He attempted a task which no other adherent of the new 'mechanical philosophy' conceived—nothing less than such a universal construction of human knowledge as would bring Society and Man . . . within the same principles of scientific explanation as were found applicable to the world of Nature." [18] With the mechanical viewpoint, the notion of bodies as bits of matter moving in space and time, Hobbes built up the scheme of human nature as a purely mechanical thing, avoiding altogether the interactionism of Des-

[18] Robertson, G. C., "Hobbes," in *Encyclopaedia Britannica*, 11th ed., 13, 552.

cartes. It is no exaggeration to say that Hobbes took the whole fabric of the seventeenth-century physical view of the world and fashioned from it a conception of human nature. Every thought, feeling, and purpose was simply internal *motion*.

It is sometimes held that his psychology is in large part Aristotelian; Aristotle gave him a "naturalism" which he could set in opposition to the "supernaturalism" of the Scholastics. Yet though Aristotle taught him a good deal, we find him making no use of the Aristotelian conception of form, preferring a mechanism like that of Democritus.

His psychology is in large part an empirical psychology. He uses the principle of motion chiefly in relation to motion as supposed to occur in the *brain*, an assumption which was supported by some evidence. And whatever may be thought of his metaphysics, his psychological observations have both a matter-of-fact empirical spirit and a richness of content very far indeed from the formalism which had characterized most psychological systems. Much of his psychological material evidently came from his own keen analysis. His work as a psychologist centers in close observation of his own mental processes, with the request that the reader "consider, if he also find not the same in himself." [19] He undertook, moreover, to show that the mind takes shape in consequence of natural forces operating upon the individual.

All experience, Hobbes held, was some special form of motion. He made, for example, no distinction between the *will* to do a thing and the doing it.[20] Appetites and fears were internal motions which led to action, and will was simply the last appetite or the last fear which in the course of deliberation precipitated overt movement.[21] Similarly, sensation was continuation of that motion which had impinged upon the sense organs, transmitting its motion through the nerves to the brain. Descartes had taught that in higher mental functions the soul, by means of the pineal gland, controlled the passage of an impulse from one nerve to another; but Hobbes did not require the intervention of the soul, for motion in the brain was sufficient.

The motion occurring within the brain substance constituted, moreover, the basis for all qualities of sensation. He proceeded, accordingly, to attack the popular conception that the qualities of

[19] *Leviathan*, Introduction.

[20] A protest against a Scholastic teaching that the internal motion was merely metaphorical.

[21] *Human Nature* (1651). 12, 2.

experience are *inherent in* the objects we perceive.[22] "There is nothing *without us* (really) which we call an *image* or colour . . . the said image or colour is but an *apparition* unto us of the *motion*, agitation, or alteration, which the *object* worketh in the *brain*, or spirits, or some internal substance of the head."[23] Moreover, after the external object has ceased to act upon the sense organ, the motion in the brain may continue. Such residual or "decaying" sensation constitutes the material of memory and imagination. As Aristotle had put it, imagination is "decaying sense."

There remains, however, the problem of the *order of events*, the "trains" of imagination and thought. This order of events depended upon the sequence of the original experiences caused by stimulation coming from the world about us. "Those motions that immediately succeed one another in the sense, continue also together after sense: insomuch as the former coming again to take place, and be predominant, the latter followeth."[24] This doctrine is basic for all associationist teaching. *Associationism* is the doctrine that we connect things in memory, in thought, and in all mental life, simply because they were connected in our original experience with them; and since our first encounters with things are by means of our senses, the associationist maintains that all the complexity of mental life is reducible to sense impressions, the elementary components of consciousness, as connected in experience. The psychologists of ancient India, as well as of Greece, had speculated along these lines; what Hobbes is here doing is vigorously modernizing the doctrine, a task brilliantly pursued by Hartley in the following century.

But we cannot predict from a given thought which one of a variety of other thoughts may follow. A thought may have been followed, in different situations, by a variety of different thoughts. There may be many competitors, each one of which has a definite claim upon the next position in a mental series. A passage in his work on *Human Nature* suggests that he believed that a knowledge of past experience is wholly sufficient to explain present associations: "The *cause* of the *coherence* or consequence of one conception to another, is their first *coherence* or consequence at that *time* when they are produced by

---

[22] The astronomer Kepler had clearly distinguished a half-century earlier between such objective reality as motion and such subjective phenomena as color. For the history of these concepts from Kepler to Berkeley, see Burtt, E. A., *Metaphysical Foundations of Modern Physical Science* (1925).

[23] *Human Nature*, II, 4. Hobbes constantly emphasizes the brain, as had some of the Greeks; but he is a good enough Aristotelian to emphasize the heart, and to give the latter a position of importance in mental life.

[24] *Leviathan*, Pt. I, Chap. 3.

sense: as for example, from St. Andrew the mind runneth to St. Peter, because their names are read together; from St. Peter to a *stone*, for the same cause." [25] But in the *Leviathan* we read: "In the imagining of anything, there is no certainty what we shall imagine next; only this is certain, it shall be something that succeeded the same before, at one time or another." [26] He failed to work out his position. Neither he nor his immediate successors realized the possibility of attaining a more adequate statement of the varieties of association. It was not, in fact, until the work of Thomas Brown, in the beginning of the nineteenth century, that this problem was fairly faced, reducing the problem of mental sequence to a large number of specific laws of association, taking into account the *competition* among experiences.

But Hobbes did take account of the vital distinction between such free or uncontrolled association on the one hand, and directed or purposive thinking on the other hand. "Mental discourse is of two sorts. The first is *unguided, without design* and inconstant. . . . The second is more constant; as being *regulated* by some desire, and design." [27] He devoted much attention to the "regulated" type, taking account of the "desire" which guides the process, and of the tendency to seek causes for consequences and vice versa. He proceeds to give illustrations of the familiar (Platonic and Aristotelian) principles of association by contiguity and similarity.

Hobbes had, then, outlined an empirical psychology in which sensation was emphasized as the source of our ideas, and had given a sketch of free and controlled association which served to explain the interconnections between the elements of experience.

LOCKE

The first great follower of Hobbes had an immense advantage over him as molder of opinion. Locke was one to attract not only the attention but the allegiance of the readers and thinkers of his era. [28] To those who had struggled for freedom, he spoke of the fitness of man to live in a free society dominated by reason and forbearance. Indeed, a primary note in his great essay is the rationality of man. Whereas Hobbes, the cynic, had wanted to fight, to argue, and to make fun, Locke spoke in the idiom of his age. Men looked askance

[25] *Human Nature*, IV, 2.
[26] *Leviathan*, Pt. I, Chap. 3.
[27] *Ibid.*
[28] *An Essay Concerning Human Understanding* (1690).

at the materialistic dogmas of "Hobbism," looked forward with Locke to a humane and enlightened social order. This conception was expressed in his discussion of politics and of education, as well as in his psychological studies which aimed to demonstrate the rationality of man and the relation of this rationality to the simpler associative laws of the mind.

Ideas, Locke noted, come from experience; [29] observation "supplies our understanding with all the materials of thinking." But ideas need not arise directly from sense impressions; they have two sources. They come either from sensation or from reflection, an "inner sense." Our minds are equipped not only with ideas directly derived from such sensory qualities as color, tone, and taste, but also with ideas derived from observing our own intellectual activity.

Locke agreed with Hobbes that "simple ideas of sensation" are the properties of experience, and not of the objects outside us which excite these ideas in us. He proceeded, however, to distinguish between "primary" and "secondary" qualities.[30] Primary qualities, such as size and motion, produce in us ideas resembling the physical stimuli which excite them. On the other hand, secondary qualities are those aspects of external objects which produce in us ideas unlike anything really existing in the external world; for example, such ideas as those of color and taste. He supposed that some aspects of experience are genuine duplicates of patterns existing in external bodies, while others bear, in fact, no such resemblance to external bodies.

Ideas, however, may be either simple or complex. The mind creates complex ideas by combining simple ideas. Many of our ideas designated by single words can in fact be analyzed in such a way as to show clearly that they are but combinations of simple sensory constituents. "Thus, if to substance be joined the simple idea of a certain dull, whitish colour, with certain degrees of weight, hardness, ductility, and fusibility, we have the idea of lead." [31] The principle was, as we shall see, far-leading. "Even the *most abstruse* ideas, how remote soever they may seem from sense, or from any operation of our own minds, are yet only such as the understanding frames to itself, by repeating and joining together ideas that it had either from

[29] The mind before all experience is "white paper." The Latin *tabula rasa* (wax tablet, smooth and ready for writing) is a familiar epitome of Locke's conception of a mind upon which experience has as yet written nothing.

[30] See page 26, footnote 22.

[31] *Ibid.*, Bk. II, Chap. XII, 6.

objects of sense, or from its own operations about them." [32] While Locke's primary emphasis is upon the capacity of man to achieve understanding of the world and of himself, he agrees that the *sequences* of ideas which appear in the mind are often irrational, being due to the mere order in which earlier impressions were made, just as Hobbes had said (page 26). Such irrational, fortuitous mental connections exhibit the "association of ideas."

Three things were needed to make a systematic psychology out of these principles. One was to lay stress upon and give content to the notions of "repeating" and "joining," which constituted the basis for integration of simple into complex experiences. The second was to show how the entire mental life could be reduced to association. The third was to postulate a physical basis for mental interconnections. All three steps were soon to be taken.

Locke's greatest contribution to psychology thus lay in making explicit the possibilities of a theory of association which should start with the data of experience and work out the laws governing the interconnections and sequences among experiences. The germ of associationism had, of course, been apparent in the work of Hobbes, which in turn went back to Aristotle. But Locke's lucid exposition of the implications of empiricism, and of the possibility, through analysis, of clearly understanding the origin and organization of ideas, gave the empirical approach an appealing and challenging quality which greatly contributed to its strength and influence.

REFERENCES

Brett, George S., *A History of Psychology*, 3 vols., London, 1914–21; Vol. 2, especially pp. 196–217

Dennis, Wayne, ed., *Readings in the History of Psychology*, Appleton-Century, 1948: Descartes and Locke

Locke, John, *Essay Concerning Human Understanding*, ed. by E. Campbell Fraser, London, 1894

Randall, John H., *The Making of the Modern Mind*, rev. ed., Houghton Mifflin, 1940

[32] *Ibid.*, Chap. XII, 8.

Chapter 3

THE EIGHTEENTH CENTURY

. . it was the natural realism of English writing which seemed to the French a new revelation of the common thoughts and emotions of common people. With a burst of enthusiasm France embraced the idea that apart from monarchs and metaphysics there are ordinary mortals and a science of man.

G. S. BRETT

THE SEVENTEENTH CENTURY had paced, with seven-league boots, the road from medieval dogmatism to the agnostic mechanism of Hobbes and the empirical rationalism of Locke. In the bright light of the new physics—so fully empirical and so utterly rational—and with every breath of the new cultural atmosphere so stimulating to the intellectual adventurer, one may expect to find the psychology of the eighteenth century all the more eager to proceed by rigorous self-observation and relentless logic. These empirical yet rational trends are evident indeed in Berkeley, Hume, and Hartley, psychologists of the "century of rationalism."

BERKELEY AND HUME

Locke's distinction between primary and secondary qualities was rejected by his immediate follower, Berkeley,[1] who showed with an indomitable logic that there are no qualities in experience except those qualities which Locke had already described as "secondary" or subjective; there are no "primary" qualities. We cannot assign to external objects a location, size, shape, mass, and movement; for we never know anything but our own experience. The whole objective world is a pure hypothesis supported by no evidence whatsoever. In analyzing our experience of a rose we encounter such qualities as redness, fragrance, softness of petals, sharpness of thorns: but

[1] *A Treatise Concerning the Principles of Human Knowledge* (1710).

these are plainly just sensations. And when we talk of external *objects* we do not know what they are; objects external to experience are nothing at all. He laid the cornerstone of that great edifice in modern philosophy, "subjective idealism," which portrays a world of experience qualities and denies, throughout, the existence of any other world. This was the logical end of the train of thought which began with Hobbes's denial that the qualities of things perceived are *in* the things themselves.

But Berkeley was eager to find some kind of unity in mental life, something that should hold these mental states together. There is no intrinsic reason why pain should follow the thrusting of the hand into fire, or why the odor of a rose should accompany the visual and tactual experience of the rose. Why do two persons see the same object or sequence of events? And what is it that holds together the collection of experiences which belong to a single mind? Experience, Berkeley concludes, is the property of the soul: the soul is the unobservable, but logically necessary, background of our experience. Furthermore, there must be an active cause for the succession of experiences, and this cause is to be found in God Himself.

This may seem to the modern reader to classify Berkeley as primarily a philosopher and a theologian; but in pursuing his problem he made an extremely important contribution to the theory of visual space perception, showing how the principle of association might be used to explain some of the most complicated facts of perception.[2] Locke had recognized that in the compounding of ideas elements might be drawn from two or more sense modalities. Berkeley went further with this analysis of the origin of compound ideas. He asked how we perceive the relative distances of objects. The retina is spread out as a surface with an "up" and a "down," a "right" and a "left," but how can we, by means of this surface, perceive a third dimension? Berkeley answered in terms of tactual experiences. Through reaching and touching, the notion of distance is associated gradually with the elements given by the retina. Touch qualities are not directly perceived when we analyze our visual perception of three dimensions: but when visual impressions are combined with tactual memories derived from reaching for objects, we find a three-dimensional quality in our objects. The retina "gives" us three instead of two dimensions. Since Berkeley used the notion of compounding sensory qualities, he became one of the founders of association psychology.

[2] *An Essay towards a New Theory of Vision* (1709).

Now appeared one who questioned the premises and conclusions, the beginning and end, of all these views which had been propounded with the confidence and perhaps the naïveté characteristic of the era. The central psychological contribution of Hume was the analysis of the stream of thought into one endlessly changing kaleidoscopic series of experiences.[3] For Berkeley a soul had been needed to bring all these experiences together, to make a coherent sequence. Hume declared that he had patiently examined his consciousness without succeeding in finding evidence for the soul. Even the thing that one calls the "self" turns out to be a group of sensations from the body. For the description of personality all that was necessary was a series of experiences. Empiricism had come to full term.

Hume took the position toward which Hobbes had groped, that psychology deals with experience as it comes to us, and not with any logical postulate of the observer as a separate entity. Hobbes had not been able to see the real issue, because there had not been a Berkeley before him to make this sharp distinction between self and experience. Hume could do it because there *had* been a Berkeley. Hume, denying the validity of Berkeley's assumption of the soul, and of God as an active cause of experience, offered a psychology which was nothing but the study of a series of experiences combining and recombining, through the natural force of association. Here arose one of the great problems which association psychology had to face henceforward: What provided the basic unity of experience? This was long before the day of a detailed physiological psychology; the idea that there was an organism that holds things together could scarcely be worked out. Associationism had become, in the hands of Hume, a means of dissecting and describing experience, dispensing with any unifying agency, whether physical or mental.

HARTLEY

By the middle of the eighteenth century associationism had thus begun to be the central point around which psychological problems revolved. But associationism as a psychological *system* is usually traced to Hartley.[4] He differed from his predecessors not so much in

---

[3] *A Treatise of Human Nature* (1739–40).

[4] *Observations on Man, His Frame, His Duty, and His Expectations* (1749). The Preface to the work makes it clear that the core of his system of thought was suggested by a "Rev. Mr. Gay," whose views on association were stated nearly twenty years earlier. Hartley's own work was not widely noticed in England till the opening of the nineteenth century.

his enunciated principles as in the clearness with which he grasped the need of a thoroughgoing physiological basis for association. He undertook to define the physical facts upon which memory images and their sequences depend. Greatly interested in Newton's study of the movement of the pendulum, he held that if certain experiences follow in a given order it means that nerve fibers must be set in *vibration* in a given order. When a stimulus arouses a sense organ, and a moment later a second stimulus arouses a second sense organ, the vibrations in the brain caused by the first are followed by vibrations caused by the second. The parts of the brain are so connected that if now the first stimulus is again presented and arouses the first brain region, the arousal of the second region follows, with no need for the presentation of the second stimulus. A series of sensations A, B, C, D forms such a pattern in the brain that later the arousal of A will set going b, c, d—that is to say, *memory images* of B, C, D. These images are produced by the vibration, on a *small* scale, of nervous tissue previously stimulated more actively.

He recognized the resemblance between motor habits—a series of acts in which, step by step, each act leads to the next—and mental activities like memory, in which a series of experiences follows in a certain order because of past experience in a certain order. There was, moreover, no distinction between sensation and image except in so far as differences in *intensity* of nerve function were concerned; the image had its seat in the *same region* which served as basis for the sensation.[5] Having found a way to explain the *succession* of ideas, it was easy for Hartley to use Locke's conception of *compound* ideas. A group of revived sensations might cohere so as to form a mental product. But this mental product was to be conceived as parallel to a physical product, a group of nerve excitations. Complex experiences were reduced to the elementary sensations which by association constituted them. In such complex experiences the component sensations may sometimes no longer be recognizable; in taking a new medicine, one may fail to recognize the components, though all of them have been experienced separately at an earlier time. He had, therefore, by physiological principles brought the whole realm of thought and of imagination into one explanatory system; clusters and sequences of sense impressions are the clue to mental life.

For Hartley, as for Locke, the child begins life without associations. But rejecting the notion of ideas derived from reflection, Hartley held that the child has simply the capacity for sensory experience. In the course of time, sensory experience, by making con-

[5] A refinement of Hobbes's statement as to the relation of image to sensation.

nections and establishing trains of association, building up complex objects of thought, becomes more and more intricate; and finally there arise systems of thought, such as philosophy, religion, and morals. Hartley had almost arrived at a complete psychical atomism, a reduction of mental life to atoms which in combination yield all observable events. He and his followers had as their goal such a thorough understanding of association as would enable them to take a number of psychical elements and show how their combination in various ways, acting according to a few simple laws, could produce every kind of psychological event. This fascinating game is one which had not yet been played with vigor and thoroughness.

THE SCOTTISH SCHOOL

Though associationism continued to thrive, another direction was open. The tendency to simplify and mechanize mental processes led to a protest against Hobbes's mechanism, and, in particular, against Hume's indifference to the claims of the soul. The protest took shape in the Scottish universities, where empiricism had made less headway than in England, and where the philosopher was alert to support the claims of established religion against impending infidelity. Skepticism might be all very well as speculation, but it had moral implications. Religion and the state, still closely allied, were alike threatened; popular education (through the parochial schools) was taken in real earnest, and public opinion could not brook an attack upon the core of its ethical and religious structure. Religious freedom was tolerated in some circles in England; respectability did not necessarily involve orthodoxy in religious thought. But Scotch Presbyterianism of the mid-eighteenth century definitely and consciously undertook to create a new philosophy to combat skepticism.

The leader was Thomas Reid.[6] He undertook to show that the skepticism of Hume was absurd, that we know perfectly well that we have minds, the capacity to perceive real things, to think, and to act rationally. Reid appealed to the practical reliability of our senses, pointing for example to Newton's studies in optics as showing the right way to approach the problem of our ability to make contact with the external world. Do we not, moreover, observe a profound difference between *reasoning* and mere *association?* Have we not intellectual powers upon which we can rely in solving problems, making it possible to understand the external world and to predict

---

[6] *Essays on the Intellectual Powers of Man* (1785).

what will happen? The child is likewise endowed with the ability to know good and evil; and we are free to choose between right and wrong. In all this Reid sought not only to undermine the basis of association psychology, but to build a new system based upon confidence in our intellectual powers: a system based upon common observation as against the subtlety—the sophistry, he maintained—of the empiricists.

Reid's teaching was characteristic of the trend of the period. For such a revolution against prevalent philosophical thought would probably have taken in the thirteenth century, or in the sixteenth, the form of an appeal to authority. Demonstration of the soul would have been effected by means of deductive reasoning. But in the eighteenth century empiricism had taken such hold that rationalism was no longer trusted; even the enemies of the empirical movement resorted to experience rather than to deductive logic as their defense. Reid says in substance: "There are the facts on which *you* rely, but look at *my* facts; they are more conclusive than yours." One of the last bursts from the dying embers of medieval dogmatism had been Berkeley's supposed demonstration of the existence of the soul. Hereafter we shall find little desire in British psychology to recur to purely rationalistic principles.

Because of its insistence upon the unity and the coherence of mental life, and because it pictured the individual as an active entity, not as a mere field in which ideas assembled and reassembled, the greatest contributions of the Scottish school were necessarily general rather than specific. It contributed little to the solution of specific problems until the school became blended to some extent with the associationist movement. But Reid and his followers had great influence, not only in Scotland but later in England, France, and the United States, because they appeared to save the individual and society from intellectual and moral chaos. In all these countries, moreover, the new doctrines came to be well known to the general reader, and not only to university students; the Scottish school became genuinely popular.

Another tendency already at work grafted itself upon the Scottish school, but also continued a separate existence in Germany: the "faculty psychology." This was never "founded," in the strict sense, at any one period; we find it implicit or explicit in the psychology of some of the ancients and some of the Scholastics. As the soul carried out the specific activities, for example, of remembering, reasoning, and volition, it made use successively of the different *faculties* of memory, reason, and will. But if one likes one may say, as is often done, that the first proponent of German faculty psychology was Christian Wolff, whose *Rational Psychology* appeared in 1734. His central doctrine is simple and intelligible: There are definite and distinct faculties or capacities of the soul; the soul enters for the time being into each activity, just as the whole body may at different times take part in widely different acts. But the soul remains a unity, never a mere sum of constituent parts. German thought remained for more than a century steadfast to this general principle.[7] For this school of psychology a *faculty* was the *capacity* of the soul to carry out a certain activity. This gives us a double enumeration of all mental processes; there is not only the specific process of remembering, but the power of remembering. The distinction is convenient. But as a system, faculty psychology merely gives names to certain functions; it cannot analyze these functions. The Scottish school and the faculty psychology shared this approach. Beginning with the soul and the various ways in which it can act, the Scottish psychologists catalogued its capacities much as the Scholastics and the German faculty psychology had done.

As associationism matured into a self-confident system (cf. page 102), it denied more and more vigorously the value of this approach. The child's mind, it asserted, was blank at birth, and only by experience learned certain ways of functioning; it had no *innate capacities* to do things. The associationists, therefore, and the faculty psychologists stood at opposite poles.

FRENCH PSYCHOLOGY

French psychology before and during the French Revolution responded directly to the tendencies in British thought.

In the work of Condillac there arose a structure even more beautiful in its simplicity than the associationism of Hartley.[8] Taking as his point of departure Locke's conception of sensation as the first source of ideas, Condillac went further and held that sensations alone are a sufficient clue to all mental life; no formulation of the principles of association, as entities, need be added to our primitive capacity for sensory experience. He asked his readers to imagine a *statue*, and to imagine what would follow if it were given sensation, say the sense of smell, and nothing more. The sum total of all possible human mental processes would follow, with need to presuppose

---

[7] Kant gave new life to the doctrine of the faculties at the same time that he elaborated his own theory of apperception (cf. page 45).

[8] *Treatise on Sensations* (1754).

no laws of association whatever. Variations in the quality of sensation, for example, would necessarily produce those acts of judgment
and comparison to which Locke referred. The fact of passing through
experiences, one after another, is a sufficient clue to the way in which
judgments and comparisons arise. Operations and functions are
not added to the elements; the elements carry out their own functions. The mind is an assemblage of parts, and these parts in their
relations explain mental functions of all describable varieties. A
point implicit rather than explicit in Condillac's system is the
assumption that pleasantness and unpleasantness are inherent in
the nature of the sensory process itself; qualities of sense are by their
very nature pleasant or unpleasant. He next assumes that pleasant
experiences are inevitably (almost by definition) prolonged and
repeated, while unpleasant experiences are as far as possible terminated. For Condillac's purposes we need consider only one of the
senses; the other senses would contribute other *qualities*, but the laws
formulated from observing them would be identical.

We may, to be sure, smile and remain unconvinced as we read
how the experience of one sensation followed by another gives us,
ipso facto, a comparison of the two, or how an inherently unpleasant
sensation constitutes directly, and without further assumptions, the
will to terminate the experience; but the logical construction comes
to the modern reader as something exquisite in its simplicity and
clarity.[9] It is the most nearly perfect modern example of *sensationism*,
the effort to reduce mental life to sensory elements. The sensationist
must indeed have a theory regarding the interaction and the succession of sense impressions, usually borrowing here from the associationist; and the associationist must agree with the sensationist's
explanations of the sensory sources of the contents of the mind. In
practice the two approaches are therefore very similar. But Condillac
marks the most radical of modern efforts to find in sensation *all* the
essential clues to psychology. This attempt to picture mental life
as an aggregate of sensory bits became one of the dominant philosophies for the remaining years of the century, until the idealistic
movement came into vigorous life again.

The success of Condillac's sensationism was due in part to the
intellectual soil of the Enlightenment, to such influences as deism

---

[9] A somewhat similar system, but with much more attention to physiology, was
offered by Bonnet (*Essai analytique sur les facultés de l'âme*, 1760). Bonnet described
memory in terms of activities in nerve fibers (in language similar to Hartley's). He
performed a rough experiment on the "span of attention." He suggested that each
quality of sensation must depend upon the specific brain area excited (cf. page 94).

and the Encyclopedist movement. The middle of the eighteenth century had been a period of heroic intellectual achievements, concentrated above all in Paris. Here the influence of scientists and historians, especially of the antiecclesiastical group, had begun to simplify the picture of human life, as the English empiricists had done, by doing away with the supernatural and by making human experience the all-sufficient object of study. The great advances of physics, chemistry, and astronomy were making for the growth of the conception of natural law so important in the economic and political policies of French statesmen both before and during the Revolution. This scientific movement was destined to reach great heights in the work of two Frenchmen who are usually thought of as figures in the history of medicine: Cabanis and Bichat. Living at the time of the French Revolution, they were the most brilliant exponents of the movement which aimed to unite the science of the nonliving with the science of living things.

Cabanis first attracted attention as a student of a problem which arose from the facts of execution by guillotine.[10] He was interested in the philanthropic question whether the guillotine hurt its victims or acted so swiftly as to be painless. By questions of this kind he was prompted to a study of reflex action (cf. Descartes, page 18) and to the formulation of a concept which has become an important principle in physiological psychology to this day. We can summarize his conception in the term "series of levels." The spinal-cord level was the simplest of a hierarchy; it carried out reflex acts in response to stimuli. At a higher level, semiconscious or semi-integrated activities were carried on; and at the highest level were such complicated functions as thought and volition.[11] Cabanis believed that unless the brain were involved there could be no mental processes, only mechanical responses. On this assumption he concluded that the guillotine was not painful; movements in the body after execution were reflexes of the lowest level.

Having postulated these levels, Cabanis went on to suggest an explanation of cerebral activities on the analogy of more elementary functions. He showed evidence that the same mechanical principles which govern reflex activity govern cerebral activity; he made use of data indicating the relation of brain disease to mental disease.

---

[10] For example, *Rapports du physique et du moral de l'homme* (1799).

[11] This conception was elaborated by Hughlings Jackson nearly a century later. Jackson supposed that the levels most recently achieved through evolution were most easily deranged, and based a psychiatric classification upon this principle (cf. *The Factors of Insanities*, 1894).

He ventured upon a systematic physiological psychology, replacing many of Condillac's assumptions by the postulation of neural functions which served as the basis for an active adjustment to environment. He suggested a genetic approach, making much of the fact of increase in mental complexity arising from increase in the complexity of the nervous system. Finally, he conceived of a social psychology, based on laws of individual behavior and social stimulation, and was led to an empirical consideration of ethics. He was thus one of the first to realize that the biological observations of the eighteenth century had clear implications for social life. Starting from reflex action, he proceeded all the way to the most complicated problem with which psychologists have to deal, human conduct in its ethical aspects.

The writings of Cabanis were contemporaneous with the work of Bichat, whose medical researches led him also to the conception of a physiological psychology. From the time of Hippocrates, medicine had recognized the body as an assemblage of *organs;* in spite of the active prosecution of research with the aid of the microscope, the intimate knowledge of the composition of these organs had not been achieved. Bichat pushed analysis into the realm of the structure of the *tissues,* and founded the science of histology. He showed that every part of the human body is composed of a few types of tissue, which combine in various ways to form the vital organs, muscles, glands, and so on. Here he came into contact with problems of neuropathology, and through these of psychopathology, viewing forms of mental disease in terms of the abnormality of anatomical and histological structure. Physiological psychology was taking shape. Descartes and Hobbes had outlined a physiological approach to psychology; Hartley had boldly attempted a physiology of association; but a thoroughgoing physiological psychology could arise only on the basis of a definite conception of the structures and the functions of the nervous system.

Another French scientist seems to sum up all these tendencies. Pinel was appointed in 1792 as director of the institution for the insane in Paris, the Bicêtre. Here he struck off the chains with which many of the insane were bound. He epitomized in this act a view which had been gaining ground steadily, the conviction that the insane are diseased: that instead of being simply queer or immoral, or in league with Satan, these individuals suffer from sick brains. Pinel epitomized on the one hand the great advances in neurology and pathology, holding that disorder in the brain meant disorder in the personality, and on the other hand the humanitarian movement, with its insistence on the mitigation of suffering. We break dramatically with the demonological conception of disease, which, although rejected by individuals in all ages, had held sway for centuries. Pinel was a practical psychiatrist of no mean ability. He won distinction in the classification of mental disorders, attempting wherever possible to correlate brain disorder with mental disease.

HUMANITARIANISM; HEDONISM; UTILITARIANISM

Pinel was representative of a wide and mounting tidal wave of humanitarianism. The nature of the trend appears in a new attitude toward the treatment of criminals. Among the factors responsible for earlier brutalities had been on the one hand the conception of original sin, and on the other hand the emphasis on the principle of the freedom of the will, which made each individual personally responsible for his wickedness. These factors added to the severity of the treatment accorded to the criminal, treatment which of course had been brutal even under the "pax Romana." Torture was in use in France until the Revolution. Violent reaction now arose against such barbarism; human dignity demanded sympathy and the impulse to correct rather than simply to inflict pain upon wrong-doers. A still wider expression of the new mood was the effort to alleviate the sufferings of the poor, and the publication of books proposing radical cures—anarchism, for example—for the inequities of human society.

Perhaps the whole movement of the Enlightenment, and in particular the humanitarian movement, had its ultimate origin, as some economists have suggested, in the discovery of the New World and in the Commercial Revolution, the bringing-in of new goods and the raising of the general standard of living. With the breakup of the feudal system and the rapid rise of democracy, merchants began to compete with the nobility for economic and political power. In the Old World the guildsmen had raised themselves into a commercial class, and even those below them had risen to positions of genuine prosperity. And in the New World Europeans found a new opportunity to escape the oppression of a landed nobility; they might claim land for themselves and take part in the establishment of a democracy. Their constant emigration contributed to a rise in wages in western Europe; with the decrease of the number of available laborers, wages rose and the condition of the poor tended to improve.

Whether our emphasis on these factors be great or small, we find the humanitarian movement widespread by the middle of the eighteenth century. Pinel expressed it in the field of medicine. It was apparent in the work of Beccaria,[12] the founder of modern criminological theory. He protested against the brutality and the futility of the heavy sentences imposed for all sorts of petty crimes; capital punishment, for example, for petty larceny seemed to him barbarous and absurd. He carried into criminology that system of thought known as psychological hedonism, which pictured each individual as motivated solely by desire for pleasure and aversion from pain. He outlined a theory of punishment which was designed to direct this human nature into conduct desired by the group. A man commits a crime only when he is impelled by a wish. A man steals bread because he is hungry; if he is terribly hungry, he steals more. If we institute a system of *graded* punishment, we may for each crime assign a punishment which will deter the individual from that act. This conception was an integral part of the humanitarian movement just considered. Had it not been for the violent repulsion against systems of torture and the use of capital punishment for dozens of crimes, such an application of hedonistic theory would not have been called for.

Closely bound up with the humanitarian movement and the eighteenth-century intellectualism were the writings of the political economists, especially the school of Adam Smith and the school of Jeremy Bentham. The French economists known as the *physiocrats* had maintained that wealth came solely from land; primarily from agriculture, and to some extent from mining, forestry, and so on. All other forms of human activity were parasitic. Soon Adam Smith in England began to see the inadequacy of such a simple formula. His *Wealth of Nations* (1776) treated the principles involved in commerce: why it is that men trade with one another, what satisfactions they obtain from exchange of goods. He grasped the need of a psychological background for economic processes, just as in his work on *The Theory of Moral Sentiments* (1759) he had already attempted a psychological explanation of fellow feeling and hence of morality. What had been a problem of mathematics with the French became a psychological problem with the English; human motives were the key to social organization.

Smith's psychology differed much from Bentham's, and while Smith retained enormous influence as an economist, the psychology and the ethics of Bentham soon won equal influence. He championed the doctrine of "ethical hedonism," the doctrine that the only individual or social good is happiness. The phrases "the greatest good of

12 *Crimes and Punishments* (1764).

the greatest number" and the "sum total of human happiness" are characteristic of the system. At the same time he insisted upon "psychological hedonism," the doctrine that all human acts are self-interested.[13] He was the first to formulate systematically this universal principle of psychological hedonism, which as we have seen (page 23) many writers had assumed, but none had thoroughly worked out. He sought to explain all social behavior in terms of conscious search for pleasure and avoidance of pain. He and his followers sought to show a way to use this self-interest motive of each individual in the interests of society as a whole; in an ideal society, individual and social good would coincide. *Utilitarianism* was the resulting doctrine that the only defensible goal of society is to provide, through the control of behavior, for the greatest good of the greatest number. Just as Beccaria had explained that if the punishment is just great enough, the individual will refrain from stealing bread, so Bentham built up the doctrine that men will work just so much for their bread; that is, they will undergo labor and suffering only if their reward is sufficiently great. In his hands this became a method of explaining not only individual conduct, but the whole organization of society. The statesman's task is to guide the social order so that each individual's conception of his own greatest good will be one with that of society's greatest good.

Bentham's theory of motivation and his desire to use this motivation for the general welfare accorded with the humanitarian movement. But paradoxically, the resulting conception of the "economic man," who is motivated solely through pleasure and pain, became a great all-encompassing dogma of the industrialists, who found in it the inescapable law of all social behavior, and hence the moral justification for every act of self-interest. The slogans of humanitarianism were often used in the rationalization of the hard practicalities of the Industrial Revolution, and even today the assumption of the self-evident and obvious correctness of ethical and of psychological hedonism runs through the thinking of "practical men" in industrial society.

But there is one more link still to be fitted in. We have tried to make clear that the dominant influence in English psychology during the eighteenth century was associationism. What was the link between associationism and these other developments? The link lay in the fact that certain things in themselves neutral become sources of pleasure and pain, and come through association to influence us

[13] Ethical hedonism does not necessarily involve psychological hedonism, nor vice versa, but Bentham embraced both.

as though they were the pleasure and pain themselves. Specifically, a piece of paper that has no use and which is not feared is neutral; but if the piece of paper has become associated with value, it becomes as *money* a direct object of satisfaction. Every symbol may be pleasant or unpleasant, according to its associations. Associationism and utilitarianism become intermingled.

A number of social and intellectual movements had now grown together. They constituted almost a systematic view of life. The Commercial and the Industrial revolutions; the development of natural science; the rise of political economy; associationism; humanitarianism; reform in the treatment of criminals and the insane; deism and utilitarianism, as well as a number of other movements, had led to a new and "naturalistic" conception of human nature. Many historians of Western culture would make the economic factors, especially those arising from the Commercial Revolution, the origin of most of the others; for our purposes it suffices to note the existence of all these factors as they molded British psychology.

Though all these movements were international, their influence on Continental psychology was considerably less than on psychology in Britain. Before the Revolution every one of these movements was clearly active in France, but no psychological system took shape such as those constructed by the associationists and the utilitarians. French psychology up to Cabanis and Bichat had merely continued the Cartesian tradition and borrowed, through Condillac and others, part of Locke's system. During the Revolution and the Napoleonic era, French thought enjoyed no such freedom for development as was vouchsafed in Britain. Although there was some psychological work in the interests of education, notably that of Condorcet, and although Pinel had led the way toward a new outlook on mental disorders, the constant war on many fronts between 1793 and 1815 inevitably stifled to some extent the development of the tendencies with which we are now concerned.

GERMAN PSYCHOLOGY: KANT

German psychology was pursuing its independent career, and had as yet been but little affected by associationism and the kindred movements noted above. It will be remembered that the "faculty psychology" of the seventeenth and eighteenth centuries had concerned itself with the various irreducible functions of the mind, maintaining that a unitary soul entered fully at different times into each one of a number of distinct activities (page 35). This conception is closely related to a view which has been widely advocated in recent years, that each function is the function not of a part or an element of the organism, but of the whole organism; every experience and every act reflects the undivided individual. The main purpose of faculty psychology was to describe the primary powers exercised by the soul: memory, reason, will, and so on. This approach was congenial to the rationalistic tendency previously noted, because functions of intellectual and moral importance were accepted at their face value and freed from the humiliation of dissection into sensory bits in the manner favored by the associationists. Faculty psychology also emphasized religious values; [14] it became essentially and mainly "idealistic." [15]

Now in the course of time this faculty psychology, with its emphasis upon the "ultimate modes of psychical functioning," expressed itself most adequately in the writings of Immanuel Kant, one of the greatest figures in the history of thought. His celebrated doctrines received their initial impetus largely from Hume's skepticism. "It was Hume," said Kant, "who awoke me from my dogmatic slumbers." Thus awakened, Kant agreed that it was impossible by deductive methods to demonstrate the reality of the soul. But we are forced, said Kant, to a new and radical analysis of our rational powers in order to discover what the mind *can* actively achieve and what it can never hope to achieve. He proceeded to find in the complexity of mental processes a variety of ultimate cognitive functions which he believed to be not further analyzable. Psychologists are especially concerned with the sanction he gave to the notion of the three great subdivisions of mental activity: knowing, feeling, and willing. Analysis of the process of knowing is set forth in his epoch-making *Critique of Pure Reason* (1781); the processes of feeling and willing, though less exhaustively treated, are handled in the *Critique of Judgment* (1790), the *Critique of Practical Reason* (1788), and elsewhere.

Though his contribution to psychology was not comparable with his contribution to philosophy—and this just because he sought the

---

[14] Much of the psychological work of Britain in the seventeenth and eighteenth centuries was done quite outside of the religious atmosphere; and English empiricism, through Condillac, was amalgamated with French agnosticism. Germany was singularly free from these powerful agnostic trends. A strong empirical tendency flourished in Germany in the late eighteenth century, but it was unable to maintain itself.

[15] "Idealism" may be defined for our purposes as that type of philosophy which emphasizes the reality and the value of mental processes which appear to be remote from or independent of physical processes.

ultimate, the transcendental, caring but little for the events of mental life as immediate data and entertaining no hope that they could become the subject matter of science—Kant's work nevertheless greatly influenced psychology. First, through his insistence on the unity of an act of perception. This attacked the very heart of associationism; many of the intellectual forces which in the nineteenth century contributed to the downfall of the associationist system are directly or indirectly traceable to Kant's emphasis upon the unity of experience. When we cognize what we call objects, as in the case of touching a solid object with the fingers, we encounter certain mental states which are apparently composed of sensory qualities; we seem to find the integration of bits of experience of which the associationists spoke. But we find these things coherent, meaningful; some operation has been performed by the mind in organizing these bits into a unitary experience.

Innate and fundamental, moreover, is the tendency to perceive in terms of space and time. A man looks and sees a tree in the world of outer space; he listens and hears a melody flowing forward in time. Locke had taught that the "primary" qualities (size, shape, motion, and so on) are independent of the observer. But all primary and secondary qualities become equally secondary to one who has assimilated Kant. Nevertheless quantitative observations are relatively free from inconsistencies in the hands of various observers. Though they fail to measure the "thing in itself," they give a systematic and orderly account of experience as qualitative observation cannot do. Kant sums up by saying that there is in any discipline as much of science as there is of mathematics. Since his time it has been the intellectual custom to believe that science deals with quantities, not with the inner quality or nature of the things measured; and that though science is a study of experience, it is subject to all the limitations of "knowledge."

Just as the ultimate nature of external things is unobservable, so the knower or inner self is unobservable; we know only phenomena, appearances. Yet the self is encountered in each act of will. The process of willing is independent of causality; the will is free. This is part of our moral nature. Kant therefore leads us back to that religious outlook which he had had to put aside in his study of the process of knowledge. He insists that the ultimate moral and religious reality lies not in the field of knowledge but in the process of the will. His adoption of a "faculty psychology" made feeling and willing each quite separable from knowledge.

The *transcendentalism* of Kant derives its name from the fact that its ultimate explanatory principles lie outside of the content of any particular experience. What is transcendental is *necessary* and *universally valid*. It was therefore in one important respect in violent conflict with empiricism; experience, taken without reference to its transcendental laws, was for Kant simply a meaningless chaos.

GERMAN PSYCHOLOGY: ROMANTICISM

Kant's transcendentalism, springing from intellectualist soil, shortly underwent profound modification in the hands of men who had much less to offer in the analysis of cognitive functions, but who reproduced more adequately the new romanticism of their age. Two streams, transcendentalism and romanticism, come together in a strange kind of unity.

German romanticism was in part an expression of the delayed impact of the Renaissance, which was beginning to produce in Germany the intellectual and moral ferment it had produced much earlier in Italy, France, and Britain. Germany had, on the whole, remained under Scholastic influences for a longer time than had Italy, France, or Britain. Experimental science, which had made rapid progress elsewhere, hardly brought an echo in Germany in these centuries, except among those educated in France. Germany was still locked in the mighty fortress of medieval culture. Now there came at last not only the influence of British empiricism through the work of Kant, but a series of profound changes in the life and the mood of the people, a rebellion against the didactic and the rationalistic.

One of the predisposing influences toward this *romantic movement* was an appreciative (or even mystical) attitude toward nature. The seventeenth and eighteenth centuries had expressed through landscape-painting and poetry a new response to the beauty of nature; and nature, rather than human institutions, was being more and more eagerly studied as the clue to the wholesome and the morally sound. What had earlier happened in Italy, and then in France and England, now began with might in Germany: a turning-away from the scholar's study into the bright day of the world outside. The love of nature and of the natural, which had reached passionate expression in Rousseau in the mid-eighteenth century, assumed in Germany toward the end of the century the form of youthful "storm and stress," which was none the less romantic when it took the majestic form of Goethe's *Faust*.

In consequence of the romantic movement there rapidly developed within transcendentalism a specific form of philosophy the whole purport of which was to show that nature is not merely a series of events but a system of interaction among spiritual entities; the events which science observes have spiritual meanings.[16] From the contact of the post-Kantian transcendentalists, such as Fichte and Schelling, with the romantic movement there arose in the early nineteenth century a philosophy which was transcendentalist in its aim, romantic in its motivation: the "philosophy of nature." It was by no means indifferent to the progress of the sciences; its leader, Oken, stimulated research, and it concerned itself constantly with newly discovered facts, especially with facts from the biological sciences. Indeed, it was dealing with the same subject matter as science, but according to a law of its own. Ultimately it proved to be incompatible with the science it imitated. We shall see that this philosophy was one of the most potent factors in the early training of some of the greatest nineteenth-century physiologists. Its psychology was necessarily vitalistic rather than mechanistic, and its center of interest lay in the fact of the richness of experience rather than in detailed analysis.

Let us review briefly these various schools with which we have been dealing so far, and see their interrelations at the beginning of the nineteenth century. First, the Scottish school, with emphasis primarily on cognitive processes which were thought to be self-evident: We can by direct observation discover that we have ways of obtaining valid knowledge. In Britain the work of the empirical school went on, under Hartley's followers on the one hand, Bentham's and the utilitarians' on the other. The French psychology was to some extent modeled upon the English, especially upon the sensationalist principles formulated by Locke. But the tradition of Descartes, especially as it related to the theory of reflex action and to a conception of bodily mechanics, had in the persons of Cabanis and Bichat led to the vision of a physiological psychology much in advance of that of Hartley. In Germany the rationalistic tendency prevailed, bearing fruit in the transcendentalism of Kant, which insisted on realities beyond experience; and on the other hand, the romantic movement appealed directly to the spiritual meaning of

---

[16] Hegel went further than this. He attempted to show that all human history is more than a succession of events; there is a spiritual thread, a series of embodiments of the "Idea."

natural events, which under transcendentalist influence inspired the philosophy of nature.

REFERENCES

Boring, Edwin G., *A History of Experimental Psychology*, Century, 1929, pp. 179–207

Brett, George S., *A History of Psychology*, 3 vols., London, 1914–21, Vol. 2

Dennis, Wayne, ed., *Readings in the History of Psychology*, Appleton-Century, 1948: Berkeley, Hartley

Ribot, Théodule Armand, *English Psychology*, London, 1873

Warren, Howard C., *A History of the Association Psychology from Hartley to Lewes*, Scribner, 1921

Chapter 4

THE EARLY NINETEENTH
CENTURY

All our thoughts [the Stoics believe] are formed either by indirect perception, or by similarity, or analogy, or transposition, or combination, or opposition.   DIOGENES LAERTIUS

WE MUST next take account of the influence of British associationism upon German thought. Transcendentalism had been gaining in momentum in Germany, but yielded to associationism in the doctrines laid down by Herbart,[1] whose significance is equally great for the history of psychology and for that of education.

HERBART

Though Herbart postulates the reality of the soul, his system of psychology is centered in those elementary bits of experience which we have heretofore called sensations. Just as Condillac and his followers had done before, so Herbart now adopted the structuralism of the English school, reducing complex mental states to combinations of elementary sensory qualities; these units by combining into groups make up our ideas. We have here a structuralism combined with a doctrine regarding the laws of association, all that is needed for a new school of association psychology. The passive linkages assumed by most of the British and French associationists were, however, replaced in Herbart's system by dynamic tendencies. The associationists had created a system very similar to a jigsaw puzzle; it was never easy to see what power put the parts together. Herbart was satisfied that the parts or bits of sensory experience served as

[1] *A Text Book in Psychology* (1816).

units, but it was clear to him that in general associationism had failed to face squarely the problem of finding an integrating principle.

Mental functions were regarded by Herbart as expressions of psychical forces, and were treated from a dynamic—and from a mathematical—point of view. Had he been more of a mathematician and less of a metaphysician, he could perhaps have constructed his beautiful associationism without reference to *forces*, the notion of which had come down from the physicists of the seventeenth century and especially from Newton.[2] But Herbart not only constructed a mathematical system to explain how bits of experience became associated; he not only showed the formulae by which we can create a calculus of the mind; he also defined the principles according to which something, as yet unknown, actively puts these parts together. He closely interwove these distinct conceptions, a mathematical system and the doctrine of an activating principle. The bits of experience coming through the senses combine with each other through the operation of certain measurable forces in the mind, as in the physical world.

Elementary bits of experience may combine harmoniously into wholes; the resulting composite ideas are closely similar to those described by Locke and Hartley. But there are also, Herbart taught, ways in which ideas may come into relation with each other through *conflict* or *struggle*. That is to say, ideas which are incapable of combining compete with one another—compete for a place in consciousness. A systematic theory of the conscious and the unconscious thus becomes necessary. Following out the dynamic implications of the system, a system in which ideas were active forces, Herbart had to show not only exactly what happens when ideas combine, but also exactly what happens when they exclude one another from consciousness. His mathematical formulae are designed to treat of the ascent of ideas into fuller consciousness and their descent from it into the unconscious. The conception of the unconscious was indeed a logically necessary result of such an analysis. Our ideas wax and wane in degree of consciousness as we observe them, and when they sink and are lost to view, we have no choice but to say that they have entered the realm of unconscious ideas. In discussing the "opposition" which leads some ideas to be ejected from consciousness by

---

[2] Burtt, E. A., *Metaphysical Foundations of Modern Physical Science* (1925).

the superior force of other ideas, he simply needed a place for those which had lost the battle, yet were destined to return.[3]

For when an idea is ejected from consciousness, it is not *lost;* it may reappear later. How does it come back? Either by the weakening of the idea which repressed it, or by its combination with an ally, a co-operating idea which may, through joining forces with it, enable it to regain supremacy in consciousness. There is thus a tendency toward the recurrence of ideas which have once been banished. No purpose was served for Herbart by trying to describe the *nature* of unconscious ideas; he insisted simply that when ideas leave consciousness they have a tendency to return. This is a clear recognition of the fact that psychology must deal not only with what is present in consciousness, but with psychological factors beyond the reach of introspection; it involves, moreover, a theory so free from ambiguities that it can be applied to the phenomena of memory and to every phase of mental conflict. As the ideas in the field of consciousness pass from it they cross a *threshold;* the same threshold is crossed in the reverse direction when the idea reappears. It was over fifty years before a more adequate description of the unconscious in terms of empirical findings was attempted.[4]

This conception of the comparability and the interdependence of conscious process with other somehow similar processes occurring outside of consciousness has been a storm center in psychology for a century. Some regard it as an unfortunate and superfluous assumption, one that is unnecessary for empirical psychology, one which clutters up psychology with confusion and contradictions. Others regard consciousness as only one of many expressions of psychological reality; indeed, many of them think that the recognition of a psychological realm far greater than the conscious realm is the great emancipating principle of all modern psychology.

Herbart had no interest in neurological formulae such as those of Hartley. He wanted a purely psychological statement without assumptions regarding echoes and re-echoes of the nerve substance. He achieved this by applying his mathematics directly to the mental processes themselves, using force and time as two of the variables which preside over the uprisings and downsittings of all the different

---

[3] Recent authors, including the psychoanalysts, point out that objects of thought do not conflict with each other because they are in logical opposition, but because they lead to divergent lines of conduct. Ideas are in conflict if they lead us to do opposite things.

[4] By Janet, James, Freud, and F. W. H. Myers. The theoretical studies by Schopenhauer and Von Hartmann seem to have been less important forerunners than the clinical work of Charcot. Cf. page 169.

bits of sensory experience in their different combinations. If we experience a series of events in a given order, the dynamic relations established between them provide the basis for subsequent experience. In place of Hartley's statement of associative sequence through patterns once established in the brain, we have in Herbart a series following in order because certain dynamic relations inherent in the ideas themselves have been set up. This conception received an impressive vindication in the experiments of Ebbinghaus upon memory a half-century later (Chapter 12).

Many of our sensory experiences are not attributable solely to a new stimulus, but to a stimulus augmenting an unconscious deposit of experience. This is equivalent in some cases to the statement that although we had not noticed a stimulus before we now have the background to notice it as soon as it is presented. We may take as an example the case of a professional tea-taster seeking and finding a particular flavor or quality. Most of us might seek in vain for a certain quality which is present, but the tea-taster has so frequently given attention to such qualities that now, when the stimulus is presented, he is able to detect it because of his accumulated past experience; it rises into his consciousness. This brings us to Herbart's most celebrated conception, the *apperceptive mass*. This comprises all those past experiences which we use when we perceive something new. In the illustration used, the perception of a certain quality in the tea is dependent upon the fact that there is a myriad of past tea flavors in the man's accumulated experience; the elements of flavor immediately find a place and are assimilated in consciousness.

Herbart applied his theory significantly to the process of learning. The child is learning, for example, the meaning of numbers. If he has observed his fingers often enough and has learned a group of words which apply to one, two, and three fingers and so on with other objects, and if we now attempt to teach him the general idea that one plus two equals three, he can assimilate this idea because he has observed it in specific cases. He can understand a map of Europe if he knows how land, water, and mountains are represented on the map of a region he already knows. His teacher builds in his mind a certain structure (say, a series of geographical symbols) and now gives him a map of Europe. Immediately all these new sensory stimuli combine with the ideas which lie already assimilated in his mind. This background of ideas constitutes the "apperceptive mass," and instead of merely gazing at the map, he apperceives it. The term "apperception" has for Herbart much the same meaning that it had for Leibnitz, with whom it began; it borrows also from Kant. The process of apperception is a combination of a number of sensory bits into a unity. But instead of emphasizing an innate unifying power, as did Kant, Herbart presupposed that a background of experience already well organized in the mind makes possible the assimilation of a new idea which could never otherwise be learned.[5] This seemingly obvious common-sense doctrine has enjoyed the most extraordinary influence in education.

A revolution in educational theory and practice was already taking place in the closing years of the eighteenth and the opening years of the nineteenth centuries. It came mainly in the form of a protest against the mechanical implanting of information. It emphasized the new idea of developing the child's inherent capacities. Rousseau, in his time, had done much to disseminate this doctrine in speaking of the natural as opposed to the artificial. The aim of education would be to bring out the natural responses of the child. But no one knew just what was "natural." It remained for Pestalozzi (at the end of the eighteenth century) and Froebel (a little later) to clarify the idea. Pestalozzi believed one must start by developing the child's ability to observe. He did not confine this doctrine to the classroom, but applied it to work on the farm, in the garden, and in the home. The implanting of information in the child's mind was reduced to a very subordinate position. Froebel carried the idea further, emphasizing the use of vivid stimuli, such as brightly colored toys, as means of attracting and holding attention, and exercising the child's capacities for dealing with things; he made much of the educational value of play, and founded the *kindergarten* as a means of making use of the "natural" in the child's development.

Herbart realized the importance of this emphasis upon observation. He saw that there were all kinds of ways of reacting to the same stimuli, depending upon the child's background. Education could make use of this principle throughout the whole course of life, starting with physical stimuli, and gradually reaching more and more complicated forms of experience. Systematic use was thus made of the doctrine of apperception. Just as counting the fingers may lead to a general knowledge of numbers, so each contact with the world gives a background for the handling of more and more complex situations.

[5] Herbart did indeed regard the soul as necessary to the coherent function and organization of mind. But from our contemporary viewpoint this seems little more than lip service to it, since the apperceptive mass sets the limits on what the soul can do, and appears to be the central agency in the process of learning and knowing.

But each idea must be offered to the child's observation only when the child, through previous observations, is ready to assimilate the new. This led to the idea of a curriculum so devised that one constantly passes from familiar to closely related unfamiliar subject matter. The entire curriculum should be presented systematically in accordance with the ability to assimilate it.

These ideas were epoch-making. Educational method became an empirical study. Herbart established an experimental school; he conducted classes for teacher training, and compared different methods of presenting school material. And although the mathematical aspirations of Herbart's work were destined to receive no great fulfillment,[6] being rejected as though by common consent, his general conception of mental organization was the basis for educational theory and experimentation for many decades, and remains influential today. He hoped to make psychology an *exact* and an *empirical* science; he failed in the former, but did much to advance the latter purpose.

Except in the case of his theory of apperception, it is difficult to appraise today the historical significance of Herbart's system. The theory of the threshold and the doctrine of conflict keep reappearing in nineteenth-century psychology; but the threshold in Herbart's sense is obscured and frequently forgotten through the different use of the concept in the writings of Weber and Fechner,[7] while modern emphasis on conflict and struggle seems to owe more to Darwinism,[8] and to psychiatric experience.

Herbart's relation to the history of associationism is unique. He was the only associationist for whom the elements of experience were measurable entities; on the other hand, his interest in the soul (with his metaphysical interest) constitutes a direct rejection of the method of most of the British empiricists. He had but little influence on subsequent associationism, which continued its course in Britain; his influence consists rather in helping to overthrow the faculty psychology, in the emphasis upon psychological factors outside of clear consciousness, and in the advancement of educational theory and method.

[6] His mathematical methods did, as we shall see (page 180), influence Ebbinghaus. He contributed also to the quantitative conception of mental abnormality, regarding mental deficiency, for example, as a matter of *degree*, levels of intelligence departing to a greater or lesser extent from the normal.

[7] See pages 80–90.

[8] Not, of course, to Darwin's conception of the conflict of organisms, but to that of dynamic patterns or "instincts" within the organism.

The German psychological literature in the age of Herbart was of considerable quantity, but most of what was written was ephemeral. Our selection of authors and tendencies must be based, as usual, upon the sole criterion of their significance in relation to our contemporary psychology.

One group, under Kant's influence, groped towards a science which would correlate data from physiology, psychology, ethics, and epistemology. They were eager to make use of the accounts of primitive cultures in relation to those more complex; the raw material of travelers' records and memoirs was woven into a system of conceptions about man in his "natural state" [9] and as a social being. There appears to have been a considerable increase during the eighteenth century of the practice of traveling for its own sake. The improvement of roads in France and later in England was important in knitting together more closely the nations of western Europe,[10] while longer journeys ceased to be ventures of discovery and became almost a part of a liberal education. The services of the traveler Von Humboldt in unifying the intellectual life of western Europe were typical. The growing knowledge of many civilizations, primitive and advanced, gave therefore an inductive basis for the work of these students of man. But they needed a theory as to how the mind works; they were forced to build some kind of bridge between the mind of the individual and the life of the group. The first vague intimation of "folk psychology" is found in this period.

One of these "anthropologists," Fries, ingeniously placed Kant's approach upon a biological, empirical foundation.[11] He agreed with Kant about the futility of hoping to know anything ultimate about reality. But the process of cognition, instead of being attributed to a soul which lies beyond experience, was for Fries a function of the constitution of the organism. Man is forced by his biological make-up to see things in a certain way. Instead of introducing a transcendental principle, we should attribute human perception and reasoning to laws inherent in organic make-up. The Kantian categories,

[9] The reader will recall that Hobbes and Rousseau, among many, had pictured a nonsocial human existence; such fervid and uncritical descriptions of primitive societies as had been offered by Montaigne served as material for Rousseau's "noble savage."

[10] Sterne, Laurence, *A Sentimental Journey:* "they order . . . this matter better in France." Goldsmith's *Traveller* is an equally celebrated expression of the tendency noted.

[11] *Handbuch der psychischen Anthropologie* (1820–21).

instead of being transcendental, are empirical. Such men as Fries helped to pave the way for skepticisms and relativities; the fear of absolutes, so characteristic of modern science (cf. page 201).

PHRENOLOGY

At the same time that these rather academic modes of thinking were going on, an extremely widespread movement was taking place which enormously exceeded in popular influence any of the writings just discussed. With the possible exception of Rousseau, none of the psychologists that we have had to consider had enjoyed what we might call a genuinely popular standing. But with the founding of phrenology by Gall in Germany early in the century,[12] a tendency began which was destined to attract wide attention.

Gall's first thesis was that the mind exhibits numerous identifiable functions; his second, that each of these is located in a specific region of the brain. The last vestige of doubt that the brain was the seat of mental life had disappeared as a result of clinical investigations. Nor was the subdivision of the brain into regions possessing independent functions original in itself. But it was one thing to suggest that memory lies in the forebrain, another to itemize the way in which supposedly fundamental traits of man, such as imitativeness, destructiveness, the poetic gift, find their appropriate seats in minute corners of the brain. Gall's list included over thirty such localized traits, and it was expanded by his followers. Thus while associationism broke up the mind into sensory particles, phrenology broke it up into functions or trait units.

Gall held that the degree to which any trait was developed depended on the hereditary development of the appropriate brain area. Such development of the brain tended to exert local pressure on the skull and to press it outward in the form of a "bump." The final assumption was that feeling the skull with the fingers can detect those regions in which there is rich endowment, and thus make possible an analysis of the individual's chief traits.

This was a fascinating game. Gall's hypotheses, with the exception of the one relating to the pressing out of the skull, seemed plausible enough at the time; but instead of seeking full clinical evidence, men went on the road to lecture and to give character demonstrations on the basis of bumps. The practice came rapidly into vogue in France, Britain, and America. In a series of lectures on "Domestic Duties" for young housewives, popular in the thirties, the well-

[12] *Introduction au cours de physiologie du cerveau* (1808).

informed young woman is warned against the hasty acceptance of the generally discussed tenets of phrenology. The continuance in popular speech today of such phrases as "the bump of locality" does not imply that those who use it are believers in phrenology; but it does show the continuance of the doctrines of faculty psychology through the vehicle of phrenological terms. The phrenological scheme reinforced faculty psychology by keeping alive the notion of independent mental functions.

Along with a theory of localization in the brain, Gall was utilizing the conception, developed by Cabanis, that the organism is equipped by nature with basic reaction tendencies in the nervous system which enable it to adjust itself. Many of the instincts, he thought, have their accompanying emotional quality.[13] This was fifty years before the publication of *The Origin of Species*, and the resulting emphasis in psychology upon instincts. Thus in relation to the idea of specialized brain areas, and in relation to the necessity for dynamic units in the study of behavior, Gall was a person of no mean significance. Nevertheless, he fared but ill in academic circles. His unverifiable assumptions and the popular degradation of his system led to the general neglect of his work among psychologists and physiologists.

THE FRENCH REVOLT AGAINST MECHANISM

As we turn to the development of psychology in France, we encounter two traditions, the tradition of Descartes and the associationist's tradition. The sturdiest figure at the turn of the century had been Cabanis, a physiologist whose emphasis upon reflex action and whose whole dynamic approach made him a worthy disciple of Descartes.

But a revolt was brewing; mechanism did not suit the intellectual climate of the Napoleonic era; an idealistic movement was rapidly coming into its own. The spirit of this revolt was largely empirical. Thomas Reid, in founding the Scottish school, had tried as we have seen to base his idealism not on dogma but on confidence in the trustworthiness of the senses. Even those who attacked the empirical findings of mechanism used empiricism as a method. The same thing is true, to some extent, of the new French idealism, in which Maine de Biran was the dominant figure.

Biran began with an attempt at empiricism: the analysis of the genesis of habit, will, and self-consciousness in the child. His chief

[13] Compare McDougall's analysis of instinct in his *Introduction to Social Psychology* (1908).

concern was the development of the self, of an individuality which is capable of integrated activity. He represented, moreover, a reaction against the mechanistic method, believing that the self is an experiencing *agent*, and something more than a series of experiences; it is a unified spiritual principle. Now the self is not at first aware of its own existence; it is not directly experienced. But, by the process of adjustment to the environment, it becomes conscious of the distinction between the self and the not-self. There are two steps in this process. Such activities as crying and movement of the limbs are first called out mechanically. They take place by virtue of those principles which Cabanis had emphasized. But when the same stimulus is repeated later, there is in the field of experience a division into two parts, the object or thing upon which we react, and the self that reacts. In other words, the exercise of will is the first and dominant principle which causes the development of self-consciousness. It is because of our reactions, especially when resistance is offered to them, that we become aware of ourselves as individuals. As activity becomes more complex, self-consciousness develops greater richness.

This is a genuinely dynamic psychology. But its importance lay in giving a new turn to French thought, rather than in providing a specific set of ideas for the use of later generations. The details of Biran's system had little influence even in France a generation after his death. Yet he remained a sort of guardian spirit constantly present with French psychology, not indeed as a stimulus to the use of the genetic method, but as an embodiment of voluntarism, emphasizing the central place of the will.

Joining in the antimechanist protest came another movement: a French version of the Scottish philosophy. For the writings of Royer-Collard, who became professor at the Sorbonne in the year 1811, were simply continuations of the work of Reid. But in giving psychology a "spiritual" interpretation,[14] the school of Royer-Collard made use of the doctrines of Biran; specifically, they emphasized the fact of activity, which the associationists had almost without exception disregarded. His voluntarism had opened the way for a psychology which could meet their requirements. The will remained dominant in French psychology for the next forty or fifty years (idealism almost necessarily clings to the will as an independent function). But no clear facts about the will were available. With Biran as their presiding genius and Royer-Collard as their recognized

---

[14] The term "*spiritualisme*," which is still in general use in French psychology, corresponds, roughly, to our "idealism."

head, French psychologists now settled down into an unimaginative and unproductive eclecticism. In the second quarter of the century the greatest figure was Cousin, whose contribution lay more in wide scholarship than in original observation. Eclecticism was so general that during the entire half-century which followed Biran French psychology may be characterized as the influenced rather than the influencing psychology of western Europe. But, as we shall see, France later did far more than its share in the development of psychiatry and in the task of bringing psychiatry and psychology together.

THE FUSION OF SCOTTISH AND ENGLISH PSYCHOLOGY: THOMAS BROWN

Thomas Brown was a representative of three schools of thought, Scottish, English, and French.[15] He was Scottish in his background, his education, and his academic position, ideally fitted for his post as Professor of Moral Philosophy at Edinburgh. He never abandoned that claim to prestige which the Scottish school had maintained through its emphasis upon the dignity of man. And he derived from the Scottish school one cardinal doctrine, the conception of a unitary substance or principle; in other words, the soul, whose affections and functions are the phenomena of psychology. The mind was not a mosaic of pieces, but a unity of substance with varying manifestations.

Yet he borrowed copiously from the associationists, and had constant recourse to their methods of observation. Beginning with the work of Brown, the Scottish school came definitely under the influence of the English tradition. The chief importance of Brown's system of psychology lay in his wise and mature development of associationist theory. Using the term "suggestion" rather than "association," he sought an empirical treatment of the problem of mental connections.

He accepted Hartley's reduction of mental connections to one basic principle, which he called "coexistence." But this basic principle manifested itself in three forms, dependent on *resemblance, contrast,* and *nearness in time and space.* But now we come to this vital problem: When one thing is somehow connected with *two* or more other things, what is it that determines each particular course of association? When, for example, *tiger* resembles both *leopard* and *lion*, why does *tiger* in some cases make us think of *leopard* and in

[15] *Lectures on the Philosophy of the Human Mind* (1820).

other cases of *lion?* Hobbes, in the middle of the seventeenth century, had vaguely seen the problem (page 26) but had given no satisfactory solution. Hartley had concerned himself with the analysis of complex life situations, but had never undertaken to show how his laws worked in the determination of particular sequences to the exclusion of others; why, for example, the same experience will prompt in the same man different ideas on different occasions. Brown, grasping the significance of the problem, undertook an analysis of the many factors determining the course of association, the celebrated "secondary laws of association." These have a peculiarly modern ring. Much of the weakness of nineteenth-century associationism could have been avoided if their importance had been recognized; it was not until the last decades of the century that German and American experimentalists discovered the necessity of taking such an analysis into account.[16]

The first four of Brown's secondary laws have perhaps the most vital significance, but all are important as modifications of the associationist tendency to oversimplify. Brown's laws are thus summarized by Warren.[17]

1. The relative *duration* of the original sensations: "The longer we dwell on objects, the more fully do we rely on our future remembrance of them."

2. Their relative *liveliness:* "The parts of a train appear to be more closely and firmly associated as the original feelings have been more lively."

3. Relative *frequency:* "The parts of any train are more readily suggested in proportion as they have been more frequently renewed."

4. Relative *recency:* "Events which happened a few hours before are remembered when there is a total forgetfulness of what happened a few days before."

5. Their coexistence in the past with *fewer alternative associates:* "The song which we have never heard but from one person can scarcely be heard again by us without recalling that person to our memory."

6. *Constitutional differences* between individuals modify the primary laws. They give "greater proportional vigor to one set of tendencies of suggestion than to another."

7. Variations in the *same individual,* "according to the varying emotion of the hour."

8. "Temporary *diversities of state,*" as in intoxication, delirium, or ill-health.

16 Notably Külpe (cf. page 227) and Calkins (cf. page 182).
17 *A History of the Association Psychology from Hartley to Lewes* (1921), p. 73.

9. Prior *habits of life* and thought—the influence of ingrown tendencies upon any given situation, however new or irrelevant the experience may be.

The general laws of "suggestion" were now seen to operate in terms, for example, of the relative *recency, frequency,* and *liveliness* of particular experiences. The emphasis on emotional and constitutional factors was also significant and quite in contrast with the associationists' usual neglect of individual differences. It was a contribution of great moment to see the need of working out such specific laws and to think in terms of the individual as a whole in the determination of each specific sequence of thought.

Brown championed Locke's position as to the presence of certain capacities of a reflective nature as well as those of a merely sensory nature. Hartley had reduced all experience to the association of sensory elements; Locke had taught that in addition to ideas derived directly from the senses, we have ideas derived from reflection upon the data given by the senses. Brown, unwilling to use the nervous system as an explanatory principle, could not regard images or ideas as mere reverberations of sensations, reducing them to faint copies of their sensory originals. The memory elements were not for him identical with the sensory elements; they were independent entities. But if two objects are observed at the same time, and if we immediately become aware of the relation between the two, this is not a sensory function; it is a function of the mind, as a mind. To perceive that one man is taller than another, or one light brighter than another, is to grasp directly a relation present in experience. This was another blow at associationism. Mental life was not a mere concatenation of sense data, but was characterized by capacities to grasp relations. This was "relative suggestion," as opposed to the "simple suggestion" by which one idea follows another by virtue of sensory experience. "Relative suggestion" was not treated as a part of perception, but was emphasized only as it appeared in such processes as comparison and judgment. These relational elements have been successively forgotten and rediscovered. Bain, for example, recognized them; German psychologists rediscovered them in various guises late in the century. They have again come into their own in connection with the Gestalt school in recent years.

In addition to these obvious influences of the Scottish and the English schools, we have to take into account the fact that Brown had immersed himself in the writings of those French philosophers who were gently but effectively reinstating idealism in opposition to the mechanistic trend of the late eighteenth century. It was noted above that the reduction of the mind by Condillac and Cabanis to simple, mechanically conceived components was in harmony with a widespread revolt against religious and spiritual interpretations. Similarly, the return of the pendulum to idealism after the French Revolution gave strength to the hands of those who sought to overthrow the mechanistic schools. The followers of Condillac were amending his system by attributing some degree of *activity* to the individual. Among their greatest names were Laromiguière and De Tracy; the former, greatly influenced by Biran's activism, influenced in turn the work of Brown. Cabanis, though himself a mechanist, had helped to point out the significance of activity in personality. An idealistic and religious turn of mind found therefore close at hand the materials for the construction of a new system. This group of "ideologists" took hold upon that polite part of society which was interested in philosophy. They would not call ideas by unpleasant names, such as "mere sensation." But they were not so direct and flamboyant as Thomas Reid; their protest was orderly and courteous. Their central principle was that mind is not a passive instrument for receiving impressions. In specific revolt against Condillac, they held that mind is essentially a thing which reacts, which has spontaneous activities of its own. But theirs was scarcely a constructive movement. It was an attempt to restore the broken handle rather than to mold a new vessel.

This philosophy had all the elements necessary to make it become popular in Scotland. It was not only in harmony with the spiritual views of the Scottish school; it had, in fact, much that had been absorbed indirectly or borrowed directly from Scotland. Its specific alterations of associationist doctrine were useful and welcome to the Scottish school. Brown mastered both Scottish and French systems; his introduction of the French viewpoint and the French critique was, in fact, an enriching influence in his own system, and responsible in part for his popularity. It was through French conceptions rather than Scottish ones that he saw how he could safely use the methods of the associationists while still rejecting their viewpoint. Regarding the soul as a living and acting entity, he could without compromise accept most of the empirical analysis of Hartley and his followers.

One point in which French influence was especially clear was his emphasis on the "muscular sensations," the sensations which give awareness of the position of the limbs, and of opposition which they may meet in contact with outside objects. Some attention had been given to the muscle sense by physiologists; its introduction into psychology was, however, chiefly the work of Brown. The muscle sense, said Brown, gives us our notion of resistance. This was an elaboration of the ideologists' position; it was similar also to the point which Biran was making, the idea that the self is, in fact, engendered by the resistance offered to the blind movements of early infancy. But Brown's treatment of the concept differs materially from Biran's. Instead of Biran's almost mystical treatment of the will, leading to self-consciousness in the child, Brown's was chiefly a simple statement of the part played by muscular sensation in giving us awareness of the solidity of material things.

Brown's chief significance lay perhaps in the fact that he served to make the Scottish school more empirical. He made the school so closely acquainted with genuinely analytical methods that it could never quite go back to the firmly implanted dogmatism of its founder. In becoming amalgamated with empiricism and associationism, it lost its identity. But in Brown's hands associationism had for the first time undertaken a specific narrative of why we think and act in the particular ways forced upon us by particular occasions, while the interaction of "ideas" was replaced by acting individuals. Psychic atomism remained, to be sure, for a while; as we shall see, it was incorporated in the thoroughgoing associationism of James Mill, with whom it reached its logical perfection and systematization. But Brown's work was the beginning of the end both of associationism and of the Scottish school. He had given new life to the bold endeavors of those who wished to analyze and systematize the furious complexity of experience. He had put an end forever to the naïve formalism and pompous barrenness of Reid's approach. At the same time his conception of personality as a unity did much to give associationism that maturity and caution through which it attained its greatest achievements in the work of Spencer and Bain.

REFERENCES

Brett, George S., *A History of Psychology,* 3 vols., London, 1914–21; Vol. 3, the opening chapters

Boring, Edwin G., *A History of Experimental Psychology,* Century, 1929, 237–50

Dennis, Wayne, ed., *Readings in the History of Psychology,* Appleton-Century, 1948: Brown

Merz, J. T., *A History of European Thought in the Nineteenth Century,* 4 vols., London, 1896

Warren, Howard C., *A History of the Association Psychology from Hartley to Lewes,* Scribner, 1921

PART TWO

The Rise of the Research Spirit

Chapter 5

SOME INTELLECTUAL ANTE-CEDENTS OF EXPERIMENTAL PSYCHOLOGY

. . . the whole conception of the Natural Universe has been changed by the recognition that man, subject to the same physical laws and processes as the world around him, cannot be considered separately from the world, and that scientific methods of observation, induction, deduction and experiment are applicable, not only to the original subject-matter of pure science, but to nearly all the many and varied fields of human thought and activity.

SIR WILLIAM DAMPIER

THE ORIGINS of experimental psychology in Germany are to be sought in the intellectual development of western Europe in the late eighteenth and early nineteenth centuries; and most of all in the progress of experimental science in France and Germany. We must turn first to the progress of the exact sciences, particularly mathematics, chemistry, and physics; next, to that of the biological sciences, especially physiology. For experimental psychology grew out of the soil of an experimental physiology which was dependent upon all of these for its existence.[1]

Experimental methods had yielded many and cumulative results in the natural sciences since the days of Gilbert and Galileo. The Newtonian mathematics had been eagerly adopted and developed in France, and became the central feature of French science. Whereas the experimental approach was more characteristic of English science, the most characteristic feature of science in France

[1] For a fuller treatment of the history of science in the eighteenth and early nineteenth centuries see Merz, J. T., *History of European Thought in the Nineteenth Century* (1896), upon which I have chiefly relied.

was the development of mathematical methods. By the middle of the eighteenth century French mathematicians had won world pre-eminence.

As early as the middle of the seventeenth century the French Academy of Sciences had found favor with Louis XIV; and from that time onward it served as a central repository of scientific methods and results, as well as a center for the mutual stimulation and encouragement of scientific men, a center not merely for France, but for the world. This was utterly unlike anything to be found in Britain or Germany. It is true that Newton took a leading part in the formation of the Royal Society in England, but it was never favored by much support. A great British astronomer of the period was forced to give part of his time to tutoring in order to get the wherewithal for his researches. The French, on the other hand, offered much encouragement to astronomical work. This matter of patronage was a prominent factor in the rapid rise of the exact sciences in France. There sprang up departmental centers for scientific study and research all over France, so that French science attained some degree of integration. Local groups had opportunities to exchange ideas with one another, and many individuals went to Paris for study. Journals were founded which served to give quick dissemination to new ideas. Such close affiliation for scientific work was not dreamed of in England, nor in Germany.[2]

But the departmental centers and the journals were dependent on an all-important element, without which French intellectual leadership would have been impossible; namely, national solidarity and a unity both political and cultural. Among the many economic factors which contributed to this national unity was the excellence of the French roads. Similarly, the improvement of English roads through the introduction of French methods in the late eighteenth century seems to have done much to knit together groups whose intellectual co-operation had previously been hampered.

Whichever of these advantages we see fit to emphasize, the pre-eminence of the French in the exact sciences was apparent. The French had borrowed to such an extent the mechanical view of the universe, founded upon Newton's work, that we begin to find literary expression of it in the mid-eighteenth century, for example in Voltaire. This gave to the reading public the unified view of the mechanical universe which had been developed by Kepler, Galileo,

[2] The German states which were parts of the empire were held together in the loosest fashion; while Prussia, though powerful, had a negligible influence as yet in the intellectual integration of the German-speaking states.

and Newton. Voltaire was almost a popularizer of Newton; he occupied himself with the task of turning over to the public that conception of the world which mathematics and physics had outlined.

This task of popularization did not, of course, really reach the masses in Voltaire's time; it spread rapidly among the elite, but it was scarcely designed for the laborer and the peasant. The French Revolution brought about an immediate change. Educators sought to dispense with traditional subjects, and to found the whole system of public instruction upon natural science. Condorcet made the point that the mathematical sciences were of immediate importance to all citizens; they strengthened the powers of observation and the capacity for clear thinking. Moreover, they were of practical value in the problems of industry and war. Engaged as France was in war with most of the powers of western Europe, the use of mathematics for artillery, and of chemistry for explosives, was sure to be emphasized. Biological science had a practical place because of its relation to the training of military surgeons. Condorcet undertook the task of educating the whole Republic in the exact sciences.

The Revolution inevitably interfered at first with research work, but it is surprising to note how much scientific investigation, even in fields not immediately practical, was carried on in France during this period of relative isolation. Some individuals suffered, but most of the scientific work in progress was publicly recognized. And Napoleon acknowledged the importance of science and mathematics, for this added to his own personal prestige as well as to the value of his engineering and artillery officers.

Some of the specific contributions of French science may serve to show its spirit. By means of the differential and integral calculus it had been possible to work out the laws of the movements of heavenly bodies more adequately than seventeenth-century mathematicians had dared to dream. A little more than a century after Newton's *Principia* (1687), Laplace published his great books on celestial mechanics. He also undertook to describe the evolution of the solar system from nebular substances (the view known as the "nebular hypothesis"). Great importance attaches to his "theory of probability." Tables showing the annual number of births, marriages, and deaths within various social groups had been in use for more than a century; but a sound mathematical understanding of the means of prediction from such tables (and of the likelihood of a variation of any given amount) was much needed. Laplace supplied the mathematical theory necessary for the first steps, so that, although his interest lay chiefly in pure rather than in applied mathematics, it was but natural that he should become statistician to Napoleon. The relatively simple conception of *quantities*, offered by Newton, was also subjected by French mathematicians to a critical analysis.

The discovery of oxygen by Priestley is another instance in which British work led rapidly to French elaboration both in theory and in practice. Almost all the chemists of first magnitude in the late eighteenth century were Frenchmen. Chemistry had been full of occult ideas; there were no unifying laws which could be quantitatively stated. It was chiefly through the work of Lavoisier just before the Revolution that an experimental quantitative chemistry came into being. In discovering, moreover, the nature of respiration (the union of carbon with oxygen), he brought chemistry into close relation with the life sciences. The scope of chemical experimentation is indicated by the founding of journals for the publication of research. This advance of chemistry in France was slow in reaching other nations, as the military situation tended to isolate France in respect to science and its applications. Furthermore, the tradition of the isolation of individual investigators from one another still held sway in Great Britain, in sharp contrast to the co-operation and centralization which characterized French research.

On the other hand, it happened through a fortunate concatenation of circumstances that early in the nineteenth century Germany began to occupy itself with chemistry and physics. Chemistry in the German universities had been very dependent on French sources.[3] Practically all textbooks in the exact sciences in use in German (as in British) universities were in French, or were translations from the French. But within the university system of Germany there began to arise shortly after the close of the Napoleonic era a group of men (some of them trained in France) who were prepared to introduce French ideas. The first decade of their work was essentially a continuation of the French tradition, but German chemistry soon acquired a distinct individuality.

Liebig founded in 1826 a university laboratory for the systematic study of chemistry. He became, indeed, the founder of a new division of chemistry; he devised suitable methods for the chemical study of some of the functions of living creatures, and for these the

---

[3] The dissemination of French science into Germany had, of course, been possible to some extent even during the Revolution and the Napoleonic era. A prominent figure in this task was Von Humboldt, whose wide travels and international spirit had done much to acquaint Germany with French problems and methods.

term "organic chemistry" came into use.[4] Borrowing freely from contemporary French work, he probably did more than any other man to give German chemistry its enviable position in the three generations which followed. Wöhler, his pupil, succeeded as early as 1828 in actually creating synthetically an organic compound, urea, and thus in throwing a bridge across the gulf which separated the inorganic from the organic.

At the same time other investigations which served to establish connections between the physical and the biological sciences were going on in many other countries. Galvani discovered (1791) the electrical current generated by stimulation of the frog's sciatic nerve. This was conceived by many to have tremendous philosophical significance. Some hastened to conclude that the intimate nature of life processes had been found, and that these processes were fundamentally different from the mechanical processes supposed to dominate the nonliving. On the other hand, mechanists derived an equal consolation from it; it proved for them that physical principles were sufficient for the explanation of life. Many men, of many philosophical expressions, were dreaming of bringing together on a scientific level those disciplines which we call physical on the one hand and those which we call biological on the other. The dream had been dreamed by many before; but these strange electrical phenomena which were actually under investigation gave new ground for the hope of unifying the physical with the biological sciences.

Other contributions bringing the life sciences into closer touch with the physical sciences came from a series of discoveries in acoustics and optics. Chladni's work in acoustics was followed by Thomas Young's celebrated studies in the wave theory of light and in the theory of retinal function.[5] Optical phenomena necessitated physiological and psychological assumptions. Young formulated a three-color theory (later supported by Helmholtz), according to which the retina is equipped with three kinds of color receptors, whose co-operative function gives the entire range of colors experienced. The Bohemian physiologist Purkinje made important observations on the brightness of color in relation to the intensity of light. From such developments followed that experimental physiology of audition and vision which was later on to play so great a role in the establishment of an experimental psychology.

[4] The term gradually acquired its present meaning: the study of the compounds of carbon.

[5] For example, *Course of Lectures on Natural Philosophy* (1807). The wave theory of light goes back to the pioneer work of Huygens, a Dutch contemporary of Newton.

THE BIOLOGICAL SCIENCES

To turn to the development of the biological sciences, attention must first be given to the classifications of species. Ray's seventeenth-century classification of species was extended by Linnaeus. Not only did Linnaeus know and classify thousands of plants (and animals), but, more significantly, he devised a *system* of classification, grouping individuals into species, and species into genera, both indicated by Latin (hence international) names. The conception of a "species" has undergone notable changes; but the Linnean system has been of inestimable value.

The work of classification was carried forward and greatly enriched by Cuvier. "To name well," he remarked, "you must know well." His many contributions extend through the Revolutionary and Napoleonic eras. They give him rank with the histologist Bichat and the physiologist Cabanis as a representative of French biology. His contribution consists first of all in carrying out Linnaeus's idea of systematically grouping organisms, and noting the elements of similarity and difference observed in members of various species and genera. He sought to make possible a classification which would not only give names to organisms, but would show their true resemblances and differences by noting which similarities were significant and fundamental, and which were superficial or without significance. In spite of the lead taken by Lamarck, Erasmus Darwin, and others, Cuvier definitely opposed the evolutionary theory (cf. page 113), which would have been most useful as a genetic method of classification. But he was an anatomist of such insight that he was able to lay down fundamental principles of wide general validity; he is generally recognized as the father of modern comparative anatomy. It is interesting to note that Cuvier relied chiefly not on the structure of bones, muscles, or sense organs, but on the central nervous system, as the most reliable single criterion in classification.

It was Cuvier's task to make a systematic survey of all the scientific work done each year; these surveys were in the form of reports to Napoleon. Together with *Eloges* delivered upon the deaths of great scientists, they mark a further advance in the establishment of central storehouses of scientific information. The group of physiologists and anatomists to which Cuvier belonged gave France—in fact, we may say specifically the city of Paris—almost as definite a position of leadership in biological science as it enjoyed in physical science.

But in the early nineteenth century a variety of forces became apparent by which a new place in the study of the biological sciences, as well as in the study of physical sciences, was won by Germany. To understand these, attention must be turned to the German university system, in which a series of important developments had been taking place during the eighteenth century.

The typical German university during the Middle Ages included three faculties: a faculty of theology, a faculty of law, and a faculty of medicine. These three faculties were virtually professional schools. No general or liberal-arts course was provided. If a student went to the university, he usually prepared himself for one of these three professions. There was a general neglect of scientific courses, except as they forced themselves into the medical curriculum. In the year 1734 a faculty of philosophy was founded at Göttingen, the aim of which was to give instruction not for the specific purpose of training for a professional career, but for the purpose of providing what we should now call a "liberal education." This involved the establishment of chairs for some subjects which had traditionally been a part of the three older faculties, and some chairs for subjects newly introduced. The faculty of philosophy included such subjects as mathematics and physics; history; history of literature; Oriental languages; as well as two chairs for various subdivisions of philosophy, and a professorship of philosophy "without special definition." Carlyle's Teufelsdröckh, professor of "things in general," would have been an ideal holder of such a chair without portfolio. This new faculty was rapidly copied all through the German-speaking world.

During the eighteenth century, science became an important part of the German university curriculum; but "science"—"*Wissenschaft*"—took on a distinctive meaning. In France, "*science*" had come to mean mathematics or "exact science." German scholars attacked the problem of phonetics and of language; they developed philological technique. They began to apply critical methods to the study of literature, developing in time, for example, the technique of Biblical criticism, and working out general principles by which it was possible to ascertain the date and the authorship of ancient manuscripts. They improved the methods of history and archaeology. They devoted themselves to the problem of evaluating historical source material. Baumgarten's attempt to found a science of aesthetics, Kant's critical approach to the process of cognition, and Hegel's revision of logic under the term "dialectic," are parts of an extensive movement already well under way; they were works of Wissenschaft just as truly as were experiments in physics.[6]

[6] But "cultural sciences" (*Geisteswissenschaften*) are of course to be distinguished from the "natural sciences" (*Naturwissenschaften*).

We may say, to put it negatively, that the reason why the French and the British had given biology and the cultural sciences a secondary place was their preference for quantitative analysis. They could approach physics and chemistry with mathematical methods; they could not understand that the biological and cultural sciences could be experimentally or mathematically approached. While the British and the French thought the physical sciences alone capable of being genuinely scientific, the Germans thought every field of knowledge could be equally scientific. Even the analysis of the knowing process itself (as Kant undertook to show) could become a systematic discipline. The application of critical methods to such a variety of subjects, and the interdependence of all these, brought it about that the German university teacher and student had but little of the departmental turn of thought which inevitably influenced the French teacher and student. The German faculty of philosophy served as a means of attaining a broad view of civilization as a whole. The German university was an engine with which to create a unified knowledge of the world.

Together with this ideal of the unity of all human knowledge there was also the feeling that the phenomena of life, as represented by the biological sciences, were to be viewed not merely in the perspective of chemistry and physics, but in their relation to all these other disciplines. No single approach could suffice in the study of so complex a thing as life; there must be some kind of unity or connection, at least in treatment if not in subject matter. There had been in both Britain and France a considerable skepticism about the possibility of building up a scientific technique for the study of living things. But in the German university the phenomena of life were subjected to the same critical treatment and seen in the same perspective as was required in any other specialty. The study of life must be undertaken from a unified philosophical world-view.

It is natural to ask how there could be uniformity of treatment in spite of the fact that there were over twenty universities in Germany, politically separated, and with each man teaching from his own point of view. Such a possibility resulted from the exchange of professors between universities and the students' habit of moving about from one institution to another, customs vitally important in the unification of German thought. It never occurred to the German student that there ought to be any local continuity in his course toward a degree. This exposure to many influences augmented the tendency to seek for a unified view of the world and the desire to see life as a whole.

One who did much to point out the unity between the sciences was Haller, the physiologist of Göttingen, who flourished in the middle of the eighteenth century. Profoundly influenced by his teacher, the Dutch physiologist Boerhaave, he sought to treat human and animal life, chemistry and physics, as a unity. He gave to German students the conception that the empirical approach—in particular, the experimental method—which the British and French were using in the physical sciences, could be applied to life processes; the notion of physiology as an experimental science was established. The importance of this conception can be realized only when we consider the extraordinary degree to which biological science had been occupied with the astrological and the occult. Even the great teacher Paracelsus, who did so much to establish a chemical view of life processes, had made extensive use of astrological principles; even the intrinsically helpful notion of humors in the blood was confused with much that was incapable of any sort of verification. Haller has been called the father of modern physiology.[7] He published a textbook which remained for three-quarters of a century the standard text on physiology for the world.[8]

But we have to consider another factor which this statement disregards. We may recall the extraordinary development of the interest which Germany of the "romantic" period showed in living things, as something distinct from the world of matter and motion. The German temperament of the time reached out toward the comprehension of life.[9] There is, of course, no need to designate this as a permanent national trait; the same general tendency was apparent in Italy during the Renaissance. One might be tempted, and not entirely without justice, to say that this is the arrival of the Renaissance in Germany. One might be tempted to say that Germany, isolated from the rest of western Europe through a series of wars and through such influences as the surviving feudalism of the Holy Roman Empire, had its awakening in the eighteenth century, so that problems of the nature of life won a prominent place outside of as well as within the university system. All this development of the biological sciences in Germany might be regarded as part of a

[7] Harvey had of course shown the way, and many clinicians had contributed important empirical studies of physiological functions, side by side with the rapid progress of anatomy.

[8] Until the publication of Johannes Müller's textbook (see page 96).

[9] Eighteenth-century France and Britain witnessed striking romantic movements. Yet the tendency to speak of the "romantic movement" as essentially German is perhaps evidence for the view suggested. But we are dealing with a question of degree.

general cultural movement. It would be out of perspective to say that the German university was the sole explanation for the rise of biology.

A familiar illustration of the German spirit of the time is the personality and career of Goethe, who was so great as a poet that few people thought of him as a scientist. But he was, in fact, responsible for two important biological contributions. He was one of the first of the moderns to put forward a theory of organic evolution; and he elaborated a significant theory of color vision.[10] In opposition to Young's three-color theory, he undertook to show that one cannot account for the facts of color-blindness, color contrast, and negative afterimages without postulating at least four primary colors. Goethe made also a number of contributions to botany which would have sufficed to render him illustrious were they not overshadowed by his position in literature and philosophy. It was not only in the universities that the growing study of life processes was manifest.

On the other hand, the main current of this development undoubtedly did flow in the universities. It reached its greatest height after the Napoleonic period in the brilliant physiological researches of Weber and Johannes Müller and their pupils. (To these men we shall later devote special attention; for the present it is important only to show their relation to the general movement indicated.) We saw above how Liebig and Wöhler worked together to found the science of organic chemistry, and how a link had been forged between the inorganic chemistry of Lavoisier and the study of life. While this was going on, botanists and zoologists sought with the aid of the microscope to discover a connection between physical principles and the principles of form which underlie the structure of living things. They were trying to do in the field of morphology what Liebig had done in the field of chemistry. A great step had already been taken in France in the closing years of the eighteenth century by Bichat's demonstration of the relation between organs and the fundamental structures (the tissues) which compose them. In Germany a new step was now taken by Schleiden, who demonstrated in 1838 that all plant tissues were made up of cells, each cell being in some respects an independent unit. Two years later Schwann succeeded in showing that the same principles held for animal tissues. The study of life processes was enormously furthered

10 *Farbenlehre* (1810).

by these two noteworthy discoveries; the knowledge of the cellular constitution of living matter greatly facilitated the analysis and classification of microscopic structures. The discovery of such structural units was of far-reaching consequence not only for anatomy but for physiology. Germany held, by the middle of the century, a position of leadership in biological science, which, as we have seen, was due very largely to a certain background of intellectual history that differentiated its specific problems from those of France and Britain.

While all this went on in Germany, there were many brilliant biological researches under way in England, in the hands of individuals who enjoyed no such co-operation and no such profound intellectual stimulus as were vouchsafed to the German scientist. The most notable of these was Sir Charles Bell's discovery of the principle of differentiation of sensory and motor nerves. Galen, to be sure, had known of sensory and motor nerve functions. But it was supposed that nerves possessed in general *both* sensory and motor functions, and it remained for Bell to show that some structures are sensory, others motor—that immediately before entering the spinal cord the sensory fibers group themselves into the dorsal, and the motor fibers into the ventral, root of each nerve.[11] He laid the foundation for a detailed study of nervous physiology in terms of the incoming and outgoing pathways. He suggested also that the division of labor might be still more detailed; that in spite of morphologic similarity the *variety* of mental functions might be based on a variety of specialized tasks carried out by many functionally distinct nervous elements.[12] The lack of scientific intercommunication across national boundaries in this period is well shown in the fact that many years passed before Johannes Müller undertook the elaboration of these two doctrines of Bell, experimentally verifying the former and stating the latter in the famous formula of "specific energies" (cf. page 93). Though Magendie, in France, did experimental work on the problem in the twenties, Bell's epoch-making discovery

[11] His *New Idea of the Anatomy of the Brain* (1811) was followed by a number of papers read before the Royal Society. See Carmichael, L., "Sir Charles Bell: A Contribution to the History of Physiological Psychology," *Psychol. Rev.*, 1926, 33.

[12] In essence, the idea is really a very old one, and the eighteenth century had revived it. Bonnet had grasped it quite clearly: " . . . there are in each sense certain fibers which are appropriate to each kind of sensation. . . . There are consequently still among the fibers of vision certain differences corresponding to those which exist among the rays."—*Analyse abrégée de l'essai analytique* (1779–83) VI, X.

regarding sensory and motor roots seems not to have been fully appreciated until Müller's time.

REFERENCES

Aside from Merz (see footnote, page 67), the most useful references are the general histories of science, such as William T. Sedgwick and H. W. Tyler, *A Short History of Science,* rev. ed., Macmillan, 1939; and also the general histories of thought, such as John H. Randall, *The Making of the Modern Mind,* rev. ed., Houghton Mifflin, 1940.

Chapter 6

THE BEGINNINGS OF EXPERI-
MENTAL PSYCHOLOGY

*The art of measurement would do away with the effect of appear-
ance. . . . They err not only from defect of knowledge in general, but of that particular knowledge which is called measuring.*

PLATO

THE RISE of the biological sciences in Germany led quickly to a
brilliant personification of the movement in E. H. Weber. He
was one of three brothers illustrious in the natural sciences.
Whereas the others devoted themselves to physical science, his own
work was centered in the physiology of the sense organs. Research
upon the sense organs and their functions in Germany, as well as in
France and England, had been confined almost entirely to the higher
senses, seeing and hearing. His work consisted largely in opening up
new experimental fields, notably research upon the cutaneous and
muscular sensations, and in perceiving psychological implications
in his results.

He began shortly before 1820 to teach anatomy and physiology
at the University of Leipzig, where he remained throughout his
career. His life there was characterized by the constant publication
of new work and the stimulation of a large number of students—
medical students for the most part, for medicine held the supremacy
among the biological sciences, and physiology as an independent
science did not yet exist. Though he was more or less under the
influence of the "philosophy of nature," with its belief in spirit
expressing itself through physical symbols, this did not mar the
solidity of his experimental and theoretical work as a physiologist.

A few examples may be given of his widely varied studies in
sensory physiology. His experiments on the temperature sense led
him to formulate a theory to the effect that the experience of warmth

and cold is not dependent directly on the temperature of the stimulating object, but on the *increase* and *decrease* of the temperature of the skin. If the hand is placed in warm water, the rising temperature of the skin leads to the experience of warmth. The skin temperature may rise or fall without occasioning the experience of warmth or cold if the change is very gradual. This theory accounts well for the adaptation or habituation which makes warmth or cold less noticeable after the skin has been exposed to it for some time. One of his minor experiments aimed to determine whether liquids or gases are the true stimuli for the sense of smell. He put a 10 per cent solution of Eau de Cologne into his nose, and tilted his head so as to bring the liquid into contact with the nasal mucous membrane. Finding that no sensation of smell was received, he concluded that liquids are not direct olfactory stimuli. An instance of his work on audition was the discovery that if he held a ticking watch at each ear he was less proficient in judging whether the ticks were simultaneous than if the two watches were held at the same ear. As an example of his experiments in vision, one may be named in which he undertook to determine the smallest arc that would permit discrimination of two lines. When the lines are exceedingly close together we get the impression of one line, while if they are not so close we see two distinct lines; he measured the arc necessary for such distinction.

To several of Weber's experiments much more attention must be given. One of these had to do with the distance that must separate two stimuli applied to the skin, in order to bring about the perception of doubleness.[1] This was, of course, the same experiment within the field of *cutaneous* sensation which we noted above in the field of vision. Precautions being taken to exclude the use of vision, the subject's skin was stimulated, sometimes with one compass point, sometimes with two, the distances between the two points being constantly varied. As the distance increased with two-point stimulation, the subject passed from the impression of one clear-cut stimulus to an impression of blurring, or uncertainty as to whether there was one or two, and thence on to a state where he was quite definitely aware that there were two points of stimulation. There was, in other words, a threshold (*limen*) to be crossed before the impression of doubleness could be evoked. He established a "two-point threshold." The concept of the *threshold*, so widely used in the measurement of stimuli and the relations between them, was first

[1] Wagner, R., *Handwörterbuch der Physiologie*, III, ii, 529 f. (1846); separately published as *Der Tastsinn und das Gemeingefühl* (1849).

systematically used by Weber. Now Weber found that the two-point threshold, the distance necessary to make possible the discrimination of doubleness, varied in different parts of the body—in fact, varied enormously. It was smallest on the tips of the fingers and the tip of the tongue. It was somewhat greater on the lips, greater still on palm and wrist, and increased toward the shoulder. Further, the threshold for a given region varied from one individual to another.

In explanation, Weber put forward the hypothesis that the "sensation circles" (areas within which doubleness is not perceived) must contain a number of nerve fibers, and that unstimulated fibers must lie between the two stimulated if doubleness is to be perceived. Difficulty was encountered in the fact that subjects showed marked effects of training; the circles became smaller with practice. Other difficulties have arisen, and the theory has lost ground.[2] Weber's experimental method remains of much greater permanent significance than his explanation of his results.

Even more important, perhaps in Weber's own mind the most important of his contributions, was his examination of the muscle sense.[3] It was while exploring the muscle sense that he made the discovery with which his name is chiefly identified. Physiologists had come to recognize that sensory impulses arise not only from the outside but from the interior of the limbs. Thomas Brown had emphasized the important part which the muscular sensations play in detecting resistance offered to our movements. Weber undertook to find to what extent muscular sensations function in the discrimination of weights of different magnitude. If the subject lifted weights with his hand in such a way as to experience not only tactual sensations, but also muscular sensations from the hands and arms, he discriminated very much more accurately than when weights were laid upon the resting hand. Weber made use of four subjects whose results were quite consistent in showing the great superiority of those judgments in which the muscle sense was used. He worked with two sets of weights, the standard weight being 32 ounces in the one set and 4 ounces (32 drachmae) in the other. He later undertook another series of experiments with a standard weight of $7\frac{1}{2}$ ounces. In the latter experiment the conditions were systematically varied; the weights were, for example, applied both simultaneously and successively. In all these experiments, the fact emerged that discrimination depended not upon the absolute magnitude of

[2] The work of Blix and Goldscheider (see page 166) showed that there are many "touch spots" in each sensation circle.

[3] Published in installments (1829–34), reprinted under the title *De tactu* (1851).

the difference between two weights, but upon the ratio of this magnitude to the magnitude of the standard. Under the most favorable circumstances, the difference between the weights was correctly perceived when they bore roughly the ratio 29:30. Using touch alone, the necessary difference was roughly one-fourth of the standard weight, but again proved to be not an absolute quantity, but a fraction depending on the relative magnitude of the stimuli.

From these facts of muscular and cutaneous sensation Weber reached the conclusion that the ability to discriminate between two stimuli depends not on the absolute magnitude of the difference, but upon a relative difference which can be stated in terms of their ratio to one another. The "just noticeable difference" could be stated as a fraction which, while varying with the sense tested, was constant within a given sense modality. This led him to inquire whether there was not evidence from other sense modalities to support the general principle that discrimination depends not on the absolute difference of stimulus magnitudes but on their relation to one another. Accordingly, he undertook experiments in vision which bore on the same problem. He presented pairs of straight lines, requesting the subject to state which of the lines was longer. The results of this experiment confirmed the principle of "relativity" which he had already found. Here the fraction was even smaller than in the case of the muscle-sense experiments; visual discrimination between two lines was possible if one was from a hundredth to a fiftieth longer than the other; that is, 1 or 2 per cent. (This holds for simultaneous presentation. With successive presentation a 5 per cent difference was needed.) The fraction for a given subject at a given time was roughly constant, and independent of the length of the "standard" line. This led Weber to offer the generalization that we can lay down for *each* of the senses a *constant fraction* for "just noticeable differences."

The generalization was overbold. These experiments with visual stimuli involved to some extent sensations from the external eye muscles, and did not directly settle the question of the discrimination of visual intensities. Having become enamored with his principle, he thought he found it exemplified also in another field. Just before the period of these experiments Delezenne, who was working in the field of acoustics, had hit upon the fact that if a wire of a certain length and tension was struck, and its pitch compared with that of a similar but slightly longer wire, a constant difference in the length of the wires was necessary to make possible a correct pitch-discrimination.[4] He worked with 240 vibrations per second as a standard, and found how much higher the tone of the second tone had to be in order to enable the subject to distinguish it from the standard. Weber seized upon this observation as another instance of his law. But as Delezenne had used only one standard, Weber was mistaken in utilizing this conclusion in support of his own. From the results of all the experiments noted, Weber believed that his general principle was founded on facts from skin, muscle, eye, and ear. But though the data at hand warranted no such sweeping generalization, the effort to find by experiment a truly psychological law relating to the experiences derived from different sense-modalities marked a turning point in the history of science.

It would be hard to overemphasize Weber's importance in the genesis of an experimental psychology. His interest in physiological experimentation served to turn the attention of physiologists to the legitimacy and the importance of approaching in the laboratory certain genuinely psychological problems which had throughout history been neglected. Not only did he set problems which occupied men of the ability of Helmholtz, Fechner, and Lotze, but he himself attacked a great many of these problems, and pointed the way to their systematic study. His conception of "just noticeable differences" and his broad assumption that our responses to the world are subject to measurement have leavened the study of everything in psychology from the simplest feelings to the most complex social attitudes.

An illustration will show the extent to which he could transform the problems of the physicist and the physiologist. An experiment had been carried out in France (by Bouguer) a generation before Weber's time, in which the sensitiveness of the eye to light was measured by varying the relative positions of candles and pinholes through which light reached a screen beyond. In order to make a faint shadow distinguishable from a shadowed area adjacent to it, it was found that the illumination of the two must differ by one sixty-fourth. The problem led to no principle of any particular consequence. Yet it was in embryo the problem of "just noticeable differences." It was just such a problem as in the hands of a Weber might have become a cornerstone of epoch-making research.

It is no accident that work like Weber's came when and where it did. German intellectual history for a century had paved the way; the influence of Haller still lived, enriched by the brilliant French discoveries of the late eighteenth century, which had been adopted with new energy by the German universities in the early years of the

[4] *Recueil des travaux de la Société des Sciences de Lille* (1826).

nineteenth century. Important as it may be to plant wisely the seed of an experimental project, the soil is no less important. When Hamilton, a few years later, undertook to study experimentally some problems in attention, nothing of significance resulted in British psychology; associationism and the Scottish school were alike uninterested. The crucial point was that in Germany experimental physiology was solidly established with quantitative methods and with a wide outlook. The measurement of the cutaneous two-point threshold, the study of visual acuity, and the study of "just noticeable differences" in the field of the muscle sense were throughout envisaged in quantitative terms; and problems were so stated that they quickly became experimental in the more restricted modern sense, several different factors being varied in order to isolate the significance of each. Weber ventured, moreover, to bring together an array of results under a common law, a universal principle. Important as this law was to become as a hypothesis for voluminous research, Weber's greatest significance lies rather in his conception of an experimental approach to psychological questions, and in the stimulation of research through which ultimately a vast variety of problems other than his have been incisively studied.

FECHNER

Nothing could be more misleading than to study Fechner as a follower of Weber, as if he were simply an echo or a reflected light from the great physiologist. A moment's glance at Fechner's early life shows how soon his characteristic genius displayed itself.

He started his career as a student of medicine, and of physics and chemistry, at Leipzig, where he began to give instruction a few years later. He interested himself especially in contemporary discoveries in mechanics and electricity. His earliest writings, consisting of scientific treatises and translations from French experimental contributions, show how, as a young man, he mastered the physical sciences of his day. But he began before long a series of brief articles of purely literary design. Among these, one of the purest gems is *Das Büchlein vom Leben nach dem Tode* (*The Little Book of Life after Death*, 1836). In this he strove to show how we are, as it were, all parts of one another, living in each other so fully that as long as human life continues, no individual can die. He was studying the philosophy of Fichte and Schelling also, and beginning to give literary expression to the feelings it kindled within him. And he was deeply stirred by the "philosophy of nature," which was dominated by the desire to find a spiritual meaning in all the events of the natural order.

The source of this many-sided distribution of interests was the problem: "How can quantitative science teach us to study the human spirit in its relation to the universe? How can those exact methods which have been applied so successfully in the natural sciences be turned to advantage in the study of the inner world? How can we ever see the soul under conditions of direct and reportable observation?" As we are told by J. T. Merz:

> He became acquainted with the philosophy of Schelling, Oken, and Steffens, which dazzled him, touched the poetical and mystical side of his nature, and, though he hardly understood it, had a lasting influence on him. The simultaneous occupation with the best scientific literature of the day (he translated French textbooks such as those of Biot and Thénard, and verified Ohm's law experimentally), however, forced upon him the sceptical reflection whether, "of all the beautiful orderly connection of optical phenomena, so clearly expounded by Biot, anything could have been found out by Oken-Schelling's method?" This mixture or alternation of exact science and speculation, of faithfulness and loyalty to facts as well as to theory, runs through all Fechner's life, work, and writings.[5]

It is easy to see why Fechner was both a follower of the "philosophy of nature" and one of its most ardent opponents. He did not come to this attitude hastily; he felt about for a way. He knew vaguely what it was that he sought, but there was no movement which undertook the thing he wanted, no school with which he could affiliate. Reaching in one direction and another, he was bewildered by the complexity of the spiritual heritage, and the futility of stating and cataloguing it in the terms of those sciences in which he was at home. He began then, in a series of satirical writings under the name of Dr. Mises, to assert a negative expression of what he felt; he began to satirize mechanistic science. The attempt to bring the biological sciences into terms similar to those of mathematics and physics seemed to him to involve the repudiation of biology and psychology, because this attempt seemed to repudiate life and mind at the outset. The attempt to transfer the methods of physics and chemistry into biology and psychology meant for him a retreat from the self-evident world of life of which we are a part; it meant also the denial of the living reality of the whole universe, every fiber and atom of which was for him equally alive and meaningful.

[5] *History of European Thought in the Nineteenth Century,* Vol. II, p. 508 *n.*

From these satires it is apparent that he had not achieved in his own mind the first statement of his problem. He could not begin to solve his problem because he could not quite state it. He felt, on the one hand, the need of an exact method in order to make headway in biological and psychological science; but on the other hand the existing methods could never interpret the events which they recorded. As he groped about, satirizing quantitative science under a pseudonym, he was at the same time carrying on exact research in the field of physics—was identified, for example, with investigations into the atomic theory. While teaching in the classroom the physics of the day, he was constantly trying to see a way in which satire could be replaced by a new understanding of the subject matter of science, an understanding which would make both the human soul and the objects which it knows equally accessible to methods by which real knowledge can be amassed.

During this period Fechner suffered from a progressively severe illness; perhaps it was the sort of illness that is now vaguely called a "nervous breakdown." He persisted in increasing his difficulties by undertaking the study of positive afterimages from bright stimuli, particularly the sun. Violent pain in his eyes and partial blindness resulted, from which he did not recover for several years. The earlier disorder, complicated by the inability to read, and apparently even the inability to think clearly without great difficulty, caused something verging upon a collapse. His wife, however, brought him through this difficult time, and he gradually recovered.

As the vigorous use of his mind returned to him, he began to ponder again the relation of mental to physical processes, and the possibility of discovering a definite relation between them. One day the discovery burst upon him that there is one sort of quantitative relation observable in daily life; namely, that the intensity of sensation does not increase in a one-to-one correspondence with an increasing stimulus, but rather in an arithmetical series which may be contrasted with the geometrical series which characterizes the stimulus. If one bell is ringing, the addition of a second bell makes much more impression upon us than the addition of one bell to ten bells already ringing; if four or five candles are burning, the addition of another makes a scarcely distinguishable difference, while if it appeared with only two its effect would be considerable. The effects of stimuli are not absolute, but relative; relative, that is, to the amount of sensation already existing. It occurred to him that for each sense modality there might be a certain relative increase in the stimulus which would always produce an observable intensification of the sensation; and this ratio would hold for the entire range through which the stimuli might be made to increase. We might say, for example, that sensations increase arithmetically, according to a formula in which we need only to know the constants which determine the rate of geometrical progression for the different sense modalities. This he stated as

$$S = C \log \frac{R}{R_0}$$

where S is the intensity of the sensation, C is a constant for each of the different fields of sense, R is the intensity of the stimulus, and R_0 is the intensity of the stimulus at the threshold.

In this same period he published a sort of philosophy of nature of his own, entitled the *Zend-Avesta* (1851), its title reflecting the general incursion of Oriental thought during the middle of the century. The Persian system, with its fundamental dualism, in which good and evil center in personal beings, laid hold upon Fechner's imagination; through it the world could be seen to be really personal, really alive. It absorbed Fechner partly because it made possible the personal interpretation of the natural world, a world not seen, however, as an antithesis between natural and supernatural, but as natural and spiritual at once. This gave him the desired antithesis to the science of his day; it gave the universe a soul, or rather a plurality of souls. In the *Zend-Avesta* Fechner mentioned that he had recently discovered a simple mathematical relation between the spiritual and the physical world.

He now undertook a series of experiments on brightness and lifted weights, visual and tactual distances, to test his hypothesis regarding the relation of sensation intensities to stimulus intensities. Immediately after beginning these he happened upon the work of Weber, which had commenced a quarter-century before. Weber had shown that there appeared to be a definite law governing the relation between the intensities of stimulation and the ability to distinguish which of two stimuli was the greater. The "just noticeable difference" is a constant fraction of the standard stimulus. This principle, laid down by Weber, seemed to Fechner to be a mathematical generalization of great importance. He saw its relation to his own hypothesis. He seized upon it, made much of it, and proceeded to extend enormously the experimental work to confirm it. But the difference between Fechner's hypothesis and Weber's is immense. Weber had concerned himself with "just noticeable differences," but Fechner could be satisfied only with a mathematical statement of the relation of the physical to the spiritual world.

Fechner's formula had to be put to the test of long and arduous experimentation. He had, of course, to use two supplementary hypotheses: first, that sensations can be measured (for example, three units of loudness); and second, that there is a zero point for all sensation. Both points became the subject of endless controversy, but both, as Fechner realized from the beginning, were essential to the very core of his purpose. For in this measurement of sensation, as he explicitly stated over and over again, his one purpose was to find the quantitative relation of the objective to the subjective world. The longing to grasp the meaning of the world in terms which would articulate with the scientific methods of his day—that is, to find the relation between the qualities of experience and the quantities of science—was the thing which forced the treatment of qualities into the quantitative mold. If he laid a foundation for one great subdivision of experimental psychology, seeking to confirm his law in as many fields and through as many methods as possible, it was in the service of a struggle to find confirmation for his great conviction. The magnitude of the man is shown not only by the elaborateness and the ingenuity of the experimental approach, but by the patience and the honesty with which errors and discrepancies, pitfalls and disappointments, were recognized.

A closer examination of the most important of Fechner's psychophysical methods is necessary. Weber's law remained his guiding principle. He carried on his experiments, stimulated by Weber's discovery, for seven or eight years before he gave any account of his methods or his findings to the public. The first presentation of his work (1858) was a paper on mental measurement, a forerunner of the *Elemente der Psychophysik*, which appeared in 1860. In the *Elemente*, psychophysics was defined as an exact science of the functional relations, or relations of dependence, between body and mind. Its sphere included sensation, perception, feeling, action, attention, and so forth. He selected sensation as most susceptible of measurement at that stage of the science, and developed his methods on the basis of the fundamental principle that sensation is a measurable magnitude. That is, any sensation is the sum of a number of *sensation units*, and these units can be standardized by the aid of the correlated stimuli. The ideal of psychophysics is, of course, to measure the relation of subjective intensities to the bodily intensities which accompany them; for example, to compare sensations with brain changes. This realm of "inner psychophysics" was regarded by

Fechner as free from those inconsistencies and errors which attend "outer psychophysics," in which the stimulus rather than the bodily response is compared with subjective intensities. Outer psychophysics was accepted only because it was more immediately practicable.

Weber had, it will be remembered, used the method of "just noticeable differences." This method Fechner developed during the course of his work on vision and temperature sensations.[6] He used Weber's method of presenting two like stimuli and increasing or diminishing one of them until a difference became noticeable. Fechner, however, recommended approaching the just noticeable difference from both directions, and averaging the just noticeable differences obtained from the ascending and the descending approach.[7]

The method of "right and wrong cases," although originated by Vierordt,[8] was developed and established as a tool Fechner used in his elaborate work with lifted weights, involving over 67,000 comparisons. In contrast to the method just described, in which the stimuli vary and a constant judgment is sought (the judgment of the just noticeable difference), the method of right and wrong cases depends on constant stimuli and varying judgments. The aim of the method, according to Fechner, was to measure the difference between stimuli which was required to produce a given proportion of right judgments. Fechner found it possible, by the use of an intricate mathematical formula, to simplify the procedure of measuring sensitivity by this method. Thus, instead of arriving at the desired difference after experimentation with a number of differences, one small difference was decided upon with which the series of judgments was to be made. This difference was large enough to

[6] Fechner's insistence on the psychophysical value of the method of just noticeable differences is not justified by the results of experimentation since his time, although the *psychological* value of the method remains almost undisputed. See Titchener, *Experimental Psychology* (1905), Vol. II, Pt. 2, p. cxiii.

[7] He did not sufficiently appreciate the value of making a carefully graded approach from a difference greater or less than the just noticeable difference. This modification was made by G. E. Müller (*Zur Grundlegung der Psychophysik*, 1878), who did not however make large use of the method. Wundt worked out the method with this modification of small gradations, and extended its use under the name of the method of "minimal changes." Wundt insisted that judgments of just noticeable difference were determined under the cumulative influence of previous judgments, and that their significance was therefore psychological rather than psychophysical (*Principles of Physiological Psychology*, 1873–74, pp. 295, 326 ff.). Wundt emphasized also the method of "mean gradations," in which the subject adjusts a stimulus so that it seems midway between two others.

[8] Hegelmaier, *Vierordt's Arch. f. physiol. Heilkunde*, 1852, 11.

be recognized most of the time, but not large enough to be recognized invariably. The right, wrong, and doubtful judgments were computed to give the measure of the perceptibility of this chosen difference. The formula, based upon the theory of probability, then made possible the computation of the difference required to give the percentage of right cases desired.[9]

In co-operation with Volkmann, Fechner developed the method of "average error" (already in use in astronomy) for use in visual and tactual measurement. The procedure is based upon the recognition that errors of observation and judgment depend not only on variable factors in the situation or within the observer himself, but, most significantly, upon the magnitude and variability of the difference between stimuli required to be noticeable. This method involves the adjustment of a variable stimulus to subjective equality with a given constant stimulus. Under controlled test conditions the mean value of the differences between the given stimulus and the "error" stimulus (adjusted by the observer) will represent the subject's error of observation. When applied to lifted weights, the method is simply as follows: The subject takes an accurately measured weight as the norm, and attempts to make a second (or "error") weight equal to it. When he is satisfied of the equality of the two weights, he determines his error by weighing the second weight. The errors through many experiments are averaged to give the "average error."

Although Fechner's confidence in the psychophysical significance of his methods was not shared by his successors, and although his methods have suffered devastating criticism and provoked endless controversy,[10] his contribution, as the real creator of psychophysics,

---

[9] G. E. Müller (*op. cit.*) objected that Fechner did not distinguish between the measure of precision of the observer and the true difference required for correct judgments; he also objected to Fechner's method of disposition of the doubtful judgments by dividing them between the right and wrong judgments. He worked out formulae for the right, wrong, and doubtful cases, and measured both precision and sensitivity.

[10] "Those who desire this dreadful literature," said James, "can find it; it has a disciplinary value; but I will not even enumerate it in a footnote."—*Principles of Psychology*, Vol. I, p. 549. The historian cannot escape so easily. The principal criticisms by Müller and Wundt are contained in the works already cited, but the following are also important: Müller, *Die Gesichtspunkte und die Tatsachen der psychophysischen Methodik* (1904); Fechner, *In Sachen der Psychophysik* (1877) and *Revision der Hauptpunkte der Psychophysik* (1882). Additional references are to be found in Titchener, *op cit.*, Vol. II, Pt. 2, p. xlvii. More recent material is given in Fröbes, J., *Lehrbuch der experimentellen Psychologie*, 3rd ed., 1923, Vol. I. See also Boring, E. G. *History of Experimental Psychology* (1929), and Woodworth, R. S. *Experimental Psychology* (1938).

was of immense importance. It was largely through these investigations that Wundt was stimulated to conceive of an exact science which should study the relations of physical stimuli to mental events. Indeed, Fechner's long and careful research did much to give Wundt and his contemporaries the plan of an experimental psychology.[11]

When at last his *Elemente der Psychophysik* was published, Fechner was beginning to turn to other fields of investigation in a way that would tempt one to think that he pretended to finality, As a matter of fact, however, the work went on and on. Through his contact with Wundt and the latter's laboratory investigations and publications, Fechner was constantly occupying himself with the writing of new articles and with answering objections.

In this period he began to concern himself with a further statement of his philosophical position, and as time went on gave it more adequate expression. This statement he called "the day view opposed to the night view." [12] In it appears an insistence upon the meaning and the value of all the known universe, expressed with a lyrical beauty which moved William James many decades later to an outburst of enthusiastic welcome to a most kindred spirit.[13] The universe, said Fechner, is an organism with articulate parts, living and rejoicing in living. Each of the stars and planets, each stone, each clod of earth, has its organization, and organization means life, and life means soul. Everything is imbued with a consciousness of itself and a response to the things about it. This view Fechner carried into the foundations of a system of philosophy which is as utterly and absolutely monistic as the materialism of the nineteenth century, but as pantheistic as Hinduism. It is a far cry from this to that parallelism which says that mental processes and brain processes go on without relation, like two trains moving on tracks side by side. Fechner was assumed to be a parallelist. But for him the world had become one; the experience which men have as persons is of the very substance of the universe, all of which is throbbing with life and experience. This life we may, if we choose, study quantitatively; we may study it in the physical laboratory or in measuring the intensity of sensations.

Both experimentally and logically, therefore, Fechner's purpose seemed fulfilled. But he was not content, and, pushing forward to new worlds to conquer, he laid the foundations of the science of

---

11 Titchener, *op. cit.*, Vol. II, Pt. 2, p. xx.

12 *Die Tagesansicht gegenüber der Nachtansicht* (1879).

13 *A Pluralistic Universe* (1909), Chap. 4.

experimental aesthetics.[14] Just as he had protested against the vague symbolism of the "philosophy of nature," so he protested against the aesthetics "from above" which undertook to lay down the principles of beauty from which the beauty of the individual object might be deduced. He began to measure books, cards, windows, and many such objects of daily use, to find what quantitative relations of line are judged to be beautiful. He carried this into the study of the masterpieces of pictorial art, undertaking to find those linear relations which the artist had unconsciously used. This aesthetics "from beneath" was to offer the same humble but endlessly careful approach to the problem of beauty which the psychophysics had offered toward the mind-body problem.

As little as in psychophysics were his hopes destined to be fulfilled. Time has gratefully taken his methods and his data and gone on with them, to be sure, to a rich harvest. The problem, however, to which he sought the key was not so easily solved. The modern temper finds the union of the mystical and the scientific difficult to understand. Yet Fechner's mystical grasp upon the unity of life and of the world lives on, and in each generation finds a welcome from a few.

JOHANNES MÜLLER

In 1833 Johannes Müller became Professor of Physiology at Berlin. As an experimentalist, especially in the physiology of the senses, he ranks among the greatest of the nineteenth century; but his enduring influence is due even more to his success as a teacher and as a systematizer of knowledge. Before his time physiological experimentation was carried on by physicians and teachers of medicine, partly in connection with clinical practice and partly as an adjunct to anatomy; Müller's career marked the emancipation of physiology from the practical demands of medicine.

He was interested in a number of specific problems in sense physiology, most of all in optics. The best known of his investigations are those which dealt with the external muscles of the eye and with the problem of space perception. His researches were inspired in part by Kant's doctrine of the innate character of space perception. Kant had laid down the principle that space perception is given to us by virtue of an innate capacity; space was for Kant a mode of experience beyond which we can never hope to go. But Berkeley had prepared the way for an "empirical" theory by asserting that

[14] *Vorschule der Aesthetik* (1876).

the third dimension, as we know it, is built up through experience—it is necessary only that the different elements of the retina and the skin should be stimulated simultaneously—and Herbart had gone further, maintaining that the world of space is organized through the integration of a large number of specific experiences. The debate over "nativism" and "empiricism" which was to occupy much attention throughout the century was already in full swing when Müller approached the problem. No compromise between the two views seemed possible; they were stated in such arbitrary terms that no genetic analysis of the facts could be made. Müller put the problem in such a way as to make use of the arguments of both schools, and in a form to some extent experimentally verifiable. His position was as follows: We are endowed with a general ability to perceive space as such, but not with the specific capacities to judge distances, size, and position. We learn by experience whether a given object is within reach or not. But we could never learn such specific relations were we not endowed with a general capacity to perceive in spatial terms. Müller borrowed from Berkeley and Herbart the idea that we build up a spatial order through experience. Important in this connection was his study of binocular vision and of the nerve pathways in the chiasma.[15] We shall see later (page 147) that the problem of the empirical derivation of the spatial order (learning to judge distances, learning to recognize at what point we are stimulated, and so on) was carried further by Lotze.

Another striking contribution was the experimental study of reflex action. This was inspired partly by the teaching of Descartes, and, more immediately, by Bell's study of the functions of the spinal roots. The theory demanded experimental verification to support anatomical analysis. It was Müller who supplied the necessary data, from experimentation with frogs. He showed that reflex activity comprises three steps: (1) impulse from sense organ to nerve center via the dorsal root, (2) connection in the cord, and (3) impulse going out via the ventral root to the muscle.

The most important theoretical contribution which he offered was the doctrine of "specific energies." [16] Bell had suggested that each sensory nerve conveys one kind of quality or experience; visual nerves carry only visual impressions, auditory only auditory impressions, and so on. Müller saw the importance of such a view; if

[15] Wheatstone's discovery of the stereoscope in 1833 gave a technique for the further investigation (notably by Helmholtz) of this problem. Müller had made at least one phase of the problem amenable to experimental attack.

[16] *Elements of Physiology* (1834–40), Bk. V.

this were true, the whole nervous system could be regarded as a company of specialists, each performing its own task, but unable to take over the functions of another. Might it not be true, moreover, that the various *qualities of experience* can come to us only through the specific qualities or energies of particular nerves? Some nerves, for example, are specialized to give us vision; just as the eye is specialized to receive light, so the optic nerve is specialized to provide visual qualities in consciousness. No other nerve could ever take over these functions; these qualities in experience come from physical qualities intrinsic in the nerve tissue.[17]

It occurred to Müller that there is perhaps another way of defining specialization in the nervous system. Not the nerves, but the terminals in the brain, may give specific qualities. Perhaps the nerves function simply as a system of connections between the sense organs and the appropriate brain tissues, and perhaps the different parts of the brain are themselves specialized to provide the various qualities. Do visual qualities result directly from the stimulation of the optic nerve or, on the contrary, do they arise from the excitement of a specialized visual area in the brain, the optic nerve serving merely to transmit the various stimuli impressed on the retina? He believed both alternatives defensible, the evidence being inconclusive in favor of either. He decided, however, in favor of the theory of specific energies in the nerves themselves. This view clinical work has now disproved, but it seemed not unreasonable in Müller's time.

His whole approach was of the greatest significance for the generation which followed. It implied that the qualities of experience are given us not by the sense organs alone but by the very constitution of specialized parts of the nervous system. The reason why we have visual experience is that we have brains containing specialized tissues which give rise to that specific kind of experience. This view led to a physiological psychology in which mind and body were even more intimately related than in the systems of Hobbes, Hartley, and Cabanis. It helped to drive from the field the doctrines of Cartesian dualism and its congeners, which were indeed already dying of inanition. Whereas earlier physiological psychologists had contented themselves for the most part with showing a correspondence between brain *connections* and mental associations or *connections*, Müller's reasoning sought to find in the brain the physiological basis for difference in the elementary *modes of experience*. Whichever of Müller's alternatives be emphasized, our variety of experiences must

[17] Thus the doctrine reasserted the principle that the qualities of experience are not the qualities of an external world (see page 26).

be due to the functioning of a variety of tissues in the central nervous system. Not, of course, that such a conception put an end to all dualism in psychology. Müller's own views tended, indeed, as we have seen, to differentiate mental from physical events. But the dualisms which have taken account of Müller's principle have necessarily narrowed the scope of the "mental" to a central governing principle, the particular varieties of experience being stated more and more in terms of physiological events.

Few physiologists clearly grasped the fact that the problem of specific energies was very similar to that of local specialization within the nervous system as it had been stated by Gall and the phrenologists. Müller had seriously entertained the possibility that the different parts of the brain might have their specific qualities. We have seen that phrenology, in defending a rather similar position, fell on evil days. Flourens's experiments on the brains of pigeons,[18] leading to the conclusion that the brain acts *as a whole*, and that no local specialization exists, were generally accepted, to the discredit of phrenology; yet without in any sense dislodging either of Müller's versions of the principle of specific energies. Flourens's work put an end for the time being to what little reputation the doctrine of cortical localization enjoyed. But it did not affect Müller's position at all. He had, in fact, given preference to the alternative of specialization in the peripheral as against the central elements. His theory of specific energies remained as orthodox as did Flourens's view that the brain functioned as a whole. In the latter part of the century clinical studies (cf. page 185) led to a revival of the concept of cerebral localization, while physiological research served to discredit the doctrine of specific energies in the form preferred by Müller. Nevertheless the plasticity of the theory gave it long life, while its attempt at definiteness in the quest for neural foundations for sensory experience made it useful as a hypothesis in experimental psychology. Helmholtz's color theory and Blix's studies of cutaneous nerves are two familiar examples (see pages 140 and 166). We shall return to the localization problem on page 374.

While Johannes Müller was devoting himself to special problems of this kind, he was also concerned with the relation of physiology to other sciences. It is interesting to see on the one hand the eagerness of his research and on the other hand the perfectly clear allegiance which he felt to Kant and to the philosophy of nature. He tried to reach a philosophical understanding of physiology. One of the

[18] *Recherches expérimentales sur les propriétés et les fonctions du système nerveux dans les animaux vertébrés* (1824).

clearest illustrations of this was his long and detailed discussion of the difference between the "mental principle" and the "vital principle." It is evident, he said, that the vital principle which distinguishes living from nonliving processes must exist not only in certain parts of the body but in all the body. But the mental principle is not so widely diffused. He was inclined to accept the mental principle as distinct from the vital principle, and as residing in the nervous system and not in the other tissues. The brain was the chief seat of the mental principle. His concern with this question is important for the light it throws upon the nature of some of the problems with which physiologists were still occupying themselves a hundred years ago. Müller was drawn into the maelstrom of the controversy concerning the nature of living matter and the whole problem of vitalism, for the excitement engendered by the discovery of electrical phenomena in the living body had gained rather than lost in intensity in the opening decades of the century. The prevalent vitalism, and the bold romanticism of the philosophy of nature, left their mark upon him.

Perhaps more important than any of these things was his production of the first great textbook of physiology since Haller's time. Müller's *Elements of Physiology* (1834–40) quickly became the international standard. Since it brought together all the notable results of European research in the whole realm of physiology, it was quite naturally translated into many tongues and served as an international storehouse and authority. From a modern viewpoint the book treats both physiology and anatomy. In fact, it is interesting to see the list of tissues and organs whose gross anatomy and histology Müller knew without knowing anything about their physiology. The description, for example, of the structure of the sympathetic nervous system and the glands of internal secretion reads much like that available in contemporary handbooks; but on many pages Müller contents himself, after describing the structure, with the brief statement that the functions are unknown. In view of the breadth of outlook and the eclectic spirit in which the book was compiled, it is futile to search in it for a rigid didactic outlook. Indeed, the very fact that Müller had an impartial avidity for all sorts of physiological data did as much as any other factor to turn German physiology in the first half of the nineteenth century from its abject position under the philosophy of nature to its independent magnificence in the hands of Helmholtz. It was indeed this quality which led men like Helmholtz and Du Bois-Reymond to study with him; it was this that made his work the point from which discussion began and from which research followed, and marked him as the great master by whom all others were to be measured.

BENEKE

In Müller's era lived a number of psychologists who sought to instigate a rebellion against the prevailing transcendentalism. Greatest among them was Beneke, the caption of whose work, *A Textbook of Psychology as a Natural Science* (1832), indicated the adoption of that spirit which had guided the English associationists. He borrowed, indeed, more of their spirit than had Herbart, though with less of their content. His central problem was to define how it is that the chaos of the newborn child's experience becomes organized into a coherent unity. There had been two traditional answers to this question. The associationists had maintained that all experience comes through the senses, and that elementary experiences are associated to make the more complex forms of experience. The "nativists," on the other hand, of whom Kant was the most illustrious spokesman, had emphasized the fundamental innate ways of knowing and thinking which are ours simply by virtue of being human. Beneke rejected both interpretations. A child begins life with a capacity for a great number of single activities, but not with the complex capacities of the adult; he manifests neither perception nor judgment, neither reason nor will. He is equipped only with very *elementary* capacities of mind and body. For example, he is not born with the ability to perceive space; he is born with many part functions ("fundamental processes") which are integrated in the total process through which space perception is achieved. The same method of approach characterizes Beneke's treatment of such traditional faculties as memory, reason, and will. Beneke may be reckoned a contributor to the dissection and hence to the disappearance of the "faculties" which still throve in German psychology.

Perhaps the chief *specific* contribution of Beneke was the doctrine of "traces." His view closely resembled that of Herbart (he devoted, in fact, much attention to the refutation of the Herbartians' charge of plagiarism from their master). Herbart had taught that the ideas lying outside the field of consciousness have a *tendency* to reappear in consciousness. Similarly Beneke postulated traces by which each idea is linked to another. He refused to state this in physiological terms, and insisted on the right of psychology to treat of its laws without recourse to the data of another science. He made use of these traces to explain how an experience may be brought back into consciousness; that is, remembered. The disappearance of an idea from consciousness simply leaves a trace which serves as basis for the later revival of the idea. A present impression is capable of bringing back a previous experience. The substance of this teaching obviously differs but little from that of Herbart; but the viewpoint and the terminology are significant in their attempt to set for psychology an empirical task. For Beneke it was all-important that memory as a faculty should be dethroned; the traces were for him a simple and empirical explanation of all memory phenomena. The value of his analysis is of less interest to us than his influence in undermining the complacency of the transcendentalists.

But Beneke's task was not an easy one. So solidly entrenched was the habit of recourse to the transcendental that Beneke's book on the "foundation of a physics of morality" caused the loss of his right to teach at the University of Berlin. The Prussian Minister of Instruction explained "that it was not single passages which had given offense, but the whole scheme, and that a philosophy which did not deduce everything from the Absolute could not be considered to be philosophy at all." [19]

REFERENCES

Boring, Edwin G., *A History of Experimental Psychology*, Century, 1929; pp. 265–87

Dennis, Wayne, ed., *Readings in the History of Psychology*, Appleton-Century, 1948: Weber, Fechner

Hall, G. Stanley, *Founders of Modern Psychology*, Appleton, 1912

[19] Merz, J. T., *History of European Thought in the Nineteenth Century*, Vol. III, p. 208 *n.*

Chapter 7

BRITISH PSYCHOLOGY IN THE MID-NINETEENTH CENTURY

The sceptre of psychology has returned to this island.

J. S. MILL (on reading Bain)

ASSOCIATIONISM and the Scottish school had quarreled through the latter half of the eighteenth century without learning much from one another. The first half of the nineteenth century, however, found them borrowing so freely from one another that it becomes more and more difficult to be sure where the one stops and the other begins. This means, of course, the decline of the Scottish school and of associationism as self-contained systems. Let us look first at the Scottish school.

We shall find some interesting parallels between Britain and Germany in this period. Germany had been dominated during the interval from the time of Kant until the middle of the nineteenth century by two philosophical approaches. One was transcendentalism, its characteristic appeal being to reality beyond experience, and the second the philosophy of nature, its keynote being an attempt to interpret nature symbolically and spiritually. Here and there a man made his protest; but in psychology proper (apart, of course, from physiology) only two figures of note, Herbart and Beneke, had seriously shaken these systems. And physiology, too, as represented by Weber and Johannes Müller, was considerably influenced by the philosophy of nature and the accompanying vitalism. It did succeed in making headway on empirical lines, because physiology was an independent discipline with an objective research problem; another half-century was to pass before psychology was to have its independent position as an experimental science. Psychology as the German intellectual of 1830 knew it was a mixture of transcendentalism and the philosophy of nature. It was this psychology against which Beneke had, not very successfully, rebelled.

This same attempt to supplant the current philosophy of mind was going on in Scotland. Religious and ethical dogmatism was beginning to yield to associationism. The tendency, inaugurated by Thomas Brown, to borrow from the associationists was destined within a generation to bring an end to the independent existence of the Scottish school. Some steps in the process are suggested by the work of Sir William Hamilton.

HAMILTON

Hamilton began as a young man to be drawn toward contemporary German philosophy.[1] He studied in Germany to acquaint himself in detail with the transcendentalist movement. This transcendentalist approach he succeeded in unifying with the spiritual and ethical tradition which had been a part of his heritage as one educated in the Scottish universities. In 1836 he became the most influential teacher of psychology in Scotland. His work was distinguished equally by his mastery of the history of philosophy and by his ability to grapple with the psychological problems of his contemporaries, especially those raised by the associationists. His lectures dealt with crucial problems which the Scottish school had in general neglected. Through his fusion of German and Scottish thought, and the critical spirit he imparted to the latter, he became an organic part of the idealistic tradition of the nineteenth century.

Accepting the faculty psychology in the form advanced by Kant, Hamilton held the first principle to be the unity and activity of the mind. He refused to admit the usefulness of either the analytic or the physiological assumptions of the associationists. For him the main problem was not to explain how integrated experience is formed from past impressions, but how the underlying unitary substance manifests itself in a variety of different situations. This position gradually fused with the tradition then taking shape, which we may characterize by the general title of "British idealism," later represented by T. H. Green and Bradley. The Scottish school came to an end with Hamilton, not because his ideas died, but because they became assimilated with another movement, the idealistic movement, which was interested primarily in the conservation of the same spiritual values which we have seen in the Scottish school.

[1] *Lectures on Metaphysics* (published posthumously, 1859–60).

His greatest psychological contribution lay in a theory as to the nature of memory and association, a theory which showed in clear form the difference between Scottish and English traditions as they then existed. This conception, known as "redintegration," was to the effect that each impression tends to bring back into consciousness the whole situation of which it has at one time been a part. It will be recalled that orthodox associationists, from Hartley on, had maintained that when A, B, C, D are actual sensations following in a given order, the sensation A will, when later presented alone, be followed by the memory images b, c, and d. This meant that the only part of the field of consciousness with which the psychologists were concerned was that which lay in the center of attention. Psychology, in its whole history from the Greeks onward, had ignored Aristotle's distinction between *having* an experience and *observing* an experience—a distinction closely related to the distinction between *fringe* and *center* of consciousness. British and French psychologists were inclined to regard the stream of experience as simply the stream of items attended to. German psychologists, however, from Leibnitz onward, stressed the role of apperception (cf. page 21), with its reinterpretation of center and fringe of consciousness; and Herbart's system had been founded upon the reality of degrees of intensity of elements which are simultaneously active. From the vantage point of his study of the German tradition, Hamilton was able to formulate precisely a continuing weakness in associationism. It presupposed the existence of individual *parts* of the mind, each of which sets going another part of the mind without any unifying principle to make the parts hold together. (Brown had realized this difficulty when he objected to the term "association" because it implied that mere sequence could give organic unity.) Going further, Hamilton showed that in their statement of the sequence of mental events, the associationists had written as if the remembering mind contained (or rather, were) one *single* idea at a time. Hamilton taught that the process of perception is such that *any one* of the elements simultaneously experienced is capable, when presented later, of bringing back the *total* experience. If a person hears another pronounce a series of numbers he may, indeed, recall them in order; but he actually recalls many other details besides. Hours later, a whole constellation of memories comes back at once, as soon as the experiment with the numbers is mentioned. The subject redintegrates in memory the original situation; he recalls not a series but a pattern. Hamilton, like Leibnitz and Herbart before him, was trying to call psychologists away from their oversimplified schematizations. He saw that any given mental event is only part of a much larger whole.

Hamilton overworked his hypothesis, omitting, as Brett remarks,[2] to explain the process of *forgetting*. Memory items not only often fail to bring back their whole context, but even fail to bring back anything recognizable. Associationism could not, of course, be dislodged with a single blow; and Hamilton had clearly gone too far in neglecting both the facts of serial association and the frequent ineffectiveness or absence of the redintegrating principle. Neither Hartley's nor Hamilton's position stated the whole truth. But we still know very little about either forgetting or remembering, and such insight as we have is in part traceable to Hamilton's doctrine that association operates not through a chain of elements, but, so to speak, through a system of interconnected aspects. Bain, James, and many others have insisted on the importance of Hamilton's contribution. Even aside from his theory of memory, his emphasis upon the whole of experience, rather than upon the center of attention alone, was a means of bringing into British thought one of the most vital contributions of German psychology. The Scottish school, as such, ceases to occupy us from this moment. After Hamilton's death the school survived only in admixture with idealism, associationism, or both.

JAMES MILL; JOHN STUART MILL

James Mill, though a true Scot, and brought up under Scottish influences, identified himself with the English school, and attained the most complete and most rigorous expression of associationism.[3]

His unity of thought, and the severity and rigor of his ethics and his logic, mark him as a very unusual personality.[4] He studied theology, but quickly found himself out of sympathy with the doctrines of the Church, and became an agnostic.[5] Earning his livelihood as an editor and a writer concerned primarily with the economic and political problems of his time, he is better known as an economist and a historian than as a psychologist. His *History of British India* (1817) gave him a nation-wide reputation. His system of political economy was closely allied to that of Bentham (cf. page

[2] *A History of Psychology*, Vol. III, p. 27.

[3] *Analysis of the Phenomena of the Human Mind* (1829).

[4] The opening chapters of John Stuart Mill's *Autobiography* (1873) give a most vivid picture of his father.

[5] He arrived at a complete agnosticism of a kind which was rare even among "freethinkers"—neither affirming nor denying the existence of Deity, and convinced that "concerning the origin of things nothing whatever can be known."

41), with whom he enjoyed the closest friendship. He borrowed Bentham's pleasure-pain philosophy, the doctrine that human actions are motivated solely through self-interest. He borrowed also his ethical conceptions, the view that the wise organization of society is that which brings about the "greatest good of the greatest number." [6] In seeking to outline a comprehensive political economy, he thus included a treatment of ethical and psychological questions. In general, Mill and the utilitarians favored the principle of free exchange without government interference; they believed that individual self-interest would bring about social welfare if economic (that is, from Mill's viewpoint, psychological) laws were left to themselves.

Mill's psychology was definitely related to these other aspects of his life. In the first place, the agnosticism which had taken hold of him made him go further in his tendency to mechanistic theory than his discipleship to Hartley required. He reduced mental life to elementary sensory particles, conceding nothing to the claims of the soul. Perception was a process by which a number of bits are put together to make a single whole. At the same time, the process of association was regarded as passive. Sensations were presented in a certain order, and later, when one of these was presented, the others followed mechanically. Association depended wholly upon contiguity. There was no association by similarity or contrast. The reason why one tree makes us think of another similar tree is simply the fact that "we are accustomed to see like things together." His explanation of association by contrast was equally simple. "Dwarf" does not make us think of "giant" by virtue of contrast, but simply because both depart from, and are necessarily associated with, a common standard.

Another aspect of Mill's psychology, one destined to be of importance because of its influence on Bain, was his concern with the task of reducing complex emotional states to simple sensory terms. Following the suggestions of Hartley, he undertook a genetic and analytic study of such complex phenomena as conscience, religious attitudes, and the like. In him associationism and hedonism were thoroughly fused, and every experience was conceived to be reduc-

---

[6] The widespread suffering of the factory workers in the newly established industrial order served to make the ethical aspects of political economy particularly acute. Partly because of the migration of agricultural laborers into the cities, there was a disturbance in the food supply. An increase in the population augmented the difficulty. Practical political problems such as the repeal of the Corn Laws were considerably influenced by the agitation of the utilitarians.

ible to sensory components under the guidance of the pleasure-pain principle.

Associationism thus came to maturity. The uncompromising rigidity and consistency of Mill's system gave much to Bain and Spencer, and much of it still lives in modern psychology. But its consistency showed where its weaknesses lay, and in the generation which followed, the inevitable reaction set in. Mill, its most thoroughgoing advocate, was willing to face the most complicated aspects of life in terms of sensation and association; no one after him dared to venture so far.

The reaction against extreme associationism was evident in John Stuart Mill's notes upon his father's work.[7] Much of the economic teaching of his father he did indeed accept; in particular, he elaborated and popularized the ethical aspects of utilitarianism. Nevertheless he had at times serious misgivings about the adequacy of the pleasure-pain principle (psychological hedonism) as well as about the mechanical conception of association. In James Mill's rigid system there was no active principle, nothing but the constant addition of new experiences. For John Stuart Mill the mind was an active, not a passive, thing. Furthermore, in its activity the mind made new syntheses. Just as seventeenth- and eighteenth-century psychologists delighted in drawing analogies from the rapidly growing science of mechanics (as in Hartley's concern with vibrations), so John Stuart Mill in the middle of the nineteenth century borrowed an analogy from the increasingly popular science of chemistry. "Mental chemistry" is the most celebrated of his doctrines. By this he meant the process by which sensory elements become so fused in a new compound that the psychologist must recognize an essentially new entity, which is more than the *sum* of the constituent parts. This doctrine was by no means wholly new; Hartley had himself noted that in a new product the ingredients may be no longer observable. But it is significant in that it shows how short a life was granted to James Mill's purely *mechanical* conceptions.

BAIN

A man of greater significance for psychology than either of the Mills was Alexander Bain. He devoted much energy to grammar, rhetoric, and education; he spent much of his long life in administrative activities of one type or another; and his chief university

[7] He collaborated with Bain in the editing and republication of the *Analysis* in 1869.

position was a chair not of psychology but of logic. But in spite of this scattering of his energies he mastered the Scottish and English, as well as much of the German, psychology, and brought together a vast quantity of material, ably organized and with great originality of treatment. His two greatest works are *The Senses and the Intellect* (1855) and *The Emotions and the Will* (1859).

Bain's approach was through physiology, particularly the work of the German physiologists; he incorporated in his writings a great quantity of research material. We find, for instance, Weber's experiments on the two-point threshold and on the temperature sense. Although the titles of his two celebrated works suggest the continuation of the old subdivisions of *knowing, feeling,* and *willing,* these titles are but cloaks for associationism. It was, however, an associationism based upon physiological findings far more detailed than had been available for any previous scholar. In Bain we have for the first time physiological explanations sufficiently elaborate to be taken seriously. The psychologist was beginning to think of experimental physiology as fundamental to his science. The sense organs, the sensory and motor nerves, the brain, and the muscles were considered in detail. The reflex arc and the instincts were regarded as elements of behavior, and human acts were presented as wholes the parts of which had been studied by the laboratory method.

His view of psychology was relatively comprehensive. Its most serious gap lay in the neglect of material (then being collected by neurologists) which showed the relations of abnormal mental processes to abnormal brain processes. But he furnished a rich and vivid picture of an immense variety of mental states and processes, many of which lay within the field now defined as social psychology. He concerned himself, as James Mill had done, with the origin of those complex attitudes and sentiments which we call aesthetic, moral, and religious; these he related to his physiological principles. We may not unfairly illustrate the kind of associationism to which this method leads by citing an extreme case, his explanation of the behavior of a mother fondling her child.[8] It is clear, said Bain, that things which are warm are pleasant; so also are things which are soft; hence maternal joy.[9] (William James suggested that lonely

[8] *The Emotions and the Will,* pp. 126–40.

[9] There is nothing new under the sun. Many psychological schools today reduce maternal behavior to elements dependent on quite simple sensory gratifications. See F. H. Allport, *Social Psychology* (1924), p. 68: "The caressing which children commonly receive and solicit is associated with sensitive zone stimulation. Their cuddling of dolls and toys, and expressions of love toward these objects, have their root in the same source"; and the rest of the paragraph.

parents might be supplied with pillows heated to the necessary temperature.[10]) This was of course a logical end result of the whole approach from Hartley onward. Bain was concerned simply with carrying out to its logical implications the doctrine of association wherever it could work.

Bain was not one to deny inborn or original nature. He was, in fact, much more concerned with "instinct," innate dispositions to action, than any previous associationist, and was much interested in the mechanics of its function. Unfortunately, however, his chief contributions were written shortly before the publication of Darwin's *The Origin of Species*, and although he lived to see the spread of Darwinism, he never remodeled his psychological conceptions upon Darwinian lines. Nevertheless he was, throughout, thinking in terms of *inborn reaction tendencies*, tendencies which came to be given a role of great importance by the Darwinians.

But the best known of Bain's specific contributions is his treatment of learning and habit. Elaborating some suggestions of Spencer, he stated learning in terms of (1) random movements, (2) retention of acts which bring pleasant results, elimination of those bringing unpleasant results, (3) fixation through repetition. His maxims on habit were quoted and elaborated by James; along with some of Carpenter's observations they receive a very important place in William James's chapter on "Habit." [11] This is but one example of the position of authority which Bain enjoyed throughout the second half of the century, and the way in which his writings have been incorporated into the writings of others.

No one else had ever attempted, as he did, to cover the entire range of normal human experience in a system of psychology. Among all associationists there were efforts to get universal principles, and with Brown an important list of secondary principles had been included; but no one before Bain had tried to analyze such a wealth of *particular* situations. Everything psychological, from the experience of a man jumping a ditch to the mental operations of a creative artist, was the perfectly legitimate concern of the psychologist. No other man had been so prolific in descriptions of human experiences, so serious in trying to give a colorful and exhaustive picture of mental life. It was as if previous authors had said, "Take these key principles and you may enter any room within the house of psychology." Bain said, "Here is the key to the study, with bookshelves that reach to the ceiling; here is the key to the conference room, with a

---

[10] *Principles of Psychology*, Vol. II, p. 552.
[11] In the *Principles of Psychology*.

long table surrounded by a dozen chairs." He was interested in providing not merely an entry into every mode of experience, but an analysis of its contents. This is the chief reason why he is so readable. Never had a psychologist been so widely read in his own day. He exerted as great a personal influence in psychology as did John Stuart Mill in political economy. Associationism became through him almost "popular." But in his interest in the living unity of the person, he reflected the spirit of the Scottish school. And he did not irritate his readers, as most of the associationists had done, by the apparent crassness of a mechanistic system. He made use of physiological principles for their practical usefulness, not for philosophical purposes. He was genuinely and consistently a psychologist; he might fairly be described as the first to write a comprehensive treatise having psychology as its sole purpose.

This work of Bain in the field of physiological psychology, if we may call it such, summed up and crowned the achievements of physiological as well as of introspective work up to the middle of the nineteenth century. Another great contribution of Bain was the founding in 1876 of a journal for the publication of psychological articles. Psychological writings before this time had for the most part appeared as independent books or pamphlets, or as contributions to general philosophical or physiological journals. The journal *Mind*, although of a philosophical cast, was from the first concerned chiefly with psychological material.

In the same era Carpenter's *Mental Physiology* (1874), and the writings of Maudsley, served further to persuade the British reader that physiological conceptions were the groundwork of psychology. This idea was also becoming popular in France, especially through the writings of Ribot (cf. page 170).

But associationism ran now into stormy waters. Immediately after Bain's chief volumes there came the publication of Darwin's *The Origin of Species* (1859). The evolutionary theory substituted for associationism two definite working concepts which changed the whole background of psychology. The concept of heredity was important both for the understanding of uniformities of mental structure and for the interpretation of permanent and stable differences from one individual to another; and the idea of the adaptation of the individual to his environment became basic for every psychological problem. The biological outlook, emphasizing such concepts as the *functions* of an *organism*, had indeed been apparent in some quarters; but after Darwin the term "biological" became a symbol for a new way of thinking, in which every organ and function was understood in terms of its history and its relation to the life of the creature which displayed it. Such an approach could not have been made before Darwinian evolutionism, and could not be avoided after it. These fundamental changes made associationism, as it flourished from Hartley to Bain, untenable. The growing strength of the idealist philosophy (led by such men as T. H. Green; cf. page 100), with its emphasis on the unity and activity of mind, was indeed pressing associationism hard from its side. Just as a coalition of radicals and reactionaries may drive out a middle-of-the-road political leadership, so associationism was attacked with equal vigor by those who thought it too biological and by those for whom it was not biological enough. Not that the central doctrines of the associationists have disappeared; and not that the wealth of their specific contributions has been forgotten. On the contrary, the attention given to memory and learning in all modern psychology has inevitably involved much use of associationist contributions; for example, modern students of the conditioned reflex (page 265) have freely drawn upon associationist doctrines, while substituting for them a description in terms of overt responses rather than of "ideas." But however much associationism left behind it in these as in more subtle ways, the classical doctrine with its *explanation of all psychological events through the juxtaposition of sensory impressions* may definitely be said to have died with Bain.

SPENCER

Herbert Spencer is sometimes regarded as sharing with Bain in the last defense of associationism; it is more nearly true to say that he was the first of the evolutionists.[12] He does, indeed, seem much less important as a psychologist today than does Bain. But he had the advantage over Bain that he was an evolutionist before Darwin; as early as 1850 he had begun to write on evolution. His system attracted wide notice, so that when *The Origin of Species* was published, his own more speculative evolutionism drew strength from it. His evolutionary system has exerted more influence upon psychology than have the associationist principles which his own psychology embodies.

Spencer undertook to create a "synthetic philosophy," in which everything in the universe should be related to everything else, expressive of one developing totality. Development, whether of stars, of plants, of men, or of political institutions, involves *differentiation*

[12] *The Principles of Psychology* (1855).

followed by *integration*. In its earliest phase any growing thing is simple, uniform, homogeneous; in time there is differentiation, the emergence of recognizable and distinct parts; last of all comes integration, the articulation of the parts in a new functioning whole. Evolution is "change from incoherent indefinite homogeneity to coherent, definite heterogeneity," with constant adjustment of inner to outer relations. In the solar system, or in the embryo, or in the growth of nations, there is always a differentiation phase, then an integration phase. For psychology this meant that the increasing complexity of the nervous system was paralleled by an increasing richness and variety in the forms of experience and in the types of association. Together with increase in complexity of structure come higher and higher integrations of function. Association was regarded as an integrating mechanism by which a more and more complex type of experience becomes possible.

Spencer was the first to elaborate the conception that the mind is what it is because it has had to cope with particular kinds of environment.[13] He laid great emphasis on the adaptive nature of nervous and mental processes, and on the notion that increasing complexity of experiences and of behavior is a part of the process of adaptation. This doctrine, though part of a speculative system, was singularly similar, as we shall see, to the conclusions which followed upon all the inductive work of Darwin. A more adequate and detailed application of evolutionary principles had to wait upon the accumulation of data by Darwin and his followers. Whereas Spencer's psychology never attained the vogue enjoyed by Bain's, his evolutionary teaching contributed to the widespread adoption by psychologists of biological conceptions, especially those relating to the principle of the adaptation of an organism to its environment.

One specific psychological doctrine of Spencer attracted attention and is still well known—his theory of the relation between mind and body. We may regard the mind, said Spencer, as a series of events, and the physical processes in the brain as a series of parallel events; but both of these arise from a deeper underlying reality. This is, of course, reminiscent of Spinoza's monism (page 20). This basic reality he regarded as unknowable. He was, for practical purposes, a parallelist, like those we have already had to consider. But, unlike Leibnitz, Spencer believed that mental and physical events were intimately and organically connected; not that either was the cause of the other, but that both sprang from the same soil.

[13] Though suggestions in this direction had been given by several; for example, Lucretius among the ancients, Schopenhauer among the moderns.

REFERENCES

Brett, George S., *A History of Psychology*, 3 vols., London, 1914–21; Vol. 3

Dennis, Wayne, ed., *Readings in the History of Psychology*, Appleton-Century, 1948: James Mill; John Stuart Mill

Flügel, John C., *A Hundred Years of Psychology, 1833–1933*, Macmillan, 1933

Chapter 8

THE THEORY OF EVOLUTION

The majority naturally perished, having too weak a constitution.
                                                            HIPPOCRATES

Our present ways of living have, I think, been discovered and elaborated during a long period of time.   HIPPOCRATES

THOUGH it is common to think of evolutionism and Darwinism as synonymous, evolutionism had been one of the great recurrent forms of thought in Western civilization ever since the great panorama of cosmic development had been drawn by Lucretius the Epicurean; and on the heels of Renaissance speculations in this direction, it became an outstanding feature of the thought of the last half of the eighteenth century and of the first half of the nineteenth. Both in the field of biology and in much broader contexts, men were thinking in evolutionary terms.

The world was changing very rapidly in social organization—as was shown not only in political revolutions but in the Industrial Revolution—with profound upheavals in the life of individuals and institutions. The romantic movement expressed and disseminated the idea of diversification and progress. Thus Goethe, one of the most illustrious of the romanticists, found evolutionary conceptions useful in his studies of botany, and indeed worked out his own theory of organic evolution. The philosophy of the period emphasized more and more the fact of change and development. Among the French, Fourier constructed a theory of human destiny in terms of many thousands of years that must be spent in each stage of growth. The same tendency was expressed in Hegel's conviction that civilization had been worked out step by step according to a universal Idea.

In the scientific thought of the period two types of evolutionary teaching went on side by side: first, the theory of the evolution of the inanimate physical universe, the study of inorganic evolution;

second, the study of biological or organic evolution. Laplace developed in connection with his mechanics the theory commonly known as the *nebular hypothesis*. This sought to explain the origin of the planets through the interaction of gravitational and centrifugal forces in a rotating nebula.[1] In geology, Lyell was making investigations from 1830 to 1860 to show how rock strata were formed by a series of changes in the earth. The late seventeenth and the early eighteenth centuries had marked the beginnings of this type of research; by the early nineteenth century the data permitted a systematic and coherent demonstration that the different strata had been built one upon another in a certain sequence, occupying definite periods of time. The various organisms whose fossil remains were found in these strata must necessarily have lived at different times, in periods corresponding to the strata where the fossils were found. Lyell enunciated the theory that the earth itself had gone through an orderly series of changes, in which a chaos of elements had gradually been superseded by differentiation and separation. Thus different kinds of rock had been formed and had become relatively fixed and immutable. This form of thought was as foreign to the idea of special creation as was the Darwinian theory itself; and Lyell, though a deeply religious man, had to face serious religious opposition. He had undertaken to show that the earth itself reveals stages requiring vastly greater time than the six days allowed in the Book of Genesis. As a matter of fact, Lyell was not the first nor the last, but in terms of scientific as well as popular influence he was by far the greatest, of the geological evolutionists. He prepared the way for the habit of thinking of growth in terms of changes in living organisms. Lyell's evolutionism was, indeed, a direct stimulus to the work of Charles Darwin.

Turning to theories of the study of living things, Buffon, in the third quarter of the eighteenth century, outlined an evolutionary theory. Erasmus Darwin (the grandfather of Charles Darwin) at the close of the century stated such evolution in terms of heredity and adaptation to environment. Lamarck elaborated Erasmus Darwin's conceptions in a system which became widely and controversially known.[2] The fact that he mastered both zoology and botany, and the fact that he had made elaborate studies and published dozens of volumes on different phases of the biology of his time, gave weight to his theory and demanded for it serious consideration; and he offered a theory which faced in detail the question

[1] Kant had suggested a similar view as early as 1754.
[2] *Philosophie zoologique* (1809).

why specific cumulative changes in organisms take place from generation to generation. Lamarck's theory involved three steps. First, in confronting the physical environment, the organism has needs, meets situations to which it must adapt itself. Second, these situations demanding adjustment cause the animal to exercise certain parts of its body. Third, the exercise of a given part of the body makes that particular member develop to a point sufficiently advanced to cause the change to appear in the offspring as an acquired characteristic. We may illustrate these three steps from the passage which explains why the snake has no legs. The snake is derived from the salamander or lizard. Some of these salamanders left the water and came to marsh ground, where there was grass. Here they had to keep out of sight. In meeting this situation, legs were a hindrance, and must be dispensed with. Each generation was born with shorter and shorter legs, until the legs disappeared altogether.

Shortly after Lamarck put forth this theory, which was destined to be the greatest of the evolutionary theories before Darwin, a debate began (1830) between Saint-Hilaire and Cuvier. Saint-Hilaire championed Lamarck's doctrine of the transmutation of species (though differing from him as to its mechanism). Cuvier refused to entertain an evolutionary doctrine, simply because of the inadequacy of the evidence. And this debate was bound to be decided in scientific circles of the day in favor of Cuvier, because, in the first place, he was right—there was not enough evidence— and in the second place, because of his immense prestige.

DARWIN

This very question of the inadequacy of the evidence during the first half of the century leads, therefore, to a consideration of the task of gathering data bearing directly on the reality of evolution, as well as on the mechanism by which it was effected, a task chiefly associated with the name of Charles Darwin. Darwin's chief importance lay not in his being the first to think in terms of evolution and the struggle for existence, but in the fact that he, like Cuvier, recognized that the problem could be solved only by the accumulation of enormous and well-ordered masses of evidence.

His trip on the *Beagle* through the South Seas (1831–36) gave Darwin a magnificent opportunity to observe and collect plants and animals. Returning to England, he gave himself over to the intensive study of a few living forms. This detailed study began to lead him to inquire why it was that forms of life were so perfectly adapted to the environment in which they lived. In his notebook of 1837, he tells of his concern with the problem of selection. He had noted that out of every generation some individuals were eliminated, although apparently constructed much like their brothers and sisters. What made some die and others live? What was the mechanism of selection; how did nature choose from the many?

In 1838 he read Malthus's *Essay on Population*, a treatise written forty years before. This essay discussed the problem of the relation of the death rate to the birth rate in human societies. Asking himself whether the lot of the poor could be improved, Malthus had concluded that the improvement which might be made in the production of food would tend to follow an arithmetical progression, while increase in population would inevitably conform to a *geometrical* progression. If, for example, each family has four children, and if three of them live and have offspring, the number given by the geometrical ratio must, in time, surpass the number that can be fed. So long as one ratio is arithmetical and the other geometrical there must follow an *excess* of population. Some individuals must be eliminated in one way or another, through starvation and disease, or through war. There was no escape from these hard alternatives. It was a rather loosely worked-out hypothesis, but it had the advantage of envisaging human society in biological terms. The hypothesis that the number of offspring is usually greater than the number that can subsist implied that there must be a struggle for existence, the elimination of some and the preservation of others.

The reading of Malthus's essay, interpreted in the light of Darwin's own observations, suggested an answer to his problem. He began to outline the theory of evolution which he later published. The theory was based, in the first place, upon the fact that in most species the total number is stationary; yet there are more offspring than parents. In fishes there may be a hundred thousand eggs for each two parents; there must be an elimination of all but two individuals. This leads directly to the idea of the "survival of the fittest." An organism is "fit" if in a given environment it is well adapted to the task of getting food and warding off its enemies. It has to survive and to develop until it is able to reproduce its kind. But if there is survival of the fittest, and at the same time adaptation to the environment (which is the necessary condition of the survival itself), this adaptation to environment must mean survival of those which are fittest *in the particular environment*. If in each generation those which are fittest for the particular environment survive, and if over the years there are changes in the environment, it follows that there must be changes in the kinds of individuals which can survive. Natural selection is effected from among variations which are regularly observable among individuals of the same parentage; and with a changing environment natural selection results in the gradual production of new species ("transmutation of species"). Darwin had noticed in the South Sea Islands that certain species showed differentiation even on the same island; the struggle for existence had selected one type of individuals for the shore, another for the interior. One species, by migrating into two environments, might become, in time, two species. What caused these variations Darwin did not profess to know, and the problem, though much studied, cannot as yet be fully answered. But that they do occur is evident, and when we find them we conclude that those individuals or species which survive could not do so if they were lacking in adaptation to the environment.

After his first rough formulation of the theory, Darwin set for himself the task of collecting data on a scale large enough to permit the verification or refutation of the hypothesis, keeping a careful record of cases which seemed to count against his own view. By 1858 he had a large amount of material. In the meantime, he had achieved through a variety of publications general recognition as a naturalist. He was nearly ready to publish the book which was to advance his theory, and the supporting evidence. In that year he received a letter and a manuscript from a young Englishman in the East Indies, Alfred Russel Wallace. Through an extraordinary coincidence, Wallace, while pondering on Malthus's *Essay on Population* [3] had formulated a doctrine much like Darwin's. During an illness he had worked out in a few hours the main outlines of a very similar evolutionary theory. In sending his manuscript to Darwin he asked for his opinion as to its merit, and whether he would help him to get it published. Darwin was in a difficult position. He must be fair to the man who had prepared a statement of the theory before his own had appeared. Yet Wallace's manuscript contained no such mass of data as Darwin had collected. So he submitted Wallace's work and an abstract of his own theory to Lyell. The latter decided that both must be submitted to the Linnean Society. Some portions of Darwin's forthcoming book were read, together with Wallace's manuscript. [4] In 1859 Darwin's *The Origin of Species* was published.

[3] Which he had read a few years earlier.
[4] The joint essay was read on July 1, 1858, and appears in the *Linnean Society Journal* for that year.

Evolutionary theories were not, we must remind ourselves again, new, and even the hypothesis as to the mechanism of evolution had been in some respects anticipated. The chief significance of the book lay not in the newness of the theory, but in the mass of relevant data presented to show the reality of the transmutation of species, and the compelling force with which they commanded serious attention. A general storm was precipitated and some of the most violent battles in intellectual history took place. Spencer had prepared the intelligentsia for such doctrines; Huxley was one of the greatest of those who took Darwin's side; Haeckel saw the whole world-view inevitably involved in the theory. Though much of the resistance to the theory was on religious grounds (because of its rejection of the principle of special creation), there was at first considerable acrimony even among scientists. Many were not ready to capitulate at once. Agassiz, probably the most eminent biologist in the United States, died without accepting the evidence. By the decade of the eighties, however, the last actual opposition to the theory of evolution as such disappeared among biologists.

The influence of Darwinism upon psychology during the last quarter of the nineteenth century probably did as much as any single factor to shape the science as it exists today. Psychology was certain to become consistently more biological; mental processes tended more and more to be stated in terms of the functions served in the task of adjusting to the world. Darwin himself in *The Descent of Man* (1871) emphasized similarity between human reasoning and similar processes in the higher animals, and in *The Expression of the Emotions in Man and Animals* (1872) suggested an evolutionary interpretation of the characteristic facial and postural changes during strong emotion. The *comparative* viewpoint, although present here and there in the eighteenth and nineteenth centuries, could come into its own only when evolutionism had become the groundwork of psychological thinking. As a natural consequence, interest in animal psychology rapidly increased. Many books appeared which concerned themselves with the nature of instincts and with the phylogenetic study of intelligence.[5] Studies of animal behavior appeared in psychological journals. The great gulf established by Descartes between human and animal psychology had been bridged. The life of the organism was seen as a whole. Human psychology was to be seen in relation to all the phenomena of life.

[5] For example, those of Romanes, Lloyd Morgan, Hobhouse, G. H. Schneider.

GALTON

Francis Galton was the greatest of Darwin's immediate followers in the field of psychology. In fact, he was the first who attempted in a thoroughgoing way to apply the principles of variation, selection, and adaptation to the study of human individuals and races. He published in 1869, a decade after the publication of *The Origin of Species*, a book entitled *Hereditary Genius*, the aim of which was to show that individual greatness follows certain family lines with a frequency and a clarity that belies any explanation in terms of environment. These studies were, for the most part, investigations into family trees of eminent jurists, scientists, authors, and so on. He collected data to show that in each case these men not only inherited genius, as shown by a long line of persons before them, but that they inherited *specific* forms of genius. A great jurist comes from a family which has attained not only eminence, but eminence in the law. It was Galton's belief that there are specific legal gifts, medical gifts, and the like, transmitted by heredity. The theory presupposed that there have been, at some time in the past, variations within the human stock, and that these variations have been able to survive. Galton believed that the Darwinian principle of accidental variation about the average or norm of the group applied as much to the general and specific gifts of man as to the length of a bird's wings or the length of a polar bear's hair; and that these variations tended to persist.

Such *individual differences* had not been seriously treated before as part of the subject matter of psychology. Perhaps their neglect had been the most extraordinary blind spot in previous psychology. It was Darwinism, rather than the previous history of psychology, which brought about an interest in the problem. A few of the fragmentary studies of the subject in the nineteenth century, before Galton, may be noted. Thomas Brown had included, in his secondary laws of association, the factor of constitutional differences in persons. Herbart, about the same time, had written of differences in association accompanying various degrees of intelligence. Among experimentalists, Weber, Fechner, and Helmholtz had found individual differences, but had not studied them systematically. Galton was the first important figure in the exploration of the field.

Galton undertook also to compare the various human races in respect to their hereditary make-up, and to show that the different races have been evolved because of their adaptation to their particular environment.[6] Darwin had pointed out instances in which

[6] *Inquiries into Human Faculty* (1883).

the skin, the proportions of the limbs, and the like, are adapted to the mode of life of given races in a particular climate.[7] Galton held not only that variations occur from one individual to another, but that there may be widespread variation and selection, so that new races are evolved. He even suggested that the culture of the Greeks had been due to a favorable variation in the Hellenic stock.

So profoundly challenging and stimulating an idea was bound to lead to exaggerations. Galton's faith in the all-importance of heredity could scarcely be better indicated than in the following two passages. After reference to anthropometric studies on the "criminal type," he proceeds to these generalizations:

> The deficiency of conscience in criminals, as shown by the absence of genuine remorse for their guilt, astonishes all who first become familiar with the details of prison life. Scenes of heart-rending despair are hardly ever witnessed among prisoners; their sleep is broken by no uneasy dreams.[8]

Galton assumed that all this was biologically conditioned; individuals are born not only to peculiarities of skull or feature, not only to genius or imbecility, but to intrinsic criminalism. This is perhaps the most extreme case of neglect of the *environmental* factors which we have to consider in all our studies so far, just as associationism in general represents the most extreme neglect of the hereditary factors. The second passage indicates an even more picturesque application (or abuse) of Darwinian principles.

> I may take this opportunity of remarking on the well-known hereditary character of colour blindness in connection with the fact, that it is nearly twice as prevalent among the Quakers as among the rest of the community, the proportions being as 5.9 to 3.5 percent. We might have expected an even larger ratio. Nearly every Quaker is descended on both sides solely from members of a group of men and women who segregated themselves from the rest of the world five or six generations ago; one of their strongest opinions being that the fine arts were worldly snares, and their most conspicuous practice being to dress in drabs. A born artist could never have consented to separate himself from his fellows on such grounds; he would have felt the profession of those opinions and their accompanying practices to be a treason to his aesthetic nature. Consequently few of the original stock of Quakers are likely to have had the temperament that is associated with a love for colour, and it is in consequence most reasonable to believe that a larger

---

[7] *The Descent of Man* (1871).
[8] *Inquiries into Human Faculty*, "Criminals and the Insane."

proportion of colour-blind men would have been found among them than among the rest of the population.[9]

After establishing in *Hereditary Genius* the pedigree method of studying mental endowment (a method quickly turned to account in the study of mental deficiency, beginning with Dugdale's *The Jukes*, 1877), Galton turned to the construction of more refined quantitative methods in prosecution of the same problem. In his *Inquiries into Human Faculty and Its Development* (1883) he outlined the procedure and results of two epoch-making studies. The first was his experiment on free association, the essentials of which he had already outlined.[10] Associationism had lived its whole life without any recourse to experimental procedure. Galton undertook to study quantitatively the appearance of various types of association. He prepared a list of seventy-five words, each word on a slip of paper which he placed underneath a book. He looked at them one at a time, using a spring chronometer to measure the time it took to form two associations with the word thus drawn. The associations might come spontaneously and immediately, or only after a pause. Many of the associations were themselves single words, but there were many cases in which there came to mind not a word but a mental picture, an image; and this image had to be described. Either a word or an image satisfied Galton's definition of an "association," but all were reduced to verbal form. These associations were analyzed with reference to their probable origin in his experience; in particular, with reference to the time when the given association seemed to have been first established. One of the most definite of his discoveries related to the great frequency of associations from early boyhood and adolescence.[11] This was one of the earliest attempts to show the significance of very early life, particularly childhood, for adult personality, and to demonstrate the amount of childish material that remains. But of greater importance was the whole fresh conception of an experimental study of association. Galton's association experiment was quickly adopted with greatly improved technique by Wundt, who had just founded his laboratory in Leipzig.

A second and equally significant contribution was the publication (also in the *Inquiries into Human Faculty*) of an extensive study of

[9] *Ibid.*, "Unconsciousness of Peculiarities."

[10] "Psychometric Experiments," *Brain*, 1879–80, 2.

[11] An example of a boyhood association was the appearance of images recalling the scene of a laboratory where he had been allowed to dabble in chemistry.

"mental imagery." [12] It was carried on by questionnaire rather than by experiment; it was, in fact, the first extensive psychological use of the questionnaire. Galton put before his subjects the task: "Before addressing yourself to any of the questions on the opposite page, think of some definite object—suppose it is your breakfast-table as you sat down to it this morning—and consider carefully the picture that rises before your mind's eye. (1) *Illumination.*—Is the image dim or fairly clear? Is its brightness comparable to that of the actual scene? (2) *Definition.*—Are all the objects pretty well defined at the same time, or is the place of sharpest definition at any one moment more contracted than it is in a real scene? (3) *Colouring.*—Are the colours of the china, of the toast, bread-crust, mustard, meat, parsley, or whatever may have been on the table, quite distinct and natural?" One of the most noteworthy things about this study was its use of quantitative method. Images were arranged in serial order from 0 to 100, according to their intensity or likeness to sensation. Galton found evidence that some individuals have no imagery whatever within certain fields. Even some well-known painters reported little or no visual imagery. There were, however, some individuals for whom it was a common experience to have images nearly as intense as full-fledged hallucinations.[13] The study of imagery lent itself, as the association experiment had done, to refinement as an experimental problem; before the close of the century the investigation of imagery became a standard problem in German and American laboratories. Imagery proved to be one of the richest fields for the study of individual differences. And the attempt to get statistical control of data that could not be measured by the yardstick was highly significant for psychology. Galton's chief interest in the problem of imagery, as in most other problems, lay in the attempt to establish hereditary resemblances; he showed, for example, that similarity between brothers and sisters was greater than similarity between individuals taken at random.

Here, as elsewhere, the exclusion of the influence of differences in environment proved to be no easy matter. There was no way of excluding the influence of tradition in the family. Such environmental factors might cause resemblances even in such traits as imagery. Partially meeting the difficulty, Galton centered his attention upon the immensely significant fact of *twin resemblance* in the

[12] The imagery of several individuals had been reported by Fechner, *Elemente der Psychophysik*, Vol. II, pp. 469 ff.

[13] The Society for Psychical Research published in 1894 an elaborate *Census of Hallucinations* (*Proceedings S.P.R.*, 10).

problem of heredity.[14] Though very little of the mechanism of heredity was then understood, Galton knew that twins inherit more in common than other individuals. He collected, indeed, some remarkable anecdotes about twins who were susceptible to the same diseases, or who, though separated for months, died on the same day.

He conceived the problem of "nature and nurture" as a practical social problem, and the eugenics movement was his personal achievement. Eugenics, as Galton formulated it, aimed not merely at the elimination of the unfit, but at the general and systematic improvement of the race through the study and use of biological laws. Spencer had discussed the future of humanity in social and moral terms, taking practically no account of biological factors. Darwin had made it clear that evolution involved not merely changes in species, but actual elimination of some stocks and increase in others. Galton asked whether it might not be possible to establish a new biological foundation upon which a more adequate social organization could be constructed. This eugenic program is still of small importance as far as its social accomplishment is concerned. But it has a good deal of significance in the development of the biological approach to the study of mental traits, because this insistence upon the huge importance of the stuff of which humanity is made helped to force psychology to attain more adequate techniques for measuring such socially significant traits as intelligence.

In all this work, as we have seen in several instances, Galton was thinking quantitatively, and one step of the greatest importance to psychology was his immense contribution to the science of statistics. Statistics may perhaps be said to have come into existence in the seventeenth century in connection with the tabulation of births, marriages, and deaths, and had been greatly advanced by the discoveries by Laplace, Gauss, and others of methods of ascertaining the likelihood of errors of various magnitudes. Nineteenth-century science, in pursuit of causal relations between variables, had had to make much use of the theory of probability, wherever causal relations of a one-to-one type were not apparent. There existed, however, no standard procedure for stating the degree to which two variables were related. The first step in the creation of such an instrument, "the coefficient of correlation," was the work of Galton.

[14] Thorndike, Gesell, Newman, and many others have realized Galton's original ambition of getting the intellectual resemblance of twins into quantitative terms. See pages 370 and 399.

Suppose he wished to find the relation between height and weight. The relation was, of course, not one of perfect correspondence; there were *some* men five feet eight inches tall who were heavier than *some* who were five feet nine. Yet he could predict, with small risk of error, that the average weight of a hundred men of the first group would be less than that of a hundred men of the second. Seeking to get the relation of such variables as height and weight into quantitative terms, he devised a primitive correlation method of measuring concomitant variations. He laid off the familiar x and y axes perpendicular to one another (as in analytical geometry) and marked off units upon both of these axes. Let us consider first an ideal case, a case of perfect correspondence between the two variables: If the units of measurement for the two variables are comparable, the recorded data when entered on our graph will give us a straight line at an angle of $45°$ from the x axis. If we find an increase in height, but no increase in weight, we record the addition of a number of units on the x axis and no units at all on the y axis; there is no correlation. Intermediate between those situations are those in which the observed amounts of x and y tend to vary together, but not in a one-to-one fashion.

But the treatment of variables like height and weight is actually rather complicated. Among a hundred men there may be, for example, *several* men of the same height but of *differing* weights, and though greater height would in general mean greater weight, there would be many individuals below average weight but above average height. These exceptions to the general tendency would "lower the correlation." How was the relation to be precisely measured? Pearson, Galton's pupil, saw the application of Gauss's "theory of least squares" to this problem. He saw that in measuring a correlation we may take the products of the x and y deviations and add these products algebraically. Tending toward a positive or plus correlation is a man above average in both weight and height; tending toward a negative or minus correlation is a man above average in one and below average in the other. Pearson's formula, worked out in the last decade of the century, superseded Galton's graphic method, and made possible the statement of correlations on a scale from 0 to 1. It permitted a quantitative statement of the degree of dependence between any two measurable variables, or, of course, of their dependence upon some other factor or factors.[15]

[15] It does not prove causal relationship, but does measure the "concomitant variation" which must appear (though perhaps masked) if causal relationship exists.

EVOLUTIONISM IN THE SOCIAL SCIENCES

Evolutionism profoundly affected also the sister sciences of anthropology, sociology, and economics in many ways, tending in general to bring their subject matter closer to the interests of the psychologists, to make them more psychological. In the social sciences, as in the physical and biological sciences, the idea of evolution was already familiar; it had been a current method of approach to the phenomena of social life long before Darwin. But Darwinism gave it a force, a rational basis, a mass of empirical data, and hence a prestige which it could not otherwise have attained.

Evolutionary thinking, to use the term very broadly, appears in the work of the German travelers Bastian and Ratzel. Ratzel's volumes, published early in the latter half of the century, described human customs as ways of adjusting to various environments. This work was followed by the world-wide assemblage of data, through many scattered collaborators, by Herbert Spencer.[16] His work, however, was hardly inductive; he was concerned rather to find support for a scheme of evolution through which he believed human institutions must pass. Spencer held that social institutions pass through a definite series of *stages;* fundamental laws of development conceived in terms of his general philosophical principle (pages 108–109) were supposed to lie behind changes in economic and social structure. This was the first clear evolutionary approach to anthropological data.

The work of Tylor expressed a somewhat less extreme evolutionism.[17] Tylor's central problem, and that which stands out as his greatest contribution, is connected with the doctrine that religion has evolved from certain attributes of primitive mentality. His theory of *animism* held that primitive man universally thinks of the world as a host of animated beings. The forces of nature, and all things perceived, are friendly or inimical to man; they are quasi-personal, animate, or "besouled." No difference is made between a man, a flower, a stone, and a star, as far as their animate nature is concerned. If a man trips on a stone, giving himself an ugly fall, the stone is malevolent. Or if his fishing net brings a large catch, this must be due to the favor of some natural deity; he seizes upon the most obvious thing, perhaps the lake, to worship. Moreover, for primitive man human and animal souls are something separate from the body. Like wine which can be poured into or out of a

---

[16] *Principles of Sociology* (1880–96).
[17] *Primitive Culture* (1871).

bottle, the soul in dreams seems to him to pass into or out of the body (cf. page 5). This animism was shown to be general among primitive people, and to be important in their thinking. This was indeed an epoch-making contribution to psychological anthropology; religion and magic were given a simple and universal psychological interpretation. This doctrine of Tylor was accompanied by an emphasis upon a theory of cultural development known as "parallelism," which asserted that wherever cultures are at the same level of advancement, the same customs may arise independently among different groups. Wherever the environments of two tribes or peoples are similar, the peoples tend to develop the same adaptations.

Toward the close of the century a large amount of data came to hand whose effect was to undermine this more naïve evolutionary point of view. In particular, there was evidence to show that many of these cases of "parallelism" were due not to independent adaptation of different groups to similar environments, but to borrowing or "diffusion" between tribes.[18] The possibility of diffusion necessitated a more critical and inductive approach to each alleged instance. Another factor equally important in forcing a revision of anthropological evolutionism was the discovery that no definite series of stages through which societies pass can be found; the stages are different for different societies. The use of evolutionary conceptions had its value; its very weaknesses helped to make clear the necessity of taking account of the extraordinary variety of cultural changes, and helped to make clear to anthropologists the direction in which their discipline must move if it were to become an inductive science.

Much of the same kind of development was going on in sociology. One of the first great figures was Auguste Comte. During the second quarter of the nineteenth century he became known for a simple but definite evolutionary theory associated with a philosophy to which he gave the name of *positivism*.[19] His viewpoint was, in part, a reaction against the "idealism" of French philosophers,[20] a demand for empirical methods, for objectivity and definiteness. Comte became a colossal influence in social theory, chiefly through the efforts of John Stuart Mill. Comte's evolutionism can be summarized

[18] Moreover, many supposed cases of parallelism turned out on closer examination to involve only superficial resemblances.

[19] His first important work was *Politique positive* (1824).

[20] One aspect of the idealistic movement was the work of Royer-Collard mentioned above (page 58).

in a few words: There are three stages in human evolution: the theological, the metaphysical, and the positive. Social reconstruction is to be effected through the emancipation of mankind from metaphysics in favor of the habit of direct appeal to experience. Terse as the doctrine was, it was important for social theory, allying itself easily with other forms of evolutionism and helping greatly to substitute dynamic for static conceptions of society. Comte also inveighed against introspective methods very much in the spirit of modern behaviorism; if he had offered a program of research, he might fairly be called the first behaviorist.

Another great social evolutionist was Karl Marx, a radical critic of the contemporary political economy. The *Communist Manifesto* (1847), in collaboration with Engels, and his work *Capital* (1867), were steps in the enunciation of the "economic interpretation of history," the view that social changes result primarily from the operation of economic laws, the development of new industrial arts, and the struggle of economic classes. Marx was one among many who gave expression before Darwin to what we may call "economic evolutionism." His importance for psychology, slight at the time, became great after the Russian Revolution, as we shall see in Chapter 29.

The theory of evolution was also conspicuous in linguistic science. Max Müller stood out as one of the greatest products of the university system which, as we have seen, was the cradle of philological science in the late eighteenth and early nineteenth centuries. As an instance of German philological work in the nineteenth century may be mentioned Müller's study of the gradual differentiation of the Indo-European languages. Closely allied to such philological work was the study of the religion of early Aryan peoples, and the stages in its development as exemplified in mythology and sacred writings.

Another social science, which concerns us more closely, is the "folk psychology" of Steinthal and Lazarus. In a journal appearing in 1860,[21] they published much material relating to the folklore, customs, and religion of many peoples. Their work presupposed the existence of differences in the fundamental psychology of races, by virtue of which, for example, the Norwegian looks at things differently from an Italian or an American Indian. The elements which go to form the aggregate of what members of a race have in common psychologically they regarded as a social mind. They espoused, in fact, the theory of a "social mind" distinct from that of individuals in the social groups. They were concerned also with the problem

21 *Zschr. Völkerpsychologie und Sprachwissenschaft.*

of transition from one to another type of social mind, and the material they gathered contributed its share to the vast stream of evolutionary thinking. Their work was important also as background for the "folk psychology" and "social psychology" of the late nineteenth century, to be considered later.

REFERENCES

Darwin, Charles R., *The Expression of the Emotions in Man and Animals,* London, 1872
——, *The Origin of Species,* London, 1859
Encyclopaedia Britannica, "Charles Darwin"
Galton, Francis, *Inquiries into Human Faculty,* London, 1883
Merz, J. T., *A History of European Thought in the Nineteenth Century,* 4 vols., London, 1896

Chapter 9

PSYCHIATRY FROM PINEL
AND MESMER TO CHARCOT

Canst thou not minister to a mind diseased?   SHAKESPEARE

THE DEVELOPMENT of psychiatry during the nineteenth century may be divided into the study of and practical work with three types of mental abnormality: the psychoses ("insanity"); mental deficiency; and the psychoneuroses.

THE PSYCHOSES

Several of the common psychoses had been recognized and described during the seventeenth and eighteenth centuries. Our first concern is with Pinel, who succeeded near the end of the eighteenth century in greatly strengthening the medical as against the demonic view of mental disease (page 39). He insisted that the insane are sick, not wicked; that insanity is a disease which can in some cases be removed through removal of physical causes. He did much to encourage humane treatment for the mentally disturbed, and his work obtained immediate and wide recognition. Such views had been held before, but Pinel's authority helped to make them the established doctrine. There was practically no demonological psychiatry after his time. Pinel was more than the advocate of a new viewpoint. He was one of the great classifiers of mental disorders, working out a fairly satisfactory rule-of-thumb classification, in which the gross symptoms of many disorders were delineated. Perhaps his greatest successor was Esquirol, who assisted in the refinement of Pinel's classification. In the meantime, Moreau de Tours gave a distinctly *psychological* account of mental disorder.[1]

1 For example, *Etudes physiologiques sur la folie* (1840).

During the time of Esquirol's dominance in France, German psychiatry began to appreciate the significance of the work done, and there arose during the second quarter of the century a number of German physicians who contributed to the problem of classification. Chief among them was Griesinger, whose work was elaborate and detailed. He conceived of mental disease in the definite terms of physical pathology. Throughout the remainder of the century emphasis alternated between somatic factors and psychic factors. The importance of the somatic conception lay not only in pointing to the etiology of some of the "organic psychoses," but also in awakening physicians to the fact that insanity was *their* problem. In the generation which followed, new systems of classification were legion. (Of course the classifications took account for the most part of gross symptoms rather than of etiology.) We find, for example, good descriptions of the condition known as mania: the patient is excited and agitated, talks incoherently, and is frequently elated. Such problems as the average duration of such conditions, the existence of intellectual disorder remaining after recovery from the attack, and the like were very inadequately treated. Griesinger's work was followed by more and more subdividing of clinical types. Among his followers, the subdivision of clinical types into subheads bearing new names went so far that some classifications listed as many as three hundred mental disorders. In the third quarter of the century the pendulum began to swing back, and there was a tendency to emphasize a few main types. By the end of the century psychiatry was tending, under Emil Kraepelin's influence, to settle down to the recognition of about twenty main types of psychosis. Remarkably enough, there was throughout the nineteenth century very little recognition among physicians that normal psychology had anything to offer, and very little recognition among psychologists that mental disorder could teach them anything.

Another dominant element in the development of psychiatry was research on the nervous system. Many mental diseases had now been recognized as physical entities; for example, by the middle of the century many of the gross pathological changes in the nervous system in *dementia paralytica* (general paresis) were definitely known from post-mortem examinations. In this field, as in that of classification, German work overtook the French.

Progress in neurology was paralleled by the movement for humane treatment of the insane. This was of extraordinary importance for psychiatry, because it was the chief means by which the insane were taken from the hands of jailers and almshouse-keepers and given into the care of physicians. Before the middle of the century institutions for the insane were few and far between. Private institutions were pitifully inadequate, and society was not sufficiently interested to support public institutions. The creation of a public conscience recognizing the obligation of society to care for the insane was chiefly the work of one person, a woman subject to long illnesses and interruptions, but a person of extraordinary personal gifts. Dorothea Dix became interested about 1840 in the condition of prisoners, and made visits to the prisons and jails of her own state, Massachusetts. The conditions prevailing were unspeakable, one of the worst abuses being the incarceration of many insane and feeble-minded together with criminals of "normal" make-up. From this beginning her work extended into two fields, one the reform of institutions for criminals, the other the creation of public institutions for the insane. Her method was the arousal of public conscience and the persuasion of legislative bodies. Massachusetts, as a result of her efforts, appropriated funds for an institution for the insane; near-by states quickly followed. Miss Dix traveled down the Atlantic coast and into the Southern states, sweeping everything before her; legislature after legislature capitulated. Within thirty years twenty states had established such institutions. Always in delicate health and realizing the necessity of avoiding a breakdown, she went to England. But finding that there were no public institutions for the insane in Scotland, she proceeded to get an Act of Parliament to provide for them. "She extended her work into the Channel Islands, and then to France, Italy, Austria, Greece, Turkey, Russia, Sweden, Norway, Denmark, Holland, Belgium, and a part of Germany. Her influence over Arinori Mori, the Japanese *chargé d'affaires* at Washington, led eventually to the establishment of two asylums for the insane in Japan." [2] There are few cases in history where a social movement of such proportions can be attributed to the work of a single individual. [3]

MENTAL DEFICIENCY

In 1798 a group of French sportsmen found in Aveyron a boy about ten years old who could not talk and who appeared to be living "wild" without human contacts. (Many such "feral"—animal-like—children are known to history.) He was taken to Paris,

---

[2] *Encyclopaedia Britannica*, 11th ed., "Dix, Dorothea Lynde."

[3] Her many other extraordinary achievements—prison reform, co-operation with Howe in the work for defectives, service as Chief Nurse of the Union Armies, 1861–65—are described in Francis Tiffany's *Life of Dorothea Lynde Dix* (1890).

and turned over to Itard, an expert in the methods of training the deaf.[4] Itard was under the influence of associationist psychology, whose principle, it will be recalled, was that experience is the basis of all mental capacity, and that from experience is to be explained all mental growth. Adult intelligence is built up through the accumulation of sensory experiences. Itard saw the opportunity to put the theory to the test. Here was a boy who obviously had very little intelligence, very few ideas. Perhaps if he were given more ideas his intelligence would be raised. Itard set to work, and for five years labored to make a social being out of this pathetic foundling. He did not succeed, and reported sadly to the Academy that the boy was practically untrainable. The great Pinel had foreseen this outcome, predicting that Itard would be successful only if the boy were free from intrinsic mental defect. But the Academy refused to regard Itard's work as a failure; they were much impressed with the definite progress which he had made in helping the boy to form a number of useful habits. Itard continued to interest himself in the problem of the subnormal, until there came under his influence a young man, Seguin, who was destined to be the greatest figure in the century in the training of mental defectives. During the thirties Seguin became known for his own achievements. His emphasis was chiefly upon what he called a "physiological method," the development of the sensory and motor functions. The child was to be educated first through stimulation by bright colors, insistent sounds, and the like. He was to be trained in motor control by being made to walk along lines, upon ladders, and so on. Seguin realized that there was no hope of bringing the feeble-minded to normal intelligence; the aim must be to develop what capacities they had. In 1842 he became the head of an institution which had been established in Paris in 1828 for the training of the feeble-minded, but unfortunately he soon got into administrative difficulties and had to give up his position.

It so happened, however, that there was a large opportunity for his work elsewhere. Dr. Samuel Howe, of the Perkins Institution for the Blind in Boston, had found that blind children suffering from mental defect could not be trained by the same methods as blind children of normal intelligence. He recognized that Seguin would be a suitable person to bring to the United States to give instruction in methods of training the feeble-minded. Seguin accepted the call, and for two decades contributed abundantly both to the improvement of methods and to the movement for the establishment of

[4] *The Wild Boy of Aveyron*, trans. by George and Muriel Humphrey (1932).

institutions for mental defectives. Then, with the assistance of Miss Dix and other philanthropists, Howe succeeded in 1848 in getting an appropriation for the training of a few feeble-minded children. Institutions for the feeble-minded spread rapidly through the United States.

Following the lead of the French, a similar movement was spreading in Europe. Switzerland is of particular interest in this connection because of the prevalence along its southern frontier of the special type of mental deficiency known as cretinism. Napoleon had tried unsuccessfully to extirpate the condition (arising from thyroid defect) by the transplanting of families. The serious problem of cretinism called forth the devoted efforts of a young physician, Guggenbühl, who undertook (1842) the systematic study and instruction of these defectives, in a colony of buildings high up in the mountains. Cretinism is not found above a certain altitude. This was the beginning of the now widespread "colonial" system of caring for defectives. Saegert, in charge of an institution for deaf-mutes in Berlin, encountered a problem similar to that which Howe had had to face; mental defectives among the deaf required special methods of training. He not only worked out methods of instruction but succeeded in founding in Berlin (1845) an institution for the feeble-minded, which led to the rapid establishment of similar institutions in many of the German states. In Britain a home for mental defectives at Park House, Highgate, in 1848, was quickly followed by other publicly endowed institutions. The movement for the public assumption of responsibility for the care of mental defectives made rapid gains during the third quarter of the century and still continues.

THE PSYCHONEUROSES

That aspect of the study of the psychoneuroses which exerted chief influence upon psychology was their treatment through suggestion. The story really begins with Paracelsus, a sixteenth-century physician of varied talents who had sought, in the midst of other enterprises, to show the influence of the stars on human health. Mesmer, an Austrian student of medicine, came into contact with this view of Paracelsus about 1760, and was profoundly influenced by it.[5] The conception of magnetic influences from the stars was in the background of his mind when, a few years later, he witnessed a demonstration of cures apparently effected by the use of magnetized plates. In 1776 he encountered the demonstrations of a priest named

[5] Mesmer's disquisition *De planetarum Influxu* (1766) shows his early interest.

Gassner who convinced him that the human hand was as effective a means of magnetizing as were metal plates. The term "animal magnetism" designated this magnetic influence of the human body. Mesmer went to Paris, where, as the intellectual center of the world, all eyes were turned upon anyone who had some new idea to disseminate. He quickly attracted the patronage of patients suffering from all sorts of diseases. "Mesmerism" became a fad.

The center of his practice was the *baquet*, a tub containing magnetized iron filings around which his patients sat. Metal bars reached out from the tub in different directions. The magnetic influence was supposed to pass from the filings through the iron rods to the bodies of the patients. We have a few descriptions of what happened to these people. Some of them had "fits" or crises. After these crises a large number of them got well, at least well enough to keep Mesmer's prestige at a great height.

He was shortly confronted with severe opposition from the medical profession, which branded him as a quack. A royal commission was organized to inquire into the value of his work. This commission included the great chemist Lavoisier, and Benjamin Franklin, the ambassador of the newly constituted United States. The commission, after studying Mesmer's work, did not controvert the claims of cure; they concentrated their attention upon the theory of animal magnetism. The cures, they said, were due not to magnetism but to the patients' "imagination." As a result of this negative report, Mesmer was forced to leave Paris. But the therapeutic use of magnetized metal and of the hands continued.

The chief of Mesmer's followers was the Marquis de Puységur, who made the important discovery that it was possible to throw the patient into a quiet sleeplike state, from which he emerged to find his condition bettered. Puységur found, at Soissons, that not only human hands, but trees, could be "magnetized." If patients stood beneath these trees, cures were effected. Then Franklin tried the experiment of telling peasants that certain trees had been magnetized. Some stood under them and were cured as effectively as those beneath Puységur's magnetized trees. This was, to Franklin's mind, good evidence that "imagination" was a sufficient explanation. The followers of Mesmer, however, went on with their work.

Shortly after 1820 another period of intense popular interest in mesmerism led to a second medical investigation. The movement had spread, in the meantime, to Germany, England, and the United States, and popular demonstrations were given everywhere. Mesmerism became an international problem, from the medical viewpoint an international nuisance. The new committee spent several years studying the mesmeric methods and their results. They reported that the cures were genuine, and moreover that there were a number of extraordinary phenomena which far transcended the scope of existing medicine: the transference of thought from one mind to another without a word spoken, the reading of letters so sealed that no normal reading of them was possible, the "transposition of the senses"—seeing with the tips of the fingers, and so on—and other similar phenomena of the kind studied later by psychical research (page 205). The committee, however, drew no definite conclusion as to the nature of "animal magnetism." This report provoked the most violent dissent, not only because of its emphasis upon the genuineness of the cures but also because of the marvels that had been reported—telepathy, clairvoyance, and the transposition of the senses—which objectors regarded as cases of imposture. The easiest way to explain the cures was to say that they were all based on fraud or illusion. A third committee was appointed, which came to a conclusion more in conformity with the opinions of medical men, with emphasis upon the statement that "animal magnetism" itself was a hoax. Mesmerism fell into even more serious disrepute. It had never succeeded in getting a standing, and now it was thrown into outer darkness.

Not that it lost its popular appeal. Among British mesmerists the leading figure was Elliotson, a physician who was convinced of the value of the method and struggled to obtain a fair hearing for it from medical men. He had such faith in the mesmeric cures that he willingly submitted the phenomena to tests by skeptics. He would "magnetize" a coin; then the coin would be applied to the body of a patient, and the patient would feel better. He gave a demonstration before one of the editors of the *Lancet*, who tried an experiment closely similar to Franklin's. It was found that the only necessary condition was the patient's *belief* that a coin had been "magnetized"; Elliotson's "magnetization" made no difference. But although mesmerism had fallen low, it dropped to a still lower ebb through its association with phrenology. Since the hands had magnetic influence, it was argued that when they touched a particular part of the skull, the brain area beneath that spot would be called into function. This union of mesmerism and phrenology was defended in Elliotson's journal, the *Phreno-magnet*.

While Elliotson fought unsuccessfully for the recognition of mesmeric therapy, word reached England regarding the hundreds of successful operations performed in Ceylon by Esdaile through induction of the mesmeric trance, a procedure already used by native surgeons. Here was support for the lonely Elliotson. Yet, as it happened, the reports synchronized closely with reports from the United States of successful operations under general anesthesia (both chloroform and ether came into use in the forties), and these, being easier to accept, and to control, than was mesmerism, pre-empted the field.

But a turning point came with the work of Braid, a surgeon of Manchester. He witnessed demonstrations of mesmerism in 1841, which started him off on a long series of reflections, doubts, and experiments. He later gave a vivid account of a young woman who while in the mesmeric trance gave ample demonstration of these wonders. "Under 'adhesiveness and friendship' she clasped me, and on stimulating the organ of 'combativeness' on the opposite side of the head, with the arm of that side she struck two gentlemen (who, she imagined, were about to attack me) in such a manner as nearly laid one on the floor, whilst with the other arm she held me in the most friendly manner. Under 'benevolence' she seemed quite overwhelmed with compassion; under 'acquisitiveness' stole greedily all she could lay her hands on, which was retained whilst I excited many other manifestations, but the moment my fingers touched 'conscientiousness' she threw all she had stolen on the floor, as if horror-stricken, and burst into a flood of tears." [6] Braid was at first skeptical about the reality of the whole cycle of psychological effects which the mesmerists seemed to induce. Through his own experimentation he became convinced, however, that there were genuine phenomena to be explained, not in magnetic, but in *physiological* terms. He experimented with various methods of inducing the sleep-like state which mesmerists induced, and found that such physiological factors as muscular fatigue served a useful purpose. This physiological emphasis, coming from a surgeon in good repute who had once been a complete skeptic, was just what was needed to win the attention of the medical public. The word "hypnotism," with its emphasis upon as common and natural a thing as sleep, marked the shift in outlook; and by experimental demonstrations Braid invited the skeptic to make his own tests. Hypnotism began, shortly after the middle of the century, to be accepted by medical men. Even fifty years after Puységur's experiments, reputable physicians had been few who would accept any explanation for mesmeric phenomena other than fraud on the part of experimenter or subject or both; after Braid, the existence of a genuine hypnotic state came

[6] *Neurypnology* (1843), 135-36.

to be generally recognized.[7] Yet Braid himself came in time to see the inadequacy of the physiological hypothesis, and emphasized psychological factors.

The next great step to be made was that of Liébeault of Nancy,[8] whose celebrated clinic demonstrated therapy through suggestion over a long span of years. For Liébeault and his pupil Bernheim, "suggestion" was a name for the process by which ideas were accepted by the patient in such a way as to lead directly to new beliefs, attitudes, and conduct. Not only could temporary changes in the patient be produced, but, through belief in the hypnotist's suggestion of health, the patient seemed in many cases to be cured. Bernheim emphasized especially that hysterical symptoms (functional blindness, functional paralysis, and the like) could be understood through supposing that the subject was suggestible in respect to his inability to perform functions which no known organic condition prevented; as suggestion caused the trouble, so it could cause the cure. A man who has been in a railroad accident is amenable to the suggestion that his legs are injured; the suggestion may be given him by another person or by associations within his own mind. Paralysis of the legs ensues. These views became the cornerstone of the "Nancy school." The Nancy school developed hypnotic methods which emphasized the direct *suggestion of sleep* as a means of inducing the hypnotic trance, in place of the physiological methods initiated by Braid. Verbal suggestion was the chief method by which experimental study of hypnotic phenomena, as well as the treatment of patients, was carried on. Bernheim systematically studied a wide variety of hypnotic phenomena, such as functional anesthesias and paralyses, amnesias and hallucinations, and showed that in many patients all these effects can be produced by suggestion in the waking state.[9]

But the physiological viewpoint was not to be dislodged so easily. A few years after Liébeault's work, Charcot, at Paris, advocated a conception of hypnosis which was in clear conflict with the theory

[7] The theory of suggestion had been outlined over twenty years before by Bertrand. But he never succeeded in attracting attention to his views; for this reason Braid rather than Bertrand is of chief historical significance.

[8] *Du sommeil et des états analogues* (1866).

[9] About the turn of the century the school came under the influence of the concept of "autosuggestion." The term marked a rebellion against the assumption of the all-importance of rapport between hypnotist and patient, insisting that all suggestion is imposed by the patient upon himself. This conception marks the transition from the "Old Nancy school" to the "New Nancy school," of which Coué (for example, *La maîtrise de soi-même par l'autosuggestion consciente; conférence faite par M. Coué à Chaumont en* 1912) was the best-known exponent.

of the Nancy school. For him, hypnosis was a physiological phenomenon to be understood as one manifestation of hysteria; and hysteria was a disease of the nervous system to be compared and contrasted with various other nervous disorders. Hypnosis was, from Charcot's viewpoint, a condition peculiar to hysterics, and a method par excellence of investigating the hysterical predisposition. Charcot's eminence as a director of two great hospital services for mental disease in Paris was augmented by his introduction of clinical methods, which gave him an opportunity to become one of the greatest teachers of neurology in the nineteenth century. Thus, a century after Mesmer's arrival in Paris, hypnotic technique became a method in the study of clinical neurology at the French capital. The position of Charcot in French psychiatry and psychology is one of such prominence that we shall return to him (page 169) in our survey of French psychology toward the close of the century.

REFERENCES

Boring, Edwin G., *A History of Experimental Psychology*, Century, 1929, pp. 115–132

Bramwell, John M., *Hypnotism: Its History, Practice, and Theory*, London, 1903

Dennis, Wayne, ed., *Readings in the History of Psychology*, Appleton-Century, 1948: Mesmer

Podmore, Frank, *Mesmerism and Christian Science*, Jacobs, 1909

Zilboorg, Gregory, and Henry, G. W., *A History of Medical Psychology*, Norton, 1941

Chapter 10

GERMAN PHYSIOLOGICAL PSYCHOLOGY IN THE AGE OF HELMHOLTZ

It was the times that set the problems, but it was Helmholtz's genius that saw the problems and advanced their solution.

E. G. BORING

WE RETURN now to consider the progress of physiological psychology in Germany, which, in the hands of Weber, Fechner, and Johannes Müller had made such a magnificent beginning.

HELMHOLTZ

Hermann von Helmholtz was the son of a Prussian army officer, and was educated with a view to becoming an army surgeon. But the practice of medicine did not interest him, and he began to devote himself to physics and physiology for their own sake. Exposure to the "philosophy of nature" on the one hand, and to the exact scientific methods of his teacher Johannes Müller on the other hand, led to a rebellion against the former and an eager acceptance of the inductive and mathematical approach. Among Helmholtz's many experimental and theoretical contributions, which dealt with physics, physiology, and psychology, three are of chief interest to us: his investigations of reaction time, of audition, and of vision.

The reaction-time problem was old when he undertook it, though new as a field for physiological experiment. In the Royal Observatory at Greenwich, an assistant had lost his position because he and his chief consistently differed in recording the time of the passage of stars across the meridian. In 1822 a German astronomer, Bessel, noticed that such discrepancies held for all observers. Bessel and other astronomers found this individual variation in recording the times of transit an important source of error, and it became known as the *personal equation*. In the twenties and thirties a number of physiologists devised simple methods by which to measure such differences. The easiest explanation of the facts seemed to be that one individual reacted more quickly than another because his nerves conducted more quickly.

Not very much more than this was done until Helmholtz took hold of the problem. His first outstanding research (in the late forties) was upon the speed of conduction of nerve impulses. Little was known in this area; Müller, in fact, had thought that the speed of nerve conduction was comparable to the speed of light. Helmholtz found a method by which he could determine the speed of conduction in the motor nerves of the frog. In some experiments he stimulated a point on the nerve near the muscle, and in others a point farther away from the muscle. The difference between the time intervals from stimulus to muscular contraction in the two experimental series was the conduction time from the first point to the second. This method gave him fairly consistent results, indicating a speed of about 30 meters per second. Science was moving ever more rapidly from authoritative opinion to the ingenious discovery of precise techniques of control and measurement.

Carrying the problem further, he undertook with human subjects the study of the complete circuit from the stimulation of a sense organ to the motor response. By varying the point of stimulation he sought to ascertain variations in reaction time which would throw light on the speed of conduction in sensory nerves. These were the earliest "reaction-time" experiments as such. The results he obtained were so very inconsistent—showing enormous differences not only from one individual to another, but from one trial to the next in a given subject—that he abandoned the investigation altogether. What he was trying to do was to get a reliable measure of the speed of conduction in nerves. The individual differences which would have interested Galton so much were for him merely uncontrollable variables. Within the thirty years following Helmholtz's experiments more than a dozen investigators tried to confirm his work, reaching results most widely discrepant from one another and from Helmholtz's figures.

It was not Helmholtz, but Donders, a Dutch physiologist, who grasped the psychological significance of the problem. He undertook in the decade of the sixties, in co-operation with De Jaager,[1] a series

---

[1] *Oven den physiologischen tijd der psychische processen* (1865).

of investigations which aimed at the discovery of the various factors intervening between stimulus and response. He realized the importance of some of those psychological factors which for Helmholtz had been a nuisance and a despair. The method of applying the stimulus and the nature of the task required of the subject were of capital importance. Donders used three methods. In the first, the subject made a specific movement as quickly as possible upon the presentation of a stimulus. This was called the *a* method. Next, he was shown two stimuli, and instructed to react in one way if the first was presented, and to react in another way if the other was presented. This was the *b* method. Then the individual was again shown two stimuli; he was to react if he saw one and *not to react* if he saw the other. This was the *c* method. The time in the *c* method (for example, reacting to red light, but withholding reaction to green light) was longer than that in the *a* method (simple reaction); Donders explained this on the hypothesis that the *c* method involved not only reaction but discrimination between red and green. He thought he could measure the discrimination time by subtracting the simple reaction time from that taken with the discrimination method. Finally, in the *choice* reaction between red and green (reacting, for example, with the right hand if he saw the red light, and with the left hand if he saw the green), the time was longer than in the mere discrimination reaction, so that by the same reasoning he undertook to calculate the speed of choice. If the simple reaction was 200 one-thousandths of a second, the discrimination reaction 300, and the choice reaction 375, the discrimination time was 100 and the choice time 75 one-thousandths. In view of the originality and the ingenuity of this first attempt to measure the speed of higher mental processes, it is astonishing to see the small amount of data upon which Donders based his judgments, thirty trials or less with some of his subjects. The influence of training was disregarded. The validity of the method of subtraction has never been accepted by most investigators. One can hardly say that one process exactly fills its assigned span of time and is instantly superseded by another process when it ceases. But the work of Donders is of permanent importance in two respects: First, he showed that some of the variability of results was clearly due not to simple differences in the speed of conduction, but to central processes; second, he laid the cornerstone for the analytic study of the time relations of mental processes. He found also that the reaction time for the different senses showed characteristic differences.

But to return to the researches of Helmholtz. Our next concern is with his epoch-making investigations of vision. His great treatise on *Physiological Optics* (1856–66) drew together research findings and general principles from the physics, physiology, and philosophy of the time, and much fundamental new material discovered and interpreted by himself, in a coherent account of the process of visual perception. His part in experimental physiology and psychology is typically represented by the fact that new editions of his work, rather than new treatises, have remained the dominant reference texts of later years. Among the most important experiments he performed were those in relation to the external muscles of the eye, and among his important theoretical contributions was the statement of the mechanism by which the lenses are focused by the internal eye muscles.

Helmholtz sponsored Young's theory of color vision (page 71). According to Helmholtz, the receptors in the eye which make differential response to color are only three; separate stimulation of these three gives respectively red, green, and blue. Each type of receptor is stimulated to a maximum degree by a certain wave length, and to a lesser degree by wave lengths adjacent in the spectrum. A wave length of 526 thousandths of a millimeter, for example, has a given stimulating effect on the "green" receptor, while wave lengths of 500 and 550 stimulate it to a lesser extent. But these wave lengths stimulate also to some extent the "red" and "blue" receptors. The sensation resulting from 550 is not a faint green, but a mixture perceived as a yellowish green. He showed that these three fundamental colors may be combined in various proportions to give the various colors of the spectrum; and, when properly balanced, to give white or gray. In this scheme Helmholtz made the far-reaching assumption that there is in the brain a specialization corresponding to these three elements in the retina. There must be three kinds of activity evoked in the cortex by the activities of the three receptors; combination is a central function. The doctrine of the *specific energies of cortical areas* (the alternative raised but rejected by Müller) was essential to Helmholtz's formulation.

The theory, of course, had various difficulties to encounter; for example, in the problem of color-blindness (and of partial color-blindness). It had been discovered long before Helmholtz's time [2] that the color-blind individual of the type most commonly encountered lacks sensitivity to both red and green. Why should red and

---

[2] The pioneer contribution coming from Dalton, who gave a paper before the Manchester Literary and Philosophical Society in 1794, entitled *Extraordinary Facts Relating to the Vision of Colours*. Dalton was himself partially color-blind.

green be lost together, but leave the perception of yellow? But the difficulties were met by a series of physiological and psychological observations. For example, the facts of color contrast were ingeniously explained through a psychological principle. Take the case of a white patch seen against a colored background. This is viewed as if through a colored covering. It is not distinguished as independent, and simply as a white patch. Rather, we carry out an "unconscious inference" as to what its true color would have to be to make it look as it does through such a covering; and this would be the complementary color. Notwithstanding difficulties, the theory has proved exceedingly valuable and has in recent years served as the basis for new "three-color theories." The physical fact that three elementary colors can yield, in mixture, all color experiences has continued to influence the effort to find a theory agreeing with all psychological facts.

Helmholtz's work in acoustics is as substantial and as noteworthy as his work in optics.[3] The brilliance and the significance of his experiments are difficult to exaggerate. We may subdivide these investigations into the study of three problems: the perception of individual tones; the perception of combination of tones; and the nature of harmony and discord.

It had long been known that the pitch of a tone depends upon the rapidity of vibration of the sounding instrument. As regards the perception of individual tones, Helmholtz came to the conclusion that there is in the ear a mechanism capable of receiving all those individual variations of pitch which the hearer can discriminate. Experimentally determining the highest and the lowest audible pitch and the number of distinguishable tones between, he supposed that the rods of Corti were capable of vibrating "sympathetically" in differential response to all distinguishable tones. It was shown later by Hensen that the basilar membrane, lying in the inner ear in a conchlike form, meets the needs of the theory more adequately. It was only necessary to assume that each fiber responded sympathetically to a given wave length or pitch. For these fibers were just such as would be expected from the study of instruments with strings of different lengths corresponding to various pitches. But whereas the longest fibers in the basilar membrane are less than three times as long as the shortest, the highest audible pitch has many thousand times the vibration rate of the lowest. This point was studied by Ewald,[4] who noted that we find frequently in sympathetic vibration a

[3] *On the Sensations of Tone as a Physiological Basis for the Theory of Music* (1862).
[4] *Pflüger's Archiv*, 1899, 76, and 1903, 93.

tendency for a body to vibrate not in sharply subdivided areas, but as a whole, and in a number of different patterns. Modern methods of mapping the areas of maximum sensitivity to pitch show that there is nevertheless a progression along the basilar membrane.[5]

Helmholtz worked on the closely related problem of pitch discrimination; and upon a long series of studies in the physiology and psychology of experiences of pitch. One of his greatest experimental contributions was the discovery of what it is that makes the characteristic differences in *tone quality* or *timbre*. Everyone knew that the vibration rate of middle C on the violin was the same as that of middle C on the piano, but the difference in qualities was not understood. Helmholtz discovered the significance of the fact that every kind of musical instrument gives off not only a certain fundamental tone, but, in addition, certain overtones with vibration rates more rapid than those of the fundamental. With the use of resonators he showed that by varying the intensity of the overtones he could produce synthetically the characteristic quality of each instrument, thus establishing beyond doubt the correctness of his hypothesis.

He went on from this to a theory of discord and harmony. Discord he believed to be due to a familiar phenomenon known as "beating" —the production of throbbing sounds resulting from the simultaneous presentation of two tones of nearly the same vibration rate. Dissonance was due to the presence of beats, either between fundamentals or between the overtones of the two tones under consideration. He believed harmony was due to the absence of discord. Subsequent work showed that when the beats are "filtered out" from dissonant tone combinations they remain dissonant, and the theory is today discredited.

Helmholtz was much interested in the history of music. He showed that there had been consistent development (from Greek to nineteenth-century music) in the direction of a constantly greater complexity of relations between tones combined for purposes of harmony. To the simple octave there have been added progressively the fifth, the fourth, the major third, and the minor third; the mathematical relation of vibration rates has become more and more complex. Apparently when listeners are adjusted to one combination of tones, they are preparing for another with more complexity, so that

[5] For recent developments see Stevens, S. S., and Davis, H., *Hearing: Its Psychology and Physiology* (1938).

harmony has inevitably become more and more complicated.[6] The chief significance of the theory was its emphasis upon factors of habituation. The man who contributed most to the physiological approach to tone perception was not content to neglect the importance of educational and historical factors.

HERING

Several other German experimentalists contributed largely during the third quarter of the century to the establishment of a physiological psychology. Two are arbitrarily selected here who are known for specific contributions which still form part of the working principles of psychology as a science.

Hering contributed to several aspects of sensory physiology, including problems in the temperature sense and in optics. While Weber had taught (page 80) that the *rising* or *falling* of the skin temperature is responsible for the temperature sensations, Hering attempted to show that it is not the rising or falling, but the relative temperature of the skin, whether below or above its own "zero point," that determines the appearance of sensations of warmth and cold.[7] The familiar experiment in which one hand is immersed in warm, the other in cold, water and then both are plunged into lukewarm water, can be interpreted as well on Hering's as on Weber's hypothesis. Perhaps the skin of each hand has adapted itselt to a given temperature, its "physiological zero"; the lukewarm water is below one zero point and above the other.

Hering is chiefly celebrated for the theory of color with which he opposed that of Helmholtz. He elaborated and systematized the suggestions of Goethe [8] and Aubert,[9] and introduced improved experimental methods for the study of such phenomena as contrast, afterimage, color-blindness in the periphery of the retina. Goethe had argued that there must of necessity be four elementary colors (disregarding white and black). If, said Hering, we take white (or gray), as demonstrated by Newton, to be due to the mixture of all wave lengths, we encounter on any three-color theory serious

[6] Partial confirmation of the theory has been secured by H. T. Moore, who has shown that practice with simple intervals makes them less satisfying, while practice with intervals which are at first too complex makes them more satisfying. *The Genetic Aspect of Consonance and Dissonance, Psychol. Monogr.*, 1914, 17 (whole No. 73).

[7] "Der Temperatursinn," in Hermann, L., *Handbuch der Physiologie*, 6 vols. in 12, 1879–80, Vol. III.

[8] *Farbenlehre* (1810).

[9] *Physiologie der Netzhaut* (1865).

difficulty in explaining cases where *two* primary colors give the same white or gray. If, for example, red and green mixed give white, the blue remaining should give us together with the white an "unsaturated" blue (a tint or shade, not a pure color). It seemed to Hering that while Goethe's hypothesis must be supplemented with more psychological detail, the four primary colors must be accepted. There must be two pairs. Red and green when mixed would give gray. Each, moreover, was the afterimage of the other as well as its contrast color (the color seen as a border around the stimulus color when shown on a gray field). Similarly, in the case of blue and yellow Hering assumed that as a pair of primary colors which are thus related in afterimage and contrast phenomena, they must, when mixed in the right proportions, give gray. Now it was known that blue and yellow when mixed do give perfect white or gray, but that many familiar reds and greens when mixed give not white, but yellow. This forced Hering into the curious problem of constructing a red and green which when mixed *would* give white. The red and green thus selected are not the red and green which seem to most subjects to be pure and simple colors. We have, then, red and green, yellow and blue, together with white and black. These six primaries were regarded as having direct stimulating effect on the receptors in the eye.[10] To explain negative afterimages and color contrast, he assumed that blue and yellow light act upon one type of receptor, red and green upon a second, and white and black upon a third. In this he found an explanation for negative afterimages and color contrast. Each color was believed to produce a chemical change in the receptor just the reverse of that produced by the other color of its pair. Yellow light caused dissimilation or katabolism in the receptor; blue light caused assimilation or anabolism. Thus the same receptors might serve to communicate either blue or yellow to the brain, depending upon whether the chemical process within them is one of building up or one of breaking down.[11] In the same way, red and green, white and black, upset the chemical equilibrium in opposite directions. If any two of these opposed functions tend to

[10] The "duplicity" or "duplexity" theory, stated by Schultze in 1866, and generally accepted, asserted that there are in the retina receptors the stimulation of which gives color sensations, and other receptors whose stimulation gives colorless sensations.

[11] This assumption of anabolism in the functioning of a sense organ is overbold. Stimulation, as far as we know, regularly means katabolism, The doctrine of specific energies was likewise attacked by Hering's theory; a given type of nerve fiber could initiate either "red" or "green" impulses. So far as is known today, this is unsound.

take place simultaneously, we have gray; red and green cancel one another, leaving the gray which all light arouses through its action on the white-black substance. Blue and yellow similarly cancel. Negative afterimages were easily explained. If we gaze fixedly at red we overwork the process of katabolism and break down tissue, and the reverse process sets in, so that we experience green. The explanation of contrast was similar. Gazing at a red stimulus on a gray field causes katabolism in one retinal area and anabolism in the adjoining region.

One of the greatest successes of Hering's theory was its easy explanation of the fact that in color-blindness red and green are usually lost together, as if dependent on one type of receptor. This conquest was pushed further by the experimental investigation of the zones of the retina; the outermost zone was shown to be responsive only to white and black, the second zone to blue and yellow as well, and the central zone to all six of Hering's primary colors. The formulation of a hypothesis by which blue and yellow, red and green, were linked together in all the main problems of their relation made it immediately acceptable to a large number of psychologists. It did after all bring an extraordinary amount of order into a very chaotic field.

The theory has, however, undergone many revisions, some of which differ so much as to be designated new theories. Among these may be named that of Ladd-Franklin, which approaches the problem from the evolutionary standpoint.[12] The problem of color has led to a vast quantity of research, and a great number of color theories has been and continues to be put forward. The significance of Hering lies not in this establishment of an unchallenged doctrine, but in this introduction of a relatively simple and suggestive hypothesis which continues to stimulate new investigations.

LOTZE

In the psychological work of Lotze there was an extraordinary synthesis of materials drawn from medicine and philosophy. He was in his day better known for his masterful handling of philosophical

---

[12] In this view, white and black were the first differentiations from a primitive sensitiveness to light. White in the course of time became subdivided into blue and yellow; the end organs became specialized so that either blue or yellow wave lengths could be distinguished from those coming from the primordial "white receptors." Later on, the yellow became subdivided into red and green. This formulation had the advantage that the red and green did not need to be so selected as to give gray; familiar reds and greens, which when mixed gave *yellow*, met all the requirements of the theory in relation to contrast, afterimage, color-blindness, and so on.

and biological problems than for the specific contribution which still bears his name in psychology. Lotze studied at Leipzig, took both Ph.D. and M.D., and became Professor of Philosophy at Göttingen (1844). Within a decade he was well known as an author of both philosophical and medical works, especially of works which were *both* philosophical and medical.

Like Bain, Lotze sought to unify physiological and psychological material in a coherent system in which justice should be done both to empirical findings and to the philosopher's demand for interpretation. Unlike Bain, he was a master of the physiology and the neuropathology of his day. At the same time he contributed powerfully to the elaboration of a form of philosophy which was destined to be of considerable significance in nineteenth-century thought. It influenced such men as Wundt, and became in time a foundation principle for many psychological schools. Lotze insisted, in the first place, on the futility of trying to find mental processes which are not related to physical processes; in other words, he protested against those forms of idealism which sought to save a part of psychology from the encroachments of physics and chemistry. Psychology must deal with the organism. The nervous system and the mind must be seen in relation to each other. On the other hand, he maintained with equal definiteness that it was ridiculous to suppose that the mere existence of physical and chemical process was an "explanation" of mind. Exact science can give us no clue as to the ultimate nature of mental processes. In particular, said Lotze, the meanings of life, the significance of things about us, the reality of our pleasures and pains, the reality of our ideals and dreams, are not affected by the discovery of mechanical laws. Such an approach as this sounds like a commonplace today; its importance in Lotze's time arose from the bitterness of the controversy between those who emphasized mechanism and those who emphasized human values.[13] This approach helped to clarify the problem for the psychologist. It gave courage to those who were seeking a formulation of psychological principles based upon the natural sciences; at the same time it cut the ground from under those who easily dismissed all problems of value as irrelevant and those who denied to psychology a subject matter of its own.

Lotze made two specific contributions in addition to this general one. He studied the psychology of the emotions and was one of the first to give a detailed statement of the nature of the expressive

[13] This is of course an arbitrary selection, for emphasis, of but one aspect of Lotze's philosophy.

functions: the way in which the face and posture, as well as the pulse, breathing, and so forth behave in the various emotional states. He had, therefore, considerable influence in later formulations of the relation of emotions to bodily change (such as the James-Lange theory) and helped to prepare the way for the experimental studies of emotion which became numerous toward the end of the century.

But he is chiefly known for his theory of "local signs." [14] This was an attempt to find a compromise between the opposed views on space perception which had been constantly reiterated since the days of Kant. Herbart had made the entire spatial order the product of experience. Johannes Müller had taught that the germ of space perception is innate, but that the elaboration of the world of space, and its organization through the modes of perception known to the adult, have to be learned. He had advocated, as we have seen, a compromise view—that in spite of a primitive awareness of bodily extension much of the process of space perception depends on learning. But many who rejected transcendentalism held with Kant that space perception is purely innate. Müller's authority carried, of course, much weight. But he had not explained how a serial order is built up in the visual world so that each object is seen in a certain relation to each other object, above or below, right or left; nor had the problem of tactual space been seriously considered. These were the tasks Lotze imposed upon himself, and solved so ingeniously that the outlines of his theory still remain influential in our analysis of space perception.

Beginning with vision, Lotze conjectured that each stimulus acting on the retina caused not only a characteristic nonspatial quality such as color, but a sensation specifically related to the point stimulated, and differing qualitatively from sensations aroused by the same object when stimulating any other point on the retina. Each point on the retina had its "local sign." The nature of these local signs and of their organization into a continuum, to give the world of visual space, was stated in terms of the muscular sensations aroused when, upon stimulation, the eye turns so as to bring the stimulus to the point of clearest vision. A light striking the retina at any point causes the eye to swing reflexly to fixate the object. But the direction and the magnitude of the arc through which the eye must pass are different for each point on the retina. Corresponding to all stimulable points on the retina there is, therefore, an immense variety of "feelings of position," forming an orderly, graded series. In the course of time each visual stimulus arouses by association memories

[14] *Outlines of Psychology* (1881, prepared from his lectures), Chap. IV.

of the muscular sensations previously excited as the eye sought its fixation point. In this way stimuli which were at first nonspatial take on a spatial character. There are likewise local signs in the skin. We need only to note that in addition to the nonspatial experiences of pressure, temperature, and so on there are experiences which depend upon the region stimulated; the tension and the curvature of the skin vary from point to point. Each stimulus arouses, therefore, a number of distinct impressions, depending on location; and these, through experience and association, come to form a coherent, graded series. The order thus constituted is now associated with the world of visual space. In the case of those born blind it is necessary to emphasize the orderly series of muscular sensations in making contact with objects at various distances and in various directions from any given starting point.

Both in visual and in cutaneous space the fundamental conception was that psychological space is built up from sensations which in isolation would not be spatial, but whose order of stimulation corresponds to transition of the stimulus from one point in physical space to another. The theory was not only highly important as an application of physiological findings [15] and associationist theory to an extremely complex and baffling problem; it marked one of the boldest and most fruitful attempts to make the muscular sensations play their part in mental life.[16]

REFERENCES

Boring, Edwin G., *A History of Experimental Psychology*, Century, 1929
———, *Sensation and Perception in the History of Experimental Psychology*, Appleton-Century, 1942
Dennis, Wayne, ed., *Readings in the History of Psychology*, Appleton-Century, 1948: Helmholtz
Hall, G. Stanley, *Founders of Modern Psychology*, Appleton, 1912
Helmholtz, Hermann L. F. von, *A Treatise on Physiological Optics*, Optical Society of America, 1924–25
———, *On the Sensations of Tone, etc.*, 4th ed., Longmans, Green, 1912

[15] In particular, Weber's data on the two-point threshold, which Lotze interpreted as indicating that local signs change more rapidly in some regions than in others.

[16] Lotze's emphasis on the muscle sense in connection with vision was welcomed and carried even further by many; for example, by Wundt and Münsterberg, a generation later.

Chapter 11

WUNDT AND EXPERIMENTAL
PSYCHOLOGY

The full tide of successful experiment.   JEFFERSON

WILHELM WUNDT was probably the most comprehensive expression in his time of the scientific forces that were remaking psychology. His position as founder of the first laboratory for experimental psychology, and his huge influence as teacher of those who flocked to study there, arose largely from the fact that he was one of those men who grasp the intellectual forces that are developing about them, realize where they are tending, and undertake to bring them to fruition.

We have seen that much of the psychology of the mid-nineteenth century was incorporated within experimental physiology. The latter included such psychological problems as sight and hearing, comparisons of "sensation intensities" in the Weber-Fechner work, and the various studies of reaction time. All these types of investigation were carried on in physiological laboratories, but were beginning to be colored by a psychological cast of thought. There was in progress, on the other hand, the development of genetic method, due more to Darwin than to any other man. An evolutionary outlook had led, through Galton, to the empirical investigation of association and imagery; evolutionism also encouraged the tendency to emphasize not only cognitive processes but affective and volitional processes as well. These various tendencies were synthesized in the work of Wundt.

Wundt took his degrees of Ph.D. and M.D. at Heidelberg, and was for a time laboratory assistant to Helmholtz. He went in 1874 to the University of Zürich. He was shortly thereafter called to Leipzig as Professor of Philosophy, and there remained until his death in 1920.

In 1873–74 he published his monumental *Principles of Physiological Psychology*, containing the foundations of much of his later work. The term "physiological psychology" meant for Wundt a psychology investigated by *physiological methods*. Its emphasis was on certain aspects of the method of the physiological laboratory. A genuinely psychological experiment involved an objectively knowable and preferably a measurable stimulus, applied under stated conditions, and resulting in a response likewise objectively known and measured. But there were certain intervening steps, which were known through introspection, sometimes supplemented by instrumentation. In this formulation Wundt radically broke with the introspective psychologists from Hobbes onward. For no matter how much emphasis had been given to behavior, and to stimuli causing behavior, by such psychologists as Hobbes and Hartley (and even by men who, like Bain and Lotze, made large use of physiology), no one had grasped in its full entirety the scientific implications of stating mental events in relation to objectively knowable and measurable stimuli and reactions. Nevertheless, introspection, which had been present in rudimentary form in the experimental program of Fechner and Helmholtz, became with Wundt a primary tool of the experimental psychologist. To Wundt, the keystone of all total adjustments of the organism was a psychophysical process, an organic response approachable through both physiology and psychology. What, then, was the relation between the psychological factors and the physiological factors? The physiological psychologist was concerned with the whole series of excitations from stimulation of sense organs, through sensory neurones to lower or to higher centers in the central nervous system and out from these centers to muscles; but parallel with the physiological activities of the higher centers ran the events of mental life, known through introspection. We must therefore have psychology and physiology side by side, always beginning with a stimulus and following through to a response. Physiological psychology was, throughout, an empirical science; it was a union of the long-established introspective methods with methods borrowed from nineteenth-century physiology.

It is not an exaggeration to say that the conception of an experimental psychology was very largely Wundt's own creation. Many psychologists had insisted on empiricism, and many physiologists, as well as philosophers and physicists, had experimentally approached psychological problems. But five years after Wundt went to Leipzig— namely, in 1879—this conception of psychological method took definite form in the founding of a laboratory for psychology independent of the laboratory for physiology. This was of no great consequence so far as its immediate technical results were concerned, but it was of very great consequence in its effect on psychology. Shortly afterward Wundt began to publish a periodical, *Philosophische Studien*, containing some theoretical articles, but devoted largely to reports on the problems of the laboratory. The yearly tables of contents give a fair indication of the interests of Wundt and his school. These interests, though widely varied, were for the most part identified with problems already generally known to physiologists.

We may classify Wundt's specific contributions under two heads: first, his work as a "systematic psychologist"; second, his work as an experimentalist. His psychological system, his point of view, and the edifice which he created are presupposed throughout his detailed theoretical contributions, and in his organization and interpretation of experiments.

In accordance with his physiological viewpoint, Wundt found a place for inherited physiological mechanisms serving reflex and instinct. As far as consciousness was concerned, he assumed a one-to-one correspondence, a parallelism between an excitation of the cerebral cortex and "a corresponding" form of sensory experience. Sensations were ultimate or elementary forms of experience. Sensations were aroused when a sense organ was stimulated and the incoming impulse reached the brain. They were classified according to their modality (seeing, hearing, smelling, and so on); or according to intensity; or according to other special features, such as duration and extension. There was no fundamental difference between sensations and images. These latter were also associated with local excitation within the cortex. In addition to these two groups of elements there were qualities known as *feelings*. Under this head were to be included all qualities of experience which did not come from any sense organ, nor from the revival of sensory experiences. Just as there was a vast number of possible elementary sensations, one might not say how many possible feelings there might be. But feelings can be classified. In the fourth edition of the *Physiological Psychology* (1893) appears the "tridimensional theory of feeling," to the effect that the feelings may be classified as pleasant or unpleasant; tense or relaxed; excited or depressed. A given feeling might at the same time be pleasant, tense, and depressed.

Another type of elementary experience was accepted by Wundt in his early work. This was the feeling of innervation, the feeling we have when we set going a nervous impulse to a muscle; an experience to be differentiated from kinesthetic experience (the sensa-tions from muscles, tendons, and joints). Wundt abandoned this conception in later writings, because of the lack of introspective evidence for it. His empirical attitude was reflected in his willingness to keep changing his mind with each new volume or edition.

Sensations carry with them feeling qualities, and when sensations combine to form more complex states, a certain feeling quality results from the total. This total may again combine with another total, a new feeling resulting from this higher compound. These feeling qualities are arranged not only in patterns, in cross sections of experience in time (the experience at a given *instant*), but in cer-tain *sequences;* feelings follow certain regular orders, and these regular orders of feelings are called *emotions*. Emotions cannot be understood in terms of mere cross sections at given moments; they are charac-teristic sequences. In rage, for example, there is a characteristic series of feelings, giving a temporal pattern distinguishable from the patterns of other emotions.

Usually emotions lead into acts of *will*. Will, like emotion, is characterized by a special temporal pattern of feelings. Will itself is a series of feelings in which at first emotional elements, together with ideas, are present; then ensue peculiar feelings of "resolution," from which the overt act follows. A particular series of feelings, therefore, constitutes the act of will. The line between emotion and will is purely arbitrary, except that volition includes some feelings never found elsewhere.

The question then arises, from our genetic viewpoint, as to which of these various processes are fundamental—reflex acts, sensations, images, simple feelings, emotions, or acts of will. Wundt approached this problem from an evolutionary point of view, emphasizing the essentially adaptive nature of reflex acts (the term "adaptive" here summarizing the conception of biological adjustment). Acts which, ages ago, were the direct expression of the animal's wants have in time become mechanized, so that their essentially voluntary char-acter is overlooked. Reflex acts, from the simplest to the most com-plicated, do, in the long run, what the organism needs to do; there-fore reflex acts were, for Wundt, "purposive."

One feels here the influence of Schopenhauer, who had made the will the central point in his philosophy. Schopenhauer's most im-portant works were written early in the second quarter of the century, but it was not until past the middle of the century that his influence reached its peak. He had taught that life is essentially a struggle in which every satisfaction leads to a new struggle, implying, therefore, the impossibility of attaining real or complete satisfaction except through the annihilation of desire.[1] Schopenhauer's metaphysics had a profound influence on German thought. He had also a very specific influence on psychologists through his attention to the will. With evolutionism it became easy to think of the will as the thing that adapts us to situations, that drives us when we are not adapted.[2] With Schopenhauer the will was absolute and primal; and intelligence had been evolved simply as a means to give what the will demanded.[3] Cravings were the ultimate mainsprings of conduct.

Schopenhauer had undertaken to show that will need not be regarded as a conscious function; Wundt utilized the conception and adapted it to his own system. For Wundt the will was primal, but in evolution its activities had in some cases degenerated into the reflex response. Wundt was heart and soul a voluntarist, a believer in the purposive nature of all life, from the most primitive ameboid movement to the most abstract intellectualism. The will, though known to introspection as a *compound*, is of the very life of the organism. The feelings were indeed coming into their own in this period. Horwicz had constructed a psychology upon the basis of the affective life.[4] Bain (page 104) and Maudsley (page 107) represent the same emphasis in British psychology.

So far, we have Wundt's elements, but what of the integrating power of the organism? The first answer lies in the characteristically Wundtian doctrine of apperception. Leibnitz had distinguished between obscure perceptions and those clearly apprehended or "apperceived." French and British psychologists had in general ignored such observations, and had for the most part contented themselves with the study of focal consciousness (that which chiefly occupies attention). With Kant and with Herbart, however, apperception had been the process of assimilating and interpreting new impressions. Wundt used the term *apperception*, with slightly different emphasis, to describe the process by which the elements of experience

[1] Schopenhauer's writings reflect the thought of India just as Fechner's *Zend-Avesta* reflects that of Iran; such influences are a part of the new interest in early Indo-European philosophy and religion.

[2] Lamarck had stressed this point; Darwin's theory, despite its different emphasis, made wide secondary use of Lamarckian principles.

[3] The conception is similar to Bichat's distinction between "animal" and "vital." Compare also recent emphasis on the control of central nervous activities by visceral and autonomic processes, and the theoretical uses made of this by psychologists and psychiatrists (for example, Kempf, E. J., *The Autonomic Functions and the Personality*, *Nerv. and Ment. Dis. Monogr.*, Ser. No. 28, 1918).

[4] *Psychologische Analysen auf physiologischer Grundlage* (1872–78).

are appropriated or laid hold of by the individual; that is, drawn into clear introspective consciousness. From such appropriation follows the necessity of a term to describe the process of relating the various elements in a unity; the process was designated *creative synthesis*.[5] Many elementary experiences—sensations, images, and feelings—are organized into a whole by the process of creative synthesis. We have in all psychological processes the following necessary steps: first, stimulation; second, perception (in which the experience is present in consciousness, nothing more than that); third, apperception (in which the experience is identified, appropriated, and synthesized); finally, an act of will which sets going the reaction. Wundt's apperception enjoyed a prominent position in German psychology for decades, though vigorously attacked by Ziehen and those of a more mechanistic turn of thought; its influence was less profound and of shorter life outside of Germany.[6] Everywhere, however, Wundt's doctrine helped to awaken psychologists to the necessity of distinguishing between focal and marginal events; in other words, to a more serious study of the nature of attention. The term "apperception" has in general been discarded, while many features of Wundt's description of apperception are still current under the caption of "attention." Wundt's emphasis upon unity and activity represents, moreover, the same point of view that we saw in John Stuart Mill in the reaction against his father's extreme associationism and atomism. Wundt held that it is of the very nature of human experience to give itself organization.

In the early years of Wundt's laboratory it was chiefly he who set the problems for experimental psychology. Wundt, like Nestor, was "alive on the earth with three generations of mortal men." Born in 1832, and living until 1920, he grew up in the atmosphere of Hegel and Schopenhauer and the new experimental physiology which came to flower in the work of Helmholtz; he lived to dominate the psychology of the late nineteenth century, permanently impressing his empirical spirit upon it, and to witness in his old age the extension of his experimental methods to a range of problems vastly beyond the scope of his own somewhat limited conception.

For Wundt believed that experimental psychology must concern itself, at least for the time being, with problems which had already

[5] The necessity for such a relating process had been recognized by Lotze, who in fact described it as "creation."

[6] Though Herbartian apperception still found favor in many educational circles, James's gentle cynicism regarding all "apperception" (*Talks to Teachers*, 1897) seems to be shared by most contemporary psychologists.

been attacked and reduced to more or less quantitative form. He did not occupy himself greatly with *new* kinds of experiments. His task was chiefly the extension and systematization of studies already inaugurated. Most of his laboratory problems can be classified under a few main heads which are already familiar to the reader. First came the psychology and physiology of vision and hearing, and, to some extent, of the lower senses; much of his work in optics (latent time of the retina, studies in eye movements, and the like) represented a continuation of Helmholtz's work. A second concern of Wundt was the reaction-time experiments, as taken from Helmholtz and Donders. In this he thought he possessed a method of showing experimentally the three stages which he believed to be present in all responses to a stimulus: perception, apperception, and will. When the stimulus is presented to the subject, he first perceives it; he then apperceives it; finally, he wills to react, and from this the muscular innervation follows. Wundt's interest in the reaction-time experiment arose largely from the belief that it gave him an opportunity to verify psychological principles which were of much wider application. But data gathered by Exner,[7] Cattell,[8] Ach,[9] and others pointed to a very different conception. In practiced subjects these stages were not clearly apparent. It seemed rather that the act of will occurred in the "foreperiod" before the stimulus, while perception and apperception were to some extent "prepared in advance"— the subject knew what stimulus to expect. In some cases certain aspects of apperception might be delayed until after the execution of the movement. Another aspect of the reaction-time experiment which interested Wundt was the discovery by L. Lange in 1888 that some subjects attend to the stimulus, others to the response; the latter were found capable in general of quicker reactions.[10]

Third, Wundt encouraged in every way the experiments in psychophysics to which Fechner was still giving attention, and to which G. E. Müller had made important methodological contributions.[11] Psychophysics, in the hands of Wundt, continued to present quantitative problems. He did, however, disagree with Fechner on one crucial point. It is indeed possible, he held, to say that two stimuli seem to be of equal intensity, or that one is just noticeably different from another. But he could not admit that sensations could be

[7] Hermann, L., *Handbuch der Physiologie*, Vol. II, ii, p. 271.
[8] *Philos. Stud.*, 1886, 3, 452, and *Natl. Acad. Sci.*, 1893, 7, 393.
[9] *Ueber die Willenstätigkeit und das Denken* (1905), pp. 116 ff.
[10] *Philos. Stud.*, 4, 479.
[11] *Zur Grundlegung der Psychophysik* (1878).

measured; measurement, strictly speaking, applied only to the *stimuli.* Instead of seeking the relation between the physical and the psychical worlds, Wundt was content to regard the psychophysical method as a means of studying the relation between sensation intensities and the process of *judgment.* Stimuli have to differ to an extent which makes possible a correct judgment as to their relative magnitudes.[12] Wundt adopted a purely psychological interpretation of Weber's law, which was for him simply an example of the psychological law of relativity.

The fourth field of experimentation in which Wundt worked was the analysis of association, begun by Galton (page 119). In 1880, Wundt adapted this experiment to the needs of the Leipzig laboratory. Galton had made use of single words as stimuli, but had recorded his responses in different forms; some were single words, but others were descriptions of images of varying complexity. In the latter case a genuine classification of the responses was difficult, and their time relations were not susceptible of exact measurement. Wundt simplified the experiment, and made it a more accurate instrument, by requiring his subjects to give each response in the form of a *single word.* In conformity with his whole conception of experimental psychology, it was now possible to examine in each case the relation between stimulus word and response word.

Wundt and his pupils worked out devices for the uniform presentation of word stimuli in visual form. Auditory presentation was sometimes substituted. The desire for exact and uniform methods of presenting the stimuli, and of recording and measuring the responses, led to the use of the lip key and of the Hipp chronoscope (measuring one-thousandths of a second), and made possible a precision in time measurement which has seldom subsequently been thought necessary. Wundt then proceeded to classify the types of word association discovered when one-word stimuli were presented; they were so classified as to afford keys to the nature of all verbal association. Since Hartley there had been scores of attempts to classify the types of association; these were uniformly worked out so as to constitute a system intellectually satisfying to the psychologist. Even Thomas Brown, the most gifted of those among the moderns who attempted such analysis, never realized the simple wisdom of finding out inductively, as Wundt and his pupils now did, what the common types of association might be in that world of heard and spoken language which plays so great a part in the structure of thought.

[12] For Wundt's work in psychophysical method see also page 89, footnote 7.

Wundt recognized that Galton had hit upon a method all-important for inductive psychology.

He subdivided all word associations into two grand categories, *inner* and *outer*. The *inner* association is one in which there is an intrinsic connection between the meanings of the two words. Definitions, for example, are inner associations; the meaning of the response word is identical with or closely similar to that of the stimulus. Supraordination is a second type of inner association; when the stimulus *snake* evokes the response *reptile*, the subject has emphasized an aspect of the meaning of the stimulus word and has given it the form of a generalization; similarly, subordination (*snake—viper*) and co-ordination (*snake—lizard*) involve meaningful relations; so also do noun-adjective associations (*snake—venomous*); adjective-noun associations (*slippery—snake*); contrasts (*white—black*); and many others. Sharply distinguished from all these, the *outer* associations are those in which a purely extrinsic or accidental connection exists between stimulus and response. Contiguity in time and space are found here; if the stimulus "candle" evokes the response "box" or "Christmas," the cause is presumably to be found in the subject's habits of buying candles by the box, or of seeing them at Christmas time, rather than to any inherent similarity between the meanings. When the stimulus word itself, rather than its meaning, evokes the response, as in the case of rhymes, the association is classified as outer; so also with the very common "speech-habit" group, in which the response word completes some catch phrase of ingrained verbal habit (dog—days, fire—fly). The elaboration of Wundt's system of classification was undertaken in 1883 by Trautscholdt.[13]

Among Wundt's pupils in the early days was Kraepelin, a young physician who saw the possibility of extending Wundt's experimental method to the related field of psychopathology. Not only were mental abnormalities to be studied through experiment, and their phenomena stated in quantitative terms whenever possible, but mental abnormalities of the milder type were to be experimentally *induced*. The association method was applied by Kraepelin and his pupils to groups subjected to the effects of fatigue, hunger, alcohol, and other disturbing influences.[14] All these agencies increased the number of "superficial"—that is, outer—associations; it was as if a disorder of attention had been produced. Kraepelin's laboratory yielded also

[13] *Philos. Stud.*, 1883, 1.

[14] Kraepelin, E., *Ueber die Beeinflussung einfacher psychischer Vorgänge* (1892). Bekhterev and his pupils were carrying on similar investigations in the same period (Walitzki, *Rev. philos.*, 1889, 28).

much valuable material on the curve of work, both in relation to fatigue and in relation to other factors making for increase or decrease of efficiency. These and many other investigations, notably those upon the effect of a great variety of drugs, have not only fulfilled his hope that much could be done toward the establishment of an "experimental psychopathology," but have directly furthered the course of experimental psychology itself.

In 1894 appeared Sommer's *Diagnostik der Geisteskrankheiten*. This gave prominence to Kraepelin's approach, especially to the association test, by which Sommer thought it possible to differentiate mental disorders. In catatonia Sommer believed there appear many responses which have no real connection with the stimulus words: "irrelevant" responses (angel—spider; dark—triangle). In mania there is an exceptionally large number of outer associations, such as those arising from rhyme or assonance. These generalizations, though excessively broad, have in general been confirmed, but their value for clinical purposes is now recognized to fall far short of Sommer's hopes; Kraepelin himself was most cautious with reference to such sharp differences between the word associations of clinical types.

These four experimental fields—the psychophysiology of the senses, reaction time, psychophysics, and the association experiment —occupied Wundt and his pupils to an extraordinary degree; they comprised more than 50 per cent of all the research work published in the first years of the *Philosophische Studien*. Wundt did concern himself to some extent with child psychology, and to some extent with animal psychology, but he did no experimentation in these fields; he was at his poorest in them.

To folk psychology Wundt devoted some of his best energies.[15] Believing that "cultural products," as well as introspective reports, are a legitimate subject matter for psychology, he undertook a systematic psychological interpretation of the data of anthropology and history. His studies on the psychological interpretation of language are perhaps his best-known contributions. He emphasized the interpenetration of psychical and physiological factors in linguistic structure, protesting against that naïve psychologism to which phonetics was a mere incident, and with equal explicitness against that merely philological approach which had sought to explain all linguistic change in terms of the laws of vocal utterance. But he

[15] The first volume of the *Völkerpsychologie* appeared in 1900.

gave the weight of his authority to that trend which aimed toward the understanding of each social group through the analysis of its language, believing that the very vocabulary and grammar of a people reveal its psychic constitution. Here, as in much of his vast and scholarly work in folk psychology, his conclusions were destined to be swept away by the constant advent of new empirical material. Studies in the diffusion of language gradually made it impossible to think of language as an index to a cultural pattern or even to a specific mental make-up; [16] both the complexity and the plasticity of language seem today to call for genetic methods of analysis in which the psychological approach will be integrated with geographical and historical approaches.

In consequence of his vast learning and the many problems on which he worked, Wundt gave a unity to the field of psychology such as no one else in his day conceived. Before Wundt published his *Physiological Psychology* and established his laboratory, psychology was little more than a waif knocking now at the door of physiology, now at the door of ethics, now at the door of epistemology. In 1879, it set itself up as an experimental science with a local habitation and a name. Although he was unqualified to handle many phases of the new science, Wundt tried to bring together experimental psychology, child psychology, animal psychology, folk psychology; nothing that was psychology was foreign to him. He poured his energies into examination of nearly every corner of mental life. When he failed as an experimentalist, as he frequently did, he stimulated much research which led far beyond anything he was himself capable of imagining; and when his theories proved to be inadequate, as they frequently did, they could and did undergo transformation through laboratory work. He saw no great new vistas, as did, for example, Freud and Wertheimer; but it was after all largely through Wundt's vision that the conception of an independent inductive psychology came into being. Such a synthesis and the establishment of such an experimental movement were, of course, the natural outcome of the development of the biological sciences, especially within the German universities. Wundt was the fulfillment, not the origin, of the movement with which his name is associated. But to bring such a movement to its fulfillment, and to outline with vigor and earnestness the conception of an experimental psychology which should take its place among the natural sciences,

[16] See, for example, Sapir, E., *Language* (1921), Chap. IX.

was an achievement of such magnitude as to give him a unique position among the psychologists of the modern period.[16a]

CATTELL

The close relation between Wundt and his immediate followers has been emphasized; one cannot really distinguish between what Wundt himself did and what his pupils did. When we speak of the Wundtian laboratory we have to think of a group of individuals, drawn from many nations and speaking many languages, catching the master's enthusiasm for the creation of an experimental psychology, free both from its sister sciences and from philosophy. This viewpoint of Wundt inspired directly or indirectly a very large amount of research; and in discussing the work of individuals in the school it is a matter of opinion how far we should regard them, during their stay at Leipzig, as pursuing investigations in their own right. Work with the association test illustrates the point. Some of Wundt's pupils, however, began even while still with him the study of problems which were both envisaged and prosecuted with originality and relative independence.

Cattell may be chosen here as an exceptionally original and productive member of the Wundtian group of experimenters, while

[16a] The following comment, by Allan Fromme, seems to me so important as to warrant being reproduced word for word. But since I cannot carry out its excellent suggestion, I must simply let it stand as his comment:

"In a sense, it was a stroke of fortune in the history of psychology that a man of such enormous scholarship as Wundt was around for the synthesis of German psychology. More than any of his predecessors he was aware of the currents in America (see James's letters, as well as Lincoln Steffens' *Autobiography*), England, and probably France. As a result, he made efforts (systematic, not experimental) to enlarge the scope of psychology and give it the dignity of a discipline separate from physiology. If we permit ourselves to guess, he may have succeeded in these efforts only enough to perpetuate the work of Weber, Fechner, and Helmholtz, so that his students came to America and continued to work in this tradition. Because of Wundt's own catholicity of thought, these students came to *think* more nearly in psychological terms, but *worked* in the same physiological tradition (that is, of Weber, Fechner, et al.) which Wundt was unable to improve or from which he could break away. Sometimes I even think that Wundt was essentially the public-relations man for the early psychophysicists and that they owe their perpetuation in the history of psychology to his efforts.

"Some comment ought to be made on the domination of experimental technique over psychological subject matter typical of German experimental psychology. I think Wundt tried to do something about this but was too steeped in the tradition to be successful. Even William James—a far more imaginative person—failed to synthesize many of the currents he was exposed to and, like Wundt, tended to close an era rather than open one."

a later chapter will consider the furtherance of Wundt's systematic approach by Titchener (pages 214 ff.). Cattell's work brilliantly exemplified the spirit of the school. He succeeded in winning wide respect for the point of view and the methods which he had seen at Leipzig; he was also conspicuous for the versatility and volume of his own work, and the significance of the problems and results associated with his name. Attention will be given to his work at this point, both before considering the development of experimental psychology in Germany outside of Wundt's laboratory and before looking broadly at American psychology; in this way perhaps the conquests and the long-range significance of the Wundtian approach can be most effectively brought out. Going to the Leipzig laboratory in 1880, Cattell later became Wundt's assistant. Partly on his own initiative and partly as a result of suggestions from Wundt, he performed a series of experiments which are cornerstones of subsequent research. His return to the United States in 1888, as Professor of Psychology at the University of Pennsylvania, marked no interruption in his life as an experimentalist.

Of Cattell's many contributions the most elaborate and extensive was his investigation of reaction time.[17] At Leipzig he not only studied elaborately some physiological aspects of the problem, but gave close attention to introspective analysis (page 155). Nothing could show more clearly than this that Wundt's point of view as to the nature of psychology constituted a large part of the background of Cattell's work. The study of reaction time led to two elaborations, one the measurement of the speed of perceptual processes of various degrees of complexity, the other the use of classification methods in the association experiment—another of Wundt's favorite children. Another important contribution to the study of the time relations of mental processes was Cattell's investigation of the "span of attention."[18] He found that a subject could correctly name the number of lines shown in a brief exposure if the number did not exceed four or five; the span for letters was about the same; and it was not appreciably less for short words. For the study of the speed of perception under a variety of different conditions, Cattell made use of the gravity tachistoscope (which makes possible the sudden exposure of an object through a slit in a screen) and in conjunction with it the gravity chronometer. He measured the length of time during which a colored stimulus must act on the retina in order to be perceived as color.

[17] For example, *Philos. Stud.*, 1885, 2 and 3.
[18] *Ibid.*, 1886, 3, 94. The problem had been approached experimentally by Bonnet (in the eighteenth century), and by Sir William Hamilton.

He proceeded to study the speed of perception of letters and words. Problems in the latter field led to the invention of another method of exposing stimuli. This was a revolving drum behind a screen containing a slot which enabled the subject to read letters pasted on the drum; the speed of rotation of the drum determined the rapidity of presentation of the various letters. Cattell found that in order to name the letters correctly when they were presented one at a time as single objects, almost half a second was required. On the other hand, if he enlarged the slit so that one letter could be seen while the preceding one was being named, the time was from one-third to one-fifth of a second. In fact, as the slit was enlarged until three, then four, and then five could be seen, for the majority of the nine subjects there was a steady improvement in speed. This pointed conclusively to the factor of *overlapping:* that an individual could not only carry on simultaneously a perceptual and a motor response, but could deal at the same time with various stages in the total response to several stimuli. Cattell used the same approach in experiments on the perception and naming of colors, showing that the time required to give a color its name was shortened if the subject was allowed to have a new color in view before naming the preceding one; overlapping was again present. This recognition of the measurable nature of overlapping processes is one of Cattell's most significant achievements. As we shall see later (page 235), Bryan and Harter showed the applicability of this concept to the learning process.

These studies were part of a systematic attack on the problem of reading. Cattell presented words as well as letters, noting the variation in reading time as the words became longer and less familiar. In this work he found that the perception of whole words of moderate length took no longer than the perception of single letters; in fact, letters frequently took longer. Here he recognized the principle that such perceptual responses need not involve the serial perception of elements present in the pattern. This principle of the organization of "higher units of response" was much utilized later in experiments on learning. Illustrative also of his studies of reading was his demonstration that an individual could read his own native language at far greater *speed* than other languages which he could speak and write virtually as well. Germans, even if very familiar with English, actually read it more slowly than German; in the same way, although several experimental subjects were well trained in the classics, the speed of reading Latin and Greek was very much less than that for the native tongue. This showed that even such associations as were regarded as absolutely fixed and mechanized were capable of quantitative differentiation.

In the association experiment Cattell and Bryant employed the classification method as described above (page 157).[19] In the major contribution in this field there were about five hundred subjects. The responses were classified according to the frequency of each response word given. In relation to each stimulus, each response word was shown to have a certain degree of commonplaceness. This was the first *frequency table*, an instrument elaborated and widely used in later investigations. Sommer utilized it for psychiatric purposes, believing that the presence in a patient's associations of a large number of rare associations was characteristic of certain disorders.[20]

The word-association method led naturally to the investigation of *controlled association*, in which the subject was required to give not simply *any* one word, but a word bearing a specific relation to the stimulus word. Despite Hobbes's and Brown's recognition of the problem, associationism had in general neglected the factor of control through the subject's attitude and the situation accompanying the chief or more obvious stimulus; experimentalists like Galton and Wundt had quite naturally failed to see the importance of such control. In these experiments Cattell made use to some extent of Wundt's classification of association. He required the subject in some cases to give a contrast word, in some a supraordinate, in others a subordinate, and so on. Cattell showed that in general such controlled association was quicker than free association. He also found that some types of controlled association were regularly quicker than others; for example, supraordinates took less time than subordinates. This was apparently because the habits of classifying— passing from a species to a genus—are in general more firmly established than are connections from a genus to any one species within it. To classify "pine" as "tree" was easy and familiar; but "tree" might arouse a variety of subordinate responses, each of which tended to inhibit all others. And just as this matter of interference delayed response, so it was easy to see why free association, offering such a wide variety of possible response, was in general slower than controlled association. The same principle emerged even more clearly in naming, for instance, a country to which a city

[19] "Mental Association Investigated by Experiment," *Mind*, 1889, 14.

[20] *Diagnostik der Geisteskrankheiten* (1894). Cattell's and Sommer's methods were carried further by Kent and Rosanoff in 1910, with 1000 normal and 247 psychopathic subjects, using 100 stimulus words (*Amer. J. Insan.*, 67, 37–96).

belonged and a city to which a country belonged. Given the stimulus word "Rome," the subject quickly replied "Italy"; whereas "Italy" might tend to arouse "Naples," "Venice," and so on with almost equal facility.

A natural outcome of all these experiments of Cattell, in which subjects differed markedly from one another, was the tendency to pass beyond the formulation of general rules and to define quantitatively the nature and significance of *individual differences*. But Wundt's concern was regularly with principles, not with questions of degree; and it was not until the nineties that the field of individual differences, which had been originally explored by Galton, became, through Cattell, a prominent part of experimental psychology. Galton, an ardent evolutionist, saw the importance of individual differences in all studies of organisms, and the inspiration of assisting Galton for a few months at the South Kensington Museum apparently made a deep and lasting impression upon the younger man. Cattell's first elaborate exploration of individual differences, as aside from the determination of general laws, was in the use of the freshman (and senior) tests conducted at Columbia in 1894.[21] This was the first battery of "psychological" tests ever given to a large number of individuals. Among these tests were measures of free and controlled association, and of simple perceptual processes, reaction time, and memory. The improvement of statistical methods in the handling of results was much needed, and methods of studying central tendency as well as variability engaged Cattell's attention.

Another field in which Cattell saw the possibilities of a new mathematical treatment was psychophysics. This work he carried out in conjunction with Fullerton, in the years immediately after returning from the Leipzig laboratory. They devised a substitute for the Weber-Fechner law. Collecting a mass of data by a variety of psychophysical methods,[22] they proceeded to formulate a mathematical generalization.[23] It postulated that the organic response to a stimulus must vary as the square root of the intensity of the stimulus. Errors of observation are included among such organic responses, and as the stimulus increases, the factors which produce errors in observation increase not directly, but as the square root of the stimulus. "The usual increase of the error of observation with the

---

[21] Cattell, J. McK., and Farrand, L., "Physical and Mental Measurements of the Students of Columbia University," *Psychol. Rev.*, 1896, 3, 618–48.

[22] "On the Perception of Small Differences," Univ. Pennsylvania Publ., *Philos. Series*, 1892, 2.

[23] "On Errors of Observation," *Amer. J. Psychol.*, 1893, 5, 285–93.

magnitude of the stimulus is accounted for in a satisfactory manner by the summation of errors." This work of Fullerton and Cattell was close enough to the general trend of psychophysical findings to be taken very seriously, but not close enough to be generally accepted.

Prominent among the later researches of Cattell were studies in the "order of merit" method,[24] and the practical use of the method in the study of *American Men of Science* (1906), which attracted attention to methods of ranking and rating personal qualities difficult to measure in the laboratory. Throughout all these investigations Cattell was clearly working further and further away from the confinements of the Wundtian method. He might be regarded as a pupil of Galton as much as of Wundt. He did, in fact, to an extraordinary extent reconcile and interweave the Helmholtz-Wundt tradition with the extramural psychology of Galton. Next to his versatility, perhaps the most striking of Cattell's characteristics as a psychologist was the constant effort to reduce everything to quantitative terms, in which general principles and individual variability won equal attention.

PARALLEL DEVELOPMENTS IN GERMAN PHYSIOLOGICAL PSYCHOLOGY

To return now to Germany. The movement begun by Wundt in 1879 to separate experimental psychology from physiology, and the founding of journals to disseminate psychological material, went on apace. Most of the larger universities soon had their psychological laboratories. Except as expressed later in the thriving laboratory at Vienna, the movement never reached large proportions in Austria. This was due partly to the fact that there were in Austria at the time several great psychologists whose interests were chiefly philosophical; they were less concerned with experimentation. Hence in thinking of German experimental psychology we must in general think more or less in terms of the German Empire.

And a great deal of psychological experimentation continued to be done in laboratories of physiology. In spite of Wundt's declaration of independence, the physiological tradition represented by such names as Weber and Helmholtz was continuing, and constantly contributing psychological data of which psychologists had to take serious account. Physiologists and physicists were, in fact,

[24] "A Statistical Study of Eminent Men," *Pop. Sci. Mo.*, 1903, 57, 359–77; "Statistics of American Psychologists," *Amer. J. Psychol.*, 1903, 14, 310–28.

contributing a great deal of important material on sensory functions. Thus in the eighties König and Brodhun published systematic work on psychophysics as such, showing that Weber's law holds for a middle range, but is quite unsatisfactory for low and high intensities.[25] The exploration of the sensory functions in the skin is another instance. At the time of the founding of Wundt's laboratory, no systematic exploration of the cutaneous senses had been undertaken. Wundt and his followers recognized, of course, that there was no such thing as a sense of touch in general, but it remained for the decade of the eighties to study intensively the sensations from the skin. This work was begun by Blix [26] and carried further by Goldscheider.[27] The latter is responsible more than anyone else for the existing technique for ascertaining the points on the skin which are sensitive to warmth, cold, touch, and pain. He heated a stylus and moved it from point to point, demonstrating that receptors for warmth are scattered irregularly throughout the skin. Similarly, cold, pressure, and pain had their sensitive "spots." Parallel with the study of the skin senses, anatomical and physiological studies were published on the kinesthetic senses, through which receptors in the muscles, tendons, and joints enable us to determine the position of our limbs.[28] Whereas the work of Wundt, centering in such questions as reaction time and association tests, set the main problems for many psychologists, these studies in the lower senses, conducted outside the Wundtian school, became by the end of the century standard laboratory investigations wherever the introspective analysis of experience was dominant.

And physiological and experimental psychology, despite Wundt's prowess and prestige, continued to be advanced by many workers who were not dependent upon him. Stumpf's *Tonpsychologie* (1883–90), for example, and his other studies of music, placed him second only to Helmholtz in the realm of acoustics. Much original experimentation was accompanied by ingenious interpretation. His theory of consonance and dissonance won special favor.[29] He emphasized the fact that tones an octave apart seem to "fuse" into one psychical unity, and that such fusion involves musical consonance.

[25] *Sitzungber. Berlin. Akad. Wissensch.*, 1888–89.
[26] *Zschr. f. Biol.*, 1884, 20.
[27] *Arch. f. Anat. u. Physiol.*, *Physiol. Abt.*, 1885.
[28] See Goldscheider, A., *Gesammelte Abhandlungen, Physiologie des Muskelsinnes* (1909).
[29] *Beiträge zur Akustik und Musikwissenschaft*, 9 pts., 1898–1924, 1.

But when one tone is sounded together with another a semitone higher, the hearer is keenly aware of the distinctness of the two tones, and at the same time finds the combination highly discordant. The degree of fusion between tones was regarded by Stumpf as the basis for musical consonance. The fact that the increasing complexity of vibration ratios is in general accompanied by decreasing consonance fits well with the theory; but Stumpf's emphasis on "fusion" makes it distinctly not a physical but a psychological theory.

Another great figure in the era of Wundt, whose best work is in no sense a reflection of Wundt's influence, is Lipps. The study of optical illusions led him to the conclusion that the observing subject tends to project himself into the pattern. A vertical line, for example, gives the observer the sense of contending against gravity, while the angles and curves of many illusions make the subject expand, bend, or whirl. The theory has very important consequences for aesthetics. A man "feels himself into" the material of visual art,[30] and the nature of the tension or relaxation which he experiences determines many aspects of his aesthetic response. A column, for example, must not have too large a capital, because this would oppress the observer with an insufferable burden; too small a capital would give him the sense of great strength devoted to a trifling task.

Stumpf and Lipps are but two of many who in Germany maintained their autonomy and continued to enlarge the boundaries of psychology. The pioneers in the experimental study of memory, Ebbinghaus (page 174) and G. E. Müller (page 181), owed little or nothing to Wundt. The work of Külpe (page 227) and his school is in a sense a part of Wundt's experimental psychology, but these students devoted themselves to problems far indeed from those which chiefly occupied Wundt. To these men we shall return later in order to trace from them certain investigations characteristic of recent psychological work.

With regard to the experimental psychology of the United States, it may be said without hesitation that in the first few years of its development it was primarily Wundtian in its outlook and approach. American psychology had hitherto been saturated with the spirit of the Scottish school; it had been dogmatic in its approach, disregarding both physiological and experimental methods. Prior to 1880, the only important American contributions were a few articles

[30] The term *Einfühlung* ("empathy") has in fact come into general psychological use. See Lipps, T., *Raumaesthetik und geometrisch-optische Täuschungen* (1897).

by William James (during the decade of the seventies).[31] But now American psychology began suddenly to be captured by the experimentalists' enthusiasm. The new psychologists who came back from Germany as pupils of Wundt carried everything before them. The first of these in order of chronology was Stanley Hall, who was also a pupil of several other physiologists and philosophers. Returning from Leipzig, he went in 1883 to Johns Hopkins, establishing the first American psychological laboratory.[32] Hall did not carry out any important original experiments during his six years at Johns Hopkins; but by founding the *American Journal of Psychology* (1887) he gave the adherents of the new psychology not only a storehouse for contributions both experimental and theoretical, but a sense of solidarity and independence. When Clark University was founded, Hall was called to be its president (1889). Two years later, he took another original step of considerable value to psychology, the founding of a journal dealing with child psychology. The *Pedagogical Seminary* (now the *Journal of Genetic Psychology*) contained much empirical work, but very little that was experimental; and a large proportion of its studies of children rested upon decidedly incomplete biographical data. But it did perform the important function of stimulating, both in psychologists and in educators, an eagerness to bring the psychology of the child within the scope of their respective fields. Hall played a leading part in founding the American Psychological Association in 1892.

Münsterberg was called to Harvard in 1892,[33] and Titchener began his career at Cornell in the same year, where Frank Angell had established a Wundtian laboratory and had gone on to found another at Stanford. In 1894 an inquiry made into the experimental psychology of the United States revealed twenty-seven laboratories. In the same year was founded the *Psychological Review*. The laboratories and journals, and the Association, furnished good opportunities for the intercommunication of ideas and for personal contact.

[31] The task of conquering the soil and devising means to utilize its vast resources, the possibilities for the acquisition of land, and an absorbing commercial activity, had kept philosophy and pure science at a low level. The United States had made some significant contributions to physical science (for example, through Franklin and Henry), but mostly in relation to its application to industry. It would probably not be forcing the point about practicality to recall that whereas psychology as a science had amounted to very little in this country, the practical task of care for mental defectives and the insane had offered through Howe and Dix an opportunity for American leadership.

[32] His pupils there included Jastrow and Dewey.

[33] Where James had done some psychological experimentation even before the opening of Wundt's laboratory.

The most important single factor in saving American psychology in this period from becoming essentially a branch of Wundt's laboratory was the influence of William James. American psychology, as the early journals show, was indeed interested in many problems not strictly experimental, but it was James who did most to give psychologists a broad and flexible definition of their field, in which the whole wealth of human experience was welcomed for investigation. Before long we shall be considering James's contributions in greater detail.

French psychology, during the middle of the century, had been eclectic and sterile, except in psychiatry, to which continual and important contributions had been made. Associationism and physiological psychology found an able exponent in Taine,[34] but psychiatry continued throughout the century to be the field of the greatest French contributions. Such contributions continued to stress the approach through hypnosis. As early as 1870 Richet had reported that consciousness may be split, that one conscious activity may be out of contact with another conscious activity of the same person. Several other medical men made similar reports in the seventies. Charcot, becoming in 1878 the head of the women's hospital for mental disorders at Paris, and shortly afterward head of the men's hospital for the same maladies, established in them the clinical method in psychiatry; he demonstrated mental disorders before groups of physicians and students, lecturing on them and illustrating methods of treatment.

In particular, Charcot emphasized the relation of hypnotic suggestion to the phenomena of hysteria. The Nancy school had taught that hypnosis was a special case of normal suggestibility (page 135). Charcot, while conceding the great importance of suggestibility, clung to a physiological theory. He came, as we have seen (page 136), to the conclusion that hypnosis and hysteria were the same thing, or, more precisely, that hypnotic sleep was a phenomenon of hysteria, which could be induced only in persons of hysterical make-up. In this conception he emphasized, of course, the phenomena of "deep" hypnosis. He undertook to classify hypnotic phenomena according to various stages. The hysterical subject was put through a series of stages in which he showed a variety of symptoms classifiable in three main groups: lethargy, catalepsy, and somnambulism. Lethargy is the state in which the patient is drowsy; catalepsy, that in which there is loss of consciousness, inactivity of the limbs (usually with rigidity), sometimes with complete forgetfulness of the state afterward; and somnambulism, a state in which

[34] *On Intelligence* (1870).

one may carry on a complex activity of which he afterward has no recollection. These three states were regarded by Charcot as fixed phases through which the hypnotic subject must pass. The Nancy school protested that these three stages were themselves dependent on specific suggestions; that the number of stages and the symptoms of each varied with the subject's expectations. They continued to challenge Charcot's identification of hysteria with hypnosis; and emphasizing *light* hypnosis, they claimed to hypnotize more than 80 per cent of all subjects.

Among Charcot's pupils, Pierre Janet was especially interested in dissociation, the splitting of personality.[35] This led to a systematic conception of personality as an integration of ideas and tendencies. In normal personality the integration is relatively stable and constant; hysteria is characterized by imperfect integration, lowered "psychic tension," which in extreme cases may result in the cleavage of the individual into two or more "alternating personalities." During the eighties and thereafter, Morton Prince and others began to make the French work popular in the United States,[36] while William James incorporated much of it in his writings. In Britain, Braid (page 134) had already prepared the way, and the work of the Paris and Nancy schools was easily assimilated.

A dominant figure, alert to all the newer British and German trends and fully expressive of the medical and psychiatric approach of French psychology, was Ribot. Though a contributor to many fields, Ribot is perhaps best known for his writings on psychopathology, especially the *Diseases of Memory* (1881) and *Diseases of Personality* (1885). He represented the fusion of two streams, psychiatric practice and mechanistic theory. The mechanistic physiological psychology inaugurated by Hobbes and La Mettrie had deeply colored medical and psychological thought. Exemplified by Ziehen [37] in Germany and by Maudsley [38] in Britain, it took vigorous form in the writings of Ribot, who made brain physiology and brain disease the basis of personality and its disorders. Ribot's desire for an empirical psychology, and his familiarity with the German work, made him a logical candidate for the position of director of the first French psychological laboratory at the Collège de France, to which, a decade after the founding of the Leipzig laboratory, he was appointed.

[35] *The Mental State of Hystericals* (1892); *The Major Symptoms of Hysteria* (1907).
[36] *Nature of Mind and Human Automatism* (1885).
[37] *Introduction to the Study of Physiological Psychology* (1891).
[38] *Physiology and Pathology of Mind* (1867); *Body and Will* (1884).

This was followed immediately by the establishment of a psychological laboratory at the Sorbonne. Here Alfred Binet began his career. He was in his early years a student of hypnosis. He and Féré published a series of experiments on *Animal Magnetism* (1886), in which the chief interest lay in the investigation of hyperesthesia during hypnotic trance. The importance of the work lay mainly in the separation of hypnotic practice from its clinical surroundings, opening the way toward its utilization by experimental psychologists. Binet served later as editor of the *Année psychologique*, founded in 1895. He was a lifelong student of personality, making pioneer studies of individual differences; for example, in the response to suggestion,[39] and of abnormalities portrayed in handwriting;[40] and became best known for his studies of the thought processes. His *Psychology of Reasoning*, appearing in 1886, was followed by a long series of empirical studies of specific kinds of thinking; for example, the thinking of mental defectives, and of chess-players and lightning calculators.[41] The experimental investigations of thinking, in which his two little daughters served as subjects,[42] belong to a period when his rigid associationism was being washed away by evidences of unity, activity, ego function, in normal and abnormal alike. It was his feeling that instead of approaching the big and the complex through the little and the simple, it was imperative to confront the big and the complex directly. It was in this spirit that he conceived the problem of testing intelligence; we shall return later to this task of his later years (page 354).

Binet's collaborator, Féré, made other notable contributions in this period. In 1888, he discovered the electrical phenomena in the body associated with emotion, to which the name *psychogalvanic reflex* was applied (page 332). He also conducted important experiments on fatigue, devising the first ergograph for the measurement of muscular energy expended. The latter experiments are associated with his celebrated doctrine of dynamogenesis,[43] which emphasized the function of stimuli in liberating energy within the organism; muscular contractions were increased even by apparently irrelevant stimuli. We may say that by the end of the century French experimental psychology, though still far behind the German, had dis-

---

[39] *La suggestibilité* (1900).
[40] *Les révélations de l'écriture d'après un contrôle scientifique* (1906).
[41] *La psychologie des grands calculateurs et joueurs d'échec* (1902).
[42] *L'étude expérimentale de l'intelligence* (1903). See Varon, E., *The Development of Alfred Binet's Psychology*, Psychol. Monogr., 1935, 46 (whole No. 207).
[43] See, for example, *Sensation et mouvement* (1887).

played its own intrinsic genius through several men of the first caliber.

Psychology in Italy in this period was modeled to some extent upon that of Germany, and never attained proportions to make it comparable with Italian neurology and psychiatry. Few laboratories were founded. Child study, however, as we shall see later (page 391), made new strides. Considerable work was done on the physiology of the emotions. Though much of this was of a purely descriptive character, Mosso was one of the first to study physiological changes experimentally induced by fear and excitement.[44] The Netherlands, Belgium, Switzerland, and the Scandinavian countries were responsive to the new trends; new laboratories reflected the Wundtian outlook. But French psychiatric interests were strong at Geneva, where Flournoy significantly contributed to the study of dissociation and suggestion.[45]

Experimental psychology was received but slowly, and with little enthusiasm, in Britain. In spite of Galton's genius, and his marked influence upon Wundt and Cattell, British psychology made small use of his methods. It was not until the appearance of Karl Pearson that there was any Galtonian psychology to speak of; and with Pearson and his school, Galton's *statistical* methods enjoyed much greater favor than his *experimental* methods. With the death of associationism had died much of the British physiological psychology that had accompanied it. Leadership in psychology was captured by the school of which James Ward was the leading representative.[46] This had two points of great advantage over associationism. It emphasized the unity of human experience and behavior, as against discrete and isolated functions; it emphasized activity and adjustment, and found the evolutionary approach highly congenial. The evolutionary point of view came to fulfillment in this school as easily and naturally as in Spencer and Galton. Toward the close of the century, nearly all British psychologists freely utilized evolutionism in relation to both man and animals; Romanes and Lloyd Morgan

---

[44] *La paura* (1884).

[45] *From India to the Planet Mars* (1900).

[46] His article on "Psychology" in the ninth edition (1886) of the *Encyclopaedia Britannica* was of great importance. "The article clearly challenged the associationists to show cause why they should continue to exist. No one wished to deny the value of the laws of Association as true for some aspects of consciousness and some of its connections; the question here put to the issue was whether 'association' should be regarded as the bedrock of all mental complexity and unity, or whether it was a minor affair dependent upon some larger and deeper conception of unity." —Brett, *History of Psychology*, Vol. III, p. 229.

devoted attention especially to mental evolution and to the concepts of instinct and intelligence. Such animal experimentation as was done was inspired much more by Darwin than by Wundt. Evolutionism became, in fact, the dominant tendency. The first British psychological laboratory was at Cambridge; here C. S. Myers attained eminence as an experimentalist. Other laboratories followed from time to time, but laboratory studies made up only a very small fraction of the psychological output of the period.

This total picture shows rather wide geographical differences, some of which remain today. German and American psychology at the end of the nineteenth century were emphasizing the experimental approach; French psychology, the psychiatric; British psychology, the evolutionary and comparative. In later chapters it will become evident that these national differences in emphasis have tended to become less clear-cut, but that they are still of importance.

REFERENCES

Boring, Edwin G., *A History of Experimental Psychology*, Century, 1929, pp. 310–44

Brett, George S., *A History of Psychology*, 3 vols., London, 1921; Vol. 3

Dennis, Wayne, ed., *Readings in the History of Psychology*, Appleton-Century, 1948: Wundt

Henmon, V. A. C., and others, "The Psychological Researches of James McKeen Cattell," *Arch. Psychol.*, 1914, No. 30

Ribot, Théodule Armand, *German Psychology of Today*, Scribner, 1886

Varon, Edith J., *The Development of Alfred Binet's Psychology*, *Psychol. Monogr.*, 1935, 46, No. 207

Wundt, Wilhelm, *Principles of Physiological Psychology*, 2 vols, Macmillan, 1873–74

Chapter 12

EARLY STUDIES OF MEMORY

We clearly understand by this what memory is. It is nothing else than a certain concatenation of ideas, involving the nature of things which are outside the body, a concatenation which corresponds in the mind to the order and concatenation of the modification of the human body. SPINOZA

THE DECADE of the eighties marked the first systematic experimental investigation of learning and memory. There had indeed been a little fragmentary investigation of memory and allied processes before that; a close approach to experimental work on memory was Galton's comparison of childhood associations and adult associations in his own mind. There had been a little animal experimentation in the field of learning, concerned, for example, with the attempt to find out whether certain acts were instinctive or learned. The material was inadequate to establish any general principle regarding the learning process. In general, psychologists were thinking in terms of learning versus forgetting, making a sharp line between what was learned and what was not learned, between what was forgotten and what was not forgotten. They were not yet thinking in quantitative terms; they took no account of degrees of learning and degrees of forgetting.

EBBINGHAUS

The whole character of the problem was changed by Ebbinghaus, who (1879–84) subjected both learning and forgetting to quantitative treatment.[1] This was one of the greatest triumphs of original genius in experimental psychology. For the first time, moreover, experimental psychology undertook, with an attempt to introduce the safeguards and precautions of scientific procedure, a psycho-

[1] *Memory* (1885).

logical problem which was not simply an adjunct to physiology.[2] The great bulk of Wundt's experimental procedure had been borrowed from physiologists. The field of experimental psychology changed immediately as Ebbinghaus entered it; his conceptions and methods soon came to be as characteristic of the "new psychology" as were those of Wundt.

Glancing through the offerings of a Paris bookstall, he had happened upon Fechner's *Psychophysik*, and had been electrified by it. What Fechner had done through strict and systematic measurements for a science of psychophysics, he would do for memory study. His first step was the adoption of certain statistical methods through which the accuracy of observation was to be gauged by the extent to which various observations agreed (that is, the study of variability about the mean). This principle, furthermore, was stated in terms of the symmetry of the curve of errors. Such symmetrical curves, said Ebbinghaus, give us reason to believe that we are dealing with variable errors, not with constant errors. Variable errors can be disregarded; for if observations are sufficiently numerous, such errors in one direction from the mean should cancel those in the opposite direction. Bringing this method into psychology, he reduced psychological material to that department of the language of science which speaks in terms of averages and probable errors of observation.[3] In so doing, he atoned in part for the fact that he made use of only one experimental subject, himself. He got rid, to a large extent, of variable errors. Of course the *constants* due to his own personal idiosyncrasies remained.

His second great innovation was the elimination of another group of variable errors which may be called qualitative rather than quantitative—the *meanings* of things learned. We cannot by any possible process of analysis take account of the varieties of meaning that attach to words as they are learned and forgotten. Ebbinghaus wished to find materials entirely or at least relatively free from meaning. One can do this more effectively in German than in English; over two thousand nonsense syllables can be constructed in German by the utilization of two consonants separated by a vowel. At one stroke Ebbinghaus solved a problem which had con-

[2] Psychological experiments performed outside the physiological laboratory had inevitably been amateurish and crude; even Galton's association experiment illustrates the point.

[3] Fechner's psychophysical methods had expressed the closest previous approach to such a conception; but Ebbinghaus borrowed not so much from Fechner as from contemporary physical science.

fused students of psychology, particularly associationists, for centuries.[4] The extraordinary complexity of factors which make for meaning was in considerable measure excluded. These nonsense syllables were of unequal "difficulty," but when combined in groups their differences could be treated as variable errors of the type described.

Whereas Galton and Wundt had measured the time relations of the process of association initiated by a single verbal stimulus, Ebbinghaus devoted himself to the formation of *series* of connections. Instead of studying associations already formed, he investigated the steps in the formation of associations; he presented for memorization a series containing many syllables which were to be learned in their order. An important contribution here was the standardization of the rate of presentation. This was set at two-fifths of a second per syllable.[5] Throughout his experiments he made the general conditions of the experiment as constant as he could, experimenting at the same hours from day to day, and keeping his regimen and habits as regular as possible. The reader who takes cognizance of the vast quantity of work to which he subjected himself may well inquire whether his interest remained constant throughout; the Herculean task has never been fully repeated.

One of his first problems was the effect of varying the length of the series to be learned, finding how the number of readings necessary for memorization increases with the length of the list.[6] He found that under ordinary conditions he could learn seven, frequently eight, nonsense syllables at one reading. This was the first systematic measurement of the "memory span." A sudden and immense increase occurred in the time required as he increased the number of syllables to nine, ten, and beyond. For example, instead of merely increasing 25 per cent in passing from twelve to fifteen syllables, the labor required was much greater.

Ebbinghaus suffered from an intellectual blind spot which is comprehensible when one recalls the cardinal tenets of associationism. Associationists, with few exceptions, had disregarded the possibility that mind is anything more than a series of impressions con-

[4] "It is not too much to say that the recourse to nonsense syllables, as means to the study of association, marks the most considerable advance, in this chapter of psychology, since the time of Aristotle."—Titchener, *A Text-Book of Psychology*, pp. 380–81.

[5] In spite of the many systematic variations of procedure, he failed to study the effect of varying the speed of presentation.

[6] Memorization was construed in his first experiments as that to the point of two perfect repetitions; in the later series, to the point of one perfect repetition.

tributed by experience, the possibility that it may *actively* adjust itself to its tasks.[7] Ebbinghaus made no distinction between mere rereading on the one hand and the process of active recall on the other. He read through the lists passively until he thought he knew them; he then forced himself to recall them, and wherever necessary he prompted himself. In some of these series he knew the list perfectly without prompting, and in other cases he might prompt himself several times. We cannot tell to what extent he made use of forced recall of material. He was saved from failure only by his statistical method, which, with so much material, presumably caused this factor of active recitation to operate (at least in most of his problems) as a variable rather than as a constant error. It must, however, have tended in general to shorten the learning time. Not until the early years of the present century (see page 245) was the importance of this principle of active recitation recognized.

The "memory-span" experiment was a direct development of Ebbinghaus's study of the influence of varying the length of a series. In 1887, Jacobs published a further investigation of the memory span with a number of subjects, the first intensive study of the problem.[8] The method was adopted by Cattell and others, and has been in wide use ever since.

Ebbinghaus's next problem was the influence of repeated reading after the attainment of the capacity for perfect repetition; that is, the influence of *overlearning*. He wished to know what happened when, after he had learned a series completely, he continued to study it. This involved his conception of memory as a matter of *degree;* he sought to measure the *strength* of the connections established between observed items. Instead of relying upon the distinction between learned and unlearned material, he introduced the celebrated "saving method," which undertakes to measure how much labor is necessary to bring back what has once been known. Suppose we learn two lists of forty-eight syllables each, and then allow twenty-four hours to pass. We may then find that from the first we can recall two-thirds of the syllables, but that it takes twenty repetitions to regain the whole list; from the second list we may recall the same number of *items*, but it may take thirty repetitions to complete the series. Ebbinghaus realized that he could get a better test of reten-

---

[7] Herbart had, indeed, explicitly recognized *activity;* yet he failed to utilize the concept so as to draw a distinction between what is actively recalled and what is effortlessly brought back by new stimulation. For him, activity belonged to *ideas;* the distinction between active and passive *learning* was disregarded.

[8] "Experiments on 'Prehension,'" *Mind*, 12.

tion by measuring the amount of work needed to relearn than by measuring the gross amount of material recalled. There is, of course, room for difference of opinion as to the best single test of memory in any given case; in fact, Ebbinghaus's methods did much to make it clear that memory is not a single process, and that a variety of methods is needed because of the variety of problems presented.

The use of the saving method made possible also a determination of the value of various amounts of overlearning, by measuring the relation of overlearning to saving. If it takes twenty repetitions to get the list of syllables, how many more repetitions are necessary to retain it twenty-four hours? Ebbinghaus recognized that there is not only a stage just below the point of knowing the material, but a stage just *above* knowing it, so to speak. These are the convex and the concave sides of the same problem; the formation of linkages between terms is not an all-or-none matter, but a question of degree. Now the amount of overlearning was compared directly with the amount of saving manifested in relearning. Knowing how much work would ordinarily be required after a given interval to relearn material which had been just learned and no more, it was possible to show how much more quickly the material could be relearned if it had in the first place been overlearned. The ratio of overlearning to saving turned out, in Ebbinghaus's data, to be roughly a straight-line relationship. Additional units of overlearning produced, after a twenty-four-hour interval, fairly uniform amounts of saving. With nonsense material under the conditions stated the number of repetitions saved was consistently about one-third of the number of repetitions in overlearning.[9]

One of the great triumphs of the saving method was the quantitative examination of the process of forgetting. From a standard mass of memorized material, decrements due to the lapse of various intervals of time could be computed. Having learned a list, for example, requiring fifteen repetitions, Ebbinghaus could find how much work it took, say twenty-four hours later, to bring back that list to the point of perfect repetition, so that he could go through it without aid. In this way he obtained the material for his "curve of forgetting," which showed that forgetting was extremely rapid in the first few minutes, considerably less rapid in the next few hours, and even less rapid in the next few days. It became at last almost a straight line, asymptotic to the x axis upon which time intervals were measured. This method established definitely a quantitative basis

---

[9] This linear relation held up to sixty-four repetitions; the nature of the curve above that point was not ascertained.

for the study of forgetting, and therefore of retention. The curve was extremely simple mathematically, stated in a form of very general validity. The exact form of the curves of forgetting, plotted by Ebbinghaus for his own data with himself as subject, has not, of course, proved adequate for other data and for other observers. These qualifications do not, however, affect the general form of the curve, which has been abundantly verified: an initial drop, gradually becoming less steep in asymptotic form.

The method was capable of application to meaningful material, and Ebbinghaus later compared this with nonsense material in order to determine whether the form of the curve still held good. He memorized many stanzas from Byron's *Don Juan*, and ascertained the amount of material retained after varying intervals, using the saving method. The same *general* shape of the curve was found for the meaningful as for the nonsense material, though the fall was less rapid throughout. He went back to this problem twenty-two years later, and relearned many of these stanzas, having in the meantime given them no further rehearsal. Comparing these with new stanzas memorized, he found an appreciable difference in learning time; the saving method revealed some retention over the twenty-two-year period.[10] This result could scarcely be explained on the basis of mere familiarity with particular words in the text. For in another connection he directly attacked the question whether the familiarity of elements in memory material altered the form of the curves or not. He made up lists in which each syllable was familiar to him, and found that the lists were just as hard to learn as lists of equal length containing unfamiliar syllables. It seemed to be the *connections* which were significant in the learning process. It appeared then that connections established in meaningful material enjoy very long life.

Another of his contributions which has been recognized and used on a large scale was the study of the most effective distribution of working time; the question whether a given amount of time yields a larger return when given uninterruptedly to the memorizing of material, or when broken up into shorter periods with rest intervals between. Is it better, for example, to give an hour all at once to incessant repetition of a task, or to break it into periods of two half-hours separated by an interval, or into four fifteen-minute periods? Ebbinghaus found that "spaced" repetition was decidedly to be preferred to continuous and "unspaced" repetition. He did not ascertain the optimum interval between work periods; but such

[10] *Grundzüge der Psychologie*, Vol. I (1905).

evidence as we have indicates that the twenty-four-hour interval, which he used, was a good choice.[11]

Finally, he sought to answer the question whether associations are ever formed according to any other pattern than A—B—C—D, the letters representing items learned, and the dashes associations or linkages. Hartley had asserted that if a series of elements A, B, C, D is learned, there is a tendency for A to recall faint images, b, c, and d, which are memories of the original elements. Now, said Ebbinghaus, we know from Herbart's work and his mathematical formulae (which Ebbinghaus almost alone of all psychologists took rather seriously) that there are associations not only from A to B, but also from A to C and from A to D. There are ideas rising into consciousness and disappearing again; there may be several present above the threshold at once. There may be in the process of learning more than two items undergoing linkage at a given moment; several terms, A, B, C, D, may be in consciousness at once, and many linkages may be in the process of formation. At a given moment A may be about to disappear from consciousness while B is, so to speak, at its zenith; C is rising into clear consciousness while D is only vaguely present. A moment later A has disappeared, B is declining, C is at its zenith, and D is rising. Any two items present in consciousness tend to form linkages. Hence there may be not only remote forward connections such as A—C and A—D, but backward associations such as D—C and even C—A. Ebbinghaus undertook to find out empirically whether connections were actually formed as the theory demanded. Taking nonsense lists which had once been learned, he constructed from these *new* lists in which every *second* syllable was used, A, C, E, G. Similarly, lists were formed by taking every third item of a learned list A, D, G . . . and so on to the point of selecting every eighth syllable. Now he found that he could learn the new list (made up by skipping every second syllable and so on) more rapidly than comparable nonsense material that was new. For him this proved that when he had originally learned the list A, B, C, D he had actually formed associations not only from A to B and from B to C, but from A to C, and the like. Herbart was vindicated. Psychologists smiled and waved Herbart aside; but the results were interesting. By the saving method Ebbinghaus showed that the linkage of A with C was more effective than that of A with D; and that the strength of the linkage consistently decreased with the number

[11] Perkins, N. L., "The Value of Distributed Repetitions in Rote Learning," *Brit. J. Psychol.*, 1914, 7, 253–61.

of syllables skipped until, with the skipping of seven syllables, the curve approached the base line.

Similarly, he constructed lists of nonsense syllables in an order the reverse of the one used in the original learning. He found that he could learn these more quickly than comparable material which was new, thus apparently showing that when learning the list in the first place he had established connections also from B to A, from C to B, and so on. And he constructed lists in which both backward association and skipping were to be tested—such as E, C, A. Even these lists were more effectively learned than was new material.

Various objections have been raised, and subsequent experimental work has shown that such results may in some cases be attributed to the tendency to revert unwittingly to syllables several steps earlier in the series, or, in successive repetitions, to anticipate syllables which are still several steps away. But some of this work, utilizing meaningful material, can scarcely be said to count against Ebbinghaus's findings with nonsense syllables, and it is by no means certain that these objections dispose of the problem.

The place of Ebbinghaus in the history of psychology is not, however, confined to the issue of finding a way to investigate memory. His determination to develop a refined technique, to control everything that could be controlled, and to reduce everything to quantitative form vividly exemplified the incursion of the physical-science methods into psychology; it set a new direction for psychology as dramatically and as clearly as did anything in the era.

G. E. MÜLLER AND THE EXPANSION OF THE NEW PROGRAM

Ebbinghaus's memory work inspired a great deal of further investigation. G. E. Müller, working now with one and now with another collaborator, improved some of the methods of Ebbinghaus, and attacked many new problems. Müller and Schumann, for example, devised a method for the uniform presentation, upon a revolving drum, of nonsense syllables for memorization, so that the rate of presentation could be systematically varied. An exposure slot makes it possible for the subject to observe one syllable in one unit of time. Another improvement in Ebbinghaus's methods was the devising of lists of nonsense syllables which were found in practice to be of approximately equal difficulty.

While such modifications in method were being made, Müller and many others contributed new experiments and results. It was found by W. G. Smith in 1896 that early and late syllables were fixated much more quickly than those in the middle of a series.[12] Steffens discovered shortly thereafter a principle which has been much utilized.[13] She demonstrated the futility of trying to break up long passages of meaningful material into short passages for memorizing; material was found to be better learned when read through from beginning to end than when learned in parts and pieced together. The task of fitting together the different parts when learned separately was very wasteful of time. The experiment has been repeated by many students, the majority of whom have confirmed the reality of this advantage of "whole learning" over "part learning" in most individuals. It was pointed out, however, shortly thereafter, that it is sometimes worth while to stop and repeat more difficult parts of the list.[14] And it naturally made a difference whether the individual had to memorize a *list* so that it could be recited without prompting, or whether his task was simply to recall as large a number of elements as he could. With the latter procedure, the method of "retained members," the advantage of "whole learning" was not apparent.

One of the most important of these extensions of Ebbinghaus's procedure consisted in the study of individual connections or linkages; emphasis was withdrawn from "serial" learning and given to association between pairs of elements. To this end, Calkins devised a method of presenting, both visually and auditorily, *pairs* of items, the items having no obvious meaningful relation; for example, a pair might consist of a word and a number.[15] Her first use of the method was to study the influence of primacy, recency, frequency, and vividness. By demonstrating the influence of these factors in assisting her subjects to recall the second item of each pair, she gave experimental confirmation to some of those "secondary" laws of association which Thomas Brown had enumerated three-quarters of a century before (page 60). Pairs early and late in the series were compared with those in the middle; frequently presented pairs were contrasted with those less frequently shown; variation in size and color of type gave to some items special vividness. The method was shortly afterward adopted and developed by Müller and Pilzecker.[16] Performance was measured in terms of the number of cases in which the second term

---

[12] "The Place of Repetition in Memory," *Psychol. Rev.*, 3.

[13] *Zschr. f. Psychol.*, 1900, 22.

[14] Pentschew, C., *Arch. f. d. ges. Psychol.*, 1903, 1; Ephrussi, P., *Zschr. f. Psychol.*, 1904, 37.

[15] *Association, Psychol. Rev., Monogr. Suppl.*, 1895, 1.

[16] *Zschr. f. Psychol., Ergänzungsb.*, 1900, 1.

could be recalled when the first term was presented. The new method of "paired associates" was applicable to a study of many sorts of variables appearing with each association to be formed.[17]

During the twenty years which followed the experiments of Ebbinghaus, research was dominated by his concepts, and concerned primarily with the extension of his methods. Nevertheless, it began to be more and more evident that a simple associationism could not account for what happened. It was discovered that the way in which the individual learns depends on his attitude or purpose. The task the individual undertook determined the manner of learning; if, for example, the syllables were simply read through without the purpose of learning them, very little connection between them was formed.[18]

Indeed, one main result of the long series of memory studies, especially those of Müller, was to reveal the great variety of devices spontaneously adopted by the memorizing subject to facilitate his difficult task. Rhythmical and other groupings, similarities and other relationships observed, even in nonsense materials, and meanings of all sorts read into the material, make the memorizing process very different from a passive or receptive establishment of contiguities. It has been urged (as by Poppelreuter)[19] that all memory experiments have really been examining "higher" or more complex processes than the simple formation of associations.[20]

REFERENCES

Brett, George S., *A History of Psychology*, 3 vols., London, 1914–21

Ebbinghaus, Hermann, *Memory*, Teachers College, Columbia University, 1913

James, William, *The Principles of Psychology*, 2 vols., Holt, 1890; Vol. I, pp. 643–89

Ladd, G. T., and Woodworth, R. S., *Elements of Physiological Psychology*, Scribner, 1911; references to Ebbinghaus, G. E. Müller

[17] Ebbinghaus himself later introduced the "prompting method" for this purpose (*Grundzüge der Psychologie*, Vol. I, p. 648). The subject is prompted whenever he falters.

[18] Müller, G. E., and Schumann, F., *Zschr. f. Psychol.*, 1894, 6; see also below, page 247.

[19] *Zschr. f. Psychol.*, 1912, 61.

[20] This much-needed paragraph was added by R. S. Woodworth.

Chapter 13

THE INFLUENCE
OF NEUROLOGY, 1860–1910

*The rapidity with which [the neurone theory] won its way
among all classes of students is notable in scientific history.*

LADD AND WOODWORTH

WUNDT's experimental psychology and the era of memory study called necessarily for all available data on the neurological functions involved in sense perception and in learning. By the beginning of the present century, in fact, a general tendency prevailed to think of learning in terms of certain current neurological doctrines; these doctrines became in many quarters even more popular than the new memory methods. We must take account here of certain striking neurological advances made during the nineteenth century and at the beginning of the twentieth, which were of great importance to physiological psychology in general and to the theory of learning in particular.

In the middle of the nineteenth century, in spite of the work of such men as Bain and Lotze, relatively little detailed information regarding the physiology of the nervous system was available for psychological purposes. The hope of a physiological psychology, repeatedly uttered in the eighteenth century, had so far resulted in but meager data of a type really useful in the explanation of specific psychological events. But from about 1860 on there occurred a series of discoveries in neurology which began to exert important influences on psychology.

CORTICAL LOCALIZATION

It will be recalled that Johannes Müller (page 93) had discussed the question of the localization of function within the cerebral cortex. Further studies during the twenties and thirties as to the definite localization of speech functions led in 1861 to the declaration by Broca that injuries to the third frontal convolution of the left hemisphere were the cause of motor aphasia, the loss of voluntary speech.[1] This statement of Broca attracted attention, and soon came into wide acceptance. This was the first case of definitely accepted cortical localization for a specific function, antedating by twenty years the definite location of any of the sensory centers, and antedating by ten years the *experimental* demonstration of the location of the motor functions.[2] In 1870 work was published by Fritsch and Hitzig on the localization of motor functions in the cerebrum of the dog.[3] Stimulation of the region immediately in front of the Rolandic fissure was found to elicit movements of the limbs.

During the period of the seventies and eighties this work of mapping cerebral localization was carried on extensively. One of the most significant contributions was that of Ferrier, who succeeded in working out the localization of motor functions in the brains of monkeys; this proved to be similar to that found for the dog.[4] Ferrier did more than explore the motor area in order to find out how the subdivisions of the motor cortex were arranged; he and others began to contribute much to the localization of *sensory* functions. Not content with the mere tracing of sensory fibers through their devious paths to the cortex, they made use of the technique of cutting sensory fibers and determining whether the visual, auditory, or other functions were affected. In this work, in general fairly accurate, Ferrier made some errors, in the localization, for example, of the visual center; where pathways are so intricate, it was only natural that errors should result from unwittingly interfering with fibers considerably removed from the point chosen for the incision. A number of experimentalists were soon in the field, and such errors were rapidly corrected. Grünbaum and Sherrington were soon exploring the brains of anthropoid apes.[5]

This kind of research made it possible to say in a general way that there are regions in the cortex which have specific functions. The whole problem of cortical localization stood in a new light as compared with the middle of the century. By 1885 or 1890 the main cortical centers for sensation and (voluntary) movement were worked

[1] *Bulletins de la Société Anatomique.*
[2] First in the dog, subsequently in other mammals. See page 374.
[3] *Arch. f. Anat. u. Physiol.*
[4] *Functions of the Brain* (1876).
[5] *Transactions Pathol. Soc. London*, 1902, 53, Pt. 1. See also Sherrington, C. S., *The Integrative Action of the Nervous System* (1906).

out for mammals to the general satisfaction of most critics. Partly by the use of analogy, but chiefly through clinical studies and anatomical research, similar localization within the human brain won general acceptance. It became a matter of agreement that the area immediately in front of the fissure of Rolando is uniformly motor and that the post-Rolandic area serves the "general senses" of warmth, cold, touch, and pain. The visual center was assigned to the occipital lobe and the auditory to the temporal lobe. A region near the olfactory bulb was recognized as the olfactory lobe. The center for taste was not (and has not yet been) clearly determined. The evidence indicated that simple sensory and motor functions are performed by both hemispheres, symmetrical areas having like functions. The results from tracing fibers and those obtained from the extirpation and cutting of fibers were consistent.

Many writers carried cortical localization much further. Wernicke [6] and others helped to define the types of aphasia on the hypothesis that there is a specific cortical localization for each type (disorders in reading, in writing, in talking, and in understanding spoken language). They described, for example, patients who had lost the ability to read—that is, to *understand* printed symbols— without manifesting any other language disturbance. This disorder was attributed to a specific lesion so circumscribed as to leave the rest of the brain unaffected. Hinshelwood, among others, believed that the centers for visual memory are distinct from those for visual sensation.[7] Destroy the visual center and the patient still has visual memories; destroy the visual memory region and the patient may have the capacity to see, without recognizing what he sees. While in general rejecting this simple localization of memory functions, many neurologists and psychologists came to the conclusion that certain lesions can disturb perception without affecting sensation. Hence the doctrine that perceptual functions are carried out not by the sensory centers themselves, but by regions adjacent to them. This fitted in well with the theory that co-ordinating or integrating centers for motor functions lie adjacent to the motor area in the pre-Rolandic region. Many clinical and anatomical studies were being made in this period, which seemed in general to confirm the view.[8]

A closely related problem was the task of tracing sensory fibers through the spinal cord and brain stem to the cortical sensory areas.

---

[6] *Der aphasische Symptomencomplex* (1874).

[7] *Letter, Word, and Mind Blindness* (1900).

[8] The evidence from post-mortem examination was scarcely definite, in view of the extraordinary irregularity of lesions and the scarcity of "pure" aphasic types.

Pathological cases helped greatly to clarify and interpret anatomical research; injuries to the nervous system could be directly compared with losses of specific sensory functions. Animal experimentation also added much; if certain fibers in the cord were cut and certain functions were consistently lost, it was possible to say with fair certainty what functions the fibers served. The discreteness of these functions seemed to call for the discovery of separate pathways serving their respective functions. Pain and temperature pathways, for example, were satisfactorily traced.

THE NEURONE THEORY

Another field of research important for psychology was the intensive study of the general anatomy and physiology of nerve cells. Histological methods, such as the staining of normal and injured nerve tissue, made possible not only the tracing of fibers but the observation and classification of many types of cells previously unrecognized. One of the most important steps taken in this direction was the method of staining used by Golgi, in Italy. A common view that the various parts of the nervous system are all anatomically connected did not seem to be confirmed by the evidence from staining, or from other methods utilized during the seventies and eighties. Staining methods seemed to indicate that nerve cells are anatomically distinct from one another; there appeared, at least in higher animals, no clear cases of fibers passing from one cell into another. This led students of the subject to gravitate toward the view that each nerve cell is in some way connected physiologically, but not anatomically, with other nerve cells. Cells are capable of influencing one another, but each cell carries on independently such functions as nutrition and self-repair. Other evidence to the same general effect was obtained from the embryological researches of His. The problem of His was to determine whether the nerve cells arise, so to speak, from one another, or whether each one pursues from the beginning an independent development. He showed that each nerve cell is from the time of its appearance until completely developed an *individual*, not sharing in the life of the other cells except in deriving its nutrition and so on from a common source. This was important in confirming the belief that the most significant relation between nerve cells was to be found not in their anatomical interconnections, but in the ways in which they might influence one another in function. This view, developing largely from the work of Ramón y Cajal, was named by Waldeyer the *neurone theory* in

1891.[9] This was one of the most important neurological contributions for the history of psychology. It brought together numerous evidences as to the nature of nervous physiology which psychologists could use. Its central conception was the anatomical independence of nerve cells, and their physiological interconnection at junction points or *synapses*.

We may best understand the influence of the theory upon psychology by considering briefly the kind of neurophysiology upon which psychologists had been relying. Many psychologists had exploited the nervous system as an explanatory principle for mental life, but explanation of the part played by the nervous system in *specific* mental processes had inevitably been extremely vague. Let us choose for illustration the work of one French and one American psychologist. Ribot in *Diseases of Memory* (1881) regarded these as the product of disordered brain functions. But he thought in terms of gross lesions, not in terms of the disorganization of microscopic or ultramicroscopic elements, such as connections between one nerve cell and another. Even the concept of the difference between organic and functional psychoses was at that time impossible; the importance of gross injuries to the brain was overemphasized, simply because the significance of ultramicroscopic changes could not be clearly stated.

Similarly, a comparison of William James's chapter on "Habit" (in his *Principles of Psychology*) with statements of the physiology of habit current a few years *after* the acceptance of the neurone theory, shows how great was the revolution in the theory of learning.[10] James was trying to think in neurological terms. He sought to find how it was that a series of connections could be made between different parts of our bodies, one movement leading to the next; but he worked without any clear conception as to the mechanism by which one nerve cell might influence another. The same lack of definite neurological concepts with which to work is apparent in James's theory of association. In his chapter on "Association," he offered a theory as to the neural functions involved in all the sequences of mental life. He suggested that if any two points in the cerebral cortex are simultaneously active, the two centers tend to "drain" into each other. Pathways are thus established, which later are traversed when either center is excited. If we *see* a man and at

---

[9] *Deutsch. Med. Wochenschr.*, 18.

[10] James borrowed a great deal from Meynert. Meynert's scheme postulated that habit was based upon the interconnection of brain areas, without making clear the mechanism of such connection.

the same time *hear* his name, a linkage is established which later enables either experience to recall the other. *Successive* association was explained in similar terms, a hypothesis being added to the effect that when one area is excited immediately *after* another, the energy drained from the first to the second is greater than the quantity drained from the second to the first. This presupposed, of course, an "irradiation" of energy in the cortex which need not involve motor discharge; it was therefore a necessary supplement to James's theory of habit. But it did not tell *how* the disturbances in one nerve cell could affect another nerve cell.

The neurone theory gave both the theory of learning and the theory of association a much more definite and usable form. The theory teaches that each nerve cell is an individual which carries on its own life as regards nutrition and other metabolic functions. The connection between one nerve cell and another is, as we saw, by means of the synapse, or junction point. The synapse is not a fibrous connection, but a point at which the nervous impulse is relayed from one nerve cell to the next. But the terminal or end brush of a neurone A may be in close proximity to the receiving organs, or dendrites, of *many* other neurones, B, C, D . . . so that according to the theory, the actual pathway A—B or A—C or A—D . . . depends upon the physiological properties of the synapse at the time. There may, of course, be synaptic connections so intimate that they cannot be broken by anything. Such would be cases of reflex action so firmly established as to be practically unmodifiable. Some of the reflexes of the spinal frog would, perhaps, represent the extreme of unmodifiability. At the opposite extreme, or limiting case, there may be synapses in which there is an equal predisposition for the impulses to go in any one of a great number of directions, the choice between the alternatives depending on slight and momentary factors, such as variations in the blood supply. These conceptions make possible a theory of learning in terms of modification of the synapse. Between these two extreme cases there are conceived to be behavior patterns less rigid than the one and less plastic than the other, so that an original disposition may have sufficient plasticity to permit the reorganization of nervous pathways as the result of experience. This view makes possible the formulation of the learning process in terms of the building-up of resistance at certain points and the breaking-down of resistance at others; and the patterned or organized functioning of many synapses jointly involved in a complex total. These aspects of the neurone theory, developed and systematized by many physiologists and psychologists, seemed to be of immediate value for the psychology of learning and for many other problems. They were rapidly accepted and came into general use in the first years of the twentieth century.

SHERRINGTON

The next great step, after Waldeyer's neurone theory, in inducing psychologists to think in neurological terms, was the work of Sherrington during the opening years of the century, described in his *Integrative Action of the Nervous System* (1906). Fundamental conceptions for neurophysiology were defined and in many cases experimentally verified, frequently with reference to psychological implications. The experimental study of the reflex arc in normal and decerebrate mammals underwent, with Sherrington, a series of refinements. When a single stimulus was too weak to elicit a motor response, the repeated application of the same weak stimulus was found to be capable, by "summation," of traversing the threshold, throwing the reflex into full swing. But simultaneous, as well as successive, stimuli might co-operate with or "facilitate" one another. When a stimulus at one point was too weak to set the reflex going, a stimulus at another point might, although itself also too weak, join forces with the first, evoking the response. In other cases, a stimulus which would ordinarily evoke a reflex response was found to be "inhibited" by another stimulus. Such "facilitation" and "inhibition," already familiar to physiologists,[11] were elaborately analyzed, and definite evidence was offered to show their relation to the functions of the synapse. Both processes seemed to be effected by synapses intermediate between receptor and organ of response; on reaching a synapse two pathways might either aid or interfere with one another. "Reciprocal inhibition" was demonstrated in numerous instances; the innervation of extensor muscles involved not only the inactivity but the *lowered tonus* of the flexor muscles of the same limbs. The process by which one pathway was opened served also to block pathways leading to opposed action.[12]

The supposition that facilitation and inhibition are synaptic functions was greatly strengthened by Sherrington's study of the effect of fatigue and drugs. A bit of nerve tissue containing no synapses proved

[11] Especially through the work of S. Exner, *Pflüger's Archiv.*, 1882, 28.

[12] McDougall's "drainage theory" of reciprocal inhibition (*Physiological Psychology*, 1905) held that when A–B and C–D are antagonistic reflexes, A–B, while functioning, draws off the energy of C, so that the response D is inhibited; fatigue in the pathway A–B makes possible the sudden activity of C–D, draining the energy from A.

quite insusceptible to fatigue, whereas regions containing synapses could conduct only for a brief period without the occurrence of fatigue. Certain drugs were found to block off an impulse quite effectively if applied to a region containing synapses, while regions containing none were practically unaffected. Other drugs, instead of increasing, greatly reduced synaptic resistance.

All this work, then, confirmed for psychologists the extraordinary importance of the synapses for facilitation and inhibition in higher processes. The nature of synaptic function, however, was not disclosed by Sherrington's methods. An interesting line of inquiry is associated with the names of Nernst,[13] Lillie,[14] and Lucas: [15] Theoretical and experimental conditions alike suggested that the nerve current is a "wave of depolarization" which passes along the nerve fiber whenever a stimulus disturbs the delicate balance of positive and negative ions produced in the metabolism of the nerve. An instant after the depolarization at a given point, that point is in "refractory phase"; another instant later it is in a condition of "hyperexcitability." Each synapse was conceived to have its own refractory phase, resulting in inhibition; and its period of hyperexcitability. The hypothesis has encountered many difficulties, the problem being highly complex, and several new theories today claim the field.[16] Such a view was illustrative, however, of the advances of physiological chemistry, and the growing insistence that the synapse should be conceived in such terms as to throw genuine light upon the phenomena of facilitation and inhibition. To such problems we must briefly recur at a later point (page 380).

REFERENCES

James, William, *The Principles of Psychology*, 2 vols., Holt, 1890

Ladd, G. T., and Woodworth, R. S., *Elements of Physiological Psychology*, Scribner, 1911; opening chapters

Merz, J. T., *A History of European Thought in the Nineteenth Century*, 4 vols., London, 1896

Sherrington, C. S., *The Integrative Action of the Nervous System*, Yale University Press, 1906

[13] *Arch. f. d. ges. Physiol.*, 1908, 122.

[14] "The Relation of Stimulation and Conduction in Irritable Tissues to Changes in the Permeability of the Limiting Membranes," *Amer. J. Physiol.*, 1911, 28; *Protoplasmic Action and Nervous Action* (1923).

[15] *The Conduction of the Nervous Impulse* (1917).

[16] See, for example, Fulton, J. F., *Physiology of the Nervous System* (1938).

Chapter 14

WILLIAM JAMES

*He always left the impression that there was more; that he
knew there was more; and that the more to come might, for all
one knew, throw a very different light on the matters under discussion. He respected his universe too much to believe that he could
carry it under his own hat. These saving doubts arose from the
same source as his tolerance and respect for his fellow man. The
universe, like one's neighbor, is never wholly disclosed to outward view, and the last word must be a consent that the other
should be itself.*   R. B. PERRY

WHILE succeeding to an extraordinary extent in bringing
together the work of the Scottish, English, French, and
German schools, William James gave to each a color and a
reinterpretation through which a sort of unity was achieved. But
thorough as his scholarship was, the man rather than the schools
spoke through his pages, in the delineation of a psychology which was
not so much an interweaving of traditions as it was a new creature.

Though he thought of becoming a painter, and despite his bent
toward philosophy, he was drawn to the study of medicine and
became a teacher of physiology at Harvard. His work involved no
sharp line between physiology and psychology; in fact, his earliest
interests included problems in sense physiology. He was pursuing psychological problems in his little laboratory as early as 1875. From
these beginnings followed his career in psychology and philosophy.

The journal *Mind*, founded in 1876, contained in its first volume
an article from his pen. In the next ten years a series of articles under
his name appeared in this and in other magazines. Much of this
material was destined to be incorporated later in the *Principles of
Psychology* (1890). From these studies and from his letters [1] it is not

---

[1] *The Letters of William James*, ed. by Henry James (1920).

hard to see what major forces were acting on his thinking. He was a terrific reader, attaining a very unusual degree of erudition and range of information. He was deeply absorbed in the Scottish as in the associationist psychology, and in that mixture of the two which flourished in Britain in the middle of the century. Here, as elsewhere, his philosophical and religious nature seized what it could use.[2]

There were also many strong and obvious German influences. German experimental work influenced James enormously, in spite of his animus against what he called "brass-instrument" psychology. Notwithstanding his feeling that the laboratory method tended to become the dissection of dead minds, he devoted nearly two hundred pages in his *Principles* to the experimental findings of men such as Helmholtz and Wundt. It is clear that James regarded the Leipzig movement as a source of much usable material, but not at all, as the Wundtians considered it, as offering a new Constitution for Psychology. Of the three figures Helmholtz, Fechner, and Wundt, he was least partial toward Fechner; he was deeply appreciative of Fechner's *philosophy*, but he held the upshot of his experimental work to be "just nothing." The methods of Helmholtz and Wundt interested him enough to cause him to invite Münsterberg, a representative of the new experimental psychology, to become his colleague at Harvard. In spite of James's acknowledged prejudices, he sought empirical material wherever he could get it. One has the feeling that as he adopted the German methods and results a sense of duty impelled him. The chapter on "The Perception of Space" reads like the work of a man who finds a disagreeable task to be done and "faces the music." It was for him the kind of experimental problem which could hardly have been undertaken in a country "whose natives could be bored"; but it gave facts, and ardent empiricist that he was, he had to have facts wherever they lay. To the Hegelian movement and other idealistic trends James reacted with strenuous and prolonged protest. To him they seemed wordy and without substance; they represented the "thin" rather than the "thick" in philosophy.[3] German philosophy influenced him by way of greatly accentuating his inclination toward "radical empiricism." His psychological outlook was a protest against both German and British "absolute idealism."

[2] His father's religious earnestness (for example, his devotion to Swedenborg) profoundly influenced him; a curious combination of personal mysticism and New England matter-of-factness is apparent throughout his work.

[3] *A Pluralistic Universe* (1909), p. 136.

The same reverence for factual material which James showed in relation to German psychology was liberated and given new life by French psychology. He thought something really important had been discovered by French psychiatric research. He was deeply interested in the work of Charcot, Janet, and others who had studied hysteria, hypnotism, and dissociation; he believed that such studies had something fundamental to teach about the structure of personality. He gave much attention to Janet's evidence that there may be parts of personality functioning unknown to our introspective consciousness.[4] This discovery seemed to James to be of great moment, indicating that personality is not the little circle of events upon which the light of introspection is thrown, but represents various levels or strata which may be as genuinely psychological as the superficially apparent. He felt that dissociation, or splitting of personality, made it possible to study at different times elements in personality which take their turns in controlling individual conduct. The mental events which go on outside the patient's consciousness might as a rule be regarded as "secondary personalities," real selves distinct from the self which is at the time in control. There are, nevertheless, James believed, *some* mental events outside of personal awareness which are not a part of any *self:* Janet's "organic memories." These questions of subconscious or unconscious mental life seemed to James to be among the central issues for psychology.

So much for the academic influences. At least as important were the personal and social influences: the progressivism and optimism of an America grown strong and turbulent; the warmth and the deep comradeships which at every time in his life were his in all his family relationships; the semi-invalidism, the heartbreaking long periods of bad eyes, aching back, nervous fatigue, which made him seek—and find—a philosophy of spontaneity, of free creativeness, in which healing could be achieved. Of all the nineteenth-century currents most fundamentally congenial to him, because so closely related to such needs, the most important was evolutionism; an evolutionism which meant creativeness through struggle, the primacy of the immediate task to be done over any abstraction which is a step removed from life.

"THE PRINCIPLES OF PSYCHOLOGY"

The contract for *The Principles of Psychology* was signed in 1878, when James was thirty-six years old; he was forty-eight when the

[4] *The Principles of Psychology* (1890), Vol. I, pp. 227 ff.

book was published. Several of the chapters had in the meantime appeared in periodicals, but *The Principles* burst upon the world like a volcanic eruption. In commenting upon his extraordinary book, there is a great temptation to introduce it as a great new "system" of psychology. Perhaps, however, the term "system" is misleading; for just as Wundt was the systematic psychologist par excellence, so James might be called the *un*systematic psychologist par excellence. He was very much less occupied with the problem of creating order and system than with the task of giving the reader something to feed upon. The chapters of *The Principles* are not built into a structural unity; that James was fully aware of this is clear from his Preface. We can tell which chapters were borrowed from British sources (note, for example, the relation of Bain and Carpenter to James's chapter on "Habit"). The three chapters on "perception" (the perception of "Time," "Space," and "Things") were taken largely from German sources. The chapters on "The Emotions," "Will," "The Stream of Thought," and "Necessary Truths," while utilizing contemporary material, were in large part original.

Having emphasized the fact that the chapters do not set forth a true "system," we shall not have to ask regarding the *elements* out of which, according to James, the mind is composed; he was not interested in such a question. Wundt had informed us that experience is composed of three main types of elements: sensations, images, and feelings, three categories which survived in the psychology of the "structuralists" (page 214). But "feeling" meant for James anything we feel like making it mean. We have certain feelings as we look at our watches, others as we are told we shall die tomorrow. James neither classified nor minutely analyzed such feelings.

The analytic method, in fact, seemed to him to be unwarranted; experiences simply are what they are, and not groups of elements which we can constrain ourselves to detect through introspection.[5] The introspective discovery of discrete elements does not prove that they were present *before* their observation occurred. For Locke, father of structuralism, the taste of lemonade (for example) would have consisted of sourness, plus coldness, plus sweetness, plus tactual sensations from the tongue, and so on. Even for Wundt (in spite of "creative synthesis") there were several distinct afferent neural pathways, which brought in the various sensations one by one, so that the sensory elements appeared separately in consciousness and were combined into a percept. James taught that this was a thor-

[5] *Ibid.*, Vol. I, pp. 157 ff.

oughly distorted picture. The psychologist, he thought, reads into an experience what he thinks should be there. Suppose a tea-taster trains himself to discriminate in a flavor elements which to most observers are fused into an unanalyzable blend. From James's viewpoint, the fact that this individual taster can analyze his experience does not prove that the separate analyzed elements are present in the consciousness of everyone who tastes the compound. To make such an assumption is to be guilty of the "psychologist's fallacy."

Just as we cannot break up a given mental content into pure sensory elements, the attempt to subdivide consciousness into a series of temporally distinct phases is unwarranted. We cannot talk about one thing leading by association to the next, as one clock tick succeeds another. There is, on the contrary, a continuous flow, a "stream of thought," and each of the entities ordinarily studied by psychologists is nothing more than a cross section arbitrarily taken out of the stream. James Mill, Spencer, and Bain had all emphasized the constant flux of consciousness, believing that it was quite impossible to describe a momentary cross section of experience except in terms of the stages just preceding it. Bain had written: "To be distinctly affected by two or more successive impressions is the most general fact of consciousness. We are never conscious at all without experiencing transition or change." [6] James, accepting and elaborating this view, held that the process of analyzing experience into temporal pigeonholes is just as absurd as the psychologist's fallacy. Mental life at any time is a unity, a total experience, flowing and changing as does a stream.

A great deal in this stream of consciousness is not easily grasped in introspective terms; much of it is vague, incoherent, intangible. A large part of it is marginal. James made much of what he called *transitive* as opposed to *substantive* states. Thought contains not only stopping places that are easily observed, but transitional states so vague and fleeting that they have escaped the attention of most psychologists. Psychologists have taken cross sections of the stream of thought at the substantive points; they have neglected the vague, the fleeting, the indefinite. If, for instance, we should say, "Substantive states do not constitute the entire subject matter of psychology," probably the word "of" would play a transitive, not a substantive, role. James suggested here that one of his tasks was to restore to consciousness the vague, indefinite, and unsubstantial. But he was not alone. The same conception was apparent in other

[6] *The Senses and the Intellect*, 2d ed., p. 325.

revolts against structuralism (to which we shall devote attention a little later), and soon became a subject for experimental study.

The evolutionism, the dynamism, the creativeness, that pervade James can best of all be portrayed in his own words as he grappled with one of the problems closest to his heart: the nature of the will. The following is from his account of the will, and his classification of the *types of decision*.[7] "The first may be called *the reasonable type*. It is that of those cases in which the arguments for and against a given course seem gradually and almost insensibly to settle themselves in the mind and to end by leaving a clear balance in favor of one alternative, which alternative we then adopt without effort or constraint. . . . In this easy transition from doubt to assurance we seem to ourselves almost passive; the 'reasons' which decide us appearing to flow in from the nature of things, and to owe nothing to our will. . . . In the *second type* of case our feeling is . . . that of letting ourselves drift with a certain indifferent acquiescence in a direction accidentally determined *from without*. . . . *In the third type* . . . it . . . often happens, when the absence of imperative principle is perplexing and suspense distracting, that we find ourselves acting, as it were, automatically . . . in the direction of one of the horns of the dilemma. . . . 'Forward now!' we inwardly cry, 'though the heavens fall.' " The fourth form of decision "comes when, in consequence of some outer experience or some inexplicable inward charge, *we suddenly pass from the easy and careless to the sober and strenuous mood*. . . . The whole scale of values of our motives and impulses then undergoes a change . . . all 'light fantastic' notions lose their motive power, all solemn ones find theirs multiplied many-fold." In the fifth "we feel, in deciding, as if we ourselves by our own wilful act inclined the beam. . . . The slow dead heave of the will that is felt in these instances makes of them a class altogether different subjectively from all the three preceding classes. . . . Whether it be the dreary resignation for the sake of austere and naked duty of all sorts of rich, mundane delights, or whether it be the heavy resolve that of two mutually exclusive trains of future fact, both sweet and good . . . one shall forevermore become impossible, while the other shall become reality, it is a desolate and acrid sort of act, an excursion into a lonesome moral wilderness."

For James, the will is, moreover, a crucial point at which all mechanistic interpretation fails. His disbelief in the possibility of a purely mechanical statement of personality was apparent, as was his belief in the substantial reality of psychic forces which could

[7] *The Principles of Psychology*, Vol. II, pp. 531–34.

not be stated in neurological terms. James has been accused of inconsistency regarding the mind-body relation. It is true that he repeatedly asserted that psychologists must dispense with the soul as a datum for their science; but on the other hand we find him saying that there seems to him some integrating and organizing force beyond the separate experiences, which looks like personality or soul, holding in cohesion and in integrated action the many disparate functions.[8] The inconsistency is in fact quite apparent if we contrast the treatment of "The Stream of Thought" with the discussion of "Will." In the former, thought is, so to speak, self-propelling, the self appearing as an experienced entity but not necessarily as a reality beyond experience. In the latter, volition exhibits in certain cases the intervention of an entity not explainable in terms of the elements preceding the decision.[9] James's heart was plainly in the doctrine of interaction between soul and body. He tried most of the time to think in monistic terms, using a neurological terminology, but did not believe such an approach to be ultimate. We shall see later, in connection with his studies of religious experience, other instances of his disbelief in the finality of mechanistic, or in fact of any rationalistic, methods.

The most celebrated and influential of James's theories (and he was prolific in theories) had to do with the emotions. Since the publication of Lotze's *Medical Psychology* (1852), a great quantity of descriptive work on the physiological aspects of emotion had been published. Such descriptions were inevitably rather sterile, most of them being based on no carefully controlled data, and presented without reference to any distinct and verifiable hypothesis. Little critical thinking had been done as to *what emotions were:* popular terms like "fear" and "rage" served as starting points for detailed description of what various parts of the body do in such states. In a first critical endeavor to determine the relation between what was called emotion on the one hand and its physiological expression on the other, James published in *Mind* in 1884 an article on this problem, which was included six years later in *The Principles of Psychology.*[10] In this article he undertook to bridge the gap between emotions and the expressive movements which attend them; he sought to show that emotions have no existence whatever apart from such physiological changes. Each emotion, he held, is nothing but a

[8] *The Principles of Psychology*, Vol. I, p. 181.
[9] His position was more fully stated in his essays, "The Dilemma of Determinism" and "The Will to Believe," in the volume bearing the latter title (1897).
[10] Vol. II, p. 449.

product of the reverberation of physiological changes in the body. This was a flat contradiction of the common assumption that emotion precedes physical expression. Whereas it is customary to think that "we lose our fortune, are sorry, and weep; we meet a bear, are frightened, and run," James maintained that we lose our fortune, cry, and are sorry; see the bear, run, and are afraid. And not only does the arousal of physical responses precede the appearance of the emotions, but our feeling of bodily changes as they occur *is* the emotion.

"Emotion" is a name for certain experiences which are produced by vigorous bodily response, especially response of viscera and muscles. In James's first statement of this he was unfortunate in stressing the *somatic* muscles, particularly the gross changes involved in such acts as running when we are afraid; but his whole treatment showed that he meant to include and to emphasize visceral changes too. (In most of the many elaborations of the theory by other writers, visceral factors have been given great prominence.) James urged that if we analyze out the various bodily reverberations in emotion— the tension of muscles, the fluttering of the heart, the coldness of the skin, and the like—there will be nothing left of the emotion. His view was epoch-making, not only in that it reversed the order in which emotion and physiological changes were said to occur, but in its reduction of emotion to a problem whose core is physiological. He sought in clinics and in hospitals the evidence which might tell decisively in favor of his view, and found a few cases in which a disorder of visceral processes did indeed present anomalies of emotion. But the evidence was not satisfactory. Objectors to the James theory run into the hundreds; but we have here a view destined to be of enormous influence among psychologists, the starting point for nearly all modern theory regarding the emotions, as well as the stimulus to much research. We shall return to the problem on page 384.

In 1885 a strikingly similar view was independently offered by the Danish physiologist Carl Lange, who described the physiology of fear, rage, and the like, and arrived at the conclusion that emotions are based simply and solely upon such physiological changes.[11] For him, the nineteenth-century distinction between mentally aroused and physically aroused emotions was meaningless; in fact, it was difficult to find any emotions which were not "physically

---

11 *Om Sindsbevaegelser* (1885); *Ueber Gemüthsbewegungen* (1887). Lange's theory was in large part derived from Malebranche (*Recherche de la vérité*, 1674), who was in turn indebted to Descartes.

aroused." Bodily changes, especially those of the vascular system, not only gave rise to, but wholly determined, the nature of each emotional state. The general similarity of this to James's view led to the habit of designating as the "James-Lange theory" the assertion that emotions are simply the manifestations in consciousness of a tide of sensory impressions from skeletal muscles, viscera, and other organs.

James's theory of memory is likewise historically important. There had been two dominant theories of memory since the seventeenth century. The first was the faculty psychologists' notion that memory is an ultimate power of the soul or mind. If you cultivate your powers of memory, you can have better memory for *everything*. The second, that of the associationists, held that memory is simply a name for the process by which experiences are reinstated through re-excitement of their physical basis in the brain. Most associationists would say that each person's memory for a given event is a straightforward result of associative laws: frequency, recency, vividness of associations, and so on. In the faculty psychology memory was one unitary function; in the association psychology memory was a loose name for an indefinite number of separate events by which an indefinite number of experiences might be reinstated through association. James suggested a view intermediate between these extremes. Retentiveness, he suggested, is a general property of brain structure, and varies from one individual to another. On the other hand, retention of a given item depends not simply upon the individual brain, but also upon practicing a *specific* brain pathway. And he conducted a series of experiments to find out whether the memorizing of certain kinds of poetry would improve the memory for poetry in general— whether the practice of some memory functions would aid others, as was assumed by those who argued that the classics, or ancient history, would "strengthen memory." He came to the conclusion that general retentiveness could not be improved by training; practice in learning one sort of material was of no value in learning other material. This pioneer investigation was followed shortly by a variety of similar inquiries, the majority of which supported James's contention that there is, in the strict sense, no such thing as general memory training. The problem as to the unity or multiplicity of memory functions had been brought to clear focus. This was the only historically important *experimental* investigation which James carried through.

James's evolutionism has been emphasized; the theory of the emotions made phylogenetic sense, and all human processes were conceived of in terms of their inheritance from an animal ancestry. Symptomatic of the evolutionary point of view was James's catalogue of the instincts. The first catalogue of human instincts and reflexes made on a careful empirical basis was that of Preyer (1880, see page 390). James accepted and greatly extended Preyer's list of human instincts. He included such widely separated things as hiccoughing and hunting. Protesting against the view that man, by virtue of his reason, is but poorly equipped with those instincts that impel animal life, James asserted that man has more instincts than any other animal. In the years since James's list of instincts was presented a great number of similar catalogues have been compiled.[12]

But one contribution, which has not received much attention from psychologists, is especially interesting as an illustration of the much more profound and radical way in which evolutionary principles had taken hold of James's thinking. It is the last chapter of *The Principles*, entitled "Necessary Truths and the Effects of Experience." In this he maintained that there are two ways in which experience may give us what we call knowledge. Some things are imposed upon us arbitrarily; in the strict sense, we "learn" them. We learn, for example, that water freezes at 32° Fahrenheit. The freezing point might as well be 28°; in fact it does vary from one region to another. Such facts are arbitrary. They are dinned into us by their regularity and inevitableness. The child has to collect such knowledge step by step. On the other hand, there are many things which "have to be" so, because of the very structure which evolution has given our minds. Geometrical relations and logical principles are of this sort. The logical structure is what it is because of the structure of the universe, and because of the nature of the minds which have developed in creatures living within it.

This points to a fundamental cleavage in our mental processes between those constructed in the evolution of the race and those constructed in the lifetime of an individual. The necessary truths that seem to us so inevitable are inevitable only because our minds cannot transcend their biological constitution.[13] They are not inevitable in any absolute sense. Here is evident the effect of the evolutionary teaching that mind is the product of adaptation to environment. James works out here for us in some detail the view that our minds are biological weapons, given to us because through countless ages our ancestors were selected by virtue of their possession of certain

[12] A new era in the problem was marked by McDougall's *Introduction to Social Psychology* (1908); to this development we shall return later (page 403).

[13] Cf. Fries, page 55.

modes of reaction to the universe. But for truths which are not thus "necessary" a plastic nervous system is needed, which will enable us to learn the arbitrary facts of every day. James did not, perhaps, fully realize the implications of his point of view. Non-Euclidean geometry had been under construction for over half a century, and both from it and from new movements in physics and logic have arisen in recent years grave questions as to just what these "necessary truths" are. That mind is biological seems true enough, but just what limits are set upon it by this fact it is extremely difficult to define.

We cannot attempt here a further account of the great variety of brilliant passages of description and analysis given in *The Principles*. We shall, however, return to James's treatise from time to time as we consider recent developments which owe much to him.

"THE VARIETIES OF RELIGIOUS EXPERIENCE"

As he worked on *The Principles*, James was clearly turning more and more to philosophical pursuits, but he continued through the nineties an active interest in new psychological developments, especially in medical psychology. His own health, always delicate, was clearly a factor in his constant effort to understand how psychological factors can work for health and illness. After an injury to his heart in 1898, and a recurrence of a period of abysmal fatigue, he set sail for Europe in 1899, aiming to prepare and deliver in Scotland the Gifford Lectures on "natural religion." On the ship he broke down, and in Europe he passed through a long and terrible twilight of half-life before he gradually regained the ability to speak and to write. At last, in 1901, came the lectures on *The Varieties of Religious Experience* (published in 1902).

The "psychology of religion" had begun to take shape a few years before, the child of cultural anthropology and of the new study of individual growth to which Stanley Hall gave such an impetus. A primary factor had been the collection, by E. D. Starbuck, of a mass of manuscripts on religious experiences, especially religious conversion. This intensive study of the psychology of conversion formed a part of the groundwork upon which James developed his lectures. James used also much historical material on religious experience, particularly records of the lives of great mystics and religious leaders.

He began with a challenge to those who delighted in probing the relation of the morbid to the religious. He took serious account of the work of authors who had emphasized the frequency of mental abnormality among religious leaders; but he insisted that the question of mental instability throws no light upon the *value* of experience —the existential approach to religion leaves open the question of its significance.[14] As a problem in psychology, George Fox's aberrations have nothing to teach us regarding the beauty and power of his message. The intense and dynamic person, though ill-balanced, may be a genuine leader, and in a field where emotion is such a vital factor, disintegration may alternate with significant achievement. The achievement may be worth more than the cost of the neuropathic signs that come with it. There is, however, a deeper significance in this relation of religion to psychopathology. James was concerned to show that our whole system of values in regard to social experiences has been woefully narrow; that if we are going to understand civilization at all, we must stop the uncritical use of the terms "normal" and "abnormal," and abandon the tendency to fling aside things that do not harmonize with smooth, easy-rolling, everyday experience. He constantly recurred to this protest against the habit of making stability of mind the criterion of social worth.

James outlined two fundamental types of religious experience. The first is the religion of "healthy-mindedness," in which the world is taken as a joyful place to live in, with the conviction that all that appears evil is incidental or irrelevant in the face of fundamental goodness. This religion of healthy-mindedness cannot understand misery and despair; it is in accord with the widespread nineteenth-century movement of mental healing through belief in the *unreality of sickness*.[15] He expressed little respect for this attitude, believing that it involved direct rejection of undeniably real and omnipresent anguish. "Civilization is founded on the shambles." If we refuse to recognize this fact, we blind ourselves to deep and terrible realities.

In contrast with healthy-mindedness is the religion of the "sick

[14] He was frankly and deeply interested, for example, in the use of drugs in inducing mystical states; the physical factors did not for him involve the exclusion of the claims of mysticism.

[15] James appears to have appraised the strength of the movement more justly than his contemporaries; witness the extraordinary wealth in recent years of popular psychology which "radiates sunshine" and the conviction that health is to be had for the asking. The vogue of the New Nancy movement (page 135, Coué) seems largely attributable to the same source. The urge for a "healthy-minded" denial of the existence of evil has, to be sure, spread far beyond the limits of religion as such; methods which in the nineteenth century were largely tinged with religious coloring have in recent years become methods of "strengthening one's will," or making one's personality "magnetic" with a view to practical success.

soul." The personal narratives of disillusionment and despair which he quotes remind one of those morbid states in which the individual feels that something is fundamentally wrong not only in his own inner life, but in the world itself. This view, James urges, is more comprehensive than that of the healthy-minded; it faces the whole of life and finds a need for some kind of conquest of evil, or some reconciliation in which evil can somehow be made to contribute to the good. The sick soul cannot understand why the same universe creates both kindness and bitterness, but struggles both to understand the universe and also to grasp the relation of himself to the world. He finds himself striving toward the attainment of happiness, or the happiness of his fellows; yet he commits acts which cause distress to himself or to those whom he loves. He finds himself in a tortured relation both with his world and with his own nature. Wherever the self conceives the powers controlling the universe in personal terms, the evil within one's individual nature is felt to be a violation of one's relation with the universe; sin inflicts suffering upon God Himself. The conflict within the self must somehow be resolved. The soul feels itself torn into two parts, and must be integrated. It tries in vain to find satisfaction in "the senses." This leads to a crisis, and this crisis necessarily takes the form of a struggle involving the ejection of some parts of the personality from the realm of consciousness.[16] Suddenly a solution is reached in which the individual *identifies himself* with what he feels to be good, abandoning his interest in all those dominating satisfactions which appear to be in conflict with his new purpose. Conversion represents a transformation of the self, in which petty aims are subordinated. Conversion, therefore, is the unification of the self through absorption in one group of ideals which evoke such profound devotion that conflicting forces lose their potency.

The last third of *The Varieties of Religious Experience* is devoted to a study of mysticism. James regarded mysticism as that form of experience in which we come into contact with elements in the universe which we cannot grasp through sensory or intellectual processes; as James puts it, it is a window into an invisible world, a way of seeing into realities which are ordinarily hidden. After describing several aspects of mystic experience—such as the fact that to the mystic it is ineffable, and that it takes on the character of complete

[16] The concept of the subconscious had been so widely heralded by Carpenter, Von Hartmann, Janet, F. W. H. Myers, and James's own earlier writings that the assumption that disturbing tendencies were forced into the subconscious was a matter of course.

and absolute reality—he comes to two generalizations as to the content of these states. First, mystic experiences are regularly optimistic, not in the carefree manner of the healthy-minded, but through the *conquest* of despair; they reveal the universe as ultimately good. Second, they represent the world as *unified*. To be sure, James goes on in characteristic fashion to give exceptions, describing the mysticism of despair and conflict. But this typical optimism and sense of unity are for him crucial in determining both the claims of mysticism to validity and the significance of mysticism for the world of values. These aspects of mysticism serve to show that notwithstanding the multitude of religious backgrounds from which mysticism arises, mystics do nevertheless seize upon something which is more than the product of time and place. They achieve for the individual a sense of grasping the meaning of the whole universe, and hence an authority which is absolute. James went the whole way in maintaining that the mystic experience is a genuine, valid way of getting into touch with aspects of the world that one cannot otherwise apprehend. But though the authority of the experience is absolute for the individual, and though full sympathy may be extended to those who live with such a faith, James regards such experiences, by virtue of their very ineffability, as authoritative only for those to whom they directly come.

INTEREST IN PSYCHICAL RESEARCH

In 1882 there was founded in England the Society for Psychical Research, which was to investigate alleged supernormal psychic phenomena, such as telepathy and clairvoyance, hauntings, and communications with the dead. James played a large part in the founding in the United States of an organization for the same purpose (1884); he was active for many years in the examination of evidence for telepathy and for communication with the dead, and acquainted himself at first hand with a great variety of psychic manifestations. This interest, which absorbed his eager attention throughout his life, resulted in some of the most earnest writings he ever penned; indeed, few of his philosophical or psychological writings surpass in vigor and personal self-realization his "Report on Mrs. Piper's Hodgson-Control" [17] and his review of Frederic W. H. Myers' *Human Personality and Its Survival of Bodily Death*.[18] He was early convinced of the reality of telepathy, or communication from

[17] *Proc. Soc. for Psychical Research*, 1909, 23, 1–121.
[18] *Ibid.*, 1903, 18, 22–23.

one mind to another by other means than the mediation of the senses.[19] Whether we can have communication with the dead remained with him a purely open question, while he constantly insisted on the legitimacy and great importance of the matter.

JAMES'S PHILOSOPHY

The distinction between psychology and philosophy was never sharp for James, and even when he was working on *The Principles of Psychology* he was making philosophical history; but after the publication of *The Principles* most of his energies went into problems with which American psychologists, proud of their new science, had rather little commerce. Some of his studies dealt with the analysis of the ultimate basis of knowledge: how it is that our minds can know anything, how we can get in touch with reality. The popular notion of the correspondence between an external and an internal world seemed to him misleading. He found at various times three different solutions to his problem. He became identified with three schools of thought, all of which have ventured upon a theory of knowledge, and have had something to say also of the mind-body relation. His *Pragmatism* (1907) and *The Meaning of Truth* (1909), though expressly representing a compilation and a revision of earlier teachings rather than a new school, mark the beginning of that contemporary pragmatist school which places its emphasis upon the relativity of knowledge, the impossibility of obtaining absolute truth, and the essentially adaptive nature of all thought. Another school which is heavily indebted to James is neorealism. In his essay "Does Consciousness Exist?" James puts forward the view that the world, in so far as we can ever know it, consists simply of things that are perceived; mind is not an independent function which knows these things, but comprises the same entities.[20] Mental events and physical events are distinguishable only through the fact that the order in which events are perceived depends not simply upon the events at a given point in space but upon the life of the organism. This view, already sketched by Mach,[21] offered no escape to those who had admitted Mach's premises; it followed that "consciousness" does *not* exist, but is simply a loose name for the fact that events are related not only to time and space but to the life of the experiencing organ-

[19] See, for example, "What Psychical Research Has Accomplished," in the volume *The Will to Believe*. The article is a compilation of three previous papers.
[20] *J. Phil., Psychol., and Sci. Meth.*, 1904, 1.
[21] *Contributions to the Analysis of Sensations* (1886).

ism. Nor can "consciousness of" events change their character. But usually two persons take part in different events, and in this their personal identity consists. Neorealism, which arose chiefly among a group of American philosophers early in the present century, has developed these conceptions to take account of many corollaries which James was disposed to neglect. Among the difficulties which have engaged closest attention are the problem of error (especially in relation to hallucinations, illusions, and delusions), and the analysis of mental events which do not at first blush seem to be identical with physical events; for example, feeling and will. Behaviorism, as we shall see (page 262), naturally found in this doctrine much that was congenial. Holt succeeded in defining consciousness itself in terms of an adjustment of the organism,[22] and in subsuming both cognition and volition under the head of muscular response. The behaviorist's dismissal of all "mental" events was most easily supported by the adoption of the neorealist contention that there really are no events to be added to the events of which physical science takes account. While behaviorism has in general declined to enter into discussions of epistemology, it has often tacitly,[23] and sometimes explicitly,[24] affiliated itself with this form of psychophysical monism.

Another solution for the mind-body problem was offered by James in the form of a new variety of dualism.[25] The interaction of soul and body had been recognized in *The Principles*. The brain, he suggested, may be not the *basis* for mental life, but merely the agency which *transmits* psychic realities into the terms which organisms use in their relations to their environment. The idea that psychic events have a genuine domain of their own, not explicable through biological concepts, appears again, as we noted, in his discussion of mysticism (page 204). He felt that something of immense value could be learned from phenomena which appeared to him to indicate that the organism comes into contact with superbiological forces. The relation of man to reality seemed to include much that was not to be found in the biological structure of personality.

In evaluating James's place and influence, account must be taken of his role as teacher, and of the American and European readiness to respond to his writings. During his period of service as Professor

---

[22] *The Concept of Consciousness* (1914).

[23] See Watson, J. B., *Psychology from the Standpoint of a Behaviorist* (1919).

[24] Holt, E. B., *The Freudian Wish* (1915).

[25] *Human Immortality* (1898).

of Psychology at Harvard until 1897, and during the following years, in which his chief energies were given to philosophy, he enjoyed as pupils a large number of those who have become eminent as psychologists in the present century.[26] In every corner of the globe where psychology was known, his name was one to conjure with. Tens of thousands read *The Principles* and hundreds of thousands, as college students, the one-volume *Briefer Course*. For a long time it seemed silly to remark that James was America's greatest psychologist, for in the judgment of scholars and of laymen alike, any second to him was a poor second. But it must be remembered that even at the height of his powers he rejected the trends that were most popular in American psychology; and to the later popular trends, such as that toward the measurement of intelligence, he turned a deaf ear. It is not surprising that as the ocean of time has closed over him he has become one of the immortals, one of the eternal spirits, rather than a presiding genius moving with the newer trends. European psychologists, reading fewer things and rereading them more times, less concerned with being up-to-the-minute, very much less concerned with the winning of prestige by performing beautiful experiments like those of the biologists, have in recent decades known James better than his countrymen; they have always invited his spirit to the feast when any great new psychological venture, empirical or theoretical, was to be broached. To many Americans, he remains "back there," framed in time; to most Europeans, he marches on. Some may feel that European psychology is too somnolent to take note of anything that has occurred in the field since 1890; others, that American psychology is too immature, too gadget-minded, to be resonant to its greatest figure. There is, of course, some measure of truth in both judgments. Putting it all less invidiously, the research tools which he distrusted have become the chief keys to a technical world for which he had no taste. Whatever the reasons, his pages speak to a generation of American psychologists whose interests and problems are in large part foreign to his own. Today they feel they should read him as a "classic." How he would have hated that word!

All this is vaguely sensed by those thoughtful Americans who are not professional psychologists: artists, physicians, men of affairs; the writers and the readers of novels, essays, plays; those who roam widely and speculate freely upon the infinite fullness, complexity, subtlety of human experience. It has become a part of our desper-

[26] Among his pupils were Angell, Calkins, Healy, Sidis, Thorndike, Woodworth, Yerkes, and many others whose names are familiar.

ately solemn growing up to put away the yen for these wider horizons. As it learns to walk, science must attend to the "hayfoot, strawfoot," its ordered mastery of the terrain just ahead. But the question is whether, in forgetting the vistas, the feet are necessarily planted in a direction that leads to major discoveries. In forgetting James one may feel that one's scientific conscience may come to rest. Yet it would be worth while, sometime, for the general historian of science to tell us just what happens when science forgoes the concern with the teeming richness and immediacy of personal experience.

REFERENCES

James, William, *The Letters of William James,* ed. by Henry James, 2 vols., Little, Brown, 1920

———, *The Principles of Psychology,* 2 vols., Holt, 1890.

———, *The Varieties of Religious Experience,* Longmans, Green, 1902

Matthiessen, Francis O., *The James Family: A Group Biography,* Knopf, 1947

Perry, Ralph Barton, *The Thought and Character of William James* 2 vols., Little, Brown, 1935

Chapter 15

STRUCTURAL AND FUNCTIONAL
TYPES OF PSYCHOLOGY

> *At all events [say the Stoics] an image is contemplated in a
> different light by a man skilful in art from that in which it is
> viewed by a man ignorant of art.* DIOGENES LAERTIUS

A s we turn now to the psychology of the twentieth century, in
which the wealth of material will require that each topic,
considered individually in its turn, be brought up to the
present period, it will be well to get a brief over-all view of the forces
that were at work or in the making. A short sketch of national
differences in psychological interest was given in commenting on
the rise of the laboratory movement (pages 149 ff.); here we may
attempt a more specific characterization of men and their projects,
and instead of simply summarizing what was said earlier, make
mention of many other figures hitherto unnamed who, already at
work in 1900, belong primarily to the twentieth century. Imagine
an observer on a high parapet above the world, armed with a
telescope which could pick out all the psychological doings as the
twentieth century began. What could the observer have seen?

In the German universities, many eager devotees of the new experimentalism: Wundt at Leipzig, at sixty-eight going strong, and
delving into folk psychology as he kept an eye on the young experimentalists; Ebbinghaus at Breslau, ardent associationist, concerned
with memory and with intelligence and its testing; G. E. Müller at
Göttingen, likewise indefatigable student of memory, dean of psychophysicists; Stumpf at Berlin, experimental analyst of music;
Stern at Hamburg, who was destined soon to create a great new
place for child psychology and for psychological applications to law
and industry; Külpe at Würzburg, about to launch a new experimental movement dealing with attitudes and thought processes.

Everywhere the new experimentalism could be seen creeping into education, too, and into psychiatry. If the man at the telescope was not too rigidly and narrowly an experimental psychologist, he would also have discerned many other lively figures whose reflective energies served to define new psychological problems: men like the physicist Mach, who asked searching questions about sensations; the philosopher Dilthey, who rejected associationism and stressed the unity, the structural wholeness, of the process of *understanding;* over the border, in Austria, the former priest Brentano, who saw in psychology the study of psychological *acts* rather than of *states;* and sitting behind his patient's couch, the thoughtful physician Sigmund Freud, for whom dark and unspeakable things were becoming both clear and communicable.

Glancing northward to the Scandinavian lands, our observer would have noted the scholarly and thoughtful Höffding, and the active laboratory worker Lehman, at Copenhagen, and a few very limited beginnings elsewhere. Turning eastward to the Russian Empire, he would have espied an occasional idealist philosopher continuing some of the German traditions, and two indomitable and hard-driving physiologists, Bekhterev and Pavlov, whose studies of reflexes were soon to make history. In northern and central Italy he would have seen a few drawing their inspiration from Wundt; he would have seen Mosso and his physiological colleagues concerned with fatigue and with the emotions; Lombroso and the anthropologists concerned with body types related to personality. Madame Montessori was building educational practice around the stimulation of the senses and the encouragement of activity. In German-speaking Switzerland were psychologically minded psychiatrists; in French-speaking Switzerland the traditional concern for educational psychology was expressed by Claparède, who was active also in the laboratory; while Flournoy made pioneer studies of dissociated states and strange utterances in the "language of Mars," and gave psychical research his sustained attention.

In France, while medical men in the provinces contributed occasional psychological papers to hospital gazettes, and hypnotic practice continued at Nancy, almost everything psychological was centered in Paris. There Ribot interpreted British and German psychology to his countrymen and carried on the great tradition in medical psychology; Pierre Janet had achieved eminence through his sustained and judicious study of hysteria and his many contacts with physiological, experimental, and social psychology; Alfred Binet was delving into the nature of dissociation and suggestibility;

of the thought processes and of intelligence. In Belgium a research interest in child psychology was already apparent; in the Netherlands the laboratory movement was supplemented, in the person of Heymans, by interest in the general psychology of individual differences.

In the same matter of individual differences, Francis Galton, across the Channel, was finding in Karl Pearson a worthy successor, where biometric and statistical prowess so greatly influenced psychology that a whole new branch of quantitative work—factor analysis (page 364)—came into being. English and Scottish universities interpreted the associationist, evolutionist, and Scottish traditions in their own ways. Ward was busy studying deep dispositions unknown to consciousness. Frederic W. H. Myers, in the last years of his life, was still struggling with the theory of the "subliminal self," with the nature of genius and the creative; Stout was lucidly portraying psychology as the study of the processes of knowing, feeling, and striving; and the young physician McDougall, rebelling against associationism, was beginning to ask whether Darwinian evolutionism and the primitive strivings of all animal life could receive justice in a psychological system. Sully was writing of child psychology; Hobhouse and Lloyd Morgan of animal intelligence, instinct, and learning.

As he turned his instrument toward the Western Hemisphere, he would have noted dozens of new American laboratories where preoccupations were similar to those he had seen in Germany. Among the persons and centers of activity typical of the new era were the scholarly Titchener and his Cornell laboratory, with its rigorous experimental studies of introspective problems; Stanley Hall and genetic psychology at Clark; Baldwin and genetic psychology at Princeton; Cattell, at Columbia, turning more and more from Wundtian studies to studies of individual differences, and across the street at Teachers College the young Thorndike, fresh from Harvard, with his new curves and theories to show how his cats had learned to solve problems; Calkins, experimentalist and student of the self, at Wellesley; Jastrow at Wisconsin and Pillsbury at Michigan, interested in studies of the cutaneous and kinesthetic senses. At Chicago John Dewey taught a James-like philosophy of wholeness of activity and of adjustment. At Yale, Ladd, a philosopher who had written a *Physiological Psychology* in the new mode, had brought in Edward Scripture as experimentalist just as James had brought in young Münsterberg to run the Harvard laboratory. At the University of Pennsylvania an observer would note a new thing in the world, a

"psychological clinic" for the study of the psychologically handicapped. In Canada he would have seen British traditions loyally
followed; in the rest of the New World he would have seen psychology still an aspect of philosophy and of education, with much
reliance on French sources. In India, China, and Japan he would
have found huge masses of psychology embedded in the ancient
systems of wisdom, but not as yet distilled into a form with which
the research-minded Occident could easily cope.

But what about the general spirit, the basic credo of all the new
psychology, as contrasted with all the old? Must we necessarily
remain content with this piecemeal geographic or panoramic view
of men and enterprises; is there no possibility of seeing the forest
despite the trees, no means of grouping and articulating these impressions? Grouping and organizing is indeed possible, and it shall
be attempted. The only danger is that the reader will attach too
much importance to one rather than another equally legitimate
method of organizing.

There is some reason to believe that the *best* (but not by any
means the *only possible*) take-off point is to ask how psychologists
conceived the fundamental task of psychology as a science. It may
be legitimate to say, in the broadest possible terms, that most
psychologists who were concerned with such questions were influenced primarily by the methods and concepts of the physical
sciences as they then existed. Now the traditional method of the
physical sciences was to discover, by analysis, the particles of which
wholes are composed, and then to formulate laws relating to the
interaction of such particles. The atomic theory in chemistry had
powerfully confirmed the belief that this is the method of science par
excellence. A psychologist who wanted to be a scientist would inevitably find in the sensationist and the associationist traditions a close
parallel to the world view of the physical sciences. If introspection
reveals sensations and other mental elements, and if the study of
association, or memory, or attention, can reveal the form of the
interrelation of such elements, the scientist's program is mapped out.
And it is not the fact of individual differences, but universal laws
like the laws of physics, that interest the scientist.

To many psychologists, however, such questions about *elements*
and *interconnections* had taken on a completely new meaning after
Darwin. It was not that there was anything wrong about seeking
elements and connections, but that everything looked very different
when one asked about *functions*, especially the functions of whole
things such as animals and plants, which, in the evolutionary strug-

gle, have survived not as organs, nor as tissues, but as going concerns about which one always has to ask: How is this activity related to adaptation and to survival? Here individual differences achieve fundamental importance. The issue could not be resolved by debate. The issue of loyalty to the method of analysis, as contrasted with loyalty to the evolutionary approach, was likely to be decided by reference to different conceptions of science, and to orientation to different kinds of facts. Indeed, as Hollingworth has suggested,[1] such issues regarding the question as to which facts are basic are to be decided partly by the predispositions of psychologists toward one rather than another form of sense experience.

By and large, the people who, about 1900, wanted to write a psychology in terms of primary forms of experience and the inter-relations of sense experience, may be called *structuralists*, though later their dominant figure preferred to write *existentialists;* those who stressed adjustment and adaptation were known in those years as *functionalists*. These two "psychological schools," in the extreme form noted here, were American products; Europe was destined to yield new psychological schools at a later period.

TITCHENER AND STRUCTURAL PSYCHOLOGY

The acknowledged leader of the structuralists was Titchener,[2] whose system and whose experiments have been generally recognized as constituting him the spiritual successor to Wundt. Completing his training at Leipzig and coming to the United States, he became at Cornell in 1892 the director of a psychological laboratory which served as a model in the study of those problems which Wundt had attacked. The unlimited erudition of his four-volume *Experimental Psychology* (1905) was paralleled by the systematic training which taught students how to introspect and to make systematic reports on events introspectively observed. For psychology dealt with experience from the point of view of the observer.

Titchener's structuralism may be regarded as a rigorous simplification of Wundt's. Mental states are made up of sensations, images, and feelings. But the only "simple" feelings are pleasantness and unpleasantness, other feeling states being in reality compounds or

---

[1] Hollingworth, H. L., "Sensuous Determinants of Psychological Attitude," *Psychol. Rev.*, 1928, 35, 93–117.

[2] For example, "The Postulates of a Structural Psychology," *Philos. Rev.*, 1898, 7, 449–65; "Structural and Functional Psychology," *ibid.*, 1899, 8, 290–99; *A Textbook of Psychology* (1909–10).

"sense feelings." "Apperception" is discarded, but "attention" is the process by which sensations or images take on greater "clearness." "Meaning" is simply the context in which a mental structure appears; if it has any further signification, the problem concerns logic and not psychology. Among the main problems of such structuralism are: the elements and their attributes, their modes of composition, the structural characteristics of familiar types of compounds, the nature and role of attention. These problems appear in the work of Titchener's laboratory, work which, though constantly inspired and directed by his interests, has been published under the names of his pupils. The list of Titchener's personal publications gives, therefore, no suggestion of the wealth of material produced. His pupils established themselves at many universities; many of them came together with him annually to exchange research reports. After his death in 1927, this group, incorporated as the Society of Experimental Psychologists, has carried on much as it had during his lifetime.

A few specific problems may serve to indicate the range of Titchener's interests and contributions. Here we find several systematic studies of sensations from skin and viscera.[3] He was concerned with the question of "mixed feelings":[4] the question whether pleasantness and unpleasantness may exist in consciousness at the same instant. He was much interested in the later report by Nafe that feelings are essentially sensory, not as independent and distinctive as they seem to be.[5]

Geissler examined the various degrees of clearness involved in attention.[6] Is there in attention a gradual transition from maximal to minimal clearness, or are there a number of definable "steps"? The reports of some subjects indicated two distinct levels, focal clearness and marginal clearness. Other subjects reported several levels of clearness. Here, as elsewhere, subjects trained in introspection were used; Titchener took seriously only the testimony of subjects who had learned to introspect; that is, to observe and describe accurately the mental states experienced. And while individual differences between subjects were sometimes revealed in introspec-

---

[3] Boring, E. G., "The Sensations of the Alimentary Canal," *Amer. J. Psychol.*, 1915, 26, 1–57.

[4] *The Elementary Psychology of Feeling and Attention* (1908).

[5] Nafe, J. P., "An Experimental Study of the Affective Qualities," *Amer. J. Psychol.*, 1924, 35, 507–44.

[6] Geissler, L. R., "The Measurement of Attention," *Amer. J. Psychol.*, 1909, 20, 473–529.

tion, Titchener remained convinced that science was concerned with general laws, not with individual differences.

It must not be concluded that all the Cornell material relied upon the adequacy of verbal report. This is evident in an ingenious experiment dealing (in part) with the relation of percept to image.[7] Perky seated her subjects in a dark room before a screen. She asked them in some experiments to "project" upon a screen images of familiar objects named to them, such as apple, banana, knife. Unknown to them, in some experiments she threw a faint picture upon the screen. The subjects were usually unaware that a "real" picture had been added; some of them made the comment, in such cases, that their imagery was especially good that day. In another series of experiments, a picture was actually projected and the subjects were asked to observe it. Unknown to them, the illumination of the faint image was sometimes reduced to zero, so that no objective picture remained. Nevertheless, most subjects continued to "see" the picture, quite unaware that no illumination came to them from the screen. Not one of the twenty subjects could consistently differentiate between images and faint sensations. The desire to find clear points of difference between sensation and image must apparently be tempered by the recognition that under special conditions the two phenomena may be indistinguishable.[8] Such a result as this objective failure in reporting the presence or absence of an external object is of interest to all experimental psychology, whether it stresses introspection or not.

FUNCTIONALISM

In contrast to such emphasis upon the problems of mental structure, there had arisen long before 1900 a widespread demand for a more intensive study of problems of function. We have seen that James was unsympathetic toward the attempt to analyze states of consciousness into elements. He was but one of a large number who in the closing years of the nineteenth century expressed the feeling that "mind" should be not a structural but a dynamic concept. Many psychologists began to shift their emphasis from states to processes. In fact, the change of emphasis was followed by a change

[7] Perky, C. W., "An Experimental Study of Imagination," *Amer. J. Psychol.*, 1910, 21, 422–52. The experiment described is preliminary to a comparison of memory images with those of imagination.

[8] See, for example, Read, C., "On the Difference between Percepts and Images," *Brit. J. Psychol.*, 1908, 2, 323–37.

in the whole conception of what psychology is. In place of the analysis of experience, many sought to substitute statements of the ways in which the mind functions, especially in relation to the life of the whole organism. So many individuals toward the close of the century exhibit these tendencies that this book can give only a kaleidoscopic view of the transition, arbitrarily selecting elements from the writings of several whose systems are widely divergent.

A few years before the publication of James's *Principles of Psychology* there had appeared Höffding's *Outline of Psychology* (1887). Höffding used as keys to psychology not ultimate *states of experience*, but ultimate *types of mental activity*. This was, in a sense, a return to faculty psychology. The faculty psychology has been buried repeatedly and has come from the grave, put on its apparel, and gone on again. For faculty psychology is in essence a method of stating mental processes in a few main categories. But an important distinction must be made. For convenience we say that we remember, we decide, we judge, we compare; but these may be either names for ultimate and distinct functions or merely useful labels for complex activities which require further study. This points to one respect in which Höffding regarded his approach as differing from the faculty psychology of earlier centuries, especially medieval and early German psychology. Höffding was content to lump together many specific acts under one common name; he did not presuppose a formal potency by virtue of which the acts described took place. For him, there existed the same three kinds of activity which had been so frequently named by the faculty psychologists—knowing, feeling, and willing. Each type, instead of being *part* of the personality (as the associationists had it), was a way in which the whole personality acted.

His treatment of cognitive functions was the one from which we derive least that is original; we can pass over it with the statement that the experimental methods and results of examination into sensory functions were accepted and sympathetically treated. The study of feeling and willing are more significant. Höffding gave descriptions of complex affective processes such as those relating to religion and ethics, but gave them in terms of physiological as well as of introspective psychology. These complex processes were approached genetically. His treatment of the will may superficially appear to be based chiefly on Wundt's concept of the will; but there is an important difference. Wundt, taking an evolutionary viewpoint, had made the will a central and primordial reality; but in his hands it had nevertheless suffered the inevitable fate of reduction to a series of feelings. With Höffding, however, we find that the will cannot be analyzed into more elementary forms of experience. The will is, in fact, an elementary and ultimate way of *acting*. Höffding undertook to go back to the beginnings of the will, as shown in the study of the evolutionary series, beginning with the lowest organisms. As a mode of action, will may show itself first in simple approaching or withdrawing, becoming more and more complex as the situations arousing it are more and more complex. The genetic approach appears also in the study of the individual child's growth from blind reflex activity (here we may be reminded of Biran's doctrine, page 57) to developed consciousness, where a variety of impulses is integrated into orderly conduct, and expressed in a conscious decision. Both in the phylogenetic and in the ontogenetic series, will was shown to be a process which cannot intelligibly be described as a mere series of states.

But the most original of Höffding's contributions was his theory of the subconscious. Here we find a definite resolution to abandon the quest for a structural knowledge of what goes on outside consciousness, together with a clear and forceful description of the significance of *processes* which lie outside consciousness. The structuralist, we may say, must take his choice between three ways of looking at the subconscious, or three assumptions as to what becomes of mental states when they lapse from the introspective field. Subconscious states may be regarded as (1) *identical in nature* with conscious states; or (2) as *conscious but impersonal;* or (3) simply as brain states, *with no mental counterpart*. This whole attempt to find the intrinsic structural quality of the subconscious is foreign to Höffding's outlook and method. For him the subconscious is essentially a name for a group of processes of which we are not aware. These processes may frequently approach or recede from the margin where they would be introspectively clear, although not changing in their essential functions. It is what they accomplish, what part they play in the course of mental events, that chiefly matters. For instance, an idea may lapse from consciousness and yet the attitude we had when it was in consciousness may remain. For Höffding, the essential thing about the subconscious is that it exists as a real group of activities; these activities may at times rise to the introspective level or lapse from it, without in any sense changing their dynamic character. "The subconscious" is a name for all activities which do not happen at the moment to be in the field of introspection. As to the question whether things outside of consciousness are the *same* as they are in consciousness, assuming that the process is the same,

Höffding adopted a complete agnosticism. We can, to be sure, discover introspectively many degrees of consciousness, from the most definite to the most obscure. Similarly, it may well be that, from the threshold or most indefinite region of consciousness all the way down to the purely mechanical process, there may exist degrees of consciousness which we cannot observe. All this, however, Höffding regarded as unverifiable and from the functional standpoint inessential.

British psychologists in this era were primarily interested in functional problems; Ward (page 172) and McDougall (page 403) were prominent examples. Stout's *Manual of Psychology* (1899) illustrates the same division of mind into a few main ways of *acting* rather than a few main types of *experience*, as noted in the case of Höffding; the process of cognition, for example, overshadows the analysis of cognitive *states*. Stout gives a discussion of memory in many ways similar to that of Herbart and Beneke, emphasizing the *disposition* of experiences to return into consciousness after a period of eclipse. When material has been memorized, the appearance of the first item in consciousness creates a disposition for the others to recur. Emphasis is not upon the structural similarity between an experience and its reproduction, but upon the tendency of experience to reinstate itself. As we have seen, associationism had suffered decline and fall largely because of the structuralism inherent in it. Stout is representative of the general tendency in late nineteenth-century British psychology to make mental activity, rather than the analysis of consciousness, the central problem. His emphasis upon conation, or striving, an emphasis shared by many other leaders in twentieth-century British psychology, is perhaps an even clearer indication of the trend toward dynamic conceptions.

The same tendency is strikingly apparent in the schools of physiological psychology. Münsterberg, who came to the United States in 1892, formulated an ingenious theory as to the nature of psychological events, in which an ultimate type of process, rather than an ultimate type of structure, was emphasized. Höffding and Stout had taught that we must look upon mind as a group of functions, but did not tell us what physiological processes to seek as correlates for mental acts. The "action theory" of Münsterberg was a clear-cut doctrine as to the physiological unit which corresponds to the simplest act in experience.[9] The theory states that when the stimulation of a sense organ leads to a conscious event and a motor response, the sensation arises not in connection with the mere excite-

9 *Grundzüge der Psychologie*, Vol. I (1900).

ment of a sensory area of the brain, but with the passage of the neural impulse from sensory to motor regions.

Structuralists had in general assumed that the neurological counterpart of psychological elements is the excitation of particular points in the cortex (cf. specific energies, page 93). The experience of pain when the finger is burned had been correlated, for example, with the specific local excitement in the general-sense area of the cortex. In visual hallucination we may perhaps suffer from something acting directly on a point within the visual area in the cortex, although neither the sensory nor the motor neurones of the usual neural pathway have been brought into action. Münsterberg asserted, in contrast to this, that all life is impulsive, tends to action. We know nothing about sensory experiences of a purely passive nature. Says Münsterberg, every experience means not simply the excitation of a sensory region in the cortex, but the passage of that excitation through the motor centers and out to the motor response mechanisms. The more open the path for motor discharge, the more clearly conscious the sensation (or other experience). Münsterberg insisted that consciousness occurs only when there is a *complete circuit* from sense organ to motor response. This theory does not necessarily exclude a structural approach to consciousness; but logical consequences are not the same as historical consequences, and the view was one of many which turned attention from states to activities, seen as a part of the behavior of the whole individual. Many whose conception of psychology differed radically from Münsterberg's have agreed that the whole sensorimotor arc is the true physiological unit for each psychological event.

Serious objections were immediately offered to that part of the theory which stated that the more open the pathway, the more conscious must be the mental process attending it. Münsterberg's neglect of reflex action was serious; for these pathways, as especially "open," ought, according to the theory, to involve clear consciousness. Another serious objection was the fact that the passage of the impulse becomes easier and easier as a habit is formed. Something which requires much effort, and is at first very clearly conscious, becomes gradually easy and smooth-running, but less and less conscious. The action theory would demand the reverse. Montague consequently suggested that the degree of consciousness is not in direct but in *inverse* ratio to the openness of the pathway from sensory to motor elements in the cortex.[10]

[10] Montague, W. P., "Consciousness a Form of Energy," in *Essays Philosophical and Psychological in Honor of William James* (1908).

A compromise between these two positions was offered by Washburn. She suggested that "consciousness accompanies a certain ratio of excitation to inhibition in a motor discharge. . . . If the amount of excitation either sinks below a certain minimum or rises above a certain maximum, consciousness is lessened. . . . The kind of consciousness which we call an 'image' or 'centrally excited sensation,' such as remembered or imagined sensation, also depends on the simultaneous excitation and inhibition of a motor pathway. The 'association of ideas' depends on the fact that when the full motor response to a stimulus is prevented from occurring, a weakened type of response may take place which we shall call 'tentative movement.' " [11] From such conceptions, Washburn built up a "motor psychology," which while making abundant use of introspective material,[12] was of a consistently dynamic character. (The "motor theories of consciousness" are still very much with us; cf. page 265).

E. B. Holt, in the same era, suggested that consciousness is simply a name for a specific kind of sensorimotor adjustment to an object.[13] To be conscious of an apple is to adjust one's eye muscles and so on to it. Consciousness is the bringing of an object into a particular relation with the organism; this specific relation is one kind of adjustment of the muscles to it. This view derives from the neorealist belief that objects outside consciousness have the same qualities as those within consciousness (page 206); cognition does not *create* the qualities which appear in experience, but simply relates them to the life of the organism. Consciousness is not something "rolled up in the skull." This concept is perhaps more radically dynamic than any heretofore named.

These are but a few illustrations to indicate that the increasing emphasis on *motor discharge* contained enough dynamite to lead to a great many explosions. The emphasis on process as opposed to structure became very evident not only in theory but in the experimental laboratory. Külpe, trained in Wundt's methods, early came to the conclusion that the relatively simple type of conscious association to which both British associationists and Wundt had given emphasis was not sufficient to explain the great variability in the types of volition found in the same individual from one experiment to another (cf. below, pages 228 ff.). The subject's behavior in the experimental situation depended not only upon elements in

---

11 *Movement and Mental Imagery* (1908), pp. 25–26.

12 This hypothesis did not in any sense involve an *attack* upon structural psychology; Titchener himself was not averse to such physiological hypotheses.

13 For example, *The Freudian Wish* (1915).

consciousness, but upon adjustments or attitudes, which might operate decisively although not present to introspective analysis. These findings regarding the reality of unconscious determinants to action undermined to some extent the structural assumptions which had come down from associationism. Even in relation to the mere reproduction of learned material, such a view was significant. But in relation to the task of adjusting to a new situation, the discovery that the course of mental life could not be understood in terms of its predecessors in the introspective consciousness involved the necessity of admitting as a real problem for psychology the study of processes outside of consciousness, and, inevitably, a shift of emphasis to more dynamic conceptions. Simply because in many cases they could not be introspectively analyzed, attitudes had to be treated as functional units.

Külpe's recognition of all this led to important consequences in the field of systematic psychology in the twenty years which followed. From it followed the experimental study of both the conscious and the unconscious aspects of "attitudes," with a view to determining to what extent the language of structuralism can describe, analyze, and classify them. This field of investigation was explored in Külpe's laboratory at Würzburg by men whose training and outlook were essentially structuralistic; and many of their findings were accepted and utilized as enrichments to structural psychology. But in accepting these findings, structuralism itself tended, so to speak, to become more functional; statics already had begun to give way to dynamics.[14] And this new department of introspective psychology, while analyzing the elements of thought, showed very clearly the need of a more adequate knowledge of the functional relations subsisting between these elements.

Shortly after Külpe's first recognition of the role of adjustment in volition came the development of the "functional psychology" of the United States. The sources of the movement are quite complex. A factor of importance had been the emergence of John Dewey in the eighties and nineties.[15] Borrowing from the general revolt against associationism in the late nineteenth century, and most of all from William James, he turned his attention chiefly to the

---

[14] A summary of the newer conception of structuralism is given in Titchener's *Experimental Psychology of the Thought-Processes* (1909), in which sensation itself is treated genetically. And Titchener insists (pp. 27 ff.) that his psychology, like Wundt's, differs from the psychology of the associationists in making sensation *processes* rather than *states*.

[15] *Psychology* (1886) was his earliest book in the field.

organism's ways of adjusting to environment.[16] At the University of Chicago in the early years of this century, when his thought was concerned primarily with social problems and with the philosophy of education, Dewey had considerable influence upon a group of younger psychologists. His junior colleague J. R. Angell soon became well known. With the help of kindred spirits, including Judd, who had studied with Wundt and had served in Ladd's department at Yale, a distinctive school developed, whose chief contribution lay in emphasis upon adjustment, and specifically, in a genetic treatment of attitudes.[17]

It happened that the revolt against the all-sufficiency of structuralism was waged on many different fronts at once. We can note the essential kinship of all these shades of opinion by comparing the functionalism of Höffding directly with that of Judd. Höffding had taught that in order to understand the will we must regard it as a *process* to be approached through a genetic treatment. Judd maintained that we cannot understand attitudes by analyzing them introspectively, but only through a genetic understanding of the functions represented by the attitudes.

Some other new experimental trends which marked a protest against the Wundt-Titchener conception of psychology will be sketched in the following chapter, but it may be best to conclude with this simple statement of the opposed aims of structuralists and functionalists, and to add a few words about the controversy as it looks from the vantage point of today.

From the standpoint of today there seems to have been scant logical necessity for this gulf that separated structuralists and functionalists of forty years ago. The structuralist recognized problems of activity and adaptation; the functionalist agreed that consciousness was interesting and important. Differences of opinion about the nature of science, and the investment of many an ego in the issue, kept the schools apart.

Functionalism did not long maintain itself as a school; but much of the emphasis lived on in behaviorism (Chapter 18) and in the increasing tendency to ask less about consciousness, more about activity—a tendency already evident in such men as Cattell and

---

[16] For example, "The Reflex Arc Concept in Psychology," *Psychol. Rev.*, 1896, 3.

[17] The treatment of motor phenomena in Judd's *Psychology* (1907) gives a summary and classic statement of the doctrines of the school. Mental processes were brought into relation with muscular adjustments which were stated not in introspective but in functional terms. The whole question whether such muscular adjustments *can* be introspectively approached will be present with us in the next chapter.

Thorndike. Structuralism, or existentialism, was eloquently defended by Titchener's posthumous volume *Systematic Psychology: Prolegomena* (1929), a volume showing that he never abandoned his primary beliefs. Many of his former pupils go on in their studies inspired by their Cornell training. But the chief issue today is how to integrate structural and functional data in relation to each psychological problem. Just as it had been evident to Aristotle that *awareness* is not necessarily the same thing as *psychological activity*, so the evolutionary psychology of today strives to conceive of awareness as one kind, but not the only kind, of adaptive psychological response.

REFERENCES

Boring, Edwin G., *A History of Experimental Psychology*, Century, 1929; pp. 402–13; 538–44

Heidbreder, Edna, *Seven Psychologies*, Century, 1933

Murchison, Carl A., ed., *A History of Psychology in Autobiography*, 3 vols., Clark University Press, 1930–36: chapters by Höffding and Judd

Woodworth, Robert S., *Contemporary Schools of Psychology*, rev. ed., Ronald Press, 1948

Chapter 16

THE WÜRZBURG SCHOOL

Shall we not, then, as we have lots of time, retrace our steps a little, and examine ourselves calmly and earnestly, in order to see what these images in us are?   PLATO

WE HAVE GIVEN some attention to the revolt against the fundamental tenets of that modern structuralism which had begun with Locke and had been perfected by associationism, by Wundt, and by Titchener. One phase of the revolt must now be more closely considered.

Among many rebellious figures one of the great pioneers was Brentano, who built up a psychology in which the "act" rather than the content of experience was central.[1] His distinction between the content of any experience and the act of experiencing, a distinction stated in a few words, is really quite involved; and to grasp it we must go back at least as far as Leibnitz's doctrine of apperception (page 21), the process by which we become conscious of our experiences. Kant and Herbart, though with personal additions to the theory, had emphasized the *activity* of mind in taking hold of the elements of experience which would otherwise have no relation to the self; we may have experience without cognizing the fact that the experience is there, and the quality of the experience is distinct from the act by which it is recognized. In Brentano's hands this conception took a more radical form. Instead of drawing a distinction between an experience and the act of recognizing that we have it, Brentano held that the distinction is to be made between the experience as a structure and the experience as a way of acting. For example, in the case of sensation there is a difference between the quality "red" and the *sensing* of "red." The true subject matter of psychology, said Brentano, is not, for example, "red," but the process of "experiencing red," the act which the mind carries out when it,

[1] *Psychologie vom empirischen Standpunkte* (1874).

so to speak, "reddens." We should perhaps substitute verbs instead of the nouns heretofore characteristic of psychology. The experience as we look at a red object is a way of behaving, and this way of behaving is to be distinguished from the quality of redness as such, which is a purely passive thing. This is rather closely related to the tendency discussed above in relation to Höffding, the change of emphasis from structure to process. Brentano's is one of the most influential systems of modern psychology. For if Brentano was right, the content of mind pointed to something outside itself ("intentionality") within the framework of the act, and mind could never be reduced to content.

Another who, though a structuralist, contributed to the same movement, was Mach.[2] He held that the world of physics and the world of psychology are the same world (cf. page 206), but that psychology must take account of certain sensations which correspond not to individual physical objects but to relations obtaining between them. If, said Mach, we see three separate spots, to each of which we react by perception, there is in our experience something more than one spot plus another, plus a third.[3] There is a relation present, and that spatial relation is just as much a quality of experience as any of the independent spots before us. In fact, the spatial quality by which we get triangularity is just as observable introspectively as any of the other elements. This can be illustrated by arranging the dots in different ways and noticing that we get different "sensations of space." Mach was structural in his way of thinking, but his emphasis was on the inadequacy of the traditional categories of sensory experience.

Following upon Mach came the work (in 1890 and thereafter) of Von Ehrenfels[4] and the school of *Gestaltqualität* (a word which we may roughly define as "the quality conferred by a pattern"). This school maintained that in all perception qualities appear which are something more than separate sensory entities, something added by the subject; namely, the quality of the configuration or form or pattern presented. For example, the quality of triangularity or the quality of squareness given in the above illustrations is typical of *all* perceptual reactions in that all percepts involve qualities dependent on the way in which sensory elements are integrated. This doctrine was in contrast to the Wundtian systematic psychology. Wundt had, indeed, recognized "creative synthesis," but the products

[2] *Contributions to the Analysis of Sensations* (1886).
[3] The point had been made by Laromiguière nearly a century earlier.
[4] *Vierteljahrsschr. f. wiss, Philos.*, 1890, 14.

created had to be stated in terms of the synthesis of the elements assumed in his system. The school of *Gestaltqualität* was concerned to show that the process of meeting a situation is more than the sum total of the elements presented by the separate parts of the situation; it has a quality given by the form of perception. A melody played in a new key may have no *element* in common with what is already known, yet be instantly recognized.

Now none of these contributions in the seventies, eighties, and nineties was expressly experimental. It remained for Külpe, as head of the experimental laboratory at Würzburg, to subject some of these viewpoints to an experimental analysis. Külpe himself had contributed to the analysis of factors which steer or drive volitional processes; [5] these factors might be either conscious or unconscious (this is the concept now often called "mental set" or simply "set").[6] Külpe's school began, at the beginning of the present century, a series of epoch-making experiments which contributed much to the antistructuralist movement we have just sketched. His laboratory at Würzburg became the center for research on an array of problems which the structuralism of Wundt's school had disregarded.

First of all came the studies of Marbe.[7] In these a situation was offered to the subject requiring him to form a judgment (as in determining which of two weights was heavier) and also a full introspective report on the processes intervening between stimulation and report. The decision was to be rendered in terms of verbal report or overt act which could be characterized by the experimenter as right or wrong; but attention was given to the thought processes which preceded the act.

Next came a method, introduced by Watt [8] and Messer,[9] of utilizing the association test to find out what thought processes occurred between the presentation of a word and the word response. These (and similar) investigations led to scattered and incoherent masses of introspective material in which there constantly appeared evidences of preoccupation with elements of experience that to the subjects did not seem to be capable of description in sensory terms. This mass of introspective material, though heterogeneous, indicated

[5] *Outlines of Psychology* (1893).

[6] His view had in several respects been foreshadowed by others. See summary in Titchener, *Experimental Psychology of the Thought-Processes* (1909), pp. 162 ff.

[7] *Experimentell-psychologische Untersuchungen über das Urteil, eine Einleitung in die Logik* (1901).

[8] *Arch. f. d. ges. Psychol.*, 1905, 4, 289–436.

[9] *Ibid.*, 1906, 8, 1–124.

the existence of a kind of experience closely similar to the transitive states which James had discussed in the chapter on "The Stream of Thought"; something to be contrasted with the substantive, the relatively discrete and independent bits of experience. These rather vague and indefinite experiences which were found to occur in the thought processes were given a name which we may roughly translate "conscious attitudes" (*Bewusstseinslagen*).[10] These states of consciousness were not reducible to simple sensations or images or feelings. Here, early in the Würzburg work, we have the emergence of elements of experience which appeared to have been disregarded by the entire school of experimental psychology under Wundt's leadership, and whose existence as a matter of fact had been generally ignored ever since the structuralism of Locke. They bore a certain resemblance to the "imageless thoughts" which Stout had mentioned in 1896.[11] These conscious attitudes included, for example, experiences of doubt and of certainty, of affirmation and of dissent. Watt emphasized also the *Aufgabe* (task or problem) which, though not necessarily present *in consciousness*, exercises a controlling influence upon the judgment or act of thought.

The Würzburg school advanced, however, to new problems. Ach proceeded to analyze the process by which decisions are reached, classifying individuals into "decision types" on the basis of their introspections.[12] He found that there are, in addition to the conscious attitudes preceding a decision, many predispositions which, although outside of consciousness, operate to control the course of thought, influences which steer toward a decision. This discovery seemed a verification of one of Külpe's conceptions which was mentioned above (page 227), and called attention, in the field of volition, to entities very similar to the *Aufgaben* found by Watt in the study of judgment. To these agencies, so important in the process of volition, Ach gave the name "determining tendencies." Recognition of such determining tendencies was closely related to the theory of meaning. Ach outlined a theory to the effect that consciousness of meaning may be carried entirely through unconscious mechanisms. If a given imaginal content of consciousness is meaningful, it is because a number of associated ideas are subexcited, though not actually brought into consciousness. Meaning itself depends on such subexcitation of associated ideas. In addition to consciousness of meaning, Ach recognized consciousness of *relation*, and certain

[10] The word was suggested by Marbe.
[11] *Analytic Psychology.*
[12] *Ueber die Willenstätigkeit und das Denken* (1905).

intermediate stages between these two groups of nonimaginal experiences.

Research upon the thought processes had in the meantime been carried on independently by Binet in France and by Woodworth in the United States. Binet's attack on the problem was not a "bolt from the blue"; he had been interested in the thought processes for twenty years. In 1886 he had published *The Psychology of Reasoning*, which from the associationist viewpoint he then held suggests that reasoning is a sort of continually changing perception. In 1903 he published a study of the thought processes,[13] a report of experiments in which his two little girls had acted as subjects (page 171). He had asked them to solve simple problems, and then to report on the mental steps taken. They told him what thoughts passed through their minds. He came to the conclusion that there was in their experience much which could not be reduced to simple sensory terms. Woodworth, in a series of experiments published four years later and continued several years thereafter, came to the same general conclusion.[14] Woodworth's chief emphasis was upon the reality of thought that was not of imaginal structure, and upon "feelings of relation." Not contenting himself with the statement that the experiences were not reducible to the traditional structural terms, he emphasized the reality of two distinct forms of meaningful consciousness, forms closely similar to those described by Ach.

There followed a new period in the Würzburg school, beginning in 1907 with the investigations of Karl Bühler.[15] These were not essentially different in purpose from Woodworth's. In fact Bühler used a method already employed by Woodworth—that of stating a question which required reflection before an answer could be given, and recording the steps involved in reaching the answer. The important thing for Bühler was the reality of nonsensory *thought* processes, a finding which had been hitherto only an aspect, not the essential purpose, of the Würzburg investigations. Bühler's work necessitated a very long period (say 5 to 20 seconds) between problem and answer, so that introspective reports were necessarily subject to much error. Largely on this score, Wundt attacked such work as undeserving of the designation "experimental." But an important difference between Bühler's work and similar Würzburg investigations lay in the fact that the shock of conflict with the Wundtian

---

[13] *L'étude expérimentale de l'intelligence.*

[14] See, for example, "Non-Sensory Components of Sense Perception," *J. Phil., Psychol., and Sci. Meth.*, 1907, 4, 169–76.

[15] *Arch. f. d. ges. Psychol.*, 1907, 9, 297–365.

methods and concepts came out much more clearly. It was Bühler, more than anyone else, who served to bring out the apparent evidence for the existence of items of experience which are not sensory. It may be hard to see why this should have been provocative of a storm, in view of the fact that the school of *Gestaltqualität* had long emphasized the relational elements in experience. But there is a new feature in Bühler's work. For all the previous psychologists the relations, after all, were only relations.[16] Even in the case of Mach's quality of "triangularity," a sensationist could say that such a spatial relation is simply a logical name for the way we react, not a name for a new quality of experience; or he could, in fact, accept Mach's description of these as *sensations of space*. But Bühler asserted explicitly that psychology must take account of new kinds of structural elements; namely, thought elements. He was trying to import into the precincts of introspective consciousness elements whose credentials had repeatedly been refused. Furthermore, these were vital elements and served in large measure as the content of the process of thinking. An American pupil of Külpe's, J. R. Angell (cf. page 223), had taken a somewhat similar position.[17]

In 1909 came Titchener's series of lectures incorporated in his book *The Experimental Psychology of the Thought-Processes*. The position here taken is of considerable historical importance. The Würzburg school had been very much on the defensive as a result of Wundt's scathing denunciation. Every student was alert to hear what a scholar of great erudition, and long experience with introspective method, had to say. His verdict was that as regards their activities in relation to determining tendencies, the defendants were innocent; indeed, he commended in the highest degree their ingenuity, versatility, and inventiveness. But on the charge of introducing methods and terms which could never form a part of systematic psychology, they were guilty. Titchener found no reason to change his view that the only elements in consciousness are sensations, images, and feelings; there was no such thing as an imageless thought. Moreover, the "conscious attitudes" of the early members of the Würzburg school, and the thought elements of Bühler, which had been expressly stated to be nonsensory, were reduced to the familiar terms of structuralism. The "conscious attitudes" were classed as highly complex integrations of sensory components, which faulty introspective technique had failed to recognize, and in so far as nonsensory meaning elements were really found, they

---

[16] Some of them were, in fact, identified with some of Wundt's "feelings."
[17] Angell, J. R., *Psychology*, 4th ed. (1908).

were the concern of logic, not of psychology. Titchener did, as a matter of fact, repeat Woodworth's experiments, finding that his own subjects did not confirm the statements of Woodworth's subjects; the experience of Titchener's observers was described in the accepted language of structuralism.

Titchener maintained that when introspection yields no clear result, the only way to get at obscure states is through a genetic study—an inquiry as to how they arose. If we go back to the earliest experience of the individual to find how conscious attitudes and thought elements began, we find that they arose largely from muscular adjustments, and hence are of kinesthetic quality. Our muscular sensations or images may be difficult to recognize, but they are all-important for the psychology of thought. The genetic approach is legitimate as an adjunct to the analytical method. The muscular nature of many attitudes is apparent if we study an individual who confronts a strange object for the first time. Attitudes and thought elements are really the last vestigial form of groups of kinesthetic and organic sensations.

The effect of Titchener's verdict was naturally to center attention on the main point of difference between his own and the Würzburg positions. The Würzburg school interpreted Titchener's lectures as indicating that they had not given enough evidence that there were such mental states as they had described. They must redouble their efforts to make the evidence more conclusive. They rallied to the defense of what they had come to regard as their cardinal doctrine. An instance of the labors of the Würzburg school to defend their position was the examination by T. V. Moore of the relation of meaning to image.[18] He presented a series of words both visually and auditorily to nine subjects. In one presentation, he gave the instructions that the subject was to lift his hand from a telegraph key as soon as the given word evoked meaning. In other experiments, the subject was to lift his hand off the key as soon as an image appeared in response to the word. Except in the case of one subject, it was found that the meanings came more quickly than the images. The time for evoking images averaged nearly a second, that for meanings about half that period. Moore concluded that meaning and image are distinct psychological elements. He therefore proceeded to postulate a structural psychology in which there were not three but four independent elements—sensation, image, feeling, and *meaning*—in consciousness.

[18] "The Temporal Relations of Meaning and Imagery," *Psychol. Rev.*, 1915, 22, 177–225.

A few words must be added about the subsequent history of the Titchenerian method. For Titchener this structural viewpoint and the exclusion of meanings became, as the result of the Würzburg investigations, even more vital than before. It became acutely necessary for him to instruct his pupils to distinguish between immediate experience (sensations, images, and feelings) on the one hand, and meanings or interpretations on the other hand. The subject must avoid the "stimulus error"; namely, the tendency to talk about the object which is stimulating him rather than to describe the observed content of experience. The subject must not say he is "angry," for this is but an interpretation of his mental state. A true description would deal simply with such elements as the kinesthetic sensations experienced, and the feelings accompanying them. The all-important distinction made by Titchener and others between experience and meaning was elaborated with the use of the German terms *Beschreibung* (description) and *Kundgabe* (meaning).[19]

A few words may be said by way of evaluation of the Würzburg movement as a whole. The concepts of attitude and set have greatly influenced all psychology. While the effort to make experimental studies of volition and thought was obviously an appropriate one, the new investigations did not provide methods which could completely fulfill the promise. Even with regard to simple sensations, images, and feelings, it was already proving difficult to get incontrovertible evidence from introspection. As to imageless thought, we have already mentioned differences between Woodworth's and Titchener's observers; and there have been instances in which Titchener's own pupils, working in later years in other laboratories, have reported data at variance with Titchener's formulation.[20] Introspection may be adequate to block out the main contours of mental events and yet fail as a precision instrument; there may be a region beyond which it is helpless to catch the delicate and fast-moving processes of thought.

None of all this, however, has in any way interfered with experimental study of thought processes from a functional viewpoint; the nature of thought may be revealed by its works. There has followed, since Bühler's time, a substantial experimental literature on many aspects of the thought processes: the formation of concepts; symbolism; the quest for missing terms or relations; the solution of mathematical, logical, aesthetic, ethical problems—all conceived in terms

[19] The terms were proposed by Von Aster, *Zschr. f. Psychol.*, 1908, 49, 56–107.

[20] Young, P. T., "The Relation of Bright and Dull Pressure to Affectivity," *Amer. J. Psychol.*, 1932, 44, 780–84.

of necessary steps to be taken and the conditions governing each such step. Some of this work, like the *Denkpsychologie* of Selz,[21] is in the Würzburg tradition, but much of it has a very different ancestry. The controversy which arose forty years ago regarding the Würzburg results has fortunately in no way prevented Külpe's movement from participating with other movements in giving rise to a rich and solid experimental psychology of thinking. Such a psychology of thinking, however, has as a rule been conceived more and more in developmental terms; or has tended to ask more and more urgently how each kind of thinking arises in the individual history, and thus to link the problem to questions of growth and of learning. There still remains a place for the kinds of questions which Külpe's school raised, in so far as introspection can be sharpened to permit reliable answers; but on the whole these questions appear today to belong rather in the context of a psychology of learning, very broadly conceived, a psychology of the total process of coping with and solving a life problem. We shall repeatedly return to these issues.

But the Würzburg movement has still another huge significance: as one of the forerunners to the Gestalt psychology initiated by Wertheimer in 1912. In a later chapter, devoted to Gestalt, we shall have another glance at the productiveness of Külpe's approach along lines which he could never have foreseen.

REFERENCES

Boring, Edwin G., *A History of Experimental Psychology*, Century, 1929; pp. 393–402

Murchison, Carl A., ed., *A History of Psychology in Autobiography*, 3 vols., Clark University Press, 1930–36; Vol. 3: Marbe

Titchener, Edward B., *Lectures on the Experimental Psychology of the Thought-Processes*, Macmillan, 1909

Woodworth, Robert S., *Experimental Psychology*, Holt, 1938; pp. 783–93

---

[21] Selz, O., *Zur Psychologie des produktiven Denkens und des Irrtums* (1922).

Chapter 17

EXPERIMENTS ON THE
ACQUISITION OF SKILL

*The first beginnings of our volitional education are of the nature
of stumbling and fumbling.*　　　　　　BAIN

IN THE CLOSING YEARS of the nineteenth century and the opening
years of the twentieth, vigorous study was first given to the
problem of the acquisition of motor skill. Memory as Ebbinghaus had conceived it had proved amenable to quantitative examination, but it now became apparent that other forms of the learning
process could be approached in the same experimental spirit as the
functions of memorizing and forgetting syllables and words.

Bryan and Harter undertook in 1897–99 a study of the stages in
learning to send and receive telegraphic messages.[1] Curves of learning were constructed, indicating the stages of progress toward mastery of the task over a period of many months. The "learning curves"
thus plotted indicated that progress was more rapid at first than
later. Progress being measured in terms of the number of units which
could be handled in a unit of time, the time devoted to learning
yielded gradually less return as the task went on. But the two men
found the learning process to be not a regular, even progression, but a
series of jumps. Learning to receive telegraphic messages was frequently interrupted by periods of no progress; in these intervals the
learning curve presented very roughly a horizontal line, to which
the name "plateau" was given.[2] No uniform duration of the plateau
or uniform interval between plateaus was apparent.

---

[1] Bryan, W. L., and Harter, N., "Studies in the Physiology and Psychology of
the Telegraphic Language," *Psychol. Rev.*, 1897, 4, 27–53; "Studies on the Telegraphic Language: The Acquisition of a Hierarchy of Habits," *Psychol. Rev.*, 1899,
6, 346–75.

[2] Such plateaus were not clearly demonstrable in the curves for "sending."

Following the principle of "diminishing returns" noted above, the learning curve was found also to reach a point where no further gains were apparent; practice merely kept the subject up to his acquired standard. This last stage was entitled the "physiological limit." But the horizontal line of the physiological limit seemed to differ psychologically from the plateaus; the plateaus did not appear to be genuine periods of *no progress*. They seemed to be periods in which the subject had reached the maximum attainable *with a given method;* but after practice had continued for a time, he was able to take advantage of a new and more efficient type of response, for which he would previously have been unprepared.

But just what is being practiced during a plateau? In one instance the subject has learned how to receive each letter of the alphabet; he handles each word as the sum of the letters composing it, interpreting the symbol for one letter and then, after a brief pause, the letter which follows. He is in the "letter-habit" stage. When the letters have been practiced long enough, the subject passes rapidly to a new system of habits in which words are grasped and received as integrated units. The subject has entered the "word-habit" stage, and the learning curve again rises. The word is a "higher unit," similar to the higher units discovered by Cattell (page 162) in his investigation of word perception. When the word habit has been mastered, the subject may pass to the phrase habit or even to the sentence habit. Some expert telegraphers were found to follow more than two hundred clicks behind a message to which they listened; they were taking in great masses of material in the form of higher units.

In immediate connection with this matter of higher units, or organization into groups or wholes, the work of Bryan and Harter showed that two or more responses might go on at once, in such a way that the first "overlapped" the second. This had been found also by Cattell in the reading of letters and words; a word might be perceived before the previous word had been enunciated. So, in receiving a message and transcribing it on a typewriter, experts were found to follow from six to twelve words after the message; higher units and overlapping were present in conjunction. The messages were received and typed not letter by letter, but phrase by phrase, or even sentence by sentence. The subject could begin a new activity while waiting to complete a higher unit.

Similar studies in the acquisition of skill were made within a few years by Swift [3] and by Book.[4] While in general confirming the conclusions of Bryan and Harter, and discovering similar plateaus, their interpretations of the significance of the plateau differed. Swift pointed out that higher units may be in the process of formation even during the plateau. Book, studying the acquisition of skill in typewriting, found that subjects frequently showed loss of interest at the beginning of the plateau, and further, that physiological observations (for example, of the pulse) indicated a lax or depressed state, which in itself seemed sufficient to account for the absence of progress. Book suggested that the plateau, far from being a period of hidden progress, was actually wasted time. Book's plateaus, similar to those of Bryan and Harter, seemed to correspond to the passage from lower to higher units.

One of Book's most important contributions related to the process of overlearning. Ebbinghaus had shown that additional memorizing beyond the amount needed for a perfect recitation at the time has a marked effect in facilitating the task of relearning; in fact, that the whole curve of forgetting for overlearned material falls off much more slowly than that for just-learned material. Book's subjects, after acquiring considerable skill in typewriting—in which, of course, a great many reactions were overlearned—dropped the problem for four months. Upon resuming practice they regained in a few days the same level of skill which had at first cost them several weeks. Book concluded that something had occurred which illustrated James's suggestion ("from an unknown German scientist") that we may perhaps learn to skate in the summer and to swim in the winter; the period of disuse was credited with "the disappearance, with the lapse of time, of numerous psycho-physical difficulties . . . interfering habits and tendencies, which, as they faded, left the more firmly established typewriting associations free to act." Though this conclusion has not commanded universal assent, the data did at least clearly demonstrate the vast importance of intensive overlearning. In terms of Ebbinghaus's "saving method," the loss during four months of no practice was exceedingly slight.

---

[3] "Studies in the Psychology and Physiology of Learning," *Amer. J. Psychol.*, 1903, 14, 201–51; "Memory of a Complex Skillful Act," *Amer. J. Psychol.*, 1905, 16, 131–33.
[4] *The Psychology of Skill with Special Reference to the Acquisition of Typewriting*, Univ. Montana Publ. in Psychol., 1908.

ANIMAL LEARNING

While these investigations were going forward in human learning, research was likewise in progress in the field of animal learning. The methods and concepts developed in animal investigations were in many ways quite different, but proved in time to contain much that was new and important for human psychology.

A word must be said about the animal psychology of the late nineteenth century. The great bulk of animal experimentation was being done by physiologists, German work being especially abundant. The physiologists were concerned with part-functions, relatively little with total adjustments. Studies in reflex action were numerous. Some experiments dealing with perceptual and instinctive functions were performed by British and American students.[5] In 1875 Spalding sought an answer to the question whether swallows fly instinctively, or *learn* to fly.[6] Swallows were placed in a small cage as soon as they were hatched; when liberated at the normal flying age, some flew without assistance. But perhaps the most conspicuous studies of animals were those of Lloyd Morgan,[7] pursued, for the most part, by the method of collecting observations rather than by controlled experiment. Galton, too, familiarized himself with the ways of wild animals. The observations of Lloyd Morgan and Galton are imbued with the evolutionary spirit, and are among the most obvious reverberations of Darwinian influence. Animals, they held, are equipped with innate mechanisms of reaction which make possible their adaptation to environment. But in most of this work there was no quantitative analysis of instinctive behavior, very little experimental isolation of variables, and no thorough analysis of animal learning.

It is therefore no exaggeration to say that Thorndike's quantitative experiments on animal learning awakened psychologists to the conception of an experimental animal psychology. His work was begun in 1897 while he was a graduate student at Harvard, studying under James. Lloyd Morgan had come to lecture at Harvard and at Clark, and had stimulated a keen interest; but what came of it, by way of general plan and specific methods, was Thorndike's own. Indeed, it is likely that the animal studies of the late nineteenth century offered Thorndike less than did the general conception of experimental psychology as the new German and American laboratories expressed

[5] See, for example, Lubbock, Sir John, *Ants, Bees, and Wasps* (1882).

[6] "Instinct and Acquisition," *Nature*, 1875, 12.

[7] For example, *Animal Life and Intelligence* (1891).

it. His first experiments were upon chicks, dogs, and cats. Shortly afterward he improvised an animal laboratory at Columbia, where, under Cattell's supervision, the work continued.

The problem most extensively studied was the nature of the animal learning curve.[8] A cat was placed, for example, in a cage which could be opened only by striking a latch or button, and a piece of fish was placed outside. Biting, clawing, and scurrying ensued, followed at last by the accidental movement which set free the animal. On a later trial the same general behavior followed, and so on in each new test. However, the total time required to get out, though fluctuating, showed a consistent tendency to decrease. When the number of practice days was indicated on the x axis and the number of minutes required to complete an act on the y axis, the learning curve was found to fall rapidly at first, then more and more gradually, until a limit, a horizontal line, was reached, indicating the animal's complete mastery of the task. Such a curve, plotted from time units, obviously corresponded to the learning curves for telegraphy currently reported by Bryan and Harter; the latter, though measuring in terms of accomplishment per unit of time, rather than in terms of time per unit of accomplishment, had pointed to the same conclusion; namely, the principle of diminishing returns with practice. Both curves were, in respect to this principle, similar to Ebbinghaus's curves of forgetting.[9] Though there were of course irregularities in the individual curves, and frequently great variations from one performance to the next, there were nevertheless no clear-cut plateaus such as those discovered in learning to receive telegraphic messages.

It appeared clear from Thorndike's curves that sudden insight into the nature of the task was rare or indeed entirely absent. There was no sudden and permanent drop in the curve indicating that the cat had "solved" the problem. The cat started with random movements, which were gradually eliminated as practice went on; the time taken to strike the latch necessarily decreased. Thorndike saw, as had Spencer and Bain (page 106), the importance of such "random" movements in leading to the discovery of the "right" movement; for this kind of behavior the term "trial and error" was soon in general use.[10] Even in the monkey, Thorndike reported

---

[8] *Animal Intelligence, Psychol. Rev., Monogr. Suppl.*, 1897, 2 (whole No. 8).

[9] All were, moreover, logarithmic curves, at least up to the physiological limit; this limit, however, seemed genuinely rectilinear rather than asymptotic to a horizontal line.

[10] See Lloyd Morgan, *Animal Behaviour* (1900), p. 139, for an early use of the term.

learning to be of this general type; he found no clear cases even of the process of "imitation." [11]

The process of learning had been regarded by most authors since Hobbes as essentially the formation of connections; those who interested themselves in physiology emphasized especially *brain connections*.[12] Thorndike accepted this approach; the functional units in behavior at a given time were for him the *bonds* between stimuli and responses. The nature of these bonds was to be understood in the light of the "neurone theory" (page 187). This general conception was utilized in the formulation of a variety of "laws of learning." These were offered in his *Elements of Psychology* (1905), and elaborated in his *Educational Psychology* (1913–14).[13] The "law of exercise" stated that the use of a given connection between stimulus and response strengthens the bond (while disuse weakens it); such factors as recency and frequency are subheads under the law. The *law of associative shifting* stated that if two stimuli are presented simultaneously, one of these eliciting a certain response, the other later acquires the capacity to elicit the same response. Another was the *law of effect*, which stated that the *satisfaction* following from an act strengthens the bond and leads to its repetition, while *annoyance* tends to weaken the bond and hence to eliminate the act.[14] All these laws had long been assumed and used, of course, as by animal-trainers; but their clear formulation was significant. (Thorndike's later revisions of learning theory will be noted on pages 275 ff.)

The first decade of the twentieth century brought a great number of experimental studies of animals. The mechanism to which Thorndike gave the name of "associative shifting" was being studied under other names (see page 255), and was shown to be present even in very lowly forms of life; on the other hand, this mechanism, rather than reasoning or insight, seemed to account even for relatively complicated types of learning. During the time of these early investi-

[11] *The Mental Life of the Monkeys, Psychol. Rev., Monogr. Suppl.*, 1899, 3 (whole No. 15). "Imitation" and "insight" have been reported by subsequent workers; cf. page 291.

[12] Hartley had emphasized motor elements in association; movements could be associated with one another as with ideas. Thorndike's view was almost identical with this doctrine, but was enriched by data from neurology, especially by the neurone theory, and by the evolutionary theory.

[13] Part of Vol. III is a revision of his book *Educational Psychology*, which appeared in 1903.

[14] Satisfaction and annoyance were conceived in terms of synaptic functions; when a pathway was ready to conduct, the process of conduction was satisfying, while annoyance might result either from the failure of a ready pathway to conduct or from the forced conduction of an unready pathway.

gations in learning there was a strong belief in the minds of most psychologists that there was a significant connection between the learning process and the thinking process. There was, on the one hand, good reason to believe that human beings learn in ways not characteristic of animals, that something different happens inside of them. On the other hand, it was natural to look for similarities between animal and human learning and to utilize as far as possible those conceptions which had proved helpful in animal experimentation. Both problems were clarified by the appearance of a number of volumes—such as Mach's *Erkenntnis und Irrtum* (1905), and Dewey's *How We Think* (1910)—which represented the thinking process as a *trial-and-error* mechanism in which human subjects manipulate situations mentally without the need for overt random movements.

LEARNING IN RELATION TO ATTITUDE AND THOUGHT

Importance must be attached to the experiments of Ruger (1910), who offered partial confirmation of the trial-and-error theory of thinking, and made extensive use of the German and American studies of "attitudes" mentioned in the last chapter.[15] He studied the process of solving mechanical puzzles, in which the subject had to disentangle and remove some part through a complex series of manual movements. In this process it was usually necessary for the subject to go through random movements or trial-and-error activity similar to that shown by Thorndike's cats. Ruger found in his twenty-five subjects much of this random exploratory behavior; a large proportion of the first solutions were genuinely accidental. Further, the subjects' reports showed that, in addition to such *overt* behavior, much trial-and-error activity was going on *mentally*. But he found that there was frequently a sudden and permanent drop in the learning curve, corresponding to a successful lead which the subject grasped clearly and continued to utilize. Such sudden drops were often due to noticing the *locus* of a difficulty.[16] In other cases the drops corresponded to more complex instances of analysis of the nature of the problem. Ruger was interested in those complex mental states where the process of "analysis" occurred; that is, recognition of similarities and differences, observation of the relation between movements hitherto disconnected, and the like. The

[15] Ruger, H. A., "The Psychology of Efficiency," *Arch. Psychol.*, No. 15.
[16] The same fact, in chimpanzee learning, had been noted by Woodworth in 1902–03. See Ladd, G. T., and Woodworth, R. S., *Elements of Physiological Psychology* (1911), pp. 552–53.

effectiveness of analysis was found to depend largely upon the subject's attitude. The conception of attitudes, while specifically borrowed from the Würzburg experimentalists, was not, as with them, that of a new kind of *structure*, but that of a way of facing the situation. Among the attitudes discovered, by far the most effective was the "problem attitude," in which the subject forgot his self-consciousness and the desire to make a good showing, and became interested in the problem itself. The problem attitude was the one most favorable to the emergence of sudden and useful insights. Even here, however, Ruger's data showed that such insights were likely to depend on similarities between the new task and a previous task successfully mastered. In other words, they were transfers from situations which resembled the one in which the subject was now working. Sudden insight, far from overthrowing the trial-and-error conception, seemed often to go hand in hand with it, arising from the reappearance of a response tendency which in a previous situation had given successful results (we shall recur to the problem on page 277 ff.).

Binet had shown certain striking similarities between perception and reasoning (page 229). Ruger and others had now ventured in the same direction. The reports of Ruger's subjects, as well as those of the Würzburg school, had in fact revealed many processes which might be classified equally well under perception, reasoning, or learning. The traditional distinctions seemed to be shaken. In the case of the German investigators the new tendency took the form of reducing the reasoning processes, in some instances, to sequences of "attitudes." Ruger, and the American "functionalist" school, made attitudes equally important for reasoning and for perception. Indeed, theoretical and experimental studies of the learning process threw such light on perception and reasoning as to make both processes seem to be classifiable as subheads under learning.

A good place to begin is the study of the transfer of training. It was often naïvely assumed (cf. page 200) that there is general strengthening of any faculty—memory, or will, or motor skill—by using it; but would a careful measurement actually reveal that anything is "strengthened" except the specific habits practiced? The earliest careful study of transfer in motor functions [17] was made by

---

[17] Fechner had reported that learning to write with one hand facilitated the process with the other hand (*Berichte d.k.-sächs. Ges. d. Wissensch., math.-phys.*, 1858, 10, 70). A. W. Volkmann had shown experimentally that the reduction of the "two-point threshold" in certain regions through training lowered the threshold in other regions (*ibid.*, 38).

Scripture and his collaborators,[18] who in 1894 trained subjects to carry out various movements with the right hand, and measured the degree of improvement in the same movement with the left hand. They found a large degree of transfer in such "cross education."

Thorndike and Woodworth, in 1901, trained subjects in such tasks as the estimation of geometrical areas and of the magnitude of weights.[19] When larger areas and weights were substituted for those used in the practice series, the transfer effects from training were slight. Such effects as did appear were interpreted as due to "identical elements" present in the practice and in the final series; these identical elements included specific habits and attitudes involved in adjustment to the task. Conclusions were stated in terms of the absence of general training in the functions involved; the elements trained were specific habits which played a part only because of the close similarity between the situations encountered. This interpretation was in accordance with Thorndike's stimulus-response psychology, and in particular with his view that learning consists in the alteration of specific bonds. Much discussion of the whole conception of identical elements ensued.[20] Ebert and Meumann undertook an experiment closely similar to that of James (page 200), testing the effect of a practice period of memorizing upon the efficiency of memorizing other material.[21] Their results seemed to show decided improvement as the result of memory training. It was pointed out by W. F. Dearborn that sufficient account had not been taken of the influence of the test material given before the practice period commenced; in fact, repeating their initial and final tests without the practice period, he found a high level of attainment in the final tests, which was attributable to the effect of the initial test.[22] Since the initial and final tests were similar, there was nothing to contradict the explanation of transfer in terms of the use of identical elements. The implications of all this for the theory of "formal

[18] Scripture, E. W., Smith, T. L., and Brown, E. M., "On the Education of Muscular Control and Power," *Studies from the Yale Psychological Laboratory*, 1894, 2, 114–19.

[19] Thorndike, E. L., and Woodworth, R. S., "The Influence of Improvement in One Mental Function upon the Efficiency of Other Functions," *Psychol. Rev.*, 1901, 8, 247–61; 384–95; 553–64.

[20] Bair, J. H., *The Practice Curve, Psychol. Rev., Monogr. Suppl.*, 1902, 5 (whole No. 19), found that the curve of a skilled act showed, from its beginning, the influence of practice in another skilled act which had some elements in common with it.

[21] *Arch. f. d. ges. Psychol.*, 1905, 4, 1–232.

[22] "The General Effects of Special Practice in Memory," *Psychol. Bull.*, 1909, 6, 44.

discipline" were clear; "perception" and "reasoning" seemed scarcely likely to be general functions capable of direct training, but names for very complex groups of activities, each activity being understood in terms of specific habits acquired by the individual.[23] Perception and reasoning were no longer clearly separable from the learning process.

The work of Fracker is of special interest, because of his success in getting rid of obvious similarities between practice material and test material.[24] He presented to his subjects a series of musical tones in groups of four. Immediately afterward, before allowing them to reproduce what they had heard, he gave four more tones, and asked them to reproduce, in order, the first group of four. Of course there was much interference, which involved the necessity that each subject should find a mnemonic device, some scheme by which to fixate the tones so as to permit recall. The individual differences were considerable; nevertheless, most of the subjects showed themselves capable of learning to reproduce the first series in spite of interference from the second. This result made possible the statement that the subjects improved in their performance by virtue of the acquisition of some specific "trick" or technique, and not as the result of formal memory training. This finding was confirmed by the fact that when the subjects turned to a new task, such as memorizing poetry, they manifested no clear gain from their previous practice in memorizing; they could not utilize their previous mnemonic devices. Many other studies of transfer have served to confirm the Thorndike-Woodworth conclusions as to identical elements,[25] although strong opposition to the view has been a prominent feature of the Gestalt psychology (pages 280 and 291).

Another field of investigation, usually treated in the same spirit, is *interference*, or the decrease in efficiency which is observable in some activities in consequence of participation in other activities. This interference was manifest in the work of Müller and Pilzecker.[26] They found that when a given pair of items, A and B, had been learned in conjunction, and an attempt was then made to link A

---

[23] For an example of the early experimental evidence indicating some transfer from one school subject to another, when closely related, see Dallam, "Is the Study of Latin Advantageous to the Study of English?" *Educ. Rev.*, 1903, 54.

[24] See Fracker, G. C., "On the Transference of Training in Memory," *Psychol. Monogr.*, 1908, 9, 56–102.

[25] See, for example, Sleight, W. G., "Memory and Formal Training," *Brit. J. Psychol.*, 1911, 4, 386–457. It must however be remembered that the term "element" is still hard to define. Cf. page 444.

[26] *Zschr. f. Psychol.*, Ergänzungsb., 1900, 1.

with C, the connection A–C might prove peculiarly hard to establish, because of interference from B. This was a statement of the problem of interference in terms of specific connections or linkages. Similar interference has been found in the study of overt motor acts. Münsterberg conducted the simple experiment of changing his watch from one pocket to another and noting how many times a day he put it into the "wrong" pocket.[27] He and subsequent investigators have reported that imperfectly formed habits tend to interfere with one another, while more thoroughly practiced acts cease to do so.

An aspect of interference which has engaged much interest is *retroactive inhibition*.[28] If immediately after a learning period the subject is confronted with a new task, his recall of the learned material is appreciably less efficient than is his recall of material followed by a rest period. The amount of interference depends on the similarity between the learned material and the task which immediately follows, but all tasks exert some inhibitory effect.[29]

But much evidence came to hand (cf. pages 228 and 247) to show that the learning process could not be regarded *merely* as a relation between stimuli and responses. The internal condition of the organism was of major importance. Thorndike emphasized "readiness." Müller and Schumann showed that the reading of nonsense syllables need not result in learning their *order*, but that when the subject's attitude is altered through the instruction to learn the syllables in order, rapid learning follows.[30] The new attitude was called the "will to learn." [31] For some, this suggestion vied with Külpe's movement in sweeping away the debris of the associationist tradition; for others, the newly emphasized attitudes were themselves associations (cf. page 269). The trend in all recent work is in the direction of showing the significance of the attitudes taken, the "control" or the "mental set" determining the formation of new associations.

A fertile field of research bearing on this question of the will to learn has been the problem of "incidental memory"; that is, memory for material which has never been consciously learned.[32] As early as

---

[27] *Beiträge z. exp. Psychol.*, 1892, 1.

[28] Müller and Pilzecker, *op. cit.* in note 26.

[29] See, for example, Robinson, E. S., *Some Factors Determining the Degree of Retroactive Inhibition, Psychol. Monogr.*, 1920, 28 (whole No. 28).

[30] *Zschr. f. Psychol.*, 1894, 6, 81–190; 257–59.

[31] By Ebert and Meumann, *loc. cit.*

[32] The problem has generally been so defined as to include many questions which have only one thing in common, the search for mental connections established without deliberate purpose.

1895 this was investigated by Cattell.[33] He gave a series of questions to Columbia undergraduates about things they had recently seen. The results pointed to the great unreliability of casual everyday observation, showing that many things frequently seen had failed to make an impression definite enough to permit of recall. Moreover, individuals were often certain of much which had no basis in fact. This experiment was repeated by Jastrow with confirmatory results.[34] Binet, using suggestion, obtained corroboration for Cattell's thesis.[35] The study took quantitative form in the work of Stern, who ascertained the increase or decrease in the number of items reported with the lapse of time after the presentation, and found a decrease in the accuracy of testimony as time elapsed.[36] He was interested in the "psychology of testimony" as a practical problem; hence not only defective memory, but the unwitting tendency to fabricate material to take the place of what was forgotten, was important. Claparède found that with the lapse of time there was a tendency to neglect the unusual and the contingent and to testify in the direction of the "probable." [37] Of course these studies, unless especially planned to meet this difficulty, leave open the question whether the results are due to failures of recall or to the failure to *notice* items in one's surroundings.[38] The question frequently appears to be not how good a man's memory is, but whether items were ever observed.

But traditional associationism was to suffer even more serious rebuffs than these. In 1907 Witasek discovered that the mere passive reading and rereading of printed matter was decidedly less efficacious than reading followed by "active recitation" in which the subject forced himself to recall what he had read.[39] This statement was reduced to clear quantitative form by A. I. Gates, who not only confirmed Witasek's conclusions, but showed that both the rate of

[33] "Measurements of the Accuracy of Recollection," *Science*, 1895, N.S. 2, 761–66.

[34] Reported by F. E. Bolton, "The Accuracy of Recollection and Observation," *Psychol. Rev.*, 1896, 3, 286–95.

[35] *La suggestibilité* (1900).

[36] *Zschr. f. d. ges. Strafrechtswiss.*, 1903, 23. See also *Beitrage zur Psychologie der Aussage*, I (1903–04), in which the decrease of suggestibility with age was demonstrated.

[37] "Expériences collectives sur le témoignage," *Arch. de psychol.*, 1906, 5, 344–87.

[38] Whatever bugbears arise when "attention" is mentioned, it would appear that the understanding of these results can come only through further investigation of the functional significance, if not, in fact, of the nature, of attention. We need to know not only the relation of attention to learning, but to the entire curve of forgetting in the case of material learned with varying degrees of thoroughness.

[39] *Zschr. f. Psychol.*, 1907, 44, 161–85; 246–82.

learning and the amount retained were increased by devoting larger and larger percentages of the learning time to recitation; even the use of 80 per cent of the time for recitation was more effective than smaller percentages.[40] It was clear that learning was at least something more than the indiscriminate formation of linkages; the ways in which such linkages were formed called aloud for investigation.

Another experiment necessitating a revision of classical associationism was the study of the role of the image in relation to the fixation and recall of complex visual stimuli—the question of the extent to which we remember by virtue of mental pictures or other reproductions of the sensory content once experienced. The experiments of Judd and Cowling were designed to find how a picture was recalled after it had been briefly exposed.[41] They found that the subject made definite attacks on the task; he would look at different points and immediately afterward recall those details that he had noticed. Each time the picture was presented, he would name a few more things observed. But never at any time was the thing photographed on the mind so that he could "read off" from his mental image what he had seen. There was no process by which he mentally saw the picture all at once, and then read off from his "mental picture" a series of details. Results equally damaging to the interpretation of memory in terms of simple imagery were obtained by M. R. Fernald.[42] She put before her subjects an arrangement of letters in both vertical and horizontal lines so as to form a square (Binet letter square). Having asked her subject to get a complete visual image of this letter square, she removed the letters. The letters could then, indeed, be named by some subjects; but when instructions were given to read, for example, from the lower right-hand corner vertically to the upper right-hand corner, or to read letters from right to left, confusion and error resulted. The subject might be able, by rehearsing the whole series, to perform even such tasks, but one thing which he evidently was not doing was reading from a clear memory image. The contrast between the reproduction of the letters in the *order learned* and the reproduction of them in any *other* order was so great as to indicate that the square was not recalled primarily in terms of mental images. The visualizer may, indeed, "see" individual letters, but he can scarcely make good his claim that he

---

[40] "Recitation as a Factor in Memorizing," *Arch. Psychol.*, 1917, No. 40.

[41] *Studies in Perceptual Development, Psychol. Rev., Monogr. Suppl.*, 1907, 8 (whole No. 34).

[42] *The Diagnosis of Mental Imagery, Psychol. Monogr.*, 1912, 14 (whole No. 58).

continues to see the square. Adherents to the theory of imageless thought found here much comfort. (All this is independent, of course, of the special case of those possessing that vivid type of imagery known as eidetic; such images may persist for hours.)

Into the chaos of theories resulting from such studies came an illuminating suggestion from Woodworth.[43] He described perception as a form of response; the "perceptual-reaction" theory postulated a process above and beyond the arousal of a group of sensations or images. It supposed that brain areas outside the sensory regions *react to* the separate sensory items in a way which the items themselves could never determine. In every perceptual experience there are sensory elements, but they do not constitute a percept unless the organism makes such a perceptual reaction. Woodworth had read to a group of subjects a series of words, instructing them to learn them in such fashion that the first word of each pair would, when presented, recall the second. But he presented the stimuli at a constant rate; the interval between A and B was identical with that between B and C. Associationists in the tradition of Hartley and James Mill might expect that the linkage from B to C would be as firmly established as the linkage A–B. But the tendency for the first term of a pair to recall its second term was actually eighty-five times as great as the tendency of the latter to recall the first term of the next pair. Woodworth concluded that the *perception of A and B as a pair* served as a basis for the connection between them. Not their proximity, not the formal will to learn, not any special attitude, but the act of perception itself established the connection. Perception was interpreted not as a state within which sensation exists, but as a reaction. "Imageless thought" might appear whenever a perceptual experience was revived without the revival of the sensory constituents.

One more departure from Hartleyan associationism must be noted in the emphasis upon total experience and its "redintegration" rather than more serial arrangement of *items* of experience. Hamilton's doctrine (page 101), adopted and used by Bain and James, and undergoing various vicissitudes in the hands of Bradley[44] and Semon,[45] has served as the starting point for much modern discussion of learning. H. L. Hollingworth uses the term "redintegration" to describe not the process by which an element *brings back* its context, but the process by which it *functions for* the situation of which it was

---

[43] "A Review of Imageless Thought," *Psychol. Rev.*, 1915, 22, 1–27.
[44] *Principles of Logic* (1883).
[45] *The Mneme* (1904).

once a part; the part acts for the whole.[46] It is evident that association (or "associative shifting") is not the *key* to such a process, but rather a special case of a principle of wide application.[47]

REFERENCES

Boring, Edwin G., *A History of Experimental Psychology*, Century, 1929; pp. 549–58

Ladd, G. T., and Woodworth, R. S., *Elements of Physiological Psychology*, Scribner, 1911; pp. 542–92

Murchison, Carl A., ed., *A History of Psychology in Autobiography*, 3 vols., Clark University Press, 1930–36; chaps. by C. L. Morgan and E. L. Thorndike

Semon, Richard Wolfgang, *The Mneme*, Macmillan, 1921

Thorndike, Edward L., *Educational Psychology*, 3 vols., Teachers College, Columbia University, 1913–14; Vol. 2

[46] For example, *The Psychology of Functional Neuroses* (1920), Chap. II; *The Psychology of Thought* (1926), p. 92 ff.

[47] Hollingworth interweaves this principle with the doctrine of the "psychophysical continuum," to the effect that the only difference between the subjective and objective worlds lies in the greater uniformity of our experience of the latter, and indicates transitional orders between the two extremes.

PART THREE

Contemporary Psychological Systems

Chapter 18

BEHAVIORISM

Dismiss therefore every idle fancy and foolish conjecture of those who confine the intellectual activity to particular locations in the body.   GREGORY OF NYSSA

THE STUDIES of the psychology of learning during the opening years of the century had not only expanded the area of experimental psychology far beyond Wundtian limits. They had tended to engender much dissatisfaction with the whole enterprise of introspective psychology, which seemed to many to be relatively sterile—at least, a much less rewarding undertaking. Learning curves, phylogenetic comparisons, studies of transfer of training, seemed to many in Germany and to even more in the United States to be much more like science, and to be closer to life problems as well. At the same time Külpe's school seemed to be undermining Wundt's and Titchener's systems; for the studies of learning were evidence that important problems existed which were inaccessible from the Wundt-Titchener approach. One of the results within a few years was a whole new school of psychology, American behaviorism, while during the same period German soil was being prepared for the new school of Gestalt psychology (Chapter 20). A third approach, psychoanalysis (Chapter 21), which within the world of psychiatry was at the same time challenging the sufficiency of the study of consciousness, and placing its emphasis upon unconscious dispositions, might be regarded as a further protest against the conception of psychology as the analysis of introspectively observable states and processes. These three protests were much more than protests against Wundt and Titchener; they were protests, taking widely varied forms, against the whole traditional conception of psychology as the analysis of conscious states. The three chapters that follow now will sketch the rise of three psychological schools which, though sharing in this protest, have taken radically different directions: behaviorism, Gestalt psychology, and psychoanalysis.

THE INTELLECTUAL ATMOSPHERE OF BEHAVIORISM

While behaviorism is expressly a psychological movement, it is an expression of a much more general movement in science (and in the philosophy of science). When it first appeared, it seemed a lonely island; but like all such islands, physical and intellectual, it proved to have many relatives, both visible and in hiding.

The growth of the biological sciences in the nineteenth century was something of a struggle between the physicalist conception (in which events can move in any direction) and the developmental conception (in which they take a direction and tend to maintain it). There were a good many attempts to dissolve the opposition between the two, and to create a sort of unidirectional physical universe, in which life should be viewed after the manner of physics, yet as developing essentially from simple to complex (cf. page 109). The mechanistic conception of life developed in the ancient world by Democritus and Epicurus, revived and given huge vitality by Hobbes and by La Mettrie, had come into eighteenth- and nineteenth-century thinking under the form of "materialism," which was to make life a special expression of forces which in their inwardness consisted simply of incessant and purposeless reorganizations of material particles. In general, despite many ingenious efforts to do away with oversimplification of the problem, those who concerned themselves with the nature of life, and of mind, found themselves forced into monistic interpretations of Democritus' type, or dualistic interpretations such as those of Plato and Descartes. Stating the problem in this guise, it gradually became more and more obvious that scientific method and the scientists' struggle to make order and clarity out of the universe pushed one, more and more, into the "materialistic" camp, and that efforts to preserve the traditional dualism resulted inevitably in one's being classified as a devotee of religion rather than of science in an era in which the "warfare of science and theology" became ever more acute. The more and more exact studies of life processes all through the nineteenth century—studies dealing with embryology and histology as well as with gross anatomy—came more and more to give coherence and conviction to this viewpoint. The disgust of Helmholtz with the "philosophy of nature" was typical of the general nineteenth-century movement of the exact sciences away from dualisms of every type, and in support of a conception of life which placed it squarely within the orbit of ordinary natural—that is, physical—law, and of mind within the scope of the law of life.

We have, therefore, the conditions which led inevitably in the late nineteenth century to a triumphant "materialism," or "mechanism," in which the problems of mind were no longer to be tolerated as such, but were to be reduced to the form of general physical problems. The phrase "mental physiology," coined by the British physician Carpenter,[1] and the pessimistic view of man's higher aspirations (as reducible essentially to brain mechanics, or even brain pathology) as formulated by Maudsley,[2] are characteristic of the movement. In the same era dogmatic mechanism flourished in Germany, notably among the pupils of Haeckel; in France and in Italy such mechanistic trends, joined with other anticlerical forces, had of course been well known since the eighteenth century, and in particular since the French Revolution.

All these predisposing factors were ready to be drawn suddenly into a new creative process, the construction of a "psychology without a soul"—indeed, a psychology which would systematically fulfill the promise of Hobbes and La Mettrie. This was to be a psychology of action rather than of thought, a psychology of physiological processes based upon the physics and chemistry of the response of living tissue. It would inevitably differ from earlier mechanistic psychology in that there would be ready at the disposal of the theorists far greater masses of material regarding the dependence of mental processes upon physiological action patterns, and it would find itself placed in a cosmic scheme following the essentially purposeless pattern of a Darwinian struggle for existence and survival of the fittest.

It was Jacques Loeb, more than any other one person, who finally formalized this mature and complete mechanistic psychology in the closing years of the nineteenth, century. The notion which gave this the specificity, the vivid concreteness, necessary to win the allegiance of eager investigators, was that of the *tropism*.[3] Just as water moves downhill, so the roots of a plant, activated by a more complex physicochemical necessity, find their way toward the center of the earth. Instead of speaking of the "lust for life" which leads the living thing to reach down toward the great mother and source of all living substances, the root is said to be essentially coerced by physical and chemical relations obtaining between it and the soil about it. There is at the same time a tendency for the portion of the plant lying above the earth to make its way upward away from the earth and

---

[1] Carpenter, W. B., *Principles of Mental Physiology* (1874).

[2] Maudsley, H., *Body and Will* (1884).

[3] *Der Heliotropismus der Tiere* (1890).

toward the sun. There are, moreover, lines of conduction within the plant which carry substances and energies from one point to another. We begin to think of the living system as physically one with the environment—not only at its periphery but at its very core. If one thoroughly understood light, warmth, acidity, gravity, and other elementary things which actually are the core of the plant's being, we should have no essential difficulty in explaining its growth, reproduction, distribution over a large area, and ultimately its whole evolutionary position in nature, in reference to the "forced movements" which its environment imposes upon it. The tropism, or turning process—turning toward or away from specific objects in the environment—becomes the key to instinct and to life in general.

Many kindred spirits in the biological sciences eagerly grasped the new theory and proceeded to develop a science of objective behavior in which the traditional problems about the nature of life were stated in terms of the tropism. Just as La Mettrie had concluded that man differs in no essential from the lower animals, so the mechanists concluded that the "forced movements" of simple animals differed in no essential way from those of plants, and that one might, if one wished, extend the interpretation upward to include man.

Many others, who declined to accept *mechanistic philosophy* as such, proceeded nevertheless to formulate the problems of response to the environment in terms of a similar emphasis upon physical factors. The turning of the eyes or of the head, or indeed the running of the animal toward or away from the sight or sound which at the moment stimulated it, was to be conceived without any reference whatever to problems of seeing or hearing or associating or learning. Indeed, one could write a psychology in terms of the tropism theory and make it as systematic as one liked. With the departure of Jacques Loeb from Germany to take up a post at the Rockefeller Institute in New York, it became possible to speak compactly of those who expressed this outlook in Germany as the "German objectivists"; the greatest names were those of Bethe, Beer, and Von Uexküll. They were interested in a biochemistry and biophysics of the living system in which it would be possible to describe the response to sound without saying anything whatever about hearing, or the response to light without saying anything at all about seeing. It was sufficient to write of phonoreceptors and photoreceptors. The fact that they were not mechanists in La Mettrie's sense was the reason why J. B. Watson [4] noted that they remained "orthodox parallelists"; that is, they admitted a place for mental processes as running parallel to

4 See footnote 11, page 259.

physical processes. It should, however, be stressed that their positive program lay entirely within the area of objective study of responses to objective stimulation.

In the same period, within the Russian Empire a new and interesting movement was afoot. It was led at first in two different research centers by two men of quite different research interests. Yet it was destined, throughout all their labors, to be accepted outside Russia as symbolic of essentially the same scientific movement.

I. P. Pavlov attracted attention at the turn of the century through his studies of the physiology of digestion, which won him a Nobel prize and wide prestige. The chemistry and physiology of the digestive processes led him, however, into behavior problems of ever greater complexity. We find less and less about digestion and more and more about the way in which the experimental animal learns to cope with various types of stimulation which mean that food is coming. Pavlov noted early, for example, that the sound of the experimenter's footsteps as he came across the floor would activate the dog's salivary response. It activated the flow of saliva not only in about the same way in which meat powder activated it, but in a way which permitted the establishment of a straightforward quantitative problem: How are the intensities of various stimuli which accompany food to be equated with the stimuli we are using as food in the course of a given experiment? If we find that meat powder in a given quantity stimulates the flow of saliva at a certain rate, as objectively measured, how can we study quantitatively the activation of "psychic reflexes"; that is, reflexes which are aroused no longer by the actual presence of the meat, but by some other type of stimulation which had been previously presented along with the meat? Pavlov sounded a tuning fork simultaneously with the application of a given quantity of powdered meat on a dog's tongue, and repeated this procedure at intervals until the tuning fork alone, without the meat, would produce a reasonably constant flow of saliva. This was the "conditioned reflex" method; the reflex was conditional upon the fact that a given stimulus had been presented together with one which was originally adequate to elicit it.

His early technique involved merely the use of a fistula in the cheek, to collect the saliva. Later he used a more elaborate method: a rubber tube connected with a fistula directed the flow upon a delicate platform resting on a spring. Each drop which fell on the platform caused a movement which was transmitted to a delicate marker upon a revolving drum, so that it was possible to record not only the number of drops but the moment at which each drop fell. This made it possible to state not only the total amount of saliva emitted in a half-minute, but its variation in ten-second intervals, and so on. The saliva meanwhile was collected as it fell from the platform. The effort to standardize conditions, to use rigid control, to eliminate sources of error, was vigorous and sustained.

During the first years of the present century many investigations were undertaken at St. Petersburg to ascertain the number of repetitions needed to build up such conditioned reflexes in the dog under different conditions, the effect of variation of the time interval between original and conditioning stimulus, the influence of other stimuli in inhibiting a conditioned reflex, and kindred problems. This problem of inhibition took on large proportions. If the conditioning stimulus A has come to cause a flow of saliva, but if now an irrelevant stimulus B is presented together with A, to what extent does the stimulus B augment or decrease the reaction? The Pavlov school found evidence that such irrelevant stimuli tend to inhibit the response, the effect varying with the nature and the intensity of the new stimulus. This led to the formulation of quite complicated problems; for example, those relating to the "inhibition of an inhibition." The conditioned-reflex method offered such extraordinary possibilities, a means of answering objectively such a host of fundamental problems in behavior, that it seemed to some investigators almost like a highroad to Paradise.

Early investigations of "discrimination"—heretofore conceived as a subjective problem, a problem of conscious response—are illustrative. Pavlov's pupils undertook to determine how well the dog discriminates tone, in terms of a *differential salivary response* to tones separated by small intervals. Suppose a tuning fork at 256 double vibrations per second is sounded simultaneously with the presentation of meat, so that, in time, the fork alone elicits a marked salivary response. Then a fork of a higher or lower pitch is sounded; saliva again flows. But the dog is not fed. When the original fork is sounded, food is given; when the other fork is sounded, food is withheld. Rapidly the dog exhibits a differential response; the salivary reflex disappears in response to the pitch which has not been attended by food. Now, continuing the use of the 256 fork together with the feeding, other forks are used whose pitch approaches closer and closer to 256, until at last a pitch is found at which the salivary response is of the magnitude which results from 256 itself; the difference between such a pitch and that of the fork vibrating at 256 measures the interval in which pitch discrimination is lacking. In the early years of the school Zeliony obtained with this method indications of very remarkable tone-discrimination, a few vibrations per second proving sufficient to cause not merely the decrease but the total disappearance of the salivary response, the number of drops falling off sharply as the vibration rate rose to 258, 260, and so on.[5] In a similar experiment on color discrimination, Orbeli reported evidence for color-blindness in the dog, hues producing identical responses so long as brightness and saturation were kept constant.[6] (At a later period Pavlov's school reported confirmation of such results, with greatly improved technique, together with much new material based upon this discrimination method.)

Now of course the conception of attaching an old response to a new stimulus was very old and familiar. Loeb had clearly described this mechanism in 1900 *(Physiology of the Brain)*, calling it "associative memory" and describing it quite objectively. Hobbes, Locke, and Spencer, among others, had described some cases of association in terms nearly objective enough to pass for descriptions of conditioned responses. What Pavlov's work accomplished in time was to suggest more fully how, upon this base, a more generalized theory of behavior could be constructed in terms of objective physiological phenomena. For Pavlov was determined to avoid all psychological problems connected with the notion of "association," and with the problem of learning as it had come down through the ages as a psychological problem. He contented himself with the formulation of what he called "conditioned reflexes"; that is, reflexes conditional upon the history of association between adequate stimuli, such as meat, and associated stimuli, such as footsteps. He rejected all appeals regarding the formulation of psychological problems and warned his students to keep away from psychology. Though he had become within a decade a hero of the rapidly developing psychology of objective-behavior study, his response to an invitation to attend the International Congress of Psychology in 1929 was that he doubted whether psychologists would really be interested in what he had to say. Persuaded at last, in his old age, he met many of those who for years had been his devoted disciples.

[5] *The Orientation of the Dog to Sound* (1905); *Contributions to the Study of Reactions of the Dog to Auditory Stimuli* (1907). See Yerkes, R. M., and Morgulis, S., "The Method of Pavlov in Animal Psychology," *Psychol. Bull.*, 1909, 6, 257–73.

[6] *Conditioned Reflexes Resulting from Optical Stimulation of the Dog* (1908).

Imbued with the same objective spirit was the indefatigable Russian physiologist and neurologist Bekhterev, pioneer in a half-dozen research areas, who in the opening years of the century was studying human learning and thought processes with objective techniques. His cardinal concept was the reflex, and the objective avenue to all higher phenomena lay in the fact that reflexes are elicited not only by the few stimuli which are in themselves adequate (for example, electric shock for retraction of the finger), but by many others which are associated with these. He showed, for example, that sights and sounds present at the time the reflex occurred could soon elicit the reflex without the presence of the original stimulus. The associationists would have regarded this as a mental process; for Bekhterev it remained a reflex. Reflex responses of the striped musculature received chief emphasis. He suggested that more complex habits might involve the compounding of such motor reflexes, and that the thought process itself, depending on inner activities of the musculature of speech, was essentially of the same character. It finally became his conviction that all the problems of psychology could be handled in this way. The theory was presented in a volume with the title *Objective Psychology* in 1907, parts of which appeared later in French [7] and in German. A decade later he used the term "reflexology." [8] Proceeding in this way, he extended his studies to include experiments on interaction in the social group, to which he gave the name "collective reflexology." [9]

No more than Pavlov was he concerned to deny the *existence* of consciousness. His whole concern was with the positive problem of writing a description of behavior in which the language of physiology would suffice. While Pavlov worked slowly and systematically in the development of a precise laboratory technique, and only after some twenty years allowed himself to be drawn into a broad systematic exposition of the nature of conditioned reflexes, Bekhterev rapidly sketched out a theory of learning through conditioning which made it possible to formulate acts of a high degree of complexity as compounds of conditioned responses. Attaching special importance to response to symbols, and emphasizing the acquisition of verbal symbols as a key to the development of the world of thought, imagination, and volition, Bekhterev constructed a complete system. A great deal of this broad system of psychology consists of special pleading for a monistic approach to the mind, as an expres-

[7] *La psychologie objective* (1913).

[8] *General Principles of Human Reflexology* (1917).

[9] Bekhterev, V. M., and Lange, M. de, *Zschr. f. angew. Psychol.*, 1924, 24, 305–44.

sion of bodily activity; but it is buttressed by a great deal of experimental and clinical material. As a plea for a point of view, his book would probably have attracted no special attention. As a cornerstone, however, of a new psychological system, in which all the higher processes were to be systematically reduced to *symbolic responses based on conditioning*, it was certainly the most original effort at monistic psychology that had appeared in the post-Darwinian era.

The aspect of the new approach which first attracted the attention of American experimentalists was the salivary-reflex method of approaching the psychology of discrimination. Yerkes and Morgulis brought this to their colleagues' attention in a general review of Pavlov's work in 1909 (see footnote 5, page 257). The use of the new discrimination technique did not, however, carry with it Pavlov's scorn for subjective analysis, nor did it eliminate from American work the discussion of the subjective side of the animal's responses. Washburn, in *The Animal Mind* (1908), devoted considerable attention to the analysis of the probable conscious states attending observed behavior. Yerkes, the most prolific in research among American experimentalists in the first years of this century, continued to employ many terms from the study of consciousness, discussing, for example, "ideational" behavior.[10]

WATSON

Now, in the spirit of the whole trend away from the concern with consciousness, an independent movement began in the work of J. B. Watson.[11] Watson was impelled, on the one hand, by his recognition of the fertility of the many new objective methods of animal psychology, to explore more and more into the nature of the learning process as a problem in the modification of *behavior*. And on the other hand, he was much disgusted by the inability of introspective psychologists, such as Titchener, Angell, and Woodworth, to demonstrate a finality with respect to imageless thought. There seemed to be great unreliability in the testimony of human subjects as to their imagery, and this seemed to give ground for doubt as to the possibility of using the image as a datum for psychology. The

---

[10] "Ideational Behavior of Monkeys and Apes," *Proc. Nat. Acad. Sci.*, 1916, 2, 639–42.

[11] Watson believed that Thorndike stimulated him much more than did the "objectivists," whose "parallelism" he contrasts with his own monistic system. (See the Preface to the first edition of the *Psychology from the Standpoint of a Behaviorist*, 1919.)

whole conception of consciousness, as Watson understood it—a stuff to be introspectively analyzed—seemed to him to involve dualism of mind and body. As an avowed materialist, Watson decided to throw overboard the entire concept of mind or consciousness, and to make both animal and human psychology the study of behavior. Modifications of behavior were to be studied in terms of stimulus-response situations, not at all in terms of conscious concomitants or neurological assumptions.

A first formulation of a behaviorist system of psychology was presented to a seminar at the University of Chicago in 1908. In 1912 came an opportunity to lecture at Columbia, on Cattell's invitation, and the result was the paper which appeared in the *Psychological Review* in 1913: "Psychology as the Behaviorist Views It." Here we have the beginnings of a psychological system which has a place for receptor functions, effector functions, and learning, but none for sensation, image, or feeling. The gauntlet was thrown down dramatically in the first chapter of his new textbook the following year, *Behavior: An Introduction to Comparative Psychology*, in which it is perfectly plain that not animal psychology alone, but all psychology, can achieve the status of science by objective definition of all its problems. The same volume affords numerous concrete examples of the concepts which he believed must be pruned away. In the "law of effect," for example (cf. page 239 above), Thorndike had maintained that if an animal does something which brings about *satisfaction*, the result is an improvement in the conductivity of the neural connections leading to the performance of the act. Acts which cause annoyance involve a decrease in neural conductivity tending to the elimination of the act. Watson objected not only to the concepts of satisfaction and annoyance, but to the claim that there was here a factor not taken account of by the principles of frequency and recency. If a cat obtains food immediately after the movement of releasing the bolt of a puzzle box, this movement is the *last* act of all that occur in the cage. Furthermore, whereas unsuccessful movements are legion, there is but one successful movement; over a number of trials the successful movement will therefore be repeated more *frequently* than any other.[12]

Some extraordinarily interesting things happened to the theory early in 1916. Watson's presidential address to the American Psy-

[12] To this it was retorted that in many cases one successful movement was promptly learned, while an unsuccessful movement, *though repeated several times in the same trial*, was eliminated. See Thorndike, E. L., and Herrick, C. J., "Watson's 'Behavior,' " *J. An. Behav.*, 1915, 5, 462–70.

chological Association in December 1915 had stressed the possibility of studying discrimination by the differential-response technique (cf. page 256).[13] But conditioning received no mention as a general clue to the learning process. That winter, however, Watson got hold of the French and German translations of Bekhterev (cf. page 258), and saw that here was just what he wanted. He began to see that his own objective psychology might well stress conditioning as the clue to all learning, and to all higher processes. So rapidly did he think out the implications that a new approach to psychopathology was offered within a few months: What we have called a sick mind is the result of a training process. The "psychopathological" dog will eat decayed meat, will avoid fresh meat; but the mystery disappears if we know the punishments which fresh meat bring him. So too, if we knew the history of our human maladjustments, we could explain them all in terms of conditioning.

With these new vistas before him, Watson turned energetically to human problems, especially to problems in infant psychology. He and J. J. B. Morgan sketched in 1917 the possibility of a psychology of personality based on early conditioning. In the winter of 1916–17 a small grant and an opportunity to work at the Phipps Clinic in Baltimore had led Watson to studies of reflexes and instinctive behavior in the newborn.

Publishing in 1919 a general textbook of psychology,[14] Watson went forward with studies of infant conditioning. In collaboration with Raynor, he first ascertained that furry animals caused no fear in children about a year old; then noted their fear of the clanging sound of a hammer on a metal bar; then struck this bar whenever the child touched the furry animal.[15] Fear in response to the animal, without the bar, was soon evident. Despite its crudeness, this experiment immediately had a profound effect on American psychology; for it appeared to support the whole conception that not only simple motor habits, but important, enduring traits of personality, such as emotional tendencies, may in fact be "built into" the child by conditioning.

While the first definitions of behaviorism were stated in rather negative terms (in terms of the exclusion of parts of the subject matter of contemporary psychology),[16] the movement was rapidly

[13] "Behavior and the Concept of Mental Disease," *J. Phil.*, 1916, 13, 589–97.
[14] *Psychology from the Standpoint of a Behaviorist* (1919).
[15] Watson, J. B., and Raynor, R., "Conditioned Emotional Reactions," *J. Exp. Psychol.*, 1920, 3, 1–14.
[16] "Psychology as the Behaviorist Views It," *Psychol. Rev.*, 1913, 20, 158–77.

developing a system of positive assumptions, and working these into a psychological system. Even in his earliest work, Watson emphasized the right of the behaviorist to think of "mental" processes as *internal* forms of behavior, the relation of language to thought being especially stressed. Indeed, one of Watson's most important theoretical contributions was the suggestion, and as time elapsed the insistence, that all the phenomena of "inner" life are in reality the functioning of mechanisms which are as objective, though not as observable, as gross muscular contractions. In particular, imagination and thought have been stated in terms of "implicit" muscular behavior, especially the behavior of the speech organs and other mechanisms which symbolize lines of overt conduct. The study of language is therefore of paramount importance for the formulation of behaviorist theory.

It is necessary, of course, to distinguish between "passive language habits" (the response to words) and "active language habits" (the use of words). The interpretation of passive language habits in behavior terms turned out to be very simple. E. B. Holt,[17] a neo-realist who early declared himself a behaviorist, put the matter well. Words, acting as substitutes for situations, *evoke the same responses* that the situations themselves would elicit.[18] The "meaning" of a word is nothing but a conditioned response to that word. We can see this plainly in the case of movements which have arisen in the history of the individual in relation to specific objects; for example, in the act of reaching. If the child reaches for a bottle and the word "bottle" is repeated many times in connection with it, the word "bottle" will in time produce in the child the specific kind of appropriate reaching movement; a conditioned response has been established. What the word "bottle" *means* is the behavior in reference to it. If bottle, glass, and pitcher have to be grasped and manipulated in different ways, the meanings are provided by the different motor responses.

But active language was a larger problem. To this problem Watson addressed himself in a paper presented to the International Congress of Philosophy and Psychology in 1920;[19] his view was later set forth in the second edition (1924) of his *Psychology from the Standpoint of a*

[17] Holt, E. B., *The Freudian Wish and Its Place in Ethics* (1915).

[18] This obvious fact was of course not put forward as a new discovery, but the grasping of its implications for behaviorism was important.

[19] In a symposium: "Is Thinking Merely the Action of Language Mechanisms?" (*Brit. J. Psychol.*, 1920, 11, 87–104.) Though Watson was not present, his paper became the subject of much discussion.

Behaviorist, and in *Behaviorism* (1925). Beginning with the random babblings of the child, any sounds that cause other persons to minister to the child's needs tend in the long run to be repeated more often than sounds which bring little or no result.[20] Consequently, the child develops, purely through such trial-and-error variations, sounds which, by approximating genuine words, bring quicker and better results. No mechanism of learning need be supposed other than those manifest in the rat's learning the maze, or the cat's learning to escape from the puzzle box. The child learns to say "da-da," and later "doll" by the same mechanism. If the word "da-da" is used and is understood by others to mean doll, it serves the purpose; the only thing necessary is that it should work. Whenever it fails to work, further trial and error occurs until "doll" is uttered.[21]

So far, we have the process by which the chief terms used in thinking—namely, words—are learned as separate units; they are now integrated, in like manner with other forms of behavior, into "higher

[20] This would, of course, be cited by Thorndike's followers as a case of the "law of effect." From the behaviorists' viewpoint we are dealing simply with the elimination of irrelevant responses (see page 260).

[21] In the view just stated, the *imitation* of words can be explained only by assuming an extraordinary amount of random activity which develops, step by step, a child's ability to duplicate what it hears or sees. But observation of the degree of successful imitation present in the second year of life suggested the need of an explanation which will not insist upon the laborious process just described, yet will avoid recourse to the theory of the "instinct of imitation." F. H. Allport (*Social Psychology*, 1924) utilized for the purpose a doctrine developed by J. M. Baldwin (*Mental Development in the Child and the Race*, 1895) a quarter-century before, the "circular reflex." Baldwin had asserted that the constant repetition of a movement might be due to the fact that each movement serves as a stimulus for its own repetition; as, for instance, when a monkey was observed to slap a surface of water over and over again. Allport assumed that the child's random utterances stimulate its auditory brain area while its motor-speech centers are still active; a connection is thus established which may lead to almost endless repetition of a sound. Such a reaction having been established between the hearing of a sound and the uttering of it, the utterance of a sound by another individual may cause, immediately, the child's repetition of it. This view seems really a supplement to the Watsonian view, rather than a direct contradiction of it. Imitation itself is regarded not as the perception of the utility of duplicating an observed act, but as a type of behavior which appears only as motor mechanisms have been practiced, ineffective acts having been rejected and effective ones gradually selected. As the sparrow *gradually* learns to approximate the songs of the canaries with which he is caged, but can, after such learning, copy a trill with sudden and dramatic success (Conradi, E., "Song and Call-Notes of English Sparrows When Reared by Canaries," *Amer. J. Psychol.*, 1905, 16, 190–98), so all imitative conduct is based on the previous mastery of the necessary elements.

units." The next step is to show how this overt language is replaced by internal language; that is, how we learn to talk to ourselves instead of talking aloud. Watson suggests that the child's vocalization is eliminated through social pressure, so that children in talking to themselves no longer talk aloud, but in a whisper.[22] Only one modification is necessary to change ordinary speech to a whisper; namely, that the vocal cords should be relaxed instead of innervated. All the rest of the speech mechanism works as before. Finally, whispering itself is eliminated, yet speech movements continue; "implicit" language activity continues in the form of constant changes in tension among the various speech mechanisms, which are duplicates of the movement involved in overt speech.

It will be recalled that several authors (cf. page 240) had described thinking in terms of mental experimentation, and had shown the close similarity between thought and overt trial-and-error behavior. Ruger had shown that a good deal of this trial-and-error activity exists in the thought processes involved in solving new and complicated problems. Now the trial-and-error mechanism, as described by Ruger, consisted, to a large extent, in the manipulation of ideas or attitudes. These processes lend themselves to construction in terms of language mechanisms. Thinking consists, therefore, for the behaviorist, of speech movements made on a very small scale, and substituted for overt acts.[23] Trial and error goes on in implicit language behavior, each word or phrase in the thinking process serving as a substitute for some act. No longer do we find "ideas," but speech movements, as the elements involved in thought.

Behaviorism, therefore, had stated the thought processes in terms of language, which, through the conditioned response, serves in place of similarly conditioned overt acts. To be sure, there must be forms of thinking which are not verbal, and these are stated by the behaviorists in terms of gesture, of movements of the hands, feet, neck, trunk, and especially of the eyes.[24] The elaborate study of eye

[22] *Psychology from the Standpoint of a Behaviorist*, 2nd ed. (1924), pp. 343 ff.

[23] Bain, Ribot, and others had described speech movements which occur in the process of thinking; but the *identification* of such movements with the thinking process is the work of Watson.

[24] But behaviorists insist that speech movements can rarely be wholly eliminated. Children seldom, if ever, succeed in completely eliminating the tongue and lip movements associated with the original printed word. The deaf and dumb use their fingers to think with: Watson has, in fact, reminded the incredulous that Laura Bridgman could be observed to talk in her sleep by means of her fingers.

movements, begun by Helmholtz, had been continued by many experimenters. The relation of these movements to the reading process had become a fertile field of inquiry early in the present century, and it was easy for the behaviorist to press such studies into his service by suggesting that memory for verbal material, as well as for events observed, may be in part the repetition of the eye movements which have occurred before, repeated in abbreviated form. Slight ("implicit") gestures and delicate eye movements co-operate constantly with speech movements in the complex processes of thought. Though the brain remains a connecting station, it is for the behaviorist no more intelligible to say that we think with the brain than to say that we walk with the spinal cord.[25]

In place of the classical doctrine of the association of ideas, behaviorism substitutes the conception of an ordered series of *motor* responses. The center of gravity is moved, so to speak, from the cortex to the periphery. The facts pertaining to "mental set," or the "motives" which give direction to the thought process, occasion no difficulty. Such mental sets are themselves, in part, a matter of verbal organization which plays its part in the total conditioning, while motives are intraorganic stimuli—"visceral tensions" or other disturbances which may give rise to verbal trial and error. They set going implicit activity just as they set going overt muscular trial and error, until some act puts an end to the tension.[26]

[25] The associationists, from Hartley on, although writing of the "association of ideas," had with few exceptions assumed that the real basis for mental connections lies in brain connections. Behaviorism undertook to get rid not only of "mental" connections, but of emphasis upon the mechanisms of cortical connection. If the neurologist wishes to study brain connections, well and good; the psychologist is concerned with observable behavior.

[26] As regards experimental evidence for the behavioristic theory of the process of thinking, many investigations (for example, Reed, H. B., "The Existence and Function of Inner Speech in Thought-Processes," *J. Exp. Psychol.*, 1916, 1, 365–90) have indeed shown a relation between the movements of the tongue and the thinking process, indicating that in some cases of silent thought the tongue actually traces the form of overt speech. The evidence seems to indicate, however, that the identity of form between "uttered" and "thought" syllables is at least very far from universal (Thorson, A., "The Relation of Tongue-Movements to Internal Speech," *J. Exp. Psychol.*, 1925, 3, 1–32). The rejoinder of the behaviorists lays stress on variations in muscular tonus too delicate to be observed, and on symbolic movements executed by other parts of the speech mechanism, or indeed of the whole body. (See also Max, L. W., "Experimental Study of the Motor Theory of Consciousness." IV. "Action-Current Responses in the Deaf during Awakening, Kinaesthetic Imagery and Abstract Thinking," *J. Comp. Psychol.*, 1937, 24, 301–44; and Jacobson, E., *Progressive Relaxation*, 2d ed., pp. 327–45.)

SPREAD OF THE CONDITIONED-RESPONSE METHOD

In the meantime, the conditioned-response *method* was beginning to be widely applied in human psychology, with profound consequences for psychological theory,[27] both within and outside the behaviorist movement. Lashley, for example, demonstrated that the conditioned salivary reflex could be elicited in human beings through the sight of chocolate candy, a small cup against the parotid gland collecting quantities of saliva which varied with the nearness of the stimulus.[28] Continuing the conditioning studies with infants initiated by Krasnogorski,[29] Mateer[30] demonstrated conditioned opening of the mouth in response to tactual contact, comparing rate of learning with intelligence level (mental age).

New possibilities of the method were likewise shown by Cason, who found that the pupillary reflex can be conditioned by the simultaneous presentation of visual and auditory stimuli.[31] A sound may in time produce those pupillary contractions which resulted originally from light. It was inevitable that profound changes in the definition of the learning process should follow from all these new studies, and that they should lead toward a restatement of the whole problem as to the mechanism by which connections between stimuli and responses are altered. They helped greatly in the effort of Watson and his followers and intellectual comrades to see their way clear to utilize these simple doctrines in the construction of the new systematic psychology which was to reduce such time-honored problems as perception, judgment, intelligence and reasoning, emotion and personality, to the more elementary forms of response. For one result of such intensive study of the conditioned response, and of the recognition of its importance for the theory of learning, has been the tendency of behaviorists to believe that *all* learning is simply conditioning, and that the conditioned response is the true *unit* of learned behavior.[32] The first formulation of behaviorism, as we saw,

[27] An early summary and bibliography appears in Cason, H., "The Conditioned Reflex or Conditioned Response as a Common Activity of Living Organisms," *Psychol. Bull.*, 1925, 22, 445–72.

[28] "The Human Salivary Reflex and Its Use in Psychology," *Psychol. Rev.*, 1916, 23, 446–64.

[29] *Ueber die Bildung der künstlichen Bedingungsreflexe bei Säuglingen* (1907).

[30] *Child Behavior* (1918).

[31] "The Conditioned Pupillary Reaction," *J. Exp. Psychol.*, 1922, 5, 108–46. See also his "The Conditioned Eyelid Reaction," *ibid.*, 153–96.

[32] Watson, *Behaviorism* (1925), pp. 157 ff.; Smith and Guthrie (*General Psychology in Terms of Behavior*, 1921), are forerunners of this view.

relied in no way upon conditioning; but it became the core, and for some psychologists the chief criterion, of behaviorist theory. (Cf. also Chapter 20.) No less important for behaviorism has been the consistent exclusion of the concept of "ideational" behavior and of the claim that animals and men are capable of sudden "insight" into situations in terms other than those of previous learning and the operation of trial and error. And emphasis on the genetic method leads the behaviorist always to inquire regarding the organism's previous conditioning.

The popularity of behaviorism in the United States became so great that a multitude of objective experiments, as well as a multitude of theories, were loosely termed "behavioristic," although little indeed of the behaviorist system was involved. Behaviorism has become in some quarters not so much a research program as a name for mechanistic psychology (essentially in accord with La Mettrie's conception of the mechanistic, cf. page 20),[33] or on the other hand has been reduced to a mere *emphasis* upon objective, as opposed to subjective, data. The description of experience known only to the subject, as in dreams, is admitted even by Watson, the interest lying ostensibly in the sleeper's implicit behavior and in his verbal reports. Indeed, the proportions of the movement would be greatly understated were we to confine the term to a set of experiments or to the program of 1914. Accurately or inaccurately, "behaviorism" means to many psychologists today any of the following:

1. The biological approach to animal and human psychology, promising that psychology shall one day make itself as objective as physical science.

2. A mechanistic or materialist view of psychology.

3. Watson's personal combination of (1) and (2).

4. Other behavior-centered systems, such as those of Tolman, Hull, and Skinner, mentioned in the following chapter.

In other words, the progeny of the behaviorism of a few decades ago are already very diverse in appearance and in disposition.

[33] "To me the essence of behaviorism is the belief that the study of man will reveal nothing except what is adequately describable in the concepts of mechanics and chemistry, and this far outweighs the question of the method by which the study is conducted."—Lashley, K. S., "The Behavioristic Interpretation of Consciousness," *Psychol. Rev.*, 1923, 30, 237–72; 329–53; the quotation is from p. 244. Such quotations might be multiplied indefinitely. For many the term "behaviorism" simply summarizes the whole trend toward "natural-science" psychology, and in particular, the trend away from psychophysical dualism. Probably the most coherent statement of *behaviorist theory* is A. P. Weiss, *A Theoretical Basis of Human Behavior* (1925); yet it was not coherence, but simple intelligible experiment, that was in chief demand.

REFERENCES

Heidbreder, Edna, *Seven Psychologies,* Century, 1933

Pavlov, Ivan Petrovich, *Lectures on Conditioned Reflexes,* International Publishers, 1928

Watson, John B., *Behaviorism,* Norton, 1924

———, *Psychology from the Standpoint of a Behaviorist,* Lippincott, 1919

Woodworth, Robert S., *Contemporary Schools of Psychology,* rev. ed., Ronald Press, 1948

Chapter 19

MODERN CONCEPTIONS
OF ASSOCIATION

*There can be indefinitely more "mind" accumulated as time
goes on, now that we have the trick.*

JAMES HARVEY ROBINSON

UNDER the title *Association Theory Today*, E. S. Robinson presented in 1932 an essay to show what had become of the classical outlines of associationist doctrine. He, among others, called attention to the fact that despite its official departure, coroner's inquest, and interment, it has gone cheerfully forward, and has in fact been able not only to maintain its own life, but to give life to many a psychological movement. Thus it inspired many of the early labors of Janet, Freud, and Jung; thus it colored early work on the conditioned response; thus it served as guide through the laborious studies of learning by Thorndike and others; and thus, though serving as whipping boy for other doctrines, it has become toughened in the process and reappeared in ever new systematic form. Guthrie holds that association is the only theory of learning that has ever been proposed; [1] and while there is no need to discuss this paradox at this point, it shows how unwilling the associationists are to agree to their own death sentence.

As pointed out earlier, most of the traditional laws of association (relating, for example, to recency, frequency, and intensity, and the effects of rewards and punishments) were taken over by behaviorism and restated in terms of objective stimulus-response relationships. If there is more emphasis upon behavioral phenomena, and less emphasis upon mental connections in the classical sense, in the learning experiments of the present century, one must still admit that it is associationism with which one is concerned. It is true that

---

[1] Guthrie, E. R., *The Psychology of Learning* (1935).

this contemporary associationism has begun to think in terms of the life of an organism whose tissues owe their very structure to the evolutionary process, and is ready at every point to manifest a rich individuality. Yet an interest in generalizations as contrasted with individual differences is surely legitimate, and if the general dynamics is essentially the dynamics associationism has always stressed, it would be arbitrary to insist that they must lose caste merely because reference to the evolutionary doctrine is not explicitly made today as was the fashion in the latter part of the nineteenth century. The huge evolutionary wave which washed over the associationists drove them from view for a while. Moist but still kicking, they reappeared as the wave moved on.

An example of contemporary associationism, in the strict sense of the word, is the study of connections made in the process of learning nonsense syllables, with major emphasis upon the reinforcing and inhibiting effects which appear when many potential connections are jointly involved. In terms of classical conceptions of the *reinforcing* effect of association, made all the more vivid by Sherrington's discussion of *summation*, and likewise the traditional principle of *interference*, made more vivid by Sherrington's discussion of *inhibition*, one finds studies of the quantitative effects of various types of reinforcement and inhibition as material is learned and as it is recalled. Typical of such an interest is the much quoted investigation by Jenkins and Dallenbach,[2] later confirmed by Van Ormer,[3] showing that during sleep little or nothing is forgotten. A subject awakened at various times in the night and required to recall nonsense material learned earlier, shows no decrement through time. He does, however, very quickly show such a decrement while remaining awake; and it becomes probable that the curve of forgetting, as classically investigated, deals with progressive interference and not with time effects as such. In the same vein are the many investigations of retroactive inhibition—the interference in recall which is evident when after a learning period one learns further material before trying to recall the first. It is the general opinion among modern associationists that the laws governing learning and recall must take account of various types of interference due to similarity in the materials.[4]

[2] Jenkins, J. G., and Dallenbach, K. M., "Oblivescence during Sleep and Waking," *Amer. J. Psychol.*, 1924, 35, 605–12.

[3] Van Ormer, E. B., "Retention after Intervals of Sleep and of Waking," *Arch. Psychol.*, 1932, No. 137.

[4] McGeoch, J. A., *The Psychology of Human Learning* (1942).

While all this type of experimental study of rote or meaningful material *learned voluntarily* by the adult human subject has maintained its place in the experimental world, there is likewise no doubt that other simple connection-forming processes, viewed objectively either in terms of the conditioned response or in some other kind of behavior language, have had even greater vogue, and that because of this vogue, the elaborate doctrines of Pavlov having to do with excitability and drowsiness, and with inhibition and the inhibition of inhibitions, have served as guides to many, both of the orthodox and of various deviant behaviorist groups. Our illustrations will have to be few and somewhat arbitrarily selected, but the dependence of contemporary work upon classical associationism on the one hand, and objective connection-forming on the other, can be easily brought out by almost any examples that might be chosen.

We might begin with Walter Hunter,[5] who succeeded early in the behaviorist era in showing that response to that which is no longer acting upon the senses—that is, response to the absent world—can be studied objectively. Place the animal or the small child in a situation from which there are several different directions in which he may move, but with only one direction leading to the food or toy which satisfies his need; let him discover that a light marks the direction which is thus to be rewarded. When he has thus been trained, throw on the light and then throw it off again before the individual is free to move. He nevertheless can, in some cases, maintain his orientation—that is, keep himself properly aimed somehow, though the light has been extinguished; when free to move, he takes the right direction. This *delayed response* involves the maintenance of orientation to an absent stimulus.

Hudgins, working closely with Hunter, has suggested that what has been called the *will* can at least in part be conceived in terms of conditioning.[6] A bright light is flashed into the eye and the contraction of the pupil measured. Now for hundreds of presentations the light is flashed by means of a device operated by the subject himself who, in strongly squeezing a dynamometer and saying the word "contract," also activates the lamp which flashes light into his own eyes. After such prolonged reinforcement, it is now only necessary that he squeeze the dynamometer and say the word "contract," and not necessary that the light be used further. The pupil still contracts. At a later stage, even uttering the word "contract" causes the

[5] *The Delayed Reaction in Animals and Children* (1913).

[6] Hudgins, C. V., "Conditioning and the Voluntary Control of the Pupillary Light Reflex," *J. Gen. Psychol.*, 1933, 8, 3–51.

pupillary contraction; and even inner or subvocal utterance of the word "contract" has a similar effect. The inner world becomes for Hunter and Hudgins the world of muscular, including verbal, activity, which operates in the form of conditioned stimuli for overt conduct. (The Hudgins experiment has proved difficult to repeat. Our interest here is in the conception and the approach.[7])

It has been an important feature of this whole modern movement to emphasize peripheral rather than central factors as far as possible. Characteristic of the trend is Guthrie's insistence that the motor phenomena observed in any conditioning experiment are themselves fundamental in reinforcing an activity in progress.[7a] He refers to "movement-produced stimuli"; that is, the types of stimulation coming from the muscles which are merged with those stimuli which have come in through other receptors at the time of the conditioning experience. Along with this emphasis upon peripheral mechanisms goes the conception that if you once know exactly what the organism has done, you know exactly what it will do a second time if it is placed in the same situation. The animal or the man tends to do in any given situation the thing which it did *last* when confronting that situation at an earlier time. A long series of varying activities ("trial and error") involves, of course, a great deal of interference or un-learning of what went before; if you systematically study the process of successive elimination and find what the animal last did when confronted by a particular field of stimulation, you know what it will do if again placed there.

This systematic objectivism and the desire to quantify elaborately the various phases of the learning process in a form involving as much as possible of the Pavlovian program has been especially character-istic of Clark Hull in the Yale University Laboratory.[8] In a long series of experiments, many of which have been elaborately treated from a mathematical viewpoint, a sustained effort has been made to reduce the more complex types of learning to the formation of associations through reinforcement. He has also emphasized another conception, only very slightly noted by Watson, Hunter, Hudgins, Guthrie, and many others of the associationist school; namely, the conception of goals—goals defined as objects which put an end to

---

[7] There had been several earlier studies of the acquisition of voluntary control over striped or unstriped musculature not ordinarily under such control. Cf., for example, Bair, J. H., "Development of Voluntary Control," *Psychol. Rev.*, 1901, 8, 474–510.

[7a] Cf. footnote 1, page 269.

[8] *The Principles of Behavior* (1943).

the tensions or needs which serve as the mainspring to activity.[9] We need no subjective definitions of goals as satisfying objects. (On the basis of close association with Hull and his experiments, Mowrer crisply defines satisfactions objectively in terms of tension reduction.[10] Needs become quiescent when the organism comes into direct contact with the goal object.) Hull undertakes to show systematically that it is contact with the goal which operates to reinforce the activities which have led to such contact, and the closer an act is to the goal, the more it is reinforced by the goal. Or, stating the matter the other way around, the more remote it is, the less effect the goal exerts upon it. There is a "goal gradient" which can thus be quantitatively defined. It is thus not very difficult to bring conditioning theory into line with the classical associationist view that rewards and punishments, pleasures and pains, act in some way to reinforce some acts and to inhibit others; goals offer rewards, and failure to reach them is punishment.

With Hull, behavior study is an objective quantitative science; both stimulation and response are measured, and their interrelation treated in terms of the most rigorous available mathematical formulation. It is nevertheless proper and necessary to set up postulates regarding the events that go on inside the organism between the stimulation and the response, and to test these postulates by constant recourse to critical experiments which show how well the behavior conforms with expectations derived from the postulates. It is hoped that one summary figure from Hull [11] (page 274) may help to convey some idea of the systematic quantitative form of the resulting behavior system.

Another approach which has much of the Pavlovian flavor, but emphasizes complex types of needs and goal orientations, is that of Razran,[12] who has shown in a long series of experimental and theoretical studies that competition between conditioned responses leads to the firm establishment of one and the obliteration of its competitor, rather than a compromise between the two. He has emphasized that the attitude or set of the subject makes a profound differ-

[9] Hull, C. L., "The Goal Gradient Hypothesis and Maze Learning," *Psychol. Rev.*, 1932, 39, 25–43.

[10] Mowrer, O. H., "The Law of Effect and Ego Psychology," *Psychol. Rev.*, 1946, 53, 321–34.

[11] Reprinted by permission of the publisher, Appleton-Century-Crofts, from *Principles of Behavior* by Clark L. Hull, p. 383.

[12] Razran, G. H. S., "Studies in Configural Conditioning: V. Generalization and Transposition," *J. Genet. Psychol.*, 1940, 56, 3–11; "Attitudinal Control of Human Conditioning," *J. Psychol.*, 1936, 2, 327–37.

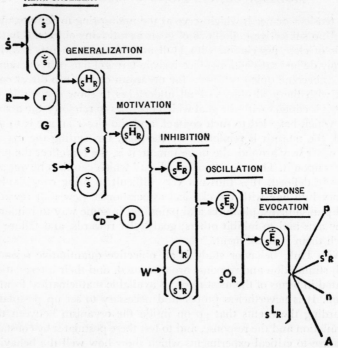

REINFORCEMENT

Diagram summarizing the major symbolic constructs (encircled symbols) employed in the present system of behavior theory, together with the symbols of the supporting objectively observable conditions and events. In this diagram $\dot{S}$ represents the physical stimulus energy involved in learning; R, the organism's reaction; $\dot{s}$, the neural result of the stimulus; $\breve{s}$, the neural interaction arising from the impact of two or more stimulus components; r, the efferent impulse leading to reaction; G, the occurrence of a reinforcing state of affairs; $_sH_R$, habit strength; S, evocation stimulus on the same stimulus continuum as $\dot{S}$; $_s\bar{H}_R$, the generalized habit strength; C_D, the objectively observable phenomena determining the drive; D, the physiological strength of the drive to motivate action; $_sE_R$, the reaction potential; W, work involved in an evoked reaction; I_R, reactive inhibition; $_sI_R$, conditioned inhibition; $_s\bar{E}_R$, effective reaction potential; $_sO_R$, oscillation; $_s\dot{\bar{E}}_R$, momentary effective reaction potential; $_sL_R$, reaction threshold; p, probability of reaction evocation; $_st_R$, latency of reaction evocation; n, number of unreinforced reactions to produce experimental extinction; and A, amplitude of reaction. Above the symbols the lines beneath the words *reinforcement, generalization, motivation, inhibition, oscillation,* and *response evocation* indicate roughly the segments of the chain of symbolic constructs with which each process is especially concerned.

ence in determining which of several possible conditioned responses will be manifest at a given time, and has continued experiments to show that patterns or configurations can serve just as well as simple stimuli in setting up conditioned responses. At a more complex level Luria demonstrated in the twenties in the Soviet Union that conditioned responses may compete and interfere either at a motor or at a symbolic level, and that very complex human adjustments (cf. page 258) can be formulated in terms of a theory similar to that of the exponents of conditioning.[13]

One other branch of conditioning work which has been highly influential in clinical and psychiatric problems is the conception of the *experimental neurosis*, conceived, as a rule, as a response to a conditioning situation involving stress. Typical here are the many studies of Liddell[14] and his collaborators, who have found under sharply defined conditions what kinds of time relations between conditioned and unconditioned stimuli give rise to what types of conflict and neurotic responses in experimental animals. Finally, conditioning theory has been brought very close indeed to a physiological formulation by experiments in which the locus of the nerve tracts involved has been specified, as by the electrical stimulation administered by Loucks and Gantt at specific points in the nervous system;[15] and in the studies by Girden and Culler showing that a drug may produce a functional block between two habit systems,[16] so that in the drugged state the animal shows conditioned responses learned in earlier drugged states, while in the drugless state he shows only responses learned in the drugless condition. From all such studies one gets the impression that physiological psychology, comparative psychology, and medicine, as well as the general theory of learning, are all leavened more and more by the method and the theoretical construction of Pavlov.

Through this whole period Thorndike, pioneer in the study of animal learning in the nineties, has continued to be a figure of immense importance. Thorndike does not lend himself easily to classification. Much of his formulation, as we shall see, is association-

[13] Luria, A. R., *The Nature of Human Conflicts* (1932).

[14] Liddell, H. S., "Conditioned Reflex Method and Experimental Neurosis," in Hunt, J. McV., *Personality and the Behavior Disorders*, 2 vols. (1944), pp. 389–412.

[15] Loucks, R. B., and Gantt, W. H., "The Conditioning of Striped Muscle Responses Based upon Faradic Stimulation of Dorsal Roots and Dorsal Columns of the Spinal Cord," *J. Comp. Psychol.*, 1938, 25, 415–26.

[16] Girden, E., and Culler, E., "Conditioned Responses in Curarized Striate Muscle in Dogs," *J. Comp. Psychol.*, 1937, 23, 261–74; Girden, E., "Conditioned Responses in Curarized Monkeys," *Amer. J. Psychol.*, 1947, 60, 571–87.

ist, or as he has preferred to say, connectionist. Learning is the establishment of connections. Here and there he recognizes that a good deal has been learned from studies of conditioning, but he has regularly insisted that the most important phenomena of learning are essentially unlike those which appear in the conditioning situation. He might be thought of as one who emphasizes subjective factors; yet as the years have gone on, his definitions have continued to become more objective. And while he has very obviously been influenced by Gestalt research and formulation, he has continued to prefer a sharply analytical procedure, even to the extent of writing quite caustically regarding many of the central Gestalt conceptions.

After a period of primary attention to the testing of human abilities in the years following World War I, Thorndike engaged again in a large program of research on human learning, a good deal of which was published in the late twenties and early thirties,[17] and some further elements of which have appeared from time to time since that date. These investigations are of the classical type (cf. Locke, page 29), in that they deal for the most part with the establishment of rote or arbitrary connections between situations and responses. They do, however, involve a great many changes of emphasis. In the earlier formula a "law of exercise" (page 239) stated that we tend to repeat what we have earlier done, by virtue of having done it. But putting subjects to work on such tasks as drawing lines of a given length, he came to the conclusion that sheer repetition was in itself in no way conducive to learning. When, however, the words "right" and "wrong" were used after the drawing of lines, the subject soon tended to do more of whatever was called right. Here we are dealing with the "law of effect," the tendency of satisfiers, such as the word "right" in this instance, to cause repetition of the acts which satisfy. The new lines of research tended to show that annoyance was in itself ineffective; it might lead to new activity, some phases of which would be right and consequently stamped in, but punishment as such proved to be as ineffective as sheer repetition.

So clear-cut did the effect of satisfaction prove to be that an ingenious experiment made it possible to bring out its effect at several stages removed from the point at which the reward was given.[18] If, for example, subjects are confronted with vertical lines which are

[17] Thorndike, E. L., Bregman, E. O., Tilton, J. W., and Woodyard, E., *Adult Learning* (1928); Thorndike, E. L., *Human Learning* (1931) and *The Fundamentals of Learning* (1932).

[18] Thorndike, E. L., *An Experimental Study of Rewards* (1933).

indistinguishable in length and are required to indicate which is the longest, being arbitrarily rewarded by the word "right" in some situations and not in others, there is not only a marked tendency to repeat those judgments which are immediately followed by "right"; there proves, upon mathematical analysis, to be both a retroactive and a proactive effect of such reward. Acts which came two steps before the reward are somewhat affected, and indeed even those which came three steps before; after the reward the first act to follow is likewise stamped in, and to a lesser degree the second one following, and to a still lesser degree even the third. All of this occurs while the subject is working rapidly ahead, unaware that these retroactive and proactive effects are at work, and of course concerned at any given moment with a specific unit of activity, not with a series of steps preceding or following. It appears from the large number of similar studies that rewards may operate in a blind fashion as reinforcers. As Postman notes, however, the problem has ceased to be the question whether rewards "stamp in" activities.[19] The question is what kinds of rewards stamp in what kinds of activities in what persons, and under what working conditions. Muenzinger was able to show that a shock may sometimes act just as a reward does; [20] indeed that a shock may stamp in both right and wrong reactions, perhaps operating as Tolman [21] and others would suggest, to "emphasize" or "alert" the animal or to make figure-ground relationships more clear. We cannot here do justice to the rich experimental and the even richer controversial literature of the law of effect. We can only point out that the floodtide of Thorndike's influence has not abated, and that even the most objective students of learning continue to deal with the stamping-in effects of rewards, albeit phrasing the situation frequently (as does Mowrer, cf. page 273), in terms of tension reduction rather than in terms of subjectively experienced satisfactions.[22]

So far our attention has been given to motor or glandular behavior modifications. Classically, however, association theory dealt also with the alteration of cognitive responses, and it is of great interest to note that the conditioning techniques and other objective procedures have been utilized likewise in recent years in the study of

[19] Postman, L., "The History and Present Status of the Law of Effect," *Psychol. Bull.*, 1947, 44, 489–563.

[20] Muenzinger, K. F., see summary in *Psychol. Rev.*, 1938, 45, 215–18.

[21] Tolman, E. C., see summary in *Psychol. Rev.*, 1938, 45, 200–03.

[22] For a recent systematic survey of this issue, challenging the automatic reinforcing nature of reward, see Hilgard, E. R., *Theories of Learning* (1947).

cognitive learning. This might take the form, as with Cason,[23] of reference to "sensory conditioning." The subject who has experienced a sensation in a particular setting will experience that sensation again when the setting is repeated. The sensory response has been conditioned. In the same way investigators have shown that the basic learning process involved in learning to perceive—that is, in trial-and-error activity followed by the reinforcement of some phases and the elimination of others, and the final integration of the rewarded phases into higher units—appears in the cognitive life just as it does in the life of motor activity. Typical here are the many studies of autistic response, such as those carried out by Sanford and others at the Harvard Psychological Clinic,[24] and the experimental data by Sherif noted elsewhere (page 412), which are explicitly pointed out by him as instances of "learning to perceive." [25] Indeed, H. L. Hollingworth had early suggested that those who argue about the reinforcing effect of rewards have overlooked a very much simpler way of formulating what happens.[26] The child who reaches for the candle flame is originally influenced by brightness and curiosity. After he has been burned he is responding to brightness and pain. The stimulus configuration has itself changed; the child is now reacting not to the brightness-curiosity combination but to the brightness-pain combination. If elements from an earlier complex recur, we react to the elements as if they were the whole which had earlier been experienced (the law of redintegration; page 247).

It is not implied by any means that all contemporary students of learning have been willing to accept the view that rewards and punishments are the essential processes in the learning situation. It is still noted that all sorts of casual connections, as between lightning and thunder, for example, get themselves established whether there are rewards or not, indeed whether there is demonstrated "motivation" to learn or not. In this connection great interest has been manifest in the problem of "latent learning"; after an organism has become familiar with various relationships in the situation, no rewards being involved, a suitable method can reveal that this period of becoming familiar with the situation greatly reduces the random-

[23] Cason, H., "Sensory Conditioning," *J. Exp. Psychol.*, 1936, 19, 572–91.

[24] Sanford, R. N., "The Effects of Abstinence from Food upon Imaginal Processes: A Preliminary Experiment," *J. Psychol.*, 1936, 2, 129–36.

[25] Sherif, M., *The Psychology of Social Norms* (1936).

[26] Hollingworth, H. L., "Effect and Affect in Learning," *Psychol. Rev.*, 1931, 38, 153–59.

ness of later activity in a learning situation, and lessens the time of learning and the number of errors made.[27] The question arises whether one continuous process of learning is going on throughout an experiment. A controversy has arisen between those who believe, in consequence of the fact that latent learning occurs, that there is continuous progress throughout the whole period of exposure to the series of experimental situations,[28] and those who believe, on the other hand, that the organism may in some experiments simply be "wasting its time," learning nothing, throughout its trial-and-error activities, until it begins to pick out what is relevant to its task, after which point the learning is real.[29]

So far, one might easily be able to make the case that Thorndike himself made, to the effect that the conditioning situation is essentially unlike the trial-and-error or random-activity situation in which some acts are stamped in by satisfying consequences. It is easy to show that in the ideal conditioning situation the organism must stay still, must be participating in only a minimum amount of random activity; usually it must be oriented toward a specific satisfier in order to get the full effect of the conditioned stimulus the experimenter uses. In most situations in life, and in such laboratory situations as maze learning, the organism is constantly changing its responses, is free to make contact with all features of its environment, and establishes for itself the elements of the figure-ground relationship which mark off the various phases of the total. There have been some, however, who have objected to this sharp distinction, and have been insistent in calling attention to the fact that this free-roaming trial-and-error activity is very difficult to control and to quantify. It might be much better if we could indeed let the animal go to work and find out how to satisfy its need, yet at the same time, if we could *limit* what it may do. It might then be possible to quantify those types of learning which, while not of the classical Pavlovian type, exemplify reward for successful activity. The long-range research program of B. F. Skinner has developed the theoretical assumptions and experimental techniques requisite to make these distinctions clear and quantifiable,[30] using, for example, a simple

[27] Blodgett, H. C., "The Effect of the Introduction of Rewards upon the Maze Performance of Rats," *Univ. Calif. Publ. Psychol.*, 1929, 4, 113–34.

[28] Spence, K. W., "An Experimental Test of the Continuity and Non-continuity Theories of Discrimination Learning," *J. Exp. Psychol.*, 1945, 35, 253–66.

[29] Krechevsky, I., "A Study of the Continuity of the Problem-Solving Process," *Psychol. Rev.*, 1938, 45, 107–33.

[30] Skinner, B. F., *The Behavior of Organisms: An Experimental Analysis* (1938).

box to house the animal and a simple horizontal bar which when depressed releases a pellet of food. It is possible to get graphic registration of the whole course of the animal's learning to manipulate the bar; to measure the relation between the frequency of bar-depressing and the intensity of hunger; to analyze the effects of various facilitating and inhibiting factors; and to study the course of extinction when bar-depressing leads to no further pellets of food. Recognizing that such activity is not conditioning of the classical type, Skinner nevertheless believes that it is properly called conditioning; the term "operant conditioning" is employed. The result has been somewhat similar to that of Thorndike's abundant work, in the sense that learning to do something and getting rewarded for doing it have been conceived as quantitative problems subject to elaborate experimental analysis. Skinner has worked also with human subjects, but the main program has been analogous to the program of Hull in its preference for simpler organisms and simpler methods.

Individual differences, of course, have been found over and over again in the analysis of all such types of data, and have often been quantified.[31] It may be worth while to note that while the curves of diminishing returns found by Ebbinghaus in the learning process and also in the forgetting process (page 178) have reappeared likewise in modern learning work, there is today much concern with individual variability. Though one can make out a good case for universally valid, quantitatively defined laws of learning and forgetting, individuality is still expressed not only in terms of deviations from central tendency, but in terms of individual ways of attacking a task, individual ways of eliminating errors and mastering problems.

As will be brought out later in the discussion of Gestalt psychology, there have been many in the modern period who have objected from beginning to end to the general formulation of learning this chapter has offered. Their approach will not be recapitulated, but the reader is reminded that Lewin (page 299) early showed that sheer successive presentation of stimuli produced no actual functional connections between them, a fact that Thorndike himself abundantly verified at a later time and which he later emphasized as the law of "belongingness." Attention might also be called to the fact that the basic conception of elements to be connected, as it appears for example in the conception of transfer of training as depending upon identical elements (page 242), has been challenged insistently. Much material has for example been brought

[31] Hilgard, E. R., and Marquis, D. G., *Conditioning and Learning* (1940).

together by Orata to show that there may be large transfer between utterly different response units and, indeed, that there may be no transfer between two situations which have numerous identical elements simply because the subject does not pick them out, recognize them, and respond to them.[32] While making a number of concessions to this approach, it has been universally recognized by the modern associationists that this abandonment of analytical detail in favor of global or integrating principles would jeopardize the whole enterprise.

While it is generally fairly easy to classify students of learning into the two main groups, those accepting the associationist tradition and those rejecting it, in favor of some Gestalt-like principle, the classification breaks down in the case of Tolman.[33] Agreeing with McDougall as to the need for a *purposive* approach and with the behaviorist as to the need for objective observations, he has emphasized, in a long-range program in comparative psychology, the structural aspects of the learning situation, the capacity of the organism to respond purposefully and selectively to its environment. He has given reason to believe that the organism perceives various objects as means toward goals; in fact, that its cognitive life is complex, orderly, and saturated with meanings, exactly as the Gestalt psychologists have maintained. In between stimuli and observed responses it is necessary (as with Hull) to interpolate a series of "intervening variables" in the light of which responses become intelligible, and the nature of these variables is to be tested by experiment. But these factors are very different from those postulated by most behaviorists. They are not easily summarized. Note for example that "behavior-supports" are "characters in the environment required by behavior acts in order that they may go off without disruption." [34] "More specifically behavior-supports divide into discriminanda (q.v.), manipulanda (q.v.) and means-end-relations." Organisms are constantly responding not just to stimuli, but to *sign-Gestalts;* and a sign-Gestalt is a "complex behavior-support, consisting of a sign object, a signified object, and a signified means-end-relation." All these concepts are systematically employed in devising crucial experimental tests and in integrating earlier work.

[32] Orata, P. T., "Recent Research Studies on Transfer of Training with Implications for the Curriculum, Guidance, and Personnel Work," *J. Educ. Res.*, 1941, 35, 81–101.

[33] Tolman, E. C., *Purposive Behavior in Animals and Men* (1932); "A Stimulus-Expectancy Need-Cathexis Psychology," *Science*, 1945, 101, 160–66.

[34] Disruption is "a breakdown and upset in behavior produced when some change, not previously met, is introduced into a given environment."

Clearly, then, stimuli do not simply *act upon* the organism; it is oriented to use them. Far from admitting that sheer satisfyingness automatically stamps in behavior, Tolman has offered a long series of experiments to show that goals serve to give meaning to the various objects in the environment, commerce with which will serve as means; sheer pleasantness and unpleasantness have no consistent and predictable end result. Electric shock, for example, may serve as an "emphasizer" (page 277). The explanation of learning in terms of conditioning is attacked on various grounds, such as the fact that the responses to the conditioned stimulus need not be at all the same as the response to the original unconditioned stimulus. Eating is an appropriate response to food, but not to an alley in a maze; one does not eat the alley, but enters it. Conditioning is not simply the establishment of a new stimulus-response connection; it is the building up of a "sign-Gestalt expectation." Even as a *physiological unit*, the conditioned response is debatable. Injury to the neural pathway of an unconditioned response, *without* injury to the pathway for the conditioned response, abolishes the response. Outstandingly important in the Tolman approach has been the insistence that living organisms set up expectations, and that they are capable of *inventive* learning. Especially influential here was the early suggestion of Krechevsky that even a rat sets up "hypotheses" about ways to solve his problem and that he tests the hypotheses as he proceeds.[35] Though failing to convince the behaviorally oriented,[36] such a conception did much to emphasize the possibility that the cognitive life of animals, as well as their motor behavior, needed to be brought into experimental contact with the psychology of human beings. Enough has perhaps been said to show why Tolman's approach is neither ordinary purposivism, nor ordinary behaviorism; and why he says that despite his own need for "*analyzed* variables," he would be proud if the Gestaltists would admit him to their fold. He is a "molar," not a "molecular," behaviorist; he seeks objectivity in the study of purposive wholes, not of physiological units.

It remains, finally, to point out that an emphasis upon behavioral components as such, without purposivism, may perfectly well be integrated with a conception of the organism as a system which in some sense functions as a whole. It is not, therefore, a paradox that among the rigidly antipurposive psychologists appears K. S. Lash-

[35] Krechevsky, I., " 'Hypotheses' in Rats," *Psychol. Rev.*, 1932, 39, 516–32.
[36] Witkin, H. A., " 'Hypotheses' in Rats: An Experimental Evaluation of the Hypotheses Concept: III. Summary Evaluation of the Hypotheses Concept," *Psychol. Rev.*, 1942, 49, 541–68.

ley, hard at work to indicate the futility of punctiform localizations in the brain as clues to specific learning processes, and eager to consider the dynamics of systems.[37] The result has been to give behavior study a theoretical flavor not very far from that of Gestalt psychology, while differing from it fundamentally in the exclusion of reference to the organism's inner world of insights and purposes. This trend is highly characteristic of contemporary work. Yet so diverse are the concepts used by different psychologists that one may find individual students of the learning process combining any two or even any three of these recurrent ideas: objectivism, the law of effect, purposivism, trial and error, wholeness.

If one had to summarize the main trend as it now exists in the middle of the century, it would almost certainly have to be to the effect that despite huge and continuous protests of strong and active personalities, the conceptions of Spencer and Bain a hundred years ago remain dominant. Under strain and stress the organism varies its responses, some of which give satisfaction, some of which do not. Here and there some associations are made through sheer intensity or through favorable circumstances without being rewarded, but in general, the psychology of rewards is the psychology of the learning process. An enormous amount of sophistication has gone into experimental and quantitative refinement of the theory of association; but the framework set up by the associationists remains.

REFERENCES

Hilgard, E. R., *Theories of Learning*, Appleton-Century, 1948
———, and Marquis, D. G., *Conditioning and Learning*, Appleton-Century, 1940
Hull, Clark L., *The Principles of Behavior*, Appleton-Century, 1943
McGeoch, John A., *The Psychology of Human Learning*, Longmans, Green, 1942
Skinner, B. F., *The Behavior of Organisms*, Appleton-Century, 1938
Tolman, Edward C., *Purposive Behavior in Animals and Men*, Century, 1932

[37] Lashley, K. S., *Brain-Mechanisms and Intelligence: A Quantitative Study of Injuries to the Brain* (1929); "Integrative Functions of the Cerebral Cortex," *Physiol. Rev.*, 1933, 13, 1–43; "Coalescence of Neurology and Psychology," *Proc. Phil. Soc.*, 1941, 84, 461–70.

Chapter 20

GESTALT

Nature is neither kernel nor shell; she is everything at once.

GOETHE

A<small>S ONE DIPS</small> into the works of psychologists in any period from the pre-Socratic to the present, one may run upon phrases which deny the possibility of explaining wholes by a study of their constituent parts. It is therefore a futile and fruitless enterprise to try to specify who first got hold of the general principle of Gestalt psychology; and it is peculiarly futile to try to guess which of the Gestalt writers were influenced, consciously or unconsciously, by this or that earlier formulation of doctrines of wholeness or structure.

It is, however, worth while to note that relationships or modes or organization are repeatedly stressed by early Greek thinkers, many of whom decried the tendency to find a primordial stuff of which the world was made, and looked rather for a law of arrangement, a principle of synthesis or order. In general, the Pythagorean answers were the most successful, and in general the history of science has shown them to be the most generally followed by men of other eras. It was, in other words, the mathematical approach to the problem of structure or organization that stood in the most fruitful and dynamic opposition to the various types of atomism or elementarism. The Platonists, of course, had taken over with enthusiasm the emphasis upon mathematics as a clue to structure, and Platonism contains many passages which may reasonably enough be regarded as foundation stones for a Gestalt theory.

In modern times—to remind the reader of a few examples already quoted—Hartley had pointed out that tastes and smells may not only combine in such a way as to give new qualities, but may be experienced in such a way that the original elements are no longer observable at all (page 33). The elements are literally lost to view.

John Stuart Mill had later made a profitable use of this conception (page 104). Alexander Bain stated expressly that this principle applies not only to momentary wholes, but to the flow of experience as well (page 196). There is no starting or stopping; there is constantly a dynamic readjustment in the structure of a complex experience which makes mechanical types of analysis peculiarly unfruitful. William James was positively obsessed with this problem, of course, and returned to it on every possible occasion (page 196). The best known of his philippics against the atomistic view is the discussion of the "psychologist's fallacy," which is simply the assumption that when one has reduced a complex to its supposed parts, the parts must have been there all the time and must have been the real key to the complex. James seldom worked out his position from an initial protest to the calm and positive assertion of a system; in fact, one feels that he would have knocked the system down if he had ever succeeded in building one. But in so far as Gestalt psychology is a protest against elementarism or atomism, this celebrated passage of James's is a clear enough forerunner. Not to tire the reader with countless examples of other forerunners, we may finally note Henri Bergson's expression of the evolutionary outlook at the turn of the century in his comment that the perceptual whole which we experience on a starlit night includes an integration of everything from the stars we observe to the brain processes which go on during the event.

But we must get down to much more specific and clear-cut examples of immediate forerunners of the German Gestalt psychology which took shape in 1912. Here we may follow Helson in noting the importance of Mach,[1] who grappled so brilliantly with the "analysis of sensations" in the eighties. While Mach had come to the conclusion that the world of sensations with which the physical scientist deals as he takes note of lights, sounds, and temperatures, is identically the same world of lights, sounds, and temperatures with which the psychologist is concerned, he did note certain relational problems which seemed to disturb the symmetry of this beautiful analysis. He noted, for example, that the arrangement of elements— say, for example, the arrangement of lines in geometrical figures— causes the emergence of different totals which are reported as squares, diamonds, and so on. He had therefore resorted (page 226) to the doctrine that there are "sensations of space," sensations which, while not pointing directly to the elements of the original experience,

[1] Helson, H., "The Psychology of *Gestalt*," *Amer. J. Psychol.*, 1925, 36, 342–70, 494–526; 1926, 37, 25–62, 189–223.

must be taken jointly with them if we are to explain the structured total.

This tour de force was followed a few years later by the more radical and adequate formulation of Von Ehrenfels (page 226). In a paper in 1890 Von Ehrenfels noted that melodies must consist of something other than a sequence of tones, since obviously one sings or recognizes the melody in other keys; and indeed (with the very dubious exception of instances of absolute pitch) one makes no absolute use at all of specific tonal *elements* which enter into the melody. One may, moreover, encounter the same "element" (say middle C) in different melodies played in different keys, and find that they differ utterly. If we can have the same elements and get a different result, and have different elements yet get the same result, where are we with regard to the reduction of experience to fixed components? Von Ehrenfels went on to conclude that over and above various sensory ingredients there must be qualities belonging to organized forms, and coined the term "form quality"—*Gestaltqualität*—to describe that which a melody or a painting or a sonnet possesses which is not given in the component tones, colors, or words. Though this is more like a real psychological theory than is Mach's, it is extraordinary that Von Ehrenfels did not really undertake to solve, any more than did Mach, the question of what to do with the *new* elements—in this case new qualities—which he had thrown into the picture. One might accuse both Mach and Von Ehrenfels of buttressing up a tottering elementarism by throwing new elements into the situation, rather than by noting the nature of the architectural problem. If there are sensations of space, then what is the relation of the sensation of space to the other sensations already present? So also with regard to Von Ehrenfels: As we specify *qualities* to be added to sensory *elements*, why do we not need to specify other qualities which result from the relations of the first qualities to the sensory elements? If qualities or relations of any sort *between elements* are to be added to primary elements, do we not find ourselves lost in an infinite regressus? Indeed, if there are form qualities which go with certain sequences of tones (melodies), these must candidly be regarded as new elements in experience.

Moreover, the Von Ehrenfels solution makes one begin to wonder whether it means anything to say that *the same melody* sounds differently in different keys. Just what do we mean by "the same"? If a voice on one occasion, a violin on another occasion, carry an air, and we note the same form quality, we have the quality reappearing when no one of the original elements is there, a resultant without any component forces. Our problem has not really been solved; all we have done is to name a quality given by each structural total so that to all intents and purposes their number is unlimited. If it is replied that this is a new structural conception, one may simply note that unless form can be more fully defined, one has no more help in explaining and predicting the outcome of a new combination of ingredients than one would have if one simply let the ingredients try to do their own work without such aid. Certainly the Von Ehrenfels principle is an honest recognition of a grave difficulty, and there can certainly be no quarrel with its statement of the facts; perceptual wholes are not made up of the kinds of sensory elements that had traditionally been described as their ingredients. But just what form actually is and what its laws are remain indeterminate.

WERTHEIMER

That is where the problem stood during the time of the Würzburg investigations of attitude and thought, described above. Eagerly prosecuting such studies of higher mental processes, Max Wertheimer and two of his experimental subjects, Wolfgang Köhler and Kurt Koffka, came upon a radically different way of viewing the whole problem. It was Wertheimer's formulation of what occurred that led in Frankfurt in 1912 to the formal inauguration of the Gestalt psychology—the psychology of form.

The problem was the perception of motion. When light is thrown through a small slit placed vertically, and a moment later through a slit inclined 20° or 30° to the right, the interval separating the two presentations may be so chosen that the shaft of light appears to *fall* from one position to the other. Wertheimer proceeded to work out quantitatively those time relations which would give (1) two simultaneous illuminated slits, (2) the experience of motion from A to B, and (3) the sense of temporal succession, the first being followed by the second, but no movement being involved. The central problem was the nature of the experience of movement, the phi phenomenon.

Now a rather good elementaristic explanation of movement had been developed by Lotze some fifty years earlier (page 147). For Lotze, the visual perception of motion depended upon the sequential stimulation of points on the retina, and hence the sequential stimulation of brain regions; a moving object caused a track of light to be made upon the retina. If, however, there is no such track of light when the eye is stationary while being stimulated successively by two lights as in the Wertheimer experiment with the phi phenomenon, Lotze's interpretation collapses. The perception of motion, argued Wertheimer, is an experience organically different from the perception of stationary lights, and no kind of serial arrangement of static stimulating points can give us this unique type of experience. The very essence of the experience is the manner in which temporal organization of two stimulations occurs. Wertheimer developed, therefore, the conception of "cross-processes" in the brain, dynamic *interactions* between the various cortical excitations which follow from the two stimulations.

Not being content with the insistence upon the reality of the experience of motion as something dynamically distinct from the awareness of position and of temporal succession of such positions, Wertheimer proceeded at once to a reformulation of the theory of wholes and parts. Just as Fechner had protested against the procedure of the philosopher from above to below (cf. page 92), so Wertheimer protested against the general modern scientific movement from below to above. We shall never achieve an understanding of structured totals by starting with the ingredient parts which enter into them. On the contrary, we shall need to understand the structure; we shall need to have insight into it. There is then some possibility that the components themselves will be understood.

This leads immediately to two laws which follow inevitably if the relation of whole to parts has been properly stated. The first is the law of membership character. The tones in a melody do not have their several fixed qualities, to which a form quality is somehow added; rather, each such tone manifests qualities which depend upon the place of the tone in the context. Such attributes, depending on the place of an identifiable component in a structure, permit no use of the conception of elements which when compounded into totals remain what they were before. Similarly, a patch of color in a landscape, far from being an ingredient in a total, depends for its value upon the context which nature, or the artist, supplies; we are working from above rather than from below. The Gestaltist insists that the attributes or aspects of the component parts, in so far as they can be defined, are defined by their relations to the system as a whole in which they are functioning.

A simple laboratory demonstration is offered by a red cross on a gray field which after twenty seconds' fixation in fair light will elicit a green border (according to the familiar dynamics of contrast, page 141). Cut out, however, a tiny notch in one of the arms of the cross. What color will the space within the notch yield to our observation? Green, says the traditional elementarist theory, for it is a part of the gray border which must take on a contrasting hue. Red, says the Gestaltist, for a cross is one of those organized wholes which forces the component materials within it, as a result of membership character, to take on the attributes supporting the structure. The Gestaltist predicts more accurately than the elementarist what will actually occur.

Proceeding further, however, Wertheimer noted that there are certain directions in which one can predict the emergence of structured wholes. Instead of simply saying with Von Ehrenfels that there is always something more than the parts, Wertheimer notes that if unstable equilibrium and unstable structure are given, which manifest certain types of inner relationships, one can predict from a knowledge of the laws of structure what kind of organization must supervene. It will be that kind of organization which is most orderly, most comprehensive, most stable, most free of the casual and the arbitrary; in a single word, that which is most good. Goodness, or as he preferred to say, *Prägnanz,* is the dynamic attribute of self-fulfillment, intrinsic in all structured totals. Glancing back at the example of the notched cross, one sees immediately that the stable, rugged, definite outlines of the arms have a far higher degree of *Prägnanz* than the chaotic, and one might even say rather irrational, lines of the notch, which disturb the simple, orderly, and stable pattern presented. These two laws, the law of membership character and the law of *Prägnanz,* are typical of many which rapidly evolved in Wertheimer's thinking. They are in general representative of Gestalt laws as a whole, laws in which one works not with an infinite number of tiny particles arranging themselves more or less independently, but with a limited, finite number of possible modes of stable organization, which because of their orderly, rationally intelligible form are capable of being discovered, and their dynamics understood.

The first task of the perceiver, then, is not to create, but to apprehend the order and meaning which is there objectively in the world. This is, so far, essentially like Platonism. There are, however, many forms or structures to be found, not all of which are of equal relevance to the perceiver. Just as perception moves from the incomplete toward that which is more nearly complete, so there is continuous dynamic selection and integration of forms. We have thus a direct transition from the psychology of perception to the psychology of thought, without involving the need of any essentially different principles. We need to grasp, first of all, the order lying in nature and waiting for our apprehension; and second, that internal order which the thinker manifests as he passes from one to another orderly form, creating new order in the succession and in the integration. The psychology of thinking already implicit in Wertheimer's earlier work became more and more important both in his own work and in that of his pupils. It was the process of thinking which intrigued Köhler (page 291) in his comparison of men with apes. It was thinking which intrigued Koffka (page 291) as he first ventured to conceive of educational psychology as the successive realization of levels of complexity, growing out of the capacity of the individual to move ever toward higher integrations rather than simply to acquire piecemeal one new response at a time. It is not in any sense accidental that during those last years of his life, when Wertheimer was endlessly burdened with the task of adapting to a new environment (after 1933 he taught at the New School for Social Research in New York), the book upon which he labored was a book on productive thinking.[2]

The basic conception which runs through this struggle to lay bare the dynamics of thought was the conception of *recentering;* the discovery of new forms of figure-ground organization in which an inadequate and ultimately disorderly mode of centering or focusing is thrust aside in favor of a newly recentered pattern—insightful and correct in the sense of mediating contact with reality, because the center as apprehended by the observer corresponds with a natural center in the objective event waiting for such discovery.

From the new viewpoint the entire domain of cognitive processes—processes of perception, learning, thinking, imagining—was to be systematically redefined in terms of the conception of Gestalt. In practice, moreover, cognitive phenomena were to be studied alongside the phenomena of affect. Emotion came to be viewed, for example, as a response involving the entire living system, rather than as a local response of the midbrain, after the manner of Walter Cannon (page 383). And impulse, instinct, and will were treated ultimately as processes involving the entire community of various aspects of a bodily tension system, and presenting no possibility that a segmental act of impulse or will could be mapped out and independently studied.

KOFFKA AND KÖHLER

The new doctrine, formulated by Wertheimer, was blazoned forth by Koffka and Köhler. They were younger than Wertheimer, and infinitely more ready to systematize publicly what was daily being

[2] Wertheimer, M., *Productive Thinking* (1945).

discovered in hundreds of fresh little experiments and communicated by Wertheimer to his friends by word of mouth. Fortunate indeed for the spread of the Gestalt doctrine was the series of circumstances which led Koffka and Köhler into the public eye. Marooned in the Canary Islands during World War I, Köhler had carried out a series of ingenious studies to test the Thorndike hypothesis that animal learning depends simply upon trial and error and upon the stamping-in of the correct responses. Working with the anthropoid apes at the Teneriffe research station, Köhler presented a series of simple problems in which the animal had to discover a way of reaching a suspended banana by placing boxes underneath it and climbing up on them, or by fitting together sticks which, when thus fitted together, would make it possible to reach the food. Köhler strove to demonstrate that apes, no less than men, come to solutions all at once by a process of integration or insight, in which not a series of separate clues taken in series, but an integrated system of clues, is responded to all at once. His reports appeared in German in 1917–24; in English in 1928, under the title of *The Mentality of Apes* (a translation of the German title would read *Intelligence Tests on Anthropoid Apes*[3]). (Although he had in the meantime written an erudite mathematical study of physical forms [4]— that is, the objective and measurable systems of forces which require consideration as systems rather than as agglomerations of particles— the volume became known only sporadically, and much later.) Koffka had in the same years published a systematic educational psychology which also soon became known. It was entitled *The Growth of the Mind* (1921; English translation, 1924). The thesis of the volume is that growth is the progressive realization of forms rather than a matter of accretion.

Though Koffka's survey article "Perception: An Introduction to the Gestalt-Theorie" had appeared in the *Psychological Bulletin* in 1922, the viva-voce introduction of Gestalt psychology into the United States occurred at the Christmas meetings of the American Psychological Association in that year, through a paper read by R. M. Ogden. The response was hesitant and uncertain; one heard the comments: "What is this Gestalt psychology?" "Is it just one more foggy German philosophy?" It soon became very evident, however, that masses of experimental materials, highly ingenious and challenging, were waiting to be assimilated along with the new theory. Through extraordinary good fortune for the movement, both

---

[3] *Intelligenzprüfungen an Menschenaffen* (1924).
[4] *Die physischen Gestalten in Ruhe und im stationären Zustand* (1920).

Koffka and Köhler were soon available to explain, at every interested American university center, what the new movement was all about, and to show its revolutionary implications. The vivid personalities and good-tempered debating tactics of Koffka and Köhler led quickly to a widening interest in the new school, and soon everybody was taking Gestalt psychology in his stride.

THE SPREAD OF GESTALT PSYCHOLOGY

There is no doubt that the enthusiasm over Watson's behaviorism as a system was a factor challenging all his opponents to discover a countersystem which had the same vitality. It was also no doubt true that the various experimental studies being carried out in laboratories charged with the maintenance of the introspective tradition called loudly for some vivid systematization that would give them the crisp and compelling form which was felt to be wanting in Titchener's rather cold and arid system. Integrations of Gestalt psychology and behaviorism were likewise attempted. In the same period appeared J. R. Kantor's organismic psychology,[5] in which the interdependence and formal unity of all organic responses is noted, but with an emphasis upon objectivism.

The Gestalt psychology became domiciled not only in American theory, but also in American laboratories. In the United States, however, it remained primarily a psychology of the cognitive processes. Those implications already noted which bore upon affective and conative processes were in this same period between the two world wars carried forward in Germany, notably at the universities of Frankfurt and Berlin. In the late twenties, Rudolf Arnheim,[6] for example, introduced Gestalt theory into the field of personality research by showing that fragments of handwriting containing the various clues which are supposedly used in gauging personality did not in fact serve any such purpose, but that the intact handwriting, with half a page or so to work with, could nevertheless give (even to a naïve observer) some capacity to tell which one of a group of scripts had been produced by a given individual. Werner Wolff was likewise beginning a series of experiments in this same period, to be continued later in Spain and in the United States,[7] in which photographs of posture, the hands, and the profile, and motion pictures of the moving body, were to be matched against one an-

[5] *The Principles of Psychology* (1924); later, *A Survey of the Science of Psychology* (1933).
[6] *Psychol. Forsch.*, 1928, 11, 1–132.
[7] *The Expression of Personality* (1943).

other and against personality sketches, demonstrating that when rather large and well-organized expressions of individuality are available, even the naïve judge attains a score significantly better than chance expectancy. In Wolff's case, the Gestalt principles were integrated with psychoanalytic principles, in the sense that unconscious dynamics was given a large place. The subject, for example, failed frequently to recognize his own expression, though dealing competently with the expressions of other persons, as if he were unable to accept certain aspects evident to other people regarding his own personality expression.

By the mid-thirties Gestalt psychology had become a complete system, with all the cardinal areas and problems of psychology undergoing redefinition in terms of the theory of form. These doctrines were coming into applied psychology, likewise notably into psychiatry and education, and were being heard of and used by social scientists such as anthropologists and sociologists. In 1933 the movement was solidly established in Germany and in the United States (hardly known elsewhere). It then became centered in the latter country, owing to the departure from Germany of Wertheimer and numerous other proponents of Gestalt doctrines, and owing, upon their arrival in the United States, to the appeal of the message which the expanding group of laboratory and clinical people brought to these shores. One encountered, particularly on the Eastern seaboard, dozens of young research psychologists who had learned to think in Gestalt terms, and who could talk interestingly, in or out of academic situations, regarding the promise of this approach; likewise, literally hundreds of clinical workers who had combined the Gestalt approach with psychoanalytic concepts in one guise or another. Gestalt psychology, then, came to be a vital new phase of American psychology, rapidly moving West as the doctrines were published and distributed in American journals, and as the eager young refugees themselves showed what a difference it made whether one did or did not utilize these new ideas.

It is not meant to imply that Gestalt psychology disappeared in Germany, or that it won an uncontested triumph in the United States. What happened in Germany after the departure of the leader and many of his followers was that the general emphasis upon wholeness and structure (which, as we saw, had been increasing for several decades) went on increasing, and that various types of applied psychology, such as graphology and the Rorschach method (already saturated with theories of wholeness), were given a larger and larger place in the various types of clinical assessment of individuals.

German psychological warfare itself made extensive use of personality testing based upon various theories of structure. That was, however, at best a rather diluted form of Gestalt psychology, when it was Gestalt psychology at all; and the amount of original experimental work done under the egis of such studies of wholeness was apparently trivial. Gestalt psychology was reduced to a very minor position in the German university system. As far as we can judge at this time, the isolation of German and Austrian scholars from those of other countries has in general impeded the recovery that might be expected since the downfall of the Nazi system, and one must conclude that the restoration of serious and systematic efforts along the lines defined by Wertheimer will prove to be a matter of some years.

In the United States, the most general tendency, except among German-trained scholars who came here as complete adherents to the system, was to regard Gestalt psychology as an interesting and valuable, but not a final or complete, solution to primary problems. Sometimes the theory was diluted to mean simply that there must always be a consideration of the multiplicity of factors working toward any given response; sometimes it was meant to signify a study of relationships obtaining between various stimuli present in the stimulus field, or various responses going on successively or simultaneously (so much, of course, any associationist would have granted). Sometimes it came nearer to the Wertheimer doctrine by emphasizing membership character and the futility of dissecting out supposedly independent elements. Occasionally it meant going the whole way, insisting that conscious or behavioral responses are intelligible only as structures or systems, and that all aspects or phases of such wholes, with their membership character, express cross sections in a dynamic flow oriented toward the completion of some purposive act.

If such a characterization is at all adequate, it means that in general Gestalt psychology has been gratefully received and grafted upon existing systems, but that it has not, except here and there on a very small scale, been espoused by American psychology as a final or fundamental solution of psychological problems.

Particularly characteristic of American psychology has been the effort, through countless experiments and clinical observations, to show that *both* piecemeal *and* organized responses occur—just as, in response to behaviorism, the prevalent tendency has been to say that both consciousness and behavior need to be studied. Typical of dozens of studies is Durkin's generalization that in problem-solving,[8] the responses made by her subjects ranged all the way from (a) blind poking about until pieces happened to fall into a correct position to (b) those responses in which a large number of separate pieces suddenly seemed to leap together into one meaningful and adequate total. There are, then, according to Durkin, and a great many of the middle-of-the-roaders, not only two basic ways of thinking—the associationist way and the insightful way—but all the theoretical possible intervening points on a continuum.

That aspect of Gestalt psychology which seems to this writer to be most fundamental and at the same time most incompletely worked out is the definition of membership character. At times one discovers in the Gestalt literature the conception that all the elements or component parts of a total need to be seen in their interrelations in order to understand the structure. On another page, however, one discovers that there *are* no elements or component parts. Each aspect or phase of the total manifests those attributes which each must possess if it is to stand at a particular point and function in a particular role; attributes which belong *to the elements themselves* are not definable. If this second statement is true, then obviously the first is far from the mark. Surely if membership character in so fundamental a sense dominates not only the locus but the very character of every ingredient, then there are no parts or elements or components, and it means nothing to say that the relations between them must be studied. The Gestaltist sometimes tries to have his cake and eat it too as he maintains that there are components which enter into structures and also that there are no components. The issue seems to stand about as it stood twenty years ago. The theory of membership character and the whole ultimate theory of the atomic or nonatomic character of psychological events remains unresolved—both as to clear theoretical treatment and as to answers from crucial experiments.

Yet every nook and cranny of psychology has been invaded with the conception of structure, or system, or interdependence; every theoretical system today either rejects atomism or admits its incompleteness, or at least apologizes for it. So huge a tidal wave cannot be "met" by a countermovement of any sort; it will have its effect. Since in general the trend is clearly in accord with general trends in physics toward fields and wholeness, and general trends in biology toward the actualization of evolutionary patterns involv-

[8] Durkin, H., "Trial-and-Error Gradual Analysis, and Sudden Reorganization: An Experimental Study of Problem Solving," *Arch. Psychol.*, 1937, No. 210.

ing the interdependence of organs, of whole individuals, and of species, this movement in psychology is fully in the modern spirit.

REFERENCES

Ellis, W. D., *Source Book of Gestalt Psychology,* Sather Gate Book Shop, Berkeley, Calif., 1938

Hartmann, George W., *Gestalt Psychology,* Ronald Press, 1935

Heidbreder, Edna, *Seven Psychologies,* Century, 1933

Koffka, Kurt, *Principles of Gestalt Psychology,* Harcourt, Brace, 1935

Köhler, Wolfgang, *Gestalt Psychology,* Liveright, 1929; rev. ed., 1947

Petermann, Bruno, *The Gestalt Theory and the Problem of Configuration,* Harcourt, Brace, 1932

Wertheimer, Max, *Productive Thinking,* Harper, 1945

Woodworth, Robert S., *Contemporary Schools of Psychology,* rev. ed., Ronald Press, 1948

Chapter 21

FIELD THEORY

. . . practically all developmental phenomena exhibit field-like characters.   PAUL WEISS

ROM time to time reference has been made in this volume to the growing tendency of nineteenth-century science to become suspicious of elements or atoms, and to doubt whether the method of analysis into such irreducible bits could ever prove satisfactory in the explanation of observed phenomena (cf. page 284). Wertheimer's theory (page 287) reflected this tendency, and field theory in psychology is sometimes regarded as its parthenogenetic child. But this view is not really sufficient; there was another parent. It may be worth while to look more directly for a moment at the outcome of such skepticism about irreducible elements, and at the form in which a new conception of scientific method was developed.

Newtonian physics had assumed infinitely divisible material bodies operating upon one another through gravitation, and through certain other secondary forces such as magnetic attraction and repulsion. Ultimately, as Einstein and Infeld have put it, the world was a question of "pushes and pulls." If one fully understood the location, the mass, the velocity, and so on of material particles, one could predict what would occur when a number of them interacted. This mode of thinking proved to be fairly adequate until well beyond the middle of the nineteenth century. The study of electromagnetism, however, gave rise in time to more and more misgivings. It was evident that a particle moving in a given direction might cause another particle to move in a direction other than that of the supposed direction of the "push." Indeed, one could not sharply localize the region in which the energy of a moving particle was expressed; it became necessary to think in terms of regions or fields through which electromagnetic forces were spread. Such fields are not aggregates of the effects generated by separate particles, each pulling and pushing in classical fashion, but must be seen in terms of new structural entities within which the behavior of individual particles may be predicted. Specifically, Clerk Maxwell, in 1875, in his studies of the distribution of electromagnetic forces, found it possible to formulate equations which no longer regarded fields as in any way the end results of distinct, individual particles, but as entities to be directly observed and mathematically treated in their own right. The era of atomism began to come to an end and particles began to be understood as aspects of field relationships.

This way of thinking invaded biology in the period between the two world wars, notably in the long series of brilliant investigations in embryology by the German investigator Spemann and his pupil and coworker Paul Weiss. It began to be evident in their studies, for example, that the various component parts of the embryonic body and of the maternal body surrounding it could not be regarded in mosaic fashion, but required the full utilization of a field theory in which chemical, thermal, and other factors were viewed as operating within a unitary matrix or field. In the effort to predict, for example, when and where a nose or an eye would appear, no system was really adequate which made use of small areas considered piecemeal; and within the living system no part could be defined in terms of what it would be were it outside the system. One transplants a few undeveloped cells into an eye socket and they become eye material; one transplants a few more into an ear region and they become ear material; but if one tries to achieve a compromise result, each cell will become completely the one or the other, not a mosaic agglutination of aspects of the two. There are thus major fields, and minor fields within them, but nothing to remind one of the juxtaposition of fragments, as was supposed in the Newtonian system.

It is within this frame of reference, notably the developments in physics, that one must understand the development of field theory in psychology. The movement began when modern physics invaded the Gestalt psychology. Indeed, as early as 1920 Köhler, in a volume dealing with "physical Gestalten," studied those distributions of energy in which field principles were evident (page 291). He specifically called attention to those experiments in physics in which the local event is determined by the entire context; in which it is impossible to specify any detail which, defined in and for itself, can then be placed in the total situation and be found to remain what it was before. So far, this gave background for Gestalt psychology; Köhler was describing Gestalten in the physical world which were analogous to perceptual responses.

KURT LEWIN

In this period the young student of mathematics and physics Kurt Lewin, who had recently returned from army service, became a vigorous and intensely creative member of the Gestalt group at the University of Berlin. He rapidly qualified himself for the role of colleague of the three senior Gestaltists already named: Wertheimer, Köhler, Koffka. At Berlin he carried out a series of studies of the dynamics of memory, in which he showed that items are linked together in memory not by virtue of "association," but by virtue of the way in which each word or nonsense syllable expresses the field organization of the experimental task as a whole (cf. page 280).

But feeling a need for a fuller utilization of what the physicists were doing, he began to think of psychological problems more and more in terms of events occurring in a kind of space which had something in common with physical space, and to think of psychological activity as a progression from one point to another within this life space, or psychological space. Here he felt the need for more adequate mathematical tools, and gave himself intensely to that branch of mathematics which deals with such types of space as are of interest for their own intrinsic spatial attributes and not for their quantitative relationships. He found what he needed in the branch of mathematics known as topology, in which one is concerned with regions and their boundaries and subdivisions, the modes of progression which are possible within them, and the possibility of transformation of such portions of space as a result of weakening or strengthening barriers. Instead of the formal quantitative laws of the individual organism conceived as a biological system, we find ourselves confronted with *psychological motion toward goals within defined regions of life space.*[1]

Our interest in quantitative problems here becomes secondary; our interest turns rather to goals toward which psychological motion occurs, the tension systems or needs which appear as vectors expressing such motion, the barriers which interfere with it, the subdivisions into subregions of life space which occur (as in the absent-minded or the dissociated), the new integration which may occur under therapy, and so on. He thus simultaneously solved two problems: first, that of transferring the field mode of thought into psychology; and second, the problem of representing graphically rather than verbally the nature of psychological impulsions, the resistance to

[1] *A Dynamic Theory of Personality* (1935); *Principles of Topological Psychology* (1936).

such impulsions, and the resulting transformations in movement toward goals.

A very simple illustration of the Lewinian mode of thought and expression appears in the case of a child wanting to go to a party and coming up against adamant refusal on the part of his parents

A

The arrow indicates psychological motion toward the goal blocked by the barrier.

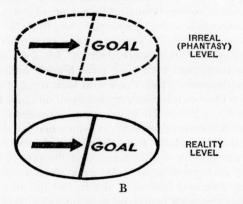

B

Finding the barrier impenetrable, the child creates a new life space at a higher level; the barrier becomes permeable. (Modified from K. Lewin)

(A). A second figure (B) portraying the same goal and the same barrier shows how the child, by "going out of the field," withdrawing into a daydream, sets up a substitute field at another level in which the barrier becomes porous, and he imagines ways in which parents can be persuaded or circumvented, and finally reaches the goal at the imaginative level.

Utilizing his dynamic approach in experimental psychology, Lewin set going two lines of research which soon became especially popular and influential. Both express the vitality of the conception of psychological needs as tension systems; that is, as systems of interrelated forces within a bounded field capable of being conceptualized as the bases for locomotion in one or another direction. The first is the study of what happens to a tension system when a reduction in tension level is permitted. The pioneer study is that of Zeigarnik,[2] who, after administering a series of tasks to her laboratory subjects, allowed them to complete some, but interrupted others before completion. She later found that the subjects were on the whole able to recall the unfinished tasks more easily than the completed ones. Subsequent research has shown that the tensions in such situations may be various and complex, but it has clearly confirmed the importance of thinking of the tension system as continuing until a means for its reduction is available. This shows, in other words, that things do not just "die down," or peter out, but remain, until something new supervenes. It is only when the task is completed that the artificially induced tension state (the "quasi-need") is put to rest. This "Zeigarnik effect" on the nature of the factors which may reduce tension has been the subject of many later investigations.

In the same years Hoppe [3] and others, set for their subjects tasks which were somewhat difficult of achievement, and studied the many factors tending to raise or lower the expectation of the individual as to what he would be able to achieve—his "aspiration level." In time, notably in the work of J. D. Frank,[4] it became customary to think of aspiration level as a definite quantitative gauge of the person's expectation regarding his own future performance; and it became the habit to treat of the difference between his aspiration and his present view of himself (his ego level) in terms of "difference scores." Such difference scores have been brought into relation to many sorts of personal variables; and it has been found, as by Gould [5] and others, that a rather accurate picture of the individual's struggle for status and his struggle to find an acceptable self is portrayed in his endless jockeying with the aspiration level so that it will neither be so high as to leave him in a perpetual state of frustration nor so low as to be overeasily attained and hence to lose its zest.

A more detailed illustration, taken from the research of Lewin and his associates after his coming to the United States in 1932, will

[2] Zeigarnik, B., *Psychol. Forsch.*, 1927, 9, 1–86.

[3] Hoppe, F., *Psychol. Forsch.*, 1930, 14, 1–63.

[4] Frank, J. D., "Individual Differences in Certain Aspects of the Level of Aspiration," *Amer. J. Psychol.*, 1935, 47, 119–28.

[5] Gould, R., "An Experimental Analysis of 'Levels of Aspiration,'" *Genet. Psychol. Monogr.*, 1939, 21, 3–115.

serve to show the radically empirical and at the same time theoretically rich nature of the approach. The hypothesis was set up by Barker, Dembo, and Lewin that the Freudian conception of regression may be restated in topological terms: regression is the loss of differentiation; therefore one may refer to "*de*differentiation." [6] We begin by showing the Lewinian conception of the mind of the newborn as essentially an undifferentiated whole. A bare circular outline may be used to portray this. Gradually, as Figure A shows,

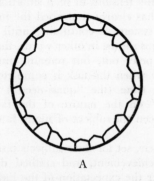 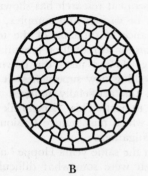

A   B

In contact with the outer environment, the undifferentiated mind of the newborn becomes differentiated at its periphery into sensory regions (things experienced) and motor regions (activities carried out). Later, an inner "world" also appears. (Modified from K. Lewin)

sensory components take shape as the child becomes aware of objects about him which he can recognize; and at the same time motor components, habitual acts, make their appearance. These events going on during the opening weeks are followed (Figure B) by the development of an inner world of memories, images, values, and purposes; in this inner world, then, we have a series of differentiations going on which make the adult infinitely more specific and at the same time more rigid than the child. The process of dedifferentiation consists of losing such differentiated subregions and reverting to the infantile condition. Now we should assume in general that frustrations, if intense enough, will cause such dedifferentiation. We have then the hypothesis: Frustration will produce a regression, meaning specifically a measurable reduction in the differentiatedness of behavior.

[6] Barker, R. G., Dembo, Tamara, and Lewin, Kurt, *Frustration and Regression: An Experiment with Children, Univ. Iowa Stud. Child Welfare,* 1941, 18, No. 1.

To test this hypothesis, children of nursery-school age whose behavior had been rated on scales indicating the degree of their "social constructiveness" while playing with a set of toys, were given a chance to observe some new and fascinating toys and to play a few minutes with them, and were then led back to the old, familiar playroom equipment. Between the child and the new toys a large wire-mesh screen was pulled down and padlocked. The behavior of most of the children in the subsequent period of observation consisted, in good measure, of responses of a rather undifferentiated sort which they had shown when much younger. Thus a child who before this experiment had used a toy telephone to carry on a conversation proved after the frustrating experience to lose this "mature behavior," and simply used the telephone as a rattle. A child who had been "writing a letter" went back to sheer scribbling. The hypothesis seems verified. A topological change occurs, in the sense of a reduction in the number and the firmness of the boundaries within the system as a whole; a dedifferentiation.

FIELD THEORY AND SOCIAL PSYCHOLOGY

Both in Germany and in the United States Lewin directed his attention largely to studies of child behavior, especially to the nature of tensions and barriers, and of the phenomena of changing response to these tensions and barriers as the child's social situation changed. During the late thirties, his association with a number of men trained in social psychology, in group work, and in youth leadership led, at the University of Iowa, to a series of monumental studies in the experimental social psychology of the child. Ronald Lippitt, Ralph White, and others joined with him in investigations of leadership.[7] Leaders who had been trained to lead according to "authoritarian," or "laissez-faire," or "democratic" patterns set up among boys' groups certain types of "social climates" or "group atmospheres," which became evident in the behavior of groups of boys with whom they worked. The five boys in each group worked at making masks in preparation for a show. They worked either under the verbal lash of a "top sergeant," or under the dull but permissive conditions of an indifferent leadership, or under conditions in which the leader, while giving directions, thought constantly in terms of

[7] Lewin, Kurt, Lippitt, Ronald, and White, R. K., "Patterns of Aggressive Behavior in Experimentally Created 'Social Climates,' " *J. Soc. Psychol.*, 1939, 10, 271–99.

the wishes and needs of the individual participant. Elaborate analyses, both of the effectiveness of the three ways of working and of the types of behaviors resulting from participation in these groups, were carried through. The aftereffects of such participation were traced in subsequent attitudes and behavior when individuals were transferred to new leaders. In short, experimental social psychology went beyond the level of research upon the socialization of the individual and directly achieved the experimental disentangling of factors involved in readiness in the group to accept this or that type of direction from one's peers and from one's leader.

A long series of similar studies in social psychology was carried out during and after World War II by Lewin and his pupils and colleagues. Some dealt, for example, with the problem of increasing the effectiveness of the war effort by changing the make-up of the group structure, and through this the morale of those engaged in war activities. Thus Alex Bavelas so set the atmosphere that a group of women industrial workers, through their own group discussion, determined upon a new level of productiveness, which they achieved and maintained.[8]

In consequence of the successful completion of such tasks, Lewin was finally invited to set up a Research Center in Group Dynamics, in which a variety of problems involving social atmospheres and leadership training were defined with a view to the reduction of tensions stemming from ethnic, religious, or other social cleavages, and a prominent place was given to industrial relationships and to leadership training. The center was established in 1944 at the Massachusetts Institute of Technology and made there a dramatic beginning.[9] This enterprise was suddenly frustrated by Lewin's death in February 1947. It is quite evident, however, that those who have been trained with him are determined to continue an ever widening series of studies of social structures and of leadership, using the community as a laboratory.

Lewin's influence on social psychology is huge, on child psychology very large, on general theoretical psychology considerable. His vitality and originality demanded respect even when his formulations were rejected, and the warmth of his intellectual companionship both brought him a wide personal following and involved him in a perpetual exchange of ideas with leaders of other movements

---

[8] See Kurt Lewin in Murphy, Gardner, *Human Nature and Enduring Peace* (1945), p. 308.

[9] Lewin, Kurt, "Action Research and Minority Problems," *J. Soc. Issues*, 1946, 2, 34–46.

and proponents of other systems. But during the last years of his life he was impressed more and more by the desperate urgency of the world situation, especially the struggle for democracy and the fascist threat to minority groups, and he gave less and less time to the development of his theoretical system and to the attempt to answer objections.

One of the commonest objections was that he was concerned with present cross sections of behavior, not with the history of how they came into being. To this he fully agreed. He believed that his system was suited only to cross sections in time, or at best to very short time durations; that it was not a genetic method, nor a method capable of application to longitudinal material. As he was fond of saying, it was an ahistorical approach: it left out the time dimension. In this sense, it could be contrasted with psychoanalysis, in which the time dimension, the genetic view, is all-important. Just how seriously this must be taken today is not clear. Let the time on the chronoscope gradually reduce to zero and try to imagine just what is "going on" in the organism in zero duration. Indeed, the typical Lewinian experiments, such as those referred to above, deal with transformations in time, as must all experiments on the functions of living individuals. Moreover, the difference between short time durations and long time durations can scarcely be elevated to a position of such tremendous importance. There is in much of Lewin's work, indeed, a concern with changes over the years: take, for example, the sketch of childhood development appearing in the figures on page 302. At this writing, it appears fair to say that Lewin's system was really competent, by means of a series of cross sections, as in any other science, to define temporal progressions.

The other main objections, of course, were (1) that he had not really shown the nonutility of the reduction of wholes into definable units; (2) that he had neglected individual differences; (3) that he had not shown that topological (or any kind of graphic) portrayal of functions was more serviceable than the current verbal and conventional mathematical methods. To all this he would certainly have said: "Look at the new experiments and results which in point of fact *did* come from the new approach." And to this the observer can only add: not the new method alone, and not the specific individual alone, but the field relation of these two—and indeed their relations to the twentieth-century world and to the psychology prevalent in that world—is what gave field theory the vitality and the productiveness it achieved.

REFERENCES

Leeper, Robert W., *Lewin's Topological and Vector Psychology: A Digest and a Critique,* University of Oregon, 1943

Lewin, Kurt, *A Dynamic Theory of Personality,* McGraw-Hill, 1935

——, *Principles of Topological Psychology,* McGraw-Hill, 1936

London, I. D., "Psychologists' Misuse of the Auxiliary Concepts of Physics and Mathematics," *Psychol. Rev.,* 1944, 51, 266–91

Weiss, Paul, *Principles of Development,* Holt, 1939; pp. 289–437

White, Ralph K., "The Case for the Tolman-Lewin Interpretation of Learning," *Psychol. Rev.,* 1943, 50, 157–86

Chapter 22

SIGMUND FREUD

Well-educated physicians, at any rate, say that we should pay
close attention to dreams. . . . The most skilful interpreter of
dreams is he who can discern resemblances. . . . As the picture
in the water, so the dream can be similarly distorted.

ARISTOTLE

I bid you, mock not Eros,
He knows not doubt or shame,
And, unaware of proverbs,
The burnt child craves the flame.

CHRISTOPHER MORLEY

WE MUST now retrace our steps to the decade of the eighties;
for we have to discuss a vast development which must be
surveyed as a unit. Indeed, the life of the founder and presiding genius of psychoanalysis has meant the continuous evolution
of doctrines which are best understood in their biographic setting.

Sigmund Freud, a young Viennese physician, was occupying himself in the late seventies with such orthodox medical investigations
as the embryology of the nervous system. He made contact with an
older man, Breuer, who was engaged in the study of hysteria and
kindred complaints. At that time hysteria was treated by many
physicians according to the methods which had been demonstrated
by Charcot; the use of hypnotic suggestion was of paramount importance. Partly through his contact with Breuer, Freud became
acquainted with the use of hypnosis as a technique for the removal
of such hysterical symptoms as functional paralysis, anesthesia, and
amnesia.

In the eighties, there came to the attention of Breuer and Freud a
case of hysteria the analysis of which contained the kernel of a new
system of treatment, and indeed a new system of psychology. A
prominent symptom of the patient, a girl of twenty-one, was a violent

repugnance to the act of drinking from a glass of water.[1] There was no evident reason for this strange aversion. The case was handled through hypnotic suggestion. While in a deep sleeplike state, the girl recalled the event from which her difficulty had arisen. It was the fact that she had seen a pet dog drink from a glass, an incident which disgusted her so violently that she feared she would display her disgust in the presence of the dog's owner. She inhibited, or repressed, her disgust, and the total experience was forced out of consciousness, so that until the time of the hypnotic treatment she had been unable to analyze the trouble. This case brought into brilliant light the possibility that though ejected from consciousness, an experience might continue to play an important part in conduct.

Shortly thereafter Freud went to study with Charcot at Paris. Charcot had a clear-cut theory of hysteria, according to which the hysterical crisis and the hypnotic trance constituted the same alteration of personality; much, therefore, of the clinical material which Freud witnessed was so presented as to suggest that hypnotic treatment bore an intimate and necessary relation to the understanding of hysteria. But Charcot made a singular remark one day that left an indelible impression on Freud's mind. A pupil had asked the master why a particular set of symptoms appeared in a particular case; Charcot replied, with animation, that such cases always had a sexual basis. And he repeated with emphasis, "Always, always, always!" "Yes, but if he knows this," said Freud to himself, "why does he never say so?" Freud states that Breuer, and the gynecologist Chrobak, had made remarks expressing the same belief in the importance of sexuality for nervous disorder; and that when reminded of these remarks, they denied making them.[2]

Freud returned to his practice in Vienna and collaborated further with Breuer. Then, learning more and more of the successful hypnotic work done by the Nancy school, he made a brief visit to observe all that he could in the clinic over which Bernheim presided. He was apparently especially impressed by the fact that posthypnotic suggestions were carried out by patients who did not know the reasons for their acts—here was clear evidence of unconscious motivation—and by the fact that when pressed to recall, the patients might, while still in the waking state, overcome their resistance and

[1] An abbreviated account of this very complicated case appears in Freud's Clark University lecture: "The Origin and Development of Psychoanalysis," *Amer. J. Psychol.*, 1910, 21, 181–218.

[2] *History of the Psychoanalytic Movement*, reprinted in *Psychoanalyt. Rev.*, 1916, 3, 406 ff.

bring back the instructions which had been given them. Freud returned again to Vienna, taking Bernheim seriously enough to translate him into German.

The use of hypnosis continued for several years to be a part of the method of Breuer and Freud. They found indeed that they could by this means detect conflicting forces which had been present in personality and had been forgotten through repression. They could lead back, by suggestion, to the recovery of these factors. They found that some apparent cures could be effected in this way, in the sense that the symptoms could be dissipated. But they discovered a serious difficulty in the use of the hypnotic method. At first the symptoms would disappear, but later other symptoms would show themselves. A paralysis might be dissipated, but six months later an anesthesia or an amnesia might appear. Hysteria could not be permanently cured through hypnotic methods. Instead of getting at the core of the trouble, they merely dispelled its manifestations. Moreover, patients sometimes fell spontaneously into a state of reverie which seemed as effective in bringing back old memories as was the hypnotic state.

Pursuing this lead, Breuer and Freud hit upon the device of allowing their patients, while in a relaxed waking state, to talk freely about anything that entered their minds, permitting their associations to lead back gradually to the sources of the difficulty. This was the "talking-out" method. In the course of therapy, patients became emotionally absorbed in the physician ("transference"), a fact which Breuer felt necessitated abandonment of the method. Freud's insistence on continuing the "talking-out" method, together with his growing conviction that sexuality was of the most vital importance for hysteria, led to a parting of the ways between Freud and Breuer.

Freud proceeded to develop this new method. He told the patient simply to attempt a narrative of his free associations; the origin of his symptoms would gradually become clear. To be sure, this necessitated the consecutive overcoming of resistances at points where the patient said that he could not think of anything more, or that he was thinking of something absurd or ugly which he hated to mention. At these points there seemed to be not so much a genuine failure of memory, through time, as an effect of the same mechanism which had been involved in the repression; namely, a resistance against the free expression of an impulsive tendency. Freud learned by experience that resistances were vitally important, and that it was at these very points that something illuminating could, through the patient's perseverance in the task, be disclosed. Resistances were especially evident where associations of a sexual nature appeared.

The "psychoanalytic" method was this use of free association; with this method, psychoanalysis as such began. Through the patient's gradual recall of the emotional episodes which precipitated the conflict, and, in particular, through the free recognition and release of pent-up emotion,[3] the struggle could sometimes be terminated and the patient's mental health restored. More adequate cooperation was secured than was possible through hypnosis, for instead of dealing with a passive subject (and all hypnotic subjects who merely follow the suggestion of the hypnotizer are passive), he had the patient's active assistance toward revealing the deeply submerged tendencies in personality.[4]

At this period (the last decade of the century) Freud had not succeeded very far in relating specific types of symptoms to specific types of conflict; nor had he any clear notion as to the period in life at which such psychopathic dispositions were at first formed. There was no reason to suppose that they necessarily involved anything more remote than emotional experiences such as were apparent in cases like that of the girl unable to drink from a glass of water. He was not as yet concerned to show an earlier origin, some predisposing cause, for such manifestations in the life of the patient. But the cure of a symptom was sometimes followed by new symptoms, and it became necessary to penetrate deeper; that is, to go farther and farther back into the patient's personal history. Adult experience seemed to call for emphasis upon the importance of childhood conflicts as basic for adult maladjustment.

Freud did, moreover, encounter many psychoneuroses in *children*. A boy, for example, was afflicted by a strange compulsion; before he could go to sleep he had to arrange a row of chairs beside his bed, pile pillows on them, and turn his face toward the wall.[5] The study of the case showed that he had been the victim of a sexual assault which had so terrified him that ever afterward a barricade

---

[3] *Abreaktion*, a part of the "cathartic method" already developed by Breuer and Freud in conjunction with hypnotic technique.

[4] Such spatial and mechanical metaphors are prominent throughout the history of psychoanalysis. James, in discussing closely similar material, said "in the end we fall back on the hackneyed symbolism of a mechanical equilibrium."—*The Varieties of Religious Experience*, p. 197. The metaphors were surely helpful at first; but with time their value has been more and more seriously challenged.

[5] *Collected Papers*, 1924, Vol. I, "Further Remarks on the Defence Neuro-Psychoses," *Neurolog. Zentralbl.*, 1896.

must be placed between the bed and the open room, and his face averted. Thus the symptoms were *symbols* of the conflict. A great variety of such symbolic symptoms were presented in Freud's essays.

A clear divergence is apparent between Freud's interpretation of symptoms and the interpretation offered by Janet.[6] Janet had indeed emphasized the reality of aspects of personality which were so dissociated as to be no longer capable of conscious control; but with Freud emphasis was laid especially upon the *dynamics* of such dissociation. The ultimate forces at work were provided by instinct; and the energy coming from instinctual forces operated outside consciousness as it did inside the conscious field. It was, he believed, only by conflict that any element or impulse could be kept outside personal awareness. But just as conflict was the explanation of dissociation, so it was held to be the clue to the particular *form* which the dissociation took, and consequently to the nature of the symptoms. The symptoms were, in a broad sense, symbols of the repressed tendencies, symbols to be understood through examination of the course of the disease. Janet had himself thought that symptoms arose from "subconscious ideas," and that amnesia involved the narrowing of the field of consciousness; but he had left the dynamics of the process almost untouched. For Freud this conception was eminently unsatisfactory;[7] in a host of cases like those already mentioned, the symptom seemed clearly to be a symbol of a specific conflict.

THE INTERPRETATION OF DREAMS

During the nineties Freud discovered that he could sometimes use another starting point for free association more fruitfully than the materials of everyday thought. He shifted his attention to the patient's dreams. Dreams had hitherto been studied in a rather haphazard fashion, though considerable attention had been given to the influence of physical stimuli,[8] especially to the position of the limbs.[9] Quite aside from its therapeutic significance, Freud's use of dreams was significant as part of the widespread movement to bring within the field of psychology materials lying outside that

---

[6] *The Mental State of Hystericals* (1892).

[7] For Janet himself it was only a provisional, and not in any sense an explanatory, formulation.

[8] For example, Maury, *Le sommeil et les rêves* (3rd ed., 1865). See also *Annales méd. psychol.*, 1854.

[9] Vold, J. M., *Expériences sur les rêves et en particulier ceux d'origine musculaire et optique* (1896).

domain of clearly conscious and observable processes which had been generally recognized as its legitimate subject matter. Freud's work on *The Interpretation of Dreams* was finally published in 1900.

Dreams he regarded as the expression of wishes. They are a means by which tendencies which have been kept out of consciousness during everyday waking life can, through symbolism, express themselves with relative freedom from interference. The dream is a dynamic expression of forces which, though repressed, are struggling to regain a place in consciousness. The dream seemed to be a beautiful illustration of the mechanism by which instinctual tendencies in conflict with the ego are manifested. The ego is a group of tendencies which have been strengthened by social—especially ethical—indoctrination, tendencies which are a part of our accepted social life, necessary in the making of a living and the building-up of a reputation. We live in a society which is intolerant of certain of our instinctual tendencies; among these, sexual (and aggressive) tendencies are prominent. Sexual tendencies are more or less constantly with us, and are subject to rigorous repression. Freud made much of the significance of dreams as symbolic representations of sex wishes.

Now there must be some factor in waking life which is not present in the dream, to explain why the dream takes on a form easily distinguished from the wish fulfillments which appear in daydreaming. It had long been known that people of orderly habits not infrequently dream of participating in burglaries, murders, and the like. Men of irreproachable character may curse like troopers in their sleep. It seemed to Freud that something in the waking life must act as a constant damper on latent tendencies which show themselves in the dream. But even in the dream there was evidence of restraint, and to this restraint he gave the name of the *censorship*. Censorship during sleep is less severe than repression during waking hours, and so allows forbidden tendencies some degree of freedom. Nevertheless, it continues in sleep to prevent the *direct* and unambiguous expression of repressed materials, forcing them to take on a disguise. This disguise or symbolism is analogous to the symbolism already noticed in the case of the psychoneurotic symptoms. But how is the dream symbolism to be interpreted?

Many dreams, especially those of children, seem to be *direct* fulfillments of wishes. A child who had eagerly wished to climb a certain mountain dreamed that he had climbed it. Another child had been boating, and was bitterly disappointed when she came to the shore;

in her dream that night she went boating again, and the trip was longer.[10] We find, Freud believes, relatively few such dreams in adults. Some common types are, however, apparent, notably "comfort" dreams. A drowsy man wishes on a cold winter's morning that he could keep his appointments without getting up; he falls asleep again and in a dream keeps the appointments. But the majority of adult dreams are not so simple; the key to them is the interpretation of symbols.

As he analyzed more and more dreams, Freud arrived at the conviction that there are, despite their infinite variety, certain striking uniformities in their contents, much greater in number than we should expect to find by chance. The dream of being in public clad only in nightclothes keeps reappearing. Dreams of flying and of being pursued are common. Freud came to believe that certain stock symbols are to be found in the dreams of all sorts of people, symbols which regularly and with very few exceptions mean the same thing wherever they appear. Many of these symbols bear an evident resemblance to the thing symbolized; this was especially emphasized in the case of sexual symbols. The interpretation of many symbols was, however, difficult, necessitating a detailed analysis of their origin. Symbols may, Freud observed, be handed on from generation to generation (the serpent has been used as a symbol of the healing art from pre-Homeric times to the present); symbols used by the social group may be accepted by the individual.

But symbolism is not the only mechanism by which repressed tendencies may appear in altered forms in the dream. The elements of the dream may be not a direct but a condensed or inverted narrative of the sequence of events unconsciously wished. The "manifest dream" is a distorted representation of the "latent dream." And whereas the latent dream is a *wish*, the manifest dream appears as an *event;* the indicative mood appears, so to speak, in place of the optative. During the dream the censorship is sufficiently lax to permit the latent dream (that is, wishes struggling for fulfillment) to find expression in such a way as to escape recognition. The dream, like the neurotic symptom, is a compromise between the repressed and the repressing tendencies. The nature of such struggle and compromise is shown in the nightmare, which becomes more and more terrifying until the dreamer wakes up. The disguise covering the repressed tendencies becomes too thin, and the ego, terrified lest the repressed wishes break forth into clear consciousness, takes

[10] These cases are cited in Freud's *General Introduction to Psychoanalysis* (Hall trans., 1920), p. 102.

full control of the situation. Freud did not dismiss the evidence which shows that nightmares, as well as many other dreams, may arise from such simple physical causes as indigestion; but he regarded such explanations merely as legitimate comments on some of the materials of the manifest dream, not as an explanation of the fact of dreaming, nor of the character of the dream. Similarly, he was not concerned to deny that many elements in dreams are recollections of recent waking events, but he insisted that the particular materials chosen for the manifest dream appeared because of their effectiveness for the purpose of the latent dream. And the dream, by its disguises, actually served to *protect* sleep.

Two illustrations will show Freud's use of these hypotheses. A woman dreamed that she attended the funeral of a small nephew. She was very fond of the boy, and did not understand why she should have dreamed of his death. Analysis showed that sometime earlier she had attended the funeral of another nephew, and had met on this occasion a young physician with whom she was in love. The dream was a simple way of saying she wished that the physician would return. The manifest dream revealed but little of the latent dream. Another illustration in which the interpretation is much less simple is more characteristic of the mass of published dream analyses.[11] A young woman who had been married for several years dreamed that she went to the theater with her husband. On arrival at the theater they found the house only half filled. Her husband told her of a young woman and her bridegroom who had wished to come, but had been unable to. She thought this "no misfortune" for them. In point of fact, she (the dreamer) had recently bought theater tickets in advance, paying a surcharge for them, only to find that one side of the orchestra was almost empty, and her mind kept running upon the theme "too hasty." The meaning of the dream as given by Freud was that painful associations surrounded the incident of buying tickets *too* early, because this was symbolic of her own unconscious protest against too early a marriage.[12]

In all this intensive dream study the psychoanalytic method was kept in constant use, patients giving their free associations in relation to each dream as they lay relaxed on a couch in the analyst's

[11] *Ibid.*, p. 98. The case is here much abbreviated.

[12] Such interpretations have been, in general, difficult to support by convincing evidence. Freud and his pupils have emphasized the fact that the interpretations are frequently accepted by the patient, and play a part in the process of self-understanding which helps toward cure. But since the influence of suggestion cannot be excluded, both arguments have failed of convincingness. Freudian dream psychology has therefore been subject, among his followers, to all sorts of revisions, and has

office, and slowly discovering, under his guidance, the nature of their own unconscious mental life. In the course of such therapy many new hypotheses and many new methods came into being. In this period Freud published a book applying his working concepts to new materials, *The Psychopathology of Everyday Life* (1901). The thesis of the book was very simple in comparison with his dream psychology. Not only in neurotic symptoms, he held, but in the everyday acts of normal persons, there is evidence that any tendency which is forced out of consciousness continues to struggle for expression, and, though failing to appear in consciousness, influences thought and action. The most casual "slips" (*Fehlhandlungen*) of tongue or pen, the forgetting of familiar names, and all sorts of oddities and blunders which interfere with our deliberate purposes, reflect a real though unacknowledged motive. At a time of rather strained relations, a man's wife gave him a book which she thought might interest him; the book was promptly lost and his efforts to find it were vain. Later she exerted herself to care for her husband's mother in a serious illness. Returning home one day with enthusiasm for her devotion, he immediately found the book. The original losing of the book was a symbolic expression of the fact that he had lost his affection for his wife. He had forgotten the book because it was a token of her. Similarly, through regaining his affection for her, the obstacle to recalling the whereabouts of the book was removed.

The psychoanalytic method, its application to dream material, and the study of *Fehlhandlungen*, were worked out by Freud before psychoanalysis became a school or a movement. Freud worked alone, in fact, until the beginning of the new century. His observations were frequently published several years after they had been made; the indifference of the public gave him a leisure which he felt saved him from the pressure later exerted upon him as the leader of a school.[13] But in 1902, a group of medical men in Vienna began to join with him in a seminar for the study of psychoanalysis. Psychoanalysis became, in a few years, a "movement" of wide proportions.

been one of the aspects of his system selected for especially vigorous attack by psychologists who have demanded experimental confirmation of his major tenets. The method of free association, with or without the use of dream material, did unravel the skein of many a tangled personality; but the question remained open whether this was chiefly due to Freud's interpretation of symbols or simply to his emphasis on the importance of conflict and repression—an emphasis which, aside from all theories of symbolism, led the patient to struggle toward a rediscovery of the forgotten episodes underlying his troubles.

[13] *History of the Psychoanalytic Movement, Psychoanalytic Rev.*, 1916, 3, 418.

In the same period Freud published his contribution to the theory of wit.[14] In this he emphasized the role of wit in suddenly liberating repressed impulses, "letting the cat out of the bag." The practical joke is funny in so far as there is genuine antagonism against the victim; jokes upon pompous or self-righteous persons or upon "hated rivals" are funny, while jokes against the helpless are merely brutal. Humorous stories, moreover, can be classified in respect to the type of impulses released. One group of stories resembles the practical joke: persons or institutions toward which a forced deference is maintained may be seen stripped of their dignity. Another group comprises puns, the explanation of which shows beautifully the ambition of the Freudian teaching to become no mere commentary on emotional life, but a genuine system of psychology. The pun is funny because it frees our minds from a particular kind of restraint; namely, that constraint which logical thought and the forms of grammar impose upon us. We are forced to use the same old words with the same old meanings year in and year out.[15] Through using words in an unaccustomed sense, the punster and his hearers are released from the strain of being logical. Anything that allows the sudden release of pent-up energies gives a sudden, in fact an explosive, satisfaction.

Wit is, however, merely one of many ways in which the mind constantly seeks freedom from restraint. Early in life the child learns the stern necessity of thinking for practical purposes, the "reality motive." [16] He continues, however, the simple and satisfying habit of letting his thoughts roam at times where they will. The struggle against accepting a painful reality may show itself in a tendency to interpret our own conduct and motives as we should wish them to be. This process of finding "good reasons" for acts of which we are covertly ashamed has been given by Ernest Jones the name of "rationalization." [17] If the behavior of others suggests that they entertain an unfavorable attitude toward us, we may resort to other "defense mechanisms"; [18] we may strive to put ourselves in a favorable light or to convince ourselves that their approval means nothing. And childish thought is *omnipotent;* thinking of a thing makes it occur.

[14] *Wit and Its Relation to the Unconscious* (1905).
[15] Unless we use them as Humpty Dumpty did.
[16] See, for example, *Beyond the Pleasure Principle* (1921).
[17] "Rationalization in Everyday Life," *J. Abn. Psychol.*, 1908, 3, 161–69.
[18] Similar, of course, to the defense of the neurotic against his repressed impulses; the idea of defense has been emphasized throughout the history of psychoanalysis.

THE LIBIDO THEORY

Through these years came thick and fast a series of contributions regarding the theory of sexuality, which remain fundamental in Freudian psychoanalysis. He had, as we noted, observed psychoneuroses whose origin lay in childhood. Further study of such material constantly drove him farther back into individual history, to the point of attaching paramount importance to the sexual life of early infancy. In the earlier years, he was often content to trace a symptom, a slip of speech or the like, back to some repression in adult life; but in subsequent work, repression came to be regarded not simply as the result of the conflict of present forces, but as the most recent manifestation of a history of conflict which went back to an origin in the sexual life of the little child. An early elaboration of much of this system of thought was presented in *Three Contributions to the Theory of Sex* (1905); the extension of the doctrine appeared in a long series of books and articles. Most of this material was obtained from the study of adults, especially neurotic adults, whose memories were carried back by the psychoanalytic method to earlier and earlier stages in their development. Confirmation of some of the hypotheses obtained was, however, sought through the psychoanalysis of children.[19]

From such analytic material, as well as from many scattered observations as to the ways of infants and children, Freud roughly outlined certain stages in individual sexual growth.[20] In early infancy there appears a wealth of response to which the term "sexual" may be applied. It had long been suspected, for example, that such habits as thumb-sucking have something to do with sexuality. Freud found, however, nothing in the infant which could be characterized as a specific sex impulse; on the contrary, sexual manifestations were so extraordinarily "polymorphous" that it seemed wiser to use the term "sexuality" to mean the whole bundle of dispositions which are connected with the love life, whether associated with the organs of sex or not. Even the "perversions" of adult life—for example, sadism—are simply continuations and elaborations of infantile responses. And even the dominating and submissive tendencies are regarded as aspects of sexuality. Very important is the child's discovery of the topography of his body, and therewith a group of satisfactions; this leads to the fixation of habits in which

---

[19] See, for example, *Analyse der Phobie eines fünfjährigen Knaben* (1909).
[20] See, for example, *General Introduction to Psychoanalysis*, pp. 277 f.

the child's affections are directed to his own body instead of toward another individual. This stage is designated "autoeroticism." [21]

Now the rather diffuse sexuality of early infancy undergoes a series of repressions and modifications. The person most intimately associated with the infant's sex feelings, as well as with the satisfaction of his hunger, is of course the mother. In the course of time, Freud believes, the little boy learns that the father is not only a competitor for the mother's affection, but may, and frequently does, interfere in the child's close intimacy with the mother. Both of the parents, and society in general as well, make it plain to the boy that he may not have undisputed possession of his mother; and the father is in fact not only the competitor, but the stern incarnation of discipline. Love for the mother, Freud contends, must be in some way repressed, while the father, though still an object of affection, is at the same time hated. Remembering the myth of Oedipus, King of Thebes, who had slain his father and married his mother, Freud called this infantile pattern the Oedipus complex, "complex" being a general term for a constellation of affectively toned ideas which have been repressed. To a somewhat similar mechanism in the girl, the name "Electra complex" was given. Both the psychoanalytic evidence and the reasoning based upon it are so complicated that our brief summary must be especially inadequate at this point. It is, however, important to remember that the picture is profoundly modified by the child's tendency to "identify" himself in some degree with each of his parents.

But the child's love energy, or *libido*, may come in time to be attached to his whole body; and this "narcistic" (or "narcissistic") stage is characterized by self-absorption and vanity, one's mental as well as physical attributes becoming objects of affection. The social situation ultimately forces the child to find another love object. He chooses individuals like himself; that is, those of his own sex. This "homosexual" stage, in which children show strong attachment chiefly to playmates of their own sex, gives place at last to devotion to the opposite sex; and this passage to the "heterosexual" stage synchronizes with the rapid physical changes of early adolescence.

From the character of these stages it is evident that the sexual impulse was regarded as of an extremely vague and indefinite character, which knows no set forms of behavior. Only when the indi-

[21] Freud calls this "the happy term invented by Havelock Ellis." This is but one of many contributions for which Ellis's work has been welcomed by psychoanalysts. (See Ellis, "Auto-erotism: A Psychological Study," *Alienist and Neurologist*, 1898, 19, 260–99.)

vidual has passed through various stages can his affections undergo
fixation of a stable and normal type, involving integration of the
many components in the "primacy of the genital zone." But the
attachments—"cathexes," literally "investments"—made in each
stage are not completely obliterated during progress to the next, and
herein much of the distress of adult life resides. Moreover, whenever
adjustment at a given stage fails, one tends to "regress" to a previous
stage which brought satisfaction. The rejected lover turns to his
old friends. Such flight away from an adult level of adjustment plays
an important part in that escape from reality which characterizes
many psychoses. But most of all, the attachments of infancy persist.
Not only does the young man often seek a wife resembling his
mother; a filial attitude is also evident as a component in adult love.
The word "infantilism" is one of the major indices to the Freudian
psychology.

But regression is only one of *many* mechanisms through which a
conflict may be resolved. *Sublimation* is the discovery of a substitute
object for the libido, some channel of expression which, by its close
association with the one sought, will give partial satisfaction. The
arts and sciences give vicarious satisfaction; civilization itself is in
large part the creature of energies which have been diverted from a
sexual outlet. Freud was deeply interested in demonstrating in the
work of creative artists the presence of materials reflecting the unconscious sexual fantasies of the artist.[22] Even in the first years of
psychoanalysis, Freud sought to understand the origins and the
consequences of the endless restraint which man puts upon his
instinctual tendencies; and this emphasis upon the unconscious instinctual materials in complicated cultural phenomena became more
and more prominent. Not only marriage and the family, but myth
and folklore, religion and ceremonial, science,[23] literature, music,
pictorial and plastic art, and most other cultural phenomena, are
full of materials for psychoanalytic study.

The first to offer a psychoanalytic interpretation of anthropological
data was Abraham,[24] but Freud welcomed this extension of method,
and contributed substantially to it. His comparison of the "ambivalence" of the sacred and the unclean with similarly ambivalent
attitudes encountered among neurotics (and others) has provoked

[22] *Leonardo da Vinci* (1910).
[23] The curiosity motive implicit in science is regarded by Freud as emanating
largely from childish curiosity regarding sex.
[24] *Traum und Mythus* (1908).

much discussion.[25] His comments, however suggestive, do not appear to have won general assent from the only group qualified to judge of them; namely, the anthropologists. But we shall return to this problem (page 422).

Now we come to Freud's interpretation of some of the phenomena which had throughout his career been the central problem for direct study, the neuroses. Nearly all of these he continued to attribute to sexual conflict. The Freudian interpretation of *obsessions* may be represented by an illustrative case.[26] A woman came to Freud suffering from a distressing obsession, an idea which she knew to be foolish, but which nevertheless she could not dispel. She felt that her husband was disloyal to her. The woman had recently seen a young and attractive officer with whom she had become infatuated. Being unwilling to acknowledge the fact, she had "projected" it to her husband. Such a process is somewhat similar to the act of rationalization, by which we explain our conduct in such terms as to free us from the sense of guilt. In contrast with obsessions, *compulsions* are overt *acts* through which an affect, or rather the defense against it, constantly symbolizes itself; many patients, like Lady Macbeth, wash their hands in an effort to wash away feelings of guilt. *Phobias*—morbid, irrational fears—present a somewhat similar mechanism. Some phobias are not sharply distinguished from compulsions; the fear of dirt (misophobia), for example, may provoke excessive hand-washing. The fear masks a repressed desire which the patient cannot recognize. The repression, and the belief that repression is the major cause for the persistence of the difficulty, distinguish such explanations sharply from the simple "conditioned response" explanations of Bekhterev and others.[27] In "conversion hysteria" the repressed affect is "converted" into a specific symptom, such as a paralysis, contracture, anesthesia, or amnesia. The unconscious protest, for example, against seeing what is painful may lead to a functional blindness.

Let us stop to take stock of the meaning of psychoanalysis as sketched up to this point. About halfway through his long career (1914), Freud wrote a *History of the Psychoanalytic Movement* which may be cited here in reference to our need to characterize what had been accomplished up to the time of World War I. Of very great interest is his insistence upon the functional significance of *transference*, a process by which the patient transfers to the physician

---

[25] *Totem and Taboo* (first published in *Imago*, 1912–13, 1–2).

[26] *General Introduction to Psychoanalysis*, pp. 213 ff.

[27] *La psychologie objective* (1913).

the love or hate which as a small child he gave to his father.[28] Utilizing the transference, the analyst is able, in completing his task, to
give the patient such self-understanding that he or she may be freed
from the transference and regain wholesome affection for a previous
love object or freely bestow it upon a new one. Transference is
prominent in any Freudian analysis. It is natural that in discussing
such a complicated system of thought, now one, now another element should be emphasized as the true keystone of the whole structure. For some it is infantilism, for others sexuality, and for some,
indeed, infantile sexuality. For some it is the unconscious, for others
symbolism. We must for the present content ourselves with the fact
that for Freud himself, in this essay, the starting points from which
a truly psychoanalytic system proceeds, and without which it should
be described by some other name, are *resistance* and *transference*.[29]

EGO THEORY

But if the reader will permit a very gross oversimplification in the
portrayal of so long and so rich a life as that of Sigmund Freud, one
might be forgiven for saying that the primary energies of the man
from the eighties until about 1912 or 1913 were given to the nature
of unconscious dynamics, and in particular to the libido and its
many indirect expressions, but that from about 1912 on until his
death in 1939 Freud seemed more and more concerned to correct
the faulty balance which the system had somehow developed, and
concerned himself more and more with integrative functions and
with the membership of the individual in society. This meant an
increasingly close concern with the origin and development of moral
and cultural systems, with man as a creature of culture rather than
primarily as a bundle of drives; perhaps, in a single word, with the
ego. *On Narcissism* (1912); *Group Psychology and Analysis of the Ego*
(1920); *The Ego and the Id* (1923); *Inhibition, Symptom, and Anxiety*
(1927)—this series of books and papers, paralleled and supplemented
by many others both on ego theory and on the further development
of the libido theory, indicate a consistent effort to discover exactly
how the impulsive and instinctual forces are ordered and directed
by man in such fashion as to make possible some sort of stable social
living, with some sort of rationality and self-control. While a summary of so vast a development can of course not be attempted here,

---

[28] See the chapter on "Transference" in Freud's *General Introduction to Psychoanalysis.*

[29] *History of the Psychoanalytic Movement.*

it may be worth while to note some of the primary implications of this sequence of studies. The account which follows will not arrange the contributions from a purely chronological viewpoint, but will attempt to give the conception of a system of ideas which changed gradually rather than abruptly. It will be noted that some fundamental aspects of ego theory had been clearly sketched even in the first decade of the century.

First, we must stress the fact that the diffuse and almost unbounded energy of the libido is conceived to be early attached to specific objects. It may, so to speak, be invested either in the persons or things of the outer world, or in the body of the individual. Even before birth there is a primitive libidinal attachment to one's warm and comfortable form; and while after the moment of birth it is caught in a maelstrom of buffets and pressures, the infant finds nevertheless a certain stability and satisfying quality in his own outer surface and his own inner vital processes. Even at the adult level, one's own body is a refuge, and in some persons the *chief* refuge; the extraordinary myth of Narcissus defines with great beauty the overwhelming satisfaction which may come to the frustrated or frightened spirit as the beauty of line and surface and of vocal cadence begin to stand out against the chaos or the threat of an uncertain background. The beginnings of self-love are established as this investment or cathexis upon the infant's own person is formed.

Through contact with his mother, moreover, and through love of her, he begins to feel himself one with her, to share her feelings, to view the world through her eyes, to identify with her. Identification with his father also occurs. He is becoming a person; he begins to show some degree of self-awareness and of awareness of the experience of other persons. Moreover, while as a newborn infant he found that his cries and gestures brought relief, he knew not how (that is, magically), he has become well aware before the end of his first year that he must adapt to an external reality. It is he himself who must pull the strings; he must manipulate the world directly. This involves *reality testing;* a function of the *ego*—an *executive* function, as contrasted with the blind instinctual functions.

Self-love or narcissism is heavily stressed. During infancy, however, cathexis upon the mother is just as fundamental; for she offers satisfaction of the infant's libidinal cravings. But in addition to these types of libidinal expression, there are others, notably those which arise from satisfaction of the various sensitive areas of the body, such as the skin of the breast and the abdomen, and those connected with the orifices of the body, particularly with the mouth, the sexual apparatus, and the lower colon and anus. Here the primitive satisfactions which are involved in rubbing are complicated by the fact that tension thus built up cannot be adequately resolved. An obvious example is that of thumb-sucking, which does not really satisfy, but leads to a perseverative effort, and hence to a prolongation of a partially satisfying and partially frustrating activity. Interference with any of these three types of activity—typical in our culture are forcible weaning, punishment for masturbation, and rigid toilet training—involves the accumulation of tension and hence of suffering, and calls for some indirect means of escape. At the same time, being essentially social, they involve the arousal of hostility toward the parents as agents of a repressive disciplinary control.

From these first conceptions regarding interference with the pleasurable contact with the sensitive zones sprang Freud's first paper on character types (1906), continued in later studies, and elaborately developed by his pupil in Berlin, Karl Abraham. The essential theory is that character in the adult tends to be a persistent quest for that which has been forcibly frustrated in infancy. Forcible weaning, for example, may lead to a disposition to demand a continuous excitation of the mouth area and a need for eating, drinking, smoking, talking, and every other kind of lip and mouth activity. In a still broader sense, such an orally centered character shows the need to re-establish a relation of dependence, a relation of parasitism, which momentarily gives relief from that chronic, unconscious sense of oral deprivation for which no true relief can ever be found. This is an exemplification of the general thesis that infancy is a period of very special vulnerability, and that profound and permanent effects follow from the frustration of infantile needs, as well as from intense infantile fears.

In connection with Freud's conception of scattered zones of special sensitiveness, emphasis was placed upon matters of the growth and the education of the sexual impulse. At first, sexuality is diffuse; it is virtually identical with a pleasure-seeking tendency, though there are many part-impulses craving satisfaction, each being relatively isolated from the rest. The parents, as disciplinary agents of the social group, interfere with this "polymorphous perverse" preoccupation with scattered erogenous zones, and repression occurs. Especially intense is the little boy's fear of punishment, or even mutilation, at his father's hands, because of the Oedipus situation. The long period of conflict connected with love for the father and fear of his punishment leads finally to the acceptance of the inexorable law regarding the infraction of rules, particularly those involving the primitive outflow of affections. From this point forward there prevails for some years a period of relative blockage of all direct libidinal expression: the latency period. At puberty there is a revitalization of the infantile libidinal responses, which are now given a heterosexual direction, partly as a result of the consolidation of infantile experiences with the newly given energies of adolescence. The persistence of the earliest primitive polymorphous perverse response-tendencies into a later period of life is conceived to lie at the basis both of overt perversions and of unconscious residues regarded as fundamental in paranoia and in various other psychoses. It is obvious in all this that adult sexuality is regarded as something which is achieved in consequence of a long series of struggles and compromises rather than as something given in biologically unalterable form.

But as psychoanalysis went on, another prominent factor in the child's struggle to cope with his instinctual needs became apparent. He feels himself threatened, but there is nevertheless a way out of this terrifying situation, and even a way to repress the hostility to the father. As he identified with his mother, so, because father is near and masculine and strong, and lovable too, he identifies with him also. As we have seen (page 321), the ego is partly based on identification processes. But now, identifying with the parents *in their disciplinary role*—that is, looking upon oneself as a sinner in need of control and repression—causes the ego to undergo a cleavage into two distinct parts. One part deals with everyday realities of getting ahead in this world, and is clothed with the realistic responsibilities of doing what one needs to do for the sake of self-preservation. On the other hand, the assumption by the child of the parental disciplinary viewpoint toward sexual sinfulness develops into that which we call a "conscience." This is a derivative of the ego, but, being morally superior to it and capable of coercing it, it is called the *superego.*

Together with this derivation of the superego we need a new terminology to define the original blind libidinal forces. This terminology was partly supplied by Freud's pupil Groddeck, who wrote in 1922 a book with the curious title: *The Book about the It (Das Buch vom Es).* That which precedes all personal existence, that which is pure, purposeless blind tension within the living system, is the "it" or *id.* The developing sense of one's own individuality, and the struggle to maintain it, is derived of course from this fund of id energy, but takes on the personal form which we call ego. In turn the morally superior subdivision of the ego appears as the superego. The superego now becomes in the subsequent work of Freud a primary factor in maintaining cohesion and continuity in human groups.

The observations which led to these new conceptions in the years 1920–27 are of extraordinary interest. In the light of his work with hypnosis, Freud had first concluded that the real tie between hypnotist and subject lies in the libidinal relationship: and by analogy, libido draws and holds groups and crowds together. The cardinal principle explaining social psychology lies not, as Le Bon would have it, in some debasement of human rationality, but in the libidinal ties which members of the human family have for one another, and in particular for him who stands in a leadership relation; that is, *in loco parentis*. This reminds one of the child's helplessness in relation to his omnipotent father, and at the same time his blind faith that help can miraculously be given.

One needs, then, in studying the helpless neurotic sufferer, to pursue the symptoms and the free associations to see what is limiting their freedom of action and keeping them helpless. Very illuminating in showing how Freud reached the conception of the superego is a case of *astasia abasia*, the loss of power to stand or walk. When the bedridden patient tries to rise and stand on the floor, he crumples up. One such patient's free associations led quickly from floor to *ground* (both are *Boden* in German) and from ground to earth, and from earth to Mother Earth. Now the pattern is clear. He fears to touch Mother Earth. Such associations are common: they point, in the context of the Oedipus complex, to the mother taboo and the fear of too great an intimacy with the person of the mother (or here, even the mother symbol).

We now face a dilemma. *Whence* comes the source of this patient's illness? Shall we say first that the trouble comes from the ego? This is nonsense, for the man wants to get well and his ego is oriented toward a return to normal life. Is the trouble then in the id? This is nonsense, for the id is pure impulse and cannot be pathological. No, the data indicate that it is actually a part of the ego, not the whole ego; indeed, it is an *unconscious part* of the ego; for there is a struggle to keep out of awareness the real meaning of contact with the floor. Consequently, we must conceive the ego to be divided against itself, to be a reality-testing system and at the same time a system of repressive, moralistic control. It was this observation which was central in the definition of the superego.

Having thus defined these three fundamental systems within the mental apparatus—the id, the ego, and the superego—it became

Freud's task to view the infinite variety of types of integrations which these components may manifest. The superego may succeed at times in controlling even the joined forces of id and ego, as one finds in the melancholic patient an overwhelming sense of guilt; or at times ego and superego may join forces successfully against the id, building up a tightly constrained, yet somehow workable system in which day-by-day responsibilities are adequately met, with some loss of adequacy as well as of personal zest, yet with adaptation to social demands.

In the matter of resistance, we are reminded that one *resists* that which *threatens*, and to note that protection of oneself against threat has always been prominent in psychoanalysis. Indeed, for many, the heart of the psychoanalytic system consists in the various devices described by Freud under the general term "defense mechanisms." Just what is defending itself against what, and by what means, was often uncertain in the early days; but the gross outlines of a defensive attitude and a defensive technique became as clear at the psychological level as they are in situations involving physical defense of the body against attack. Whereas in his earlier work Freud was content to stress the fact that the individual defended himself against painful memories, it became more and more clear with the growth of the ego theory that the process of defense was carried out *by* the ego, and that it served the purpose of defending the ego against the direct confrontation of painful situations, primarily those involving parental disapproval and consequently *guilt*. What functioned in the little child as fear of punishment or mutilation became in the older individual fear of recurrence of those thoughts which were laden with a sense of guilt and shame. It would be true of both earlier and later psychoanalytic theory to say that the ego develops a series of defenses for remaining ignorant of guilty acts, tendencies, interests, and thoughts.

These defenses need now to be described. While Anna Freud, shortly before her father's death, defined ten modes of ego defense, we shall here be content with summary descriptions of a somewhat smaller number. Following from the general logic of ego and id, we have to take account of *projection* and *introjection* as devices for the direct alteration of the way in which one's own self-love is safeguarded. What is regarded as unworthy and guilt-laden is projected upon another person; that is, it ceases to be one's own, and becomes an attribute permitting the moral condemnation of another. Especially common is the removal of hostile impulses which when projected upon another person enable the individual to suffer from feelings of persecution rather than from awareness of his own desire to attack and persecute others. A reverse process, introjection—originally related to direct oral incorporation of the mother's breast—is the assignment to oneself of that which actually belongs to another; it stems partly, also, from the original impulse of the child to attribute strength, bigness, and general adequacy to himself and to make himself like an adult in so doing. This process, like so many other psychoanalytic processes, involves actually the fusion of different dynamic phases at different times. The little child apparently experiences the nursing situation as one of actual incorporation of the warm, strong, and protective mother. As teeth develop, oral activity may become a power-seeking activity as well as a nourishment-seeking activity, and the biting of the breast may take the form of incorporation which is objectively aggressive. In the same way, the child experiences the impulse to incorporate the father within himself, and may at the same time fear that the father will bite him, either in the sense of sexual mutilation or in the sense of devouring him. Consequently, when later on he becomes aware of the need to make of himself something which is strong and big, these primitive acts of oral aggression and these impulses to oral assimilation may lead easily into the form of a desire to bring the big and strong within oneself. (That is exactly what a weak person who enjoys the companionship of a strong person may do; namely, to pretend that the strength and the bigness actually invade and pervade his own personality.)

The mechanism of *repression*, originally recognized as a matter of the ego versus the impulses in the unconscious, became more and more a matter of superego function, the ego usually joining forces with the superego in holding at bay those impulses which could not be deflected or transformed. Following from such repressions is, of course, the everyday device of denial of the true basis for one's acts, discovering that they spring solely from noble motives. This is the process of *rationalization* (page 316). If the stings of guilt are such as to make any perception of one's adult selfhood unbearable, one may return slowly or rapidly to the age of childhood, or even to a period prior to the development of moral categories, and we have *regression*. The mechanisms of *displacement* and *substitution* have to do with the discovery of objects in the world toward which one may without guilt entertain this or that feeling, thus disguising from oneself the identity of those toward whom such feelings are really entertained. Finally, the fullest transformation of unacceptable impulses may occur in *sublimation*, in which scientific, artistic, or other socially laudable activities serve as channels for libidinal or aggressive tendencies which cannot be directly expressed.

The critical reader will see that all these mechanisms of defense, which of course had been understood by the Greek tragedians as well as by Shakespeare and Ibsen, are still crudely formulated, particularly with regard to the question: What is defending what against what, and by what means? But answers to these questions began to emerge more and more clearly from 1913 on, in consequence of the series of papers on the ego (page 321). It became more and more evident that the dynamic system of activities concerned with probing reality, and making realistic adjustments to life demands, must continually cope with the threats which the living organism had experienced, and with those threats or acts of moral condemnation which, even when not leading to physical injury, were nevertheless intrinsically painful. We may therefore conclude from psychoanalytic studies that the reality-oriented functions are defending the whole living individual both against physical danger and against threat, and even against all that would remind him of danger or threat.

We find ourselves here, then, in the area of organized social control based on discipline, the area of sublimated activities which are permissible; that is, in the area of cultural phenomena. Freud remained essentially skeptical of any solution of the problem of freedom and discipline—"civilization" and its "discontents" were inseparable. Blind impulse was never a cure for anything. Yet order had somehow to be found by pitting impulse against impulse.

The issue was in fact greatly complicated by Freud's conviction that along with the life-giving and creative forces within the id there lies likewise in its core a destructive tendency, or death instinct, expressing itself in interpersonal aggressions and wars, and even in the unwitting urge of the individual to escape from life and return to the infinite peace of the inorganic. There can be, he feared, no real and ultimate equanimity and poise in civilized living. There may, nevertheless, be better societies and worse societies; and Freud came to feel more and more during the events in Europe in the thirties that psychoanalysis had a social as well as a personal message, which might in time be so developed as to bring some measure of healing to the tragedy of the era.

The spread of psychoanalytic doctrine throughout the world may be subdivided roughly into the following periods: 1. Its dissemination through the medical circles of Vienna from Freud's *The Interpretation of Dreams* (1900) until the organization of an international psychoanalytic effort as expressed throughout the German-speaking world in the organization of international congresses of psychoanalysis. 2. The growth and consolidation of psychoanalysis from this period until the break with Jung and Adler in 1911 (page 337). 3. The "closing of ranks" among those orthodox psychoanalysts who were determined to cling to Freud's leadership. 4. The time of the dramatic extension of psychoanalytic theory during World War I to British, and later to American, psychiatry (as a result of the bad results of treating war neuroses as cases of "concussion," and so on). Among British medical men, there occurred from 1916 to 1918 the rapid development of functional, especially psychoanalytic, conceptions of neuroses. In 1918 there occurred, in consequence both of war experience and of the able leadership of the mental-hygiene movement by Clifford Beers, a large-scale invasion of American psychiatry by psychoanalytic modes of thinking. 5. During the twenties, the further spread of psychoanalysis within American medicine, while also the popular mental-hygiene literature became rapidly suffused with a Freudian coloring.

Of importance in this movement were two books. The first was Freud's own *General Introduction to Psychoanalysis* (translated by G. Stanley Hall in 1920), widely read by the American public as well as by psychologists and their students. The second was Bernard Hart's *The Psychology of Insanity*, which, through many editions, has remained the most effective and most widely read of all the popular primers of psychoanalytic dynamics.

But popular psychoanalytic literature was soon at flood tide. All reading and thinking Britons and Americans had become roughly familiar with the implications of psychoanalysis by the end of the twenties, and the only question was how far one went in defining the role which the new doctrine was to fulfill. Many went as far as J. Arthur Thomson who, in *The Outline of Science*, as early as 1921 presented psychoanalysis as the sum and total of "modern psychology." Others regarded the new movement as extravagant and fantastic, insecure as to its factual foundations, and lurid as to its interpretations; yet they grudgingly admitted the significance of an approach in terms of unconscious dynamics, and in terms of clinical as well as experimental findings.

It is true that in general the public was inclined to be interested in the pathological rather than in the everyday phenomena; that it was interested in the queer, the exotic, the bizarre, the intense, and the cruel, rather than in the types of everyday struggle to keep going which concerned Freud in *The Psychopathology of Everyday Life*. The public did, however, fully understand from the very beginning that Freud stood squarely for his original thesis that sexuality in its various aspects is the central problem of all life and all adjustment, and they understood quite clearly that the rift between Freud on the one hand and Jung and Adler on the other was related to such an emphasis on the role of sexuality. If one notes that the popular acceptance or rejection of Freud's theory of sex was itself colored by irrational factors of romanticism or moral disapproval, the same was certainly true regarding the professional reaction of many psychiatrists and psychologists to the same issue.

In the matter of recourse to well-defined and well-controlled *facts* as the ultimate basis for appraising psychoanalysis, it is odd to note Freud's own skepticism in 1920 as to what could be done by such methods of objective testing. Yet there has been in recent years a steady increase in experimental output and in the feeling that experimental approaches are intrinsically no more out of place or difficult to apply here than in most phases of the study of personality and of social relationships. When Sears had the task in 1943 of surveying "objective studies of psychoanalytic concepts," he was able to point to over a hundred such investigations, and certainly there are more in the last few years than there had been in any comparable period prior to 1942.[30] The psychoanalytic method has not only become a general way of looking at human beings, but has within the same years become a system of explicit hypotheses inviting critical examination by the methods developed in experimental biology. We shall return in later chapters to the contact of psychoanalysis with the social sciences and with the biological sciences, respectively, as they have taken shape in the last few years.

REFERENCES

Bernfeld, S., "Freud's Earliest Theories and the School of Helmholtz," *Psychoanal. Quart.*, 1944, 13, 341–62
Freud, Sigmund, *Collected Papers*, 4 vols., London, 1924–25
———, *The Interpretation of Dreams*, Macmillan, 1910
———, *New Introductory Lectures in Psychoanalysis*, London, 1933
Healy, W., Bronner, A. F., and Bowers, A. M., *The Structure and Meaning of Psychoanalysis*, Knopf, 1930
Sachs, Hanns, *Freud, Master and Friend*, London, 1944
Wittels, Fritz, *Sigmund Freud*, Dodd, Mead, 1924
Zilboorg, Gregory, and Henry, G. W., *A History of Medical Psychology*, Norton, 1941

[30] Sears, R. R., "Survey of Objective Studies of Psychoanalytic Concepts," *Soc. Sci. Res. Coun. Bull.*, 1943, No. 51.

Chapter 23

THE RESPONSE TO FREUD

A man lives not only his personal life, as an individual, but also, consciously or unconsciously, the life of his epoch and his contemporaries.   THOMAS MANN

IMMEDIATELY upon the appearance of Freud's *The Interpretation of Dreams*, C. G. Jung of Zürich became greatly interested, and put himself eagerly in touch with the new movement. He was especially interested in the possibility of integrating the new method with the methods which had developed in the psychological laboratories of the German-speaking world.

He thus conceived the possibility of a large-scale objective and experimental testing program relating to certain aspects of Freud's theory, and in collaboration with Riklin and others, undertook systematic investigations of unconscious dynamics by means of the association test (cf. page 156), combined with various physiological methods which would reveal unconscious conflict. Starting with classical association theory, Jung undertook to define submerged mental contents very much as Herbart had done, with emphasis upon those clusters of emotionally toned ideas which had been shown by Freud to be the source of continued suffering. To these clusters Jung gave the name *complexes*. One of his methods, then, became the use of a systematic association test in the exploration of repressed complexes. In hysteria, for example, words were presented which led not to simple everyday associations, like *black-white*, but to marked delay in response, or to repetition of the stimulus word, or to coughing, sighing, blushing, stammering, or other "complex indicators," the true nature of which would become evident to the psychiatrist either through further probing with the test or through the familiar psychoanalytic procedure. Jung believed that an experimental technique such as the association test would serve as a starting point for certain analyses, or as a method for short-cutting the length of the analytic procedure. Jung gave sustained attention also to the question of personality typing in the association test, undertaking to show how hysterics differ from normals, and indeed how educated people differ from uneducated, mature from immature, men from women.

By far the best known of these many studies with the association test were those which dealt with the detection of crime. The theory was very simple. A group of accused persons may all be frightened during the period of police examination, but, so to speak, only the guilty know *exactly* what to be frightened at. On the occasion of a theft at one of the Zürich hospitals, words representing the objects within a stolen purse, mixed in with words of indifferent affective value, were presented serially to the various suspects. In the case of only one individual there was repeated evidence that words referring to the specific contents of the purse elicited a type of response which other "indifferent" words in the test did not elicit. Dramatically, the culprit, a nurse, confessed as soon as she became aware of the results of the test.[1] The primary meaning of such results, as far as psychologists are concerned, has been the fact that the types of unconscious motivation and of blockage described by psychoanalysis have become amenable in some degree to experimental examination.

Parallel to these extensive experimental studies, Jung gave his attention to the application of basic psychoanalytic theory. As early as 1907, he formulated a conception in which physiological and psychoanalytic factors were studied in intimate association. It had been evident that Freudian theory would sooner or later lead to a full characterization of dementia praecox as a faulty form of investment of the libido. Jung in 1907 (and Abraham in the following year) stressed the inward turning of the libido, the development of a morbid attitude of self-absorption, from which would follow an inability to make normal social contacts. For Jung, however, the psychoanalytic formulation was simply the first step in a more

---

[1] These crime-detection techniques have become excessively common, partly as demonstrations in elementary psychology courses and partly as an adjunct to police-court procedures. In more recent years, however, they have usually been accompanied by physiological techniques somewhat less crude than in Jung's time. The galvanic skin reflex has been systematically studied in connection with the word associations given, and marked galvanometric deflections have usually been encountered in connection with disturbing words. Blood-pressure changes have been used in the same way. In the Soviet Union Luria has in the same way studied physiological upheavals occurring in accused persons in connection with specific stimuli—in one case studying murderers shortly after their arrest, and in another case studying persons accused of political "deviations."

comprehensive theory. Faulty adjustment to life demands leads, Jung suggested, to a biochemical disorder, so that in time the morbid absorption in oneself leads to a deterioration of bodily processes, involving toxic effects injurious to the central nervous system. The actual deterioration of many patients in later stages of dementia praecox thus becomes a *psychosomatic* expression of a pathological libidinal process. This approach was hailed by Freud.

Immediately after this contribution, we find Jung joining Freud in the symposium at Clark University at Worcester, Massachusetts, organized by G. Stanley Hall in 1909, and marking in fact the introduction of the American public to psychoanalytic theory. Here, after Freud had outlined "The Origin and Development of Psychoanalysis," Jung spoke on "The Association Method," [2] making clear and vivid the use of the association test and the integration of psychoanalytic and experimental techniques. Upon returning to Europe after this occasion, Jung was invited again to speak in the United States, and accepted; Freud in the same period declined a similar invitation. Freud speaks with asperity in later years about a letter Jung sent to him from the United States in which it was made clear that the American public was eager to accept psychoanalysis when freed of its "overemphasis" upon sexual factors. This was, of course, one of various early intimations that Freud had regarding Jung's unwillingness to accept the psychoanalytic system as Freud saw it.

A number of other factors contributed to a break between them. One that Freud himself emphasized was bad feeling over the presidency of one of the international congresses. Another, stressed by Jung, was a difference of opinion regarding the ultimate definition of the libido and of its relation to early trauma. For Freud, in those years, the libido was sexual, and when injury to the infantile libidinal impulse was experienced, there was trauma or shock, involving lifelong consequences. Jung disagreed on two counts: First, he came to believe that the libido was simply a life process taking different forms at different periods—taking, for example, the nutrient form in infancy, the form of play and casual friendly interaction in subsequent years, and a heterosexual form only after puberty. Second, he came to the opinion that trauma is of no real importance in itself, but is used by the individual patient as a device for compelling attention and pity, or whatever it is that the patient wishes to achieve. If we understand the present needs of the patient, and the purposes which, as a living system, he is fulfilling in consequence of those needs, we shall find that the trauma is simply one of many items in his experience which he plays up or plays down in the service of these purposes. A girl, for example, who had behaved hysterically when she heard a team of horses on the road—rushing ahead of them instead of quietly withdrawing to one side—proved upon analysis to be behaving hysterically as a device for being picked up and taken to the nearest house, where there was every reason to believe that she would be cared for by a man whom she loved.[3] These two fundamental changes in orientation led to a sharp break, and the setting-up of an independent system of therapy known thereafter as "analytical psychology."

One fundamental difference between Freud and Jung lay in the approach to individual differences. With Freud, the attempt was made from the very beginning to find universal dynamics applicable to each case. Interest in fundamental individual differences was secondary; indeed, it did not come sharply into focus until the time of his study of character types in the middle of the first decade of this century (page 323), and never became the center of his system. Despite the recognition of heredity in predisposing toward one or another character type, Freud was always concerned primarily with a conception of instinctual life and the dispositions of energies applicable to all human experience. With Jung, on the other hand, there was a prominent place for that heavy emphasis on typology, that grouping of persons into basic types, which was so characteristic of nineteenth-century philosophy.

The great tradition, traceable at least as far back as Hippocrates' conception of body types, came to the fore in various anatomical and physiological types used in German medicine, and was dramatically taken over in Italy by the school of "criminal anthropology." The aim of such systems was to simplify and clarify those fundamental modes of interrelation or structuring of traits which constitute the "pure types" from which each individual may in minor ways deviate. The conception is comparable to that of pure elements or pure compounds in chemistry, which may be infrequently realized in nature, but which constitute fundamental reference points for the understanding of the confused and amorphous realities, the mixtures and contaminations, of which everyday life is so full.

On the basis of such conceptions Jung early turned the libido theory to account.[4] There were for him two fundamental types, the extravert and the introvert, who were congenitally predisposed to

[3] Jung, C. G., *The Theory of Psychoanalysis*, *Nerv. and Ment. Dis. Monogr.*, 1915, No. 19.

[4] *Psychological Types* (1920).

the outer and the inner manifestations of the libido. The extravert was primarily concerned with social relationships in which a rich fulfillment of libidinal needs could be found; the introvert, preoccupied with his own inner world of fantasy and bodily activity, was relatively incapable of such outgoing social participation. This conception, which "caught" like wildfire in psychiatry, in psychology, and in the mind of the general reading public, was shortly elaborated by means of a subdivision of mental operations into four fundamental activities: sensing, feeling, thinking, and intuiting— operations into which the libido may flow, in such a way that each of these four processes may be brought into relation either to external or to internal objects. There may thus be a sensing extravert, and a sensing introvert, and so on. From this followed a rather intricate conception of the structure—one might even say the geometry—of the mind, in which the four fundamental activities have their locus and their mode of contact with the other activities.

Comparable to the polarity of the extravert and the introvert is likewise the polarity of true and of make-believe individuality, the *persona* and the *socius*, what one might call the inner self and the social pose. There is likewise the polarity of the essentially masculine and the essentially feminine, the animus and the anima, found (in accordance with the theory of bisexuality) in all individuals, the man unconsciously expressing feminine and the woman masculine attitudes along with those attitudes which are accepted at the conscious level. While the practitioners of the Jungian school do of course make continuous integrated use of the rather complicated structural system thus developed, it should be stressed that the only aspect of Jung's doctrine which has really taken hold in psychology in the narrow sense is the original extravert-introvert typology.

As regards therapy, and education with a therapeutic cast, there is again fundamental cleavage between Jung and Freud. Freud remained to the end essentially a medical practitioner operating on the basis of natural science. However speculative his doctrines might be, they proceeded from nineteenth-century monistic conceptions of the mind-body relation, and regarded mental processes in all their aspects as expressions of an evolutionary reality residing in the tissues of the living organism. For Jung, however, emphasis on the conception of spiritual forces and a spiritual destiny became prominent in the early years, and became more and more prominent as the decades went by. The title of one of Jung's most influential books, *Modern Man in Search of a Soul* (1933), indicates quite exactly the direction in which he made his own protest against the natural-

ism of Freud—expressed in caustic language by Freud himself in
earlier years in a reference to the period in which Jung was a
psychoanalyst and did not yet aspire to be a "prophet." Jung replied
to this, and all other implied accusations, by an extraordinary chapter in which he said that it is right for each investigator to tell the
world candidly what he finds in his own soul; and that just as Freud
has so faithfully described the animality and violence he finds in
his own, so he, Jung, has the obligation to report the aspirations, the
boundless thirst for the divine, which he and many of his patients
have experienced.

Judgment as to the degree of importance to be attached to emo·
tional cleavages as profound as this becomes, of course, partly a
question of individual temperament and taste. It would be a mis-
take, however, to imply that for purposes of world psychology the
naturalistic is the *only* important trend visible to the naked eye, or
that the philosophical controversy of nineteenth-century naturalism
and idealism is at an end. The naturalistic outlook is still an item
of faith rather than just the forced acceptance of a simple fact, and
in a number of important works, such as Müller-Freienfels' *The
Evolution of Modern Psychology* (1935), it is made clear that one can
find as much in support of, as in opposition to, Jung's conception
that the really important forces lie outside the sphere to which
biology (or economics) possesses the keys. There has been a continuous hammering by numerous physicists at the same issue in recent
years. The problem is the general direction of the long-range philosophical trend of a society which has gone through paroxysmal
changes in ideology in the last few centuries; and it is only here and
there, as among the Watsonian behaviorists and among the Marxists, that one is willing to predict with finality what the scientific
outcome must ultimately be.

ADLER

Among the young medical men who joined Freud's seminar in
the earliest years of this century was Alfred Adler, who apparently
from the beginning regarded himself as a junior colleague rather
than as a disciple of the master. Drawn early by the strictly biological
aspects of Freud's doctrine, he sought to expand and develop one
cardinal thesis which Freud had already defined: the nature of the
process of *compensation*. In the case of incomplete sexual development,
Freud had noticed a basic need to compensate for the deficiency.
The individual might become in some ways more "masculine" or

more "feminine" than anatomical or physiological factors could warrant. The process lay at the very bottom of the problem of psychosomatic relationships, for the developing tissues pointed to those deficits which were experienced by the individual as marking his inadequacy.

Why not, said Adler, extend this doctrine of defect, and of compensation for defect, to cover every type of constitutional limitation? He drew attention to the tendency for a lung or a kidney to do extra work if the corresponding organ was injured; the tendency of one eye to become more acute if the other was defective; the tendency to develop a hypertrophy of function, a secondary acuteness, wherever sense organs fell short of normal adequacy. But among all the organs of compensation for civilized man there is a primary emphasis upon the central nervous system, for man's adaptation to social living is largely a question of learning how to cope with the demands of others and with social requirements. Whereas, therefore, compensation at the biological level appears in animals, most of the significant types of compensation in man are conscious or unconscious efforts to make good where one is socially inadequate.

The thesis up to this point, appearing in a publication entitled *A Study of Organic Inferiority and Its Psychical Compensation* (1907), was accepted by Freud and his followers as a significant contribution to ego psychology. For four more years Adler went on developing this conception, showing more and more devices by means of which inadequacy—physical, intellectual, or social—was "compensated for" through overt behavior, through symptoms, or through a broad technique for dominating a hostile environment. He developed the thesis to a point where compensation became not a peripheral, but the central, clue to neurosis.

In 1911, according to Wittels (and Freud appears to endorse the story),[5] Adler requested of the seminar the opportunity to develop an orderly thesis regarding the role of compensation. Consent was given and several consecutive meetings of the seminar were devoted to this purpose. At the end of the last presentation, one of Freud's followers offered a motion to the effect that since Dr. Adler was "not in sympathy with psychoanalysis," he be asked to withdraw from the seminar. Apparently the motion was formally seconded and passed, and Adler together with nine of his associates (in a total group of perhaps thirty-five physicians) withdrew. Immediately thereafter Adler formally established his school of *individual psy-*

---

[5] Wittels, F., *Sigmund Freud* (1924).

chology, which began to develop its own postulates and to publish its own journal.

Individual psychology, as defined, is founded first upon the conception that the experience of life in the newborn child is one of weakness, inadequacy, and frustration. He finds big, strong, active people who go marching about; who decide what they want to do, and do it; upon whose tenderness or pity he must rely if he wants to be nursed or picked up or dried or amused. He is a little, helpless object, to whom this or that specific want, such as that for food or for a maternal embrace, is altogether secondary to the primary want to control one's own activity, to be oneself and liberate oneself from the domination of this big, inscrutable world. Power, in other words, is the first good, just as weakness is the first evil; and compensation becomes simply a name for the struggle of the individual in the direction of power. It is relatively easy for the child to discover the things that endear him to his parents or the things which shock them, and it is not surprising, in view of the biology of sexuality, that both the tendency to be pleased and the tendency to be shocked are manipulated by the child very much as the analysts describe. The essential clue, however, is compensation for inferiority.

The child develops, as a rule, a rather consistent and workable method of compensating—a method depending upon his own situation, the personalities of his parents, their age and economic status, the presence and attributes of brothers, sisters, grandparents, and so on, in the home. Later the nature of neighborhood and community pressure determines what it takes to get over being a helpless little baby; determines whether one is to become a brat, a braggard, a delinquent, a mamma's boy, a poor little thing for whom everyone is sorry, and so on. Individual personality takes shape as a device for coping with the frustrations of infantile experience.

The essential technique of each individual for coping with such difficulties becomes more and more generalized and consolidated, and becomes the "style of life," destined, as a rule, to persist. If the parent for whose sake the device is developed suddenly dies, or if one moves to a neighborhood in which the early technique can no longer be used, one may have to abandon the established style of life and begin all over again; and from this fact serious difficulties— everything from blushing or stammering to a psychotic episode— may develop. Running through all this description is the basic assumption of continuity of purpose. The power objective of the individual may take on different masks from time to time, but it remains the real generator of every specific activity. Since this is the case, it follows that in a long-drawn-out psychoanalysis the patient is playing a game to hoodwink the physician. Free associations on a couch are usually less painful than admission that one is out for power; but they serve the purpose. By costing the family a good deal of money, one can dominate them too. For Adler all that was necessary was that physician and patient sit vis-à-vis and face realities directly and, as a rule, bluntly.

The most interesting of Adler's specific contributions to individual character study are those which have to do with position in the family; that is, with order of birth, and with the relations of siblings. The "only child" not only dominates the father and mother during the entire growing-up period, forcing them to adapt their previously rather free existence to his own needs, but also carries over into the school and the community a number of the habits which have worked well at home. This may mean that some of the frustrations are peculiarly acute when it proves impossible to handle the teacher as one handles one's parents; but at the same time it may mean that a number of the same techniques which prove capable of transfer—such as hyperintellectualism and hypermaturity, a readiness to get along with grownups rather than with children, and so on— become consolidated as a permanent personality attribute. The second-born child has at first the experience of dominating the household which was originally the privilege of the eldest, but in addition he is capable of dethroning the firstborn from a position of both power and affection, and instead of mastering two people, he finds a way to master three. The youngest child in a rather large family not only enjoys at first a rather large domain in which his control can be exercised, but learns with peculiar poignancy the satisfactions of being little, helpless, cute, and perhaps even pitiful. One is permanently the baby of the family, and in addition one reminds the parents continually of the days when they had little children, and draws them back to their youth with an appeal few can resist.

These brief paragraphs perhaps show how far we are from the biological emphasis of Freudian psychology and from the biological orientation of Adler's own earlier work. More and more the nature of the social pattern of which the growing individual is an aspect comes into focus. It is hardly surprising to learn that individual psychology became during the twenties essentially a theory of group action, a theory applied to delinquency, to the classroom situation, and to social movements. To two of the social movements Adler devoted special energy: feminism and socialism.

Rejecting root and branch the entire Freudian conception of basic masculine and feminine psychology, Adler pointed to the fact that biological differentiation is relatively unimportant until it has been exploited for the purposes of power. Just as Veblen in *The Theory of the Leisure Class* (1899) had developed the conception of masculinity as essentially a social rather than a biological phenomenon, the basis of which he calls the "predation" of one individual upon another, so Adler undertook to show that masculine and feminine psychologies are sheer artifacts of a social order in which patriarchal family status is accompanied by military, economic, and political power. The struggle of the modern woman in the direction of masculinity has nothing whatever to do with anatomical deficiencies or compensatory activities of the sort which he himself would have stressed in 1907. It has everything to do with the dislocation in traditional feminine roles, and the double pressures upon contemporary woman to enter the existing masculine orbit and to remain at the same time in the earlier wifely and motherly orbit, with high probability that the satisfactions from neither will be really complete.

Socialism, in the same way, became for Adler a direct and necessary expression of response to a fundamental frustration which falls to the lot of most people living in an industrial civilization. For most men and women removed from the immediate satisfactions of contact with the soil or the artisan's delight in seeing the labors of his own hands, there is a world of routine, mechanical activity which is intrinsically meaningless, and during which one is dominated either by a man whom one does not know or by a machine whose function and ultimate objective one does not understand. There is no escape except in full democratic participation in the planning and in the control of processes of production. We constantly find ourselves emerging with an essentially socialistic conception regarding the incompatibility between human nature and the existing social order. It might be argued, of course, that man can adapt himself to any kind of a social order; but with Adler the experience of weakness and the need for power as a compensatory device is so fundamental that there is only one means of satisfaction: a social order in which each man's compensatory struggle can be integrated effectively with that of each other man. Men would thus collectively dominate some natural difficulty; through "social feeling" rather than through hostility they would achieve a livable social reality.

It became rather obvious that in so far as the Marxists of central Europe were concerned with psychology at all in the period between the two world wars, they would incline to Adler rather than to

Freud or Jung. It was not simply that Freud had himself written caustically on the matter of Marxism; it had a strong positive basis in the fact that Adler's was the first psychological system in the history of psychology that was developed in what we should today call a social-science direction. While much effort has been evident in the gradual adaptation of Freudian psychoanalysis to the findings of cultural anthropology (cf. page 342), and the resultant struggle to align a biological scheme with a system of compelling social forces, the Adlerian system slipped so casually and easily into a social frame of reference that one would never think it necessary to write a book showing how individualistic and social-science conceptions are to be reconciled.

THE INFLUENCE OF THE CULTURAL SCIENCES

These summaries may perhaps help in some very slight degree to give perspective for that very great change in psychoanalysis itself which began in the late twenties, developed strikingly during the thirties, and flowered into such prominence in the forties—the reorientation of many Freudian psychoanalysts, with the aim of making the system applicable to men of all cultures and of all historical periods, yet capable of providing an organic continuity from the study of individual tension systems to the study of the dynamics of social interaction and social change. Not at all that Adler acted as prime mover in the process; on the contrary, it was the habit of the Freudians to ignore him. The forces which easily and naturally operated on Adler's very simple system in the second decade of the century began to operate on the very much more complicated Freudian system later; and the Freudian system, having crystallized in an earlier form, had to be broken up, melted down, rearranged, in order to provide a workable system for those interested in solving the newer problems of the relation of personality to the structure of culture.

Freud had early given attention to the psychoanalytic interpretation of the behavior of primitive peoples. In *Totem and Taboo* (1910) a parallel is drawn between neurotic and primitive attitudes. Attempts in ethnological field work to apply Freudian doctrines, however, encountered one difficulty after another, while providing at the same time some excellent confirmations of the general Freudian position regarding the role of unconscious dynamics. Thus Malinowski, in a series of studies of the Trobriand Islanders of the western Pacific, noted that the taboos were of a type fundamentally different from those found among Europeans (the sister rather than the mother being a primary taboo object); yet unconscious mechanisms operated to influence not only the formation of symptoms, but also the general structure of character.[6]

Shortly thereafter, in the middle twenties, Margaret Mead made a field study to test various hypotheses about "storm and stress" as a fundamental and necessary aspect of adolescent development (page 410). Her material, obtained from a study of Samoan girls, indicates no such turmoil in making the adolescent transition in Samoa, and suggests that perhaps a good deal of what is sometimes ascribed to the basic biology of the growth process is due rather to the nature of the social pressures applied to the child.

Neither this nor her other early ethnological studies can be regarded as Freudian in any very useful sense. During the thirties, however, Mead, in collaboration with Bateson (page 422), studied in Bali the influence of infantile frustration upon adult character structure, in a fashion running parallel to psychoanalytic character studies. In the same period a group of ethnologists worked closely with the analyst Kardiner in the preparation of a series of studies dealing with personality formation among various primitive peoples, using a modified Freudian psychodynamics as a clue. It would be absurd and meaningless to attempt to give chronological priority to one or another of these studies. The Mead-Bateson material from Bali was finally published in 1942, though various interesting intimations of the new approach had appeared earlier in journal articles. The Kardiner approach appeared in 1940 in a volume entitled *The Individual and His Society* and was followed in 1945 by another entitled *The Psychological Frontiers of Society*. It should be noted that while the Mead-Bateson study contains many references to Freudian theory and assumes on the reader's part a familiarity with Freud and psychodynamics, there is not very much use here of symbol interpretation, the primary task being the problem of accounting for the passivity, "withdrawnness," and bodily grace of the Balinese on the one hand, and their violent and orgiastic behavior on certain special occasions on the other. With Kardiner, however, an essentially Freudian conception of basic bodily tensions is followed through, with a good deal of emphasis upon psychoanalytic mechanisms and upon the role of symbols in developing philosophies of life and those forms of interpersonal relations which dramatize and

[6] Malinowski, B. K., *Argonauts of the Western Pacific* (1922); *Sex and Repression in Savage Society* (1927).

indirectly satisfy the basic needs which have been both molded and frustrated in infancy.

It should be stressed that in these modern ethnological studies the classical methods of obtaining the history of the group and of the individual by interviewing informants and observing the daily round of activities have been supplemented by the use of projective tests (page 423), such as free drawing, free painting, Thematic Apperception Test, and Rorschach; and that in several cases experts with these projective techniques have made "blind analyses" of the projective products and have written descriptions of the culture and of individual members of the group which have fitted well the general cultural and biographical picture prepared by the ethnologist.[7] We have therefore a multidimensional approach to the deep-level psychology of primitive groups.

But a third and a fourth psychoanalytic approach to the problem of deep-level interpretation of culture awaits emphasis: During the thirties Erikson began to note among the Sioux and other American Indian groups a number of types of symbolic activity which could only be interpreted by reference to unconscious dynamic forces; and at the beginning of the decade of the forties he turned his attention to a straightforward psychoanalytic interpretation of the extraordinary ritual of the Yurok Indians of northern California.[8] He was, for example, able to demonstrate that the annual cycle of activities connected with the coming and going of the salmon in the river, which constituted the nucleus of the life of the Yurok, lay at the very center of their world of mythology and fantasy, and that the passage of the salmon into the river from the sea had been assimilated by the tribe to the passage of food into the alimentary canal of the individual eater of the salmon. Life had been systematized in terms of the regenerating function of that which passes into a central canal which may be stopped up, and the opening and closing of which constitutes the primary punctuation in the sentence of life. One begins to see the possibility of a joining of hands between analysts in the field, as was Erikson in this instance, and ethnologists with analytic training on the other, the latter turning over their records to analysts for interpretation; and, co-operating with both groups, experimenters and projective testers working with personality studies contributed by the ethnologists. With deep-

[7] Oberholzer, E., in Du Bois, C. A., *The People of Alor* (1944).

[8] Erikson, E. H., *Observations on the Yurok: Childhood and World Image*, Univ. Calif. Publ. Amer. Archaeol. and Ethnol., 1943, 35, No. 10.

level personality study a new dimension is being added to the research upon the social order and upon social change.

FROMM AND HORNEY

But even within the heart of psychoanalytic practice with patients in our own culture, there has occurred an active movement against the biological assumptions of Freudian psychoanalysis and an effort to conceive psychoanalytic problems in terms of social dynamics. Those who represent this tendency have come to feel that the primary factors operative both in neuroses and in the shaping of the normal personality are those which spring from conflicting cultural pressures, or from demands upon the individual in response to which nothing really satisfying and adequate can be done.

It is difficult to specify at what point this "left-wing" movement in psychoanalysis began. It is different from the many "splinter groups" which developed within the Freudian system itself in earlier years. Many of these splinter groups were concerned with differences in the technique of dream interpretation. Others, such as the strong group led by Otto Rank, asked whether analysis should go on until the patient wanted to stop it or should stop at a point specified in advance by the analyst. Rank was especially concerned with the patient's attitude (for example, his activity or passivity) and with the analyst's determination to study and rectify the *relationships*, the social world, of the patient. Such questions were questions of method; they were not centered in the question of Freud's biological theory. But the new movement with which we are now concerned arose from the basic conviction that the Freudian system of biological assumptions was ill adapted to the study of men under industrial society, that it was much less effective in contemporary American urban centers than in the Vienna of a half-century ago—or even of twenty years ago—in which the patriarchal family still supplied most of the background with which the individual analyst had to deal.

It was Erich Fromm who sketched, in the middle thirties,[9] a theory of "authority and the family" which challenged the postulates regarding the father-son relationship so prominent in the Oedipus complex. Fromm began to raise questions regarding the cultural diversities of expression, and even regarding the ultimate cultural origins of various types of character formation. Believing that the psychoanalytic mechanisms would be of real value in the study of all

[9] See Horkheimer, M., "Studien über Autorität und Familie," *Schr. Instit. Sozialforsch.*, 1936, 5.

cultures—that is, that all cultural groups would show the basic phenomena of repression, projection, rationalization, and so on—he maintained that the specific content of the neurosis, and indeed of the individual personality pattern, depends largely upon the type of social pressure first applied in early life. Fromm made these ideas the common property of a series of seminars and of other groups of physicians and psychologists with whom he was associated.

Contemporaneously, Karen Horney began to stress, as a staff member of the New York Psychoanalytic Institute, the role of various social factors in neuroses, and began to challenge the biological functions of the Freudian system.[10] She and her pupils felt themselves stifled in the orthodox atmosphere. Without going into personalities, it is sufficient to note that the system departed so far in the social direction that it experienced, as had Adler's thirty years earlier, a need to strike out on its own path. Horney and her associates accordingly began openly to carry out analysis without an instinct theory, and without any assumptions regarding the inevitable rise of an ego and a superego as a result of instinctual repressions and conflicts, and began to emphasize the nature of urban industrial society and the broader contributions of our whole culture as a basis for the "neurotic personality of our time." Partly in consequence of a wide therapeutic following and partly in consequence of a series of vivid and compelling publications, Horney has found herself the leader of a social school of psychoanalysis in which the psychoanalytic tools and fundamental psychodynamic assumptions are retained in so far as one can retain them without laying any stress whatever upon fixed, inalienable biological trends or instincts. She does not, of course, deny, any more than Adler had, the reality of the life of instinct. But she has stressed, as did he, the social form which the instincts are given, and the fact that they are made to conflict with one another not through the operation of inevitable forces, but because society plays them against one another.

From what has been said, it should be clear why the Adlerians accuse Horney of plagiarism, and why she in turn insists that Adler's method—which, as we have seen, makes short shrift of the whole psychoanalytic technique and procedure—is superficial, a short cut which may often guess right, but which lacks the solid foundations required of theory and practice in the study of personality. It is sufficient for present purposes to indicate that Horney, with all the weapons of psychoanalysis, has been treading the path of social interpretation upon which, more naïvely and impulsively,

10 *The Neurotic Personality of Our Time* (1937); *New Ways in Psychoanalysis* (1939).

Adler had ventured in earlier years. It goes almost without saying that the yield from the Horney technique is richer; it also goes without saying that a certain blunt simplicity, as exemplified in Adler, may have been of great value in its time in calling attention to neglected realities.

While this is no place for a systematic critique, whether of orthodox analysis or of any modern derivative, it is worth while to note how the orthodox Freudians view the new movement.[11] They wish to know: Just what are the original bodily activities which are frustrated in society, or which are pitted against one another in the way described by the left-wingers? Just as Adler never quite explained why weakness has to be painful, and why it is that one cannot quietly and happily accept a dependent role (as indeed some people do), so the left-wing psychoanalytic movement seems to the orthodox to fail in explaining what the forces are which are socially molded into such tense and harrowing forms. Surely the individual cannot be artificially made to demand this or that type of satisfaction unless he has a craving which would be satisfied thereby. One can scarcely develop a theory of famine until one has a theory as to why food is needed. One can scarcely develop a theory of "ego needs" until one has explained why human beings have so passionate a demand for recognition or for status. Freud, as has been noted, attempted to solve the ego problem by reference to such conceptions as narcissism, in which instinctual energies are early devoted to one's own physical person. Without any instinctual forces waiting to be deflected in one direction or another, it is hard for the orthodox practitioners to see where the energy comes from which does so much work in the neurotic personality. And the orthodox Freudians cannot see how the newer questions basically affect the complex technical task of psychoanalytic therapy.

But, as many psychiatrists have pointed out, the orthodox and the newer statements are two aspects of a reality which need not be so hopelessly obscure. Like the little child in Hans Andersen's story of the Emperor's new clothes, they are not afraid of saying the obvious. Perhaps all human beings develop quite early in life some preoccupation with their own bodies, some need to defend the body against injury, and at the same time a primitive capacity for warm, outgoing response which inevitably is bestowed upon one's own person just as it may be upon any other available object. The result would be a need to enhance and defend the self.[12] Sometimes these

[11] Cf. Fenichel, O., *The Psychoanalytic Theory of Neurosis* (1945), 586–89.

[12] Cf. Sullivan, H. S., "Conceptions of Modern Psychiatry," *Psychiatry*, 1940, 3, 1–117.

primitive tendencies are frustrated, and very complicated and devious means of defense must be found. Ultimately, however, the mainsprings of what Adler calls compensatory activity may be traced to these simple mechanisms. In the same way the main outlines of the psychoanalytic system may be reduced to the perpetual struggle to enhance and defend the self. The one difficulty which the leftwing analyst would find in this formulation would lie in its oversimplified statement of the nature of social frustrations to the process of self-enhancement. One might therefore quite appropriately accept their suggestions by spelling out in considerable detail the different ways in which different societies frustrate primitive self-enhancing tendencies, and the various ways in which the lovable picture of the self which the child has had a chance to build up is mutilated by reproof or by social ostracism. In the meantime everything that has been discovered by Freud regarding methods of plumbing unconscious dynamics can continue to be used—and joined with data from experimentation and projective methods—in a socially oriented psychoanalysis. This appears in general to be the aim, for example, of the William Alanson White Institute of Psychiatry.

It appears likely, moreover, that what is already happening in psychiatry, in psychiatric social work, and in the deep-level study of our own society by sociologists and group workers will in time happen in the more academic formulation of personality problems; namely, that the various systems will be forced to shed some of their dogmatic trappings, and be reduced to a relatively orderly and uniform pattern in which the primary role of the self, and of activities centered around it, will be placed in the central position which Freud, as early as 1913, suggested it might require. This would of course mean the end of naïve "drive psychology," and its replacement by an "ego psychology" oriented toward the study of conflict and of the means of escaping it and achieving integration.

REFERENCES

Adler, Alfred, *The Practice and Theory of Individual Psychology,* Harcourt, Brace, 1924

Bellak, L., and Ekstein, R., "The Extension of Basic Scientific Laws to Psychoanalysis and to Psychology," *Psychoanal. Rev.,* 1946, 33, 306–13

Fromm, Erich, *Escape from Freedom,* Farrar and Rinehart, 1941

Horney, Karen, *The Neurotic Personality of Our Time,* Norton, 1938

Jung, Carl G., *The Psychology of the Unconscious,* Moffat, Yard, 1916

Lorand, Alexander S., ed., *Psychoanalysis Today,* Int. Universities Press, 1944

Murphy, Gardner, and Jensen, Friedrich, *Approaches to Personality,* Coward-McCann, 1932

Myerson, Abraham, "The Attitudes of Neurologists, Psychiatrists, and Psychologists toward Psychoanalysis," *Amer. J. Psychiat.,* 1939, 96, 623–41

Woodworth, Robert S., *Contemporary Schools of Psychology,* rev. ed., Ronald Press, 1948

PART FOUR

Some Representative Research Areas

Chapter 24

THE MEASUREMENT
OF INTELLIGENCE

Reason, however, in the sense of intelligence, is not found equally in all animals, nor in all men.　　　　ARISTOTLE

IT CANNOT be emphasized too strongly that the central idea of nineteenth-century biology, and hence of all studies within the life sciences, was the Darwinian conception of the transmutation of species. Certain biological sciences, such as experimental physiology, maintained themselves for a considerable period in the soil of the nineteenth-century physicalist conception (page 253). It made no difference whether you worked forward or backward in the time dimension, and you were not concerned with individual variability (variability meant accidents, or errors). There was no real aim in experimentation except the ordering of data with reference to those patterns of time and space with which physical science was already dealing. The point of view, as the modern terminology would put it, was "ahistorical." Just as the events in the world of astronomy or physics were supposedly of the same fundamental type whether appearing in the ninth century or in the nineteenth, so events in the living body were fundamentally of the same order whether they occurred in mice or in men; or whether they occurred in embryo mice or in embryo men; or, indeed, whether they occurred in embryo mice or in octogenarian men. Developmental problems were real, but incidental. Indeed, biological laws were themselves static abstractions. Although the time dimension entered in, it was, so to speak, the time dimension of a few seconds or hours, as in the respiratory or the diurnal cycle, just as the photographer is concerned with time when he sets his shutter for a shot of a race today and does the same thing at the races tomorrow.

The evolutionary approach changed all this. It made it necessary to conceive that life processes might be going on today in a form essentially different from those which occurred before, because of a higher level of complexity reached; and it made it possible to think of unidirectional trends which are irreversible. Life thus became a historical, and not simply a physical, problem. The life sciences accordingly began to be infected more and more with the urge to answer the question: What can a given specific biological event tell us which no other event in nature could tell us, and in which no amount of experimental control of present conditions could adequately serve? From this point of view, even the life sciences which dealt with ahistorical problems (such as problems of present structure) rather than with historical problems were gradually drawn into the vortex of the historical or evolutionary method of thinking.

It was the interaction of the historical or evolutionary approach on the one hand, and on the other hand the physicalist approach, with its delight in accurate time-space measurements, that led to the systematic study of individual differences toward the close of the century. The reconciliation came slowly. For several decades after the publication of *The Origin of Species*, individual differences continued to be of trivial and secondary importance wherever the ahistorical or physicalist approach prevailed.

This appears to be the primary reason why psychology was so slow to respond adequately to Galton's studies. The experimental systems of Wundt and of Ebbinghaus, children of the physicalist type of experimental physiology and of associationism—both of them nearly tone-deaf to evolutionary issues—tended to slight the individual. (Ebbinghaus had the personal ingenuity to devise a means of measuring intelligence: the completion test; [1] that is, fill in the blanks: the —— sets in the ——; or, if the subject has been exposed to Homer, —— dragged —— around the walls of ——. But those who responded to the new experimentalism were, in general, pure physicalists in approach.) This was in general true of the new German systems, and of those in other lands which descended from them. It was true with a vengeance regarding Titchener's school at Cornell, which enjoyed exceptional prestige largely because it was so squarely, so massively, based upon the huge foundations of an analytical method which had been derived from experimental physics. It was not individual perversity which led it to reject systematic studies of individual differences; rather, it was the meaning of the physicalist

[1] *Zschr. f. Psychol.*, 1897, 13, 401–59.

conception as a whole. Titchener indeed made absolutely explicit that it was the analytical and essentially static conception of James Mill, the ahistorical reconstruction of psychological totals from fixed mosaic pieces, that first inspired his own approach to psychology, just as a few years earlier it had been the physicalist conception of Herbart which inspired the systematic quantitative investigations of Ebbinghaus.

But we have noted (page 117) how Francis Galton grasped the implications of the evolutionary outlook for psychology, and made his ingenious experimental contributions to this area of research. Galton, an extramural, leisure-time devotee of the life sciences, a typical far-ranging amateur so characteristic of British science, saw where the arbitrary limits of the prevalent laboratory psychology lay. As Cattell is said to have remarked, had Galton been an academic psychologist, he would have made no great contribution. Cattell himself, inspired above all by Darwinism, and delighted with the opportunity to work with so great a Darwinian as Galton, saw exactly how and where the evolutionary approach was to be fused with the physicalist conception of exact time-space measures of living functions. It was therefore Cattell who defined on a large scale the place of quantitative studies of individual differences in the new psychology.[2] Measuring the speed of retinal response, he asked how the responses varied from person to person; studying the differences between free and controlled associations, he sought to obtain data from enough subjects to get a picture of human variability. Turning from these rather hasty and incomplete investigations to variability in other functions, shortly after his return to the United States he plunged into a systematic examination of individual differences in sensory and in motor tasks, such as the difference in the time required to name colors, or to read words.

The use of tests of simple sensorimotor and associative functions was continued, especially in the United States. Kirkpatrick, working with a large number of subjects, compared such mental-test scores with achievement as shown in other ways, for example, with schoolwork.[3] In 1903 Kelly and in 1906 Norsworthy compared, by means of such tests, normal and defective children.[4] The results indicated

[2] Henmon, V. A. C., and others, "The Psychological Researches of J. McK. Cattell," *Arch. Psychol.*, 1916, No. 30.

[3] Kirkpatrick, E. A., "Individual Tests of School Children," *Psychol. Rev.*, 1900, 7, 274–80.

[4] Kelly, R. L., "Psychophysical Tests of Normal and Abnormal Children," *Psychol. Rev.*, 10, 345–52; Norsworthy, N., "The Psychology of Mentally Deficient Children," *Arch. Psychol.*, No. 1.

that the feeble-minded tended to do distinctly less well than the normal, but that there was a fairly even transition from the lowest to the highest scores. In Norsworthy's language, the feeble-minded were not a "species"; the more intelligent of the feeble-minded could not be sharply distinguished from the least intelligent of the normal.

BINET AND INTELLIGENCE TESTING

But the scene shifts now to France. During the nineties Binet had occupied himself with attempts to devise suitable measures of intelligence. In 1904, the year after Binet's publication of his experimental study of the thought processes, the Minister of Public Instruction appointed Binet as a member of a commission on special classes in the schools. When children were failing in the schoolwork for their age, it was important to differentiate between the mentally deficient and the indifferent or lazy. In collaboration with Simon, Binet undertook the task of devising tests suited to the immediate practical task of detecting and measuring mental defect. They offered in 1905 a set of tests arranged from the simplest to the most difficult, but without further standardization.[5] Among these were tests requiring the naming of designated objects, the comparison of lengths of lines, the repetition of digits, the completion of sentences, and the comprehension of questions.[6] In 1908 this scale was revised,[7] practical experience having shown that some of the tests were harder and others easier than was at first supposed. Another very important change was introduced. The tests were arranged according to the age levels, experimentally determined, at which the average child performed them successfully, from three to twelve years inclusive. A child's *mental age* was the level which he attained on this scale; the child of six might be able to pass the tests for seven or eight, or only those for age four or five. This scale was translated and adapted for American use by Goddard in 1910.[8] In the following year Healy and G. M. Fernald published a set of tests which at once became widely known.[9]

[5] *Année psychol.*, 1905, 11, 163–336.

[6] De Sanctis published a short scale of mental tests in the year following, *Annal. di. neurol.*, 1906, 24 (1).

[7] *Année psychol.*, 1908, 14, 1–94.

[8] Goddard, H. H., "A Measuring Scale for Intelligence," *Training School*, 1910, 6, 146–54.

[9] Healy, W., and Fernald, G. M., *Tests for Practical Mental Classification*, *Psychol. Monogr.*, 1910, 13 (whole No. 54).

Binet offered another revision of his scale in 1911, the year of his death.[10] His steady progress in the devising of tests was accompanied by indecision and changes of opinion regarding the essential characteristics of intelligence. Among the definitions of intelligence he suggested at one time or another, probably the most characteristic of his trend of thought is one in which not a single capacity but a combination of three different capacities was emphasized. Intelligence, he suggested, is the ability to understand directions, to maintain a mental set, and to apply "autocriticism" (the correction of one's own errors).

The problems of intelligence testing began to attract attention in Germany, where Meumann had already conducted pioneer investigations. Stern made an important contribution to method by suggesting a change in the calculation of test scores.[11] Binet had been content to measure subnormality by subtracting mental age from chronological age. Stern urged that the absolute retardation in years was of less importance than the relative retardation; and he suggested the use of the *intelligence quotient* (IQ), obtained by dividing the mental age by the chronological age. He showed, moreover, that this quotient is fairly constant from year to year for most children.

Another important step in technique was Terman's revision of the Binet scale.[12] His "Stanford Revision" of 1916 was based upon work with a thousand subjects, and standardized in the form of tests for age levels from three years to eighteen (the sixteen-year-old tests were devised for adults, while the eighteen-year-old tests were for "superior" adults). Many of Binet's tests were placed at higher or lower age levels than those at which Binet had placed them, and new tests were added. Each age level was represented by a battery of tests, each test being assigned a certain number of month credits. It was possible, therefore, to reckon the subject's intelligence quotient, as Stern had suggested, in terms of the ratio of mental age to chronological age. A child attaining a score of 120 months, but only 100 months old, would have an IQ of 120 (the decimal point is omitted). This intelligence quotient was found by Terman, as by Stern, to be fairly constant from year to year.[13]

[10] *Année psychol.*, 1911, 17, 145–201.

[11] Stern, W., *The Psychological Methods of Testing Intelligence* (1912).

[12] *The Measurement of Intelligence* (1916).

[13] *The Intelligence of School Children* (1919). Marked variation in IQ has, however, been reported by Woolley, H. T., "The Validity of Standards of Mental Measurement in Young Childhood," *School and Society*, 1925, 21, 476–82, and by others. See page 370.

The Stanford Revision, by far the most widely used of individual tests of intelligence, was itself revised by Terman and Merrill in 1935. There are numerous other American revisions of the Binet tests. Kuhlmann's revision,[14] including tests below the three-year level, places less emphasis on language factors than the Stanford scale. One other early revision must be noted, the elaborate and systematic work of Burt,[15] adapted especially for use in Britain.[16] The various revisions of the Binet-Simon tests have, for the most part, been used with children. In view of the great demand for individual tests suitable for adults as well as children, great clinical importance attaches to the more recent development of the Wechsler-Bellevue test,[17] which not only meets this need but explicitly offers a variety of graded tests to determine the intellectual level of the subject in each of a number of distinct functions.

The necessity for "performance tests" for those suffering from linguistic (or sensory) handicaps had already been met by the Seguin, Witmer, and Healy form boards. Holes of various sizes were, for example, to be filled by appropriate blocks. The *standardization* of performance tests and the construction of scales for mental age occurred very shortly after Terman's work. The Pintner-Paterson scale makes use of such materials as a Healy test consisting of dissected pictures which are to be reconstructed,[18] and many similar tests in which the recognition of spatial relations is emphasized. A great many performance tests and a considerable number of performance "scales" are now in use, of which one of the best known is the Minnesota battery of tests of mechanical ability,[19] involving for example the capacity to put together a number of two- or three-dimensional pieces to make a specified whole. The results from such performance tests, however, have made it clear that the ability to manipulate things is scarcely the same as the ability to manipulate words (or other symbols).

Notwithstanding the very large number of children examined in schools and clinics by the Stanford test immediately upon its publication, it was not civil but military experience which made clear the

[14] *A Handbook of Mental Tests* (1922).

[15] *Mental and Scholastic Tests* (1921).

[16] Some differences between British and American test usage, as in the case of coinage, are inevitable. Burt's revision, however, is not a mere adaptation of any American scale.

[17] Wechsler, D., *The Measurement of Adult Intelligence* (1939).

[18] *A Scale of Performance Tests* (1917); *Memoirs of the National Academy of Sciences*, 1921, 15.

[19] Paterson, D. G., and others, *The Minnesota Mechanical Ability Test* (1930).

fact that such an extensive testing program called, in many cases, for *"group tests"* rather than *"individual tests."* In 1917 psychologists devised for use in the United States Army a group scale Alpha for literate English-speaking recruits, and a group scale Beta for illiterates and non-English-speaking recruits.[20] The Alpha comprised a "following-directions" test, arithmetic and information tests, and much other verbal material; the Beta, though of a paper-and-pencil variety, emphasized the subject's ability to grasp spatial and other nonverbal relations which could be visually represented. Shortly thereafter, the use of group tests in surveys of the public schools became frequent, and many tests for different age levels were prepared. The educational uses of intelligence tests [21] in the United States are reflected in hundreds of titles in psychological and educational journals, and cannot even be summarized here. Among the most important of such uses are, first, the classification of pupils in accordance with their intelligence, in order that pupils widely separated in mental age may not be forced into the same group, and second, the examination of the probable cause for poor scholarship, so that (as the French authorities wished) laziness may be distinguished from dullness. In general, group tests are more frequently used for classification, and individual tests for the analysis of maladjustment. The devising of satisfactory tests for the higher levels of intelligence has necessarily proved difficult, but has attained a degree of success sufficient to cause many American colleges to utilize such tests for the classification of applicants for admission and for other administrative purposes. Extraordinarily high reliability and general suitability for intellectually gifted adults has characterized Thorndike's test CAVD (so called because completions, arithmetic, vocabulary, and following directions are tested), which offers items of all degrees of difficulty so that every human being reaches his ceiling or limit in each function.[22]

SOME REPRESENTATIVE FINDINGS

Taking the more successful tests as reasonably adequate measures of intellectual ability, a little attention may be given to typical comparisons of persons classified according to age, sex, race, and occupation.

[20] *Memoirs of the National Academy of Sciences*, 1921, 15.
[21] And of many "educational" and "achievement" tests.
[22] Thorndike, E. L., Bregman, E. O., Cobb, M. V., Woodyard, E., *The Measurement of Intelligence* (1925).

First, as to the relation of ability to age. In 1908 Binet established his "mental-age" scale, which gave a cross section of certain abilities found in children at age levels from three to twelve years. In the Stanford Revision Terman added tests for the period from twelve to sixteen years and made sixteen the level of "intellectual maturity." The assumption that the intelligence of most individuals does not progress beyond the sixteen-year level was based upon data from high-school students and adults. This general assumption was crystallized in the standardization of the sixteen-year-old tests as tests for adults.[23] But data obtained in the United States Army in 1917–18 strongly suggested that this sixteen-year level was too high.[24] Several hundred soldiers took both the Stanford-Binet test and the Alpha test, making it possible to equate the scores on the two tests. Knowing what Stanford score corresponded to each Alpha score, it was possible to conclude from the vastly more extensive testing work in the Army that the average mental age of the white draft was somewhat under fourteen years. This did not, of course, indicate how much variability may exist in the age of attaining one's intellectual maturity; it meant simply that the average intelligence of a fair sample of white male adults proved to be equal to the average intelligence of schoolchildren between thirteen and fourteen years of age. In 1919 Doll undertook a study of over five hundred children from 9.5 to 15.5 years of age,[25] from whose test scores he concluded that "on the average, or for 50 per cent of presumably unselected cases, intelligence growth is practically complete at 13 years." This level was generally accepted for some time.[26] But on account of selective factors operative in the school population beyond fourteen, it proved difficult to gather satisfactory data on the variations in the exact form of the maturity curve. Considerable change of opinion occurred in later years as a result of the data of Thorndike,[27] Thur-

---

[23] The eighteen-year-old tests, or tests for the "superior adult," were defensible either on the hypothesis that *some* individuals gain in intelligence beyond sixteen, or on the supposition that the unusually bright person may obtain a score which, because it does not fall within the scale, necessitates a higher standard (which for convenience takes the form of a higher age level).

[24] *Memoirs of the National Academy of Sciences*, 1921, 15; Brigham, C. C., *A Study of American Intelligence* (1923).

[25] Doll, E. A., "The Average Mental Age of Adults," *J. Appl. Psychol.*, 1919, 3, 317–28.

[26] Much discussion ensued as regards the educational and political implications of such alarming unintelligence.

[27] "On the Improvement in Intelligence Scores from Fourteen to Eighteen," *J. Educ. Psychol.*, 1923, 14, 513–16.

stone,[28] and others, indicating that measurable intelligence continues to increase even to eighteen years or beyond (more and more slowly, of course). Most studies agree in showing a gradual decline thereafter, the rate of the decline depending on the function tested. And the decline may be counteracted for a long time by specific training and experience. While Miles' data indicate decline in all functions after early maturity,[29] Thorndike's data on *Adult Learning* (1928) show that (among those whose occupations keep them alert) the decline in learning ability during the middle years is very slight.

While the literature on "sex differences" in intelligence and special abilities is voluminous, the extent of such differences appears in most investigations to be very slight, if indeed any difference exists. Binet's standards were constructed for age levels irrespective of sex, and the work of Terman and many others has justified this procedure. The point has been made that the somewhat earlier adolescence of girls would lead us to expect some superiority of girls over boys in the neighborhood of ten to twelve years of age, this disadvantage disappearing when both sexes have attained mid-adolescence; but even this temporary difference is small. Many tests for adults have indicated a slight superiority in the average score of men, but the fact that the information items have usually been drawn largely from masculine pursuits appears to explain the findings.

With reference to special abilities and disabilities, however, some fairly large and significant differences have been reported. Early work with rating scales and numerous studies of excellence in school subjects indicated some sex differences in interest and capacity, such as are reflected by feminine superiority in spelling and geography, masculine superiority in history and mathematics. Even where the reported sex differences are of great magnitude, it has as yet proved impossible to determine their relation, if any, to biological factors, in view of the cultural preference for some traits in boys, others in girls. There seems reason to believe that special abilities and disabilities are, like intelligence, "normally distributed," being merely ends of the distribution curve.[30]

The study of race differences in intelligence has engaged the attention of many psychologists, especially in the United States. Studies indicating no clear differences between the sensory acuity of primi-

---

[28] "A Method of Scaling Psychological and Educational Tests," *J. Educ. Psychol.*, 1925, 16, 433–51.

[29] Miles, W. R., "Age and Human Ability," *Psychol. Rev.*, 1933, 40, 99–123.

[30] See Hollingworth, L. S., *Special Talents and Defects* (1923), p. 45.

tive peoples and that of advanced peoples were reported very early in the present century.[31] The first systematic experimental comparison of the intellectual capacities of races was that of Woodworth at the St. Louis Exposition in 1904.[32] The Seguin form board was found useful in studying the "performance-test" ability of racial groups from all over the globe. Woodworth's conclusions were that in general the average abilities of the different races differed but little, while overlapping was large; the only exception was the case of the Negritos, whose abilities averaged distinctly less than that of other races.

The study of Negro intelligence in the United States has received much attention. Beginning about 1910, attention was drawn by several students to the widespread retardation of Negroes in the schools, and several studies of Negro children and adults were made with intelligence tests shortly thereafter. Ferguson, using four familiar tests of mental ability (of which he regarded the completion test and the analogies test as the most satisfactory), found large and consistent intellectual inferiority in the average attainment of several hundreds of Negro children as compared with white children.[33] Ferguson's conclusions as to the relation of Negro intelligence to white intelligence appeared confirmed by the study of Negro recruits in 1917–18.

Meanwhile, with the advent of the Stanford Revision of the Binet scale, a series of studies of Negro intelligence by this method began to appear. The results have indicated with fair consistency that Negro children and adults average below the whites. But the difficulties of properly evaluating environmental factors, which are especially acute in view of the inferior economic status of the Negro, soon began to be emphasized, as by Arlitt.[34] Of importance in this connection and as a check upon all earlier studies was the work of Peterson.[35] He undertook to eliminate not only the verbal handicap

[31] Rivers, W. H. R., "Observations on the Senses of the Todas," *Brit. J. Psychol.*, 1904, 1, 321–96. Rivers's summary, "pure sense acuity is much the same in all races," is based on earlier work together with his own, and has not been overthrown by subsequent research.

[32] Woodworth, R. S., "Racial Differences in Mental Traits," *Science*, N. S., 1910, 31, 171–86.

[33] Ferguson, G. O., "The Psychology of the Negro," *Arch. Psychol.*, 1916, No. 36.

[34] Arlitt, A. H., "On the Need for Caution in Establishing Race Norms," *J. Appl. Psychol.*, 1921, 5, 179–83.

[35] Peterson, J., *The Comparative Abilities of White and Negro Children, Comp. Psychol. Monogr.*, 1922, 1 (Ser. No. 5); Peterson, J., Lanier, L. H., and Walker, H. M., "Comparisons of White and Negro Children in Certain Ingenuity and Speed Tests," *J. Comp. Psychol.*, 1925, 5, 271–83.

which had been thought responsible for some of the reported race differences, but, in addition, the speed factor, which may well play a large part in differentiating races. In the "disc-transfer" method, for example, Negro and white children of various ages were allowed to manipulate discs to form a predetermined pattern, their movements being governed by the rules of a game similar to "The Fox and the Goose and the Bag of Meal," but more complex. White children were found to work more rapidly, but when accuracy of performance irrespective of speed was measured, a significant degree of white superiority did not appear. A rather similar thing was soon found by Klineberg,[36] using a battery of performance tests with Yakima Indian boys. The Indian children at all age levels worked more slowly than the whites, but they made fewer errors. This reminds one of the statement of Franz Boas,[37] to the effect that racial differences in intelligence may consist not in differences in intellectual endowment, but in the types of activity emphasized by different cultures. Indeed, a series of later studies by Klineberg has shown that the grossly inferior test scores of rural Negro children are not characteristic of urban Negro children; and that Negro and white children in the same schools are very much alike.[38] Yeung,[39] Darsie,[40] and others have published studies of the intelligence of Mongolian groups, from which it appears clear that children who speak Chinese or Japanese at home tend to be inferior to whites in tests involving the use of English, but that on nonlanguage tests no significant differences exist.

The Army Alpha and Beta tests offered some information regarding the intelligence of subdivisions of the white race. On the Army tests, both verbal and nonverbal, immigrants from the British Isles and from Canada gave scores closely comparable to those of American-born whites; German and Scandinavian immigrants averaged slightly lower; while Italians, Poles, and Russians tended to make distinctly lower scores. In the absence of satisfactory data on these groups when tested in their own countries, opinion is divided between three interpretations: These results may be significant of

[36] Klineberg, O., "Racial Differences in Speed and Accuracy," *J. Abn. and Soc. Psychol.*, 1927, 22, 273–77.

[37] *The Mind of Primitive Man* (1911).

[38] Klineberg, O., "Cultural Factors in Intelligence-Test Performance," *J. Negro Educ.*, 1934, 3, 478–83.

[39] Yeung, K. T., "The Intelligence of Chinese Children in San Francisco and Vicinity," *J. Appl. Psychol.*, 1921, 5, 267–74.

[40] Darsie, M. L., *Mental Capacity of American-Born Japanese Children, Comp. Psychol. Monogr.*, 1925, 3 (Ser. No. 15).

genuine racial differences; they may be due to the "sampling" which all immigration involves; they may be due to varying degrees of difficulty in meeting the test situation in America. There appears to be a drift toward the third interpretation. Testing ten large groups of preadolescent boys in western Europe, and comparing those of Nordic, Alpine, and Mediterranean stock, Klineberg found no significant differences attributable to the stock as such.[41]

Many of the difficulties found in the study of race differences occur also in the study of occupational differences. Here again the Army data mark the beginnings of extensive study of the problem, and here also subsequent studies have confirmed the results. A definite "intellectual hierarchy" was discovered, corresponding closely to an "occupational hierarchy" popularly recognized. The intelligence of (Taussig's) five major "noncompetitive groups"—(a) professional, (b) semiprofessional and higher business, (c) skilled, (d) semiskilled, and (e) unskilled—follows in the order named, though with much overlapping. A more detailed analysis makes possible a similar comparison of specific occupational groups, for example, carpenters with teamsters. A fairly close relation has appeared between economic status and intelligence. Burt,[42] English,[43] and others [44] early showed that children classified according to the social status of their parents form a similar hierarchy, though again with considerable overlapping. The whole problem of the relation of inheritance to intelligence besets us here (page 366). In the meantime the empirical level of intelligence is socially important, and has been greatly emphasized in vocational guidance, industrial-personnel work, the treatment of children who are in difficulties, and many other problems.

THE THEORY OF INTELLIGENCE

The development of the technique of testing, especially for practical purposes, was for a time so rapid in the United States that relatively little attention was given to the analysis of the nature of

[41] Klineberg, O., "A Study of Psychological Differences between Racial and National Groups in Europe," *Arch. Psychol.*, 1931, No. 132.

[42] Burt, C., "Experimental Tests of General Intelligence," *Brit. J. Psychol.*, 1909, 3, 94–177.

[43] English, H. B., *An Experimental Study of the Mental Capacities of School Children, Correlated with Social Status, Psychol. Monogr.*, 1917, 23 (whole No. 100).

[44] For example, Pressey, S. L., and Ralston, R., "The Relation of the General Intelligence of School Children to the Occupation of Their Fathers," *J. Appl. Psychol.*, 1919, 3, 366–73.

intelligence. Terman emphasized the ability to think conceptually.[45] Thorndike has emphasized the relative independence of each specific function, and the conception that intelligence is not "homogeneous"; [46] intelligence might be regarded as the sum total of many distinct functions. Such a multifactor theory is in sharp contrast to those unifactor theories (for example, that of Ebbinghaus) which regard intelligence as a single function. The fact that the various tests of abilities do not correlate perfectly with one another has seemed to present serious difficulties for any unifactor theory.

Yet the great advance of testing technique, and in particular of statistical method in connection with it, soon brought into great prominence a theory offered by Spearman as early as 1904.[47] It is necessary, Spearman believed, to take account in every human ability of two factors, one general and one specific. General ability, or G, plays some part in nearly every human activity. In some activities, such as science, philosophy, and executive tasks, success depends largely upon this general factor. In other functions, such as skill in many of the arts and crafts, the importance of general ability is much less marked, success depending on much more specific aptitudes. Each individual possesses many such specific abilities, each one of which may, like G, be measured. Every activity, in fact, calls into play at least one special ability, or S, while nearly all demand also the use of G. Tasks in which G is relatively important may be said to involve G in greater "saturation" than those in which it plays a minor part. G can never be directly measured, but through the study of correlations many functions involving G may be compared in such fashion as to make its indirect measurement possible. It is possible, Spearman suggested, to think of G as a general fund of cortical energy, each S representing a special cortical area to which G may be mobilized.[48]

[45] "Intelligence and Its Measurement: A Symposium," *J. Educ. Psychol.*, 1921, 12, 127–33.

[46] See, for example, *Educational Psychology*, Vol. III (1914). There is, of course, a close relation between the theory of intelligence and the theory of the transfer of training (see page 241). Thorndike, for example, would regard any two intellectual functions as entirely distinct except in so far as they possess *identical elements*.

[47] Spearman, C. E., "General Intelligence Objectively Determined and Measured," *Amer. J. Psychol.*, 1904, 15, 201–93. See also "The Theory of Two Factors," *Psychol. Rev.*, 1914, 21, 101–15, and *The Abilities of Man: Their Nature and Measurement* (1927).

[48] He later suggested that G may consist of the capacity to "educe relations"; for example, to find how loyalty is related to treachery, or to educe "fundaments," as in stating what stands in a relation of opposition to loyalty (*The Nature of Intelligence and the Principles of Cognition*, 1927).

But as was early pointed out, for example by Woodrow,[49] there may be, intermediate between general ability and each of the special abilities, a level of abilities less general than the one and less specific than the other. Between ability in addition and general intelligence there may lie, for example, an all-round numerical ability. Such all-round numerical ability would be, if substantiated, a *group factor*. Evidence for such group factors in verbal, numerical, spatial, and other tasks rapidly increased as the new approach was used.

But this called for new methods. The standard method introduced by Spearman was that of "tetrad differences," a simple mathematical procedure which disentangled a primary or general factor from the various specific factors which surrounded or complicated it. Conceived in geometrical terms, each specific may overlap each other specific, or may overlap the general factor; yet all are mathematically capable of isolation. During the 1920's, there developed, primarily in the United States, a series of further mathematical approaches for the isolation and measurement of individual attributes. These methods, known as methods of *factor analysis*, undertook to disentangle very complex masses of data in which many types of functional components were teased out from the intercorrelations of test scores. Thus one may utilize the intercorrelations between test scores of a dozen functions, such as vocabulary, eye-hand co-ordination, pitch discrimination, and attempt to find out how many fundamental abilities or capacities have to be assumed to explain the test scores, and in what strength or saturation each such factor appears.

The largest influence at work in this field is that of L. L. Thurstone, who, together with his pupils, has developed the best-known factorial methods and applied them in dozens of problems.[50] He has made it abundantly clear that the raw scores obtained from tests are usually unsuitable, in that they do not point clearly to the simplest group of assumptions that might be made about the organization of abilities. One might visualize the situation by saying that instead of measuring people's height and weight, one might be so unfortunate as to have to measure the length of their shadows. It is therefore necessary to rearrange the data so that they measure not shadows, but height. This conversion of raw scores to a new numer-

[49] Woodrow, H. H., *Brightness and Dullness in Children* (1919).
[50] Thurstone, L. L., *The Vectors of Mind* (1935); *Primary Mental Abilities, Psychometr. Monogr.*, 1938, 1.

ical form is called rotation of axes,[51] and it is from many such rotations, until the best and simplest fit is obtained, that one proceeds to derive factors.

It has been shown that factors are of value when they point to definable psychological functions; that is, when psychologically meaningful names for the underlying abilities can be found. Thurstone points to verbal, numerical, spatial abilities, and so on. On the other hand, some factors appear to be statistical artifacts for which really useful names are hard to find; and in a few instances experimental work with large numbers of subjects, as in training them to carry out certain intellectual processes, has not only raised the level of some of their abilities but has eventuated in a new and unsuspected interrelation of abilities, necessitating new factors. The result is to make a good many psychologists uncertain as to whether the factors, however real and useful, are really irreducible or unchangeable. Functional units they often are, but structural components in the mind they may very well fail to be.

Despite such difficulties, factor analysis is more and more used as a way of finding what a group of tests is actually testing; as a way of determining fundamental differences between the effective capacities of various groups which must carry out certain defined military or industrial operations; or as devices for showing the gradual development of those interrelations of abilities which we typically find at the adult level. Of interest here are a series of studies conducted by Garrett and his pupils. These appear to indicate that the mind of the small child is relatively undifferentiated (that is, that almost any intelligence-test items will correlate substantially with any other intelligence-test items); that a differentiation goes on rather rapidly during the elementary-school period, so that tests come to fall more and more into natural groups, each distinct and more or less independent of the rest. There is found at nine years of age, for example, verbal ability as distinct from mathematical ability, and at fourteen still further differentiation of the mind into distinct abilities—like the differentiation of a tree trunk into a number of boughs or branches. Though there does remain some broad pervasive or general ability which runs through all the items of a test battery measuring intellectual competence, the process of progressive specialization or differentiation of the mind seems to

[51] Usually the assumption is made that each of the factors is uncorrelated with the others. Visualizing the matter geometrically, we may say that each factor is at right angles to each of the rest. But there are, of course, other possible working assumptions which may at times be warranted.

continue through the college years; the senior student has developed a series of intellectual skills, such as his attack on mathematical problems or his special skill in literary criticism, but rather little can be concluded about his competence in history or economics. It is stressed by Garrett and others that constitutional factors in the pattern of maturing, as well as environmental pressures, may tend to produce such increasing specificity, or departmentalization of the mind.[52]

THE INHERITANCE OF INTELLECTUAL ABILITY

The psychologist's preoccupation with measurements of intelligence has been accompanied by an intensive study of the inheritance of intellectual endowment. Research on the inheritance of mental traits has very naturally seen its most rapid development in relation to intellectual inheritance, rather than in relation to those aspects of personality which have yielded more slowly to quantitative attack. Perhaps 90 per cent of all the work done in the field of mental inheritance has concerned itself with intelligence.

As early as 1869 Galton had undertaken to show in his *Hereditary Genius* that superior intelligence is inherited. His method, the study of lines of descent and of collateral branches, a procedure known as the *pedigree method*, was adopted in 1877 by Dugdale, who (though himself an environmentalist) showed in *The Jukes* the continuance of mental deficiency within the family stock for several generations.[53] Many investigations of mental deficiency by the pedigree method followed, of which perhaps the best known is Goddard's *The Kallikak Family* (1912).

The pedigree method has been subject to some suspicion, because of the inaccuracy of the historical and questionnaire methods upon which it relies. Many other traits have, however, been suggestively studied in the same way, and within recent years the use of questionnaires has been supplanted to some extent by more direct case studies of the living individuals concerned. Such a combination of case method with pedigree method in the study of children of unusual ability is found in the work of Terman and his collaborators.[54]

---

[52] Garrett, H. E., "A Developmental Theory of Intelligence," *Amer. Psychologist*, 1946, 1, 373–78.

[53] In 1916, the work was brought up to date by Estabrook, A. H., in *The Jukes in 1915*.

[54] Terman, L. M., *Genetic Studies of Genius*, 3 vols. (1925–30).

But the status of the whole problem of mental inheritance has been greatly affected by the rediscovery, about 1900, of Mendel's laws of inheritance. Mendel had discovered, a little past the middle of the nineteenth century, a series of fundamental laws of heredity. First, in studying plants such as the sweet pea, he found that individuals of unlike color yielded hybrid offspring resembling one parent much more than the other. The color of one parent was "dominant." Now when such hybrids were mated, 25 per cent of their offspring reverted to the color which had disappeared in the first hybrid generation; 75 per cent showed the "dominant" character. It was evident that the "skipping of generations" need no longer remain a mystery. It was important to distinguish between "body plasm" and "germ plasm," and to look in the latter for the elements (now known as *genes*) which, in ever varying combinations, give rise to the diversities of body structure.

This view seemed to imply that a large number of changes which occur from generation to generation can be explained not by the influence of changes occurring in the body, but by the reshifting of elements in the germ cells. In the eighties and nineties Weismann showed clearly that the germ cells preserve a continuity of their own; [55] that each germ cell can be traced back in its lineage to other germ cells, and that germ cells are rather remarkably free from influence from the vicissitudes of the body which has enclosed them. This conception has been of profound import for all studies of heredity; its significance for psychology has been seen in the rigid exclusion of explanations of mental life in terms of "ancestral experience" and "ancestral habits." Changes from generation to generation were now explained in terms of variations within the germ cells themselves. Later De Vries and others pointed out that the germinal material might undergo sudden *mutation*, and that a new species might arise as the result of such germinal changes. [56] This made it possible to think of changes in species not so much in terms of slight variations, such as Darwin had emphasized, as in terms of sudden and permanent alterations.

With this work of Weismann and De Vries, and with the rediscovery of the Mendelian principles, an attempt was made to apply Mendelian concepts to the phenomena of human heredity. Davenport urged, for example, that both mental deficiency and certain defects in self-control are true Mendelian traits. [57] The complexity of

[55] For example, *The Germ Plasm* (1893).
[56] De Vries, H., *Die Mutationstheorie* (1900).
[57] *The Hill Folk* (1912); *The Feebly Inhibited* (1915).

the mental traits whose hereditary principles are sought, and the difficulty of accurately gauging environmental influences, have prevented most of these contributions from attracting wide attention. A large mass of material was, however, collected by Goddard on the subject of the inheritance of mental deficiency, with results which aroused much discussion.[58] His more than 1700 cases were scrutinized with respect to the Mendelian formula. Inspection of the figures suggested the hypothesis that mental defect not due to accident or illness is a Mendelian trait recessive to normal intelligence. He then undertook to verify the hypothesis by determining whether it was possible to "predict" the status of the children of the mating of two individuals whose family trees had been studied. The results appeared clearly to confirm his hypothesis. But in this, as in most such investigations, the population had, without clear warrant, been grouped into two sharply contrasting subgroups, disregarding the gradations of intelligence. The major objection to Goddard's findings has arisen from considerations relating to the "normal distribution" of intelligence—the fact, already noted, that the feeble-minded do not constitute a separate "species," but are simply those individuals whose intelligence lies below an arbitrarily selected point on a distribution curve. All that we know about heredity forces us to think of intelligence as depending not on one but on many genes, and consequently to think of mental defect as an expression not of one specific germinal defect but of a much more complex genetic composite.

But with the refinement of intelligence tests, and with the increasing recognition of the importance of statistical methods, a more satisfactory approach to the problem of the inheritance of intelligence has been offered. It began to be clear that studies of the inheritance of human abilities would have to proceed from accurate data on intellectual level, and that they would have to include systematic studies of the degree of resemblance of child and parent, the degree of resemblance between child and foster parent (where the resemblance might be due at least in part to environmental factors), and direct quantitative comparison of intellectual level with the socioeconomic level of the home. In view of the complexity (and the prejudice) usually encountered in dealing with human material, there had to be likewise systematic animal-breeding experiments, in which the possession of superior or inferior ability could be experimentally followed through from one generation to another.

[58] *Feeble-mindedness: Its Causes and Consequences* (1914).

All these lines of research were undertaken in the 1920's, and have made extensive progress since that time.

In the matter of human heredity, the classics are the investigations of Burks,[59] and of Freeman, Holzinger, and Mitchell,[60] supported by several subsequent investigations. In general, the method was to study the effect of environment by comparing the intelligence-test level of children with that of foster parents, and in another series with that of true ("own") parents—noting how much closer the parent-child resemblance was in the latter case, where nature and nurture worked together, than in the former case, where nurture was the primary or sole factor causing resemblance. This fundamental method was eked out by comparing children adopted early in life with those adopted later, and by considering the degree to which selective placement might have brought children into homes more or less at their own intrinsic intellectual level. Stripping aside all subtleties and complications, we may note that both investigations showed the marked influence of home environment; but both showed also that home environment, instead of wielding unlimited power over the children, operated within definite limits set by the child's original capacity. Freeman and his collaborators emphasized a rather environmentalistic approach and Burks a rather hereditarian approach, and their quantitative data are in many ways noncomparable. It is by no means clear sociologically that the California situation (Burks) was comparable with the Illinois situation (Freeman); and that the Illinois study controlled selective placement as well as the California study. It is not clear whether the measures of socioeconomic status were adequate. We may safely draw only the broad conclusion that the potential represented by a child's hereditary capacity may be actualized more fully in a stimulating environment than in a cramped and inhibited environment. If we try to speak more precisely, we find Leahy's study confirming—and more than confirming—Burks's emphasis upon heredity,[61] since almost all of her observed similarity of children to foster parents is reasonably traceable to home environment, and the total of such resemblance

[59] Burks, B. S., "The Relative Influence of Nature and Nurture upon Mental Development: A Comparative Study of Foster-Parent Foster-Child Resemblance and True-Parent True-Child Resemblance," *Yrbk. Natl. Soc. Stud. Educ.*, 1928, 27, 219–316.

[60] Freeman, F. N., Holzinger, K. J., and Mitchell, B. C., "The Influence of Environment on the Intelligence, School Achievement, and Conduct of Foster Children," *Yrbk. Natl. Soc. Stud. Educ.*, 1928, 24, 103–218.

[61] Leahy, A. M., "Nature-Nurture and Intelligence," *Genet. Psychol. Monogr.*, 1935, 17, 235–308.

is very slight. On the other hand, a series of much-debated studies has emanated from the State University of Iowa, where Wellman and others have pointed to the stimulating effect of educational opportunities enjoyed by specific groups,[62] with increases in intelligence quotient which are sometimes cumulative and of spectacular magnitude over the years. Technical flaws have been pointed out in all these studies, and recent years have witnessed an even more intense controversy over the Iowa studies than prevailed earlier with respect to the California and Illinois studies.

Partly because of local loyalties to one's own research group, partly because of the general preference for a "biological" or a "social-science" view of human nature, and very largely because of a difference of opinion regarding the improvability of human nature, the nature-nurture issue has generated much heat along with the light. On the whole, the environmentalists regard themselves as humanitarians free from the false aristocracy of those who stress innate differences—differences not only between individuals but, when taken at their first value, differences also between social classes. Indeed the environmentalists have not hesitated to refer to biological emphasis as reactionary or even fascistic. On the other hand, the proponents of a biological approach insist that sober facts, rather than humanitarian wishes, must be the guide, and frequently point out that the hopes of humanity may actually be most effectively placed in specially endowed individual leaders who, wherever they are found, must be fully understood, respected, and cultivated, and even more so in a democracy than in a more tightly controlled social system. It is obvious that arguments of these types are not likely to carry much conviction with those of an opposing cast of mind, and that the importance of defining quantitatively the degree to which each kind of human stock can be functionally bettered by good homes and good education is as great as is our ignorance regarding the best way to solve the problem.

At the same time, a considerable number of very specific approaches have yielded some very concrete results. Newman and his collaborators have shown that identical twins, even when separated in early infancy, tend to resemble one another rather closely in intelligence—more than one would expect to find with fraternal twins.[63] In the case of individual children undergoing emotional

[62] Wellman, B. L., "Iowa Studies on the Effects of Schooling," *Yrbk. Natl. Soc. Stud. Educ.*, 1940, 39 (II), 377–99.

[63] Newman, H. H., Freeman, F. N., and Holzinger, K. J., *Twins: A Study of Heredity and Environment* (1937).

deprivation or emotional blockage, Woolley showed, as early as 1925, that emotional release and free stimulation could cause rapid increases of 20 or 30 points in intelligence quotient. Data of this sort have accumulated, particularly in the hands of psychiatrists and clinical psychologists who have worked intensively with small numbers of individuals whose emotional problem was rather fully defined. From such studies it appears that part of the beneficial effect comes from a gradual setting-free of attitudes of confidence, with resulting ability to use such wits as one has; and that the very atmosphere of a test situation itself, by being made more permissive, may offer a free rather than a hostile challenge and permit the mobilization of latent capacities. Parallel to such studies are others indicating the marked and prompt effect of dietary changes, such as those permitting better utilization of sugars, and finally a limited number of studies showing that many children are carrying around within them a considerable deficit or penalty as a result of organic or metabolic disorder. Since we do not know how prevalent these defects are, or the degree to which each is amenable to treatment, all that we can appropriately say is that the atmosphere today seems to favor a much more modest and empirical attack on such immediate problems, and that broad quantitative generalizations about the nature-nurture relations in the general public are less and less frequently heard. And finally, if it be really true, as the factorial studies suggest, that intelligence is a composite of many things, it may prove to be fruitful to shift the whole attack, giving special attention to the problem of inheritance of the specific measurable capacities—making use in each study of parent-child resemblance, twin-twin resemblance, and of longitudinal data on the way in which each such capacity reflects the influence of specific environmental factors.

REFERENCES

Binet, Alfred, and Simon, Théodore, *A Method of Measuring the Development of the Intelligence of Young Children,* Courier Company, 1913

Guilford, J. P., *Psychometric Methods,* McGraw-Hill, 1936

Mann, C. W., "Intelligence Test Standardization" in Harriman, P. L., ed., *Encyclopedia of Psychology,* Philosophical Library, 1946; pp. 286–304

Murchison, Carl A., ed., *A History of Psychology in Autobiography,* 3 vols., Clark University Press, 1930–36: Spearman and Terman

Peterson, Joseph, *Early Conceptions and Tests of Intelligence,* World Book Company, 1925

Terman, Lewis M., and Merrill, Maud A., *Measuring Intelligence: A Guide to the Administration of the New Revised Stanford-Binet Tests of Intelligence,* Houghton Mifflin, 1937

Wolfle, Dael L., *Factor Analysis to 1940,* University of Chicago Press, 1940, Psychometric Monog., No. 3

Woodworth, Robert S., *Heredity and Environment: A Critical Survey of Recently Published Material on Twins and Foster Children,* Soc. Sci. Res. Council Bull., 1941, No. 4

Chapter 25

PHYSIOLOGICAL PSYCHOLOGY

The nature of the mind and soul is bodily.   LUCRETIUS

Or something that the things not understood make for their uses out of flesh and blood.   MASEFIELD

PHYSIOLOGICAL PSYCHOLOGY meant for Wundt a psychology pursued by physiological *methods*. But the fact that he and his school devoted considerable attention to physiological mechanisms supposed to be fundamental for mental processes, and the fact that the Wundtians who spread from Leipzig to other laboratories at the end of the last century enthusiastically shared this interest, meant that the term "physiological psychology" soon came to be equivalent to the investigation of psychology in terms of the physiological *foundations* of experience and behavior. Indeed, a large part of the work of such men as Helmholtz, Ribot, and James had been devoted to physiological functions as clues to psychological functions. The new psychology became more and more dependent upon current physiological research.

Attention was given chiefly to the central nervous system, since the cardinal hypothesis was the dependence of experience upon cortical activity, and cortical activity was conceived to be merely the highest expression of a general dynamic which lay within the central nervous system. The original conception of Cabanis to the effect that the mental and moral life of man was a reflection of activity at the various levels of the central nervous system was fulfilled in the physiological psychology of the early years of this century.

Waldeyer's neurone theory (page 187) had soon won general acceptance. Since there were a number of neurones between any stimulated sense organ and any responding muscle, the core of the physiological problem was the nature of the action at the synapse which connected one neurone with another. Here lay, many believed, the answer to the problem of variations in response to a given stimulus, and variations in the kinds of stimulation that may arouse a given response. In this context the monumental work of Sherrington appeared, an extensive experimental program of research upon the functional interdependence of reflex systems,[1] surveyed above on pages 190–91.

The outline of neurophysiology sketched by Sherrington was soon generally regarded as the central achievement in this area. The result, on the whole, was to confirm the habit of reducing the complicated to the simple. Despite Sherrington's assertion that the simple reflex was a "convenient abstraction," and that the nervous system was an integrating system, many psychologists understood Sherrington's findings to mean that the explanatory base for all psychological phenomena lay in the fundamental phenomena of reflex action, with the principles of summation, facilitation, and inhibition as adequate supplementary concepts which could well care for the phenomena at the highest level.

This position could not be maintained for long. The advent of Gestalt psychology in 1912, of Gelb and Goldstein's studies of the brain-injured of World War I in 1919, of Henry Head's studies in 1923 of aphasia, and of Lashley's various investigations of cortical localization in the twenties, led to the gradual decline of the conception of the nervous system as a composite structure made up of functioning elements. Increasing emphasis was placed upon phenomena at the highest integrating level, which were conceived to make the simple reflex actually a very *inconvenient* abstraction, and upon organismic laws, embodiments of principles at a high emergent level, requiring emphasis on the integrating process itself, rather than primarily on the components which had to be integrated. All these studies call for consideration. But they also lead us into the vexed question of cortical localization, so that we shall now have to bring our story of the localization problem (page 184) up to date.

CORTICAL LOCALIZATION

Ever since Hippocrates locked mental activity in the brain, a bold medical practitioner could be found in any era who would lock memory in one lobe of the brain, fantasy in another, the will in a third; who would compartmentalize soul and body alike. This practice was revitalized in the Middle Ages and the Renaissance, and seemed on the whole to comport well with studies of the nervous

[1] Sherrington, C. S., *The Integrative Action of the Nervous System* (1906).

system carried out in the eighteenth century. By the end of that period, medicine had been doing what an Egyptian surgeon had done at the time of the great pyramid-building; namely, describing exactly the paralysis and contracture of certain muscles which followed from cranial injuries of this or that type.

The French physician Dax had made some notes on brain localization in 1825, and medical men went on speculating along this line despite the fact that, as noted above (page 95), the experiments of Flourens on the brains of pigeons had failed to support any theory of localization. But there was also the evidence of Bell and of Müller (page 93) indicating at least certain neural centers for specific sensory activities. How could one reconcile the data on sensory centers with Flourens's data on mass action in the brain? Reconciliation was perhaps out of the question. But the log jam to the flow of fresh thought in the matter was removed in 1861 by Broca, who unwittingly applied a certain "shock therapy" to the medical profession by his explanation of aphasia in terms of a dramatically exact localization of the function of speech.[2] Motor speech, said Broca, is located "in the posterior portion of the third left frontal convolution." This is an area over which one could place a quarter-dollar; so that Broca represents the most extreme conceivable antithesis to the mass-action hypothesis of Flourens.

Fortunately there followed almost immediately thereafter the determination to test the conception of localization by experiments on the brains of monkeys. These investigations by Fritsch and Hitzig in 1870 gave results parallel to some fragmentary results obtained by military surgeons in operating upon the brains of men wounded in the Franco-Prussian War, and pointed clearly to the fact that excitation of certain portions of the brain gave rise to specific localized muscular contractions.[3] Within a few years the studies with monkeys were supplemented by data from chimpanzees, and later from other anthropoid apes. By the middle eighties the work had been brought into clear alignment with the data from post-mortem studies of cases of human brain injury. It began to be more and more clear that in the higher mammals, at least, there is a general allocation of motor functions to the frontal lobes of the brain, just anterior to the fissure of Rolando, of auditory functions to the temporal lobes, and of visual functions to the occipital lobes. The senses which are served by sense organs not concentrated in the head but scattered through the body (the "general senses" which mediate touch,

[2] Broca, P., *Bull. de la Société Anatomique* (1861).
[3] Fritsch, G., and Hitzig, E., *Arch. f. Anat. u. Physiol.*, 1870.

pain, warmth, and cold) were found to be localized just behind the fissure of Rolando. Moreover, the motor area proved capable of certain further subdivisions. Certain areas gave rise to arm movements, others to leg movements, and so on; and in the same way, some subdivisions of function within the various sensory centers seemed to be well established.

By 1890 such doctrines of cortical localization were well defined and generally accepted. James's *Principles of Psychology*, for example, gives the conception of localization as just stated, while various medical observers went much further. Hinshelwood specified, for example, areas for the reading of English which were separate from those involved in reading French, as shown by the loss of one function without the loss of the other function in certain cases of brain pathology.[4] Such doctrines of precise localization integrated well with the neurone theory, in which specific neural tracts underlay specific psychological functions, and in which a modification of the neural connections served as the basis for the learning process.

Gradually, however, partly as a result of more sophisticated methods of examining the brain and partly as a result of conceptions of the unity of the organism (as represented after 1912, for example, in the Gestalt viewpoint), data began to take on a somewhat different form early in the present century. Marie rejected Broca's approach and regarded aphasia as an expression of a generalized brain condition.[5] As early as 1907 there are some suggestions in the work of Franz that cortical localization is not rigid and absolute; [6] and in the later work of Lashley and Franz there were suggestions that a function may be mediated on one occasion by one neural area and on a different occasion by another area.[7] From these studies emerged a long series of investigations by Lashley,[8] beginning in the early twenties, the general purport of which has been to point to the dynamic interrelatedness of all aspects of the nervous system; to challenge the fixed structural basis for any given act; and to raise questions which go to the heart of the problem of cortical localization (and therefore of specific energies) and of atomism, whether of psychological function or of bodily structure.

[4] Hinshelwood, J., *Letter, Word and Mind Blindness* (1900).

[5] Marie, P. Cf. Moutier, F., *L'aphasie de Broca* (1908).

[6] Franz, S. I., "On the Functions of the Cerebrum: The Frontal Lobes," *Arch. Psychol.*, 1907, No. 2.

[7] Lashley, K. S., and Franz, S. I., "The Effects of Cerebral Destruction upon Habit Formation and Retention in the Albino Rat," *Psychobiol.* 1917, 1.

[8] For example, Lashley, K. S., *Brain Mechanisms and Intelligence: A Quantitative Study of Injuries to the Brain* (1929).

Lashley's investigations with rats, monkeys, and other animals brought out the fact that the classical localizations which had been accepted might have to be modified where lower mammals were concerned; that even in the monkey the extirpation of specific motor areas permitted rapid reappearance of function, so that one might have to think of a number of different cortical areas as indifferently capable of serving a given activity. The older conception of "vicarious" function—the notion that a cortical region might take over a task in which it had heretofore played no role—was supplanted by the conception that regions playing a small role in a given activity might, when occasion demanded, take on a more important role, or indeed the primary role. Thus extirpation of part of the pre-Rolandic motor area, while causing temporary paralysis, nevertheless permitted rapid recovery of function, apparently under dominance of other regions.

In the case of the rat, the conception of diffuseness of localization was pushed much further. Indeed, it became evident from many extirpation experiments that no one region was all-important to the execution of any specific sensory or motor task. The removal of the visual cortex, for example, while causing temporary blindness, was followed after a few weeks by recovery of some visual functions, served by other regions. A large amount of such extirpation research led to the view that at least in the rat the important thing is not the locus of injury, but the gross amount of injury done: cortical loss up to about 15 per cent of the total meant no measurable loss of function, whereas from that point on, the more pervasive the injury, the more profound the disorganization of the habit system under investigation. The various parts of the brain, Lashley suggested, were *equipotential*.

By the end of the 1920's Lashley had gone far in his emphasis upon equipotentiality—upon the absence of point-for-point localization and upon the importance of brain dynamics as a whole. Indeed, his presidential address to the American Psychological Association in 1929 emphasized the interdependence of functions as a general biological law. He pointed with admiration to experiments in which a sponge squeezed and flattened beyond all recognition had reconstituted itself into its original form. He reminded psychologists that in their attempt to find sharply localized centers and sharply isolable functions they had lost something of the ground plan of the organism.

It has of course been pointed out by many that such findings in the rat may have no specific bearing upon localization at a more

complex level, in view of the progressive specialization in more and
more complex organisms. It may well be that localization of function is more precise in the human brain. Indeed, the newer evidence
that the retina is "projected upon" the cortex, a specific point in
the former corresponding to a specific point in the latter,[9] has been
accepted by Lashley. In the evolutionary sequence increasing complexity has in general accompanied specialization in cortical activity—a doctrine reminiscent of Jackson's theory of levels (page
38). Nevertheless if the principle of interdependence is sound, if in
general the function of a living system must be interpreted by reference to the dynamics of the system rather than by reference to the
dynamics of the component parts, this must make a difference in
human experimental and clinical studies. If, concretely, one wants
to explain a blurring of vision, or an inability to differentiate tones,
by referring to pathology of the brain, one must make use of a
general principle which is sound and consistent with what one knows
about living systems in general. Here the new approach may be
important even if it contains misconceptions; indeed in all psychology, fundamental errors have over and over again been tracked
down and removed not by more minute attention to technique, but
only by broadening the scientific vista with a view to encompassing
all the relevant facts.

At this point, one turns inevitably to our major source of information regarding the total activity of the human brain; namely, the
study of brain disorder resulting from disease or from industrial or
military catastrophe, and in particular the cases classically known
as aphasia. Here the results obtained in England by Henry Head,[10]
and in Germany and in the United States by Gelb and Goldstein,[11]
led to a converging philosophy of neural function. Head found himself unable to use effectively Broca's conception of specific localization and specific functions in specific brain areas, and found himself
drawn to a conception of relations between certain broad types of
speech activity and certain ways or forms of brain activity. In the
same way, Gelb and Goldstein, studying the brains of men suffering
from gunshot wounds in World War I, found that the whole visual field would be recast if a slight injury was inflicted upon the
visual area. It was not a question of cutting out, so to speak, one
part of the visual field; rather, it was a question of forcing upon the

[9] Polyak, S. L., *The Retina* (1941).

[10] *Aphasia and Kindred Disorders of Speech* (1923).

[11] Gelb, A., and Goldstein, K., *Psychologische Analysen hirnpathologischer Fälle auf
Grund von Untersuchungen Hirnverletzter* (1920).

impaired organism a completely new way of giving structure to the perceived world. If, for example, the brain area supposedly serving the region of the fovea is shot away, the result is not the loss of foveal vision, but rather the development of a "pseudo-fovea" in another region. There must be focusing, there must be sharp figure-ground differentiation, if anything like human seeing is to go on. What is seen, moreover, must be meaningfully organized. Suppose a man has suffered a local "micropsia," so that part of the world appears abnormally small. When looking at a cross which lies partly in the area of micropsia, he does not see *part* of the cross reduced in size, but sees all of it large or all of it small. Organizing tendencies dominate any punctiform activities which may be going on here and there.[12]

In the same way, in the case of intellectual functions Goldstein showed that specific errors do not necessarily follow upon local injury; rather, the shattered or broken individual reduces the level of his activity, attempts less, and finds a way of coping with life at a reduced level. The organism must always "come to terms" with the environment. Instead of reacting "mosaic-fashion" to specific brain losses, the organism makes a patterned response in a qualitatively distinct mode of adjustment.

While proponents of these "organismic" doctrines have derived much comfort from such studies as those of Gelb and Goldstein and Head, the students of nerve conduction, of transmission across the synapse, of facilitation and inhibition, and of the effects of degeneration of pathways, have in general gone on their way, finding out more and more in detail what the biophysics and the biochemistry of the elementary processes appear to be. With an occasional gesture toward recognition of the organismic issues, those who have preferred to prosecute research through the traditional analytic procedure have continued for the most part deaf to the newer emphasis; while those who have espoused the new approach have tended to

---

[12] Wertheimer's original study of the perception of motion (page 287) emphasized the inadequacy of the conception of point-for-point localization within the cerebral cortex—not only the conception that an association depends upon the communication of impulses from one point to another, but even the conception that there is a constant relation between a given punctiform excitation in the cortex and a given elementary mode of experience. Wertheimer himself had used the phrase "cross processes" to describe modes of functional interconnection which were themselves the primordial bases for experiences not further reducible. In other words, instead of the specific energies of cortical spots (page 94), one had to begin to think of the functional importance of modes of cortical activity conceived in larger patterns.

push aside the material gathered within the analytical frame of reference. There have been rather few who have recognized that stubborn facts are available in large quantity from both types of investigations; [13] and that not merely a philosophy of the organism, but even a very modest research approach to the problem of drive, learning, perception, and thinking must take into account the various types of empirical evidence offered. A homely example is the fact that the man under local anesthesia whose brain is being operated upon can very roughly define the type of experience elicited by electrical stimulation of the "general sense" areas (page 375); he can state whether warmth, cold, touch, or pain is involved. This would seem to give support to the traditional theory of specific energies. In the same breath, however, one must add that the patient's reports are vague; they are not like reports on warmth, cold, touch, and pain which he would give if he were delicately using the finger tips. Moreover, not quite the same report is given on successive stimulations of the same point; and furthermore, there is abundant evidence that he is *interpreting* or giving meaning to raw sensory material, perhaps in the manner in which a person born blind and for the first time (through surgical aid) capable of seeing does something more than baldly describe raw sensory material. Such patients have various perceptual habits which have developed in terms of the use of the other senses; and when they are first given the sense of sight they give to the impressions received some degree of meaning based on such earlier experiences. These experiences with electrical excitations of the brain can just as well be used to support an organismic conception. They cannot, of course, be used to support any theory of equipotentiality of the cortex; but they point up the fact that one utilizes all that one has. One comes to terms, as well as one can, with the meaning which a stimulus has for one. These two schools of thought derive equal comfort from such observations, and neither seems to learn very much from the other.

[13] An example of the integration of the two approaches appears in the work of Paul Weiss: *Principles of Development* (1939); "Autonomous versus Reflexogenous Activity of the Central Nervous System," *Proc. Amer. Philos. Soc.*, 1941, 84, 53–64; Weiss is equally attentive to biological detail and to field principles. In connection with problems of specific energies (page 94) in nerve cell and muscle, he suggests for example a "resonance theory." As C. T. Morgan summarizes it: "A muscle has a specific functional property. It induces the nerve associated with it to take on a similar functional property and thus to be in 'resonance' with it. This specific property of the nerve fibre acts in the central nervous system to 'select' nervous impulses 'intended' for the muscle in question and to let others go by."—*Physiological Psychology* (1943), p. 135. But we cannot embark here upon a survey of neurophysiology.

The same difficulty in making themselves intelligible to one another occurs in connection with functional shifts in the brain centers for activity, of the sort quoted above from Lashley's work with the monkey. If the extirpation of the region is followed within a short time by the reappearance of the old activity through the utilization of a new functional center, or through the development of a rather unimportant secondary center to a position of central importance, this fact may be used by the atomist to bring out the highly specific localization of each cortical process; for without a center, the activity cannot be set going. At the same time, one may plead equally well that the law of the organism takes priority over the law of any of the parts, and that what fails in local or short-range terms may succeed in long-range terms. The issue is so fundamental that we shall return to it, and reflect on it further, in the concluding chapter (pages 444–45).

But before leaving the central nervous system, two other important tools of research require emphasis: the electroencephalogram and mathematical biophysics. It became possible during the twenties to attach electrodes to the scalp in such a way that the rapid changes in voltage between such points could be magnified and recorded, and these records have already contributed a great deal both to the specific local physiology of the cortex during states of concentration, relaxation, sleep, and so on and to the more formal understanding of patterning of many concurrent events through the cortex as a whole.[14] In the meantime Rashevsky and others have defined ways of stating mathematically the overall functioning of the brain in perception, learning, thinking, and so on in the form of hypotheses to be tested by recourse to present—and future—experiments.[15]

THE AUTONOMIC NERVOUS SYSTEM

Physiological psychology was at first chiefly concerned with the central nervous system. But two factors were destined to extend the field in short order. The first had to do with the discovery of the functions of the autonomic nervous system; and the second, with the investigation of the behavior significance of the endocrine glands. The autonomic nervous system, recognized during the nineteenth century as a series of ganglia and fibers not enjoying the pro-

[14] Cf. Lindsley, D. B., "Electroencephalography," Hunt, J. McV., *Personality and the Behavior Disorders*, 2 vols., (1944); Vol. II, pp. 1033–1103.

[15] Rashevsky, N., "Outline of a Physico-Mathematical Theory of the Brain," *J. Gen. Psychol.*, 1945, 3, 82–112.

tection of vertebrae and skull which was offered to the central nervous system, represented seemingly unimportant masses of tissue which might be related to the distribution of the blood, and to other vegetative activities. Late in the nineteenth century, however, studies of fear (page 172) began to suggest that the autonomic nervous system is important through its activation of unstriped muscles and glands, and that a great deal of the visceral activity to which the James-Lange theory and other theories of emotion pointed could be understood only by a systematic study of this autonomic system.

In the second decade of the present century, Walter Cannon drew attention to the role of the autonomic nervous system and the endocrine glands in the life of the emotions and in the process of adapting to stress and danger.[16] The effects upon psychology and psychiatry were rapid and profound. E. J. Kempf, in 1918, called attention to the fact that incoming impulses from the vital organs set going many of those strivings to which the term "personality" is applied, and that a peripheral rather than a central view of the seat of personality was therefore warranted.[17] Dozens of specific problems in normal and pathological material began to be defined as one asked specifically how the autonomic nervous system functioned in cases of emotional imbalance, in the gradual change from childish to adult modes of emotional integration, and in the effects of disease in causing prolonged personality disorder—in cases, for example, of injury to the basal ganglia, as by epidemic encephalitis. The question arose how far one could explain alterations of temperament by referring strictly to central-nervous-system activities without reference to the disturbance of autonomic function. Even in the classical studies reported by Head of emotional change after brain-stem injuries, the psychiatrists and the psychologists began to ask whether these effects were not at least in some measure due to resulting disturbance in autonomic function.

A tug of war developed between those who wished to assign a larger and larger role to the autonomic system in the production of those phenomena which we label feeling and emotion and those, on the other hand, who were still content to think of feeling and emotion, and indeed of all forms of consciousness, as directly dependent upon central-nervous-system activity. A very obvious compromise view was, of course, espoused by many; namely, the view that it is when the disturbance within the autonomic system has directly or

---

[16] *Bodily Changes in Pain, Hunger, Fear and Rage* (1915).
[17] Kempf, E. J., *The Autonomic Functions and the Personality* (1918).

indirectly given rise to cortical changes that consciousness is affected. But in spite of such compromises, the practical question of the degree of importance of the autonomic system for the understanding of the affective life remained; and it is no exaggeration to say that the study of the emotions by psychiatrists and psychologists has been to an extraordinary degree the study of the known or presumed functions of the autonomic system. It is not only the advanced graduate student, but the beginner as well, who is shown diagrams of the autonomic nervous system, is carefully introduced to the distinction between the sympathetic system involved in rage, fear, and pain and the parasympathetic system, involved primarily in vegetative activities.

This shift of emphasis was due more to Cannon than to any other individual. Indeed, his volume *Bodily Changes in Pain, Hunger, Fear and Rage*, appearing in 1915, revolutionized the whole attitude toward the emotions, turning the attention of psychologists to certain physiological conceptions which might bring order out of chaos, both in their own research and in their clarification of problems for their students. Aside from the studies of hunger, which had been published in 1911, the volume dealt essentially with the role of the autonomic nervous system and of the adrenal glands in mobilizing the body for struggle. Take, for example, the cat lying placidly digesting her dinner. The barking dog brought near leads to the cat's spitting, bristling, and arching her back, while physiological instruments show the increase in blood pressure, in blood sugar, reduction of coagulation time of the blood, and other indices of marked increase of activity in the adrenal glands. These activities put the organism "on a war footing." They are conceived basically to be functions of the sympathetic division of the autonomic system, and the sympathetic division may therefore be regarded as fundamental in emotions—that is, when the term "emotion" is restricted to the struggle or emergency type of behavior.

But instead of drawing conclusions involving a "peripheral" view of emotion, Cannon emphasized the initiating role played by the central nervous system in the rage experience, and by implication in the other emergency reactions. He showed, for example, that the excitation of parts of the brain stem appeared to give rise to ragelike behavior, and he argued that the outgoing and glandular effects simply followed in the train of this activity in the central nervous system. Similarly, his pupil Bard, on the basis of extirpation experiments, assigned the center for rage to the hypothalamus. In other experiments. Cannon surgically separated the sympathetic nervous system from the rest of the functioning animal, and found that while the activities of the animal were somewhat impaired, this cutting-off of impulses innervating the viscera in no way interfered with its capacity for the rage responses. Taking the James-Lange position, then, as the classical *peripheralist* position, Cannon and Bard strongly upheld a *centralist* view—the view that if one knows what is happening in the central nervous system, one has the key to the phenomena of rage, the autonomic effects being chronologically and logically secondary.[18]

It is true that Masserman,[19] Arnold,[20] and others have given grave reasons for doubting Cannon's localization of the emotions. The fact remains, however, that the interest of twentieth-century psychologists in the autonomic system and its relation to the endocrine glands is still largely formulated in Cannon's terms.

The endocrine glands were anatomical curiosities for medical men, not the seat of known physiological functions, until about the middle of the nineteenth century. In 1855, Addison described the clinical picture of tuberculosis of the adrenal glands, and several other well-defined clinical descriptions became available in subsequent decades. But just what the glands do and how they are interrelated continued a mystery. For example, even though various types of goiter had been known throughout the history of Western medicine, the physiological role of the thyroid remained unknown. Just before the turn of the century, the clinical consequences of thyroid defect, with some suggestions regarding thyroid therapy, were pointed out; and in 1914 Kendall attained chemical isolation of thyroxin, a major constituent in the thyroid secretion. These stages, through the anatomical, through the clinical, to the biochemical can be roughly traced in regard to each of the endocrine glands. Most of this is entirely outside of the scope of a volume such as the present one, but the point should be stressed that the development of biochemistry was the thing chiefly wanting before any reasonably complete definition of endocrine functions could be undertaken.

After World War I rapid strides were made in endocrinology. Unfortunately, there appeared a series of rather exaggerated and

[18] Bard, P., "Emotion I: The Neuro-humeral Basis of Emotional Reactions," in Murchison, C. A., ed., *Handbook of General Experimental Psychology* (1934), pp. 264–311.

[19] Masserman, J. H., *Behavior and Neurosis* (1943).

[20] Arnold, M. B., "Physiological Differentiation of Emotional States," *Psychol. Rev.*, 1945, 52, 35–48.

overimaginative studies of the endocrines, some of which were in popular form. They were well described by H. E. Starr as "certain manuals of information and misinformation which enable the laity to diagnose glandular imbalance with the finality of a palmist or a phrenologist." It was in this form that the psychologist had to cope with the problem. Often he played up the Cannon findings on the adrenals and the newer knowledge of the role of thyroxin in the stimulation of the growth of the central nervous system, with perhaps a few vague remarks about the relation of glands to the process of sexual maturing. Often, however, he was tempted to leave the whole problem out of account, as consisting of a mixture of wild guesses and sheer charlatanism. This latter attitude was, in fact, so widespread that the inclusion of endocrinology within the sphere of physiological psychology was long delayed. One may glance, even now, through the contemporary treatises on the subject of physiological psychology and be amazed to see the scant treatment given to such very fundamental problems as the interrelations between the various glands which are responsible for general and for sexual growth and differentiation.

PSYCHOSOMATICS

Contemporary physiological psychology can no longer be sketched in terms of the nineteenth-century framework, in which one begins with physiological explanatory principles and works from these to specific psychological events which are to be explained. Physiological psychology used to be a one-way street from the physical to the mental. Sometimes one espoused psychophysical parallelism, body and mind being two aspects of the same reality. Sometimes mental phenomena were conceived as "epiphenomena"—shadows, ghosts, or phosphorescent emanations derived from, but not reacting upon, their physiological bases. A completely new conception began to be well defined in the third decade of the present century: the conception that the storm and stress, the wear and tear, of life's difficulties involve physiological derangement which may, under certain conditions, lead to visible anatomical or histological damage. This is the conception of psychosomatic medicine, a conception heralded in a number of papers by psychoanalysts in the early twenties, and reaching such vast proportions by the thirties as to warrant a compilation by Flanders Dunbar, including hundreds of references.[21]

---

[21] Dunbar, H. F., *Emotions and Bodily Changes* (1935).

Her volume was followed just before World War II by the appearance of a journal: *Psychosomatic Medicine.*

Many of the modern studies still seem derived from a tendency to think in terms of one-way streets—this time, however, from the "mental" to the "physical." But there are also numerous instances in which the psychiatrist has been able to conceive his problem in "circular" terms, noting an initial weakness or predisposition due to genetic or early disease factors, which predispose the individual to one or another type of strain, worry, or other personality difficulty, these finally causing "organic" (that is, visible) damage. Such damage, in turn, has been at times conceived as the basis for the elaboration and accentuation of the emotional or other disorder, which would have been less serious in a context of organic health.

Finally, some of the analysts have brought to bear the full weight of Freudian theory in indicating that a specific region, especially a diseased or an injured region, may be invested with libido, and may in consequence involve, through its ill-health, continuous ill-health at the mental level. Through the unconscious interplay of attitudes with reference to this region or organ, there may be "feed-back" into the patient's mental life of various sensory impressions which are too intense to be taken in one's stride, or which give rise to two or more conflicting types of impulses. Physiological psychology becomes, in such a context, the study of systems of physiological responses, of which some are reflected in consciousness, others not. But with all that, psychosomatic medicine continues to study action "from mind to body" rather than "from body to mind."

An example of the rearrangement of horse and cart which typifies the main effort of psychosomatic medicine lies in the studies of those endocrine disorders in which a psychic shock or conflict precedes an endocrine dysfunction. Before World War I, it was general practice to derive various personality deviations from endocrine deviations. Graves's disease (toxic hyperthyroidism), for example, gave rise to apprehensiveness and restlessness. More and more clearly it has emerged from clinical data that in most such cases there is a long period of manifest apprehensiveness and restlessness before the onset of hyperthyroidism. Another example appears in the multitudinous current studies of gastric ulcer of various sorts. In one series of studies, as typified in the work of Carl Binger and his collaborators,[22] a long struggle in childhood and adolescence to break away from parental

[22] Binger, C. A. L., Ackerman, N. W., Cohn, A. E., Schroeder, H. A., and Steele, J. M., *Personality in Arterial Hypertension, Psychosom. Med. Monogr.*, 1945, No. 8.

domination, together with terror lest one should actually make a sharp break with one's parents, gives rise at the crisis point to a marked elevation in blood pressure, becoming chronic in the form of arterial hypertension. Some types of gastric ulcers likewise often appear to arise from prolonged unconscious struggle in relation to the process of eating. The overdependent child, for example, who would like to eat in and out of season, may develop chronic rubbing of the stomach walls against one another—a type of activity fundamentally different from normal peristaltic action.[23] In one case studied by Wolff and collaborators, an exposed stomach wall was studied hour by hour in relation to the emotional shocks of the individual patient, who remained ambulatory and available for constant observation.[24] The actual hyperacidity, hypermotility, and hyperemia which regularly accompany a condition predisposing to ulceration was observed, and it became possible not only clinically but also experimentally to demonstrate that this ulcerative process was controllable from control of the emotional life.

One might expect from such studies a renewed effort at some sort of rational formulation of functional mind-body interdependence, if not some more high-flying philosophical solution of the mind-body problem. Actually, however, no such happy consummation can be noted. We continue to have our parallelisms, interactionisms, and so on. To be sure, there is a great deal of insistence about the unity of the organism. But having verbally created the unity, one says that the psychogenic condition *causes* the organic damage, or vice versa; or one says that in view of the unity of the organism as a whole, one must see how psychic processes *reflect* physical processes. Nothing much really seems to be going on by way of an attempt at a clean formulation of how there can be such a thing as a mind in relation to a body, or how there can be a body in relation to a mind. In view of the fact that profound efforts to get a respectable and well-ordered philosophy of mind-body relations go back as far as Spinoza, and that philosophers with the necessary technical training in epistemology have done a good deal of serious work in recent decades, it is a bit sad that neither the psychiatrists nor the psychologists have taken time off to take note of what has been said.

Probably the most serious of strictly contemporary efforts to cope with the mind-body problem are those of the Gestaltists, using the

[23] Alexander, F. "The Influence of Psychologic Factors upon Gastro-intestinal Disturbances: A Symposium," *Psychoanal. Quar.*, 1934, 3, 501–39.

[24] Wolff, H. G., "Disturbances of Gastrointestinal Function in Relation to Personality Disorders," *Ann. N. Y. Acad. Sci.*, 1943, 44, 567–68.

conception of isomorphism.[25] Here the mental and the physical, though not treated as one and the same event, are treated as events having the same structure or form. Thus, in the study of visual perception one might find that the space-time pattern which we subjectively experience has exactly the same structure as the space-time pattern which emerges from a study of the physics of retina and brain. We can actually predict in some degree the nature of visual illusions by knowing the distribution of bodily electric currents. Some success has attended such efforts; in some measure a new unity of mind and body—and that of a quantitative sort—is being discovered. The main task, however, is that of a coherent theory as to "the mind and its place in nature," and this remains about where it has remained for the last few hundred years. Most psychologists appear to feel that the problem is inaccessible to science, or at least to the science of today.

REFERENCES

Cannon, Walter B., *Bodily Changes in Pain, Hunger, Fear and Rage*, Appleton, 1915

Dunbar, Helen Flanders, *Emotions and Bodily Changes*, 2nd ed., Columbia University Press, 1938

Goldstein, Kurt, *The Organism*, American Book Company, 1939

Halstead, Ward C., *Brain and Intelligence: A Quantitative Study of the Frontal Lobes*, University of Chicago Press, 1947

Lashley, Karl S., *Brain Mechanisms and Intelligence*, University of Chicago Press, 1929

———, "Coalescence of Neurology and Psychology," *Proc. Amer. Philos. Soc.*, 1941, 84, 461–70

Morgan, Clifford T., *Physiological Psychology*, McGraw-Hill, 1943

Murchison, Carl A., ed., *A Handbook of General Experimental Psychology*, Clark University Press, 1934

[25] Köhler, W., *Dynamics in Psychology* (1935).

Chapter 26

CHILD PSYCHOLOGY

At every period of human civilization, we find care, education and instruction of the child . . . now we suddenly discover beside what deep mysteries and riddles we have wandered blind and deaf for thousands of years.　　　WILLIAM STERN

THERE were scattered evidences during the seventeenth and eighteenth centuries that children were coming into their rights as individuals, as something more than unfinished men and women. Comenius published a children's picture book. Children's stories and verses, such as *Mother Goose*, began to appear. Rousseau's delight in the natural, the free, the spontaneous, meant new interest in what children did. Late in the eighteenth century Tiedemann published some biographical observations of childhood growth.[1] Pestalozzi, pioneer of progressive education (page 53), had kept a three-weeks record of the behavior of his little son. The conception that education must be founded on the study of child psychology took shape in Froebel and Herbart; and much the same spirit was evident in the work for the mentally handicapped (page 130). When the evolutionary movement and experimental physiology began to bring their forces to bear, child psychology came into its own. The evolutionary theory added markedly to the interest in children as children, for one could see in individual growth a great deal that showed the nature of life processes and their tendency to move ever toward the more complex; and it was no accident that Darwin himself was one of the first to take systematic notes on the day-by-day development of a child.[2]

The beginnings of systematic and serious child psychology date

[1] *Beobachtungen über die Entwicklung der Seelenfähigkeiten bei Kindern* (1787).

[2] Darwin, C. R., "A Biographical Sketch of an Infant," *Mind*, 2, 877. See also Taine, H. A., *Philos. Rev.*, 1876, 1.

from the work of Preyer in Germany.[3] Preyer studied, among other things, the tendency to imitate, and the earliest expressive functions. Children were sometimes included among the experimental subjects at the Leipzig laboratory. But above all it was Stanley Hall who made child psychology a field for a new international enthusiasm. In 1891 he founded the *Pedagogical Seminary*, a magazine devoted to the study of children, and in his gathering of observations on children's ideas, attitudes, and personalities a body of systematized information began to appear to show what children were like. "Evolutionary" this work certainly was, with a vengeance, for it not only used Darwinian conceptions, but when necessary forced them into the data. It found, for example, in the recapitulation theory—the theory that the individual recapitulates the history of the race—an explanation of the "big-injun" war parties which often characterize the play of preadolescent American children. Evolutionary likewise was his vivid and systematic study of physical growth, and his effort to explain the psychology of adolescence and early adulthood as consummations deriving from organic changes within the body.[4]

If one compares Hall's studies of religious conversion, defined in terms of the organic needs of the growing individual, with the highly competent studies of comparative religion going on in the same era, one realizes the extraordinary one-sidedness (the neglect of human culture) of even the best evolutionism of the period. Though there was ethnological evidence which showed the variability of human experiences over the face of the globe, the biological view nevertheless attempted to show why religion among ourselves must for physiological reasons take a particular form, with practically no awareness that two aspects of the same biosocial reality were being studied. Hall's approach to adolescence represents, therefore, both the strongest and the weakest of what the evolutionary science of his era had to offer.

Continuing to act as the chief mentor of the new interest, Hall met at the Chicago World's Fair in 1893 a number of visiting psychologists from Europe, among whom he stimulated a vivid interest in the prosecution of researches in this area. British, French, and German studies began rapidly to show his great influence.

A movement of international importance followed directly. Two years later, Sully, founder of the new British Association for Child Study, published his widely popular *Studies of Childhood*. A similar

[3] Preyer, W. T., *The Mind of the Child* (1881).
[4] Hall, G. S., *Adolescence*, 2 vols. (1910).

organization for child study was shortly formed in Paris, and kindred organizations were established in several other cities of France. Binet's studies of the thought processes of his children (page 229) were carried out shortly thereafter, and in 1904 he began to devise those intelligence tests (page 354) for "young children" from which such a vast quantity of research in the psychology of both children and adults has followed. In Germany the movement took more precisely an educational form, in close connection with the school system. Emphasis was placed upon classroom experimentation. One of the leaders was Meumann,[5] whose use of mental tests in the schools stimulated much subsequent research. The child-study movement rapidly spread to the Scandinavian countries, to Belgium and the Netherlands. In Italy the movement found its way already prepared by years of excellent medical and biological study of the child,[6] while in Switzerland, always eminent in educational contributions, the expressly psychological features of the movement were welcomed. In the United States attention was given especially to the study of the learning process and to the measurement of the various attainments of the schoolchild (for example, spelling, reading, handwriting).

Studies of learning, of practice and fatigue, of the optimum conditions for work, and, above all, of individual differences, transformed the nature of the relations between psychology and education. A comparison of Bain's *Education as a Science* (1878) with Claparède's *Experimental Pedagogy* (1905), and Thorndike's *Educational Psychology* (1913–14), shows at a glance the advent of a new discipline, an "educational psychology" the literature of which is too vast for any sort of summary here.

Shortly thereafter, two excellent studies involving day-by-day records of children appeared. Millicent Shinn's *The Biography of a Baby* instantly became, and remains, a great landmark of simple, faithful, well-proportioned observations of a child's growth,[7] in which even a considerable amount of Victorian sentimentality regarding the opening of the little mind and so on cannot blind the reader to the solid workmanship and faithful regard for realities which attended the observation of the child through the first year of life.

[5] *Zschr. f. exp. Pädagog.*, 1905. His *Haus- und Schularbeit* (1914) included pioneer studies in the influence of the classroom situation upon the child's capacity for study.

[6] Melzi, De Sanctis, and Ferrari were among the leading spirits in this movement, about the turn of the century. Marro's *La pubertá* was published in 1897.

[7] *The Biography of a Baby* (1900) is a popular abbreviation of her *Notes on the Development of a Child*, Univ. Calif. Stud., 1893.

K. C. Moore did a scholarly study in the same era,[8] which helped a good deal toward the development of an objective classification of types of childhood activity.

From these new marks of interest in child psychology came great comfort and aid to the "progressive-education" movement, launched by John Dewey at the turn of the century. Child psychology was to give rich factual material on the emotional, impulsive, and intellectual attributes of children, which would aid the democratic processes in the schools, and would permit the individualizing of the school tasks, so that fulfillment rather than frustration would arise in the process of learning. Tasks were to be geared to an actual knowledge of what the child was ready for, and wanted to do, at each period in his development. At the same time there followed from the new interest the impulse to measure objectively whatever was going on; to measure intellectual levels, types of fatigue, and the like, progress in schoolwork, the role of rest and play periods, and all those conditions with which the scientific-minded teacher and school superintendent must cope. As has been noted, the development of objective tests of intelligence and aptitude was well under way, but the launching of a formal child psychology did much to hasten the process.

Likewise in the same era began the intensive effort to be of service to maladjusted children through the inauguration of studies of individual children in terms of discrepancies between their potential abilities and the level at which they were expected to work. In 1896 Witmer established at the University of Pennsylvania the first "psychological clinic." Witmer's aim was primarily to study individual children, to discover what obstacles lay in their paths, and to help them find a way. Though he made use of such limited intelligence tests as already existed (notably form boards), the emphasis was on the biographical approach. The development of tests of all sorts inevitably became, however, a larger and larger part of the clinician's task. William Healy took a leading role both in the development of new performance tests, which could be used in cases where a verbal test would be difficult to administer, and in showing the ways in which the clinician must integrate a testing program with his biographical and medical studies of the child. Child psychology, owing to such labors as these, was tending by about 1915 to become a system of devices for throwing into relief the difficulties a child might have with reading, with arithmetic, or

[8] *The Mental Development of a Child, Psychol. Rev., Monogr. Suppl.*, 1896, 1 (whole No. 3).

even with paying attention, or with getting on with people. Research in the field of child psychology had a place also for studies in pure or general psychology—for example, in comparing memory span or learning in children with that found in adults—but problems of individual adaptation were primary.

The scene shifted dramatically when, in 1916, J. B. Watson, whose behaviorism was almost at its zenith, was given a small sum at the Phipps Clinic in Baltimore to study the behavior of the normal new-born infant. As was noted earlier, these studies dealt with the question of innate behavior, and also with the process of conditioning. Important as they were in calling attention to the behaviorist research program, they were also of the greatest possible importance in directing attention to the possibility of a scientific study of the "human young." The "mental-hygiene" movement, centered largely in children's needs, was likewise just getting into high gear. Experimental studies of children were soon drawing widespread support from foundations and universities. Institutes of Child Welfare were soon flourishing at many American universities; and by sheer force of manpower, equipment, and money for research, they gave child psychology an "objective" or "behavioral" emphasis from which it has hardly as yet recovered. One may, for example, compare the enormous quantities of objective and scientific data on human growth, development, and learning achieved in the United States in the last twenty-five years with the investigations characterizing the work of the University of Hamburg and the University of Geneva, where, respectively, William Stern and Jean Piaget defined their new approaches. Even at the zenith of their scientific contributions, neither Stern nor Piaget had a staff comparable in size with that of one American Institute of Child Welfare. In reference, therefore, to the work of the last quarter-century, we shall have to think in terms of geographical differences, glancing first at European work, then at American.

For while research in child psychology in the United States took predominantly the direction of behavior study, with emphasis upon growth and development, upon quantitative studies of the learning processes in childhood, and upon adaptation to home and school situations, European lines of research continued to be guided in large part by preoccupation with the great traditional questions about the mind of the child, such as had characterized the work of Pestalozzi and Preyer. Just as Stern in the opening years of the century sought to introduce us to the world in which the child lived—the picture of the world as the child sketches it—so the greatest investigators in Britain and on the Continent have continued to be concerned in more recent decades with the evolution of the child's own outlook, the development of his own perspective.

At Vienna, where Karl Bühler had for years been known as a contributor to the theory of intellectual development, Charlotte Bühler began in the mid-twenties a series of long-range experimental studies of infant and child psychology.[9] What does the little child see, or hear; how rapidly and in what ways can he learn to differentiate between faces and voices? How does he express a relation of ascendancy or submission to other children? Together with this experimental child psychology went the development of intelligence tests and a sociological study of the preschool child and the child of school age. Vienna became one of the great research and training centers in child psychology.

PIAGET

Also typical of modern leadership in such investigations is Jean Piaget, of the University of Geneva.[10] Having at his command the facilities of the Institut Jean-Jacques Rousseau, he began to systematize the methods of observing children at play, contriving experiments for the solution of key questions and, above all, developing the clinical interview as a semistandardized device for testing children between the ages of two and fourteen with respect to their ways of envisaging the world around them. With a constantly changing staff of coworkers, he has published from 1923 to the present no less than nine volumes containing the rich harvest of these interviews and experiments.

The key concept which runs through all this material appears in the first of these volumes, *The Language and Thought of the Child*. This is the concept of *egocentrism*. The child develops only very slowly awareness of self; until he perceives himself as distinct from the environment he cannot recognize the subjectivity of his own outlook. Things *are* as they seem to be. To this acceptance of one's own viewpoint as conveying absolute reality the term "realism" is applied. The two concepts may be illustrated by reference to a little experiment in which small children are individually placed near a table upon which stands a huge relief map of the Alps. Around the walls of the room are photographs showing how the Alps would look

[9] *Kindheit und Jugend* (1928).
[10] *The Language and Thought of the Child* (1923); *The Child's Conception of the World* (1929); *The Moral Judgment of the Child* (1932).

to observers stationed at different points on the mountain trails. Doll figures are placed here and there in the mountains, and the child is asked to indicate how the mountains would look to the doll as it is placed here or there. The small child reports that the mountains would look as they do to him as he is standing beside the table. There is just one way in which the mountains *can* look, and that is the way in which they look to me.

From such egocentrism and realism follows a third conception: that of *participation*, in which one fails so completely to distinguish oneself from that which is external that one attributes life, mind, and purpose to all that one encounters. As one rides one's bicycle, the distinction between one's thought of the tires and the actual tires themselves is so vague and blurred that one dare not think of them as punctured, lest the puncture automatically occur. Childish magic and the ceremonial control of distant or future events are explained in terms of this quality of participation. This is, of course, analogous to Freud's conception of the omnipotence of thought (page 316); but it occurs for Piaget not by virtue of Freudian dynamic principles, but because a differentiation between self and not-self has not as yet occurred.

Practically the whole panorama of intellectual development in the small child is viewed by Piaget in terms of the gradual emancipation of the individual from the egocentric mode of thought. In the use of language, in the understanding of the forces of nature, and in terms of his first grappling with such psychological concepts as those of the dream, or the meaning of words, or the bases of moral judgment, the problem is always to trace the nature of the initial egocentrism and the specific ways in which egocentrism is outgrown a step at a time. The dream, for instance, permits the clear differentiation of a series of stages, beginning with one in which the dream, as a physical entity, comes in through the window and lies down on the bed beside the child; through various stages of semiphysical existence in which the dream still occupies space; then on to a final stage in which the dream is a process carried out by oneself.

Emphasis is placed in Piaget's *The Child's Conception of the World* upon the tendency to find analogies between oneself and the forces of nature, analogies which lie in the impossibility of dissociating oneself from the world. By virtue of egocentrism, the child finds that the cold wind which beats in his face is hostile, while the warm sun is generous. In the same way, the tree is sorry when the warm sun sets, and the rivers rejoice when the ice melts and sets them free in the spring. From this *animistic* tendency, similar to the animistic tendenues of primitive peoples, there is slow and arduous emancipation. To the small child, anything that moves has life. Later, there must be movement that is self-initiated, and finally, there must be activity that is purposive.

In many ways, the greatest stroke of genius in Piaget's work has to do with his primary venture into social psychology, *The Moral Judgment of the Child*. This investigation, influenced by the French sociological studies of ethics, is a systematic effort to define the stages through which judgments of right and wrong pass in a child from about two to about fourteen. Piaget begins by studying "the rules of the game." He becomes expert in the children's chosen games, learning how to make a good shot at marbles and a duffer shot. He wants chiefly to find out what is regarded by the child as a *fair* or an *unfair* thing.

We may illustrate the stages he discovered in the evolution of moral judgment by the following scheme: The little child of two or three tosses the marbles with great delight; his pleasure derives from sheer physical functioning. If asked at the end who has won, he says, "I won and John won and we all won." Competitive standards and man-made rules are not as yet clear. At four or five years, the fact of rules begins to be understood. You must draw a square of given proportions, you must stand outside it, you must pitch one marble at a time, and if your own marble, instead of hitting and displacing your opponent's marble, goes out of bounds, you have lost. Rules here are absolutely sacred. No one could possibly change them. (When the boys in Geneva are told that the boys over in Neufchâtel play differently, the only reply is "Those guys over there never did understand marbles anyway!" We have then, as Lerner remarked, egocentrism at the social level, or *sociocentrism*.)

At seven or eight the rigidity of these rules begins to give way. It is now permissible to alter the size of the square, or even to step on the line, provided all contenders follow the same rules. We have left the area of "moral realism," in which the moral world is a rigid, external structure, and have entered the area of reciprocity, where social relationships are the basis of lawmaking. Finally, beyond such reciprocity comes a stage in the preadolescent period in which more subtle personality factors become matters of weight. The nearsighted boy may stand nearer than the others, just as in the sand-lot ball game in the United States the crippled boy may bat, though someone else must run the bases for him. Reciprocity, says Piaget, is "colored by considerations of equity." One has achieved *autonomy* in so far as one recognizes the personal meanings and values rather than the sheer objective situations with which one must cope if ethical behavior is to be rationally defined.

No systematic repetition of Piaget's system of inquiries has been undertaken. Here and there an investigation throws some light on the question of the universal validity of his findings. It must be recognized that the terminology has proved to be rather slippery, making repetition difficult. A second difficulty lies in the fact that in so far as the methods are repeatable, they suggest that the age levels reported by Piaget are consistently too high; at least, American children pass a given developmental point much earlier than do the Swiss children. Third, there comes the question whether the stages described by Piaget are truly stages in child development as such, or are primarily stages in the development of children's thinking in response to certain specific cultural processes. Take, for example, the question of animism. Both Swiss and American children are subjected from their earliest years to animistic stories. Sun and wind contend to see which can make a man take off his coat; indeed, even the most objective forces of nature like sun and moon are referred to as "he" and "she," and are sometimes represented with eyes, nose, and mouth. How could children be anything but animistic when exposed to this view of nature? Margaret Mead notes that one of the peoples of the southwest Pacific show no such personifying tendencies.[11] On the other hand, Dennis and his collaborators have reported findings confirmatory of Piaget from American Indian tribes, under conditions which make it doubtful whether exposure to the white man's culture can be the explanation.[12] As matters stand now, the question of the role of biological and cultural factors in determining such stages may be regarded as indeterminate.[13]

THE INFLUENCE OF PSYCHOANALYSIS

We turn now to the influence of psychoanalysis upon child psychology. It will be recalled that Freud's attention had early been directed to neurosis in childhood, and that a theory of infantile sexuality had been formulated even before his celebrated study of the

[11] "An Investigation of the Thought of Primitive Children with Special Reference to Animism," *J. Roy. Anthrop. Inst.*, 1932, 62, 173–90.

[12] See for example, Dennis, W., and Russell, R. W., "Piaget's Questions Applied to Zuni Children," *Child Developm.*, 1940, 11, 181–87.

[13] Piaget has more recently been at work on problems relating to the very earliest phases of child development—the elementary awareness of the infant, the first modes of quantitative thinking, and the like.

phobia of a five-year-old child (page 317). Psychoanalytic studies of children were, however, few and fragmentary until the 1920's. Anna Freud early presented a systematic view of child analysis.[14] Play techniques were initiated by Melanie Klein,[15] David Levy,[16] and others in the 1930's for direct observation of personality dynamics in small children (with action as a substitute for verbalization) within a psychoanalytic frame of reference. By allowing the child to manipulate toys representing father, mother, brother, sister, and self, and by allowing, in a permissive atmosphere, the expression of sexual and other conflicts, it was possible to enrich the psychoanalytic theory of sexual development, and in some measure to test experimentally the adequacy of its formulations. To the late twenties and early thirties belongs Isaacs' stimulating study of the aggressiveness of small children,[17] while Anna Freud went on with systematic studies of the ego and the mechanisms of defense.[18] The psychoanalysis of children became during the thirties a widespread and most fruitful field of investigation.

Even more important for the history of psychology was the merging of psychoanalytic ways of thinking with other approaches to the study of childhood growth, particularly the study of the emotions, dreams, and fantasies of children, whether such studies were pursued as parts of a clinical concern for the mental-hygiene needs of children or as integral parts of research projects. More and more one finds the literature of child psychology peppered with investigations of unconscious dynamics, in which the child rather than the adult is the center of interest. It is hard today to imagine a child psychology devoid of psychoanalytic coloring, for even the most objective of behavior analysis is heavily indebted to psychoanalytic conceptions.

STUDIES OF GROWTH

Despite these European influences, the term "child psychology" has an essentially different meaning to most American psychologists. Shortly after World War I, in consequence of the awakening public interest in child welfare, the availability of foundation support, and the behaviorist movement, large-scale objective studies of child development got under way in the United States. Very characteristic

---

[14] *Einführung in der Technik der Kinderanalyse* (1927).

[15] *The Psychoanalysis of Children* (1932).

[16] Levy, D. M., *Studies in Sibling Rivalry* (1937); *Maternal Overprotection* (1943).

[17] Isaacs, S., *Social Development in Young Children* (1933).

[18] *The Ego and the Mechanism of Defense* (1936).

indeed have been the elaborate studies of the behavior of the new-born conducted at Ohio State University, and the growth studies at the universities of California, Iowa, and Minnesota. A pioneer enterprise, early assuming large proportions, has been the ambitious, long-range research program under Arnold Gesell at Yale, where norms of infant development, follow-up studies of individuals, and detailed analyses of specific behavior sequences (such as the development of the prehension patterns) have been published in large number. These and many other research centers have turned out voluminous data on the earliest emotional and motor responses, and the learning processes, of normal children, especially under the favorable conditions afforded by the rapid development of nursery schools for children from two to four years of age.

The nature-nurture problem has especially interested many child psychologists (cf. page 366). Gesell and Thompson used identical twins as an experimental and a control in stair-climbing and in the grasping of a small cube.[19] McGraw taught one infant twin to roller-skate and to climb a steep slide; his brother remained untrained.[20] Jersild, among others, showed that equal training made dissimilar children even more dissimilar in measurable skills, suggesting the huge role of constitutional capacities.[21] Foster children have been compared with "own" children in their degree of intellectual resemblance to the parents in whose home they were reared, and experience in nursery school and institutions has been brought into relation to IQ changes (page 369). Gifted individuals have been studied in large numbers (cf. Terman and collaborators, page 366); thus L. S. Hollingworth studied a group made up entirely of children of exceptional intelligence. The process of conditioning in childhood (as noted on page 266) has been analyzed in infancy and at other ages, while the psychology of trial-and-error learning, learning by imitation, learning by observation, and so on has attracted as much attention as similar work with adults (page 234 ff.).

All three of the primary areas with which we have been concerned here—behavior study, the study of the child mind, and the study of unconscious childhood conflicts—have tended in recent years to provide a large place for longitudinal (as compared with "cross-

---

[19] Gesell, A. L., and Thompson, H., *Learning and Growth in Identical Infant Twins: An Experimental Study by the Method of Co-twin Control*, Genet. Psychol. Monogr., 1929, 6 (whole No. 1).

[20] McGraw, M. B., *Growth: A Study of Johnny and Jimmy* (1935).

[21] Jersild, A. T., *Training and Growth in the Development of Children: A Study of the Relative Influence of Learning and Maturation*, Child Devel. Monogr., 1932, No. 10.

section") methods. Whereas only a few years ago it was adequate to slice through the behavior or the fantasy life of a few hundred children, with appropriate "samples" at each age level, it has more and more come to be recognized that individual variability in many functions is so complex as to make this approach rather precarious. Characteristic of modern longitudinal approaches is Macfarlane's Guidance Study at the University of California, the Adolescent Growth Study at the same institution, the Cambridge-Somerville Youth Study in the Boston area, the Fels Foundation longitudinal study at Antioch College, and other more modest investigations in which the same individuals are pursued relentlessly through one school and community after another. The Rorschach test (page 423) is applied to a group of children all the way from five or six to sixteen or eighteen, as the Fels study has done; or, on the other hand, the studies take a more complex over-all pattern, the "personality as a whole," and pursue this pattern in all its ramifications year by year in relation to a changing social setting. There is no doubt that such studies are more realistic, less prone to abstraction, than cross-section studies. Whether they will, however, actually reveal laws and principles which are of greater scientific validity (as is hoped on behalf of all the existing methods, including those of Piaget and Freud) remains to be seen. The longitudinal methods are so rich and complex and, it must be admitted, so far from clear in terms of methodological assumptions, that they still have before them the task of defining hypotheses about growth and learning that can be fully validated.

Quite aside, however, from their specific contributions to methodology and to the accumulation of facts, the longitudinal studies have the advantage that they point the way toward the integration of conceptions from biology, social psychology, psychoanalysis, and the general psychology of personality. As we shall see in the discussion of ethnological problems later on, it is only when a full-bodied picture of the individual is provided and then considered longitudinally in terms of the life span that one can really take hold of the problem of integrating the appropriate scientific disciplines.

To talk about interdisciplinary research, or wisely integrating the best from many different scientific fields, has become a very trite and threadbare ideal in recent years; the real question is just *how* such an integration can be used to permit deeper insights and more accurate predictions than could be achieved by the best methods of a single discipline. It is in the longitudinal studies primarily that workers have been forced to check against one another the assumptions from different disciplines, and to work through the grubby problem of integrating a physical examination, a personal interview, a documentary analysis, a testing program, and a series of experimental procedures carried out against the backdrop of family, community, and culture as a whole. Child psychology, as the storm center in which all these forces gather and are observed, represents therefore the best proving-ground for the conception that these disciplines really can be integrated.

REFERENCES

Carmichael, Leonard, ed., *Manual of Child Psychology*, Wiley, 1946

Gesell, Arnold L., and Ilg, F. L., *Infant and Child in the Culture of Today*, Harper, 1943

Jersild, Arthur T., *Child Psychology*, 3rd ed., Prentice-Hall, 1947

Murchison, Carl A., ed., *Handbook of Child Psychology*, rev. ed., Clark University Press, 1933

Piaget, Jean, *The Moral Judgment of the Child*, Harcourt, Brace, 1932

Psychoanalytic Study of the Child, a journal; current volumes

Werner, Heinz, "Genetic Psychology, Experimental," in Harriman, P. L., *Encyclopedia of Psychology*, Philosophical Library, 1946, pp. 219–36

Chapter 27

SOCIAL PSYCHOLOGY

A few strong instincts, and a few plain rules. WORDSWORTH

It is not consciousness that determines life, but life that determines consciousness. MARX

FROM the time of Aristotle until late in the nineteenth century, psychology was a study of individual minds. The problem of group interaction or interpersonal relations was a problem for the historian, the moralist, or the jurist, and—especially during the eighteenth and nineteenth centuries—for the political economist. We saw in the case of Hobbes, Rousseau, and Bentham how theories of individual motivation led into conceptions of the nature of society; but there was no social psychology worthy of the name until the nineteenth century drew near to its close.

The beginnings of social psychology in the modern sense came through the growth of psychiatry, and in particular through the work of the Paris school and the Nancy school—for, as the reader will recall, Charcot had defined the hysterical disposition, and Liébeault the nature of suggestibility, in such a way as to provide a scaffolding for a naturalistic conception of the relations of leaders and followers. It was exactly at this point that Tarde defined the "*laws of imitation*," the first truly modern work in social psychology.[1] It was in these same terms that Sighele defined the "criminal crowd" two years later,[2] and that Le Bon wrote his monumental studies of crowd psychology.[3] A glance through Tarde's work, or that of Le Bon, will make evident how heavily these authors drew upon studies of pathological suggestibility. It was, in other words, the work of the clinic that gave the working conceptions from which the theory of the

[1] Tarde, G., *Les lois de l'imitation* (1890).
[2] Sighele, S., *La coppia criminale* (1893).
[3] Le Bon, G., *The Crowd* (1895).

crowd mind was derived. These theories were of importance chiefly in their contradiction of the classical rationalistic conceptions which underlay not only political economy, but also all of the major theories of social conduct. Even Descartes's "passions" had turned out to be the result of calculations of inherent pleasure and pain in the various possible courses of action. For this reason, there must be added emphasis upon the importance of Darwinism, with its consistent underscoring of blind and impulsive factors in adaptation to the environment. It was in a soil prepared by Darwin that studies of pathological suggestibility led to a nonrationalistic social psychology.

MC DOUGALL

It was in this era of transition that the work of William McDougall took shape. Trained in the Scottish and English schools, he found himself, as a Darwinian, profoundly dissatisfied with all rationalistic assumptions. In later years, he told with some emotion how he had been seated at dinner next to a self-sufficient personage who, in kindness to the younger man, had asked his area of interest. When the personage heard the word "psychology," he commented: "Oh yes! Association of ideas, and all that sort of thing. Very important!" To this McDougall inwardly replied, "Very *unimportant*, he means!" From that time forth he began to muse more actively upon the question of making psychology really important, by getting to the mainsprings of conduct which had so long been forgotten. He would, in other words, become a student of the dynamic and irrational foundations of behavior.

Such foundations he found in the instincts provided through natural selection. There had been, as a matter of fact, in the early days of Darwinism, a series of exquisitely clear inventories of animal instincts, several of which had shown the relation of human instincts to those at a prehuman level. Much theoretical work, however, remained to be done to throw the instinctive or impulsive life into orderly shape. McDougall took hold of an aspect of instinct theory which was as much in need of clarification as was the physiological core of emotion defined by James and Lange (page 198). The two problems—the problem of instinct and the problem of emotions—were to be solved simultaneously, and at the same time the problem of specific strivings toward specific ends, the problem of conation.

The thesis is stated in McDougall's *An Introduction to Social Psychology* in 1908. By a single clear and brilliant stroke, he defined instinct in terms of successions of processes always occurring in a given order. 1. There is an innate tendency to perceive a situation in a given way; there is, for example, an innate tendency of the chick to perceive the hawk's shadow in a specific way. 2. Such perception is followed immediately by an appropriate affective or emotional response—appropriate in the sense that survival is possible only for those in whom such affect follows. We have, then, our chick perceiving the hawk's shadow as a danger sign, and experiencing fear. 3. The experience of fear, classified as an emotion, leads physically on into the impulse to escape; it is only among those who strive to escape that survival is possible.

Natural selection has provided all three of the essential innate tendencies. Each instinct, then, involves a perceptual, an emotional, and a striving aspect, or, in slightly more rigorous language, a cognitive, an affective, and a conative disposition.[4] Every instinct contains, therefore, an emotional core, and every emotion is the core of an instinct. Since man, like all higher animals, has instincts, McDougall had thus laid an instinctive foundation for social life. Social life springs not from suggestibility nor from the association of ideas, nor indeed from any of the phenomena observed at a surface level in the clinic. On the contrary, social life springs from dynamic sources—the instincts with which man is equipped. *An Introduction to Social Psychology* is appropriately a study of the instincts which underlie social behavior.

The instincts, however, are at first rather nonspecific. One may fear many things or be curious about many things. In time, however, the instinctive activities come to be called out more and more consistently in relation to those specific situations which have habitually elicited them. One has become specifically curious about fire, or about the seats of authority in the community in which one lives, and potentially, therefore, one may become a primitive engineer or a primitive politician.[5] For McDougall, however, there are typically two or more instincts focused or canalized in a given direction. One has for one's father both love and fear, and in the authoritarian family the two are so intimately fused that one cannot easily observe the separate components. The term "sentiment" is used by McDougall as the center and core of the habit system of the social individual; for in social development a person has developed fusions

---

[4] Here we have the recurrence of the threefold division of mind; cf. Kant, page 44.

[5] The same conception of progressive narrowing of drives is considered by Janet under the term "canalization" and by Freud under the term "cathexis" (cf. page 319).

of specific instinctive responses in regard to most of the people and institutions around him.

Of special importance, of course, is the sentiment related to the perception of oneself. This system of attitudes toward oneself McDougall calls the *self-regarding sentiment*. It is from this sentiment that organized, continuous membership in the social group chiefly derives. Self-regarding sentiments are the key to those sustained and persistent activities to which we give the term "will," and they are likewise the basis for self-respect and moral order.

Along with the instinctive basis for social behavior and the theory of sentiments, one finds in McDougall an emphasis upon various broad classes of social response to which the terms "suggestion," "imitation," and "sympathy" are given. Here, as heretofore, an attempt is made to find an instinctive basis; for example, suggestion is related to the instinct of self-abasement.

The appearance of McDougall's book marked the beginning of a new era in social psychology; it swept everything before it. About one new edition a year appeared during the following twenty years, and well over a hundred thousand copies were disposed of, largely in college classes. More important, psychologists and social scientists in general came rapidly to accept a dynamic or a Darwinian approach to problems of social behavior. Lists of instincts were coined right and left, for example by Thorndike in *The Original Nature of Man* and by Woodworth in *Dynamic Psychology* (1918). Economists such as Veblen found themselves carried forward by the new tide,[6] and new volumes dealing with World War I and its aftermaths were laden with interpretations of the world predicament in terms of the clash of instincts. To this category belongs Wilfred Trotter's *Instincts of the Herd in Peace and War* (1916). The instinct doctrine became the center of social psychology. As Bernard made clear in 1926,[7] the term "instinct" was applied, more and more loosely, to almost any type of uniformity in human conduct to which some sort of hereditary basis might, with or without evidence, be assigned.

It was into this situation that Dunlap hurled in 1919 the first of the "anti-instinct" bombshells. This was actually a statement indicating that behind all McDougall's views lay a *purposive* definition of instinctive activity. If at the animal or early childhood level impulsive acts occur which can hardly be attributed to a clear purpose, and if a strictly biological view of such impulses be taken, the dissection of human social life into purposive or goal-seeking

---

[6] Veblen, T., *The Instinct of Workmanship* (1916).

[7] Bernard, L. L., *Instinct* (1926).

activities may become an attempt to explain the observable by reference to the unobservable. For a period of nearly ten years thereafter, anti-instinct writings of various types flooded the journals, with more and more emphasis upon the vagueness and the incompleteness of the evidence that this or that type of behavior is actually inborn, and with more and more specific experimental demonstration that animals and children may actually be molded to do a great deal which differs fundamentally from what we ordinarily find them doing. The result was to leave social psychology toward the end of the twenties without any generally accepted theoretical basis, and without any common agreement as to the kinds of entities or principles to which the complexities of social life should be reduced. At the same time, however, two movements were serving to bring into relief alternative conceptions of human nature, and a series of new devices for the gathering of authentic information. The latter, consisting of a revision in the *methods* of social psychology, are simpler and may be considered first.

THE RISE OF EXPERIMENTAL METHOD

Just before the outbreak of World War I, Walther Moede had written an extraordinary little pamphlet on "experimental group psychology." In it he suggested that groups be constituted in various ways for laboratory investigation, with appropriate variables under control, so that the effects of group membership upon thinking, feeling, and action might be sharply defined. He began some investigations, which were inevitably delayed, and which did not actually appear in published form until 1920.[8] These investigations dealt with the influence of group membership upon various types of intellectual operations, such as association and imagination, in a group of boys and young adults. Unwitting imitation of what was being done by others and unwitting response to the quantity and quality of work being done by others were systematically studied. He showed, for example, that in his experimental situation the individual in the group thought of words in the chain-association reaction more rapidly than he did when alone. He came also to problems of full-fledged competition, as, for instance, the influence of competition between teams as compared with the influence of competition between single individuals.

These investigations were known to Hugo Münsterberg at Harvard, who had himself carried out a few years earlier a pioneer study

[8] *Experimentelle Massenpsychologie* (1920).

showing that individuals in the classroom influence one another in reporting upon an objective situation, such as the number of dots appearing on a screen. Under the influence of Münsterberg, and through him, of Moede, F. H. Allport began at Harvard and continued elsewhere an extraordinarily fruitful series of investigations on the influence of the group upon the individual.[9] He showed, for example, as had Moede, that one associates more rapidly in the group—"social facilitation"—but he was also able to show that when the quality of a more complex reasoning process is investigated, group membership seems in general to depress quality while adding to quantity. He also investigated the problem whether membership in the group tends to force individuals into more central and less extreme judgments. There are likewise in Allport's work a series of studies of individual reaction to facial expressions shown in photographs, and the ways in which the individual learns to interpret such expressions.

Systematic experimental work in social psychology was thus definitely launched. It is true that highly competent investigations of a strictly experimental type had already been carried out—for example, by H. T. Moore, in gauging the relative effect of expert opinion and majority opinion upon the moral and aesthetic judgments of students.[10] The fact remains, however, that such investigations had been sporadic and without much influence until Allport brought together a group of interrelated experiments and showed the revolutionary implications of the experimental method for the study of group behavior. His *Social Psychology* (1924), in which these experimental methods and their results were for the first time made generally available, is full of clear and practical implications for broader problems. The investigations of the quantitative gain and qualitative loss of work in the presence of others are, for example, defined in such fashion that individualistic implications for education are drawn.

Allport's experimental methods have been emphasized first in order to make clear that there was something decidedly new, exciting, and interesting to take the place of the rather formal, schematic outlines which had been laid down earlier. For Allport himself, however, there were two other notes to be sounded, and each of them as important as that of experimental method. One was an objective behavioral approach essentially similar to that of J. B. Watson, with

[9] *Social Psychology* (1924).

[10] Moore, H. T., "The Comparative Influence of Majority and Expert Opinion on Individual Judgments," *Amer. J. Psychol.*, 1921, 32, 16–20.

emphasis upon observable reflex tendencies in the newborn rather than upon theoretical constructs like the McDougall instincts; the other was an insistence that social psychology is not a study of group minds but of *individuals* in social situations.

The "prepotent reflexes" of the newborn are classified by Allport under six heads. It is the conditioning of these reflexes which constitutes the objective basis for social growth and for the interaction of group members. Complex types of social behavior are systematically reduced to this type of formulation. Indeed, one of the most original chapters in Allport's book has to do with the explanation of crowd behavior in terms of the reflex on the one hand and "social facilitation" on the other. Individuals are not rendered helpless in crowd situations. There is no "crowd mind"; there is no subservience of the individual to the mass. The same thing which people want when they are considered as individuals they also want when they are in the group situation. But social facilitation accentuates their wants. Words are used which touch off the appropriate behaviors in situations in which alternative suggestions are wanting. The men who participated, for example, in the "massacre" in the Illinois mines in the period after World War I were not just "swept off their feet"; they were hungry and frightened men who knew exactly what attitudes they held toward strikebreakers, and who when the strikebreakers were brought in to take over the available jobs, reacted by mutual interstimulation. The fact that they had weapons and knew how to use them, and that they were organized physically and verbally for the threat, shows how far they were from the true embodiment of plasticity in the hands of outside forces.

The Allport formulation succeeded swiftly in dominating American social psychology, partly through its experimental approach and partly through its behavioral emphasis. In later studies Allport went on to demonstrate that "institutional behavior"—the response of individuals to institutional patterns—is quantitatively distinguishable from noninstitutional behavior.[11] In the former case, most people conform; and those who do not conform to the institution may be ranged on a J-curve. Fewer and fewer people appear on the chart as one moves further and further to the right from the point which indicates absolute conformity.

11 Allport, F. H., *Institutional Behavior* (1933); "The J-Curve Hypothesis of Conforming Behavior," *Publ. Amer. Sociol. Soc.*, 1934, 28, 124–25.

Another theoretical contribution consists in the definition of the interactions of individuals as an "event system," [12] in which one defines and measures the degree to which each person actually contributes toward a social goal to which he is verbally committed, as compared with the degree to which he believes himself to be so contributing. Instead of speaking of mass trends or of leadership and followership, one defines the rate at which each person is responding in each of these two respects. We find, therefore, in the work of Allport a systematic and extensive reduction of social-science phenomena to the phenomena of individual behavior.

THE INFLUENCE OF ANTHROPOLOGY

In the meantime, the conception of ingrained action tendencies was taking a beating. The instinct theory, already in serious trouble, was being belabored by another force as hostile to it as was the movement in the behavioristic direction. This was the growth of a type of cultural anthropology which had begun to emphasize the cultural molding of the individual. Social psychology had for the most part been a psychology of the nineteenth- and twentieth-century man of the Western world. Here and there, to be sure, there were gestures of recognition of the meaning of cultural diversity for the child's personality. But the general assumption seems to have been that the difference between societies would be found to lie only in specific content—for example, in the particular things that are said or believed or feared or done—while in general the dynamics of human nature would remain everywhere the same. But in the decade of the twenties came a series of hammer blows directed at the conception that human nature as we know it is to be found in the same form everywhere. Studies of cultural diversity began to show that both content and form—both the specific thing done and the way of doing it, both the specific belief and the feeling tone associated with the belief—bear the marks of cultural arrangements.

Following shortly upon Malinowski's study of the psychology of the Trobriand Islanders (page 341), the first of these investigations to capture the imagination of psychologists came from the pupils of Franz Boas, who had himself suggested in *The Mind of Primitive Man* (1911) how profoundly the basic psychological processes reflect adaptation to the environment. The whole approach became more

[12] Allport, F. H., "An Event-System Theory of Collective Action, with Illustrations from Economic and Political Phenomena and the Production of War," *J. Soc. Psychol.*, 1940, 11, 417-45.

concrete upon the publication of Margaret Mead's *Coming of Age in Samoa* (1928). This volume was a straightforward test of the familiar hypothesis, coming from Western studies of childhood, that the "storm and stress" of adolescence is due to the rapidity of puberty changes, and that society must reconcile itself to the difficulties entailed by storm and stress. This hypothesis could easily be tested by choosing a preliterate society in which transition to adulthood is taken casually, and is in fact gradual, not signalized by any special excitement, affect-laden ritual, or frightening system of taboos. Study of girls before, during, and after puberty in Samoa failed to reveal anything much by way of storm and stress, and the conclusion was therefore reached that in earlier formulations a biological explanation had mistakenly been given to a phenomenon which was essentially cultural.

Quite aside from the question of the acceptance or the rejection of the thesis of this volume, American social psychology was struck as if by a blinding force. Could we, in fact, describe the laws of social psychology at all until we had an infinitely bigger cultural basis from which to work? This volume of Mead's was followed immediately by a companion study, *Growing Up in New Guinea* (1930), in which emphasis was laid upon the hard, competitive, commercial mode of living obtaining among the Manus people, who in their regulation of many types of behavior in childhood, adolescence, and early adulthood produce constraints and rigidities utterly different from the casual attitudes of the Samoans. Then followed, from the pen of Mead and many others, a series of further demonstrations of profound cultural molding of personality. To these studies we shall recur on pages 422–23.

The instinct theory had already been weakened by Dunlap and the anti-instinct movement and by Allport's conception of conditioned reflexes. From the cultural studies first described came in full force a cultural relativism which undertook to make environmental forces, especially cultural forces, nearly all-sufficient in the determination of personality and of its readiness for community living. Social psychology had to make concessions here to the social sciences, just as in McDougall's days it had made concessions to biology. In the late twenties the psychologist began to throw in the phrase "in our culture" after every generalization about human conduct, just as he had begun, in the earlier twenties, to put quotation marks around the word "instinct." Obviously an aching void had been created, and new conceptions gathered around the edges, waiting to be drawn into the vortex. It was clear that a new conceptual system soon had to take shape.

In the meantime, and before it took shape, the late twenties and the early thirties were periods of great activity in the gathering of empirical data by the methods of experimental social psychology, with an enormous amount of careful work on the formation of attitudes in children, on the effects of participation in various types of social groups, and in the formulation of more and more adequate methods for sampling and experimenting upon various types of response to education, or to propaganda, or to family membership, or to other types of social pressure. It was, in fact, during these years that Bruno Lasker introduced us to the first careful studies of race attitudes in childhood,[13] and that Horowitz measured accurately the development of one representative attitude (attitude toward the Negro) from the kindergarten all the way through the school years, with appropriate samples and quantitative data at each age level.[14] Thurstone,[15] and later Likert,[16] developed scales for the measurement of the *intensity* of attitude; scales which became very serviceable in the more precise definition of individual variation in prejudice, or radicalism-conservatism, and so on, or response to various types of opinion-making forces. It was in these same years that public-opinion research took on its modern form through the fact that George Gallup and others, from 1932 on, developed greatly improved methods of sampling, in such a way that the important social variables, such as age, sex, economic level, education, could be appropriately represented in the total sample. To the same period belong large-scale experimental studies of propaganda, with more and more recognition of the fact that what is sociologically a rather simple problem becomes psychologically a very intricate one, in view of the great individual differences in susceptibility to propaganda, in view of the facts that many individuals move in a direction opposite from that intended, and that all sorts of subtle personality factors appear which can only be fully understood by recourse to clinical or experimental methods.

[13] *Race Attitudes in Children* (1929).

[14] Horowitz, E. L., "The Development of Attitude toward the Negro," *Arch. Psychol.*, 1936, No. 194.

[15] See for example Thurstone, L. L., "The Measurement of Change in Social Attitudes," *J. Soc. Psychol.*, 1931, 2, 230–35.

[16] Likert, R., "A Technique for the Measurement of Attitudes," *Arch. Psychol.*, 1932, No. 140.

SHERIF

In this period of seething activity and conflicting theoretical formulations, many began to turn to the great systematic psychologies for their key to the specific problems of social psychology. A psychoanalytic version of social psychology was already available (page 319). Gestalt formulations began to appear (page 293), and field theory made successful invasions of the area in the persons of Kurt Lewin and J. F. Brown.

But one thing that was urgently needed if these and other empirical studies were to be brought into a unified, systematic form was a definition of the nature of social responses so formulated as to bring laboratory studies into full alignment with observations made in the field. It was a Turkish student working at Harvard and at Columbia who achieved these definitions and formulated within their frame of reference a research program. Muzafer Sherif,[17] while still in Ankara, had begun to note the influence of the group upon the individual at the level of his social *perception:* the fact that the individual learns to *perceive* as a member of his cultural group must perceive. At Harvard and at Columbia he used the autokinetic effect—the apparent movement of a point of light in the dark. The effect is governed by factors of previous learning and of present attitude. Placing his experimental subjects in the company of others, he showed that the individual is progressively molded into the group's way of seeing the movement. In other experiments he perceives the rates of tapping, or the degree of excellence of literary passages, as they are defined for him by group participation. Under group conditions of work, the norms and variabilities which had characterized the individual when alone were rapidly forced in a direction determined by others in the group. It is possible after each session to trace the degree to which each individual had given up his own autonomy of judgment in favor of the central tendency of the group as a whole. The curves indicate the convergence, or, as Sherif calls it, the "funnel-shaped relationship" which characterizes indoctrination into group norms. In another study he showed the utility of the autokinetic phenomenon in measuring relationships of prestige; [18] a naïve subject accommodated herself to the leadership role played by a more experienced person.

[17] *The Psychology of Social Norms* (1936).
[18] "An Experimental Approach to the Study of Attitudes," *Sociometry*, 1937, 1, 90–98.

These data from laboratory experimentation were combined with anthropological materials showing that in general the individual's perceptual habits are adaptations to current cultural habits. It soon became apparent that the redefinition of social psychology in perceptual terms may have the most profound implications for the study of language, family life, religion, politics, and indeed all social behavior. Behavioral interaction was to be studied not in conditioned-reflex terms as such, but at the level of molding of the cognitive processes. Throughout the presentation, Koffka's conception of the process of perceiving was espoused and developed; namely, that the perceptual reactions are bipolar, with external structure and internal predispositions jointly determining the perceptual organization. The more rigidly defined the external structure, the smaller the play of internal factors, and vice versa. Other cognitive processes, such as recall, imagination, and thought, were of course also envisaged in cultural terms.

From this conceptual scheme and the experimental exemplification of it, there soon followed over a hundred studies in social psychology devised to bring out the determination of the cognitive life of each group member by the existing norms. Cantril and McGregor showed that the prediction of future events was determined in part by internal factors of desire and expectation, in part by the factual material available to the subject, with the same roles assigned these processes as had been assigned by Sherif.[19] Many studies of value judgments and of recall and recognition of material earlier learned followed in the wake of Sherif's investigations: for example, Clark's studies of differences between men and women in recalling material bearing on a struggle between a man and a woman,[20] and Bruner and Goodman's studies[21] of the apparent size of coins as judged by children from favored and from unfavored backgrounds. More recently Bruner and Postman have added a series of further studies in which socially significant material, such as pictures of social scenes, are shown on the screen for a very small fraction of a second, and interpretations demanded.[22] To an extraor-

[19] Cantril, H., "The Prediction of Social Events," *J. Abn. and Soc. Psychol.*, 1938, 33, 364–89; McGregor, D., "The Major Determinants of the Prediction of Social Events," *J. Abn. and Soc. Psychol.*, 1938, 33, 179–204.

[20] Clark, K. B., "Some Factors Influencing the Remembering of Prose Materials," *Arch. Psychol.*, 1940, No. 253.

[21] Bruner, J. S., and Goodman, C. C., "Value and Need as Organizing Factors in Perception," *J. Abn and Soc. Psychol.*, 1947, 42, 33–44.

[22] Several studies in press or in progress at the time of this writing.

dinary degree, the subjects read into the scenes meanings which stem from their own social orientations. A whole social psychology of attitude and of readiness for social participation of one or another sort is being written today in terms of the cognitive phenomena, with methods which have long been a part of the standard field of experimental psychology.[23]

MORENO

One other striking movement marks the development of the social psychology of the mid-thirties; namely, the system of conceptions and procedures introduced by J. L. Moreno. In his book *Who Shall Survive?* (1934) appear three cardinal ideas, each implemented by research procedures and drawn into a coherent system for the analysis of interpersonal relations.

1. First comes *sociometry*, a device for the measurement of social processes. Reduced to its simplest form, a sociometric procedure consists of the choice by each person of those persons with whom he would like to be placed, in relation to a series of activities. With whom would he like to eat, or to work, or to form a club, or to develop a community activity? Typically, individuals indicate their personal choices from first to third, or from first to fifth. Typically, as in the huge investigation carried out by Moreno and Jennings at the New York State Training School for Girls at Hudson, New York, mutual first choices are automatically put into effect; that is, individuals are actually placed with those with whom they want to be placed. Where the reciprocation is not so clean-cut—as, for example, when B is A's first choice, but A is B's third choice—one achieves the maximum adjustment which the entire mass of choices

---

[23] One may wonder, since this is so, why it should be felt that social psychology must inevitably remain less exact than physiological psychology. The factors determining the cognitive responses—for example, the interpretation of such pictures—often reach a high level of predictability, a level which compares favorably with the predictability of responses at the physiological level. If it be maintained that after all, such responses are not "real behavior," the reply is that perceiving and remembering and thinking and imagining are real behavior whenever they occur, and that if they are less rich and complex than the world outside the laboratory, the same is true of the physiological responses which characteristically have been studied in laboratories in simplified form. The conception of experimental method in social psychology is now a commonplace and a banality; the continued separation of social from experimental psychology is based more upon a habit of thinking of what social psychology used to be than upon a realistic confrontation of the present scene. There is, of course, a large field of theoretical, or even speculative, social psychology. The same is true of most subdivisions of psychology.

permits. In the Hudson study, and in others, it has proved possible to place most persons with those with whom they wished to be associated in some concrete, specified activity. The reaching out of one person to another is considered by Moreno to have a deep emotional core, to which the term "tele" is applied. Very roughly, it is tele which is measured in sociometric studies.

2. Persons may, however, "warm up" to each other; their choices may in time become more spontaneous. The second of Moreno's conceptions, developed only briefly in his book, is therefore that of *spontaneity testing*. Here two individuals are simply placed together and told to begin a conversation. The study of their verbal and postural interactions gives some conception of the background for the tele and the choice which stems from it, and throws some light on the degree of plasticity of each individual.

3. From this we come to the third major conception: *spontaneity training*. Moreno regards the individual as typically a hardened or encrusted form of what was once the flexible, or even fluid, social creature of early childhood. He has learned to do the things society demands; has built up a shell which becomes more and more difficult to pierce as social roles and obligations are more and more fully understood and mechanically accepted. A rather heroic process is then required to cut through the shell, and to permit a return to the vital and flexible attitude of a really spontaneous person. Spontaneity training has been developed chiefly in the form of the drama; a drama, however, without detailed plot, without written lines, without sharply defined roles. In the spontaneity theater one may call upon member after member of the audience to come on the stage and act out this or that role which may be educationally or therapeutically valuable either for him or for someone else already engaged in the action upon the stage. The drama is plastic and creative: it makes possible self-realization through the constant demand for a vital and meaningful response to a new situation. The neurotic may in this way relive upon the stage the harrowing struggle through which his own indecisiveness or conflict has dragged him in the last few hours. At times it may be necessary for the psychiatrist to appoint an alter ego (an assistant psychiatrist, perhaps) who will take over those functions of the individual patient's ego which the patient himself is unable at the time to realize. One may, then, witness in oneself and in those with whom one participates all sorts of unconscious dispositions and roles.

Sociometry has spread with rapidity through American sociology and social work, especially "group work," as well as psychology.

The American Sociometric Association has over a hundred members; annual sociometric meetings add vitality to the steady stream of research reports which appear in its journals. The sociometric movement has given support to that direct study of interpersonal relations to which, as we have seen (page 344), other schools of psychiatry have also given attention.

Movements such as sociometry and group work tend, in fact, to reinforce the conception that a new system of disciplines is coming into existence, dealing neither with the individual as such nor with the social structure as such, but with certain types of interpersonal relations which make the sharp distinction between psychology and sociology rather useless and meaningless. One may study for their own sake certain interactions between persons; not as symbols of social classes or social roles, but as social expressions of concrete individuals in all their literal fullness of selfhood. In the same direction tends another series of studies which began in the mid-thirties: the investigations of Kurt Lewin and his associates (page 304), which attempt to introduce experimental methods into the study of social climates or group atmospheres. One may experiment today (in the full sense of experimentation, with specification of parameters, with controls, with statistical treatment of results) just as easily and naturally in the field of social patterns as one did in 1930 in the field of individual social response to one's place in a group, and in 1900 in the field of "impersonal" response.

The viewpoint developed in this chapter is that of the psychologist concerned to expand his conception of his own field to include the problem of membership in the group. In the same era another kind of social psychology has been developing, from the viewpoint of the sociologist. In the first decade of the century John Dewey and G. H. Mead were already thinking of individual psychology as a reflection of a group process, and of the development of the self as an aspect not of growth alone but of awareness of others and of one's relations with them. Mead emphasized the role of language in the individual's induction into the group, and in making him a group member, not just an individual who joins a group. Sympathy, fellow feeling, sense of oneness with others, are primitive and compelling and have a large place in social psychology. C. H. Cooley likewise pointed out the unreality of the question whether the individual or the group comes first; the social processes of individual-in-group permit no such dissection. Eagerly drawing material from history, politics, and psychiatry, the sociologists have not hesitated to emphasize the group life of today. The sociologists have likewise done their *experiments*, and have contributed effectively to the study of attitudes and public opinion. While for a couple of decades this sociological social psychology was largely distinct from the psychologist's social psychology, the two have been moving toward each other in recent years, the psychologist gaining (as he has also gained from the anthropologist) through increasing awareness of the social nature of man's primary experiences, and the sociologist gaining through a sharpening of intellectual tools for the study of the individual.[24]

But everything that has been said here about the development of experimental methods in social psychology remains tentative and incomplete until the material gathered during World War II has been adequately digested. There is an enormous quantity of material on American soldiers' attitudes toward the war; vast amounts of data on public opinion and the direction of current changes in American thinking; thousands of hours of clinical observations of officers and men selected for various types of wartime assignments; and of clinical observations and projective-test data on the personnel of the armed forces and the Office of Strategic Services in tension-producing and other situations. There is also some material on morale and other interpersonal phenomena. Finally, the abundant wartime material on perceptual and motor responses to laboratory and field situations may also prove to have great social significance. When these and many other types of information bearing on the control and measurement of social behavior are organized and assimilated, they may make a good part of our summary seem obsolete.[25]

[24] For a survey of the origins of this movement, with suitable documentation of the part played by Dewey, Mead, Cooley, and their successors, see Young, K., in *The History and Prospects of the Social Sciences,* ed. by H. E. Barnes (1925).

[25] It may be worth while to add a word about the organization of social psychology in American institutions. For the most part, a man trained in social psychology will also be trained in the psychology of personality and in abnormal or clinical psychology. Clinical psychology, the psychology of personality, and social psychology show a great overlapping, and a large proportion of the studies appearing in clinical or in social psychology journals are not strictly classifiable either as clinical or as social, to the exclusion of the other. The huge growth of experimental method in clinical psychology serves, then, to enrich social psychology, and the converse is also true. The one factor tending to hold social psychology in line and to keep it from becoming simply a subdivision of clinical psychology is the fact that sociology, public-opinion research, and many other phases of normal group life demand so much attention as to make the clinician's concern with the maladjusted or the pathological rather remote from the life tasks of many social psychologists. We may speak, then, for the present, of overlapping but still relatively independent efforts, each destined to influence the other more and more, but almost sure to

REFERENCES

Barnes, Harry Elmer, ed., *The History and Prospects of the Social Sciences,* Knopf, 1925

Cottrell, Leonard S., "Important Developments in American Social Psychology," *Sociometry,* 1941, 4, 302–24

Karpf, Fay B., *American Social Psychology,* McGraw-Hill, 1932

McKinnon, Donald W., "The Use of Clinical Methods in Social Psychology," *J. Soc. Issues,* 1946, 2, 47–54

Murchison, Carl A., ed., *Handbook of Social Psychology,* Clark University Press, 1935

Murphy, Gardner, Murphy, Lois B., and Newcomb, Theodore M., *Experimental Social Psychology,* rev. ed., Harper, 1937; chap. 1

become so extensive in factual material and in variety of research methods as to forbid their final unification.

The following is from Allan Fromme: "I think this chapter ought to mention the importance of Thomas and Znaniecki's *Polish Peasant* and any other material which led to interdisciplinary reading, such as Lasswell's *Psychopathology and Politics;* H. E. Barnes' and J. H. Robinson's books emphasizing psychological factors in what they called *The New History;* Clark's (and others') recognition of the inadequacy of Adam Smith's psychological presuppositions; Veblen's insistence on irrational motives in his institutional economics and sociology; Durkheim's *Suicide,* and Halbwachs' follow-up, as well as the latter's *Les cadres sociaux de la mémorie;* the replacement of instinct study by attitude study, particularly as statistical methods improved; and finally R. S. Lynd's *Knowledge for What?* with specific mention of his wonderful story about the doctoral candidate in history who had no theory of psychology at all." All good! Yet I feel unequal to the task of evaluating such trends at this time, and will let this stand as Fromme has phrased it.

Chapter 28

PERSONALITY

If I could get within this changing I.   MASEFIELD

THE CLINICAL PSYCHOLOGY of the second quarter of this century tended to draw more and more both upon psychoanalysis and upon behavioristic psychology, with little apology for the blending of the two conceptions. In the twenties, for example, one might use a conditioned-response approach to the problem of compulsive stealing, yet not turn a deaf ear to the psychoanalytic demand that unconscious motivating factors be investigated. In the same way, behavioristic and Gestalt conceptions began to be combined; objective studies of maturation, language formation, and the growth of motor skills were combined with references to character structure, personality style, figure-ground relationships, and the like. The leaders of American clinical psychology, such as William Healy at the Judge Baker Foundation in Boston, never hesitated to draw concepts from any source which might prove helpful, and indeed exemplified different approaches in different research studies. Academic psychologists might at times protest against eclecticism, insisting that parts from different systems could never be made to cohere. But those engaged in diagnosis and in therapy—and indeed those engaged in correcting reading disabilities, or stammering, or enuresis—were always glad to see whether, despite all the argumentation, the ideas would not fit together at the concrete level of a problem to be solved.

It was largely in terms of this willingness to ransack all the more vital conceptual systems that the modern conception of personality study came into being. At the turn of the century, personality study meant primarily a case history, with a few sage comments interspersed here and there. As the case-study method developed in clinics, as more and more medical directors became sympathetic to psychoanalysis, as more and more psychiatric social workers were themselves analyzed, the term "case history" came to mean more and more a study conceived in terms of Freudian (or at times Rankian or Adlerian) dynamics. But in line with what was just said about eclecticism, the lingo and the modes of thought characteristic of the vigorous new experimental study of the child, dominated by the behaviorists, filtered into the clinic, to be followed by the habit of looking for systematic interrelationships in the manner favored by the equally new and vigorous Gestalt school.

Personality study came, then, to be a rather sophisticated type of case analysis based upon a search for all material capable of throwing light on personal development. Until the mid-thirties there was little readable in the new area except in manuscript form; that is, in the form of case studies in Institutes of Child Welfare and in clinics serving maladjusted children. The books on the psychology of personality appearing in the twenties and early thirties were mostly popular books on psychoanalysis, or eclectic syntheses of theory, which sometimes made a gesture toward the rapidly accumulating case records. A marked advance from the point of view of simplicity and systematic clarity was Stagner's *Psychology of Personality*, appearing in 1936; the emphasis was upon social-cultural dynamics in personality formation. This was followed immediately by a systematic integration: G. W. Allport's *Personality: A Psychological Interpretation* (1937). This volume, while inclined on the whole toward a Gestalt orientation, stressing the uniqueness and structural wholeness of the individual, makes free use also of the conceptions from psychoanalysis and from behaviorism, and indeed from medical and sociological as well as literary sources. One of its most important conceptions was that of "functional autonomy." Human activities are not just continuations of instinctive tendencies, but are "contemporary systems," autonomous and developing in their own right. In 1938 appeared H. A. Murray's *Explorations in Personality*. This presented a systematic conception based in considerable measure upon psychoanalysis, but was very extensively documented with experimental and clinical studies by Murray and his staff at the Harvard Psychological Clinic, and pointed the way to an experimental science of personality study. The psychology of personality was becoming a recognized subdivision of general human psychology in consequence of books such as these.

It is not implied that Stagner's, Allport's, and Murray's books suddenly altered the academic situation as far as interest in personality problems was concerned. The journals were carrying annually hundreds of papers on the biological foundations of personality, on early habit formation, on the measurement of adult attitude and opinion, and on many other topics relevant to personality study. It was, however, common practice to refer to the biologically oriented studies as parts of physiological psychology, and to the socially oriented ones as parts of social psychology, or even of anthropology or sociology. The time was not ready for a psychology of personality as such, allowing personality itself to become the central problem, separated for the moment from primary concern with physiology on the one hand, or from problems of the community on the other. It was the decade of the thirties which finally realized in full-fledged form the conception of personality study for its own sake.

In the meantime, the ancient conception of personality as dependent upon body type or "constitutional type" was revitalized by Kretschmer's studies suggesting that schizoid tendencies appear among the "leptosomes" of spindle-shaped build and cycloid tendencies among the "pyknics" or "well-rounded" individuals.[1] Then came the extensive and systematic studies of Sheldon and his collaborators,[2] combining body measures and ratings of personality, to define three basic constitutional components (derived from embryonic endoderm, mesoderm, and ectoderm) varying in relative prominence from person to person, and predisposing to specific personal qualities.

On page 409ff. it was noted that social psychology had been profoundly modified by anthropological studies; the same was true for personality study, and to an even greater degree. Indeed, personality study and social psychology were driven closer together, even in some respects telescoped into each other, by the pressure of the new ethnological material.

It will be recalled that two of Margaret Mead's studies appearing in the twenties had had a great effect; we shall here turn to other samples of her work especially important for the theory of personality. In 1937, Mead compared habits of co-operation and competition in thirteen primitive societies,[3] showing, with the aid of a group of ethnological helpers, the extraordinary variations in such behavior in different societies. It was shown, moreover, that no simple geographic or climatic explanation would suffice to account for the facts, and that a very rich historical and cultural system of interacting factors must be presupposed.

[1] Kretschmer, E., *Physique and Character* (1925).

[2] Sheldon, W. H., Stevens, S. S., and Tucker, W. B., *The Varieties of Human Physique* (1940); Sheldon, W. H., and Stevens, S. S., *The Varieties of Temperament* (1942).

[3] Mead, Margaret, ed., *Cooperation and Competition among Primitive Peoples* (1937).

Highly influential as a culmination of this new emphasis upon culture for the determination of personality was Mead's volume *Sex and Temperament in Three Primitive Societies* (1935). Taking note of the widespread belief that masculinity is necessarily expressed through aggressiveness, femininity through passivity or co-operativeness, she undertook to document fully the thesis that in one primitive society both sexes are highly aggressive; in a second, both sexes are highly co-operative; in a third, the women are predominantly aggressive, the men passive. Offered without any intention to minimize endocrine and other biological factors, this volume, in conjunction with many similar studies of the cultural determination of personality, brings sharply into focus the question whether biological concepts derived from animal work on the one hand, or from human work in any single culture on the other, can ever be regarded as pointing unequivocally to any thesis regarding the origins of personality characteristics. In this connection it is important to recall the psychoanalytic approaches of Kardiner, Fromm, and Horney (page 342ff.), who likewise undertook to show how profoundly the human nature of different groups may vary in consequence of cultural pressures. In these anthropological studies there is, however, recourse to direct observation which is often lacking when Freudian concepts are applied. In the study of *Balinese Character* (1942), Mead and Bateson offered prolonged and close observations not only of adults but also of children being molded into the social process (cf. page 410), documenting the entire presentation with an enormous quantity of material, including motion pictures.

But the cross-cultural method has been moving along very fast, and the demand has arisen that more complex societies be systematically studied from this vantage point. In particular, the exigencies of World War II made it imperative that systematic studies of "enemy peoples" be made to foresee where and how they would resist, what types of heroic effort could be expected under what circumstances, where morale would prove soft, and so on. A number of such studies were made, and indeed have continued to develop the conceptual scheme as they sketch the "national character" of many other literate peoples all over the globe. A sample is the study by Ruth Benedict entitled *The Chrysanthemum and the Sword*—a study of Japanese personality structure in which historical, biographical, literary, and psychoanalytic concepts are used in developing a view regarding the role of such motives as loyalty and shame in determining the normal and acceptable behavior patterns. It has, of course, proved difficult to satisfy all experts that any single one of these interpretative studies is sound. It is clear that the method remains to be developed and tested. It is nevertheless characteristic of the present era that attempts to study national character should take advantage of all the available ethnological and psychoanalytic techniques, with as much direct testing in the field as the conditions of observation allow.

PROJECTIVE TESTING

So much for the development of a conception of personality as a highly complex system of forces molded by massive cultural forces as well as by many factors specific to the individual. The most important *research device* by which the new field of personality study became enlivened and carried beyond the case-history level was that of *projective testing*. The term "projective test" is recent,[4] but the basic conception that the person projects his own individuality *into* the way in which he perceives, or takes hold of, the task had dim beginnings at the turn of the century, and it will be worth our while to follow its development rather closely.

Both French and German investigators began to notice about 1900 that individual differences in perception, recall, and other cognitive processes were expressive of differences in temperament or attitude. The pioneer here was William Stern, who studied such individual differences in relation to the psychology of testimony. It began to be evident that the fluidity of external structure and the urgency of internal demands permit each individual to perceive in a way which is characteristic of himself (cf. page 278). Of all the semistructured materials with which investigations were carried out, the most rewarding proved to be ink blots. It occurred to the Swiss psychiatrist Hermann Rorschach, about 1911, to begin a systematic exploration of the possible uses of ink blots of many types and forms in the comparison of normal, neurotic, and psychotic individuals. Investigating the responses of many individuals to dozens of different blots, he finally prepared a standard set of ten blots, some simply black upon a white ground, some utilizing also the factor of color.[5] The ten cards were always presented in a standard order. He had early noted that color is releasing to the emotional life; that the tendency to perceive only in terms of form, rejecting color, is characteristic of a concern with realistic factors; and that a tendency to

---

[4] Frank, L. K., "Projective Methods for the Study of Personality," *J. Psychol.*, 1939, 8, 389–413.

[5] Rorschach, H., *Psychodiagnostics* (1921).

perceive human forms in motion is expressive of inner, imaginative factors, the tendency to throw one's inner resources into perceptual interpretation. In the same way, he noted that the struggle to see the blot as a whole betokens an integrating attitude altogether different from the dissecting attitude which results from the tendency to take note only of detail; and he stressed that the sequence of responses—for example, the tendency, in each card, to see wholes first, then larger details, then small details—may tell something about the orderliness (or compulsiveness) of the individual. Broader dispositions, such as the originality or the banality of mind, were also easily brought out.

The test had moved rather far toward standardization at the time of Rorschach's sudden death in 1922, for hundreds of normal and mentally disturbed individuals had been studied, and the data classified. Shortly thereafter a very full "posthumous case" was published by Emil Oberholzer; he had sent a case record to Rorschach for diagnosis solely on the basis of the subject's responses to the blots. This posthumous case is merely the best known of a large number of "blind analyses" which show the degree to which the dynamic factors in these perceptual reactions may permit a complete clinical evaluation.

Graphology, or the systematic study of handwriting as a clue to personality, had been a very ancient art, slowly moving toward a higher level of scientific sophistication, and becoming rather widely recognized with the work of Ludwig Klages in Germany in the first decade of this century.[6] Through Klages's system, and later that of Pulver in Switzerland,[7] it became a center of serious research attention in Germany, France, Britain, and the Netherlands. Graphology did not succeed—and has not as yet succeeded—in achieving objective and widely accepted methods of scoring, such as were early achieved by Rorschach, nor has it met in a large way the demand for published blind diagnoses. The amount of research in graphology is, however, rapidly increasing, and studies such as those by Lewinson and Zubin point to the possibility of sharp definition and accurate measurement of impulsive, rhythmic, and other factors in the flow of script which are of value in relation to unconscious self-portraiture.[8]

When Florence Goodenough published in 1921 her "draw-a-man test," the intention was primarily to measure the degree to which a

[6] Klages, L., *Handschrift und Charakter* (1907).

[7] Pulver, M., *Symbolik der Handschrift* (1930).

[8] Lewinson, T. S., and Zubin, J., *Handwriting Analysis: A Series of Scales for Evaluating the Dynamic Aspects of Handwriting* (1942).

child demonstrates the intellectual maturity necessary to indicate the parts and relationships of body and clothing.[9] Putting artistic ability to one side, the plan was to develop a method of intelligence testing in which the diffuse scribblings of the tiny child could be followed through step by step to the full representation of eyes, nose, mouth, hands, fingers, and so on, which even the crudest drawing by an adult usually includes. This draw-a-man test has proved to be more than an intelligence test; it came over into personality study during the late thirties and forties, and while the findings have not as yet seen the light on a large scale, it is apparent that many a clinician is today exploring its projective significance.

Finger painting with small children,[10] and brush painting with either children or adults,[11] have proved in the same way to permit analysis in terms of emotional response to color, love of the definite or the vague, the sense of safety achieved in even rhythms or in symmetry, the chaos which appears in jumbled lines and surfaces. In contrast to the rather limited material with published drawings, free painting methods have rapidly come into their own in the last few years. The methods have obtained a good deal of objective validation in the personality analyses of Alschuler and Hattwick.[12] Other methods used with children consist of play with blocks, clay, and the like, and with the miniature life toys—the doll house and furniture, with human and animal figures, motorcars, trees, and so on—which are so handled and arranged by small children that their view of the world and of themselves is brought to light.[13] Picture tests have been extensively used both with children and with adults. One may, for example, "make up a story" about each one of twenty pictures shown him in the Murray-Morgan Thematic Apperception Test,[14] revealing as he does so the deeper needs and struggles which autistically control his own thought.

These are but a handful of illustrations of methods in which the cognitive or the motor expression, or the two combined, are used

[9] Goodenough, F. L., "A New Approach to the Measurement of the Intelligence of Young Children," *J. Genet. Psychol.*, 1926, 33, 185–211.

[10] Shaw, R. F., *Finger Painting* (1924).

[11] Waehner, T. S., "Interpretation of Spontaneous Drawings and Paintings," *Genet. Psychol. Monog.*, 1946, 33, 3–70.

[12] Alschuler, R. H., and Hattwick, L. W., *Painting and Personality: A Study of Young Children*, 2 vols. (1947).

[13] Lerner, E., and Murphy, L. B., eds., *Methods for the Study of Personality in Young Children*, *Soc. Res. Child Developm. Monogr.*, 1941, 6 (whole No. 4).

[14] Tomkins, S., *The Thematic Apperception Test* (1947).

to get a picture of personality as a system of interrelated dispositions. In all such studies, as L. K. Frank points out, one asks not how well an individual responds, nor how rapidly; it is not the assignment done which counts, but the way in which the personality is projected into it. Projective tests reveal the "private world" of the individual. Each person living in his own private world unwittingly portrays the structure and the feeling tone of that world, what is to be done about it, and the way in which it makes sense in relation to himself.

While the projective tests were developed in the first instance largely as an aid to psychiatric practice, by 1940 they had become standard auxiliary aids to observational analysis of child and adult personality. The development of projective testing has done more than any other single thing to give the conception of formal personality study a place in psychology, enabling personality research to stand on its own feet as a legitimate inquiry relatively independent of immediate problems of diagnosis and therapy.

These investigations, however, have suffered from one rather serious shortcoming: They usually cut cross sections through the individual life history. It has proved difficult indeed to follow through the same individuals in a longitudinal study, giving the same projective tests year after year, or at suitable intervals. One still relies largely upon the biographical study to supply longitudinal material. Sometimes such biographical analysis becomes semi-quantitative, as in the work of Chassell, who roughly estimated the intensity of various character-forming factors at various times in life.[15] Sometimes, as in the work of Sheldon and Eleanor Glueck,[16] and in the work of David M. Levy,[17] rough quantification of various factors in childhood is brought into relation to over-all adjustment level in adulthood. But longitudinal study in the strict sense requires that the same individuals be studied year after year. Several such longitudinal studies, notably the California Adolescent Growth Study, the Guidance Study of J. W. Macfarlane, the Cambridge-Somerville Youth Study, and the various studies of L. W. Sontag under the Fels Foundation, have been under way for years, but at this writing the results remain largely unpublished (cf. page 400).

In all these projective and longitudinal studies, a further shift away from the earlier behavior-centered approach has become evident. Just as it has become clear that behavior is more intelligible when the perceptual response is clear, so it has been increasingly

---

[15] Chassell, J. O., *The Experience Variables* (1928).
[16] Glueck, S., and Glueck, E. T., *Five Hundred Criminal Careers* (1930).
[17] Levy, D. M., *Maternal Overprotection* (1943).

emphasized that one perceives not just "the environment," but oneself in relation to the environment.[18] Following through on the early emphasis of Cooley and G. H. Mead upon the social factors which mold the child's way of viewing himself and reacting to this self-picture,[19] the students of projection (and indeed all students of personality) have tended more and more to stress that perception is not just a system of responses to a whole, but involves a whole in which one's observed self is a major determinant. At a still higher level of sophistication, the emphasis (as with Schilder [20]) is upon the ways in which the ego (cf. page 321) may be characterized through its unconscious devices for enhancing, magnifying, defending, blotting out, or distorting the self-image.

CLINICAL APPLICATIONS

It was noted above that pure or academic psychology finally found a place for the psychology of personality as such. On the other hand, it is equally important to note that most of the methods of personality study so far indicated, while carried out primarily at Institutes of Child Welfare or at university laboratories, have seen their major *application* in therapy. While it is impossible in a volume like this to do justice to the rapid changes in the role of psychology in clinical practice—for example, in the guidance and care of maladjusted persons—a few words seem to be needed, particularly in the matter of the relations of clinical psychology to psychiatry.

It will be remembered that the work of psychological clinics, as conceived by Witmer (page 392), consisted largely of testing, case studies, and simple, direct advice and guidance. With the development of clinics for children's problems, such as the Judge Baker Foundation in Boston and Frederick Allen's clinic in Philadelphia, under medical supervision and with increasing psychoanalytic emphasis, psychologists found themselves expected to do more and more of what the medical men wanted. This, until the late twenties, consisted mostly of administering intelligence tests; during the thirties, however, as the level of sophistication went up, there was more and more demand that personality factors be tested likewise. Beginning with D. M. Levy's pioneering studies in 1924, and Beck's dissertation at Columbia in 1930, Rorschach work began to take a

[18] Calkins, M. W., *A First Book in Psychology* (1910).

[19] Cooley, C. H., *Human Nature and the Social Order* (1912); Mead, G. H., *Mind, Self, & Society: from the Standpoint of a Social Behaviorist* (1934).

[20] Schilder, P., *The Image and Appearance of the Human Body* (1936).

more and more prominent place in the training of clinical psychologists. A few years later, Klopfer initiated a Rorschach Institute and a Rorschach Research Exchange. Rorschach practitioners were soon numbered in the hundreds. Other projective methods, such as the Thematic Apperception Test, began to be added to the equipment of clinical psychologists. Here and there they were also expected to assist in the formulation of a diagnosis; that is, to work as assistants in psychiatric tasks. Often, as at the Institute for Juvenile Research in Chicago, they contributed notably to research.

But the clinical work to be done, especially with disturbed and maladjusted children, was far more than the medical man could handle. Partly for this reason, partly because psychologists here and there took the lead, child-guidance clinics were sometimes established under the direction of psychologists. There has recently been an immense increase in the tendency to utilize psychologists in positions of autonomy with regard to clinical service to the maladjusted. Of importance here was the position of leadership won by Carl Rogers at Rochester, at Ohio State, and at the University of Chicago. His method of "nondirective therapy" [21]—finding out what the patient really wants and helping him to see his problem as a whole, rather than advising or directing him—was shared by a rapidly increasing group of psychologists, many of whom achieved positions independent of the world of medical psychiatry.

In breaking down the sectarian independence of psychology and psychiatry, a huge factor was the terrific pressure which World War II placed upon the limited facilities, both medical and psychological, available within the armed forces for men who cracked up or in other ways ran into difficulties with which they could not cope. The shortage of trained personnel, and the fact that a considerable number of medical men charged with such responsibility had little or no psychiatric training, often resulted in the assignment of heavy responsibility to junior officers or enlisted personnel who had a psychological background. Many of these men in the postwar situation have gone forward to further training, and are finding their way in great numbers into positions of clinical usefulness, often sharing not only in diagnostic but also in therapeutic programs. There are some difficulties, but in general it seems fair to say that the problem is no longer whether nonmedical psychologists should or could participate in such diagnostic and therapeutic activities, but how, under present conditions of medical education, they are to get the experience most suitable to provide for effective handling of

[21] Rogers, C. R., *Counseling and Psychotherapy* (1942).

such responsibilities. A good many of them are being psycho-analyzed; a good many are working out close relationships with medical men; a good many are participating in research in which the question of the relative effectiveness of this or that therapeutic method necessarily entails their sharing in the therapeutic program itself. All of this has had a powerful reflex effect upon academic psychology, in supplying new clinical findings for course material, in giving a new orientation to instructors, in constantly tempting instructors to become interested in clinical opportunities, and in shifting the center of gravity of that rather amorphous whole known as "general psychology."

REFERENCES

Allport, Gordon W., "The Ego in Contemporary Psychology," *Psychol. Rev.*, 1943, 50, 451–78

Angyal, András, *Foundations for a Science of Personality*, Oxford University Press, 1941

Brotemarkle, Robert A., "Clinical Psychology, 1896–1946," *J. Consult. Psychol.*, 1947, 11, 1–4

Hunt, Joseph McV., ed., *Personality and the Behavior Disorders*, 2 vols., Ronald Press, 1944

Krugman, Morris, "Recent Developments in Clinical Psychology," *J. Consult. Psychol.*, 1944, 8, 342–52

Murray, Henry A., Jr., *Explorations in Personality*, Oxford University Press, 1938

Chapter 29

AN INTERPRETATION

The world of our present consciousness is only one out of many worlds of consciousness that exist.   WILLIAM JAMES

ALL SCIENCE and philosophy must of course express in some measure the cultural stream in which they appear, as well as the more conspicuous eddies and crosscurrents of personal and local interest and ingenuity. A full-bodied history of psychology would do justice to the cultural whole. In the meantime, while manifestly unable to achieve such a standard, our last chapter may throw into focus a few of the more obvious cultural determinants which have been noted on the way, and attempt to suggest some of the reasons for the wide individual variability in response to them.

The great forces affecting psychology in the nineteenth century appear to have been: (1) the incredible development of science and of the technology built upon it; specifically the concepts that life and mind were themselves proper subject matter for science; and (2) the spread of political democracy and of universal or near-universal education. Experimental psychology arose even before Darwin, and the biological approach of Darwin and his successors, gave psychology the physical underpinning which it had wanted since the time of Democritus. Schools (and industries) wanted studies of individuals, and quantitative science showed how to begin. Respect for science became perhaps the chief hallmark of modern thinking; and the makers of psychology, sensitive to the demand and wanting the respect, moved swiftly forward to show how man himself might become the object of science. The vigor of this trend was of course the greatest in those two countries—Germany and the United States—in which science was most deeply respected.

But hardly had the challenge and the response been clearly defined when it became evident (early in the present century) that science was a larger enterprise than had been grasped. If the living individual is to be scientifically studied, so likewise is the group to which he belongs; if the interrelations of his tissues and of his sensory and motor acts are proper subject matter for science, so are the interactions of men in their linguistic, their economic, their political behavior. Preliterate, or "primitive," societies being easier to study scientifically, the endeavor first took shape there. The ethnologists began to solve their problem of method, of meaningful description, and of the formulation of laws; and sociologists, psychologists, and psychiatrists began to grasp the concepts of social science as fundamentally similar to other forms of science. This did profound things to psychology, some of which were hinted in earlier chapters, but these need more explicit analysis here.

The essence of the transition was the psychologists' beginning to grasp that the phenomena with which they had been concerned in our society were not necessarily universal expressions of human life. Just as Cattell emphasized individual differences, so now we tend to doubt the universality of what is closest to us. Cultural anthropology served to make available a comparative picture of psychological mechanisms under different cultural arrangements, and at the same time a revised conception of that very plastic and unformed human nature which could be molded into such very diverse products as were described by the ethnologists. These conceptions began to merge with those of the Gestalt psychologists, who had been noting that the individual reacts to a great deal more than the stimulus or situation which the experimentalist wants him to react to; it became evident that much which is not explicit in the situation as defined, much that is half-hidden or even completely ignored in the social context, is highly relevant. It seemed to some that to provide rigid control of the explicit situation, along with unawareness of primary but unacknowledged social determinants, was to "strain at the gnat and swallow the camel."

In consequence, those whose conception of science was modeled closely upon the norms prevailing in physiology and the other life sciences of the laboratory limited themselves more and more to problems in which those larger external factors could be ignored without very serious consequences, while those who thought of science (as did the Göttingen scholars of 1734; cf. page 73) as an enterprise adapted to all subject matters began to formulate questions that might be suitable for the new areas that were emerging.

But two additional scientific movements hit psychology at about the same time: relativity theory and operationism. The former, though a physical theory showing that all time-space measurement is relative to a frame of reference, had even greater implications for "social" behavior than for "laboratory" behavior, since it became more and more evident that all observations are relative to a context. Along with Gestalt psychology, the relativity approach emphasized that all the conditions governing an organism's response must be explicitly defined, with none left unacknowledged. Operationism, likewise grafted easily upon psychology from the flourishing growth of modern physics, insisted that all concepts be explicitly defined in terms of the concrete operations by which their places in an event are determined.[1] The meaning of this approach was quickly grasped by those whose stimulus fields were already given in time-space terms, more slowly by those whose social fields were less easily couched in this "universal language of science."

The incursion of the concepts of field theory into psychology was noted in Chapter 21; but the same tendency of the general scientific concepts of the era to invade psychology may be seen in many other ways. Closely akin to field theory, to relativity theory, and to operationism is the postulate that psychology is as much the science of the environment as the science of the organism, since it is the specific observable form of their interaction that makes psychology. Representative of this trend is not only the clinician's study of the effect of changed environment on personality and the social psychologist's study of the interdependence of personality and culture, but also the whole conception of tests of individual differences as depending for their validity upon the degree to which such tests represent the actual environments that have to be dealt with. Most radical and most systematic of the newer efforts are the experiments of Brunswik, who has pointed out that if we really wish valid laws, we must pay as much attention to an adequate sampling of the aspects of the environment as to an adequate sampling of individuals.

Take experiments in learning, for example: Do our experiments represent the world in which typical learning occurs? "Situations in which food can be found always to the right and never to the left, or always behind a black door and never behind a white one, are not representative of the structure of the environment, but are based on an idealized black-white dramatization of the world, somewhat in a Hollywood style. . . . In an effort to imitate experimentally the tangled causal texture of the environment more closely than is customary, the writer tested a variety of ambiguous environmental

---

[1] Stevens, S. S., "The Operational Definition of Concepts," *Psychol. Rev.*, 1935, 42, 517–27; Boring, E. G., "The Use of Operational Definitions in Science," *Psychol. Rev.*, 1945, 52, 243–45.

means-end relationships, using rats as subjects. . . . The probability character of the causal (partial cause-and-effect) relationships in the environment calls for a fundamental, all-inclusive shift in our methodological ideology regarding psychology. . . . Proper sampling of subjects is . . . replaced by proper sampling of objects or objectives." [2]

Yet it may perhaps be noted that one important step in the development of this type of theory is still usually left out by students of behavior in the community, just as it is usually left out by the experimental psychologist who has moved to the new vantage point. One forgets that one's own perceptual apparatus—indeed, all that one is—is an aspect of the field situation just as fully as is that of any participating member of an observed group. One forgets in the field approach the relativity to which it is so intimately related. Relativity denies any "favored position" to the observer—any position from which accuracy of observation yields that which is "true" in itself. Field theory in psychology, even more than in physics (because safeguards are as yet less explicit in psychology than in physics), involves the full coloration of the individual observer by the hue which is expressed in his field relationships. It is not clear to this writer that the field theorists of the modern era, or the social psychologists, are aware of this fact. Hints, here and there, appear; but it is a pretty safe guess that a much more radical "relativity approach," in which the observer himself is an aspect of the whole field observed, will begin to invade the psychology of the next few years. This will in some respects make the operational approach more relativistic than it is today, and at the same time will force all observations to take on such operational form as is compatible with the placing of the operations within their field contexts.

NATIONAL DIFFERENCES IN INTERESTS

In a general way these various new difficulties and problems facing modern psychology had become inescapable by the decade of the thirties. But the marked national differences earlier noted (page 210) still persisted within the general framework, and in consequence of political events became more striking. So let us attempt a closer scrutiny of the national psychologies of the modern era.

[2] Brunswik, E., "Organismic Achievement and Environmental Probability," *Psychol. Rev.*, 1943, 50, 255–72 (quotation from pp. 261, 263); "Systematic and Representative Design of Psychological Experiments; with Results in Physical and Social Perception," *Univ. Calif. Syllabus Ser.*, No. 304, 1947.

In Germany the cleavage had widened during the nineteenth century between "natural-science psychology," concerned with laboratory activities, and "cultural-science psychology," concerned with the critical and philosophical study of man in society. The latter enjoyed, on the whole, somewhat the greater prestige; but many laboratories achieved high standards of scientific competence and a rapidly increasing status in university circles, a fact marked objectively by an increasing number of students working for the doctorate. Among the cultural-science approaches should be stressed the various philosophical inquiries into the nature of knowledge and of personality, while among the laboratory inquiries should be emphasized those investigations of sense perception which we have already defined as characteristic of the work of Wundt (page 155). Remaining at Leipzig until his death at the age of eighty-eight in 1920, Wundt continued to be the dominating figure in experimental psychology. Indeed, it was from his own former pupils that many of the more important "splinter groups" developed. Though actually concerned, during the opening years of the twentieth century, with problems of encyclopedic magnitude in the area of folk psychology, language, ethics, and law, Wundt remained the master under whom were trained many of the dominant experimentalists of the new era. Closely following in importance were Stumpf, at Berlin, prosecuting studies in the psychology of music and language; Ebbinghaus at Breslau, moving forward to a systematic modern associationism based on structural elements and their interconnections; and Müller at Göttingen, pioneer experimentalist in psychophysics and in memory. Applied psychology was rapidly taking shape through the development of experimental methods of research on the learning process in the schools and experimental devices for studying mental disorders; likewise through development of systems of personality analysis, such as the graphology of Klages (page 424). These last-mentioned devices for evaluating or measuring personality were, in general, disregarded by those who still molded psychology upon physics; yet these new techniques influenced psychiatry, and gradually forced their way into the universities. In the period between the two world wars experimental psychology of the Wundtian type was, on the whole, losing the struggle to pre-empt the field of psychology.

It is not implied that the three broad movements thus described—natural-science psychology, cultural-science psychology, and applied psychology—had ever maintained a completely independent exist-ence. Indeed, efforts at integration were frequent; and one of the ablest and most original psychologists of the period, William Stern, embraced all of these movements, and others as well. His invention of a tone variator, his philosophy of the person, his systematic studies of the psychology of early childhood, his practical development of mental tests, his editing of a journal of applied psychology, his concern with experiments on testimony and legal psychology, represent not only an integration but an actual fusion of diverse trends. In the hands of men like Stern, the Psychologisches Institut, as it was called at each German university, became a beehive of many enterprises.

Here the classical outline of the elementaristic psychology of Herbart, Wundt, and Ebbinghaus were being attacked, from every redoubt, by the eager devotees of the Gestalt psychology. Characteristic also of the period was the new interest in individual differences; for example, in *psychological types*, as exemplified by Kretschmer's conception that types of mental disorder are related to somatic constitutional types, and the efforts of Jaensch to show that eidetic imagery [3] is related to endocrine constitution.

Into this busy and creative intellectual world, which continued to thrive during the Weimar Republic, the Nazi movement threw in 1933 an assassin's bomb. Not only were fanciful ideas about the psychological superiority and inferiority of races promulgated as official doctrine; not only were psychologists politically spied upon, but a great many of them, being Jewish, were expelled from university positions. They flocked in large numbers to other countries, especially to the United States, where they rapidly leavened both experimental and clinical psychology. All four, for example, of the acknowledged leaders of the Gestalt movement—Wertheimer, Köhler, Koffka, and Lewin—found new homes in American institutions. Psychology in Germany under the new regime was able to continue some of its more physiologically oriented studies, even during the war; and it did, during the war, a little research in personality here and there (not very much real research, despite the frequent reference to German psychological warfare). After the collapse in 1945, a few non-Nazis were able to make a painful renewal of effort, but at this writing it remains pitifully small.

In France the center of gravity still lay in medical psychology all during this period, where indeed it still lies today. The "grand old man," Ribot, under whom almost all dominant French psychologists had studied, continued to define his problems in medical terms, a

[3] An extraordinarily vivid type of imagery persisting long after the removal of the stimulus.

mechanistic associationist psychology providing the primary hypothesis. His pupil Dumas began in the twenties to systematize experimental psychology in a vast opus, *Traité de psychologie*, with the usual medical emphasis. Pierre Janet had already made those brilliant applications of associationism to which all the world turned in the opening years of this century, as Janet delivered his lectures at Harvard on the *Major Symptoms of Hysteria*. Personality was a synthesis of ingredients, sensory and affective, integrated in varying fashion from moment to moment as the level of psychological tension went up or down. Encyclopedic in his learning, versatile in his interests, Janet kept up in his *Journal de psychologie* a high standard of scholarship and creativeness, while turning out a remarkable series of personal contributions dealing with everything from cortical irritability to those states of "anguish and ecstasy" between which some of his patients oscillated. Alfred Binet, the only figure of importance in the French school until recently who was not medically trained, represented a range of creative interests comparable to or even surpassing that of Stern. He appeared in the 1880's as a student of experimental hypnosis; proceeded thence to a study of double and multiple personality and of psychic activity of which the individual subject was unaware; he moved forward to the experimental study of graphology and of the suggestibility and the reasoning processes of normal children. But it was the mental defective on the one hand, the lightning calculator or the chess-player on the other—the handicapped and the gifted—that most keenly interested him.

It was largely through Ribot, through Janet, and through Binet that French psychology became known to American and to British psychologists. German psychology, except as represented in the experimental laboratory of Ribot, was on the whole accepted with skepticism in France. Indeed, Binet said quite flatly that he thought all the fuss about "modern psychology" as represented by these German investigations was misplaced, in view of the vitality of personality research going on in his own country. In turn, the Germans paid very little attention to the French contributions of the era. Despite all this, experimental psychology of high rank, as in the work of Piéron, has appeared.[4]

In Britain, the distinction between the Scottish and the English psychology could still be discerned; but everywhere the Scottish emphasis upon the integrity of the individual was now well fused with a Darwinian concern with the adaptation of the individual to his environment. British psychology was evolutionary, and above all,

[4] Piéron, H., *Psychologie experimentale* (1927).

functional (page 219). The dominant psychologists were concerned with the nature of knowing, feeling, and willing, and with the role played by these functions in mediating between the living organism and its environment. Most characteristic of such functionalists was G. F. Stout, while the foremost representative of the evolutionary emphasis was Lloyd Morgan, student of instinct and intelligence at the animal level, who looked for implications of animal studies in human evolutionary psychology. It was Lloyd Morgan who, in his lectures at Harvard and at Clark University during the 1890's, had done more than any other single individual to sensitize the young American experimental psychologists to the interest and importance of animal studies in defining a broad evolutionary approach (cf. page 237). James Ward continued the emphasis of the Scottish tradition upon the unity of the mind. Sensitive to German influences, he had written a highly influential article on psychology in the ninth edition of the *Encyclopedia Britannica*, which probably did as much to define the broad trends that were remaking British psychology as any single book in the era, with the possible exception of Darwin's own *Expression of the Emotions in Man and Animals*. Francis Galton lived on in his pupil Karl Pearson, who in his new biometric laboratory carried on the measurement and statistical evaluation of individual differences. Profoundly indebted to the work of Galton and Pearson was Charles Spearman, who, as has been noted (page 363), saw the implications of these measurements for the development of a formal definition of human abilities. Substantial work in psychometrics and in factor analysis, as in the studies by Cyril Burt and Godfrey Thomson, has continued, while at the Cambridge laboratory F. C. Bartlett has made notable contributions to the study of memory,[5] and of social psychology. In recent years the Cambridge laboratory has put great emphasis on studies of skilled acts, and on fitting the machine to the man.

American psychology in the twentieth century was long dominated by the enthusiasm of the men newly trained in the German laboratories, who rapidly wrested psychology from control by philosophy in American universities, established laboratories for the study of sense perception, psychophysics, reaction time, and the learning process. The British psychology so well known to their immediate American predecessors tended to be displaced rapidly by German formulations which provided a matrix within which the new German experiments could be pursued. They learned to measure, and following Titchener, they learned to introspect.

[5] *Remembering* (1932).

It is not, however, implied that American psychology, as a whole, became "introspective." Even the study of the senses need involve no introspection of any precise technical sort. Jastrow, for example, could measure with new devices the two-point threshold of the skin, while Pillsbury could tell how much movement of a limb was needed before the movement could be reported, without encountering problems of introspection. Cattell's career in America was at no time concerned with reports on the nature of consciousness. While using the new techniques, American psychology was for the most part concerned with studies of performance. Behaviorism accentuated a trend that was already well defined, and mental tests fitted easily into the objective concern with individual differences. Psychoanalysis began to filter into psychiatry, then into psychology, in the second decade of the century. After World War I, as we saw (page 291), Gestalt psychology moved in with a bang. Then came the experimental social psychology of F. H. Allport, the cross-cultural studies of personality, the spread of Institutes of Child Welfare, and the rapid rise of factor analysis.

All of this must not be taken too abstractly. The concrete personal influence of the vivid and compelling figures imported in the thirties was Germany's loss and America's gain. It is a fact, and a very sober and tragic one, that some of the national differences have tended to become *relatively* unimportant in these recent years *not* through the enriching effects of cultural diversity but through the political and economic events which have caused psychologists to multiply and congregate in one country; far more than half of all the psychologists in the world are today in the United States.

While substantial psychological contributions have continued to come from Switzerland, Belgium, the Netherlands, Italy, Poland, and the Scandinavian countries, their relative dependence upon German, French, British, and American sources has inevitably continued; and neither Japan, China, nor India has as yet developed a strong indigenous modern movement in this area (as contrasted with the ancient wisdom of Hinduism and Buddhism). To the psychology of the Soviet Union, however, a separate section must be devoted. As contrasted with physiology (Pavlov, Bekhterev, and the rest), experimental psychology was poorly represented in the old regime. Shortly after the Bolshevik Revolution, child psychology and psychotechnics made rapid progress, while the chief theoretical developments lay in applying the Marxist doctrine of dialectical materialism. This may be sharply contrasted with Western materialism. While Hegel had found that thesis, antithesis, and synthesis must begin with the "Absolute Idea," Marx had commented that Hegel had stood philosophy "on its head," and rewrote the sequence to read: matter (first principle, or thesis) gives rise in time to mind (antithesis) in a dialectical movement which eventuates in the organic synthesis of the living system. Symbolic activities are highly characteristic of mind under cultural conditions. Lenin, developing these principles, strongly emphasized creative cultural activities at a high symbolic level. Highly original research in symbolic thinking was initiated in the twenties by Vigotsky,[6] and by Luria (page 275). The official Communist Party philosophy was as strenuously opposed to "naïve materialism" (for example, Watson) as to idealism. Workers who thought of themselves as robots, responding reflexly like machines, could never remake the social order. A great deal of controversy arose as to what kinds of psychology were truly dialectical, and a good many Russian psychologists were disciplined for approaches that were officially declared to be nondialectical. Western ideas about individual differences and about progressive education had at first been encouraged, later rejected; an especially rigorous campaign in the thirties put an end to intelligence testing and to individualistic tendencies in education (and "soft" methods with delinquent children). Psychotechnics was apparently not much developed during World War II.

The conclusion seems to be warranted that the Soviet authorities are skeptical of the whole Western approach. With dialectical materialism on the one hand, and emphasis upon social molding of the individual on the other (to the virtual neglect of all intrinsic psychological differences), the Russians appear to be determined to work out their own new psychology, free of what they regard as bourgeois preconceptions.

While it is very easy to see the role of sociopolitical factors in the psychology of the U.S.S.R., it may be a little harder, but just as intriguing an enterprise, to see it in our own recent history. Thus in a society relying heavily upon science and technology, devotion to exact science has led to the feeling that exact quantification is fundamental, so that almost automatically those problems become important which permit quantification. The conditioned response, for example, had been well known to Locke and to Spencer, but the exquisite turf-lined chamber in which the dogs' salivation could be measured drop by drop, with no interference from outside noises (something of an anomaly in Czarist Russia), opened up for Amer-

[6] Vigotsky, L. S., "Thought and Speech," *Psychiatry*, 1939, 2, 29–54.

icans a new avenue to all behavioral phenomena. For many years the rough measurement of children's intelligence had but little effect upon theoretical psychology; but the devices for scaling tests in terms of equal units of difficulty, and above all the beautiful operational clarity of a modern factorial analysis, made the organization of the mind a true object of science (a "quantitative rational science" [7]). Personality studies, even with tests whose reliability and validity could be ascertained, gained little status until the public demand for clinical services gave them strong economic support; and even today this newer field, so little resembling the world of laboratory science, has somewhat the character of a relative from the country whose pronunciation makes one wince. Psychoanalysis was for a long time an excessively crude imitation of serious science, until experimentation and operationism, and psychosomatics, made it comparatively reputable; soon, with factorial analysis of psychoanalytic mechanisms, stated as instances of quantifiable conditioning processes, it will be ready for adoption.

PARAPSYCHOLOGY

But it is of course not only the methods, but also the concepts, that must fit into the current standards. The most obvious illustration here is parapsychology (experimental studies in psychical research).[8] Since 1882, systematic work, including a good deal of experimental investigation in long-distance telepathy, had been carried out, as for example by three psychologists at the University of Groningen; but nobody bothered about it. As Titchener had said, no scientifically minded psychologist believes in telepathy; Helmholtz had earlier said that neither the testimony of all the members of the Royal Society nor the evidence of his senses would make him accept it, since it was manifestly impossible. When, in 1934, J. B. Rhine reported, along with preliminary tests under crude conditions, several extensive series of long-distance tests of telepathy and clairvoyance, making use of symbols printed on cards, there was much controversy about his statistics, which soon petered out as it became evident that the slight difference in the formula to be chosen had no bearing on the main findings. Since much of the work then and thereafter was done at long distance, the systematic emphasis on sensory cues from the cards was likewise soon dropped. Emphasis

---

[7] This phrase expresses the aim of the Psychometric Society.

[8] A condensed sketch of parapsychology by Murphy, G., appears in Harriman, P. L., *Encyclopedia of Psychology* (1946), 417–36.

upon possible errors in recording was made, and in reply many successful series reported in which triple checking of records was used. The question therefore had to be rephrased in terms of Rhine's competence. In the meantime investigators at several other American institutions and at three British universities reported extrasensory phenomena under their own specially devised conditions. But by this time the excitement was clearly dying down. The phenomena did not fit in. Perhaps they were fraudulent; perhaps these psychologists were incompetent; at any rate, the practice was not one with which one could afford to waste more time. This is about as the matter stands today. New studies appear in the *Journal of Parapsychology*, but it is not much read. There is no reason to be surprised that emotion arises in this very human situation, either among those who belabor their colleagues for prejudice or among those who resort to ad-hominem arguments. This is a very familiar story in the history of science; for one is dealing with a foreign body in the science of today, and there is trouble in digesting foreign bodies.

THE NATURE-NURTURE CONTROVERSY AS AN EXAMPLE OF CYCLES OF OPINION

But even within the cultural temper of a period there is a place for waves of changing sentiment; for fashions; for new modes; and for very large individual differences in predilection for one rather than another kind of interpretation of data. Good examples are found in the story of the nature-nurture controversy.

The reader will recall the successful revolt of the anti-instinct psychology against McDougall (page 405). Then followed a long period of social psychology, in which the pendulum swung toward nurture, and almost completely ignored the biology of the individual; but this time the swing was not so far. In time one began to stress the differing activities of biologically distinct individuals within the same cultural milieu; the actual behavior was conceived as a fusion of biological and cultural factors. To be concrete, one of the earliest recognitions of this type of reciprocity lay in Benedict's study of the social deviant—the individual incapable of accepting a normal, everyday social role.[9] Benedict undertook to show the varying modes of response available to the cultural group in assimilating and exploiting persons who deviate widely from the central tendency of their group. The wide biological variability within any group

[9] Benedict, R., "Anthropology and the Abnormal," *J. Genet. Psychol.*, 1934, 10, 59–82.

makes a few individuals at the extremes difficult to accept, but they may be accepted for special aberrant roles: the epileptic may be used for the sake of the visions which may come to him in an "epileptic equivalent" or "epileptic furor state." Individuals much more aggressive or much less aggressive than the norm prevailing at the time may be given special tasks suited to their temperament. At the same time, one must note that the kind of temperamental attribute which is nearest to the expected norm in one society may be rather far from the norm in another; an individual who is just aggressive enough in one society may be too unaggressive to carry on his task in another. From this it follows that what is abnormal is relative to the demands of a given society. Suppose, for example, one takes the factors that may predispose to intense suspiciousness, or an egocentric belief that one is entitled to all that is good. If this becomes standardized for a cultural group, or for a social class within that group, individuals who have a high degree of suspiciousness and of egocentric hostility may be normal, while the same individual in another society might be grossly abnormal. Normality is literally an ability to adapt to a norm. This approach has not gone unchallenged, of course, and it has been easy to show that certain types of deviations, such as the development of systematized delusions, are maladaptive in any and all societies; but the essential fact that personality traits spring from the relation between a given individuality and the kind of demand put upon it by society remains fundamental and of greater and greater importance in contemporary studies.

But the reconciliation thus effected is representative not only of certain areas of psychological thinking, but of the whole of it. If one looks at other contemporary studies in the hereditary-environment controversy, one finds much of the old emphasis still evident. The study of the internal regulation of behavior through chemical factors on the one hand, and through the slowly maturing integrative processes of the central nervous system on the other hand, drew attention more and more to the innate determining tendencies of the human species as a whole. Seen phylogenetically, against the background of similar developing systems at the infrahuman level, it became impossible to go on thinking and doing research in these terms while still maintaining the original position of the anti-instinct psychology. Indeed, the whole flurry, ignored by most biologists, may be regarded now as a sort of protest by psychologists against the acceptance of ready-made instincts, partly on the grounds that as portrayed by McDougall they seemed to point to vitalistic factors, and perhaps because they were not so formulated as to stimulate analytical research. With the passage of the intense wave of anti-McDougall and, in general, antivitalist feeling, instinctive mechanisms came slowly back into place. As they came back, they showed beneficial effects of the period of critical discussion. It began to be recognized that heredity and environment, as Carmichael had noted, are neither antithetical nor independent, but aspects of a single process of development, and many looked for a psychology of growth in which neither instinct nor the learning process, but reciprocities and interactions of the two, would be stressed.

The swing of the pendulum appears to be a necessary, indeed an obvious, phase in history. Both laboratory studies and the parallel development of the social sciences in this era show, like most other intellectual movements, a good deal of the dialectical. The thesis gives rise to an antithesis which is as extreme and as hard-bitten as is the original thesis. One swings from paranoid hereditarian theories to paranoid environmentalist theories, and from paranoid biological determination to paranoid social determination. The truth, instead of lying "somewhere between these two extremes," seems to lie rather in gradual assimilation of each system by the other; each one "takes the other in" until the essential truth in both systems appears in an integration. Synthesis is not a mosaic or a medley of fragments torn from the earlier systems; it consists rather in seeing the nature of the reality which expresses itself at times in antithetical forms. In the present instance one may be pretty sure that the social emphasis will in time make fuller and fuller use of the biological individuality which is socialized in a different way in the case of each individual; and will conceive of interpersonal relations as expressions of biological as well as social uniqueness in individual life histories. This will not be a compromise; the social point of view itself entails a recognition that nothing occurs which is not an expression of the individual's biological individuality, and at the same time an expression of his position, his role, his tasks, his place in the social pattern.[10]

---

[10] This will not come all at once. The concepts of heredity and of environment as independent entities are so deeply ingrained in the cultural mold that a psychologist has often returned afresh to the fray, taking a "hereditarian" or an "environmentalist" position, and maintaining his loyalty to one or the other emphasis. A symposium in 1947 in the *Psychological Review* renews the emphasis upon the instinctive factor, the gene-determined factor, in individual action patterns. We shall long hear the familiar phrases: heredity versus environment; basic traits versus socially acquired traits; viscerogenic versus sociogenic motives, and the rest.

THE ISSUE OF WHOLES AND PARTS

But the most acute of all issues in contemporary psychology seems to be the issue of *wholes and parts*, the quest for patterned structure or for the definition and functional analysis of component elements. It is in a sense the old issue of Aristotle's forms versus Democritus's atoms, but it is stated today in terms of evolutionary holism, the indivisibility of the "living system," or in terms of laboratory analysis of behavior into identifiable and measurable units. There are so many facts that call for the one approach, so many that call for the other, that at first sight one might hesitate to make a final choice between them. One may assess the spirit of modern psychology by attempting to find out why the controversy goes on.

In Chapter 25 it was noted that there is much to show that the nervous system is best understood if one first understands its parts; likewise to show that its parts are best understood if one first understands it as a whole. We had to skirt around a bog of doubts, for we were sure of two things that seemed contradictory. Actually, the same two things were known in the 1880's. Indeed, the familiar experiments with the spinal frog were used in that period both to prove the machinelike nature of reflexes and to show the evolutionary significance of activities which express the integrating dynamics of the frog's nervous system, permitting activity to go on even after one limb or another has been bound or paralyzed.

In modern biology each group may momentarily silence the other by such observations as these: 1. "It's all very well to talk of the 'real life situation' and the 'artificial' laboratory situation, but such knowledge as we have regarding vitamins, vaccines, penicillin, comes from simplification from a state of confusion found in nature. The supposedly artificial situation gets the results, and you can literally use them to save the 'life' about which you have been spouting." 2. "You use them, but how do you use them? You find under what actual conditions they work, under what conditions they fail, or interfere with life. Much that you find *in vitro* won't work *in vivo*, simply because you don't really understand the living system. It is a living system that determines whether, and how, the vitamin, or vaccine, or penicillin, will actually function."

One may begin to suspect that the basic temperamental or emotional incompatibility of the promachine and antimachine theorists has changed rather little in recent decades. One might even point out that the issue drawn by La Mettrie two hundred years ago still stands approximately as he defined it. More and more technical research gives more and more weapons to each school. The history of biology and that of psychology give no reason for believing that the question of mechanism is soluble by the mere accumulation of more and more data. Definitions of machines become more and more subtle. It is indeed difficult to imagine a crucial test which would convince any atomist that an organismic principle appears, or vice versa. Perhaps we are moving toward the view that neither formulation is very well attuned to the actual life of the organism— that perhaps life processes are so much more complicated than machine processes that it is not very useful to compare one with the other, and at the same time not very useful to insist on their ultimate discontinuity.

An example of such a view would be the view formulated by C. D. Broad under the term "emergent vitalism." [11] This is the doctrine that much that is really new develops not by the addition of a new substance, but by the emergence of attributes at one level which cannot exist at an earlier one. It should, however, be stressed that these speculations as to a possible mode of integration of the two ways of thinking are not actually *characteristic* of the temper of psychologists in general at the present time. While gratefully receiving experimental material of all sorts, they remain, by and large, determined to vindicate either the analytic approach or the organismic approach.

It may well be objected that the discussion confuses two issues. Analysis versus organicism is by no means the same as the issue between those who find in life something transcending the ordinary concepts of science and those who do not. To this, it must be replied that while this latter distinction still has some place in European psychology, it has never had much place in American psychology; and with the demoralization of European psychology in recent years, it remains to be seen whether the conflict over these dualistic kinds of vitalism is important at the moment. On the other hand, the issue between those who proceed from the small to the large and those who proceed from the large to the small continues to be a *very acute* issue; and the fact that it cannot be resolved by any present type of evidence, or by any evidence of which we can conceive, makes one wonder whether the hope, until recently entertained, of achieving an integrated view of the organism which will make use of all the sciences as its foundation has actually much chance of fulfillment in the present era.

11 Broad, C. D., *The Mind and Its Place in Nature* (1923).

But fortunately science can still go on while the warfare of ideologies continues both outside and inside the laboratories and clinics. Man has developed in recent centuries a confident hope that a series of approximations to reality can in actual fact be discovered by science, and that this is worth all that it costs. Economic or political events may, at the next turn of the road, crush all that is known in free scientific inquiry—and reduce us to technical servants of a central authority. But perhaps also the method of science applied both in laboratories and in community relations may help in some small measure to delay, or even to fend off, that threat to the spirit of inquiry, without which psychology will promptly curl up and die.

REFERENCES

Bruner, J. S., and Allport, G. W., "Fifty Years of Change in American Psychology," *Psychol. Bull.*, 1940, 37, 737–76

Brunswik, Egon, in Harriman, P. L., *Encyclopedia of Psychology*, Philosophical Library, 1946, pp. 523–37

Dwelshauvers, Georges, *La psychologie française contemporaire*, Paris, 1920

Fernberger, Samuel W., "A National Analysis of the Psychological Articles Published in 1939," *Amer. J. Psychol.*, 1940, 53, 295–97

Hall, Margaret E., "The Present Status of Psychology in South America," *Psychol. Bull.*, 1946, 43, 441–76

Hartmann, George W., and Schiller, P., "Contemporary Hungarian Psychologies," *Psychol. Bull.*, 1940, 37, 621–28

Klüver, Heinrich, "Contemporary German Psychology," in Murphy, G., *An Historical Introduction to Modern Psychology*, Harcourt, Brace, 1929, pp. 417–55

Murchison, Carl A., ed., *A History of Psychology in Autobiography*, 3 vols., Clark University Press, 1930–36

Murray, Henry A., Jr., "What Should Psychology Do about Psychoanalysis?" *J. Abn. and Soc. Psychol.*, 1940, 35, 150–75

Pratt, J. G., Rhine, J. B., Smith, B. M., and Stuart, C. E., with Greenwood, J. A., *Extra-sensory Perception after 60 Years* (1940), Holt

Razran, Gregory H. S., "Current Psychological Theory in the U.S.S.R.," *Psychol. Bull.*, 1947, 39, 445–46

Woodworth, Robert S., *Contemporary Schools of Psychology*, rev. ed., Ronald Press, 1948

Wyatt, F., and Teuber, H. L., "German Psychology under the Nazi System, 1933–40," *Psychol. Rev.*, 1944, 51, 229–47

BIBLIOGRAPHY

Primary sources are given in the text itself or in footnotes, and can most easily be traced in the name index. Secondary sources, as well as a few primary sources considered feasible for general class use, are given as "References" at the ends of chapters. Below are listed a few volumes dealing with general psychological history. When dealing with the contemporary period these must of course be generously eked out by following up the clues given in the surveys and reviews in the psychological journals, and above all by those given in the *Psychological Abstracts*.

Baldwin, James M., *A History of Psychology: A Sketch and an Interpretation*, Putnam, 1913

Boring, Edwin G., *A History of Experimental Psychology*, Century, 1929

———, *Sensation and Perception in the History of Experimental Psychology*, Appleton-Century, 1942

Brennan, Robert E., *History of Psychology, from the Standpoint of a Thomist*, Macmillan, 1945

Brett, George S., *A History of Psychology*, 3 vols., London, 1914–1921

Dennis, Wayne, ed., *Readings in the History of Psychology*, Appleton-Century, 1948

Dessoir, Max, *Outlines of the History of Psychology*, Macmillan, 1912

Flügel, John C., *A Hundred Years of Psychology, 1833–1933*, Macmillan, 1933

Hulin, William S., *A Short History of Psychology*, Holt, 1934

Klemm, Otto, *A History of Psychology*, Scribner, 1914

Müller-Freienfels, Richard, *The Evolution of Modern Psychology*, Yale University Press, 1935

Murchison, Carl A., ed., *A History of Psychology in Autobiography*, 3 vols., Clark University Press, 1930–36

Pillsbury, Walter B., *The History of Psychology*, Norton, 1929

Rand, Benjamin, ed., *The Classical Moralists*, Houghton Mifflin, 1909

———, ed., *The Classical Psychologists*, Houghton Mifflin, 1919

Ribot, Théodule Armand, *English Psychology*, London, 1873

———, *German Psychologies of Today*, Scribner, 1886

Russell, Bertrand, *History of Western Philosophy*, Simon and Schuster, 1946

Siebeck, Hermann, *Geschichte der Psychologie*, 2 vols., Gotha, 1880–84

Spearman, Charles E., *Psychology down the Ages*, Macmillan, 1937

Warren, Howard C., *A History of the Association Psychology from Hartley to Lewes*, Scribner, 1921

Williams, Robert D., and Bellows, R. M., *The Background of Contemporary Psychology*, H. L. Hedrick, Columbus, Ohio, 1935

INDEX OF NAMES

Abraham, Karl, 319, 323, 332
Ach, Narziss, 155, 228–29
Ackerman, Nathan W., ref. to publ.,
 386 n.
Addison, Thomas, 384
Adler, Alfred, 336–41, 345–47, 420;
 breaks with Freud, 329–30, 337–38;
 ref. to publ., 347
Agassiz, Louis, 116
Alexander, Franz, ref. to publ., 387 n.
Allen, Frederick, 427
Allport, Floyd H., 263 n., 407–10, 438;
 quoted, 105 n.
Allport, Gordon W., 420; ref. to publ.,
 429, 446
Alschuler, Rose H., 425
Andersen, Hans Christian, ref. to, 346
Angell, Frank, 168
Angell, James R., 208 n., 223, 230,
 259
Angyal, András, ref. to publ., 429
Aristotle, 6, 8–12, 21 n., 26, 101, 224;
 influence of, 22, 25, 27, 29; quoted,
 17, 307, 351; ref. to, 4, 176 n., 402,
 444; ref. to publ., 16
Arlitt, Ada H., 360
Arnheim, Rudolf, 292
Arnold, Magda B., 384
Aster, Ernst von, 232 n.
Aubert, Hermann, 143
Augustine, St., 11, 23

Bacon, Francis, 14
Bain, Alexander, 61, 63, 102–09, 153,
 195–96, 264 n., 285, 391; influence of,
 283; quoted, 234; ref. to, 99, 146, 150,
 184, 238, 247
Bair, Joseph H., ref. to publ., 242 n.,
 272 n.
Baldwin, James Mark, 212, 263 n.; ref.
 to publ., 16
Bard, Philip, 383–84
Barker, Roger G., 302
Barnes, Harry Elmer, ref. to publ.,
 417 n., 418

Bartlett, Frederic C., 437
Bastian, Adolf, 123
Bateson, Gregory, 342, 422
Baumgarten, Alexander Gottlieb, 73
Bavelas, Alex, 304
Beccaria, Giovanni Battista, 41–42
Beck, Samuel Joseph, 427
Beer, Theodor, 254
Beers, Clifford W., 329
Bekhterev, Vladimir Mikhailovich,
 157 n., 211, 258–59, 261, 320, 438
Bell, Sir Charles, 77–78, 93, 375
Bellak, Leopold, ref. to publ., 347
Benedict, Ruth, 422–23, 441–42
Beneke, Friedrich Eduard, 97–100,
 219
Bentham, Jeremy, 24, 41–42, 47, 102–
 03, 402
Bergson, Henri, 285
Berkeley, George, 26 n., 30–32, 35, 92–
 93
Bernard, Luther L., 405
Bernfeld, Siegfried, ref. to publ., 330
Bernheim, Hippolyte, 135, 308–09
Bertrand, Alexis, 135 n.
Bessel, Friedrich Wilhelm, 137–38
Bethe, Hans Albrecht, 254
Bichat, Marie-François Xavier, 38–39,
 47, 76; ref. to, 43, 72, 153 n.
Binet, Alfred, 171, 211–12, 229, 241,
 245, 391, 436; tests, 354–56, 358–60,
 391; ref. to publ., 371
Binger, Carl A. L., 386–87
Biot, Jean-Baptiste, ref. to, 85
Biran. See Maine de Biran.
Blix, Magnus, 81 n., 95, 166
Blodgett, Hugh C., ref. to publ.,
 279 n.
Boas, Franz, 361, 409
Boerhaave, Hermann, 75
Bolton, Frederick E., ref. to publ.,
 245 n.
Bonnet, Charles, 37 n., 161 n.; quoted,
 77 n.
Book, William F., 236

Boring, Edwin G., quoted, 137; ref. to publ., 16, 48, 63, 90 *n.*, 98, 136, 148, 173, 215 *n.*, 224, 233, 248, 432 *n.*
Bouguer, Pierre, 83
Bowers, Anna M., ref. to publ., 330
Bradley, Francis Herbert, 100, 247
Brahe, Tycho, 13–14
Braid, James, 134–35, 170
Bramwell, John M., ref. to publ., 136
Bregman, Elsie O., ref. to publ., 276 *n.*, 357 *n.*
Brentano, Franz, 211, 225–26
Brett, George S., quoted, 30, 102, 172 *n.*; ref. to publ., 4 *n.*, 16, 29, 48, 63, 110, 173, 183,
Breuer, Joseph, 307–09, 310 *n.*
Bridgman, Laura Dewey, 264 *n.*
Brigham, Carl C., ref. to publ., 358 *n.*
Broad, C. D., 445
Broca, Paul, 185, 375–76, 378
Brodhun, Eugen, 166
Bronner, Augusta F., ref. to publ., 330
Brotemarkle, Robert A., ref. to publ., 429
Brown, Emily M., ref. to publ., 242 *n.*
Brown, James F., 412
Brown, Thomas, 59–63, 81, 100–01, 106, 117, 156; ref. to, 27, 163, 182
Bruner, Jerome S., 413; ref. to publ., 446
Brunswik, Egon, 432–33; ref. to publ., 446
Bryan, William L., 162, 234–36, 238
Bryant, Sophie, 163
Bühler, Charlotte, 394
Bühler, Karl, 229–30, 394; ref. to, 232
Buffon, Georges L. L., comte de, 112
Burks, Barbara S., 369–70
Burt, Cyril L., 356, 362, 437
Burton, Robert, 16
Burtt, Edwin Arthur, ref. to publ., 26 *n.*, 50 *n.*
Byron, George Gordon, Lord, ref. to, 179

Cabanis, Pierre, 19 *n.*, 38–39, 47, 57–58, 62, 373; ref. to, 43, 72, 94
Calkins, Mary W., 60 *n.*, 182, 208 *n.*, 212; ref. to publ., 427 *n.*
Calvin, John, 23
Cannon, Walter B., 382–85; ref. to, 290; ref. to publ., 388
Cantril, Hadley, 413
Carlyle, Thomas, ref. to., 73
Carmichael, Leonard, ref. to, 443; ref. to publ., 77 *n.*, 401
Carpenter, William B., 106–07, 195, 204 *n.*, 253

Cason, Hulsey, 266, 278
Cattell, James McK., 160–65, 177, 212, 235, 245, 353, 431, 438; ref. to, 155, 172, 223, 238, 260
Charcot, Jean-Martin, 51 *n.*, 135–36, 169–70, 307–08; ref. to, 194, 402
Chassell, Joseph O., 426
Chladni, Ernst F. F., 71
Chrobak, Rudolf, 308
Claparède, Edouard, 211, 245, 391
Clark, Kenneth B., 413
Cobb, Margaret V., ref. to publ., 357 *n.*
Cohn, Alfred E., ref. to publ., 386 *n.*
Comenius, Johann Amos, 389
Comte, Auguste, 124–25
Condillac, Etienne Bonnot de, 36–39, 43, 44 *n.*, 49, 62
Condorcet, Marie-Jean A. N. de Caritat, marquis de, 43, 69
Conradi, Edward, ref. to publ., 263 *n.*
Cooley, Charles H., 416, 417 *n.*, 427
Copernicus, Nicolaus, 13–14
Cottrell, Leonard S., ref. to publ., 418
Coué, Emile, 135 *n.*, 203 *n.*
Cousin, Victor, 59
Cowling, Donald J., 246
Culler, Elmer, 275
Cuvier, Georges L. C. F. D., baron, 72, 113

Dallam, M. Theresa, ref. to publ., 243 *n.*
Dallenbach, Karl M., 270
Dalton, John, 140 *n.*
Dampier, Sir William, quoted, 67
Darsie, Marvin L., Jr., 361
Darwin, Charles Robert, 57, 112–15, 121, 149, 173, 367, 389, 430; ref. to publ., 126
Darwin, Erasmus, 72, 112
Davenport, Charles B., 367–68
Davis, Hallowell, ref. to publ., 142 *n.*
Dax, Marc, 375
Dearborn, Walter F., 242
De Jaager, J. J., 138–39
Delezenne, Charles E. J., 82–83
Dembo, Tamara, 302
Democritus, 6–8, 252; ref. to, 25, 430, 444
Dennis, Wayne, 397; ref. to publ., 16, 29, 48, 63, 98, 110, 136, 148, 173
De Sanctis, Sante, ref. to publ., 354 *n.*, 391 *n.*
Descartes, René, 17–21, 23 *n.*, 24–25, 252; influence of, 47, 57, 93, 199 *n.*; ref. to, 3–4, 38–39, 43, 94, 116, 403
Dessoir, Max, quoted, 6; ref. to publ., 4 *n.*, 16
Destutt de Tracy, Antoine L. C., comte, 62

De Vries, Hugo, 367
Dewey, John, 168 *n.*, 212, 222–23, 240, 392, 416, 417 *n.*
Dilthey, Wilhelm, 211
Diogenes Laertius, quoted, 49, 210
Dix, Dorothea Lynde, 129, 131, 168 *n.*
Doll, Edgar A., 358
Donders, Frans Cornelis, 138–39, 155
Du Bois, Cora A., ref. to publ., 343 *n.*
Du Bois-Reymond, Emil, 96–97
Dugdale, Richard L., 119, 366
Dumas, Georges, 436
Dunbar, Helen Flanders, 385–86; ref. to publ., 388
Dunlap, Knight, 405, 410
Durkheim, Emile, ref. to publ., 418 *n.*
Durkin, Helen E., 294–95
Dwelshauvers, Georges, ref. to publ., 446

Ebbinghaus, Hermann, 167, 174–81, 210, 236, 280, 352–53, 434–35; ref. to, 52, 54 *n.*, 234, 238, 363; ref. to publ., 183
Ebert, Ernst, 242; ref. to publ., 244 *n.*
Ehrenfels, Christian, freiherr von, 226, 286–87, 289
Einstein, Albert, 297
Ekstein, Rudolf, ref. to publ., 347
Elliotson, John, 133–34
Ellis, Havelock, 318 *n.*
Ellis, Willis D., ref. to publ., 296
Engels, Friedrich, 125
English, Horace B., 362
Ephrussi, Paula, ref. to publ., 182 *n.*
Epicurus, 10, 252
Erikson, Erik H., 343
Esdaile, James, 133–34
Esquirol, Jean E. D., 127–28
Estabrook, Arthur H., ref. to publ., 366 *n.*
Ewald, Richard Julius, 141–42
Exner, Sigmund, 155, 190 *n.*

Farrand, Livingston, ref. to publ., 164 *n.*
Fechner, Gustav Theodor, 84–92, 117, 120 *n.*, 175, 193, 241 *n.*; ref. to, 54, 83, 137, 149–50, 153 *n.*, 155, 160 *n.*, 164, 288
Fenichel, Otto, ref. to publ., 346 *n.*
Féré, Charles Samson, 171
Ferguson, George O., Jr., 360
Fernald, Grace M., 354
Fernald, Mabel R., 246
Fernberger, Samuel W., ref. to publ., 446
Ferrari, Giulio, 391 *n.*
Ferrier, Sir David, 185

Fichte, Johann Gottlieb, 47, 84
Flourens, Pierre J. M., 95, 375
Flournoy, Theodore, 172, 211
Flügel, John C., ref. to publ., 110
Fourier, François M. C., 111
Fox, George, 203
Fracker, George C., 243
Frank, Jerome D., 301
Frank, Lawrence K., 426; ref. to publ., 423 *n.*
Franklin, Benjamin, 132–33, 168 *n.*
Franz, Shepherd I., 376
Freeman, Frank N., 369; ref. to publ., 370 *n.*
Freud, Anna, 326, 398
Freud, Sigmund, 51 *n.*, 211, 307–30, 400, 404 *n.*; influence of, 331–47, 386; ref. to, 159, 269, 302, 395, 397, 420, 422
Fries, Jakob Friedrich, 55–56, 201 *n.*
Fritsch, Gustave, 185, 375
Froebel, Friedrich W. A., 53, 389
Fröbes, Joseph, ref. to publ., 90 *n.*
Fromm, Erich, 344–45, 422; ref. to publ., 347
Fromme, Allan, quoted, 160 *n.*, 418 *n.*
Fuller, Benjamin A. G., ref. to publ., 16
Fullerton, George S., 164–65
Fulton, John F., ref. to publ., 191 *n.*

Galen, 16, 77
Galileo, 4, 14–15, 24, 67–68
Gall, Franz Joseph, 19 *n.*, 56–57, 95
Gallup, George H., 411
Galton, Sir Francis, 117–22, 156–57, 163–64, 174–76, 212, 237, 352–53, 366; influence of, 165, 172, 437; ref. to, 138, 149; ref. to publ., 126
Galvani, Luigi, 71
Gantt, William Horsley, 275
Garrett, Henry E., 365–66
Gassner, Johann Joseph, 132
Gates, Arthur I., 245–46
Gauss, Karl Friedrich, 121–22
Gay, Rev. John, 32 *n.*
Geissler, Ludwig R., 215
Gelb, Adhemar, 374, 378–79
Gesell, Arnold L., 121 *n.*, 399; ref. to publ., 401
Gilbert, William, 14, 67
Girden, Edward, 275
Glaucon, 23 *n.*
Glueck, Sheldon and Eleanor T., 426
Goddard, Henry H., 354, 366, 368
Goethe, Johann Wolfgang von, 76, 111, 143–44; quoted, 284; ref. to, 46
Goldscheider, Alfred, 81 *n.*, 166
Goldsmith, Oliver, ref. to, 55 *n.*

Goldstein, Kurt, 374, 378–79; ref. to publ., 388
Golgi, Camillo, 187
Goodenough, Florence L., 424–25
Goodman, Cecile C., 413
Gould, Rosalind, 301
Gray, Thomas, 22 *n.*
Green, Thomas Hill, 100, 108
Greenwood, Joseph A., ref. to publ., 446
Gregory of Nyssa, quoted, 251
Griesinger, Wilhelm, 128
Groddeck, Georg Walther, 324
Grünbaum, Anton A., 185
Guggenbühl, Johann Jakob, 131
Guilford, Joy Paul, ref. to publ., 371
Guthrie, Edwin R., 266 *n.*, 269, 272

Haeckel, Ernst Heinrich, 116, 253
Halbwachs, Maurice, ref. to publ., 418 *n.*
Hall, G[ranville] Stanley, 168, 202, 212, 329, 333, 390; ref. to publ., 98, 148
Hall, Margaret E., ref. to publ., 446
Haller, Albrecht von, 75, 83, 96
Halstead, Ward, ref. to publ., 388
Hamilton, Sir William, 84, 100–02, 161 *n.*, 247
Harriman, Philip L., ref. to publ., 371, 401, 440 *n.*, 446
Hart, Bernard, 329
Harter, Noble H., 162, 234–36, 238
Hartley, David, 30, 32–34, 39, 101–02, 104, 180, 239 *n.*, 284; ref. to, 26, 36, 37 *n.*, 47, 50–52, 59–62, 94, 103, 106, 108, 150, 156, 247, 265 *n.*
Hartmann, Eduard von, 51 *n.*, 204 *n.*
Hartmann, George W., ref. to publ., 296, 446
Harvey, William, 16, 75 *n.*
Hattwick, La Berta W., 425
Head, Henry, 374, 378–79, 382
Healy, William, 208 *n.*, 354, 356, 392, 419; ref. to publ., 330
Hegel, Georg W. F., 47 *n.*, 73, 111, 154, 193, 438–39
Hegelmaier, F., ref. to publ., 89 *n.*
Heidbreder, Edna, ref. to publ., 224, 268, 296
Helmholtz, Hermann L. F. von, 71, 93 *n.*, 95–97, 117, 137–43, 149–50, 154, 440; ref. to, 83, 155, 160 *n.*, 165–66, 193, 252, 265, 373; ref. to publ., 148
Helson, Harry, 285
Henmon, Victor A. C., ref. to publ., 173, 353 *n.*
Henry, George W., ref. to publ., 136, 330

Henry, Joseph, 168 *n.*
Hensen, Viktor, 141
Heraclitus, quoted, 17
Herbart, Johann Friedrich, 49–55, 93, 101, 117, 147, 153, 177 *n.*, 180, 225, 389; ref. to, 97–99, 154 *n.*, 219, 331, 353, 435
Hering, Ewald, 143–45
Hermann, Ludimar, ref. to publ., 143 *n.*, 155 *n.*
Herrick, Charles J., ref. to publ., 260 *n.*
Heymans, Gerardus, 212
Hilgard, Ernest R., ref. to publ., 277 *n.*, 280 *n.*, 283
Hinshelwood, James, 186, 376
Hippocrates, quoted, 111; ref. to, 39, 334, 374
His, Wilhelm, 187
Hitzig, Eduard, 185, 375
Hobbes, Thomas, 19 *n.*, 21–32, 39, 60, 170, 252–53, 257; ref. to, 3–4, 33 *n.*, 34, 55 *n.*, 94, 150, 163, 239, 402
Hobhouse, Leonard Trelawney, 116 *n.*, 212
Höffding, Harald, 211, 217–19, 223, 226
Hollingworth, Harry L., 214, 247–48, 278; ref. to publ., 359 *n.*
Hollingworth, Leta S., 399
Holt, Edwin B., 207, 221, 262
Holzinger, Karl J., 369; ref. to publ., 370 *n.*
Homer, ref. to, 5–6
Hoppe, Ferdinand, 301
Horkheimer, Max, ref. to publ., 344 *n.*
Horney, Karen, 345–46, 422; ref. to publ., 347
Horowitz, Eugene L., 411
Horwicz, Adolf, 153
Howe, Samuel Gridley, 130–31, 168 *n.*
Hudgins, Clarence V., 271–72
Hulin, Wilbur S., ref. to publ., 16
Hull, Clark L., 267, 272–74, 280–81; ref. to publ., 283
Humboldt, Alexander, freiherr von, 55, 70 *n.*
Hume, David, 30, 32, 34, 44
Hunt, Joseph McV., ref. to publ., 275 *n.*, 381 *n.*, 429
Hunter, Walter S., 271–72
Huxley, Thomas Henry, 116
Huygens, Christian, 71 *n.*

Ibsen, Henrik, ref. to, 328
Ilg, Frances L., ref. to publ., 401
Infeld, Leopold, 297
Isaacs, Susan S. F., 398
Itard, Jean M. G., 130

Jackson, John Hughlings, 38 n., 378
Jacobs, Joseph, 177
Jacobson, Edmund, ref. to publ., 265 n.
Jaensch, Erich, 435
James, William, 19 n., 51 n., 91, 102, 105–06, 154 n., 160 n., 168, 170, 188–89, 192–209, 236, 285, 373; influence of, 169, 207–09, 222; philosophy of, 206–07; quoted, 90 n., 310 n., 430; ref. to, 216, 228, 237, 242, 247, 376; ref. to publ., 183, 191, 209
Janet, Pierre, 51 n., 170, 204 n., 211, 311, 404 n., 436; ref. to, 194, 269
Jastrow, Joseph, 168 n., 212, 245, 438
Jefferson, Thomas, quoted, 149
Jenkins, John G., 270
Jennings, Helen H., 414
Jensen, Friedrich, ref. to publ., 348
Jersild, Arthur T., 399; ref. to publ., 401
Jones, Ernest, 316
Judd, Charles H., 223, 246
Jung, Carl Gustav, 331–36; breaks with Freud, 329–30, 333–36; ref. to, 269; ref. to publ., 347

Kant, Immanuel, 36 n., 43–47, 55–56, 73–74, 97, 112 n., 153, 225; influence of, 53, 92, 95, 100; ref. to, 147, 404 n.
Kantor, Jacob R., 292
Kardiner, Abram, 342, 422
Karpf, Fay B., ref. to publ., 418
Kelly, Robert L., 353
Kempf, Edward J., 382; ref. to publ., 153 n.
Kendall, Edward C., 384
Kent, Grace H., 163 n.
Kepler, Johannes, 14, 26 n., 68
Kirkpatrick, Edwin A., 353
Klages, Ludwig, 424, 434
Klein, Melanie, 398
Klineberg, Otto, 361–62
Klopfer, Bruno, 428
Klüver, Heinrich, ref. to publ., 446
Köhler, Wolfgang, 287, 290–92, 298–99, 435; ref. to publ., 296, 388 n.
König, Arthur, 166
Koffka, Kurt, 287, 290–92, 299, 413, 435; ref. to publ., 296
Kraepelin, Emil, 128, 157–58
Krasnogorski, Nikolai Ivanovich, 266
Krechevsky, Isadore, 282; ref. to publ., 279 n.
Kretschmer, Ernst, 421, 435
Krugman, Morris, ref. to publ., 429
Kuhlmann, Frederick, 356
Külpe, Oswald, 60 n., 167, 210, 221–22, 227–28, 230, 233, 244, 251

Ladd, George T., 212, 223; quoted, 184; ref. to publ., 183, 191, 240 n., 248
Ladd-Franklin, Christine, 145
Lamarck, Jean-Baptiste P. A. de Monet, chevalier de, 72, 112–13, 153 n.
La Mettrie, Julien Offroy de, 20, 170, 252–54, 267, 444
Lange, Carl Georg, 199
Lange, Ludwig, 155
Lange, Maria W. de, ref. to publ., 258 n.
Lanier, Lyle H., ref. to publ., 360 n.
Laplace, Pierre Simon, marquis de, 69–70, 112, 121
Laromiguière, Pierre, 62, 226 n.
Lashley, Karl S., 266, 282–83, 374, 376–78, 381; quoted, 267 n.; ref. to publ., 388
Lasker, Bruno, 411
Lasswell, Harold D., ref. to publ., 418 n.
Lavoisier, Antoine Laurent, 70, 76, 132
Lazarus, Moritz, 125
Leahy, Alice M., 369
Le Bon, Gustave, 325, 402
Leeper, Robert, ref. to publ., 306
Leeuwenhoek, Anthony, 16
Lehman, Alfred, 211
Leibnitz, Gottfried Wilhelm, freiherr von, 4, 20–21, 53, 153, 225; quoted, 3; ref. to, 101, 109
Lenin, Nikolai, 439
Lerner, Eugene, 396; ref. to publ., 425 n.
Levy, David M., 398, 426–27
Lewin, Kurt, 280, 299–305, 412, 416, 435; ref. to publ., 306
Lewinson, Thea S., 424
Liddell, Howard S., 275
Liébault, Ambroise-Auguste, 135–36, 402
Liebig, Justus, freiherr von, 70–71, 76
Likert, Rensis, 411
Lillie, R. S., 191
Lindsley, Donald B., ref. to publ., 381 n.
Linnaeus, Carolus, 72
Lippitt, Ronald, 303
Lipps, Theodor, 167
Locke, John, 27–31, 45, 61, 195, 257, 439; influence of, 33, 36–37, 43; ref. to, 50, 225, 228, 276; ref. to publ., 29
Loeb, Jacques, 253–54, 257
Lombroso, Cesare, 211
London, Ivan D., ref. to publ., 306
Lorand, Alexander S., ref. to publ., 348
Lotze, Rudolf Hermann, 19 n., 93, 145–48, 154 n., 287–88; ref. to, 83, 150, 184, 198
Loucks, Roger B., 275
Lubbock, Sir John, ref. to publ., 237 n.

Lucas, Keith, 191
Lucretius, 109 *n.*, 111; quoted, 373
Luria, Alexander R., 275, 332 *n.*, 439
Lyell, Sir Charles, 112, 115
Lynd, Robert S., ref. to publ., 418 *n.*

McDougall, William, 19 *n.*, 190 *n.*, 201 *n.*, 212, 219, 403–06, 441–43; ref. to, 57 *n.*, 281, 408, 410
Macfarlane, Jean W., 400, 426
McGeoch, John A., ref. to publ., 270 *n.*, 283
McGraw, Myrtle B., 399
McGregor, Douglas, 413
Mach, Ernst, 206, 211, 226, 230, 240, 285–86
Machiavelli, Niccolò, 22–23
McKinnon, Donald W., ref. to publ., 418
Magendie, François, 77
Maine de Biran, Pierre, 57–59, 62–63, 218
Malebranche, Nicolas de, 19–20, 199 *n.*
Malinowski, Bronislaw Kasper, 341–42, 409
Malthus, Thomas Robert, 114–15
Mann, Cecil W., ref. to publ., 371
Mann, Thomas, quoted, 331
Marbe, Karl, 227, 228 *n.*
Marie, Pierre, 376
Marquis, Donald G., ref. to publ., 280 *n.*, 283
Marro, Antonio, 391 *n.*
Marx, Karl, 125; quoted, 402
Masefield, John, quoted, 373, 419
Masserman, Jules H., 384
Mateer, Florence E., 266
Matthiessen, Francis O., ref. to publ., 209
Maudsley, Henry, 107, 153, 170, 253
Maury, Louis F. A., ref. to publ., 311 *n.*
Max, Louis W., ref. to publ., 265 *n.*
Max Müller, Friedrich, 125
Maxwell, James Clerk, 298
Mead, George H., 416, 417 *n.*, 427
Mead, Margaret, 342, 397, 410, 421–22
Melzi, Costantino, 391 *n.*
Mendel, Gregor Johann, 367–68
Merrill, Maud A., 356; ref. to publ., 372
Merz, John T., quoted, 85, 98; ref. to publ., 63, 67 *n.*, 126, 191
Mesmer, Franz Anton, 131–36
Messer, August, 227
Meumann, Ernst, 242, 355, 391; ref. to publ., 244 *n.*
Meynert, Theodor Hermann, 188 *n.*
Miles, Walter R., 359
Mill, James, 63, 102–05, 196, 247, 353

Mill, John Stuart, 102 *n.*, 104, 107, 124, 154, 285; quoted, 99
Milton, John, 22 *n.*
Mitchell, Blythe C., 369
Moede, Walther, 406–07
Montague, William P., 220
Montaigne, Michel Eyquem de, 55 *n.*
Montessori, Maria, 211
Moore, Henry T., 143 *n.*, 407
Moore, Kathleen C., 392
Moore, Thomas V., 231
More, Sir Thomas, 22, 23 *n.*
Moreau de Tours, Paul, 127
Moreno, Jacob L., 414–15
Morgan, C. D., 425
Morgan, Clifford T., quoted, 380 *n.*; ref. to publ., 388
Morgan, [Conwy] Lloyd, 116 *n.*, 172–73, 212, 237, 437; ref. to publ., 238 *n.*
Morgan, John J. B., 261
Morgulis, Sergius, 259; ref. to publ., 257
Morley, Christopher, quoted, 307
Mosso, Angelo, 172, 211
Moutier, François, ref. to publ., 376 *n.*
Mowrer, Orval H., 273, 277
Müller, Georg Elias, 89 *n.*, 90 *n.*, 155–56, 167, 181–83, 210, 243–44, 434; ref. to publ., 183
Müller, Johannes Peter, 75 *n.*, 76–78, 92–97, 99, 137–38, 140, 147, 184, 375
Müller, Max. *See* Max Müller.
Müller-Freienfels, Richard, 336
Münsterberg, Hugo, 148 *n.*, 168, 193, 212, 219–20, 244, 406–07
Muenzinger, Karl F., 277
Murchison, Carl A., ref. to publ., 224, 233, 248, 371, 384 *n.*, 388, 401, 418, 446
Murphy, Gardner, ref. to publ., 304 *n.*, 348, 418, 440 *n.*, 446
Murphy, Lois B., ref. to publ., 418, 425 *n.*
Murray, Gilbert, 5; quoted, 9
Murray, Henry A., 420, 425; ref. to publ., 429, 446
Myers, Charles Samuel, 173
Myers, Frederic W. H., 51 *n.*, 204 *n.*, 205, 212
Myerson, Abraham, ref. to publ., 348

Nafe, John P., 215
Nernst, Walther Hermann, 191
Newcomb, Theodore M., ref. to publ., 418
Newman, Horatio H., 121 *n.*, 370
Newton, Sir Isaac, 4, 14–15, 18, 68, 143, 297–98; influence of, 33–34, 50, 67–70
Norsworthy, Naomi, 353–54

Oberholzer, Emil, 424; ref. to publ., 343 n.
Ogden, Robert M., 291
Oken, Lorenz, 47, 85
Orata, Paula Tamesis, 281
Orbeli, Leon, 257
Origen, 11

Paracelsus, Philippus Aureolus, 75, 131
Paterson, Donald G., 356
Paul, St., 11
Pavlov, Ivan Petrovich, 211, 255–59, 438; influence of, 271–73, 275, 279; ref. to publ., 268
Pearson, Karl, 122, 172, 212, 437
Pentschew, Christo, ref. to publ., 182 n.
Perkins, Nellie L., ref. to publ., 180 n.
Perky, Cheves W., 216
Perry, Ralph Barton, quoted, 192; ref. to publ., 209
Pestalozzi, Johann Heinrich, 53, 389, 393
Petermann, Bruno, ref. to publ., 296
Peterson, Joseph, 360–61; ref. to publ., 372
Piaget, Jean, 393–97, 400; ref. to publ., 401
Piéron, Henri, 436
Pillsbury, Walter B., 212, 438; ref. to publ., 16
Pilzecker, Alfons, 182, 243–44
Pinel, Philippe, 39–41, 43, 127, 130
Pintner, Rudolf, 356
Plato, 6–11, 23 n., 252; quoted, 79, 225
Podmore, Frank, ref. to publ., 136
Polyak, Stephan L., ref. to publ., 378 n.
Poppelreuter, Walther, 183
Postman, Leo, 277, 413
Pratt, James B., ref. to publ., 446
Pressey, Sidney L., ref. to publ., 362 n.
Preyer, Wilhelm Thierry, 201, 390, 393
Priestley, Joseph, 70
Prince, Morton, 170
Pulver, Max, 424
Purkinje, Johannes Evangelista, 71
Puységur, Armand M. J. de C., marquis, 132, 134

Ralston, Ruth P., ref. to publ., 362 n.
Randall, John H., ref. to publ., 29, 78
Rank, Otto, 344, 420
Rashevsky, Nicolas, 381
Ratzel, Friedrich, 123
Ray, Francis Willughby, 72
Raynor, Rosalie, 261
Razran, Gregory H. S., 273; ref. to publ., 446
Read, Carveth, ref. to publ., 216 n.

Reed, Homer B., ref. to publ., 265 n.
Reid, Thomas, 34–35, 57–58, 62–63
Rembrandt van Rijn, ref. to, 16
Rhine, Joseph B., 440–41; ref. to publ., 446
Ribot, Théodule-Armand, 107, 170, 188, 211, 264 n., 373, 435–36; ref. to publ., 48, 173
Richet, Charles Robert, 169
Riklin, Franz, 331
Rivers, William H. R., ref. to publ., 360 n.
Robertson, George Croom, quoted, 24
Robinson, Edward S., 269; ref. to publ., 244 n.
Robinson, James Harvey, quoted, 269; ref. to publ., 418 n.
Rogers, Carl R., 428
Romanes, George John, 116 n., 172–73
Rorshach, Hermann, 423–24
Rosanoff, Aaron J., 163 n.
Rousseau, Jean-Jacques, 46, 53, 55 n., 56, 389, 402
Royer-Collard, Pierre-Paul, 58–59, 124 n.
Ruger, Henry A., 240–41, 264
Russell, Bertrand, ref. to publ., 16
Russell, Roger W., ref. to publ., 397 n.

Sachs, Hanns, ref. to publ., 330
Saegert, C. W., 131
Saint-Hilaire, Auguste de, 113
Sanford, Robert N., 278
Sapir, Edward, ref. to publ., 159 n.
Schelling, Friedrich W. J. von, 47, 84–85
Schilder, Paul, 427
Schiller, Paul, ref. to publ., 446
Schleiden, Matthias Jakob, 76
Schneider, Georg Heinrich, 116 n.
Schopenhauer, Arthur, 51 n., 109 n., 152–54
Schroeder, Henry A., ref. to publ., 386 n.
Schultze, Maximilian J. S., 144 n.
Schumann, Friedrich, 181, 244; ref. to publ., 183 n.
Schwann, Theodor, 76
Scripture, Edward W., 212, 242
Sears, Robert R., 330
Sedgwick, William T., ref. to publ., 78
Seguin, Edouard, 130–31, 356, 360
Selz, Otto, 233
Semon, Richard Wolfgang, 247; ref. to publ., 248
Shakespeare, William, quoted, 127; ref. to, 320, 328
Shaw, Ruth F., ref. to publ., 425 n.

Sheldon, William H., 421
Sherif, Muzafer, 278, 412–14
Sherrington, Sir Charles Scott, 185, 190–91, 270, 374; ref. to publ., 191
Shinn, Millicent, 391
Sidis, Boris, 208 n.
Sighele, Scipio, 402
Simon, Théodore, 354, 356; ref. to publ., 371
Skinner, Burrhus F., 267, 279; ref. to publ., 283
Sleight, Walter G., ref. to publ., 243 n.
Smith, Adam, 41, 418 n.
Smith, Burke M., ref. to publ., 446
Smith, Stevenson, 266 n.
Smith, Théodate L., ref. to publ., 242 n.
Smith, William G., 181–82
Socrates, 7, 9–10
Sommer, Robert, 158, 163
Sontag, Lester W., 426
Spalding, Douglas A., 237
Spearman, Charles E., 363–64, 437; ref. to publ., 16
Spemann, Hans, 298
Spence, Kenneth W., ref. to publ., 279 n.
Spencer, Herbert, 106–09, 121, 123, 196, 257, 439; influence of, 116, 283; ref. to, 63, 104, 172, 238
Spinoza, Baruch, 18, 20–21, 109, 387; quoted, 174
Stagner, Ross, 420
Starbuck, Edwin D., 202
Starr, Henry E., 385
Steele, John M., ref. to publ., 386 n.
Steffens, Henrik, 85
Steffens, Laura, 182
Steffens, Lincoln, ref. to publ., 160 n.
Steinthal, Heymann, 125
Stern, William, 210, 245, 355, 393, 423, 435–36; quoted, 389
Sterne, Laurence, quoted, 55 n.
Stevens, Stanley S., ref. to publ., 142 n., 421 n., 432 n.
Stout, George Frederick, 212, 219, 228, 437
Stratton, George M., ref. to publ., 6 n.
Stuart, Charles E., ref. to publ., 446
Stumpf, Carl, 166–67, 210, 434
Sullivan, Harry S., ref. to publ., 346 n.
Sully, James, 212, 390
Swedenborg, Emanuel, 193 n.
Swift, Edgar J., 236

Taine, Hippolyte Adolphe, 169; ref. to publ., 389 n.
Tarde, Gabriel, 402
Taussig, Frank W., 362

Terman, Lewis M., 355–56, 358–59, 363, 366; ref. to publ., 372
Teuber, Hans L., ref. to publ., 446
Thénard, Louis-Jacques, baron, ref. to, 85
Thomas Aquinas, St., 11
Thomas, William Isaac, ref. to publ., 418 n.
Thompson, Helen, 399
Thomson, Godfrey H., 437
Thomson, Sir John Arthur, 329
Thorndike, Edward L., 121 n., 168, 208 n., 212, 237–40, 242–44, 275–77, 279–80, 363, 391, 405; CAVD test, 357–59; influence of, 259 n., 263 n.; ref. to, 224, 269, 291; ref. to publ., 248, 260 n.
Thorson, Agnes M., ref. to publ., 265 n.
Thurstone, Louis Leon, 358–59, 364–65, 411
Tiedemann, Dietrich, 389
Tiffany, Francis, ref. to publ., 129 n.
Tilton, John W., ref. to publ., 276 n.
Titchener, Edward B., 168, 212, 214–16, 221 n., 222 n., 223–25, 230–33, 251, 352–53, 437, 440; quoted, 176 n.; ref. to, 161, 259, 292; ref. to publ., 89 n., 90 n., 91 n., 227 n., 233
Tolman, Edward C., 267, 277, 281–82; ref. to publ., 283
Tomkins, Silvan S., ref. to publ., 425 n.
Tracy, de. See Destutt de Tracy.
Trautscholdt, Martin, 157
Trotter, Wilfred, 405
Tucker, William B., ref. to publ., 421 n.
Tyler, Henry W., ref. to publ., 78
Tylor, Sir Edward Burnett, 123–24

Uexküll, Jakob Johann, freiherr von, 254

Van Ormer, Edward B., 270
Varon, Edith J., ref. to publ., 171 n., 173
Veblen, Thorstein, 340, 405, 418 n.
Vierordt, Karl, 89
Vigotsky, L. S., 439
Vold, John M., ref. to publ., 311 n.
Volkmann, Alfred Wilhelm, 90, 241 n.
Voltaire, 68–70

Waehner, Trude S., ref. to publ., 425 n.
Wagner, Rudolf, ref. to publ., 80 n.
Waldeyer, Wilhelm von, 187–88, 190, 373
Walitzki, Marie, ref. to publ., 157 n.
Walker, Helen M., ref. to publ., 360 n.
Wallace, Alfred Russel, 115
Ward, James, 172, 212, 219, 437

Warren, Howard C., quoted, 60–61; ref. to publ., 48, 63
Washburn, Margaret F., 221, 259
Watson, John B., 19 n., 254, 259–66, 393; ref. to, 272, 292, 407, 439; ref. to publ., 207 n., 268
Watt, Henry J., 227–28
Weber, Ernst Heinrich, 76, 79–84, 87–89, 99, 105, 117, 143; ref. to, 54, 137, 148 n., 149, 156, 160 n., 164–66
Wechsler, David, 356
Weismann, August, 367
Weiss, Alfred Paul, ref. to publ., 267 n.
Weiss, Paul, 298, 380 n.; quoted, 297; ref. to publ., 306
Wellman, Beth L., 370
Werner, Heinz, ref. to publ., 401
Wernicke, Carl, 186
Wertheimer, Max, 159, 233, 287–91, 293–94, 297, 299, 379 n., 435; ref. to publ., 296
Wheatstone, Sir Charles, 93 n.
White, William Alanson, 347
White, Ralph K., 303; ref. to publ., 306
Witasek, Stephan, 245
Witkin, Hermann A., ref. to publ., 282 n.
Witmer, Lightner, 356, 392, 427
Wittler, Fritz, 337; ref. to publ., 330
Wöhler, Friedrich, 71, 76
Wolff, Christian, freiherr von, 36
Wolff, Harold G., 387
Wolff, Werner, 292–93

Wolfle, Dael L., ref. to publ., 372
Woodrow, Herbert H., 364
Woodworth, Robert S., 183 n., 208 n., 229, 240 n., 242–43, 247, 360, 405; quoted, 184; ref. to, 231–32, 259; ref. to publ., 90 n., 183, 191, 224, 233, 248, 268, 296, 348, 372, 446
Woodyard, Ella, ref. to publ., 276 n., 357 n.
Woolley, Helen T., 371; ref. to publ., 355 n.
Wordsworth, William, quoted, 402
Wundt, Wilhelm Max, 89 n., 90 n., 91, 119, 148 n., 149–73, 175–77, 195, 210, 217–18, 226–27, 229–30, 251, 352, 434–35; influence of, 160, 211–12, 214, 221, 223, 373; ref. to, 146, 193, 225; ref. to publ., 173
Wyatt, Frederick, ref. to publ., 446

Yerkes, Robert M., 208 n., 259; ref. to publ., 257 n.
Yeung, K. T., 361
Young, Kimball, ref. to publ., 417 n.
Young, Paul T., ref. to publ., 232
Young, Thomas, 71, 76, 140

Zeigarnik, Bluma W., 301
Zeliony, Georgii, 257
Ziehen, Theodor, 154, 170
Zilboorg, Gregory, ref. to publ., 136, 330
Znaniecki, Florian, ref. to publ., 418 n.
Zubin, Joseph, 424

INDEX OF SUBJECTS

Abilities, 276, 363, 365, 368–69, 437
  special, 97, 359, 363–66
  See also Capacities.
Abnormal psychology. *See* Psychiatry.
Acoustics. *See* Hearing.
Act psychology, 225–28
Action theory, 219–20
Active recitation, 177, 245
Activism, 58, 62, 88, 101, 225, 253
Adaptation
  biological, 107, 109, 112–15, 117–18,
    124, 152–53, 201, 214, 237, 403,
    409, 436
  sensory, 80, 143, 382
  social, 337, 413
Adolescence, 119, 318, 324, 342, 358–
    59, 386–87, 390, 400, 410, 426
Aesthetics, 73, 92, 166–67, 407
Affective processes, 153, 217, 239, 292
  See also Emotion; Feeling.
Age and mental traits, 245 *n.*, 358–59
Agnosticism, 44 *n.*, 102–03
Ambivalence, 319–20
Amnesia, 135, 307, 309, 311, 320
  See also Aphasia; Dissociation.
Analytical psychology, 334
Anatomy, comparative, 72
Anesthesia, 134–35, 307, 309, 320
Animal
  magnetism, 132–34, 171
  physiology, 93, 185–87, 375–78
  psychology, 116, 158–59, 174, 212,
    237–40, 255–61, 271–72, 275, 279–
    80, 282, 291, 437
  spirits, 18
Animism, 123–24, 395–96
Anthropology, 5, 55–56, 123–24, 158–
    59, 211, 293, 319–20, 341–44, 390,
    397, 400, 431
  influence of, 409–10, 417, 421–23, 431
Anxiety neurosis, 320–21
Aphasia, 185–86, 374–76, 378
Apperception, 21, 36 *n.*, 52–54, 101,
    153–55, 215, 225
  See also Perception.

Applied psychology, 293, 434–35
Aspiration level, 301
Association, 31–36, 50–54, 59–62, 117–
    20, 147–48, 156–58, 180–83, 188–
    89, 196, 200, 213, 221, 244, 257–58,
    265, 299, 331, 404, 406
  backward, 181
  by contiguity, 9, 27, 59, 103, 247–
    48
  by contrast, 9, 59, 103, 182–83
  by similarity, 9, 27, 33–34, 59–60,
    103, 183
  controlled, 27, 163–64, 353
  free, 27, 119, 163–64, 309–11, 314–15,
    325, 339, 353
  laws, 27–29, 33–34, 36–37, 49–50, 59–
    61, 103, 176, 269; secondary, 60–
    61, 117, 182
  tests, 119–20, 156–57, 161–64, 166,
    227–28, 331–33, 353–54
Associationism, 26–27, 32, 35, 42–43,
    49–50, 54, 59–63, 84, 97, 99–109,
    163, 169, 171–72, 176–77, 183, 193,
    200, 210–13, 219, 221–22, 229,
    265 *n.*, 281, 294–95, 434, 436
Associative shifting, law of, 239, 248
Astasia abasia, 325
Atomism, 6–7, 34, 63, 86, 285, 295, 297–
    98, 376, 381, 445
Attention, 21, 53, 84, 88, 101–02, 154,
    213, 215, 245 *n.*, 393
  span of, 37 *n.*, 161
Attitude, 21, 210, 222–23, 228–32, 240–
    42, 244, 264–65, 273–75, 319–20,
    332, 344, 386, 405, 411–12, 417,
    423
  See also Mental set.
Audition. *See* Hearing.
Aufgabe, 228
  See also Mental set.
Authority and the family, 344, 404
Autoeroticism, 318
Autonomous nervous system. *See* Nervous system.
Autosuggestion, 135 *n.*

Behaviorism, 125, 207, 223, 251–68, 271, 282–83, 292, 336, 393, 398–99, 419–20, 438
intellectual atmosphere of, 252–55
Belongingness, law of, 280
Binet-Simon tests, 354–56, 358–60, 391
Biological sciences, 15–16, 38, 47, 67, 69, 71–78, 85–86, 159, 252–54, 298, 330, 352–53, 444–45
Blood pressure, 332 *n.*, 387
Brain. *See* Cortical localization; Nervous system, central.

Canalization, 404
Capacities, 36, 61, 97, 281, 355, 359, 371
See also Abilities.
Catatonia, 158
Cathexes, 319, 322, 404 *n.*
Censorship, 312–13, 319
Character
individual. *See* Personality.
national, 422–23
reading. *See* Graphology; Phrenology.
Child psychology, 158–59, 168, 172, 210, 212, 271, 300–05, 310–11, 317–19, 389–401, 411, 420, 435, 438
infant, 33–34, 36, 261, 266, 317–19, 322–23, 338–40, 391–94, 399, 408
See also Education.
Child welfare, 427–28
Church Fathers, 10–11
Clairvoyance, 133, 205, 440
Clinical psychology, 169, 213, 293, 392, 402–03, 417, 419, 427–29, 432, 435
Cognition, 44–46, 55, 73–74, 105, 201, 206, 212, 217, 219, 221, 277, 281–82, 290, 292, 404, 413–14, 423, 437
See also Epistemology; Perception.
Color, 71, 76, 95, 140–41, 143–45, 423, 425
Color-blindness, 76, 118–19, 140–41, 143, 145, 257
Commercial Revolution, 13, 40, 43
Comparative psychology, 275
Compensation, 336–41, 347
Competition, 23, 396, 406, 421
See also Conflict.
Completion test, 352
Complexes, 318, 323, 325–27, 331, 338, 344
See also names of complexes.
Compulsions, 310–11, 320
Conation, 25, 219, 292, 404–04
See also Purposivism; Will.
Conditioned response, 108, 255–82, 320, 408, 410, 413, 419, 439–40
delayed, 271

Conflict, 50–51, 54, 152–53, 275, 301, 310–13, 317–20, 323–24, 329, 331, 345, 347, 387, 398–99, 415
Connectionism, 276
Conscience, 324
Consciousness, 18–21, 38–40, 50–52, 97–98, 195–97, 206–07, 218–24, 227–28, 251, 258–60, 263, 294, 382–83, 438
fringe of, 101
See also Unity; Unconscious.
Consonance. *See* Harmony.
Conversion, religious, 202–04, 320, 390
Co-operation, 421
Cortical localization, 95, 184–87, 283, 374–81
See also Phrenology.
Creative synthesis, 154, 195, 226–27
Cretinism, 131
Crime detection, 332
Criminology, 40–41, 118, 334
Crowd psychology, 402–03, 408
Cultural-science psychology, 341–48, 434
Curiosity, 278, 319 *n.*, 404
Cutaneous senses. *See* Pain; Temperature; Touch.

Darwinism. *See* Evolution, organic.
Death instinct, 328
Defense mechanisms, 316, 326–28, 346–47, 398
Deism, 37–38, 43
Delusions, 207
Dementia paralytica, 128
Dementia praecox, 332–33
Democracy, 40, 303, 305, 340, 370, 392, 430
Depression. *See* Manic-depressive psychoses.
Determining tendencies, 222, 228, 230, 442–43
Dialectical materialism, 438–39
Differences. *See* Individual; Occupational; Sensory; Sex.
Differentiation, 108–09, 115, 216, 302–03, 365, 378
Diffusion, cultural, 124
Diminishing returns (memory), 179, 235, 238, 280
Discrimination, 81–83, 139, 141–42, 256–57, 259, 261, 364
Displacement, 327
Disruption, 281
Dissociation, 169–70, 172, 194, 211, 299, 311, 436
Drainage theories, 188, 190 *n.*
Drawing, 276–77, 424–25

Dreams, 267, 307, 311–16, 395, 398
Drive psychology, 347, 380
  See also Instinct; Motivation.
Drugs, effects of, 158, 190–91, 275
Dualism, psychological. *See* Mind-body
  relation; Soul-body relation.
Duplicity theory, 144 *n.*
Dynamogenesis, 171

Eclecticism, 59, 419–20
Economics, 41–42, 102–03, 114, 123–25,
  403, 405
Education, 28, 34, 43, 53–54, 104, 211,
  223, 293, 389, 391–92, 407, 411,
  424–25, 430, 439
  progressive, 389, 392, 439
Educational psychology, 211, 239, 391
Effect, law of, 239, 260, 276–77, 283
Ego, 171, 312–14, 321–28, 337, 345–47,
  398, 415, 427
  alter, 415
  See also Self.
Egocentrism, 318, 332–35, 394–96, 405,
  442
  See also Narcissism.
Eidetic imagery, 435
Electra complex, 318
Electromagnetism, 297–98
Emotion, 9, 19, 61, 146–47, 152–54,
  172, 198–200, 203, 211, 266, 290,
  382–84, 398, 403–04
  expression of, 116, 146–47, 198, 390,
  437
  See also Feeling, and names of emo-
  tions.
Empathy, 167 *n.*
Empiricism, 13–15, 21–38, 44 *n.*, 46–47,
  54, 56–58, 62–63, 92–93, 99, 193
Encephalitis, 382
Encyclopedists, 38
Endocrine glands. *See* Glands.
Enlightenment, the, 37, 40
Epilepsy, 442
Epiphenomena, 385
Epistemology, 22–23, 27–28, 34–35, 43–
  44, 55–56, 159, 200–02, 206–07,
  387
Equipotentiality, 377
Escape, 319, 323, 328, 404
Ethics, 23, 40–41, 45, 98, 103, 159, 217,
  312, 326–28, 330, 395–97, 405, 407,
  434
Ethnology. *See* Anthropology.
Eugenics, 121
Event system, 409
Evolution, inorganic, 111–12
Evolution, organic, 54, 76, 106–26, 149,
  153, 172–73, 197, 200–02, 212–14,

  217–18, 237, 253, 270, 285, 295–96,
  335, 351–53, 389–90, 403, 405,
  430, 436–37, 444
  in the social sciences, 123–26
  theory of, 111–26
Exercise, law of, 239, 276
Existentialism. *See* Structuralism.
Experimental method, 14, 81–82, 237
Experimental psychology, 3–4, 67–98,
  137–87, 211, 221–24, 227–28, 233,
  237–39, 255–67, 300–03, 332–33,
  406–09, 430, 434, 436, 438
  See also James, William, Index of
  Names.
Expression, facial, 293, 407
  See also Emotion; Personality.
Extraversion, 334–45
Eye movements, 140, 155, 264–65

Facilitation
  biological, 190–91, 374, 379
  social, 407–08
Factor analysis, 212, 364–66, 437–38,
  440
Faculty psychology, 35–36, 43–45, 54,
  56–59, 100, 200, 217, 326
Family, authority and the, 344, 404
Fantasy. *See* Imagination.
Fascism, 305
Fatigue, 157, 171, 190–91, 211, 391–92
Fear, 23, 25, 172, 198–99, 261, 320,
  322–24, 382–83, 404
Feeble-mindedness, 130–31, 353–54,
  368
Feeling, 25, 44–45, 88, 105, 151–52, 154,
  195, 212, 214–15, 217–18, 228, 230–
  32, 260, 335, 382, 406, 437
  tridimensional theory of, 151
Feelings, mixed, 215
Feminism, 339
Field theory, 297–306, 412, 432–33
Folk psychology, 53, 125–26, 158–59,
  210, 434
Forgetting, 102, 174, 178–79, 236, 238,
  245 *n.*, 270, 280, 315
  See also Memory.
Form psychology. *See* Gestalt psychology.
Free will, 18, 40, 197
Frustration, 301–02, 322–23, 338–40,
  342–43, 346–47, 392
Functional psychology, 222–24, 420,
  437
Functionalism, 213–14, 216–24, 241

Gastric ulcers, 386–87
Genetic psychology, 38–39, 55–56, 212,
  217–19, 230–33
  See also Behaviorism.

Genius, 117, 212, 366
Gestalt psychology, 61, 233, 243, 251, 276, 280–96, 298–99, 374, 376, 387–88, 412, 419–20, 431–32, 435, 438
Gestaltqualität, 226–27, 230, 286
Glands, 382–85
  endocrine, 96, 381–86, 435, (pineal) 18–19, 25, (thyroid) 384–86
Goals, 272–73, 281, 299–300, 405–06
Graphology, 171, 292, 424, 434, 436
Greek philosophy and psychology, 4–12, 26, 284
Group intelligence tests, 357
Group psychology, 303–04, 321, 339, 406–09, 412–16
Growth, 233, 389–93, 398–401, 443
Guilt complex, 320, 326–27

Habit, 18, 33–34, 57, 61, 106, 188–89, 220, 242–43, 275, 404
Hallucinations, 5, 120, 135, 207, 220
Handwriting, 171, 292, 424, 434, 436
Harmony, 142–43, 166–67
Hearing, 71, 79–80, 82–83, 86–88, 137, 141–43, 151, 155, 166–67, 185–86, 254, 266, 285–87, 378
Hedonism
  ethical, 41–42, 103
  psychological, 19, 22–24, 41–42, 103–04
Heredity, 107, 112, 117–22, 129–30, 334, 362, 366–71, 441–43
  Mendelian laws of, 367
  See also Evolution, organic; Instinct.
Heterosexuality, 318, 324, 333
Higher units of response, 162, 235–36
Homosexuality, 318
Humanitarianism, 40–43, 127–31, 370
Hunger, 22, 157, 255–56, 280, 318, 383
Hypnotism, 134–36, 169–71, 194, 211, 307–10, 325, 436
Hysteria, 135–36, 169–70, 194, 211, 307–09, 320, 331–32, 334, 402, 436

Id, 324–26, 328
Idealism, 31, 37, 44, 57–58, 61–62, 100, 102, 108, 124, 146, 193, 211, 336, 439
  See also Transcendentalism.
Ideas, 28–29, 47 *n.*, 49–53, 61, 97–98, 264, 439
  complex, 28, 33–34, 49
  See also Association; Imagery; Thought.
Identification, 318, 322, 324
Ideologists, 62–63
Illusions, 167, 207
Imagery, mental, 33, 61, 119 *n.*, 120,

151, 154, 156, 195, 214–16, 221, 228, 230–32, 246–47, 259–60, 302
  eidetic, 435
Imagination, 9, 26, 132, 262, 290, 335, 374, 398, 400, 406, 413, 414 *n.*
Imitation, 239, 263 *n.*, 390, 399, 405–06
  laws of, 402
Impulses, 19, 22–23, 197, 220, 290, 299–300, 311, 316, 321, 326–28, 384, 386, 403–06
Individual differences, 60–61, 81, 117–18, 138, 164, 171, 212–16, 228, 243, 270, 280, 301–03, 305, 334–35, 352–53, 359, 365, 370, 391, 411, 423–24, 431–33, 437–39
Individual psychology, 337–41, 416
Inductive psychology, 159
Industrial Revolution, 42–43, 111
Infantilism, 319, 321
Inferiority feelings, 337–38
Inhibition
  biological, 190–91, 221, 256, 270–71, 274, 374, 379
  psychological, 244, 273–74, 321
Innervation, 151–52, 155, 190
Insanity. *See* Psychoses.
Insight, 239, 241, 267, 283, 290–91, 295
Instinct, 22, 54 *n.*, 57, 105–06, 116, 151, 201, 212, 237, 261, 290, 311–12, 319, 321, 324, 328, 334, 345–46, 403–06, 409–11, 437, 442–43
Institutional behavior, 408
Intellectualism. *See* Rationalism.
Intelligence, 116, 153, 210, 212, 266, 355, 371
  inheritance of, 366–71
  measuring. *See* tests below.
  quotient (IQ), 355–62, 399
  tests, 171, 210, 352–66, 391–92, 400–01, 427–28, 435, 438–40
  theory of, 362–66
Intentionality, 226
Interactionism, psychophysical, 18–21, 24, 47, 198, 207, 288, 387
  See also Mind-body relation; Soul-body relation.
Interference, 243–44, 270, 272, 312, 323
Introjection, 326–27
Introspection, 125, 150, 194–95, 212–16, 218, 221–33, 251, 259–60, 292, 437–38
Introversion, 334–35
Intuition, 335
  See also Instinct.
Isomorphism, 388

James-Lange theory, 20, 147, 200, 382, 384, 403

Journals, psychological, 68, 107, 151, 168, 171, 192, 386, 390, 436, 441
Judgment, 18, 37, 87–90, 97, 156, 227–28, 266, 407, 412–13
  moral. *See* Ethics.

Kinesthetics, 79, 81–83, 147–48, 152, 166, 199–200, 207, 212, 223 *n*., 231–32, 262, 265, 272, 373–75, 380 *n*., 382
Knowledge. *See* Cognition.

Language, 73, 125, 158–59, 186, 262–65, 416, 419, 434
  See also Aphasia; Association tests; Word association.
Learning, 9, 22, 33–34, 52–54, 106, 108, 162, 174–83, 188–90, 200–01, 212, 233, 251, 258–83, 290, 376, 380–81, 391–93, 399–400, 432–34, 437, 443
  laws of, 106, 239, 260, 276, 280, 283
  motor skills, 234–48
  See also Association; Habit; Memory.
Letter perception, 162, 235, 246–47
Libido, 317–22, 332–35, 386
Limen. *See* Threshold.
Local signs, 147
Localization, cortical. *See* Cortical localization.

Manic-depressive psychoses, 128, 158
Marxism, 336, 340–41, 438–39
Materialism, 252–55, 267, 438–39
  dialectical, 438–39
  See also Mechanism.
Mathematics. *See* Quantitative methods; Statistics.
Maturity
  biological, 419
  emotional, 390
  intellectual, 358–59
Meaning, 175–76, 179, 183, 215, 228–29, 231–32, 262–63, 281, 414
Measurement, 79, 352, 431–32, 437
Mechanism, 18–21, 24–26, 34, 57–58, 61–62, 71, 85, 104, 146, 154, 170, 253–54, 267, 444–45
  See also Materialism.
Medicine, 16, 39, 73, 79, 84, 145, 275, 329, 375–76
  See also Psychiatry.
Membership character, law of, 288–89, 294–95
Memory, 9, 26–27, 33–35, 37 *n*., 44, 51–53, 60–62, 97–98, 101–02, 108, 167, 174–84, 186, 200, 210, 213, 219, 234–48, 270, 299, 302, 309, 312, 374, 413, 414 *n*., 423, 434, 437
  incidental, 244–45

Memory—(Cont.)
  span, 176–77, 393
  tests, 242–44
  See also Faculty psychology; Forgetting; Imagery; Learning.
Mental
  age, 354–58
  chemistry, 104
  deficiency, 54 *n*., 119, 129–31, 157–58, 168 *n*., 171, 353–54, 366–68, 389, 436
  disorders. *See* Psychoneuroses; Psychoses.
  healing, 203
  hygiene, 329, 393, 398
  imagery. *See* Imagery.
  physiology, 253
  set, 227, 244, 273–75, 355
  tests. *See* Intelligence tests.
Mesmerism, 131–36
Micropsia, 379
Mind, 9, 18, 25, 28 *n*., 37, 44, 50, 62, 104, 146, 195–97, 201–02, 216–17, 219, 291, 388, 439
Mind-body relation, 6, 10–11, 20–21, 92, 109, 198, 206–07, 260, 335, 385–88
Monism, 6, 18–19, 21, 91, 109, 198, 206–07, 259, 335
Morals. *See* Ethics.
Motion
  perception of, 287–88, 379 *n*.
  psychological, 24–26, 299–300
Motivation, 22–23, 41, 103, 197, 274, 278, 316, 319 *n*., 419
  See also Drive; Instinct; Mental set; Will.
Motor psychology, 221
Muscle sense. *See* Kinesthetics.
Music, 142–43, 166–67, 210, 434
Mutation, 367
Mysticism, 85, 92, 193 *n*., 203 *n*., 204–05, 207

Nancy school, 135–36, 169–70, 203 *n*., 211, 308, 402
Narcissism, 318, 321–23, 346
National psychologies, 422–23, 433–40
Nativism, 93, 97
Naturalism, 11, 25, 46–47, 335–36
Nature-nurture controversy, 121, 370, 399, 441–43
Nature, philosophy of. *See* Philosophy.
Nazism, 294, 435
Neorealism, 206–07, 221
Nerves, 33, 81
  sensory and motor, 77, 93–95, 105
  See also Nervous system, central; Neurone theory.

Nervous system
autonomic, 381–85
central, 17–19, 25–26, 33, 38–39, 72, 93–95, 128–29, 146, 150, 188, 219–21, 337, 373–78, 381–85, 442
Neurology, 184–91
Neurone theory, 187–90, 239, 373–74, 376
Neurophysiology, 374
Neuroses. *See* Psychoneuroses.
Nonsense syllables, 175–81, 183, 244, 270, 299

Objectivism, 17, 269–77, 281–83, 330–31
See also Behaviorism.
Obsessions, 320
Occupational differences, 362
Oedipus complex, 318, 323, 325, 344
Olfaction. *See* Smell.
Operationism, 431–33
Optics. *See* Sight.
Order of merit, 165
Organismic psychology, 292
Overlapping, 162, 235
Overlearning, 177–79, 236

Pain, 10, 19, 23, 37, 41–43, 103–04, 166, 186–87, 220, 273, 278, 376, 380, 383, 403
Parallelism
cultural, 124
psychophysical, 20–21, 91, 109, 151, 254–55, 385–87
Paralysis, 135, 307, 309, 320
Paranoia, 324
Parapsychology, 440–41
Participation, 395, 411, 414–16
See also Group psychology.
Pathways, neural, 77, 93, 186–90, 200, 220–21, 376, 379
Pedigree method, 119, 366
Perception, 21, 31, 45, 55, 61, 88, 97, 101, 103, 153–55, 161–64, 186, 195, 226–27, 229, 235, 241, 243, 247, 266, 278, 289–92, 380–81, 388, 404, 414 *n.*, 423–24, 427, 437
social, 412–13
space. *See* Space.
time. *See* Time.
See also Aphasia; Apperception; Epistemology; Gestalt psychology; Insight; Relations.
Performance tests, 356, 392
Personal equation, 138
See also Individual differences.
Personalism, 435
Personality, 63, 170–71, 194, 197–98,

207, 211, 217, 261, 266, 292–93, 310–11, 332, 338, 342–47, 366, 382, 386, 398, 400, 410–11, 417 *n.*, 419–29, 432, 434–36, 438, 440, 443
expression of, 293
split. *See* Dissociation.
testing, 294
Perversions, 317, 324
Philology. *See* Language.
Philosophy of nature, 47–48, 79, 84–85, 92, 95–96, 99–100, 137, 252
Phobias, 307–08, 320, 398
Phonetics, 73, 158
Phrenology, 56–57, 95, 133–34
Physical science, 13–15, 33, 50, 67–71, 74–76, 83–86, 137, 140–43, 166–67, 252, 286–87, 297–99, 351–52
Physiocrats, 41
Physiological limit, 235
Physiological psychology, 39, 47, 71, 94, 107, 137–48, 150, 165–67, 169, 184–91, 219–22, 275, 373–88
See also Nervous system.
Physiology, experimental, 67–68, 76–77, 83, 92–97, 99, 105, 134, 149, 198–200, 237, 438
Plateaus, 234–36
Platonism, 14, 27, 238, 284, 289
Play, 333, 390, 392, 398
Pleasure, 10, 19, 23, 37, 41–43, 103–04, 273, 403
See also Affective processes; Feeling; Hedonism, psychological.
Positivism, 124–25
Practice. *See* Learning.
Prägnanz, 289
Pragmatism, 206
Primitive cultures. *See* Anthropology.
Probability, theory of, 69, 90, 121
Projection, 326–27, 345
Projective testing, 343, 417, 423–28
Propaganda, 411
Psychasthenia. *See* Compulsions; Obsessions; Phobias.
Psychiatry, 38–40, 54, 59, 127–36, 157–59, 169–73, 194, 211, 293, 382, 386–87, 402, 427–29, 434, 438
Psychical research, 205–06, 211, 440–41
Psychoanalysis, 51 *n.*, 251, 305–47
influence of, 397–98, 400, 419–20, 438, 440
See also Psychiatry.
Psychogalvanic reflex, 171
Psychologist's fallacy, 196, 285
Psychometrics, 437
Psychoneuroses, 131–36, 310–11, 320, 344–45, 397
experimental, 275

Psychoneuroses—(Cont.)
See also Psychiatry, and names of neuroses.
Psychopathology, 157–58, 170, 310, 315, 329
　religion and, 203
Psychophysics, 88–92, 155–56, 158, 164–66, 175, 207, 210, 434, 437
　inner, 88–89
Psychoses, 39–40, 43, 127–29, 157–58, 169–71, 188, 194, 324, 329, 332–33, 386, 434, 436
See also names of psychoses.
Psychosomatics, 333, 337, 385–88, 440
Psychotechnics, 438–39
Public opinion, 411, 417
Punishment, 23, 41, 269, 273, 276, 278, 323, 326
Purpose. *See* Conation.
Purposivism, 152–53, 281–83, 302, 405–06
Pythagoreans, 7, 14, 284

Qualitative psychology, 286–90
Qualities, primary and secondary, 28, 30, 45
Quantitative method, 13–15, 45–46, 50–53, 54 *n.*, 68–70, 74, 81–84, 86–92, 137–48, 174–83, 234–38, 255–59, 272–75, 279–83, 287–92, 352–72, 439–40

Race psychology, 117–18, 125–26, 359–62
Racial attitudes, 411, 435
Rage, 152, 198–99, 383
Random movements. *See* Trial and error.
Rationalism, 27–28, 34–35, 47
Rationalization, 316, 320, 327, 345
Reaction time, 137–39, 155, 158, 161–62, 164, 166, 437
Reading, 162–63, 177–79, 235, 245–46, 265, 392
Reality
　escape from, 319, 323, 328, 404
　motive, 316
　testing, 322, 325, 328
Reasoning, 9, 34–35, 44, 55, 97, 116, 171, 197, 239, 241, 243, 266, 407, 436
Recapitulation theory, 390
Recentering, 290
Reciprocity, 396–97, 414–15, 443
Redintegration, 101–02, 247–48, 278
Reflexes, 18–19, 38–39, 47, 93, 105, 151–52, 189–90, 201, 211, 218, 220, 237, 266, 374, 408, 444
　circular, 263 *n.*

Reflexes—(Cont.)
　conditioned. *See* Conditioned.
　prepotent, 408
　psychogalvanic, 171
Regression, 302, 319, 327
Reinforcement, 270–74, 278
Relations, perception of, 61, 82, 221, 226, 228–29, 240–41, 286
Relativity, 82, 86–87, 431–33
Religion, 5–6, 10–11, 34, 62, 123–24, 217, 252
　psychology of, 202–05
Renaissance, 4 *n.*, 12–16, 22, 46, 75
Repression, 309–14, 317–20, 323–27, 331, 345
Resistance
　biological, 81, 189
　psychological, 299–300, 308–10, 321, 326
Response, higher units of, 160, 235–36
See also Conditioned response.
Rewards, 269, 273, 276–83
Romanticism, 46–48, 75, 111
Rorschach test, 293, 343, 400, 423–24, 427–28

Sadism, 317
Satisfaction, 260, 273, 276–79, 282, 316–19, 322–23, 340, 346
Saving method, 177–79, 236
Schizophrenia, 332–33
Scholasticism, 25, 35–36, 46
Science, 12–17, 38–40, 45–47, 67–98, 252, 430–34, 439–40, 445–46
Scottish school, 34–36, 47, 57, 59–63, 84, 99–102, 212
　influence of, 107, 167, 192–93, 436–37
Self, 32, 57–58, 194, 198, 204, 212, 346–47, 394–95, 416
　subliminal, 212
See also Consciousness; Ego; Egocentrism; Personality.
Sensationism, 36–38, 213, 230
Sensations, 25–26, 28, 31–33, 37, 49–52, 60–63, 79–91, 101, 103, 147–48, 151–56, 185–87, 195–96, 211, 213–16, 221, 225–26, 228, 230–32, 247, 260, 278, 285–86
　measuring, 88–89, 91
Sensory differences, just noticeable. *See* Psychophysics.
Sentiment, 404–05
Set, mental, 227, 244, 273–75, 355
Sex
　differences, 332, 335–37, 340, 359, 413, 422
　impulses, 22
See also Libido; Sexuality.

Sexuality, theory of, 308–30, 333, 338, 397–98
Shame, 326
Shock, 277, 282, 333–34, 387
  therapy, 375
Sight, 9, 71, 79–84, 87, 89, 92–95, 137, 140–41, 143, 147–48, 151, 155, 167, 185–86, 246, 254, 266, 285, 287–88, 378–79, 388, 435
  See also Color; Space perception.
Sign-gestalt, 281–82
Skepticism, 7, 10, 32, 34, 44
Skills, motor, 234–48, 419, 437
Skin sensitivity, 80–83, 143, 148, 166, 215, 438
Sleep, 134–35, 312, 314, 381
Smell, 36, 80, 151, 186
Social psychology, 22, 39, 323, 341–47, 400, 402–18, 432–33, 437–38, 441–43
  field theory and, 303–04
  See also Folk psychology
Social sciences, 293, 330, 431, 443
  evolutionism in the, 123–26
Socialism, 339–41
Sociocentrism, 396
Sociometry, 414–16
Sophists, 7, 10
Soul, 5–12, 18–20, 25, 31–32, 34–36, 43–44, 59, 62, 86–87, 91, 198, 253, 335–36
Soul-body relation, 5–12, 19, 198, 207
Space perception, 45, 92–93, 97, 147–48, 193, 230, 285–86, 388
Specific energies, 77, 93–95, 140, 380
Speech. *See* Language.
Spiritual values, 47–48, 58, 62, 84–85, 87–88, 100, 335–36
  See also Mysticism; Religion; Transcendentalism.
Spiritualisme, 58 *n.*
Spontaneity testing and training, 415
Stanford Revision (of Binet-Simon test), 355–60
Statistics, 69–70, 121, 139, 164–65, 172, 175–80, 212, 363, 368
Stimulus error, 90, 164–65, 232
Stimulus-response psychology, 239, 242, 244, 255–67, 269, 294
  See also Behaviorism.
Stoics, 49, 210
Structuralism, 49, 195, 197, 214–16, 219–31, 293–96
Struggle. *See* Conflict.
Subconscious. *See* Unconscious.
Sublimation, 319, 327–28
Substitution, 319, 327
Suggestibility, 211, 402, 404, 436

Suggestion, 59–61, 171, 245, 309, 314 *n.*, 405
  See also Hypnotism; Mesmerism.
Summation, 190, 270, 374
Superego, 324–27, 345
Suppression. *See* Inhibition; Repression.
Symbolism, 43, 232, 258–59, 275, 311–14, 320–21, 325, 342–43, 439
Sympathy, 405, 416
Synapses, 188–91, 373–74, 379
Systematic psychology, 151, 221, 224, 226, 353

Taboos, 325, 341–42, 410
Taste, 186, 195–96
Technology, 439
Telepathy, 133, 205–06, 440
Temperature sense, 79–80, 89, 143, 148, 166, 186–87, 285, 376, 380
Tension, 300–01, 304, 323, 417
Testimony, psychology of, 245, 423, 435
Tests
  completion, 352
  draw-a-man, 424–25
  group, 337
  memory, 242–43
  performance, 356, 392
  projective, 343, 417, 423–28
  vocabulary, 364
  See also Association tests; Intelligence tests.
Thematic Apperception Test, 343, 425, 428
Thought, 25–27, 31–34, 171, 196, 198, 210, 212, 227–33, 240, 258, 262–65, 289–90, 335, 354, 380–81, 395, 406, 413, 414 *n.*
  imageless, 228, 230, 232, 247, 259
  transference. *See* Telepathy.
Threshold, 51, 54, 190, 219
  two-point, 80–81, 84, 87, 105, 438
Time perception, 45, 196–97, 287–88, 388
Topology, 299–303, 305
Touch, 80–82, 87, 148, 166, 186, 266, 375–76, 380
Traces linking ideas, 97–98
Transcendentalism, 45–49, 97–100
Transfer of training, 241–42, 251, 280–81, 363 *n.*
Transference, 309, 320–21, 339
Trauma, 333–34
  See also Shock.
Trial and error, 238, 240, 263–65, 267, 272, 278–79, 283, 291, 399–400
Tropism, 253–54
Twins, 120–21, 370–71, 399
Typology, 228, 332, 334–36, 421–22, 435

Unconscious, 21, 50–52, 194, 212, 218–19, 227–28, 251, 293, 308–47
Understanding, 28–29, 211
Unity of consciousness, 31, 35–36, 43–46, 53, 58–59, 63, 100, 108, 172, 437
Utilitarianism, 42–43, 47, 103–04

Values, 302, 413
  See also Spiritual values.
Vision. *See* Sight.
Vitalism, 47, 71, 96, 442–43
  emergent, 445
Vocabulary test, 364
Volition. *See* Will.
Voluntarism, 58, 153

War neuroses, 329, 428
Wholeness, 211–12, 283–89, 293–96, 420, 444–46
Will, 11, 18, 25, 35, 44–45, 57–58, 97, 105, 152–54, 197–98, 217–18, 221, 227–28, 232, 241, 271–72, 290, 374, 405, 437
  freedom of the, 18, 40, 197
  See also Conation.
Wish fulfillment, 312–13
Wit, 316
Weber's law, 81–82, 84, 87–89
  See also Psychophysics.
Word association, 156–57, 162–64, 231, 235, 247, 262–65, 299, 331–32
Work, 179–80, 391, 406–07, 412